Mustang 1964¹/₂ - 1973
Restoration Guide

Tom Corcoran and Earl Davis

motorbooks

First published in 1998 by MBI Publishing Company and
Motorbooks, an imprint of MBI Publishing Company, 400 1st
Avenue North, Suite 300, Minneapolis, MN 55401 USA

Motorbooks titles are also available at discounts in bulk quantity
for industrial or sales-promotional use. For details write to
Special Sales Manager at MBI Publishing Company, 400 1st
Avenue North, Suite 300, Minneapolis, MN 55401 USA.

To find out more about our books, join us online at
www.motorbooks.com.

ISBN-13: 978-0-7603-0552-2

Printed in China

Contents

Acknowledgments 4

Introduction 5

Chapter 1 Data Plates and Decals 6

Chapter 2 Exterior 24

Chapter 3 Interior 88

Chapter 4 Engine 129

Chapter 5 Drivetrain 212

Chapter 6 Suspension, Brakes, Steering, Wheels and Exhaust 248

Chapter 7 Wiring and Electrical Systems 307

Chapter 8 Options 340

Chapter 9 1971–1973 Mustangs 352

Index 448

Acknowledgments

A book of this size represents the work of many people. We have been fans of the 1965–1973 Mustangs most of our lives. Still, we found plenty to learn while assembling this volume. Donald Farr, Ford titles Group Editor, Automotive Performance Group, Petersen Publishing Company, gave us our first opportunities at Dobbs Publishing Group to get paid for having this hobby. Our former editor at Mustang Monthly and Super Ford, Larry Dobbs, founder of Dobbs Publishing Group, provided a work environment that encouraged investigations into the details and fun of restoring Mustangs.

The Product Analysis and Publications Department, Parts and Services Division, Ford Motor Company, granted us permission to extract and reformat valuable vintage information from the *Ford Car Master Parts and Accessories Catalog.* For this we are grateful. Much of the information in the huge catalog is difficult for the average hobbyist to decipher, but, as you read this, the massive volume may still be available. Send your inquiries regarding the availability and cost of the catalog (#FPS 7635-A&B) to B.U.D. Co., P.O. Box 27146, Detroit, MI 48227.

Several people offered direct support beyond the call of duty, especially in assembling the first edition: Barbara Fahrenholz and Debbie Miller patiently and meticulously entered chart data on their computers; Rob Reaser and Tom Wilson, our former associates at DPG, offered understanding and assistance; the late Jim Osborn of Jim Osborn Reproductions in Lawrenceville, Georgia (770-962-7556), provided the top notch decals and tags; Harvey Hester, Rob Reaser, Franette Abercrombie, and Adrian Hoff contributed expert darkroom work; Dinah George assisted greatly with computer knowledge; and our family members, Diane Davis and Sebastian Corcoran, endured months of strained schedules and late nights. Special thanks go to Mark Houlahan, Lyle Johnston, John Boisonault, and Dinah George for their assistance in compile the 1971–1973 addendum included in this second edition.

Many car owners, club members, automotive journalists, restorers, and parts vendors have helped to shape our ideas regarding the Mustang hobby. We have managed to learn from practically every hobbyist we've met over the past 20 years. The world of Mustangs has become a significant hobby and a fertile atmosphere for the founding of hundreds of small related businesses. We owe thanks to everyone we've met over the years, especially Bob Aliberto; Paul Newitt (author of the fine *GT/California Special Recognition Guide*); Brant Halterman of Virginia Classic Mustang, Inc., Broadway, Virginia; Steve Bennett and Bob Twist at California Mustang, Industry, California; Creed Stammel at C.J.'s Pony Parts, Harrisburg, Pennsylvania; Al Sedita of Classic Auto Air, Tampa, Florida; Bob Perkins of Perkins Restoration, Juneau, Wisconsin; Teresa Vickery; Steve Statham; Tom Daniel; Gregg Cly; Lauren and Paul Fix of Classic Tube, Lancaster, New York; Frank and Corky Reynolds; Bruce Weiss; and the many owners of the Mustangs photographed for this book. A special thanks must be offered to the officials and members of the Mustang Club of America for setting standards of restoration and judging that improve the automobiles and encourage the hobby participation of thousands of individuals around the world.

Tom Corcoran
Earl Davis

Introduction

The *Mustang 1964 1/2-1973 Restoration Guide* is intended to be a foundation for the disassembly, rebuilding, restoration, reassembly, research, authentication, and detailing of a top-notch collectible car. Throughout this volume can be found information, both major and trivial, to assist any hobbyist in locating, identifying, matching, and, if needed, swapping or substituting original Ford parts in the course of a restoration.

Authentication is always a challenge in the process of analyzing a 30-year-old car, and the 325 charts in this book will serve as a helpful guideline for both beginners and veterans. It is important to note that the first edition of this book covered model years 1964 1/2 through 1970. This second edition includes a sizable 1971-1973 addendum (Chapter 9) to provide information important to an expanding and deserving segment of the Mustang hobby. To make things easier for readers, the 1971-1973 chapter sections match the first eight original chapters. In many cases the charts and exploded views of the early chapters apply to the later Mustangs covered in the addendum. The authors have tried, in as many cases as possible, to refer the 1971-1973 reader to specific applicable charts and line drawings that appear in the first eight chapters. You may have to compare sections from the first and second editions in order to answer questions and identify parts, but you'll find we've done our utmost to provide a complete reference guide.

Throughout the book the reader will notice that some parts, especially exterior trim and components, will be identified by both a photograph and an exploded line drawing, while most suspension, drivetrain, and "out-of-sight" parts will be identified by a part number, dimensions, and a line drawing, plus further descriptions and applications where needed. Certain parts are difficult to photograph in a manner that communicates needed information; it is also the way the world of Mustangs works. If you are restoring a 1966 GT and need a gas cap, you should not need the gas cap part number to order one. Experienced Mustang parts vendors know what a 1966 GT gas cap looks like and, by referencing the photo in this book, you will too. If, however, you need to identify a part you already own, or need a particular attaching bracket for a power steering hose, both you and the vendor can eliminate confusion by having a part number handy. This book will provide such information.

Let us also mention that over the years many components listed in this book have been deleted and consolidated with similar and adaptable parts in order to streamline Ford's procurement, storage, and distribution process. Some part numbers listed may not represent the factory original pieces for vintage Mustangs and Shelbys. Nevertheless, the ability to identify any part included in the construction of a Mustang can simplify identification and communication in regard to parts purchases, swaps, trades, and shopping.

Please understand that the numbers shown in most exploded line drawings indicate unit base numbers only and cannot be presumed to be complete part numbers. For example 8005 is the base number for all Ford radiators. The prefix and suffix of the actual part number would identify the correct model, year, body type, engine type, application, and so on. Additionally, while Ford still manages to stock parts that are listed for vintage Mustangs, there is no guarantee that any or all of the parts listed throughout this book will be available through the Ford dealer network.

Finally, we must point out that the three assembly plants for Mustangs and Shelbys in San Jose, Dearborn, and Metuchen were often inconsistent in their procedures and parts suppliers. Also, there was no guarantee that the "correct" part–any number of brackets, for instance–was placed on a car during its original assembly. For example, if the supply of Mustang-correct air cleaners went dry, the plant did not shut down. Instead, compatible air cleaners from Fairlanes could have been installed over a period of days until the proper pieces were back in stock. Throughout this book, primarily in the exploded component views, you will see the word "typical." These drawings generally cover several models and styles and should not be used as absolute guidelines to authenticity.

The hobby of restoration is, by and large, an enjoyable pastime. The main point is to have fun, and we trust that this book will make it easier for you to fulfill your desire to own and drive a vintage Mustang. So, have fun, and don't quit. There is a light at the end of the tunnel.

Chapter 1

Data Plates and Decals

VIN/Data Plate Decoding System

The coding system for Mustang identification involves four distinct areas, each using alphanumeric series and direct codes.

The VIN format remained consistent through early Mustang production. The data plate took different forms over the years, with coded items such as paint and interior colors changing from year to year (as well as the style of the plates and labels). The body buck tag, used on some but not all Mustangs, combined data and intra-plant guidelines; and the broadcast sheets, single pieces of paper, also provided assembly-line instructions for many Mustangs.

We have yet to completely decipher all body buck tag and broadcast sheet codes, but the VIN and data plate system shown here is straightforward.

The charts for applicable exterior body colors is included in Chapter 2 on Exteriors; the chart for interior trim code is included in Chapter 3 on Interiors.

Note that 1964-1969 warranty plates (or data plates), located on the lock face of the driver's door, could have been shaded with a black or a gray background. In 1964 and 1965, a black plate indicated a vehicle painted with M30J Non-Acrylic Enamel; a gray plate indicated a vehicle painted with M32J Acrylic Enamel. From 1966 to 1969, a black warranty plate identified a vehicle painted with M32J Acrylic Enamel, and a gray plate indicated a vehicle painted with M30J Non-Acrylic Enamel.

Vehicle Identification Numbers

By Federal law, every vehicle produced or sold in the United States must have a Vehicle Identification Number, VIN. The Mustang's coded number indicated the model year, production plant, body style, engine code, and consecutive assembly-line unit number. Each of the three plants that produced Mustangs had its own series of consecutive unit numbers; a 1966 Mustang from the Metuchen plant could have a VIN ending in 112233, and a completely different Mustang made in Dearborn could have those same final six digits. The makeup of the VIN remained constant through the first generation of Mustang manufacture.

The first position on the left of the VIN is the final digit of the model year; the number 7 would indicate a 1967 Mustang. (Note that the number 5 could indicate either the 1964½ or the 1965 model.)

The second position from the left indicated the assembly plant code. Dearborn cars received an F; Metuchen cars a T and San Jose cars an R.

The next two numbers, the third and fourth positions from the left, provided the body serial code. For 1965 and 1966 models, 07 meant hardtop, 08 meant convertible, and 09 indicated a fastback. For 1967 through 1970, the numbers were 01 for the hardtop, 02 for the fastback, and 03 for a convertible. Additionally, in 1970 (through 1973), 04 indicated a Grandé and 05 meant a Mach 1.

The next letter, in the fifth position from the left, identified the engine in the car (see charts in this chapter and the Engines chapter).

The final six digits were the consecutive assembly line unit number.

To clarify this decoding system, analyze VIN 6T08A211150. It is a 1966 convertible built in Metuchen, with an A-code, or 289-4V, engine, and consecutive unit number 211150. A Mustang with VIN 0F05M157894 would be a 1970 Mach built in Dearborn with a 351-4V engine.

Engine Compartment Decals

One of the biggest problem areas for the final detailing of any Mustang or Shelby restoration is the correct selection and placement of engine compartment decals. The easiest and most effective way to determine the individual needs of any car is to view similar cars at a concours exhibition such as a Mustang Club of America or Shelby American Automobile Club national event.

Experienced restorers are another good source for information, and the decals shown on the following pages represent a major portion of the Mustang needs, but there is always a chance that your car requires additional markings for correctness. Our main source for these decals and stickers was Jim Osborn Reproductions, Inc., 101 Ridgecrest Drive, Lawrenceville, GA 30245, (404) 962-7556.

We recommend diligent research and careful confirmation before buying and applying any decal or application label. Bear in mind that the three Mustang assembly plants did things in different ways, even from year to year in the same plant, and consistency from car to car, from model to model, and from week to week was not a Ford Motor Company hallmark.

Mustang Warranty Plate Date Codes

From 1965 to 1969 an alphanumeric code above or below the word "Date" identified the day and month a vehicle was built. A code of 17K meant the 17th day of October. Beginning in 1970, the date code was shown in "10/70" format at the upper left corner of the warranty label.

Code	Month, First Production Year
A	January
B	February
C	March
D	April
E	May
F	June
G	July
H	August
J	September
K	October
L	November
M	December

Code	Month, Second Production Year
N	January
P	February
Q	March
R	April
S	May
T	June
U	July
V	August
W	September
X	October
Y	November
Z	December

Note: Confusion often clouds the date codes of the 1964½ and 1965 Mustangs. At the outset of Mustang production, in March 1964, the codes began with C, D, E, and so on. In January and February 1965, the letters A and B were used, but were followed by Q for March and the remaining second-year codes through August (V).

1965-1970 Mustang Body Style Codes

Code	Years	Body Style	Interior Designation
63A	1965-1968	Fastback	Standard Interior, Bucket Seats
	1969-1970	SportsRoof	Standard Interior, Bucket Seats
63B	1965-1968	Fastback	Luxury Interior, Bucket Seats
	1969-1970	SportsRoof	Luxury Interior, Bucket Seats
63C	1968	Fastback	Standard Interior, Bench Seat
	1969-1970	Mach 1	Mach 1 Interior, Bucket Seats
63D	1968	Fastback	Luxury Interior, Bench Seat
65A	1965-1970	Hardtop	Standard Interior, Bucket Seats
65B	1965-1970	Hardtop	Luxury Interior, Bucket Seats
65C	1965-1969	Hardtop	Standard Interior, Bench Seat
65D	1968-1969	Hardtop	Luxury Interior, Bench Seat
65E	1969-1970	Grandé	Grandé Interior, Bucket Seats
76A	1965-1970	Convertible	Standard Interior, Bucket Seats
76B	1965-1970	Convertible	Luxury Interior, Bucket Seats
76C	1965-1967	Convertible	Standard Interior, Bench Seat

1964-1970 Ford Motor Company DSO Codes

These two-digit numbers indicated District Sales Offices. Certain DSOs began and ceased operation in the middle of model years. Often a Mustang will have a DSO code that was not officially in use until the next year.

Code	Years	Location
11	1965-1970	Boston
12	1965-1966	Buffalo
13	1965-1970	New York
14	1965-1966	Pittsburgh
15	1965-1970	Newark
16	1967-1970	Philadelphia
17	1967-1970	Washington DC
21	1965-1970	Atlanta
22	1965-1970	Charlotte
23	1965-1966	Philadelphia
24	1965-1970	Jacksonville

Code	Years	Location
25	1965-1970	Richmond
26	1965-1966	Washington DC
27	1967-1968	Cincinnati
28	1967-1970	Louisville
31	1965-1966	Cincinnati
32	1965-1970	Cleveland
33	1965-1970	Detroit
34	1965-1968	Indianapolis
35	1965-1970	Lansing
36	1965-1966	Louisville
37	1967-1970	Buffalo
38	1967-1970	Pittsburgh
41	1965-1970	Chicago
42	1965-1968	Fargo
43	1965-1966	Rockford
43	1967-1970	Milwaukee
Code	Years	Location
44	1965-1970	Twin Cities
45	1965-1968	Davenport
46	1969-1970	Indianapolis
47	1969-1970	Cincinnati
51	1965-1970	Denver
52	1965-1968	Des Moines
53	1965-1970	Kansas City
54	1965-1970	Omaha
55	1965-1970	St. Louis
56	1969-1970	Davenport
61	1965-1970	Dallas
62	1965-1970	Houston
63	1965-1970	Memphis
64	1965-1970	New Orleans
65	1965-1970	Oklahoma City
71	1965-1970	Los Angeles
72	1965-1970	San Jose
73	1965-1970	Salt Lake City
74	1965-1970	Seattle
75	1967-1970	Phoenix
81	1965-1968	Ford of Canada
83	1965-1970	Government
84	1965-1970	Home Office Reserve
85	1965-1970	American Red Cross
89	1965-1970	Transportation Services
90-99	1965-1970	Export

1964-1970 Mustang Axle Codes

Code	Years	Axle Ratio	Remarks
0	1967	2.79:1	
1	1965-1967	3.00:1	
	1968	2.75:1	
	1969	2.50:1	
2	1965-1967	2.83:1	
	1968	2.79:1	
	1969-1970	2.75:1	
3	1965-1967	3.20:1	
	1969-1970	2.79:1	
4	1967	3.25:1	
	1968	2.83:1	
	1969-1970	2.80:1	
5	1965-1967	3.50:1	
	1968	3.00:1	
	1969-1970	2.83:1	
6	1965-1967	2.80:1	
	1968	3.20:1	
	1969-1970	3.00:1	
7	1968	3.25:1	
	1969-1970	3.10:1	
8	1965-1966	3.89:1	
	1968	3.50:1	
	1969-1970	3.20:1	
9	1965-1966	4.11:1	
	1968	3.10:1	
	1969-1970	3.25:1	
A	1965-1967	3.00:1	Limited Slip
	1969-1970	3.50:1	Limited Slip
B	1965-1966	2.83:1	Limited Slip
	1969-1970	3.07:1	Limited Slip
C	1965-1967	3.20:1	Limited Slip
	1969-1970	3.08:1	Limited Slip
D	1967	3.25:1	Limited Slip
	1969	3.91:1	Limited Slip
E	1965-1967	3.50:1	Limited Slip
	1968	3.00:1	Limited Slip
	1969	4.30:1	Limited Slip
F	1965-1966	2.80:1	Limited Slip
	1968	3.20:1	Limited Slip
	1970	2.33:1	Limited Slip
G	1968	3.25:1	Limited Slip
H	1965	3.89:1	Limited Slip
	1968	3.50:1	Limited Slip
I	1965	4.11:1	Limited Slip
J	1969	2.50:1	Limited Slip
K	1969-1970	2.75:1	Limited Slip
L	1969	2.79:1	Limited Slip
M	1969-1970	2.80:1	Limited Slip
N	1969	2.83:1	Limited Slip
O	1969-1970	3.00:1	Limited Slip
P	1969	3.10:1	Limited Slip
Q	1969	3.20:1	Limited Slip
R	1969-1970	3.25:1	Limited Slip
S	1969-1970	3.50:1	Limited Slip
T	1969	3.07:1	Limited Slip
U	1969	3.08:1	Limited Slip
V	1969-1970	3.91:1	Limited Slip
W	1969-1970	4.30:1	Limited Slip
X	1970	2.33:1	Limited Slip

1965-1970 Mustang Data Plate Transmission Codes

Code	Years	Transmission Type	Remarks
1	1965-1967	Three-speed Manual	2.77:1
1	1968-1970	Three-speed Manual	
3	1966-1967	Three-speed Manual	3.03:1
5	1965-1967	Four-speed Manual	
5	1968-1970	Four-speed Manual	2.78:1

Code	Years	Transmission Type	Remarks
6	1965-1966	C-4 Automatic	
6	1967-1970	Four-speed Manual	2.32:1 Close Ratio
U	1967-1970	C-6 Automatic	
W	1967-1970	C-4 Automatic	
X	1969-1970	FMX Automatic	

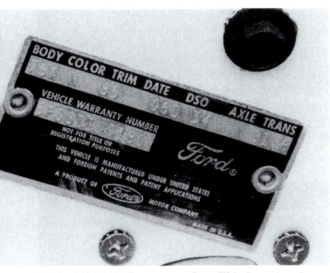

Typical 1964-1965 warranty plate. This data plate from a 1964¹/₂ Mustang tells us that the car is a standard interior convertible (76A), with Wimbledon White exterior paint (M); a red vinyl interior (85); a scheduled build date of April 6, 1964; destined for Indianapolis (DSO 34); with a 3.00:1 open rear end, C-4 automatic transmission (6), and a D-code 289ci four-barrel engine (the D in the 5th position of the eleven-character VIN).

This 1966 convertible's warranty plate was installed above the latch mechanism. This seeming inconsistency was not unusual on Ford production lines.

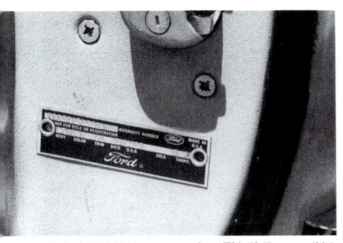

Typical 1966-1969 warranty plate. This 1967 convertible's driver's door data plate has engine code A in the fifth position of its eleven-character VIN. That indicates the 289ci four-barrel engine, and the car might be called an A-code car. Many Mustangs have had their driver's side door replaced, and are missing this plate. Reproductions can be obtained but for many such data is lost.

Using the data decoding system, a Mustang owner can determine that this K-code, Deluxe interior, Silver Frost 1966 fastback has a black vinyl interior, 3.50:1 limited slip rear end, and a four-speed manual transmission. Its scheduled build date was September 8, 1965, and its destination was Chicago.

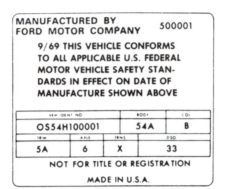

In 1970 Ford replaced the metal warranty plate with a Safety Standards Certification Label that included the VIN and applicable vehicle data codes. This example is typical of the labels in use in 1970 and later.

Prior to 1968, a Mustang's VIN was stamped atop the left front inner fender. Only in 1968, as shown here, did the official VIN appear on an aluminum plate riveted to the passenger-side upper dash adjacent to the windshield glass.

Mustang VIN Body Serial Codes, 1965-1970
These numerals are the third and fourth VIN positions.

Code	Years	Body Style
0 1	'67-'70	2-Door Hardtop
0 2	'67-'70	2-Door Fastback (SportsRoof, '69, '70)
0 3	'67-'70	2-Door Convertible
0 4	1970	2-Door Hardtop, Grande
0 5	1970	2-Door SportsRoof, Mach 1
0 6	n/a	Not used.
0 7	'65-'66	2-Door Hardtop
0 8	'65-'66	2-Door Convertible
0 9	'65-'66	2-Door Fastback

Beginning in 1969 the official stamped aluminum VIN plate was riveted inside the windshield in the driver's side of the Mustang.

Special warranty plates were created for the 1969-1970 Boss 429 and Shelby Mustangs. Ford noted that these cars were Special Performance Vehicles, and gave the Shelbys identifying DSO codes. Kar Kraft, the company that performed final assembly of the Boss 429, also affixed an identifying plate above the Special Performance Vehicle data plate.

This VIN plate, on a 1970 Boss 302, is located on the driver's side.

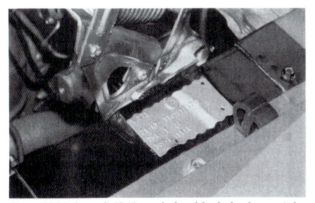

From 1964 through 1968, underhood body buck tags (also called build plates, build sheets, and broadcast sheets) were attached to all Metuchen-built cars, some Dearborn-built cars, and, it is thought, no San Jose-built cars. The tags provided instructions to assembly-line workers so that special options, special orders, and build exceptions could be noted on each vehicle. This body buck tag, on a 1967 convertible, indicates the assembly-line sequence number, beginning build date, VIN, exterior paint code, interior color code, convertible top color code, and a note to install clear rather than tinted glass. Metuchen tags, through 1967, generally had wavy edges; workers acknowledged their instructions by punching small holes of varying shapes in the tags.

In 1968 the body buck tags tended to have straight edges. According to best-guess decoding, this Metuchen-built fastback received power brakes, dual exhaust, and the GT package (including suspension). Because all 1968 Shelbys originated at Metuchen, most have this style body buck tag.

This Silver Frost 1966 convertible was built in Metuchen on February 18, 1966, with a black Deluxe interior, black top, A-code 289ci engine, remote mirror option, factory air conditioning, and an untinted windshield.

The ultimate prize for a restorer is a bona fide copy of a Mustang's original sales invoice or window sticker. Both show the vehicle's VIN, as well as the standard and optional features on that particular car.

FoMoCo

GENUINE ACCESSORIES

PERMANENT TYPE ANTI-FREEZE

(Do Not Over Fill Radiator)

PROTECTION _____°F

DATE _____

NUMBER OF QUARTS_____

𝕲𝖚𝖆𝖗𝖆𝖓𝖙𝖊𝖊𝖉 All Winter Anti-Freeze Protection

The Ford Dealer listed on the reverse side warrants that this cooling system is guaranteed for all winter anti-freeze protection as noted on dealership repair order provided that the owner of the vehicle maintains the cooling system in a water-tight condition. This warranty is given in lieu of all other warranties expressed or implied. The obligation of the dealer is limited to the installation of such additional Genuine FoMoCo Anti-Freeze as may be necessary to maintain the guaranteed degree indicated on top portion of this tag and to referenced repair order.

The 1964-1970 Mustang FoMoCo Antifreeze tag.

NEAR THE RADIATOR FILLER NECK

YOU'RE FULLY PROTECTED FOR TWO YEARS AGAINST ANTI-FREEZE LOSS

Ford Permanent Anti-Freeze is a top quality, highly concentrated formula with a long lasting, rust inhibiting agent. A minimum quantity provides protection down to the required temperature level.

For this reason it is possible to offer an exceptionally liberal guarantee which protects your anti-freeze investment...

IF THE ANTI-FREEZE LOSES ITS DEGREE OF PROTECTION DUE TO ANY DEFECT IN THE ANTI-FREEZE...

(SEE COMPLETE DETAILS ON REVERSE SIDE)

FORD FULL STRENGTH
TWO YEAR PERMANENT ANTI-FREEZE

has been added to the cooling system of this vehicle as follows (see Guarantee on other side):

No. OF QUARTS_____PROTECTION_____°F

OWNER'S NAME_____

ADDRESS_____

MODEL_____

CAR MILEAGE_____

The 1967-1972 Mustang Ford Antifreeze tag.

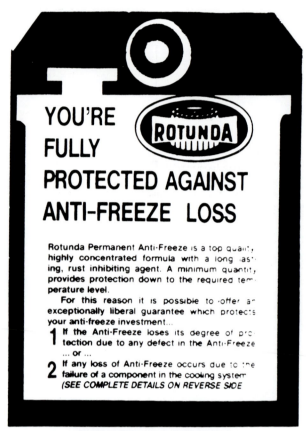

YOU'RE FULLY PROTECTED AGAINST ANTI-FREEZE LOSS

ROTUNDA

Rotunda Permanent Anti-Freeze is a top quality, highly concentrated formula with a long lasting, rust inhibiting agent. A minimum quantity provides protection down to the required temperature level.

For this reason it is possible to offer an exceptionally liberal guarantee which protects your anti-freeze investment...

1 If the Anti-Freeze loses its degree of protection due to any defect in the Anti-Freeze ... or ...

2 If any loss of Anti-Freeze occurs due to the failure of a component in the cooling system *(SEE COMPLETE DETAILS ON REVERSE SIDE)*

ROTUNDA FULL STRENGTH
ALL-WINTER PERMANENT ANTI-FREEZE

has been added to the cooling system of this vehicle as follows (see Guarantee on other side):

No. OF QUARTS_____PROTECTION_____

OWNER'S NAME_____ _____

ADDRESS_____

MODEL_____

CAR MILEAGE_____ DATE_____

The 1964-1966 Mustang Rotunda Antifreeze tag.

WHEN REFUELING: · Check engine oil ONLY add same type oil as recommended under oil change ONCE A MONTH: · Check battery fluid level. Check coolant-antifreeze level. DO NOT OVERFILL. Fill only to 1" below bottom of filler neck at operating temperature. ONLY add same type antifreeze as that used for coolant change.	EVERY 6000 MILES OR 6 MONTHS: · Change oil and oil filter. ONLY use 10W-30 GRADE OIL (for temperatures above -10°F.) labeled. "Meets or exceeds car makers requirements sequence tested M.S." Use ROTUNDA Oil Filter for best service.
ANTI-FREEZE-COOLANT: · Change every 36,000 miles or 2 years. Cooling system originally protected to -35°F. · ROTUNDA permanent antifreeze mixed 50-50 with water gives -35°F. protection.	CRANKCASE VENTILATION SYSTEM: · Service periodically in accordance with directions in the Owner's Manual.

ALWAYS USE GENUINE FORD MOTOR COMPANY REPLACEMENT PARTS THAT BEAR THESE INSIGNIA

ROTUNDA **FoMoCo** ⊕ **AUTOLITE**

FOR COMPLETE SERVICE RECOMMENDATIONS SEE OWNER'S MANUAL

The 1965-1966 Mustang Service Specifications decal.

The 1967-1969 Mustang Service Specifications decal.

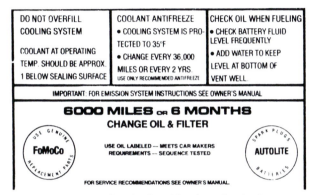

The 1964 Mustang Service Specifications decal (chrome).

The 1970 Mustang Service Specifications decal.

IMPORTANT
This engine equipped with Autolite parts

Specify Autolite

AIR CLEANER NO. C90Z-9600-H ELEMENT NO. FA41

The 1969 Mustang Boss 302 and 428CJ non-Ram Air Autolite Parts Air Cleaner decal.

IMPORTANT
This engine equipped with Autolite parts

Specify Autolite

AIR CLEANER NO. C9AF-9600-F ELEMENT NO. FA41

The 1969-1970 Mustang 428CJ Ram Air Autolite Parts Air Cleaner decal.

IMPORTANT
This engine equipped with Autolite parts

Specify Autolite

AIR CLEANER NO. DOZE-9600-N ELEMENT NO. C7SF-9601-A

The 1970 Mustang Boss 302 Autolite Parts Air Cleaner decal.

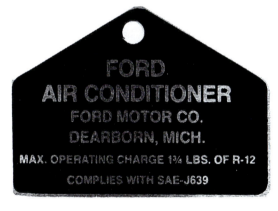

The 1964-1970 Mustang Air Conditioner Compressor Aluminum tag.

The 1968-1975 Mustang Autolite Parts Air Cleaner decal.

The 1966 Mustang Disc Brake Master Cylinder decal.

CAUTION-FAN

The 1968-1969 Mustang Caution Fan decal.

CRANKCASE VENTILATION SYSTEM

THE CRANKCASE VENTILATION SYSTEM ON THIS ENGINE SHOULD BE SERVICED PERIODICALLY IN ACCORDANCE WITH INSTRUCTIONS IN OWNER'S MANUAL

SEE YOUR DEALER

The 1964-1966 Mustang Crankcase Vent Air Cleaner decal.

IMPORTANT: COOLING SYSTEM IS PROTECTED FOR -35°F. FOR PROTECTION BELOW -35°F ADD ROTUNDA PERMANENT TYPE ANTI-FREEZE. FOR YEAR AROUND PROTECTION USE A 50% MIXTURE OF ROTUNDA ANTI-FREEZE AND WATER FOR ADDITIONAL FILL.

The 1964-1966 Mustang Cooling System Info decal.

The 1964-1966 Mustang Oil Filler Cap decal.

Ford 6000 Mile or 6 Month Lube sticker.

WARNING

YOUR NEW CAR IS EQUIPPED WITH FRONT DISC BRAKES. RIDING WITH A FOOT RESTING ON THE BRAKE PEDAL CAN RESULT IN RAPID LINING WEAR, POSSIBLE DAMAGE TO THE BRAKES, AND REDUCED FUEL ECONOMY.

DEALER: LEAVE TAG IN PLACE AND CALL TO ATTENTION OF PURCHASER.

C5SA-2B182-A   Printed in U.S.A.

The 1965 Mustang Disc Brake Warning tag (for interior of car).

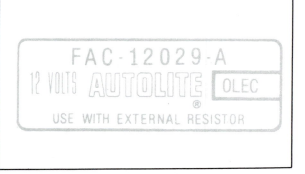

The 1965-1972 Mustang Coil decal.

The 1964 Mustang Coil decal.

The 1965-1966 Mustang non-Air Conditioning Voltage Regulator decal.

The 1964 Mustang non-Air Conditioning Voltage Regulator decal.

The 1968-early 1970 Mustang non-Air Conditioning Voltage Regulator decal.

The 1965-1966 Mustang w/ Air Conditioning Voltage Regulator decal.

The 1964 Mustang w/ Air Conditioning Voltage Regulator decal.

The 1967 Voltage Regulator decal.

The 1968-1971 Mustang Hi-Performance Voltage Regulator decal.

1968-early 1970 Mustang w/ Air Conditioning Voltage Regulator decal.

The 1964-1968 Mustang Autolite Spark Plug Air Cleaner decal.

The 1964-1966 Mustang 6-Cylinder Autolite Spark Plug Air Cleaner decal.

The 1967 Mustang Disc Brake Master Cylinder decal (chrome).

The 1964-1972 Mustang Autolite Sta-Ful Battery tag.

The 1969-1970 Mustang Boss 429 Valve Cover decal.

The 1969-1970 Mustang Boss 302 Valve Cover decal.

The 1965-1970 Shelby Accessory Ventra-Flow Air Cleaner decal.

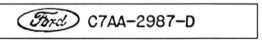

The 1967-1970 Mustang Air Conditioner Clutch decal.

The 1967 Mustang Air Cleaner Part Number decal (typical).

The 1964-1973 Mustang Air Cleaner front decal.

The 1964-1966 Mustang Air Conditioner Dryer decal.

The 1967-1968 Mustang Air Conditioner Dryer decal.

The 1969 Mustang Air Conditioner Dryer decal.

The 1970 Mustang Air Conditioner Dryer decal.

BATTERY OK

CHARGE READING	DATE	BADGE

The 1964-1966 Battery Test OK decal (for inner fender).

The 1964¹/₂ Mustang 170ci Air Cleaner decal.

The 1965-1968 Mustang 200ci Air Cleaner decal.

The 1968-1969 Mustang 250ci Air Cleaner decal.

The 1966 Mustang Sprint 200 Air Cleaner decal.

The 1967-1968 Mustang Sports Sprint Air Cleaner decal.

The 1964¹/₂ Mustang 260ci Air Cleaner decal.

The 1967-1968 Mustang 289ci Air Cleaner decal (red/black checks).

The 1965-1966 Mustang 289ci Air Cleaner decal (white/black checks).

The 1967 Mustang 289-4V Air Cleaner decal (red/black checks).

The 1965-1966 Mustang 289-4V Air Cleaner decal (white/black checks).

The 1964-1967 Mustang 289 High Performance Air Cleaner decal.

The 1968-1969 Mustang 302 High Performance Air Cleaner decal.

The 1967-1968 Mustang 390 High Performance Air Cleaner decal.

The 1968-1969 Mustang 302-2V Air Cleaner decal.

The 1968-1969 Mustang 302-4V Premium Fuel Air Cleaner decal.

The 1969 Mustang 428-4V Premium Fuel Air Cleaner decal.

The 1969 Mustang 351-2V Air Cleaner decal.

The 1968 Mustang 428-4V Premium Fuel Air Cleaner decal.

The 1969 Mustang 351-4V Premium Fuel Air Cleaner decal.

The 1967 Shelby Cobra Powered by Ford Air Cleaner decal.

The 1967-1969 Mustang 390-4V Premium Fuel Air Cleaner decal.

The 1970 Mustang 250ci Air Cleaner decal.

The 1970 Mustang 302-2V Regular Fuel Air Cleaner decal.

The 1970 Mustang 302-4V Air Cleaner decal.

The 1970 Mustang Boss 302 Air Cleaner decal (green).

The 1969 Mustang Boss 302 Air Cleaner decal (orange).

The 1970 Mustang 351-4V Premium Fuel Air Cleaner decal.

The 1970 Mustang 351-2V Regular Fuel Air Cleaner
decal.

The 1969 Shelby 351ci Ram Air Air Cleaner decal.

The 1969-1970 Shelby 428ci Cobra Jet Ram Air Air
Cleaner decal.

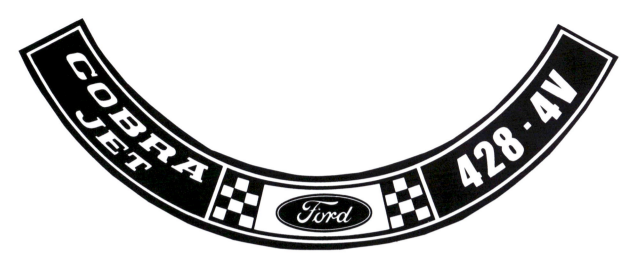

The 1969-1970 Mustang 428ci Cobra Jet Air Cleaner decal.

Chapter 2

Exterior

For many years experts and devotees have tried to analyze the appeal and success of the Ford Mustang. They also have tried to define the reasons for its long-term popularity. After all the discussion is over, one word applies: Style.

It is amazing that the unibody structure of the Mustang sprouted from the Ford Falcon, a somewhat staid design of the late 1950s. In the interest of reducing development costs for the Mustang, Ford engineers built upon the existing Falcon platform and drivetrain. Fortunately, the exterior styling did not suffer for those mechanical requirements. Even the interior used only a few Falcon items such as the door handles, instrument cluster, and heater box.

Mustang Style came from several years of development, effective judging of consumer demographics, a legendary intra-company design contest, the edicts of Lee Iacocca, and the known appeal of the long-hood, short-deck early Thunderbirds. The Mustang was to have a rear seat, sporty performance, and a lively appearance. Ford succeeded beyond its most optimistic sales forecasts, and the public took the Mustang to heart.

Looking back through the early years, Mustang design clusters into three groups: the 1964½ through 1966 models, the 1967 and 1968 models, and the 1969 and 1970 Mustangs. Those were the days when some form of annual design change came out of Detroit but, looking back to the end of World War II, such two- and three-year clusters were common at Ford.

Many of the exterior trim items depicted in this chapter will fall into those three groupings. Antenna bases, rearview mirrors, and bumpers will not differ in the 1967-1968 group, for instance, but most exterior badges and trim, the wheelcovers, and the grilles will allow a viewer to differentiate between each model year.

Introducing the Mustang

Even though the basic concept and design of the Mustang was well established prior to its April 1964 introduction, the 1964½ model was a hurried attempt to combine older components with fresh styling and to get a product out the door quickly. For that reason, many Falcon components are found on the earliest Mustangs. A number of those parts were phased out during the changeover to the 1965 Mustang (along with the introduction of the alternator and several engine changes), but many parts were used into the 1965 model year. These minor carryovers represented assembly-line economies: existing stock was used until supplies ran out, then newer components were phased into the production process. Many changes were due to the Mustang's ability to sell and to achieve its own image. Once its success seemed inevitable, designers felt compelled to make the Mustang even more distinctive.

Several exterior identifiers can help an observer spot a 1964½ Mustang. The top of the grille surround falls off at a 45-degree angle before angling another 45 degrees downward toward the sculptured louvers. Where the hood meets this angle, its edge also is beveled. An obvious carryover from the Falcon was the 13in wheel. A four-ply 6.50x13 tire came standard on all six-cylinder Mustangs plus all eight-cylinder models without the optional handling package (except for air-conditioned cars which received a four-ply 7.00x13 tire). Mustangs with the handling package received 6.50x14 tires during 1964½ production or, optionally, 5.90x15s. The 15in wheel was phased out in late August 1964. This standard wheelcover with its optional three-bladed spinner was offered for 13in wheels until the mid-summer 1964 changeover to the 1965 Mustang. A nearly identical wheelcover with spinner continued in the 14in size throughout the 1965 model year.

When the Mustang was introduced in April 1964, Ford felt the need to tie the Mustang name to the manufacturer. Hence the hood letters F-O-R-D, and a number of other smaller components which related both to Falcons and to full-size Fords. By 1967 the Mustang had attained its own (strong) identity, and there was no need for the word Ford trim on the hood.

The marketing of the Ford Mustang has been long regarded as a public relations masterpiece. America was teased about the product for weeks, then the print and broadcast media became saturated with "lifestyle" advertising and aggressive promotion. Dealership point-of-sale efforts and word of mouth added impetus to the craze. The week that Ford introduced the Mustang at the 1964 World's Fair in New York, both *Time* and *Newsweek* featured the new car in cover stories. The Mustang looked like no other American automobile. It was one of the first cars to show body color (on the valances) below the bumpers, and the effect made the car seem lower and more sporty. Ford's tremendous promotional campaign was boosted by the naming of the Mustang as the official 1964 Indianapolis 500 Pace Car.

Less than one month after the introduction of the Mustang, Ford offered their 289ci 271hp four-barrel V-8 engine. The Hi-Po option set the tone for the Mustang's performance image, and the marque was off and running.

1964½-1965 Mustang Exterior Paint Codes

Data Code	Color Name
A	Raven Black
B*	Pagoda Green
D	Dynasty Green
F*	Guardsman Blue
H	Caspian Blue
J	Rangoon Red
K	Silver Smoke Grey
M	Wimbledon White
P	Prairie Bronze
S*	Cascade Green
U	Sunlight Yellow
X	Vintage Burgundy
Y*	Skylight Blue
Z*	Chantilly Beige
3	Poppy Red
5	Twilight Turquoise
7	Phœnician Yellow

Colors marked with an asterisk were offered only on 1964½ Mustangs. All other colors carried through the 1965 model year.

1965 Mustang Exterior Paint Codes

Data Code	Name of Color
A	Raven Black

Data Code	Name of Color
B	Midnight Turquoise
C	Honey Gold
D	Dynasty Green
H	Caspian Blue
I	Champagne Beige
J	Rangoon Red
K	Silver Smoke Grey
M	Wimbledon White
O	Tropical Turquoise
P	Prairie Bronze
R	Ivy Green
V	Sunlight Yellow
X	Vintage Burgundy
Y	Silver Blue
3	Poppy Red

1966 Mustang Exterior Paint Codes

Data Code	Name of Color
A	Raven Black
F	Arcadian Blue
H	Sahara Beige
K	Nightmist Blue
M	Wimbledon White
P	Antique Bronze
R	Ivy Green
T	Candyapple Red
U	Tahoe Turquoise
V	Emberglo
X	Vintage Burgundy
Y	Silver Blue
Z	Sauterne Gold
4	Silver Frost
5	Signalflare Red
8	Springtime Yellow

1966 Special Order Colors (No codes)
Medium Palomino Metallic
Medium Silver Metallic
Ivy Green Metallic
Tahoe Turquoise Metallic
Maroon Metallic
Silver Blue Metallic
Sauterne Gold Metallic
Light Beige

1967 Mustang Exterior Paint Codes

Data Code	Name of Color
A	Raven Black
B	Frost Turquoise
D	Acapulco Blue
E	Beige Mist
H	Arcadian Blue
I	Lime Gold
K	Nightmist Blue
M	Wimbledon White
N	Diamond Blue

Data Code	Name of Color
Q	Brittany Blue
S	Dusk Rose
T	Candyapple Red
V	Burnt Amber
W	Clearwater Aqua
X	Vintage Burgundy
Y	Dark Moss Green
Z	Sauterne Gold
4	Silver Frost
6	Pebble Beige
8	Springtime Yellow

1967 Special Order Colors (No codes)
Playboy Pink
Anniversary Gold
Columbine Blue
Aspen Gold
Blue Bonnet
Timberline Green
Lavender
Bright Red

1968 Mustang Exterior Paint Codes

Data Code	Name of Color
A	Raven Black
B	Royal Maroon
D	Acapulco Blue
F	Gulfstream Aqua

The 1964¹/₂ Mustang gas caps were not attached with a wire bail. From the introduction of the 1965 Mustangs, the bail was standard.

Data Code	Name of Color
I	Lime Gold
M	Wimbledon White
N	Diamond Blue
O	Seafoam Green
Q	Brittany Blue
R	Highland Green
T	Candyapple Red
U	Tahoe Turquoise
W	Meadowlark Yellow
X	Presidential Blue
Y	Sunlit Gold
6	Pebble Beige

1969 Mustang Exterior Paint Codes

Data Code	Name of Color
A	Raven Black
B	Royal Maroon
C	Black Jade
D	Pastel Grey
D	Acapulco Blue*
E	Aztec Aqua
F	Gulfstream Aqua
I	Lime Gold
M	Wimbledon White
P	Winter Blue
S	Champagne Gold
T	Candyapple Red
W	Meadowlark Yellow
Y	Indian Fire
2	New Lime
4	Silver Jade
6	Acapulco Blue*

Note: All Mach 1 Color Codes ending in 5 denote flat black hood paint.

*Acapulco Blue is shown as both code D and code 6 on two conflicting vintage Ford reference charts.

1970 Mustang Exterior Paint Codes

Data Code	Name of Color
A	Black
C	Dark Ivy Green Metallic
D	Bright Yellow
G	Medium Lime Metallic
J	Grabber Blue
K	Bright Gold Metallic
M	White
N	Pastel Blue
Q	Medium Blue Metallic
S	Medium Gold Metallic
T	Red
U	Grabber Orange
Z	Grabber Green
1	Calypso Coral
2	Light Ivy Yellow
6	Bright Blue Metallic

The 1964¹/₂ Mustang nameplate that adorned the lower front fenders measured 4³/₈in long. It was lengthened to 5in at the beginning of the 1965 model year.

It was common for components and options such as this version of the spinner wire wheelcover to be shared by other Ford models.

Four out of the available six full disc wheelcovers installed on 1964¹/₂ Mustangs were manufactured in both 13in and 14in sizes, including this rare base cover with spinner.

Because it was a completely new model and had barely achieved its own identity, the 1964¹/₂ Mustang was adorned with Ford corporate insignias and logos. For example these early spinner wire wheelcovers bore the vintage Ford crest in their centers.

A distinctive feature indicating a true 1964¹/₂ Mustang is this bevel on both sides of the grille opening. The bevel matches the contour of the unique 1964¹/₂ hood.

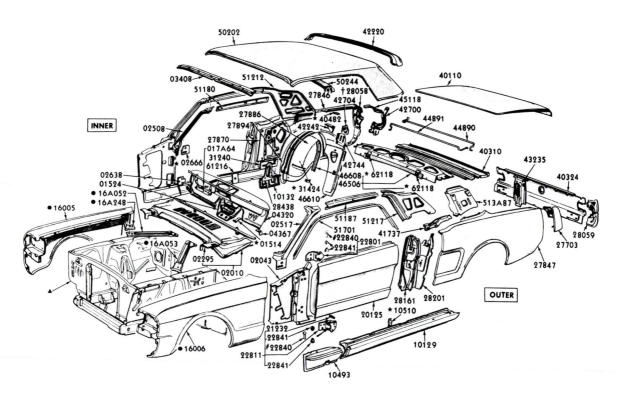

The 1965-1966 Mustang hardtop upper-body structural components and sheet-metal panels.

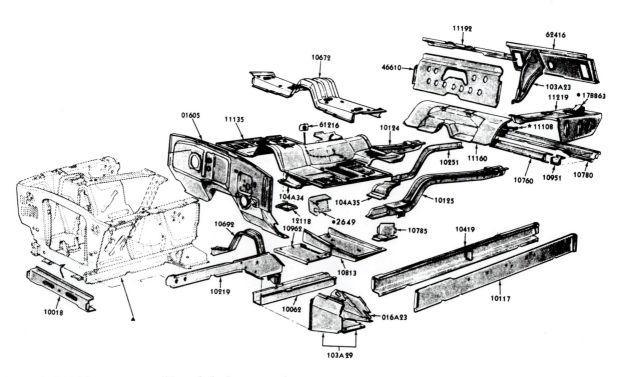

The 1965-1966 Mustang convertible underbody structural components and sheet-metal panels.

28

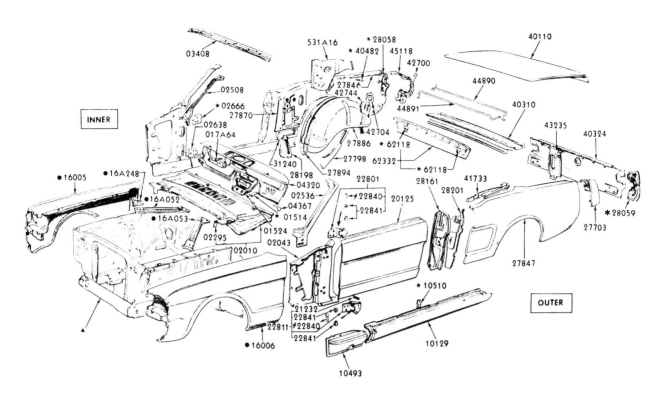

The 1965-1966 Mustang convertible upper sheet-metal panels and structural members.

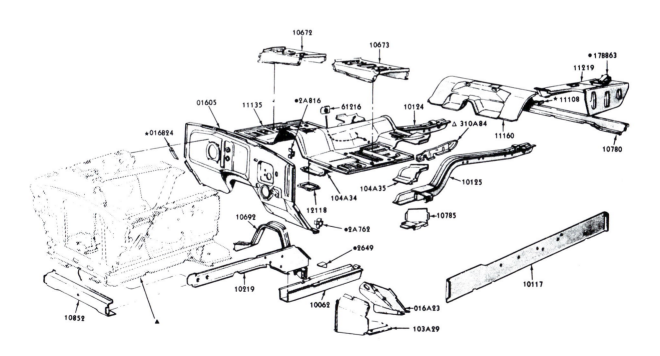

The 1967-1970 Mustang SportsRoof and 1967-1969 Mustang hardtop underbody sheet-metal panels and structural members.

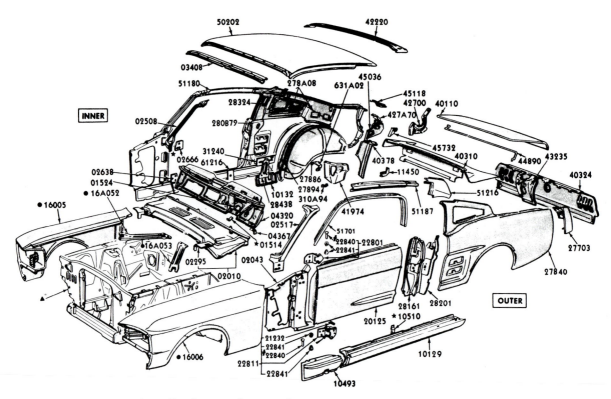

The 1967-1968 Mustang SportsRoof upper-sheet-metal panels and structural members.

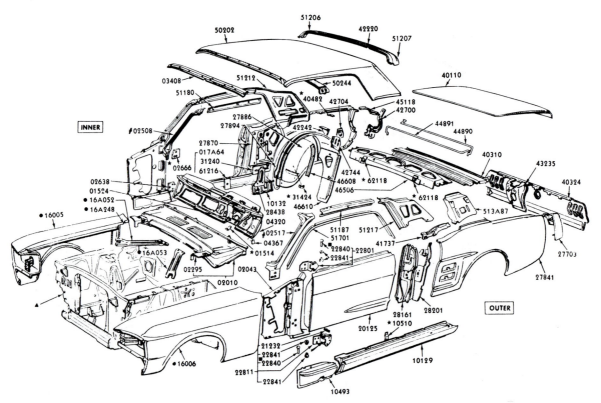

The 1967-1968 Mustang hardtop upper-sheet-metal panels and structural members.

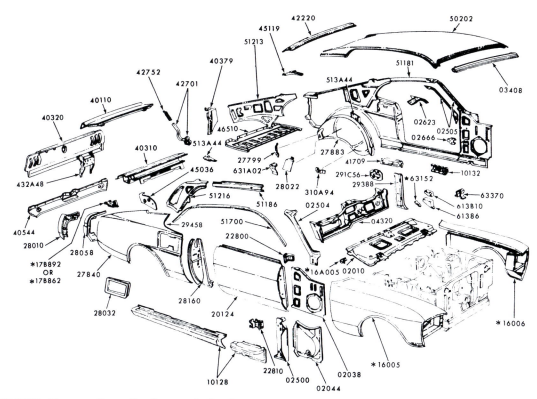

The 1969-1970 Mustang SportsRoof upper-body sheet-metal panels and structural members.

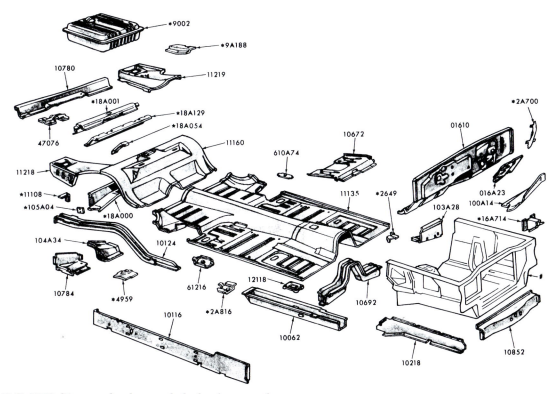

The 1969-1970 Mustang hardtop underbody sheet-metal panels and structural members.

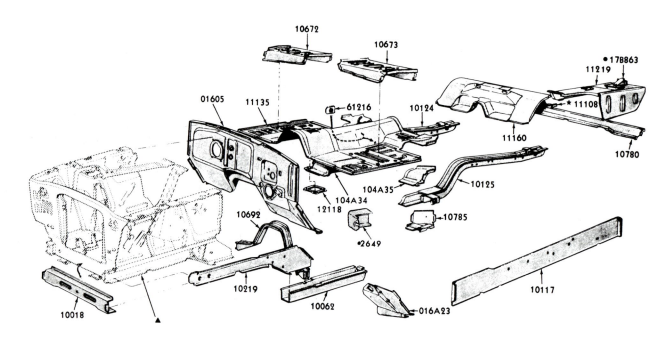

The 1965-1966 Mustang SportsRoof and hardtop under-body structural components and panels.

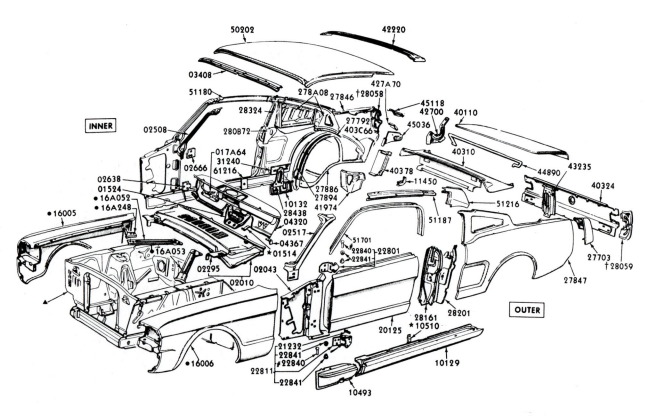

The 1965-1966 Mustang SportsRoof upper-body structural components and sheet-metal panels.

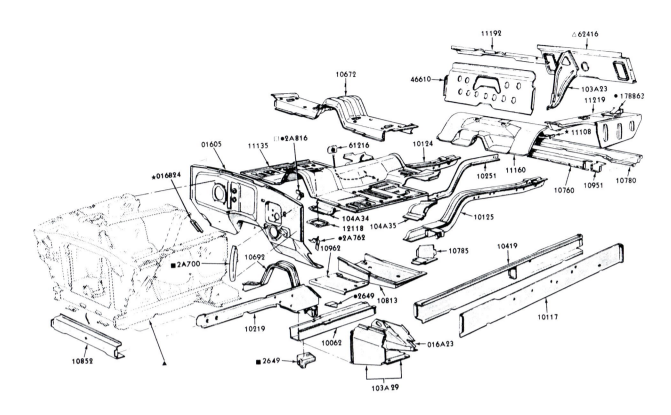

The 1967-1968 Mustang convertible underbody sheet-metal panels and structural members.

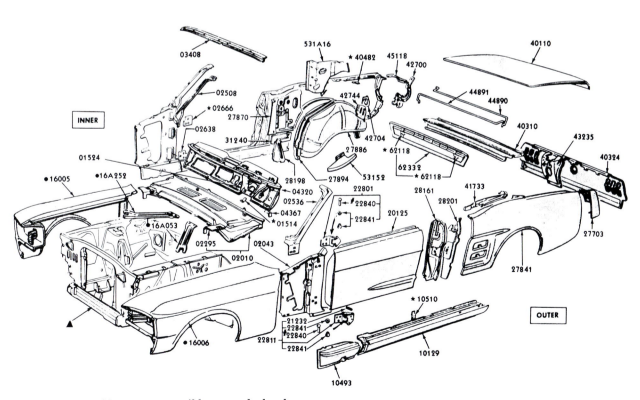

The 1967-1968 Mustang convertible upper-body sheet-metal panels and structural members.

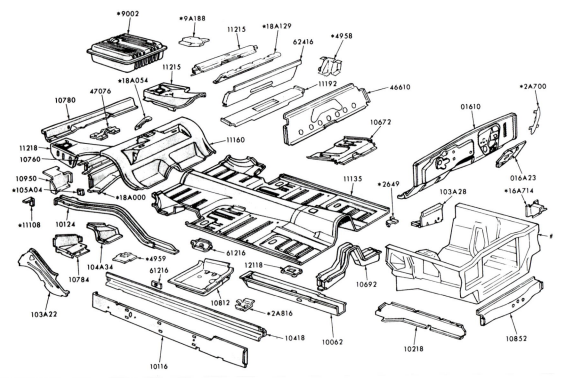

*The 1969-1970 Mustang convertible underbody sheet-metal
panels and structural members.*

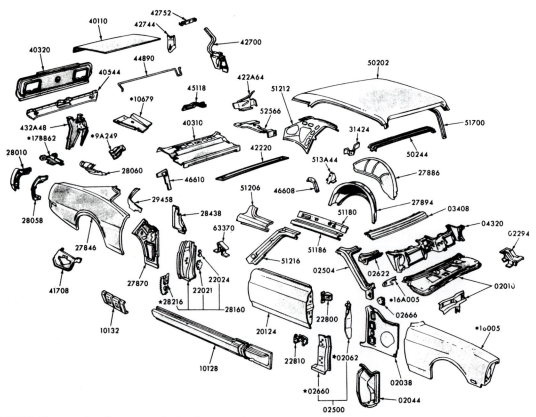

*The 1969-1970 Mustang hardtop upper-body sheet-metal
panels and structural members.*

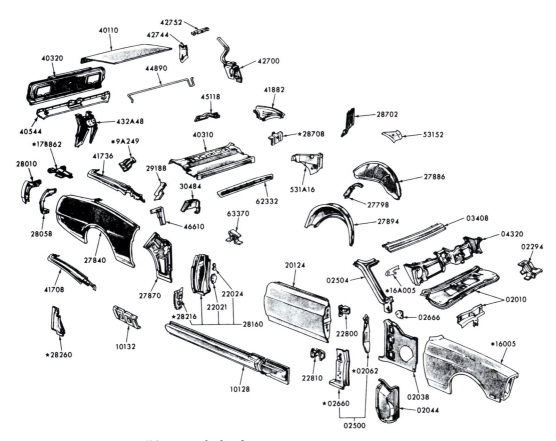

The 1969-1970 Mustang convertible upper-body sheet-metal panels and structural members.

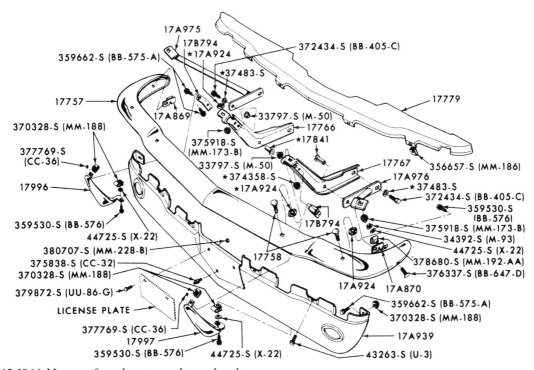

The 1965-1966 Mustang front bumper, valance, brackets, and related mounting hardware.

*The standard 1965 grille with argent-colored honeycomb
screen and conventional running horse and corral.*

*The 1965 GT grille had blacked-out screen and foglamps at
the ends of the bars.*

The 1966 GT grille uses the 1965 light bar on a blacked-out screen.

The 1966 grille loses the bars extending from the corral and replaces the screen with horizontal chrome strips.

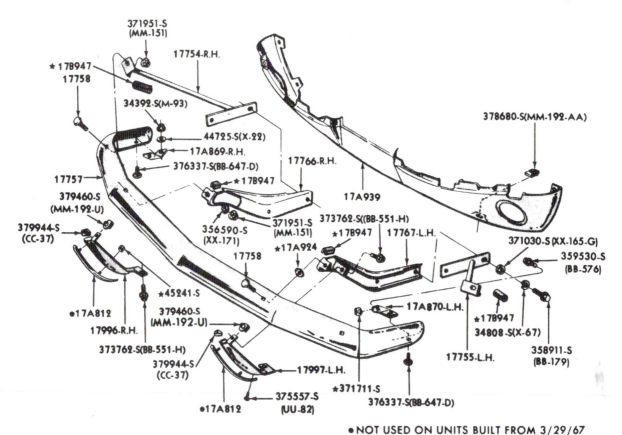

371951-S
(MM-151)

★17B947
17758

17754-R.H.

34392-S(M-93)

44725-S(X-22)

17A869-R.H.

376337-S(BB-647-D)

17757

379460-S
(MM-192-U)

379944-S
(CC-37)

●17A812

17996-R.H.

373762-S(BB-551-H)

379944-S
(CC-37)

●17A812

375557-S
(UU-82)

★45241-S

379460-S
(MM-192-U)

17758

356590-S
(XX-171)

371951-S
(MM-151)

★17B947

★17A924

17766-R.H.

17A939

373762-S((BB-551-H)

★17B947

17767-L.H.

17A870-L.H.

17997-L.H.

★371711-S

376337-S(BB-647-D)

378680-S(MM-192-AA)

371030-S(XX-165-G)

359530-S
(BB-576)

★17B947

34808-S(X-67)

17755-L.H.

358911-S
(BB-179)

●NOT USED ON UNITS BUILT FROM 3/29/67

*The 1967-1968 Mustang front bumper, valance, brackets,
and related mounting hardware.*

*As in previous years, the 1967 Mustang GT grille includes a
blacked-out screen and foglamps.*

The standard 1967 Mustang grille reinstates the horizontal bars.

A 1968 GT California Special sets a pair of rectangular foglamps in front of a plain blacked-out screen.

The 1968 Mustang GT grille simply adds foglamps to a
standard grille.

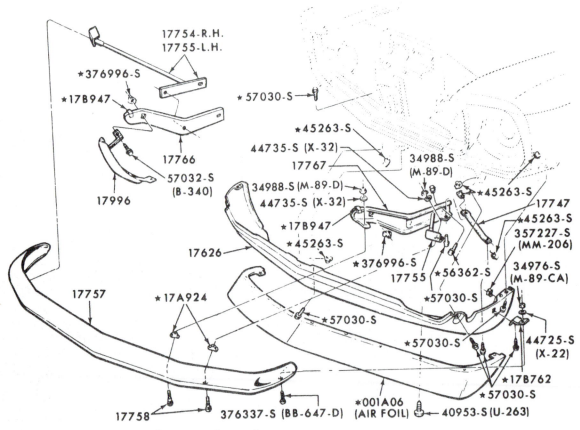

17754-R.H.
17755-L.H.
★376996-S
★17B947
★57030-S
17766
★45263-S
57032-S
(B-340)
44735-S (X-32)
17996
17767
34988-S
(M-89-D)
34988-S (M-89-D)
★45263-S
44735-S (X-32)
17747
★17B947
★45263-S
17626
★45263-S
357227-S
(MM-206)
★376996-S
34976-S
(M-89-CA)
17757
17755
★56362-S
★17A924
★57030-S
★57030-S
44725-S
(X-22)
★57030-S
★57030-S
17758
★17B762
★57030-S
376337-S (BB-647-D)
★001A06
(AIR FOIL)
40953-S (U-263)

The 1969-1970 Mustang front bumper, valance, front
spoiler, and attaching hardware.

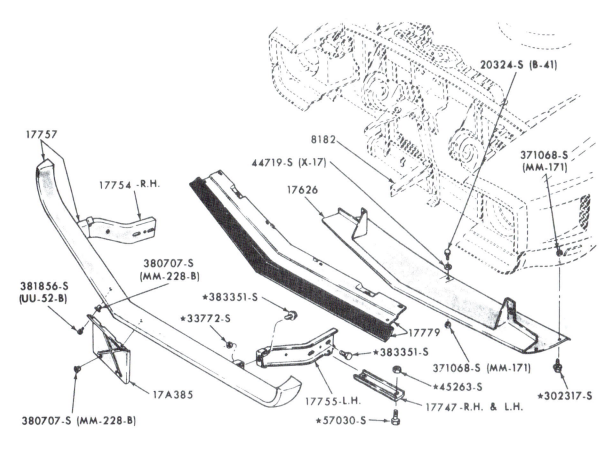

17757

17754 -R.H.

380707-S
(MM-228-B)

381856-S
(UU-52-B)

★383351-S

★33772-S

17A385

380707-S (MM-228-B)

★57030-S

17755-L.H.

17747-R.H. & L.H.

★45263-S

★383351-S

17779

371068-S (MM-171)

★302317-S

8182

44719-S (X-17)

17626

20324-S (B-41)

371068-S
(MM-171)

The 1969-1970 Shelby Mustang front bumper, valance, and attaching hardware.

The 1969 grille emblem, inner headlight, and chrome grille trim.

The 1970 Mustang headlight door with fake scoop.

The running horse and tri-colored bar emblem is located at the center of the grille in 1970.

The grille emblem was deleted from the 1970 Mach 1 grille, and replaced by two outboard sport lamps.

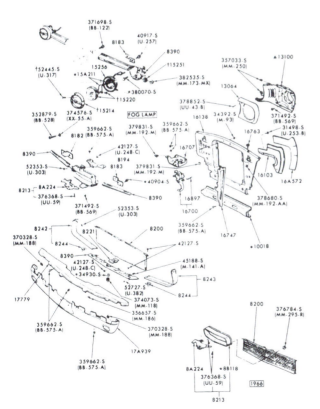

The 1965-1966 Mustang grille, stone shield, lower valance, headlight bucket, radiator-core support, GT light bar, and related hardware.

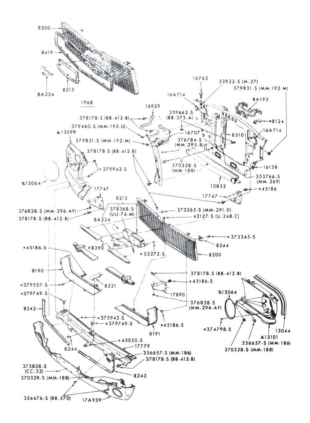

The 1967-1968 Mustang grille, fender extension, valance, trim, radiator-core support, and attaching hardware.

43

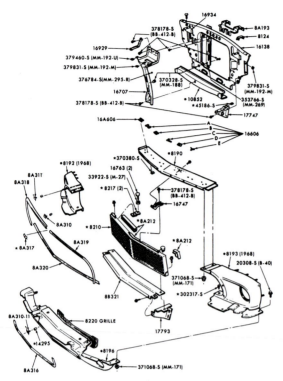

The 1967-1968 Shelby Mustang grille, fender extension, valance, header panel, radiator-core support, and attaching hardware.

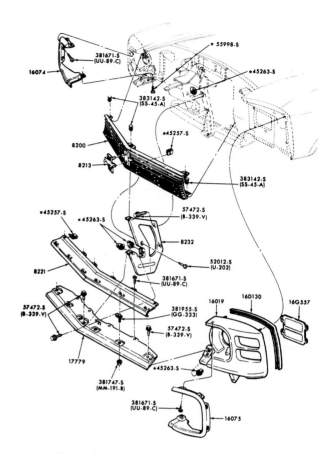

The 1970 Mustang grille, fender extension, stone shield, trim, and related hardware.

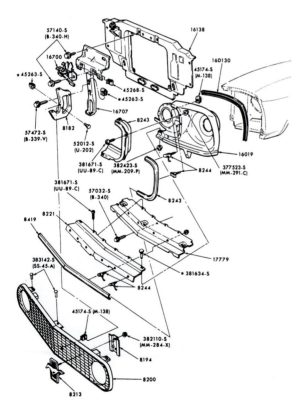

The 1969 Mustang grille, headlight bucket, stone shield, hood latch, radiator-core support, and related hardware.

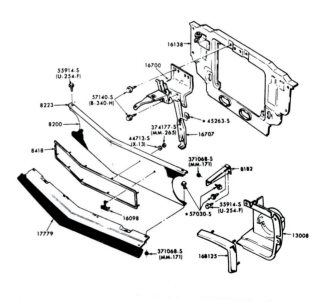

The 1969-1970 Shelby Mustang grille, stone shield, headlight bucket, hood latch, radiator-core support, and attaching hardware.

44

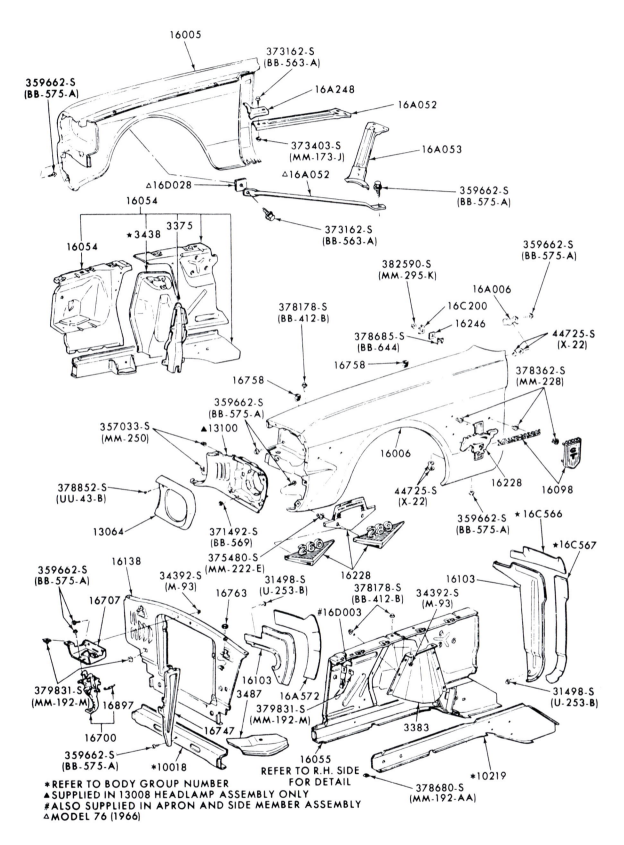

16005

373162-S
(BB-563-A)

359662-S
(BB-575-A)

16A248

16A052

373403-S
(MM-173-J)

16A053

△16D028

△16A052

359662-S
(BB-575-A)

16054

16054 ★3438 3375

373162-S
(BB-563-A)

382590-S
(MM-295-K)

359662-S
(BB-575-A)

16A006

16C200

16246

44725-S
(X-22)

378178-S
(BB-412-B)

378685-S
(BB-644)

16758

16758

378362-S
(MM-228)

359662-S
(BB-575-A)

357033-S
(MM-250)

▲13100

16006

16228

16098

378852-S
(UU-43-B)

44725-S
(X-22)

359662-S
(BB-575-A)

★16C566

13064

371492-S
(BB-569)

375480-S
(MM-222-E)

260

289

★16C567

16228

16103

16138

359662-S
(BB-575-A)

34392-S
(M-93)

16763

31498-S
(U-253-B)

378178-S
(BB-412-B)

34392-S
(M-93)

16707

16103

31498-S
(U-253-B)

#16D003

379831-S
(MM-192-M)

16897

16103

3487

16A572

379831-S
(MM-192-M)

3383

16700

16747

16055

*10219

359662-S
(BB-575-A)

*10018

REFER TO R.H. SIDE
FOR DETAIL

378680-S
(MM-192-AA)

★REFER TO BODY GROUP NUMBER
▲SUPPLIED IN 13008 HEADLAMP ASSEMBLY ONLY
#ALSO SUPPLIED IN APRON AND SIDE MEMBER ASSEMBLY
△MODEL 76 (1966)

The 1965-1966 Mustang front fenders, aprons, and related parts.

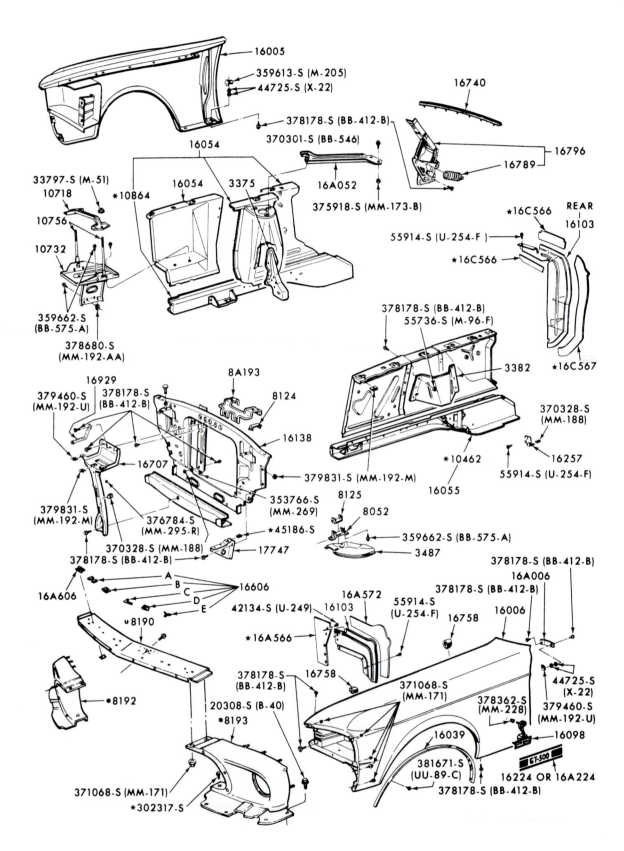

The 1967-1968 Shelby Mustang front fenders, aprons, and related parts.

46

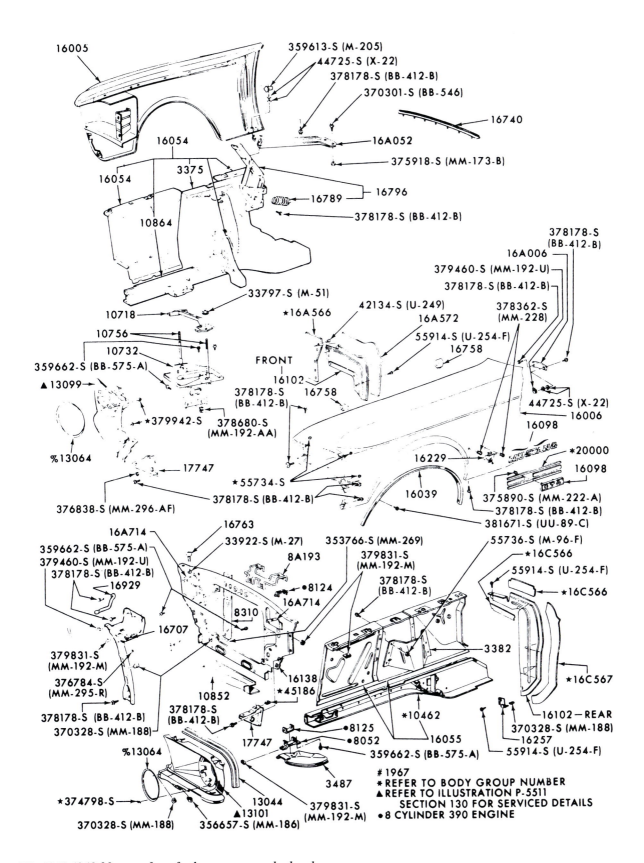

16005

359613-S (M-205)
44725-S (X-22)
378178-S (BB-412-B)
370301-S (BB-546)

16740

16A052

375918-S (MM-173-B)

16054

3375

16054

16796

16789

378178-S (BB-412-B)

10864

378178-S
(BB-412-B)

16A006

379460-S (MM-192-U)

378178-S (BB-412-B)

378362-S
(MM-228)

33797-S (M-51)

42134-S (U-249)

16A572

55914-S (U-254-F)

16758

10718

10756

*16A566

10732

FRONT

359662-S (BB-575-A)

16102

378178-S
(BB-412-B)

378680-S
(MM-192-AA)

16758

44725-S (X-22)

16006

16098

▲13099

*379942-S

*20000

16098

%13064

16229

MUSTANG

17747

16039

375890-S (MM-222-A)

376838-S (MM-296-AF)

*55734-S

378178-S (BB-412-B)

378178-S (BB-412-B)

381671-S (UU-89-C)

16763

16A714

33922-S (M-27)

353766-S (MM-269)

55736-S (M-96-F)

359662-S (BB-575-A)

8A193

379831-S
(MM-192-M)

*16C566

379460-S (MM-192-U)

55914-S (U-254-F)

378178-S (BB-412-B)

●8124

378178-S
(BB-412-B)

*16C566

16929

16A714

8310

16707

3382

379831-S
(MM-192-M)

*16C567

376784-S
(MM-295-R)

16138

378178-S (BB-412-B)

*45186

16102—REAR

370328-S (MM-188)

10852

378178-S
(BB-412-B)

*10462

370328-S (MM-188)

%13064

17747

●8125

16055

16257

●8052

55914-S (U-254-F)

359662-S (BB-575-A)

*374798-S

13044

379831-S
(MM-192-M)

#1967
✱ REFER TO BODY GROUP NUMBER
▲ REFER TO ILLUSTRATION P-5511
    SECTION 130 FOR SERVICED DETAILS
● 8 CYLINDER 390 ENGINE

370328-S (MM-188)

3487

▲13101

356657-S (MM-186)

*The 1967-1968 Mustang front fenders, aprons, and related
parts.*

47

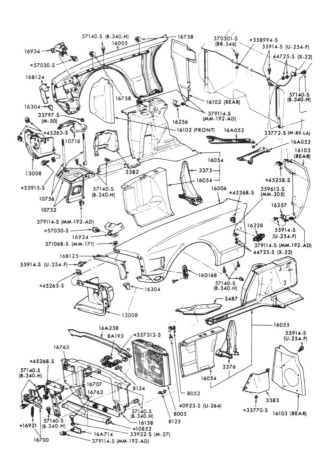

All 1965-1968 Mustangs (except 1968 Shelby Mustangs) equipped with a radio were outfitted with a standard round-base telescoping antenna mounted on the right front fender. The 1968 Shelby Mustang antennas were mounted on the right rear fender.

The 1969 Shelby Mustang front fenders, aprons, core support, and related parts.

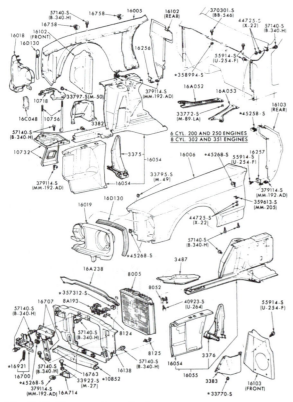

The 1969 Mustang front fenders, aprons, core support, and related parts.

A rectangular base telescoping antenna was installed on all 1969-1970 Mustangs equipped with a radio. Deleting the standard radio was an option for all years and models. The lower shaft of OEM rectangular-base antennas is teardrop shaped (viewed from above) to create an aerodynamic image. Replacement units have a round mast.

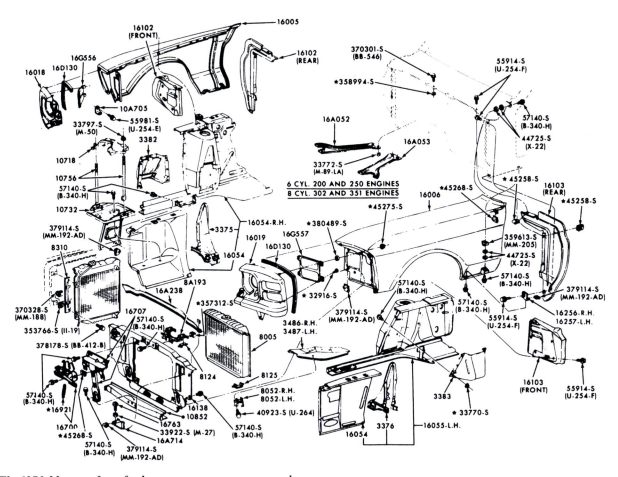

The 1970 Mustang front fenders, aprons, core support, and related parts.

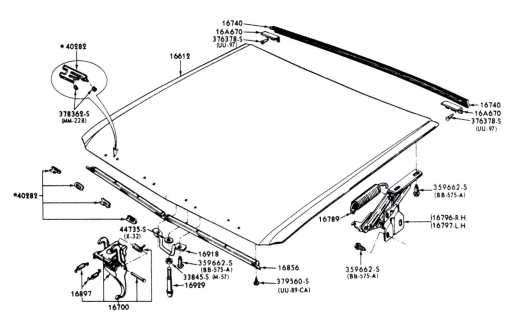

The 1965-1966 Mustang hood, hinges, latch, and related parts.

Hood louvers with integrated turn signal indicators were a popular 1967-1968 Mustang option.

Race-inspired hood pins and locks were popular in the late 1960s. Chrome hood posts with linchpin clips were standard equipment on Mach 1s for 1969, and flush-mounted twist-locks (shown) took their place in 1970.

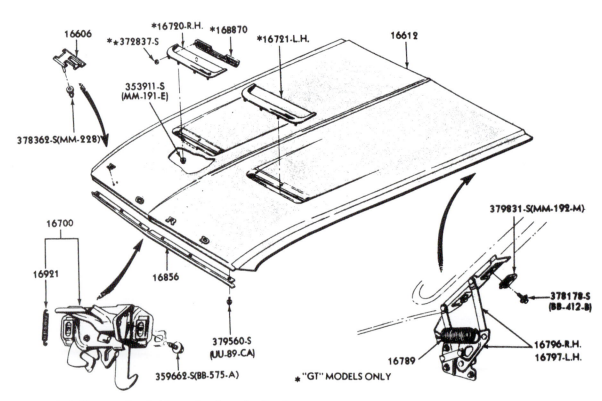

The 1967-1968 Mustang hood, hinges, latch, and related parts.

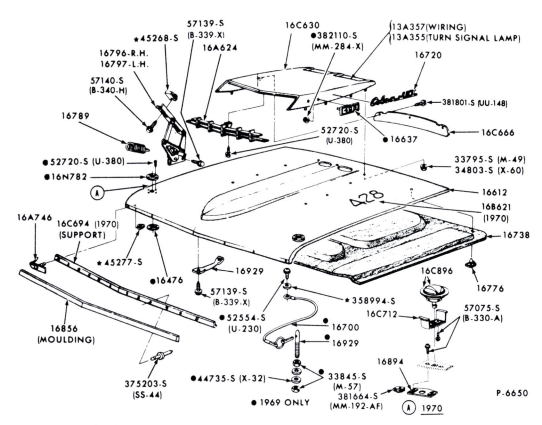

The 1969-1970 Mustang hood, hinges, scoop, and related parts.

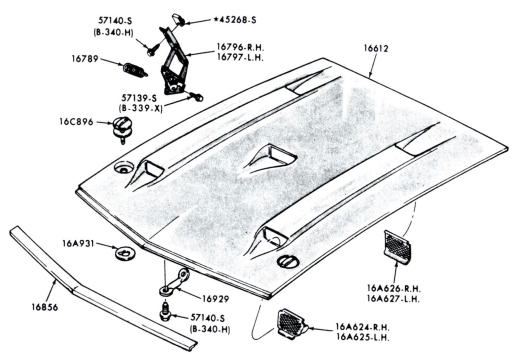

The 1969-1970 Shelby Mustang hood, hinges, and related parts.

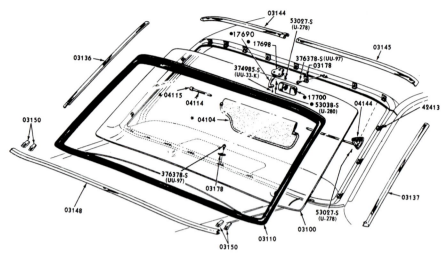

The 1965-1968 Mustang hardtop and fastback windshield, gasket, trim, and related parts.

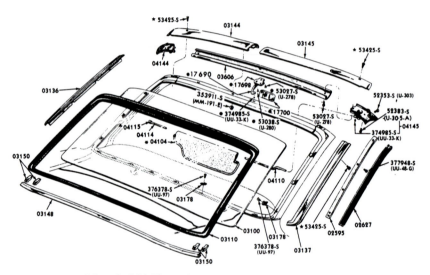

The 1965-1968 Mustang convertible windshield, gasket, trim, and related parts.

MUSTANG INSIDE REAR VIEW MIRROR APPLICATION CHART

YEAR	PART NUMBER	DESCRIPTION
65/66	C7OZ-17700-C	Day/night - 2.38" x 10" - 1/4" flat across shank for set screw mounted - vinyl covered
67	C7AZ-17700-F1A	Day/night - 2.42" x 10" - 1/4" flat arm for bolt mounted - black vinyl covered
67	C7AZ-17700-F1B	Less mounting arm - breakaway type - blue Day/night - 2.45" x 10" - diam. 1/2" - ball mounted - black vinyl covered less mounting arm
68	C7AZ-17700-E1K	Less mounting arm - cement-on type
70		Day/night - 2.45" x 10" - undetachable mounting arm - black vinyl covered

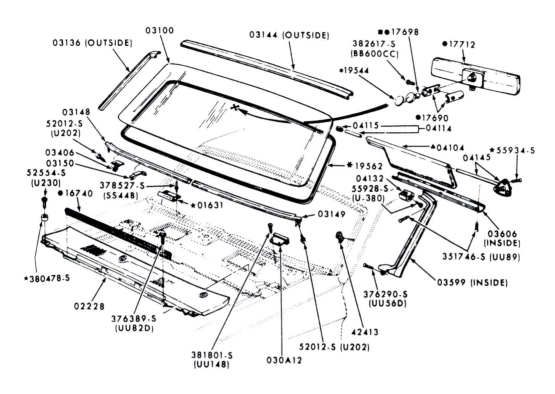

The 1969-1970 Mustang hardtop and SportsRoof wind-shield, gasket, trim, and related parts.

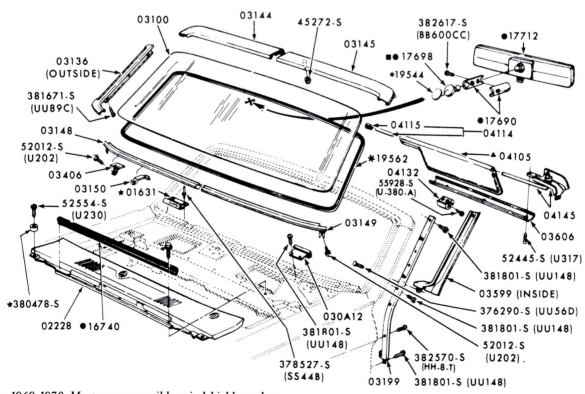

The 1969-1970 Mustang convertible windshield, gasket, trim, and related parts.

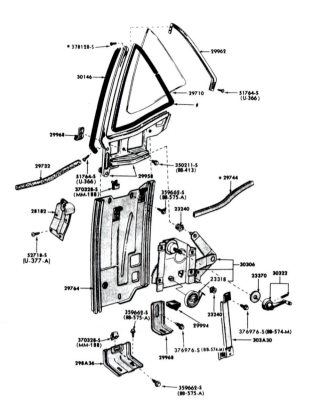

The 1965-1966 Mustang hardtop and convertible quarter window, regulator, and related parts.

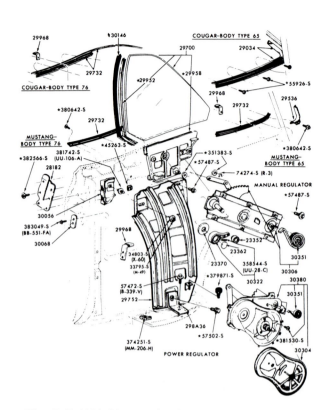

The 1969-1970 Mustang hardtop and convertible quarter window, regulator, and related parts.

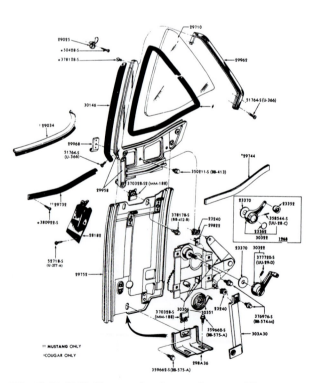

The 1967-1968 Mustang hardtop and convertible quarter window, regulator, and related parts.

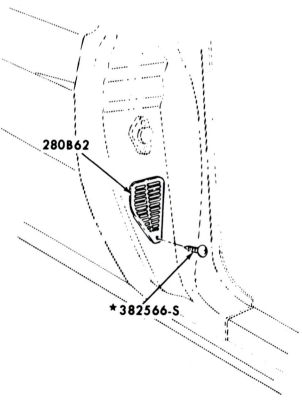

The 1970 Mustang quarter-panel pressure-release vent.

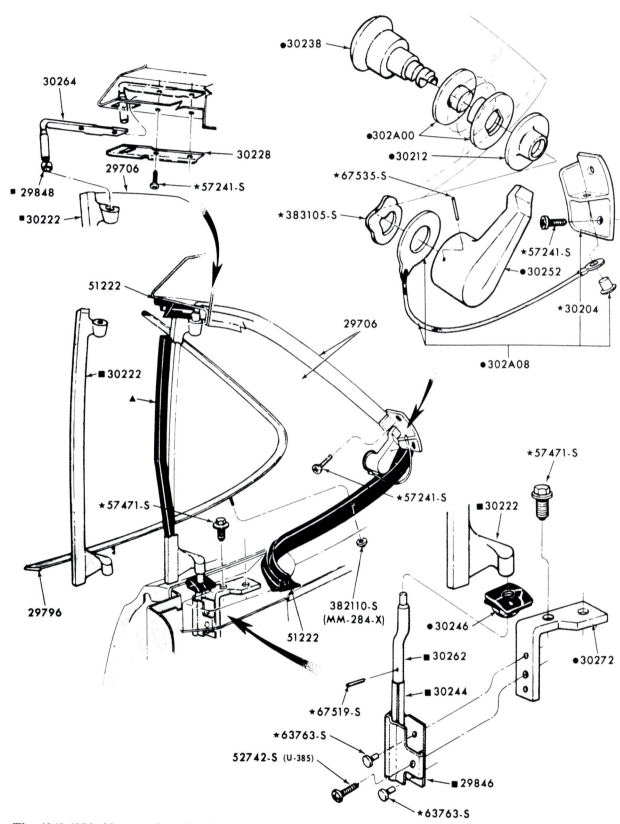

30264

●30238

●302A00

●30212

★67535-S

★383105-S

30228

29706

■ 29848

★57241-S

■30222

★57241-S

●30252

★30204

51222

●302A08

■30222

▲

29706

★57471-S

■30222

★57471-S

★57241-S

29796

382110-S
(MM-284-X)

●30246

51222

●30272

■30262

★67519-S

■30244

★63763-S

52742-S (U-385)

■29846

★63763-S

*The 1969-1970 Mustang SportsRoof quarter window,
latch, weatherstrip, and related parts.*

55

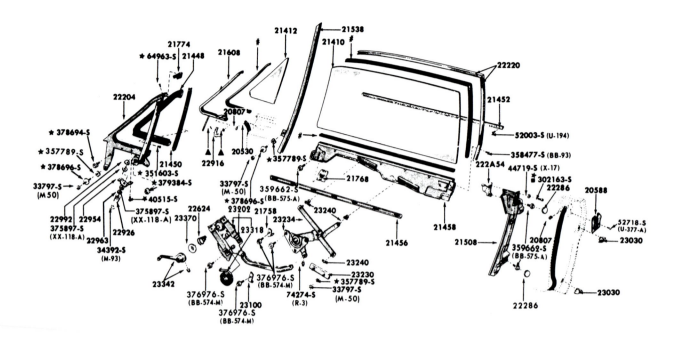

The 1965-1966 Mustang door window, window regulator, vent wing, and related hardware.

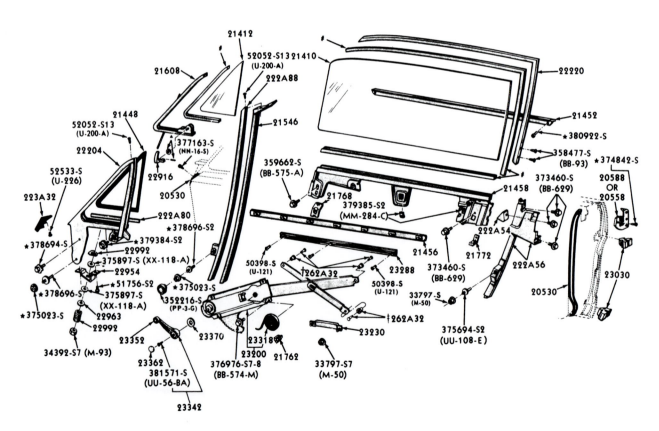

The 1967-1968 Mustang door window, window regulator, vent wing, and related hardware.

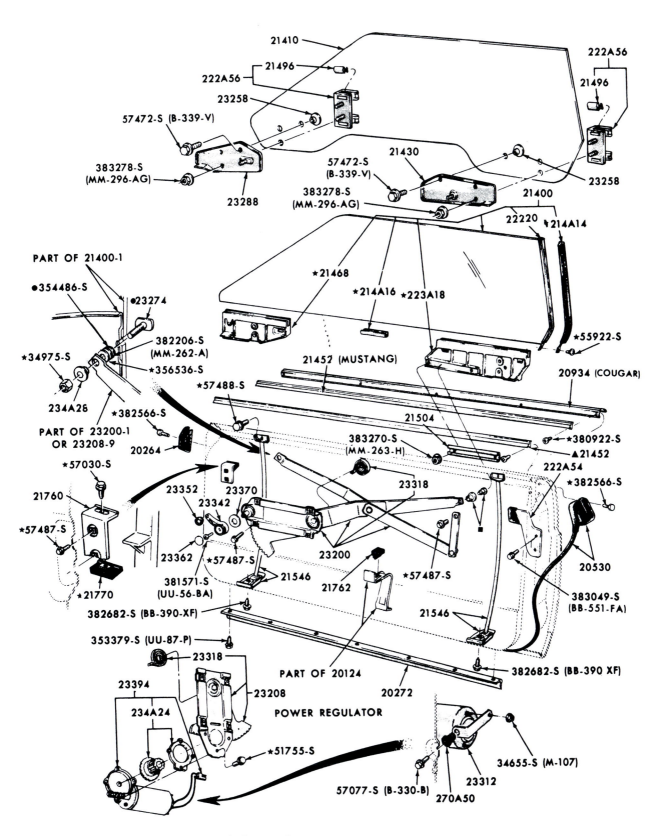

The 1969-1970 Mustang door window, window regulator, and related hardware.

57

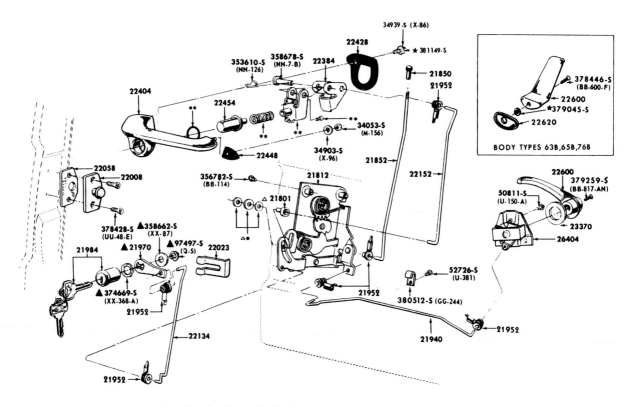

The 1965-1966 Mustang door handles, latch, and related hardware.

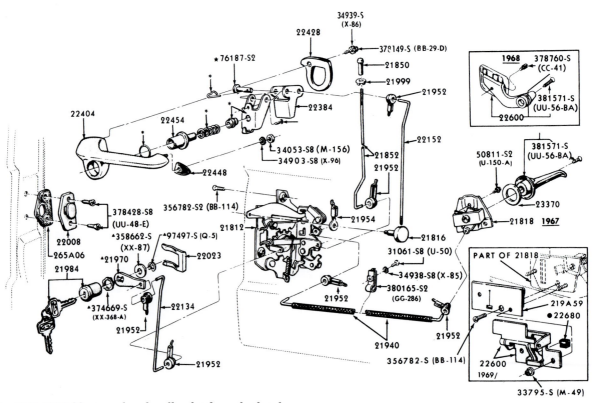

The 1967-1970 Mustang door handles, latch, and related hardware.

58

Functional rear-facing fresh air vents adorn the sides of all 1965-1968 Mustang fastbacks. The 1965-1966 louvers (shown) have five large openings.

The 1967-1968 fastback louvers are more numerous than the 1965-1966 models, and less pronounced.

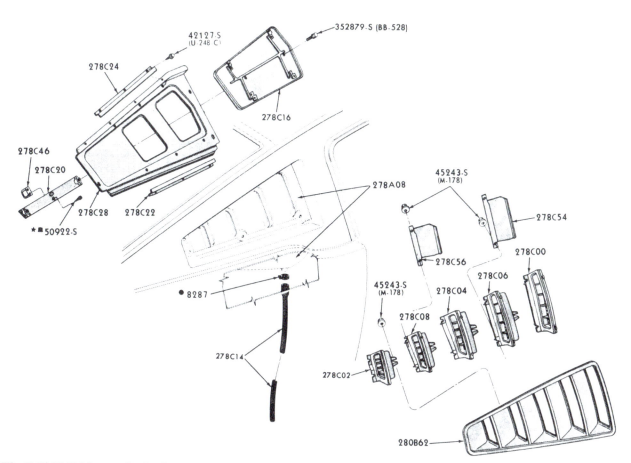

The 1965-1966 Mustang fastback rear-quarter vent louvers, hardware, and trim.

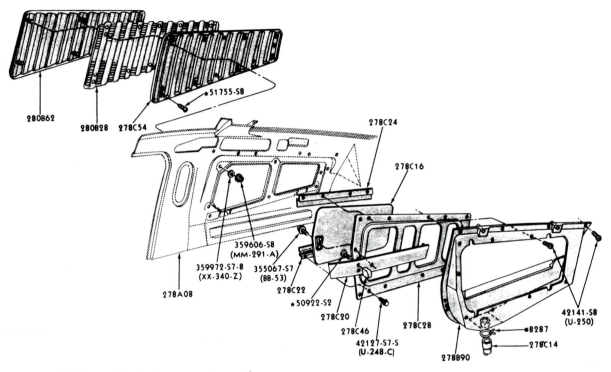

The 1967-1968 Mustang fastback rear-quarter vent louvers, hardware, and trim.

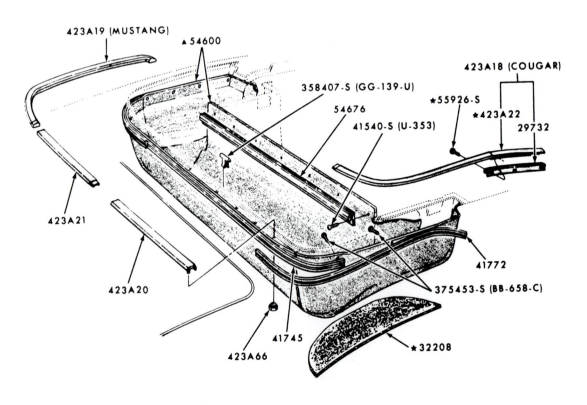

The 1969-1970 Mustang fastback rear window, gasket, and window molding.

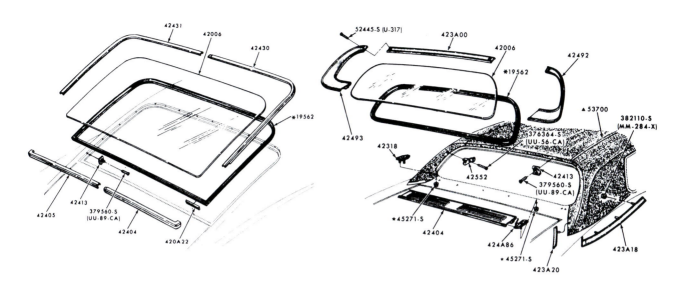

The 1969-1970 Mustang convertible-top well liner, rear belt moldings, and related parts.

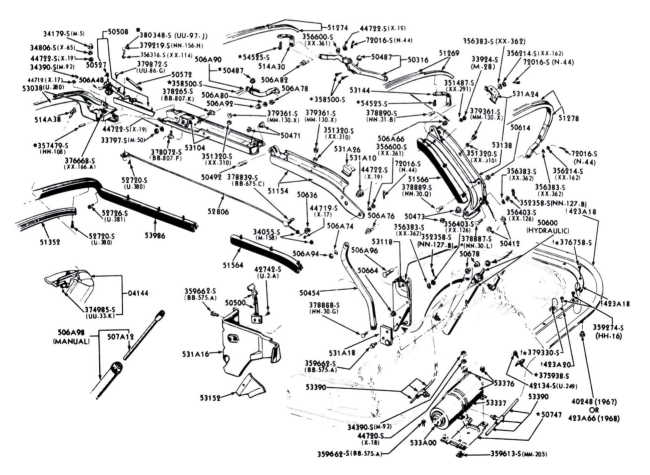

The 1965-1968 Mustang manual and power folding-top components, brackets, and hardware.

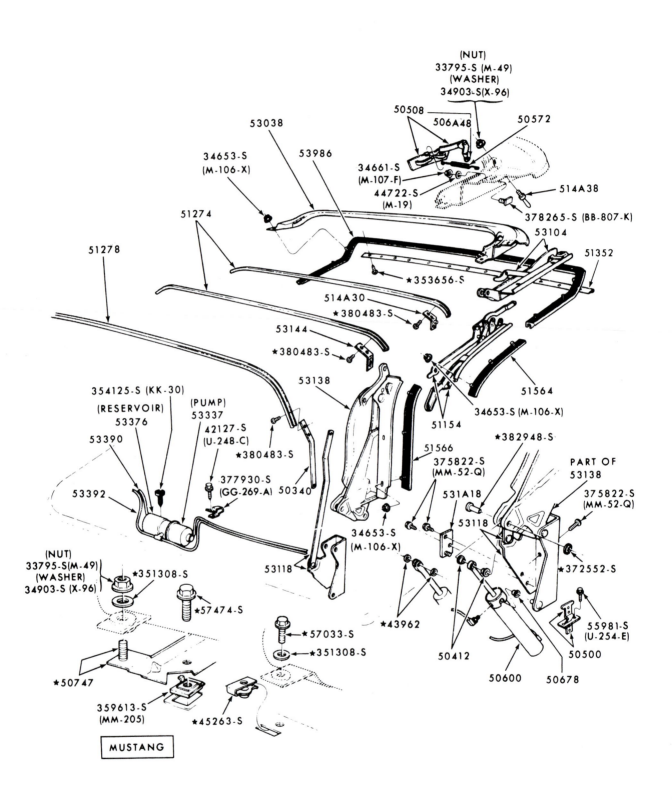

*The 1969-1970 Mustang power folding-top components,
brackets, and hardware.*

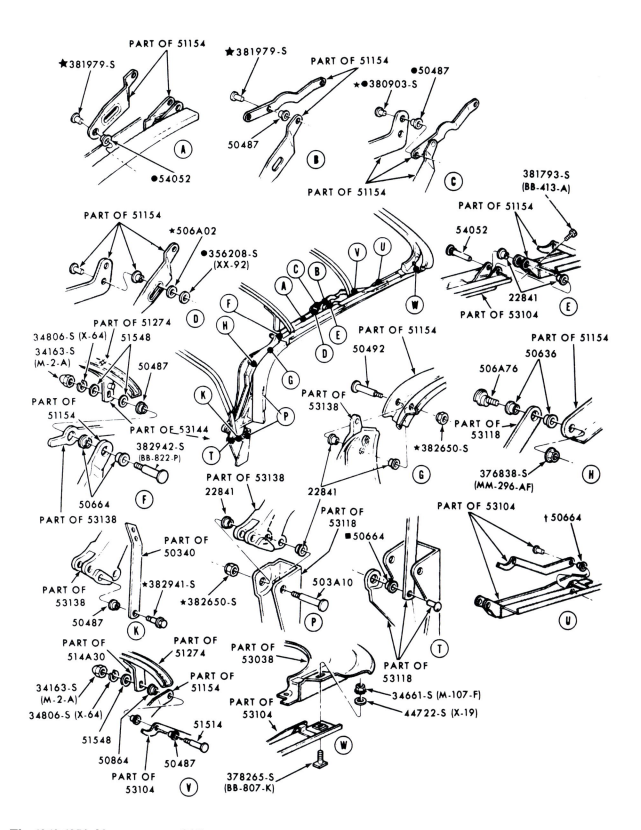

The 1969-1970 Mustang power folding-top components, brackets, and hardware (continued).

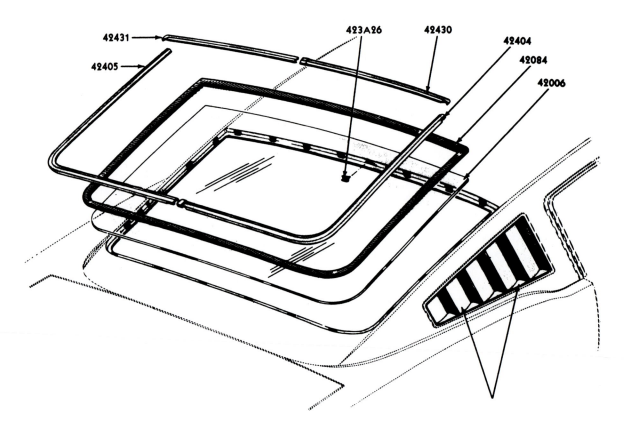

The 1965-1966 Mustang SportsRoof rear window, gasket, and window molding.

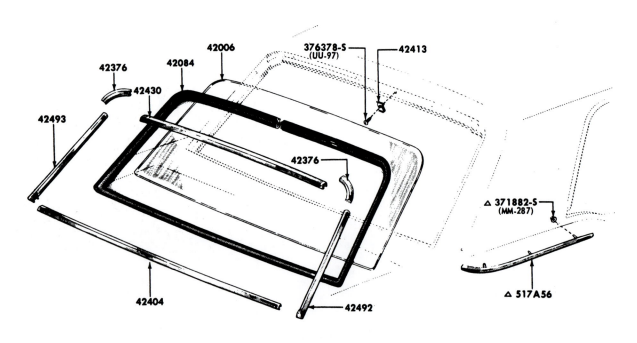

△   USED WITH VINYL ROOF COVER OR TUTONE PAINT

The 1965-1966 Mustang hardtop rear window, gasket, and window molding.

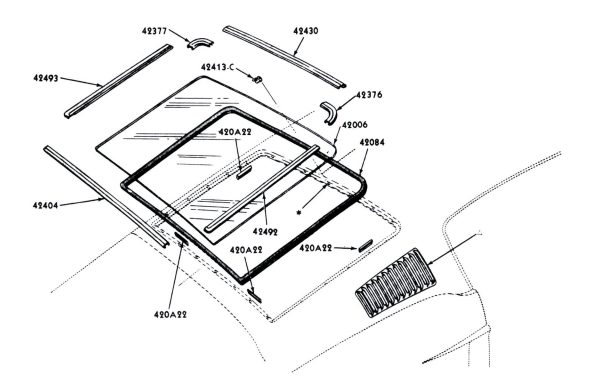

The 1967-1968 Mustang fastback rear window, gasket, and trim.

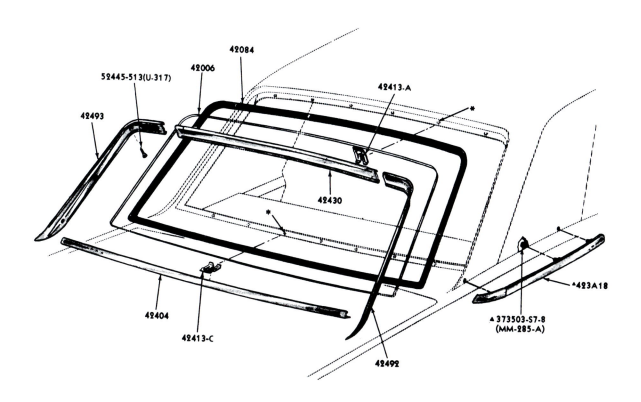

The 1967-1968 Mustang hardtop rear window, gasket, and trim.

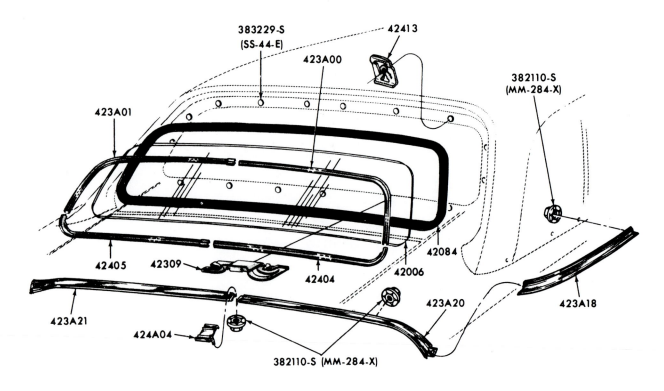

The 1970 Mustang hardtop rear window, gasket, and trim.

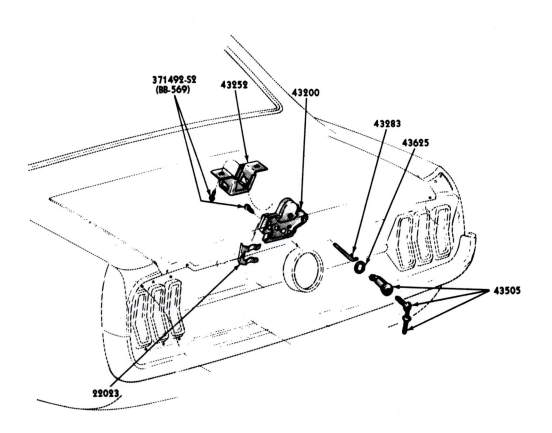

The 1967-1970 Mustang luggage compartment door latch and related parts.

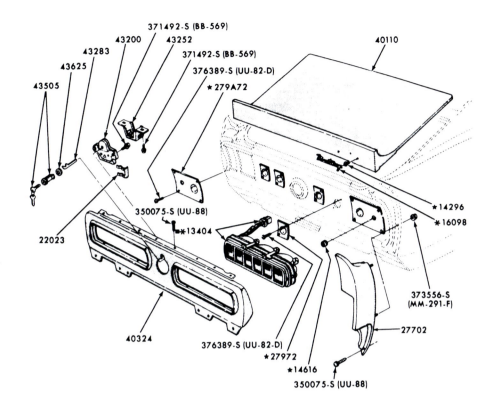

371492-S (BB-569)
43200
43252
43283
43625
371492-S (BB-569)
43505
376389-S (UU-82-D)
★279A72
40110
350075-S (UU-88)
★13404
★14296
★16098
22023
373556-S (MM-291-F)
40324
376389-S (UU-82-D)
★27972
★14616
350075-S (UU-88)
27702

The 1968 California Special GT Mustang luggage compartment lid, fender extension, taillight, rear tail panel, luggage compartment latch, and related hardware.

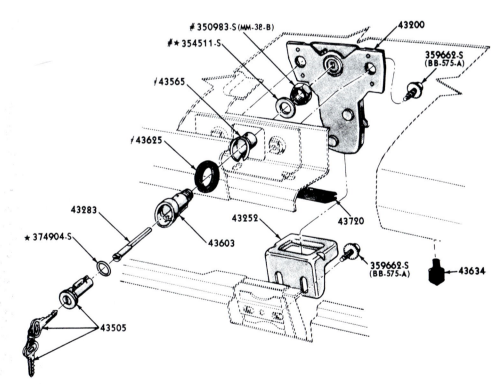

#350983-S (MM-38-B)
#★354511-S
43200
359662-S (BB-575-A)
∤43565
∤43625
43283
43252
43720
★374904-S
43603
359662-S (BB-575-A)
43634
43505

The 1965-1966 Mustang fastback luggage compartment door latch and related parts.

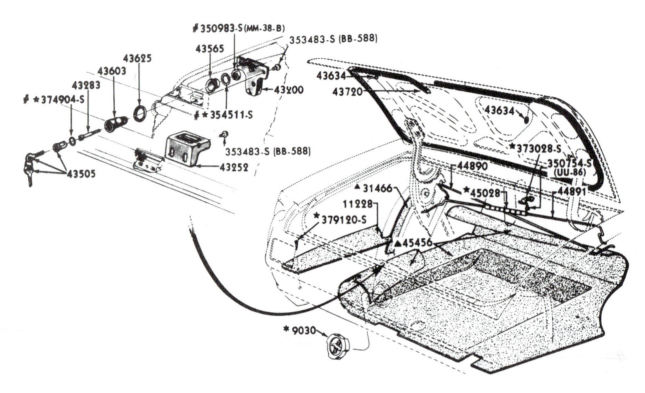

The 1965-1966 Mustang hardtop and convertible luggage compartment door latch, trunk floor covering, and related parts.

All 1966 Mustangs equipped with the GT package received a special gas cap (the 1965 GT received a standard Mustang gas cap). On this 1966 version the recessed letters in the Ford name were painted black while the word Mustang was in red. The raised GT letters are centered in a spun-aluminum disc and the remainder of the cap is chrome.

The three-fingered standard twist-off gas caps installed on all 1967 non-GT equipped Mustangs resembled a wheelcover spinner. The intricate plastic center retains the FORD MUSTANG inscription encircling the traditional running horse logo.

The 1967 was the first year for the optional pop-open gas cap. On GT Mustangs, the embossed running horse logo is replaced by the letters GT. The 1967 GT pop-open cap also was used on 1968 Mustang GTs.

A non-GT pop-open cap was available in 1968. The unique embossed logo is centered on a brushed-aluminum disc.

An optional ribbed rear grille panel was available on 1967 Mustangs equipped with the Exterior Decor Group.

The same standard twist-off gas cap is installed on all 1969 and 1970 Mustang body styles except Mach 1, GT, and Shelby.

The standard twist-off gas cap for 1968.

The 1969 GT Mustangs received their own unique pop-open gas cap with its gear-toothed center disc and traditional GT lettering.

Mach 1 pop-open gas caps were outfitted with the running horse logo set atop a tri-colored bar.

The 1970 Mach 1 pop-open cap is similar to the model used in 1969. A flat tail panel (between the taillamps) was brought back for 1970. It was the first year since 1966 that the tail panel was not concave. Mach 1s and cars optioned with the Exterior Decor Group received a honeycomb rear panel.

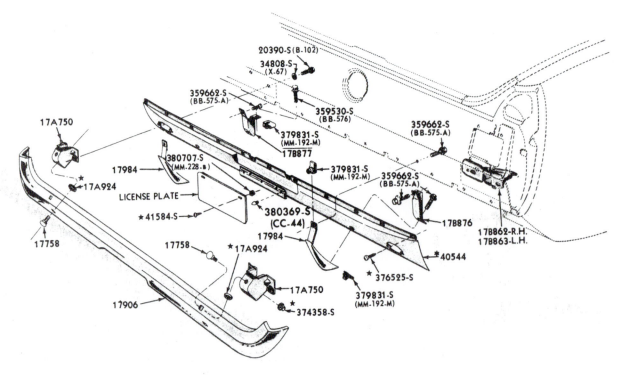

The 1965-1966 Mustang rear bumper, valance, brackets, and related mounting hardware.

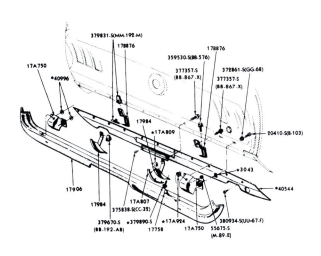

The 1967-1968 Mustang rear bumper, valance, brackets, and related mounting hardware.

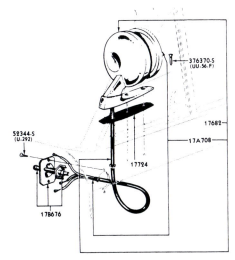

The 1965-1966 Mustang driver's side remote-control rearview mirror.

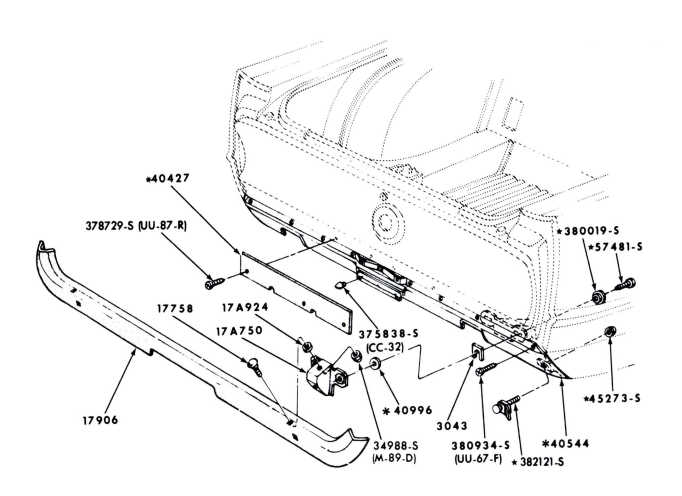

The 1969-1970 Mustang rear bumper, valance, brackets, and related mounting hardware.

MUSTANG OUTSIDE REAR VIEW MIRROR ASSEMBLY APPLICATION CHART

Year	Type	Part Number	Description	I.D. Number
65	1	B5AZ-17696-A	Conical shaped, not replaced	C3RA-17682-D
65/66	2	C1SZ-17696-B	Universal type, round head	C5DB-17682-C
65/66	5	C5AZ-17696-F	Rectangular head	C5AB-17682-C,F C5OB-17682-C
65/66	6	C3RZ-17696-A	L.H., universal type, round head. Kit.	
67	12	C7AZ-17696-D	Trailer towing mirror, R.H. or L.H. fender mounted. Kit.	
65	12	D3AZ-17696-B	Trailer towing mirror, R.H. or L.H. fender mounted. Kit.	
68	9	D4AZ-17696-A	Kit. R.H. or L.H., manual, rectangular head.	
67/68	9	D4AZ-17696-B	L.H., manual, rectangular head.	C7AB-17683-A C7TB-17683-U C7TB-17683-AB C8AB-17683-B
67	5	C7AZ-17696-E	L.H. - remote control - door mounted	C7AB-17683-B,D C7AB-17683-G,H C7AB-17683-J C7OB-17683-B
67/68	5	C8AZ-17696-A	R.H., rectangular head, companion to L.H. remote control mirror.	C7AB-17682-D,E C8AB-17682-C C8DB-17682-A C8GB-17682-A,B C8GB-17682-C,D
68	5	C8AZ-17682-D	L.H., remote control, rectangular head.	C8AB-17683-D
69	5	C9ZZ-17682-B	L.H., remote control, rectangular head for non-Mach 1 SportsRoof & Conv.	C9ZB-17683-D C9ZB-17683-F
69	9	C9ZZ-17682-D	L.H., remote control, rectangular head except Mach 1 & Grandé	C9ZB-17683-A
69	13	C9ZZ-17682-C	L.H., remote control, racing type head. Before 2/24/69	C9ZB-17683-CW C9ZB-17683-EW
69	13	C9ZZ-17682-E	L.H., remote control, racing type head. from 2/24/69	C9ZB-17683-GW
69/70	13	C9ZZ-17682-A	R.H., manual, racing type head.	C9ZB-17682-AW C9ZB-17682-BW
70	5	DOZZ-17696-A Consists of: DOZZ-17682-A C9ZZ-17724-B C8SZ-17B733-B C7SZ-17B732-B (2) 382879-S45 382031-S100 57259-S2 382930-S	L.H., remote control, rectangular head. Mirror assembly Gasket Plate Nut No. 10 screws (24 x 1") Clip assembly No. 8 screw/washer (32 x .75") Clip-wiring	
70	13	DOZZ-17682-B	L.H., remote control, racing type head.	DOZB-17683-BW
70	5	DOZZ-17682-A	L.H., remote control, rectangular head.	DOZB-17683-C

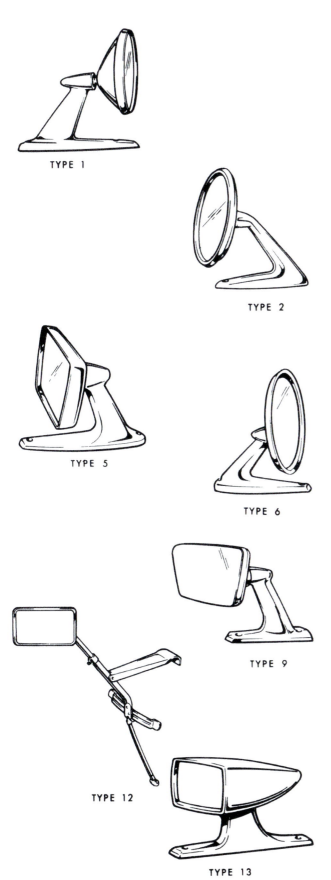

TYPE 1

TYPE 2

TYPE 5

TYPE 6

TYPE 9

TYPE 12

TYPE 13

The 1965 Mustang outside mirrors.

The standard driver's side rearview mirror installed on late 1965 and all 1966 Mustangs was an adaptation of a common mirror used on many other Ford cars. A conical-shaped mirror was installed on early 1965 Mustangs.

A passenger's side non-remote mirror was an inexpensive option on 1965 and 1966 Mustangs. It is actually a driver's side mirror mounted on the passenger's side door.

The base of the optional remote driver's side mirror mounts more toward the rear of the door compared to the standard non-remote mirror. The vent wing should just clear the mirror's head when opened.

In keeping with the times, standard mirrors went rectangular for 1967. This is the optional passenger's side non-remote mirror available for all 1967-1968 Mustangs. As with earlier standard mirrors, this was simply a driver's side mirror mounted on the passenger's side.

Bullet-shaped racing mirrors color-keyed to the exterior body color were a popular Mustang option in 1969-1970. The package included both driver's side and matching passenger's side mirrors, and was available on all body styles. The driver's side mirror is remotely controlled.

The optional Deluxe passenger's side mirror for 1967-1968 Mustangs resembled the driver's side remote mirror but was adjusted manually.

The unique passenger's side racing mirror is a visual reverse image of the driver's side mirror, but is adjusted manually.

Standard outside mirrors for 1969-1970 Mustangs were similar in design to the 1967-1968 rectangular part. The base and stem were contoured to accommodate the change in body style. Unlike earlier standard mirrors, this design will not mount on the passenger's side door. A driver's side remote-control mirror with a rectangular head was also an option for 1969-1970 Mustangs.

The familiar running horse over the red, white, and blue striped bar, and block letters spelling MUSTANG made up the standard lower front fender logo for all late 1965 and 1966 Mustangs. Early 1965 lettering measured 4³/₈in long, and the later emblem was lengthened to 5in.

A GT badge and large separated letters spelling MUS-TANG bordered by a racing stripe replaced the traditional lower fender logo on models optioned with the Sports Handling Package.

The 1965 and 1966 non-GT fastback Mustangs were identified as 2+2 models. A special 2+2 fender emblem accompanied the Mustang fender lettering.

The 1965 and 1966 Mustangs equipped with V-8 engines boasted their cubic inch displacements with special upper front fender badges. The displacement, 260 or 289, is positioned above a wide chrome V, Ford's longtime symbol for a V-8 engine.

A black and chrome checked placard with the words HIGH PERFORMANCE engraved along its upper edge indicated a 271hp, 289ci engine was nestled under the hood.

Combining the 289 HiPo engine with the popular GT Sports Handling Package option makes for a desirable and collectible package. Interest goes up if the car is a convertible or fastback.

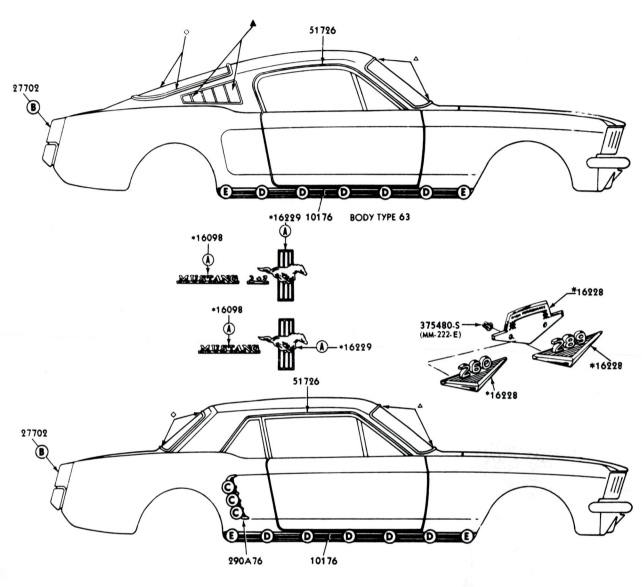

51726

27702 Ⓑ

Ⓔ Ⓓ Ⓓ Ⓓ Ⓓ Ⓓ Ⓔ

*16229 10176   BODY TYPE 63

*16098 Ⓐ   Ⓐ *16229 10176

MUSTANG 2+2

*16098 Ⓐ   MUSTANG   Ⓐ *16229

*16228

375480-S
(MM-222-E)   *16228

260   289

*16228

51726

27702 Ⓑ

Ⓒ
Ⓒ
Ⓒ

Ⓔ Ⓓ Ⓓ Ⓓ Ⓓ Ⓓ Ⓔ

290A76   10176

BODY TYPE 65 , 76

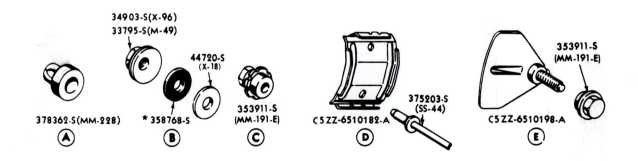

34903-S(X-96)
33795-S(M-49)

44720-S
(X-18)

353911-S
(MM-191-E)

378362-S(MM-228)   *358768-S   353911-S
(MM-191-E)   C5ZZ-6510182-A

375203-S
(SS-44)

C5ZZ-6510198-A

Ⓐ   Ⓑ   Ⓒ   Ⓓ   Ⓔ

*The 1965-1966 Mustang fastback and hardtop body side
molding, trim, and attaching hardware.*

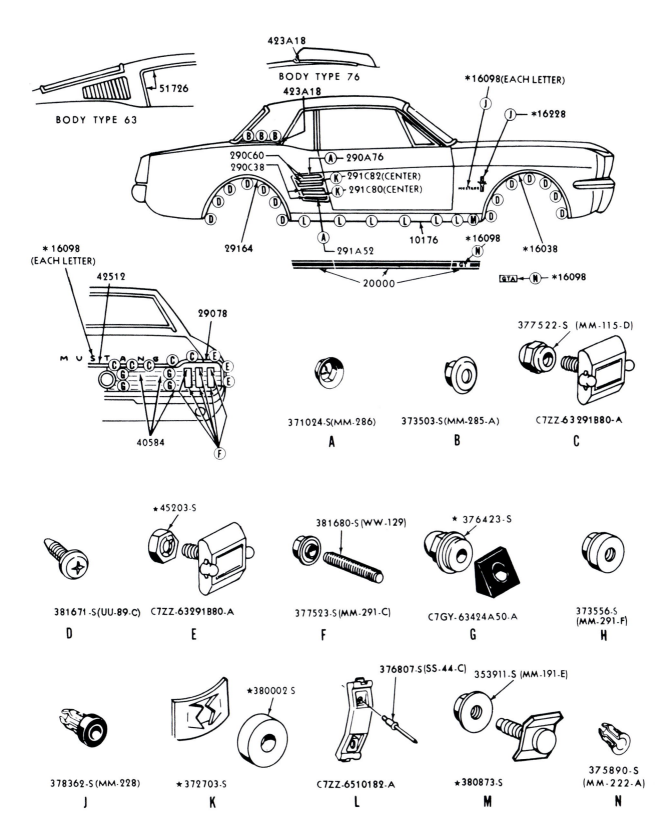

51726

BODY TYPE 63

423A18

BODY TYPE 76

423A18

*16098(EACH LETTER)

J

J —*16228

290C60

290C38

A — 290A76

K -291C82(CENTER)

K -291C80(CENTER)

*16098
(EACH LETTER)

42512

29078

29164

A

291A52

10176

*16098

*16038

N

20000

GY

GTA ← N — *16098

MUSTANG

40584

371024-S(MM-286)

A

373503-S(MM-285-A)

B

377522-S (MM-115-D)

C7ZZ-63291B80-A

C

381671-S(UU-89-C)

D

★45203-S

C7ZZ-63291B80-A

E

381680-S(WW-129)

377523-S(MM-291-C)

F

★376423-S

C7GY-63424A50-A

G

373556-S
(MM-291-F)

H

378362-S(MM-228)

J

★380002 S

★372703-S

K

376807-S(SS-44-C)

C7ZZ-6510182-A

L

353911-S (MM-191-E)

★380873-S

M

375890-S
(MM-222-A)

N

The 1967 Mustang body side molding, trim, and attaching hardware.

The block letters changed again in 1967, but the running horse logo remained the same as the standard lower fender treatment for Mustangs equipped with six-cylinder engines.

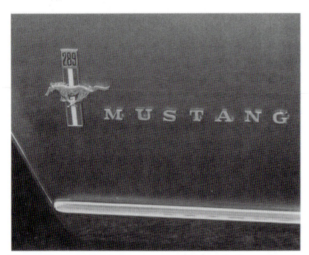

The cubic inch displacement was displayed above the tri-colored bar on 1967 and 1968 Mustangs equipped with V-8 engines.

The 1967 Mustangs equipped with the GT option received a special lower fender badge bordered by a racing stripe. In 1967 cars designated simply GT had manual transmissions. In that year only, the designation GTA was given a GT with an automatic transmission.

The straight GT stripe went away in 1968, as did the GTA designation. The Sports Handling Package option was indicated by a simple rectangular GT badge on each front fender.

The 1968 was the first year the Mustang fender emblem was written in script. The cubic inch displacement of V-8 powered Mustangs was still perched above the tri-colored bar.

Ford engineers added 0.130in to the 289 engine's 2.87in stroke and created a 302ci engine. Then, in the middle of the production year, it was installed in 1968 Mustangs. The 302 had completely replaced the 289 by the beginning of the 1969 model year.

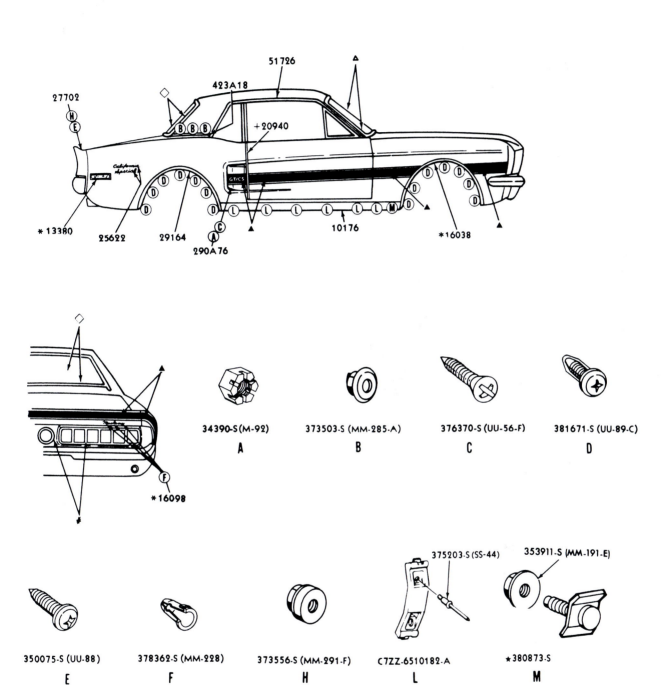

27702

51726

423A18

+20940

*13380

25622

29164

290A76

C

A

10176

*16038

34390-S (M-92)
A

373503-S (MM-285-A)
B

376370-S (UU-56-F)
C

381671-S (UU-89-C)
D

*16098

350075-S (UU-88)
E

378362-S (MM-228)
F

373556-S (MM-291-F)
H

375203-S (SS-44)

C7ZZ-6510182-A
L

353911-S (MM-191-E)

*380873-S
M

*The 1968 California Special GT Mustang body side and
rear molding, trim, strips, and attaching hardware.*

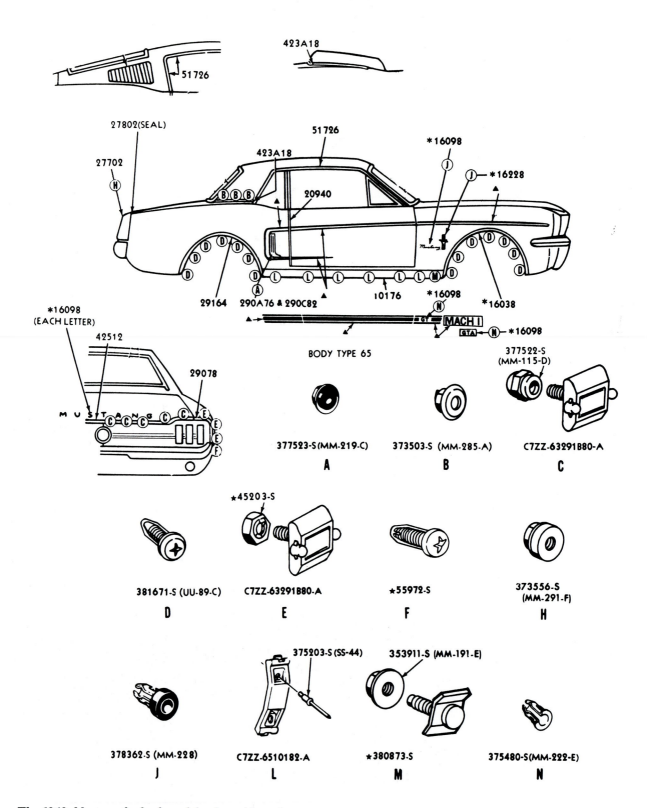

51726

423A18

27802(SEAL)

51726

*16098

27702

423A18

20940

*16228

27702 H

B B B

*16098
(EACH LETTER)

42512

29078

29164   290A76 & 290C82

10176   *16098

*16038

MACH 1

*16098

BODY TYPE 65

377522-S
(MM-115-D)

377523-S (MM-219-C)

A

373503-S (MM-285-A)

B

C7ZZ-63291B80-A

C

★45203-S

381671-S (UU-89-C)

D

C7ZZ-63291B80-A

E

★55972-S

F

373556-S
(MM-291-F)

H

375203-S (SS-44)

353911-S (MM-191-E)

378362-S (MM-228)

J

C7ZZ-6510182-A

L

★380873-S

M

375480-S(MM-222-E)

N

The 1968 Mustang fastback and hardtop side and rear molding, trim, strips, and attaching hardware. Note: Mach 1 was proposed in 1968 but never built.

The Mustang script was hollowed out and painted for 1969. The 351 Windsor engine also made its debut in 1969. The 351 and the 390 engines were designated with a numeric placard located just below the front fender script on standard models.

The 1969 Mustangs equipped with the Sport Handling Package did not have a traditional GT badge on the lower front fenders, but the straight lower body stripes reappeared.

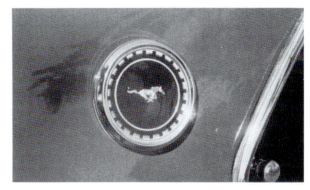

Ford copied the center of a 1969 twist-off gas cap to make this SportsRoof quarter panel medallion. Pieces are unique to each side of the car in order to keep the running horse always facing toward the front.

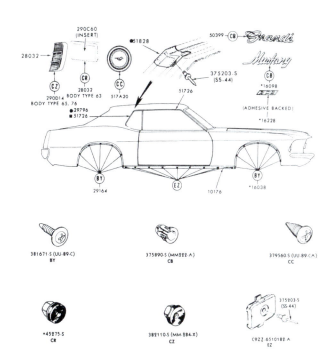

The 1969 Mustang body side molding, trim, and attaching hardware.

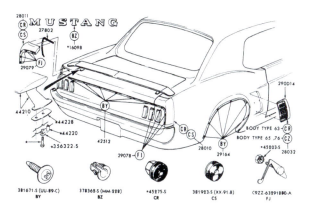

The 1969 Mustang rear spoiler, trim, and related hardware.

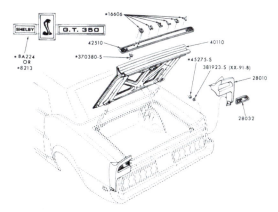

The 1969-1970 Shelby rear deck, trim, and lettering.

The Grande option converted a 1969-1970 Mustang hard-top into a luxury car.

Boss 302 Mustangs were labeled with taped letters in conjunction with tape stripes.

In 1970, a Landau vinyl roof was standard equipment on the Grande. A full vinyl roof was optional.

In 1969, "Boss 302" appeared in a C-stripe located on the car's sides. In 1970 (shown), "BOSS 302" was included in the Z-stripe that started at the leading edge of the hood.

In 1970, the Mustang script appeared just above the wide louvered rocker panel that was standard on the Mach 1.

The mighty Boss 429 had the most subdued insignia when compared to other Mustangs. An outlined "Boss 429" tape decal located on the front fenders was the only warning.

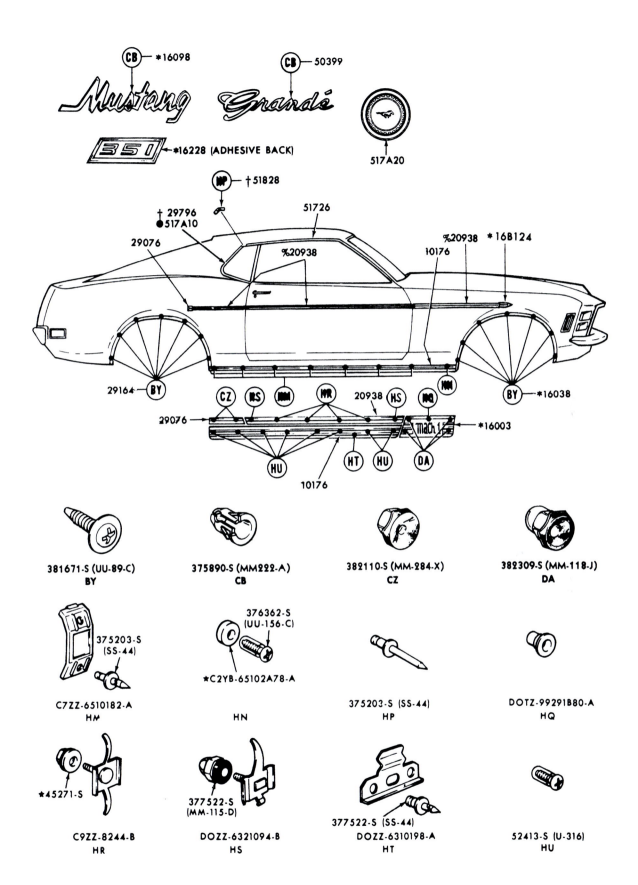

CB — *16098
CB — 50399

Mustang Grande

351 ← *16228 (ADHESIVE BACK)

517A20

NP — †51828

† 29796
● 517A10

29076

51726

29076

%20938

%20938   *16B124

10176

%20938

10176   *16B124

29164   **BY**

CZ **RS** **MM**   **HR**   20938 **HS**   **MM**   **BY** — *16038

29076   *16003

10176

HU   **HT** **HU**   **DA**   Mach 1

Mach 1

381671-S (UU-89-C)
BY

375890-S (MM222-A)
CB

382110-S (MM-284-X)
CZ

382309-S (MM-118-J)
DA

375203-S
(SS-44)

376362-S
(UU-156-C)

*C2YB-65102A78-A

375203-S (SS-44)
HP

DOTZ-99291B80-A
HQ

C7ZZ-6510182-A
HM

HN

*45271-S

377522-S
(MM-115-D)

377522-S (SS-44)

52413-S (U-316)
HU

C9ZZ-8244-B
HR

DOZZ-6321094-B
HS

DOZZ-6310198-A
HT

The 1970 Mustang body side molding, trim strips, and
attaching hardware.

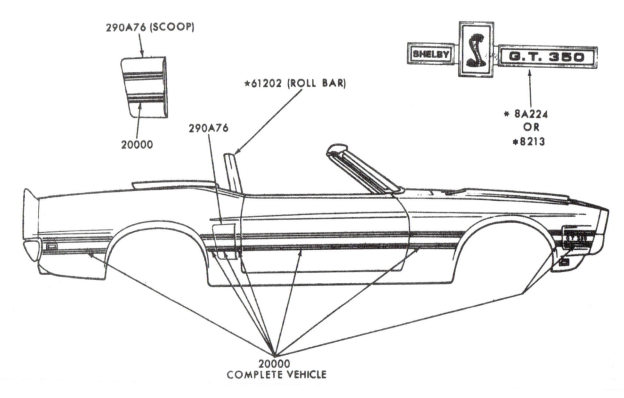

The 1969-1970 Shelby Mustang body side molding, trim, stripes, and lettering.

Rear quarter or body side trim was changed year by year, and therefore provided a good way to determine the model year of the car. The 1965 Mustangs sported a scalloped chrome strip; 1966 Mustangs (shown) had a ribbed bar with three fingers extending toward the front of the vehicle. Chrome rear quarter ornaments were deleted from fastbacks and all GT models in 1965 and 1966.

In 1967 the chrome rear quarter trim gave way to painted louvers that resembled scoops. These louvers were not deleted on GT equipped cars.

A thin vertical bar set in a body-colored bezel decorated Mustang rear quarters in 1968. These ornaments were also included on GT cars.

Ford dealers in Colorado and its adjacent states offered their own version of the popular California Special in 1968. The High Country Special carried a 51 DSO code and was available only as a hardtop. The High Country Special, primarily hardtops, also had been available through DSO 51 in 1966 and 1967, with special factory colors and ornamentation.

The GT C-stripe was a popular option in 1968. Bright rocker panel molding was standard on all 1968 Mustang models.

One of the Mustang trademarks, the sculptured body side recess, disappeared in 1969. A chrome simulated rear-facing scoop set in a body-colored bezel took its place.

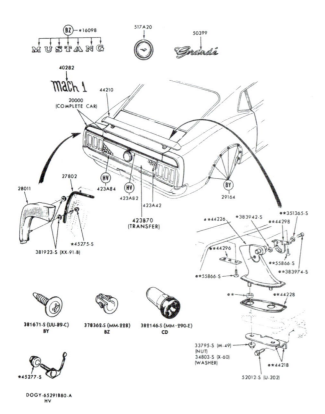

The 1970 Mustang rear spoiler, trim, moldings, and lettering.

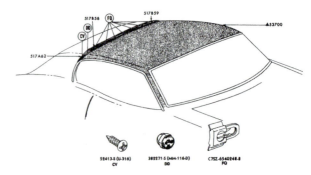

The 1970 Mustang SportsRoof vinyl roof molding and attaching hardware.

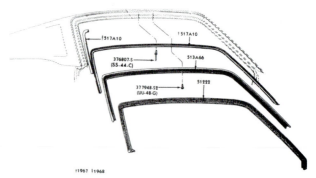

The 1965-1968 Mustang fastback roof side moldings and weatherstrips.

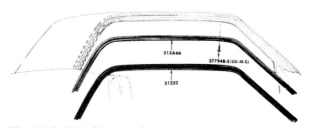

The 1965-1968 Mustang hardtop roof side moldings and weatherstrips.

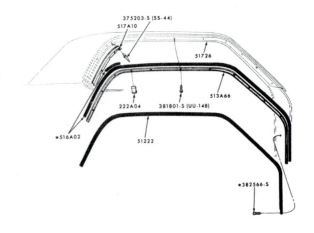

The 1969-1970 Mustang hardtop roof side moldings and weatherstrips.

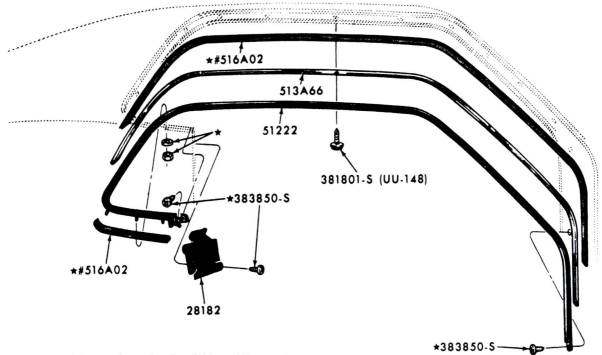

★#516A02

513A66

51222

381801-S (UU-148)

★383850-S

★#516A02

28182

★383850-S

*The 1969-1970 Mustang SportsRoof roof side moldings and
weatherstrips.*

Chapter 3

Interior

Few have openly recognized that a major appeal of the Mustang to its owners over the years has been its interior design. Basically grouped like Mustang exteriors in their 1965-66, 1967-68, and 1969-1970 similarities, the interiors always have held a personality and uniqueness all their own. From a plain bench seat decor with standard upholstery and an AM radio in 1965 to a full luxury pleated and woven bucket seat Mach 1 interior with woodgrain trim and piping on the floor mats, Mustang interiors have made it possible for owners to feel truly at home in their own cars.

The reader should note that this chapter will not include shifters (to be found in Chapter 5 on Drivetrain), steering wheels (to be found in Chapter 6 on Suspension), or instrument clusters (to be found in Chapter 7 on Wiring).

A huge percentage of the money spent in Mustang restoration is devoted to rejuvenating interiors. The restorer is always wise to check with concours experts and reputable parts vendors before spending money for interior components and upholstery. Small details such as the texture and grain of vinyl upholstery, the composition of the carpet material, the accuracy of seat belt retrofitting, and proper colors of interior paint are best researched before a mistake is made. It is suggested that anyone restoring a Mustang for the first time obtain the California Mustang (800-854-1737) publication, *How To Restore Your Mustang*, available from Classic Motorbooks (800-826-6600) in order to view color chips for carpet and upholstery.

Use this chapter for the correct placement of hardware, the proper assembly sequence, model-specific components, authentication of swap meet and used parts, restoration continuity, and selection of optional upgrades.

MUSTANG INSTRUMENT CLUSTER HOUSING APPLICATION CHART

Year	Model	Description	Part Number
65		Only w/ clusters w/ charge indicator light and oil pressure warning light.	C5ZZ-10838-A
65		Black camera case finish; only w/ clusters w/ ammeter and oil pressure gauge.	C5ZZ-10838-C
65,66		Wood grain finish; only w/ clusters w/ ammeter and oil pressure gauge.	C5ZZ-10838-B
66		Black camera case finish; only w/ clusters w/ ammeter and oil pressure gauge.	C6ZZ-10838-A
67	Std. interiors	Black camera case finish; includes lenses.	C7ZZ-10838-C
67	Deluxe interiors	Brushed aluminum; includes lenses.	C7ZZ-10838-B
68		Camera case.	C8ZZ-10838-A
68		Wood grain.	C8ZZ-10838-B
69	Except Mach 1 & Grandé.	Black leathergrain	C9ZZ-10838-A
69	Mach 1 & Grandé.	Light teakwood, not replaced.	C9ZZ-10838-B
69	Mach 1 & Grandé.	Dark teakwood.	C9ZZ-10838-C
70	Except Mach 1 & Grandé.		D0ZZ-10838-A
70	Mach 1 & Grandé.	Dark teakwood.	D0ZZ-10838-B

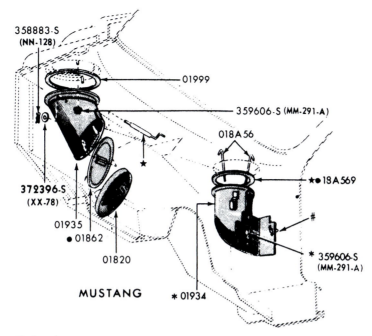

The 1965-1968 Mustang ventilating ducts.

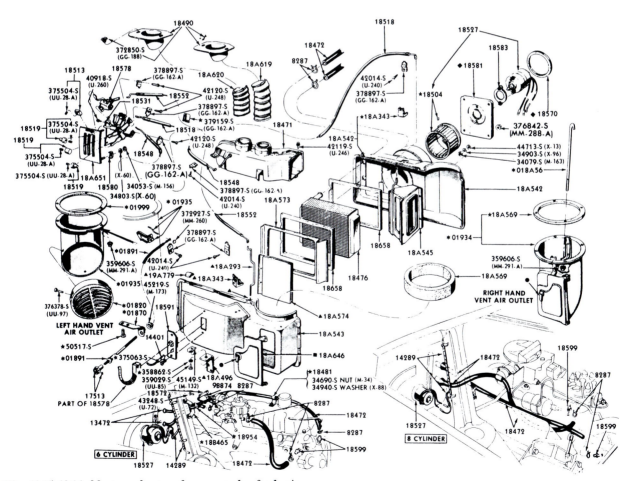

The 1965-1966 Mustang heater, fan, controls, fresh-air vents, and related hardware.

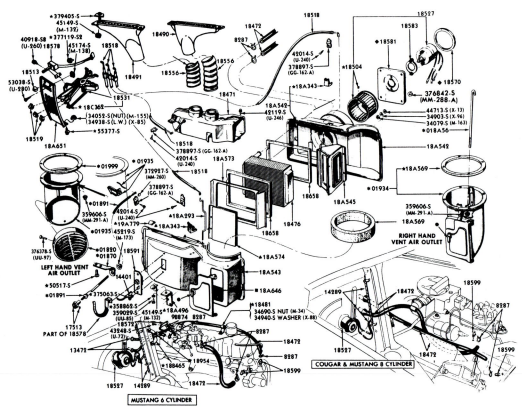

The 1967-1968 Mustang heater, fan, controls, fresh-air vents, and related hardware.

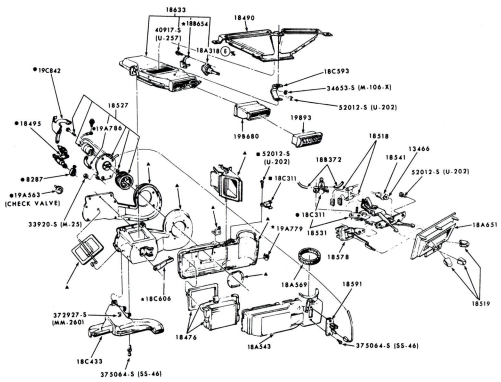

The 1969-1970 Mustang heater, fan, controls, fresh-air vents, and related hardware.

MUSTANG INSTRUMENT PANEL GLOVE COMPARTMENT APPLICATION CHART

YEAR	NOTES	PART NUMBER	DESCRIPTION
65/66		C5ZZ-6506010-A	
67/68		C7ZZ-6506010-A	Without hang-on air conditioning
69/70		C9ZZ-6506010-A	Without air conditioning
65/66		C5ZZ-6506024-B	With air conditioning
69			Includes retainer, spacer, socket and rivet
		C9ZZ-6506010-A2K	Rear - Aqua
		C9ZZ-6506010-A2B	- Blue
		C9ZZ-6506010-A1G	- Ivy gold
		C9ZZ-6506010-A1Y	- Nugget gold
		C9ZZ-6506010-A1D	- Red
70	1	DOZZ-6306010-D	Rear - Black
		DOZZ-6306010-B	- Blue
		DOZZ-6306010-F	- Ginger
		DOZZ-6306010-A	- Green
		DOZZ-6306010-E	- Red
		DOZZ-6306010-C	- Tobacco
70	2	DOOZ-6306010-K	Rear - Black
	3	DOOZ-6306010-H	- Blue
		DOOZ-6306010-M	- Ginger
		DOOZ-6306010-G	- Green
		DOOZ-6306010-L	- Red
		DOOZ-6306010-J	- Tobacco
70	4	DOOZ-6306010-R	Rear - Black
		DOOZ-6306010-P	- Blue
		DOOZ-6306010-T	- Ginger
		DOOZ-6306010-N	- Green
		DOOZ-6306010-S	- Red
		DOOZ-6306010-Q	- Tobacco

Notes:

1. Before 9/2/69
2. From 9/2/69
3. Before 12/1/69
4. From 12/1/69

The AM radio was the most popular option in 1965 and 1966. An AM/FM radio and AM with Stereophonic 8-track tape player were also available.

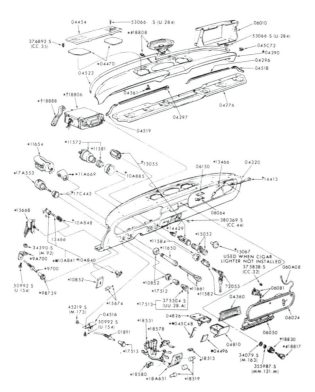

The 1965 Mustang instrument panel and related parts with indicator lights.

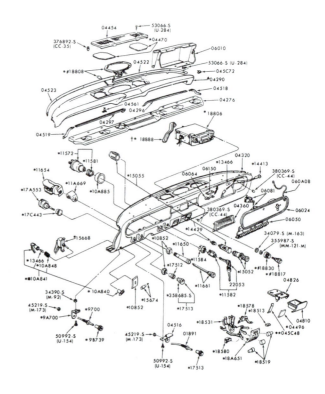

The 1965-1966 Mustang instrument panel and related parts with gauges.

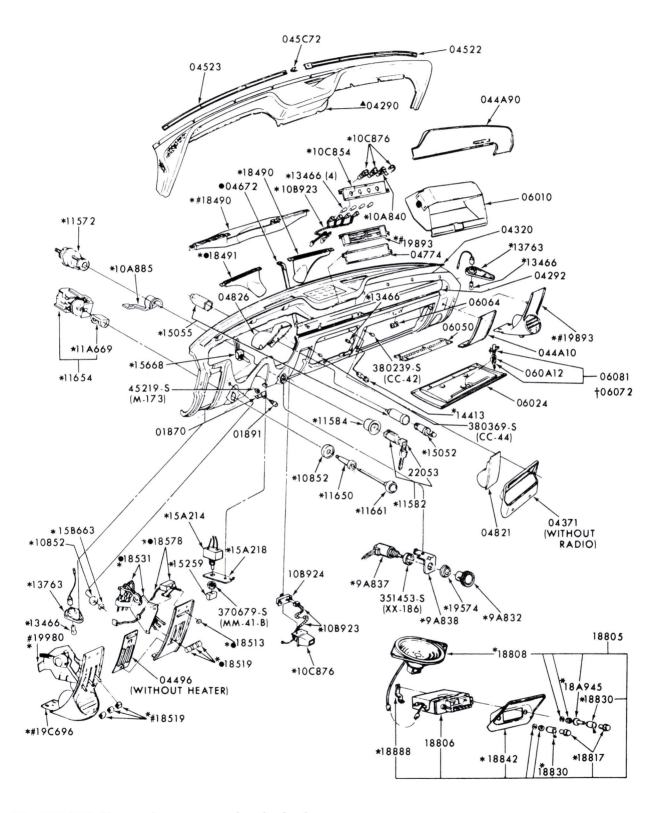

The 1967-1968 Mustang instrument panel and related parts.

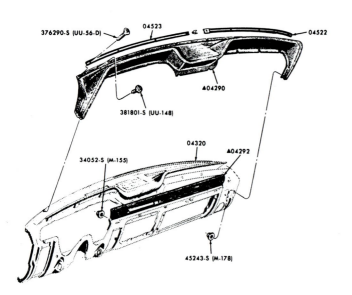

The 1967-1968 Mustang dash pad and attaching hardware.

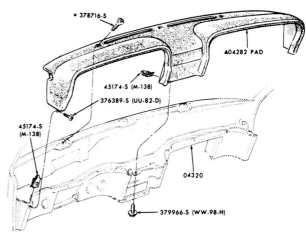

The 1969-1970 Mustang dash pad and attaching hardware.

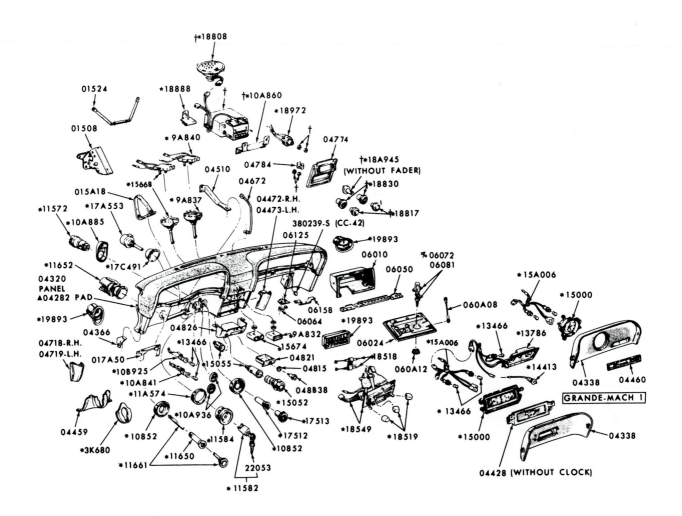

The 1969-1970 Mustang instrument panel and related parts.

94

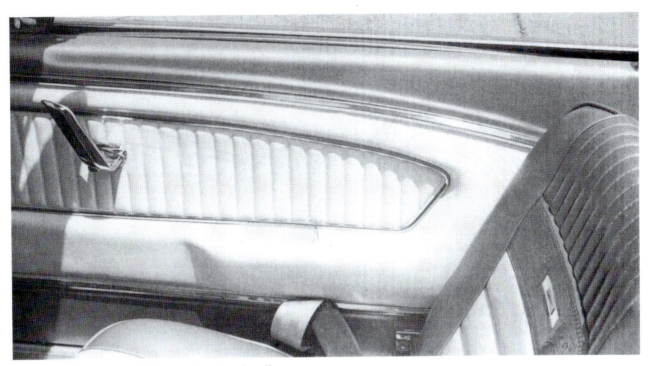

Sculptured door panels and Thunderbird door handles were part of the Interior Decor option.

Early Shelby Mustang interiors, like this 1966 model, are simple and business-like. Except for a woodgrain wheel and dash-mounted tachometer, 1965-1966 Shelbys retained the standard black Mustang interior.

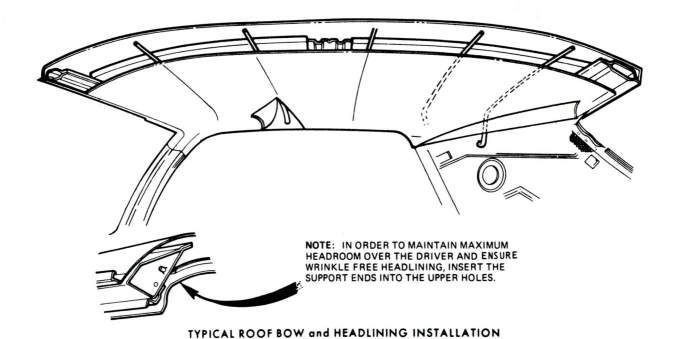

NOTE: IN ORDER TO MAINTAIN MAXIMUM HEADROOM OVER THE DRIVER AND ENSURE WRINKLE FREE HEADLINING, INSERT THE SUPPORT ENDS INTO THE UPPER HOLES.

TYPICAL ROOF BOW and HEADLINING INSTALLATION

A typical Mustang hardtop roof bow and headlining installation.

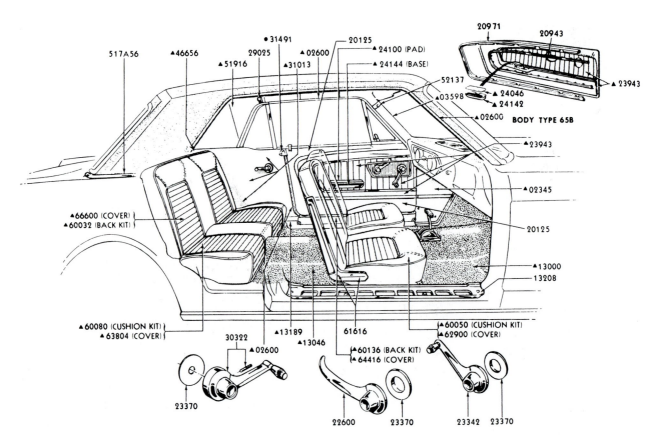

Typical 1965-1966 Mustang hardtop interior trim and related parts.

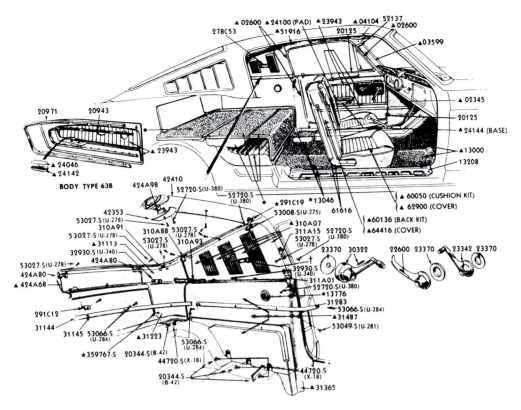

Typical 1965-1966 Mustang fastback interior trim and related parts.

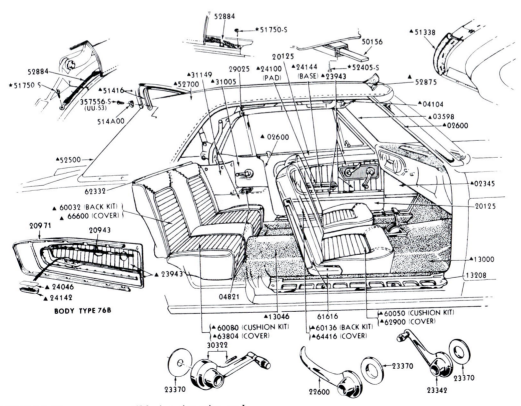

Typical 1965-1966 Mustang convertible interior trim and related parts.

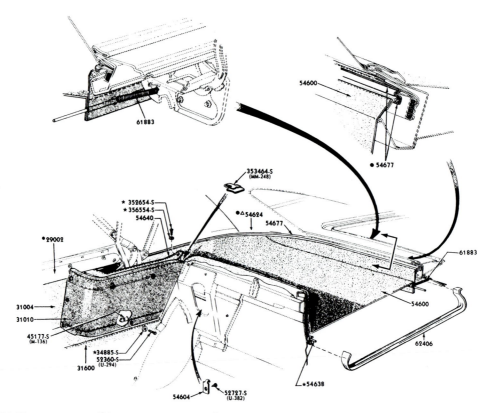

The 1965-1966 Mustang convertible top compartment trim and related parts.

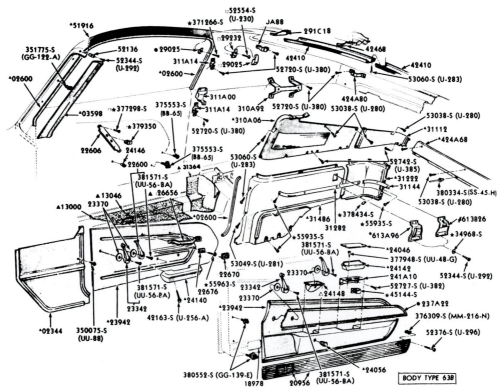

The 1967-1968 Mustang fastback door and quarter trim panels and related parts.

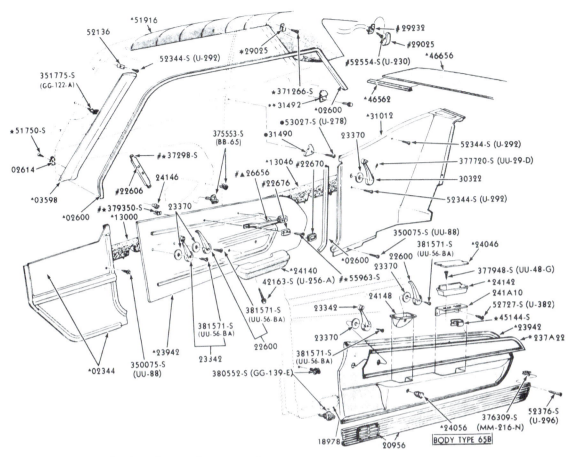

The 1967-1968 Mustang hardtop door and quarter trim
panels and related parts.

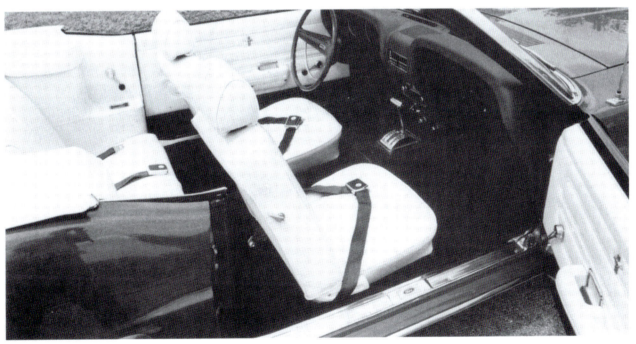

A white standard interior provides an attractive contrast in
this beautifully restored 1969 Mustang convertible.

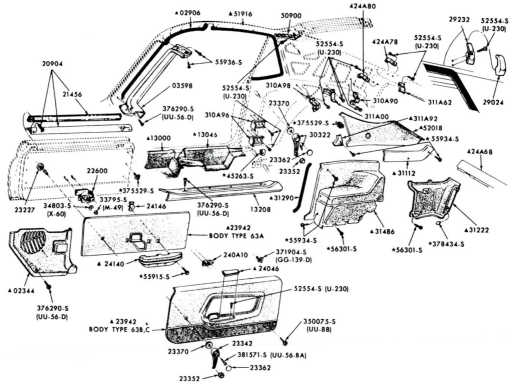

The 1969-1970 Mustang SportsRoof door and quarter trim panels and related parts (with fold-down rear seat).

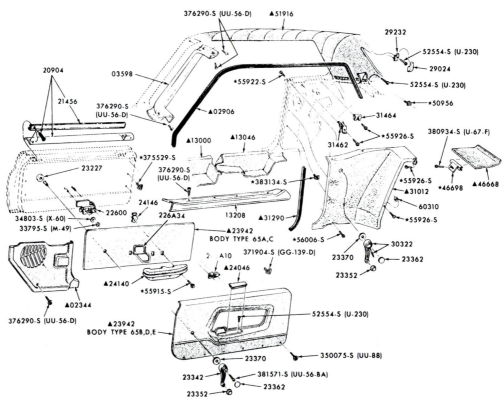

The 1969-1970 Mustang hardtop door and quarter trim panels and related parts.

100

The Deluxe interior was standard in 1969-1970 Shelby Mustangs. This 1969 model is also equipped with a tilt wheel and air conditioning.

A Deluxe interior, which included molded door panels with woodgrain inserts and a carpeted kick panel, was standard equipment on all 1969-1970 Mustang Mach 1s.

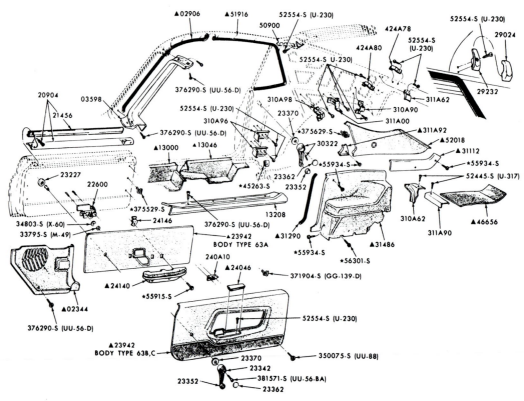

The 1969-1970 Mustang SportsRoof interior trim and related parts (with fixed rear seat).

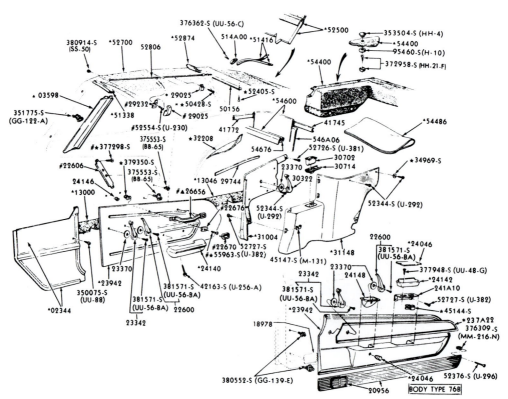

The 1967-1968 Mustang convertible door and quarter trim panels and related parts.

Mustang Interior Trim Scheme Codes, 1965

Code	Body Type	Trim Scheme
22	63A,65A	Medium blue crinkle all vinyl
22	76A	Medium blue crinkle all vinyl
25	63A,65A	Red crinkle all vinyl
25	76A	Red crinkle all vinyl
26	63A,65A	Black crinkle all vinyl
26	76A	Black crinkle all vinyl
28	63A,65A	Light ivy gold crinkle all vinyl
28	76A	Light ivy gold crinkle all vinyl
29	63A,65A	Medium palomino crinkle all vinyl
29	76A	Medium palomino crinkle all vinyl
32	65C	Medium blue crinkle vinyl all vinyl
32	76C	Medium blue crinkle vinyl all vinyl
35	65C	Red crinkle all vinyl
35	76C	Red crinkle all vinyl
36	65C	Black crinkle all vinyl
36	76C	Black crinkle all vinyl
39	65C	Medium palomino crinkle all vinyl
39	76C	Medium palomino crinkle all vinyl
42	63A,65A	White crinkle all vinyl with blue
42	76A	White crinkle all vinyl with blue
45	63A,65A	White crinkle all vinyl with red
45	76A	White crinkle all vinyl with red
46	63A,65A	White crinkle all vinyl with black
46	76A	White crinkle all vinyl with blue
D9	63A,65A	White crinkle all vinyl with palomino
D9	76A	White crinkle all vinyl with palomino
F2	63B,65B	White crinkle all vinyl with blue
F2	76B	White crinkle all vinyl with blue
F5	63B,65B	White crinkle all vinyl with red
F5	76B	White crinkle all vinyl with red
F6	63B,65B	White crinkle all vinyl with black
F6	76B	White crinkle all vinyl with black
F7	63B,65B	White crinkle all vinyl with turqouise
F7	76B	White crinkle all vinyl with turqouise
F8	63B,65B	White crinkle all vinyl with ivy gold
F8	76B	White crinkle all vinyl with ivy gold
F9	63B,65B	White crinkle all vinyl with palomino
F9	76B	White crinkle all vinyl with palomino

Body Type Codes
63A Fastback, Standard interior
63B Fastback, Deluxe interior
65A Hardtop, Standard interior
65B Hardtop, Deluxe interior
65C Hardtop, Bench seat option
76A Convertible, Standard interior
76B Convertible, Deluxe interior
76C Convertible, Bench seat option

1966 Mustang Interior Trim Scheme Codes

Code	Body Type	Trim Scheme
22	63A,65A,76A	Light blue crinkle vinyl and medium blue rosette pattern vinyl
22A	65A,76A	Light blue crinkle vinyl and medium blue crinkle vinyl
25	63A,65A,76A	Red crinkle vinyl and red rosette pattern vinyl
25A	65A,76A	Red crinkle all vinyl
26	63A,65A,76A	Black crinkle vinyl and black rosette pattern vinyl
26A	65A,76A	Black crinkle all vinyl
27	63A,65A,76A	Light aqua crinkle vinyl and medium aqua rosette pattern vinyl
27A	65A,76A	Light aqua crinkle vinyl and medium aqua crinkle vinyl
2DA	65A,76A	Parchment crinkle all vinyl
32	65C,76C	Light blue crinkle vinyl and medium blue rosette pattern vinyl
35	65C,76C	Red crinkle vinyl and red rosette pattern vinyl
36	65C,76C	Black crinkle vinyl and black rosette pattern vinyl
62	63B, 65B	White crinkle vinyl and light blue crinkle vinyl
62A	65B	White crinkle vinyl and light blue crinkle vinyl
64	63B,65B,76B	Parchment crinkle vinyl and medium emberglo crinkle vinyl
64A	65B	Parchment crinkle vinyl and medium emberglo crinkle vinyl
65	63B,65B,76B	Red crinkle all vinyl
65A	65B	Red crinkle all vinyl
66	63B,65B,76B	Black crinkle all vinyl
66A	65B	Black crinkle all vinyl

Code	Body Type	Trim Scheme
67	63B,65B,76B	White crinkle vinyl and light aqua crinkle vinyl
67A	65B	White crinkle vinyl and light aqua crinkle vinyl
68	63B,65B,76B	White crinkle vinyl and light ivy gold crinkle vinyl
68A	65B	White crinkle vinyl and light ivy gold crinkle vinyl
C2	65C,76C	Parchment crinkle vinyl and parchment rosette pattern vinyl
C3	65C,76C	Parchment crinkle vinyl & parchment rosette patt. vinyl w/ burgundy
C4	65C,76C	Parchment crinkle vinyl & parchment rosette patt. vinyl w/ emberglo
C6	65C,76C	Parchment crinkle vinyl and parchment rosette patt. vinyl with black
C7	65C,76C	Parchment crinkle vinyl and parchment rosette pattern vinyl with aqua
C8	65C,76C	Parchment crinkle vinyl & parchment rosette patt. vinyl w/ ivy gold
C9	65C,76C	Parchment crinkle vinyl & parchment rosette patt. vinyl & parchment
D2	63A,65A,76A	Parchment crinkle vinyl & parchment rosette patt. vinyl with blue
D2A	65A,76A	Parchment crinkle all vinyl with blue
D3	63A,65A,76A	Parchment crinkle vinyl & parchment rosette patt. vinyl w/ burgundy
D3A	65A,76A	Parchment crinkle all vinyl with burgundy
D4	63A,65A,76A	Parchment crinkle vinyl & parchment rosette patt. w/ emberglo
D4A	65A,76A	Parchment crinkle all vinyl with emberglo
D6	63A,65A,76A	Parchment crinkle vinyl and parchment rosette patt. vinyl w/ black
D6A	65A,76A	Parchment crinkle all vinyl with black
D7	63A,65A,76A	Parchment crinkle vinyl & parchment rosette patt. vinyl with aqua
D7A	65A,76A	Parchment crinkle vinyl with aqua
D8	63A,65A,76A	Parchment crinkle vinyl & parchment rosette patt. vinyl w/ ivy gold
D8A	65A,76A	Parchment crinkle vinyl with ivy gold
D9	63A,65A,76A	Parchment crinkle vinyl & parchment rosette patt. vinyl w/ palomino
D9A	65A,76A	Parchment crinkle vinyl with palomino
F2	63B,65B,76B	Parchment crinkle all vinyl with blue
F2A	65B	Parchment crinkle all vinyl with blue
F3	63B,65B,76B	Parchment crinkle all vinyl with burgundy
3A	65B	Parchment crinkle all vinyl with burgundy
F4	63B,65B,76B	Parchment crinkle all vinyl with emberglo
F4A	65B	Parchment crinkle all vinyl with emberglo
F6	63B,65B,76B	Parchment crinkle all vinyl with black
F6A	65B	Parchment crinkle all vinyl with black
F7	63B,65B,76B	Parchment crinkle all vinyl with aqua
F7A	65B	Parchment crinkle all vinyl with aqua
F8	63B,65B,76B	Parchment crinkle all vinyl with ivy gold
F8A	65B	Parchment crinkle all vinyl with ivy gold
F9	63B,65B,76B	Parchment crinkle all vinyl with palomino
F9A	65B	Parchment crinkle all vinyl with palomino

Body Type Codes

63A	Fastback, Standard interior	65C	Hardtop, Bench seat option
63B	Fastback, Deluxe interior	76A	Convertible, Standard interior
65A	Hardtop, Standard interior	76B	Convertible, Deluxe interior
65B	Hardtop, Deluxe interior	76C	Convertible, Bench seat option

1967 Mustang Interior Trim Scheme Codes

Code	Body Type	Trim Scheme
2A	63A,65A,76A	Charcoal black crinkle all vinyl
2B	63A,65A,76A	Light blue crinkle vinyl and dark blue crinkle vinyl
2D	63A,65A,76A	Red crinkle all vinyl
2D1	65A	Red crinkle all vinyl
2F	63A,65A,76A	Medium saddle haircell all vinyl
2F1	65A	Medium saddle haircell all vinyl
2G	63A,65A,76A	Light ivy gold crinkle vinyl & medium ivy gold crinkle vinyl

Code	Body Type	Trim Scheme
2G1	65A	Light ivy gold crinkle vinyl & medium ivy gold crinkle vinyl
2K	63A,65A,76A	Light aqua crinkle vinyl and dark aqua crinkle vinyl
2K1	65A	Light aqua crinkle vinyl and dark aqua crinkle vinyl
2U	63A,65A,76A	Paster parchment crinkle all vinyl
2U1	65A	Paster parchment crinkle all vinyl
4A	65C,76C	Charcoal black crinkle all vinyl
4B	65C	Blue all vinyl
4D	65C	Blue all vinyl
4U	65C,76C	Pastel parchment crinkle all vinyl
4U1	65C	Pastel parchment crinkle all vinyl
5A	63B,65B	Charcoal black crinkle vinyl & charcoal black knitted vinyl
5U	63B,65B	Pastel parchment crinkle vinyl & pastel parchment knitted vinyl
6A	63B,65B,76B	Charcoal black crinkle all vinyl
6B	63B,65B,76B	Light blue crinkle vinyl and dark blue crinkle vinyl
6D	63B,65B,76B	Red crinkle all vinyl
6F	63B,65B,76B	Medium saddle haircell all vinyl
6G	63B,65B,76B	Light ivy gold crinkle vinyl & medium ivy gold crinkle vinyl
6K	63B,65B,76B	Light aqua crinkle vinyl and dark aqua crinkle vinyl
6U	63B,65B,76B	Pastel parchment crinkle all vinyl
7A	63A,65A	Charcoal black crinkle vinyl & charcoal black knitted vinyl
7U	63A,65A	Pastel parchment crinkle vinyl & pastel parchment knitted vinyl

Body Type Codes

63A Fastback, Standard interior
63B Fastback, Deluxe interior
65A Hardtop, Standard interior
65B Hardtop, Deluxe interior

65C Hardtop, Bench seat option
76A Convertible, Standard interior
76B Convertible, Deluxe interior
76C Convertible, Bench seat option

1968 Mustang Interior Trim Scheme Codes

Code	Body Type	Trim Scheme
2A	63A,65A,76A	Charcoal black crinkle vinyl and charcoal black kiwi pattern vinyl
2AA	63A,65A,76A	Charcoal black crinkle vinyl and charcoal black kiwi pattern vinyl
2B	63A,65A,76A	Light blue crinkle vinyl and dark blue kiwi pattern vinyl
2BA	63A,65A,76A	Light blue crinkle vinyl and dark blue kiwi pattern vinyl
2D	63A,65A,76A	Dark red crinkle vinyl and dark red kiwi pattern vinyl
2DA	63A,65A,76A	Dark red crinkle vinyl and dark red kiwi pattern vinyl
2F	63A,65A,76A	Medium saddle crinkle vinyl and medium saddle kiwi pattern vinyl
2FA	63A,65A,76A	Medium saddle crinkle vinyl and medium saddle kiwi pattern vinyl
2G	63A,65A,76A	Light ivy gold crinkle vinyl and medium ivy gold kiwi pattern vinyl
2GA	63A,65A,76A	Light ivy gold crinkle vinyl and medium ivy gold kiwi pattern vinyl
2K	63A,65A,76A	Light aqua crinkle vinyl and dark aqua kiwi pattern vinyl
2KA	63A,65A,76A	Light aqua crinkle vinyl and dark aqua kiwi pattern vinyl
2U	63A,65A,76A	Pastel parchment crinkle vinyl & pastel parch. kiwi patt. vinyl & black
2UA	63A,65A,76A	Pastel parchment crinkle vinyl & pastel parch. kiwi patt. vinyl & black
2Y	63A,65A,76A	Light nugget gold crinkle vinyl & light nugget gold kiwi pattern vinyl
2YA	63A,65A,76A	Light nugget gold crinkle vinyl & light nugget gold kiwi pattern vinyl
5A	63B,65B	Charcoal black crinkle vinyl and charcoal black clarion knitted vinyl
5AA	63B,65B	Charcoal black crinkle vinyl and charcoal black clarion knitted vinyl
5B	63B,65B	Light blue crinkle vinyl and dark blue clarion knitted vinyl
5BA	63B,65B	Light blue crinkle vinyl and dark blue clarion knitted vinyl
5D	63B,65B	Dark red crinkle vinyl and dark red clarion knitted vinyl
5DA	63B,65B	Dark red crinkle vinyl and dark red clarion knitted vinyl
5U	63B,65B	Pastel parch. crinkle vinyl & pastel parch. clarion knit. vinyl w/ black
5UA	63B,65B	Pastel parch. crinkle vinyl & pastel parch. clarion knit. vinyl w/ black
6A	63B,65B,76B	Charcoal black crinkle vinyl and charcoal black kiwi pattern vinyl

Code	Body Type	Trim Scheme
6AA	63B,65B,76B	Charcoal black crinkle vinyl and charcoal black kiwi pattern vinyl
6B	63B,65B,76B	Light blue crinkle vinyl and dark blue kiwi pattern vinyl
6BA	63B,65B,76B	Light blue crinkle vinyl and dark blue kiwi pattern vinyl
6D	63B,65B,76B	Dark red crinkle vinyl and dark red kiwi pattern vinyl
6DA	63B,65B,76B	Dark red crinkle vinyl and dark red kiwi pattern vinyl
6F	63B,65B,76B	Medium saddle crinkle vinyl and medium saddle kiwi pattern vinyl
6FA	63B,65B,76B	Medium saddle crinkle vinyl and medium saddle kiwi pattern vinyl
6G	63B,65B,76B	Light ivy gold crinkle vinyl and medium ivy gold kiwi pattern vinyl
6GA	63B,65B,76B	Light ivy gold crinkle vinyl and medium ivy gold kiwi pattern vinyl
6K	63B,65B,76B	Light aqua crinkle vinyl and dark aqua kiwi pattern vinyl
6KA	63B,65B,76B	Light aqua crinkle vinyl and dark aqua kiwi pattern vinyl
6U	63B,65B,76B	Pastel parchment crinkle vinyl & pastel parch. kiwi patt. vinyl & black
6UA	63B,65B,76B	Pastel parchment crinkle vinyl & pastel parch. kiwi patt. vinyl & black
6Y	63B,65B,76B	Light nugget gold crinkle vinyl & light nugget gold kiwi pattern vinyl
6YA	63B,65B,76B	Light nugget gold crinkle vinyl & light nugget gold kiwi pattern vinyl
7A	63B,65B	Charcoal black crinkle vinyl and charcoal black clarion knitted vinyl
7AA	63B,65B	Charcoal black crinkle vinyl and charcoal black clarion knitted vinyl
7B	63A,65A	Light blue crinkle vinyl and dark blue clarion knitted vinyl
7BA	63A,65A	Light blue crinkle vinyl and dark blue clarion knitted vinyl
7D	63A,65A	Dark red crinkle vinyl and dark red clarion knitted vinyl
7DA	63A,65A	Dark red crinkle vinyl and dark red clarion knitted vinyl
7U	63A,65A	Pastel parch. crinkle vinyl & pastel parch. clarion knit. vinyl w/ black
7UA	63A,65A	Pastel parch. crinkle vinyl & pastel parch. clarion knit. vinyl w/ black
8A	63C,65C	Charcoal black crinkle vinyl and charcoal black clarion knitted vinyl
8AA	63C,65C	Charcoal black crinkle vinyl and charcoal black clarion knitted vinyl
8B	63C,65C	Light blue crinkle vinyl and dark blue clarion knitted vinyl
8BA	63C,65C	Light blue crinkle vinyl and dark blue clarion knitted vinyl
8D	63C,65C	Dark red crinkle vinyl and dark red clarion knitted vinyl
8DA	63C,65C	Dark red crinkle vinyl and dark red clarion knitted vinyl
8U	63C,65C	Pastel parch. crinkle vinyl & pastel parch. clarion knit. vinyl w/ black
8UA	63C,65C	Pastel parch. crinkle vinyl & pastel parch. clarion knit. vinyl w/ black
9A	63D,65D	Charcoal black crinkle vinyl and charcoal black clarion knitted vinyl
9AA	63D,65D	Charcoal black crinkle vinyl and charcoal black clarion knitted vinyl
9B	63D,65D	Light blue crinkle vinyl and dark blue clarion knitted vinyl
9BA	63D,65D	Light blue crinkle vinyl and dark blue clarion knitted vinyl
9D	63D,65D	Dark red crinkle vinyl and dark red clarion knitted vinyl
9DA	63D,65D	Dark red crinkle vinyl and dark red clarion knitted vinyl
9U	63D,65D	Pastel parch. crinkle vinyl & pastel parch. clarion knit. vinyl w/ black
9UA	63D,65D	Pastel parch. crinkle vinyl & pastel parch. clarion knit. vinyl w/ black

Body Type Codes

63A Fastback, Standard interior	65B Hardtop, Deluxe interior
63B Fastback, Deluxe interior	65C Hardtop, Bench seat option
63C Fastback, Bench seat option	65D Hardtop, Bench seat luxury option
63D Fastback, Bench seat luxury option	76A Convertible, Standard interior
65A Hardtop, Standard interior	76B Convertible, Deluxe interior

1969 Mustang Interior Trim Scheme Codes

Code	Body Type	Trim Scheme
1A	65E	Charcoal black corinthian vinyl & charcoal black hopsack pattern cloth
1AA	65E	Charcoal black corinthian vinyl & charcoal black hopsack pattern cloth
1B	65E	Light blue corinthian vinyl and light blue hopsack pattern cloth
1BA	65E	Light blue corinthian vinyl and light blue hopsack pattern cloth

Code	Body Type	Trim Scheme
1G	65E	Dark ivy gold corinthian vinyl and dark ivy gold hopsack pattern cloth
1GA	65E	Dark ivy gold corinthian vinyl and dark ivy gold hopsack pattern cloth
1Y	65E	Light nugget gold corinthian vinyl & light nug. gold hopsack patt. cloth
1YA	65E	Light nugget gold corinthian vinyl & light nug. gold hopsack patt. cloth
2A	63A,65A,76A	Charcoal black corinthian vinyl and charcoal black kiwi vinyl
2B	63A,65A,76A	Light blue corinthian vinyl and light blue kiwi vinyl
2D	63A,65A,76A	Dark red corinthian vinyl and dark red kiwi vinyl
2G	63A,65A,76A	Dark ivy gold corinthian vinyl and dark ivy gold kiwi vinyl
2Y	63A,65A,76A	Light nugget gold corinthian vinyl and light nugget gold kiwi vinyl
3C	63C	Charcoal black corinthian vinyl and charcoal black clarion kitted vinyl
3AA	63C	Charcoal black corinthian vinyl and charcoal black clarion kitted vinyl
3D	63C	Dark red corinthian vinyl and dark red clarion knitted vinyl
3DA	63C	Dark red corinthian vinyl and dark red clarion knitted vinyl
3D1	63C	Dark red corinthian vinyl and dark red clarion knitted vinyl
3W	63C	White corinthian vinyl and white clarion knitted vinyl
3WA	63C	White corinthian vinyl and white clarion knitted vinyl
3W1	63C	White corinthian vinyl and white clarion knitted vinyl
4A	63A,65A	Charcoal black corinthian vinyl and charcoal black clarion knitted vinyl
4D	63A,65A	Dark red corinthian vinyl and dark red clarion knitted vinyl
4D1	63A	Dark red corinthian vinyl and dark red clarion knitted vinyl
5A	63B,65B	Charcoal black corinthian w/ charcoal black ruffino & clarion knit vinyl
5AA	63B,65B	Charcoal black corinthian w/ charcoal black ruffino & clarion knit vinyl
5B	63B,65B	Light blue corinthian vinyl w/ light blue ruffino & clarion knit vinyl
5BA	63B,65B	Light blue corinthian vinyl w/ light blue ruffino & clarion knit vinyl
5D	63B,65B	Dark red corinthian vinyl and dark red ruffino and clarion knitted vinyl
5DA	63B,65B	Dark red corinthian vinyl and dark red ruffino and clarion knitted vinyl
5G	63B,65B	Dark ivy gold corinthian w/ dark ivy gold ruffino & clarion knit vinyl
5GA	63B,65B	Dark ivy gold corinthian w/ dark ivy gold ruffino & clarion knit vinyl
5W	63B,65B	White corinthian w/ white ruffino & clarion knitted vinyl w/ black
5WA	63B,65B	White corinthian w/ white ruffino & clarion knitted vinyl w/ black
5Y	63B,65B	Lt. nugget gold corinthian w/ lt. nug. gold ruffino & clarion knit vinyl
5YA	63B,65B	Lt. nugget gold corinthian w/ lt. nug. gold ruffino & clarion knit vinyl
6A	76A	Charcoal black corinthian vinyl and charcoal black clarion knitted vinyl
6D	76A	Dark red corinthian vinyl and dark red clarion knitted vinyl
7A	76B	Charcoal black corinthian w/ charcoal black ruffino and corinth. vinyl
7AA	76B	Charcoal black corinthian w/ charcoal black ruffino and corinth. vinyl
7B	76B	Light blue corinthian vinyl with light blue ruffino and corinthian vinyl
7BA	76B	Light blue corinthian vinyl with light blue ruffino and corinthian vinyl
7D	76B	Dark red corinthian vinyl with dark red ruffino and corinthian vinyl
7DA	76B	Dark red corinthian vinyl with dark red ruffino and corinthian vinyl
7G	76B	Dk. ivy gold corinthian vinyl w/ dk. ivy gold ruffino & corinthian vinyl
7GA	76B	Dk. ivy gold corinthian vinyl w/ dk. ivy gold ruffino & corinthian vinyl
7W	76B	White corinthian vinyl with white ruffino and corinthian vinyl w/black
7WA	76B	White corinthian vinyl with white ruffino and corinthian vinyl w/black
7Y	76B	Lt. nugget gold corinthian w/ lt. nugget gold ruffino & corinth. vinyl
7YA	76B	Lt. nugget gold corinthian w/ lt. nugget gold ruffino & corinth. vinyl
8A	65C	Charcoal black corinthian w/ charcoal black ruffino & clarion knit vinyl
8AA	65C	Charcoal black corinthian w/ charcoal black ruffino & clarion knit vinyl
8B	65C	Light blue corinthian vinyl w/ light blue ruffino & clarion knit vinyl
8BA	65C	Light blue corinthian vinyl w/ light blue ruffino & clarion knit vinyl
8D	65C	Dark red corinthian vinyl and dark red ruffino and clarion knitted vinyl
8DA	65C	Dark red corinthian vinyl and dark red ruffino and clarion knitted vinyl
8Y	65C	Lt. nugget gold corinthian w/ lt. nug. gold ruffino & clarion knit vinyl
8YA	65C	Lt. nugget gold corinthian w/ lt. nug. gold ruffino & clarion knit vinyl
9A	65D	Charcoal black corinthian w/ charcoal black ruffino & clarion knit vinyl
9AA	65D	Charcoal black corinthian w/ charcoal black ruffino & clarion knit vinyl
9B	65D	Light blue corinthian vinyl w/ light blue ruffino & clarion knit vinyl
9BA	65D	Light blue corinthian vinyl w/ light blue ruffino & clarion knit vinyl

Code	Body Type	Trim Scheme
9D	65D	Dark red corinthian vinyl and dark red ruffino and clarion knitted vinyl
9DA	65D	Dark red corinthian vinyl and dark red ruffino and clarion knitted vinyl
9Y	65D	Lt. nugget gold corinthian w/ lt. nug. gold ruffino & clarion knit vinyl
9YA	65D	Lt. nugget gold corinthian w/ lt. nug. gold ruffino & clarion knit vinyl
DA	63B,65B	Charcoal black corinthian vinyl and charcoal black clarion knitted vinyl
DAA	63B,65B	Charcoal black corinthian vinyl and charcoal black clarion knitted vinyl
DD	63B,65B	Dark red corinthian vinyl and dark red clarion knitted vinyl
DDA	63B,65B	Dark red corinthian vinyl and dark red clarion knitted vinyl
DD1	63B	Dark red corinthian vinyl and dark red clarion knitted vinyl
DW	63B,65B	White corinthian vinyl and white clarion knitted vinyl with black
DWA	63B,65B	White corinthian vinyl and white clarion knitted vinyl with black
DW1	63B	White corinthian vinyl and white clarion knitted vinyl with black

Body Type Codes

63A SportsRoof, Standard interior
63B SportsRoof, Deluxe interior
63C SportsRoof, Mach 1 option
65A Hardtop, Standard interior
65B Hardtop, Deluxe interior

65C Hardtop, Bench seat option
65D Hardtop, Bench seat luxury option
65E Hardtop, Grandé option
76A Convertible, Standard interior
76B Convertible, Deluxe interior

1970 Mustang Interior Trim Scheme Codes

Code	Body Type	Trim Scheme
3A	63C	Charc. black corinth. vinyl w/ charc black clarion knit & corinth. vinyl
3B	63C	Medium blue corinthian w/ medium black clarion knit & corinth. vinyl
3E	63C	Vermillion corinthian w/ vermillion clarion knit & corinth. vinyl
3F	63C	Medium ginger corinthian w/ med. ginger clarion knit & corinth. vinyl
3G	63C	Med. ivy green corinth. w/ med. ivy green clarion knit & corinth vinyl
3W	63C	White corinthian w/ white clarion knit & corinth. vinyl w/ black
AA	65E	Charcoal black corinthian vinyl & black houndstooth pattern cloth
AA1	65E	Charcoal black corinthian vinyl & black houndstooth pattern cloth
AB	65E	Medium blue corinthian vinyl & medium blue houndstooth pattern cloth
AB1	65E	Medium blue corinthian vinyl & medium blue houndstooth pattern cloth
AE	65E	Vermillion corinthian vinyl and vermillion houndstooth pattern cloth
AE1	65E	Vermillion corinthian vinyl and vermillion houndstooth pattern cloth
AF	65E	Medium ginger corinthian vinyl & med. ginger houndstooth pattern cloth
AF1	65E	Medium ginger corinthian vinyl & med. ginger houndstooth pattern cloth
AG	65E	Med. ivy green corinthian & med. ivy green houndstooth patt. cloth
AG1	65E	Med. ivy green corinthian & med. ivy green houndstooth patt. cloth
BA	63A,65A,76A	Charcoal black corinthian vinyl and charcoal black ruffino vinyl
BAA	63A,65A,76A	Charcoal black corinthian vinyl and charcoal black ruffino vinyl
BA1	63A	Charcoal black corinthian vinyl and charcoal black ruffino vinyl
BB	63A,65A,76A	Medium blue corinthian vinyl and medium blue ruffino vinyl
BBA	63A,65A,76A	Medium blue corinthian vinyl and medium blue ruffino vinyl
BE	63A,65A,76A	Vermillion corinthian vinyl and vermillion ruffino vinyl
BEA	63A,65A,76A	Vermillion corinthian vinyl and vermillion ruffino vinyl
BF	63A,65A,76A	Medium ginger corinthian vinyl and medium ginger ruffino vinyl
BFA	63A,65A,76A	Medium ginger corinthian vinyl and medium ginger ruffino vinyl
BG	63A,65A,76A	Medium ivy green corinthian vinyl & medium ivy green ruffino vinyl
BGA	63A,65A,76A	Medium ivy green corinthian vinyl & medium ivy green ruffino vinyl
BW	63A,65A,76A	White corinthian vinyl and white ruffino vinyl with black
BWA	63A,65A,76A	White corinthian vinyl and white ruffino vinyl with black
BW1	63A	White corinthian vinyl and white ruffino vinyl with black
CE	63B,76B	Vermillion corinthian vinyl and vermillion spectrum stripe vinyl
CE1	63B,76B	Vermillion corinthian vinyl and vermillion spectrum stripe vinyl

Code	Body Type	Trim Scheme
CF	63B,76B	Medium ginger corinthian vinyl & medium ginger spectrum stripe vinyl
CF1	63B,76B	Medium ginger corinthian vinyl & medium ginger spectrum stripe vinyl
EA	63B,76B	Charcoal black corinthian w/ charcoal black clarion knit & ruffino vinyl
EA1	63B,76B	Charcoal black corinthian w/ charcoal black clarion knit & ruffino vinyl
EB	63B,76B	Medium blue corinthian vinyl w/ med. blue clarion knit & ruffino vinyl
EB1	63B,76B	Medium blue corinthian vinyl w/ med. blue clarion knit & ruffino vinyl
EG	63B,76B	Med. ivy green corinth. w/ med. ivy green clarion knit & corinth. vinyl
EG1	63B,76B	Med. ivy green corinth. w/ med. ivy green clarion knit & corinth. vinyl
EW	63B,76B	White corinthian vinyl w/ white clarion knit & corinth. vinyl w/ black
EW1	63B,76B	White corinthian vinyl w/ white clarion knit & corinth. vinyl w/ black
TA	63B,65B	Charcoal black corinthian w/ charc. black clarion knit & corinth. vinyl
TAA	63B,65B	Charcoal black corinthian w/ charc. black clarion knit & corinth. vinyl
TA1	63B,65B	Charcoal black corinthian w/ charc. black clarion knit & corinth. vinyl
TB	63B,65B	Medium blue corinthian vinyl w/ med. blue clarion knit & corinth. vinyl
TBA	63B,65B	Medium blue corinthian vinyl w/ med. blue clarion knit & corinth. vinyl
TB1	63B,65B	Medium blue corinthian vinyl w/ med. blue clarion knit & corinth. vinyl
TGA	63B,65B	Med. ivy green corinth. w/ med. ivy green clarion knit & corinth. vinyl
TG1	63B,65B	Med. ivy green corinth. w/ med. ivy green clarion knit & corinth. vinyl
TW	63B,65B	White corinthian vinyl w/ white clarion knit & corinth. vinyl w/ black
TWA	63B,65B	White corinthian vinyl w/ white clarion knit & corinth. vinyl w/ black
TW1	63B,65B	White corinthian vinyl w/ white clarion knit & corinth. vinyl w/ black
UE	63B,65B	Vermillion corinthian vinyl and vermillion spectrum stripe vinyl
UEA	63B,65B	Vermillion corinthian vinyl and vermillion spectrum stripe vinyl
UE1	63B,65B	Vermillion corinthian vinyl and vermillion spectrum stripe vinyl
UF	63B,65B	Med. ginger corinthian & med. ginger spectrum stripe & corinth. vinyl
UFA	63B,65B	Med. ginger corinthian & med. ginger spectrum stripe & corinth. vinyl
UF1	63B,65B	Med. ginger corinthian & med. ginger spectrum stripe & corinth. vinyl

Body Type Codes

63A	SportsRoof, Standard interior	65B Hardtop, Deluxe interior
63B	SportsRoof, Deluxe interior	65E Hardtop, Grandé option
63C	SportsRoof, Mach 1 option	76A Convertible, Standard interior
65A	Hardtop, Standard interior	76B Convertible, Deluxe interior

The 1965 standard Mustang interior features unique molded door panels and all-vinyl seat upholstery. Front seat belts were optional in 1965.

Standard 1966 interiors, like this example in Parchment, were simple yet comfortable. Seat belts were standard equipment in 1966.

*A folddown rear seat was included as standard equipment
on all fastback models through 1968. This 1968 Mustang
fastback has a black standard interior.*

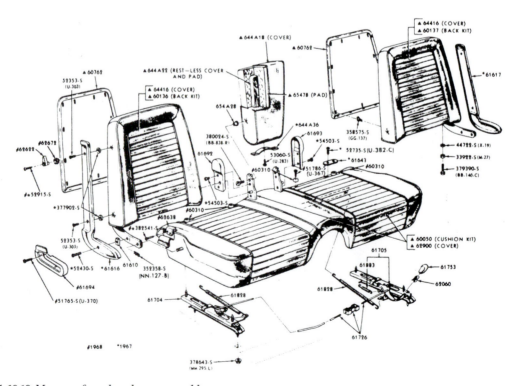

The 1965-1969 Mustang front bench seat assembly.

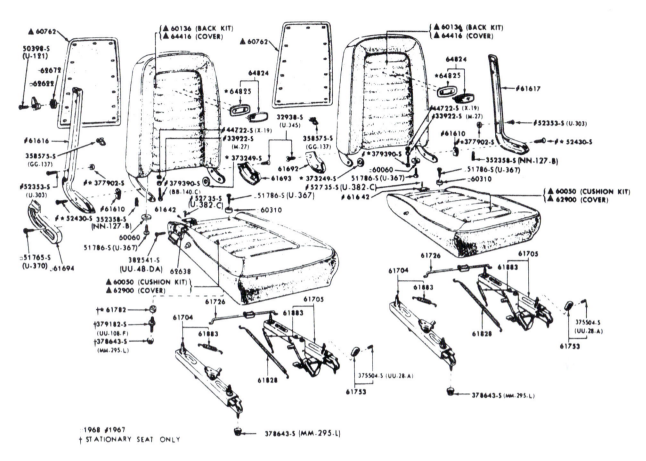

The 1965-1966 Mustang, 1967 Mustang (standard interior), and 1968-1969 Mustang front bucket seat assembly.

The 1968 standard seats have more padding and a seatback lock—yet another safety feature.

This 1966 Mustang convertible is equipped with the Interior Decor Group and air conditioning.

The optional Interior Decor Group included these unique seatbacks embossed with running horses.

This 1965 hardtop has a white standard interior, optional seat belts with retractors, and a Rally-Pac.

Standard interior for 1965 placed a pleated seat cushion inside smooth vinyl bolsters. Rear seat belts were a dealer-installed option in 1965.

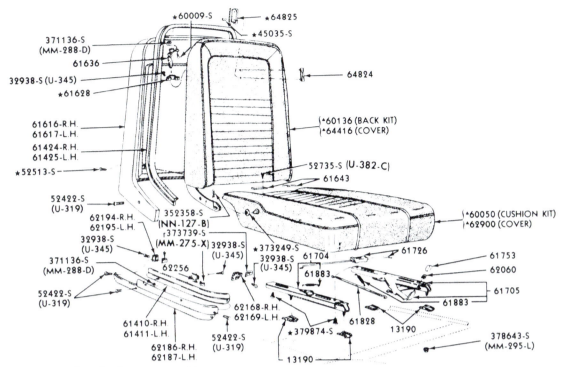

The 1967 Mustang front bucket seat assembly.

A Parchment front bench seat in a 1966 Mustang.

This two-tone Deluxe interior is in a 1967 convertible.

A full-width bench seat with center armrest was a Mustang option through 1969. This is a front bench seat in a 1967 convertible. Until 1968, a bench seat was available only with standard interior. In 1968 and 1969 a Deluxe bench seat option was offered.

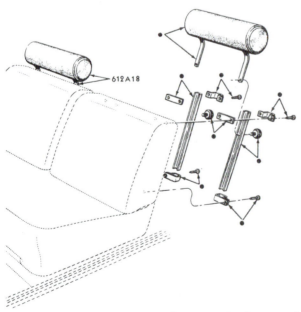

Optional 1966-1967 Mustang front seat headrests and related parts.

The full-length console for 1967 is attractive and functional. Its front compartment has a roll-top door and inside courtesy lamp.

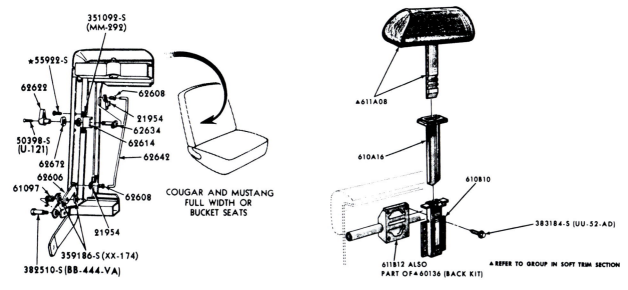

The 1968 Mustang front seatback latch assembly.

The 1969-1970 Mustang front seat headrest assembly.

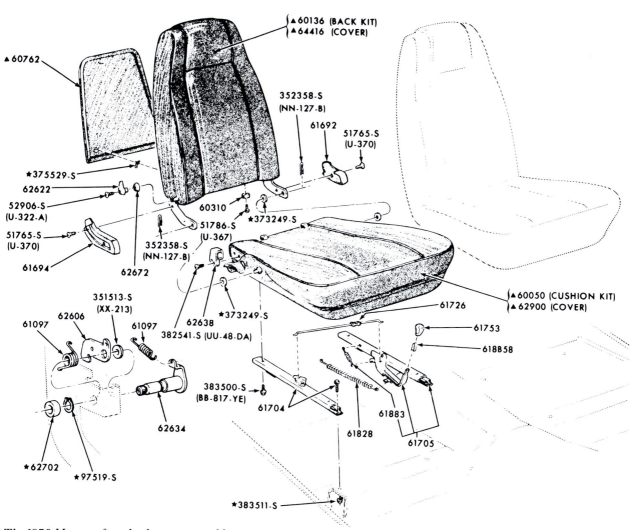

The 1970 Mustang front bucket seat assembly.

MUSTANG FRONT SEAT BELT ASSEMBLY APPLICATION CHART

BODY TYPE	PART NUMBER (less suffix)	R/N	AQUA	BLACK	BLUE	BUR-GUNDY	EMBER GLO	IVY GOLD	PARCH-MENT	RED
1966 *										
63, 65	^C6OZ-62611A72	N	◊	GAB	◊	◊	◊	◊	◊	CAC
	^C7OZ-62611A72	R		B1A	B1B				◊	
Right	#C7OZ-76611A72	R		A1A	◊					
Left	#C7OZ-76611A73	R	DAF	A1A	◊			◊		
Before 3/28/66	#C6OZ-62611A72	R	DAF	DAB	GAD		GAG		◊	GAC
3/28 - 5/16/66	#C6OZ-62611A72	R	◊	GAB					◊	GAC
From 5/16/66	#C6ZZ-65611A72	R	DAF	DAB	◊		DAG	DAE	DAJ	DAC
76	^ C6ZZ-76611A72	N	◊	DAB	◊	◊	◊	◊	◊	◊
Before 5/16/66	#C6ZZ-76611A72	N	◊	EAB	◊		◊	◊	◊	◊
From 5/16/66	#C6ZZ-76611A72	N	◊	EAB	◊		◊	◊	Grandé	◊

BODY TYPE	PART NUMBER (less suffix)	R/N	AQUA	BLACK	BLUE	SADDLE		IVY GOLD	PARCH-MENT	RED
1967 *										
63, 65	#C7ZZ-65611A72	R	◊	D1A	◊	◊		◊	◊	◊
76	#C7ZZ-76611A72	N	◊	A1A	◊	◊		◊	◊	◊
	^ C7ZZ-76611A72	N		B1A	◊				◊	
63,65 exc. Shelby GT350/500	^ C7ZZ-65611A72	R		B1A	B1B				◊	
63 Shelby GT350/500	S7MS-65611A72-A		Includes emblem							

BODY TYPE	PART NUMBER (less suffix)	R/N	AQUA	BLACK	BLUE	NUGGET GOLD	IVY GOLD	PARCH-MENT	RED
1968									
63,65 exc. Shelby GT350/500	+C8WZ-65611A72		B1K	B1A	B1B		B1G	B1U	B1D
76 exc. Shelby GT350/500	+C8ZZ-76611A72	N	◊	E1A	◊	◊	◊	◊	◊
	@D1TZ-10611B60			E					

BODY TYPE	PART NUMBER (less suffix)	R/N	AQUA	BLACK	BLUE	SADDLE	NUGGET GOLD	IVY GOLD	RED
1969									
63,65	+C9ZZ-65611A72	R	F2K	F2A	F2B	F2F	F2Y	F2G	F2D
76	+C9ZZ-76611A72	N	◊	B1A	◊	◊	◊	◊	◊
Ctr. & rear seat	+C9AZ-62611A72	N	K1K	K1A	K1B		K1Y	K1G	K1D

BODY TYPE	PART NUMBER (less suffix)	R/N	BLACK	BLUE	GINGER	GREEN	PARCH-MENT
1970							
63,65	D0ZZ-65611A72		J	G	H	K	F
	«D0ZZ-65611A72	R	N				
76	D0ZZ-76611A72	N	B	A	E	C	

R/N: Retractable or Nonretractable harness

*   Includes attaching parts
^   With fingertip release
#   With push button release
◊   Use black
+   Chrome and plastic buckle
@   Plastic buckle
«   Standard buckle - plastic covered

Body Type Codes:
6 3 Fastback/SportsRoof
6 5 Hardtop (incl. Grandé)
7 6 Convertible

MUSTANG REAR SEAT BELT ASSEMBLY APPLICATION CHART

BODY TYPE:	PART NUMBER LESS SUFFIX	COLORS and PART NUMBER SUFFIXES:							
1966		EMBER-GLO		BLUE	IVY GOLD	PARCH-MENT	RED		TOB-ACCO
Before 1/3/66 *	^C6AZ-62613B84				DAE		DAC		DAK
From 1/3/66 to 5/16/66 *	#C6AZ-63613B84	@		EAD		EAJ			EAK
From 5/16/66 *	#C6ZZ-65613B84	BAG		BAD		BAJ			
1967		AQUA	BLACK	BLUE	IVY GOLD	PARCH-MENT	RED	SADDLE	TOB-ACCO
Exc. Shelby	#C7AZ-62613B84	A1K	A1A	A1B	A1G	A1U	&	A1F	&
GT 350/500	+C7AZ-62613B84		B1A	B1B		&			
1968		AQUA	BLACK	BLUE	IVY GOLD	PARCH-MENT	RED	SADDLE	NUGGET GOLD
Exc. Shelby	=C8AZ-62613B84		C1A	C1B		&			
GT 350/500	~C8WZ-65613B84	A1K	A1A	A1B	A1G	A1U	A1D	A1F	A1Y
1969									
Rear & aux. seat	Refer to group 611A72-3								
1970		GINGER	BLACK	BLUE	GREEN	PARCH-MENT			
	DOMZ-76613B84	E	A	B	H	J			
	>DOAZ-62613B84		A						

* Includes attaching parts
@ Use C7AZ-62613B84-A1D
^ With fingertip release
\# With push button release
= Plastic buckle
& Use black
~ Chrome and plastic buckle

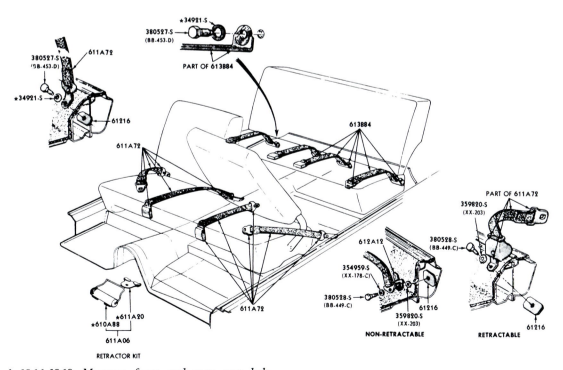

Typical 1966-1969 Mustang front and rear seat belt installation.

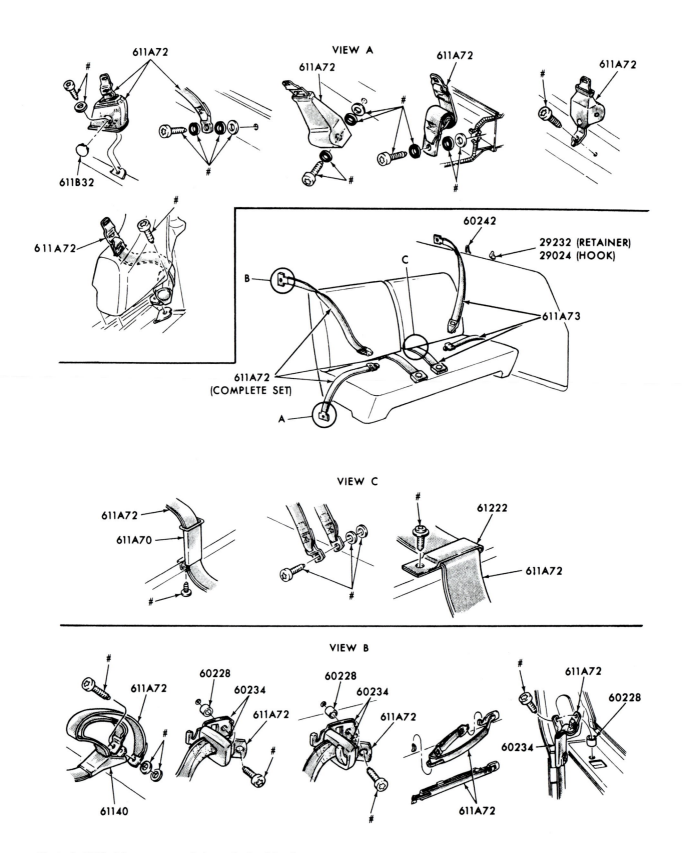

Typical 1970 Mustang seat belt and shoulder harness installation.

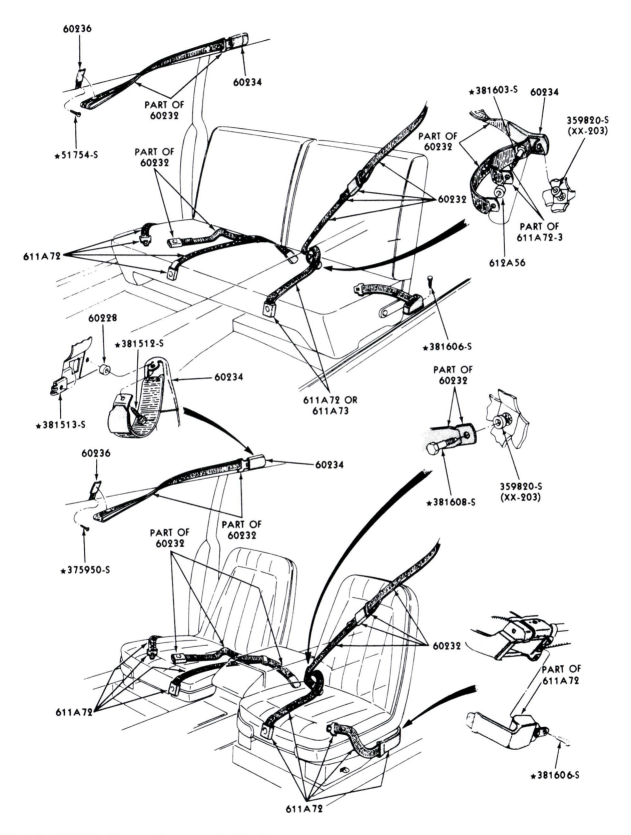

60236

60234

PART OF
60232

★381603-S   60234

359820-S
(XX-203)

PART OF
60232

PART OF
60232

60232

★51754-S

PART OF
611A72-3

611A72

612A56

60228

★381512-S

60234

★381606-S

★381513-S

PART OF
60232

611A72 OR
611A73

60236

60234

359820-S
(XX-203)

PART OF
60232

PART OF
60232

★381608-S

★375950-S

60232

PART OF
611A72

611A72

611A72

★381606-S

*Typical 1967-1969 Mustang front seat shoulder harness
installation.*

119

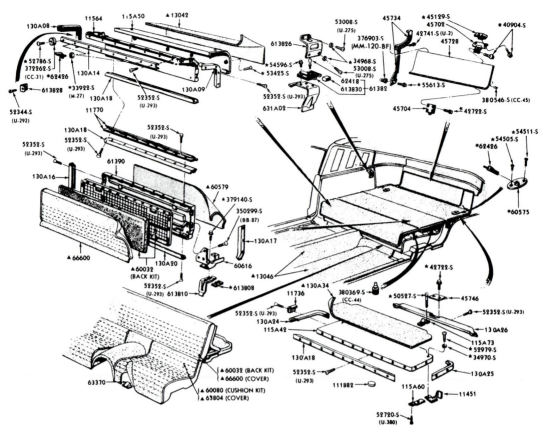

The 1965-1966 Mustang fastback fold-down rear seat assembly.

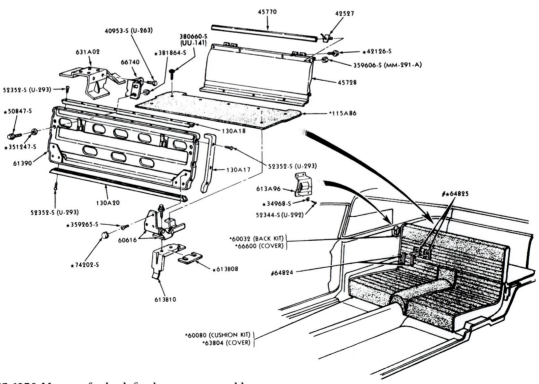

The 1967-1970 Mustang fastback fixed rear seat assembly.

120

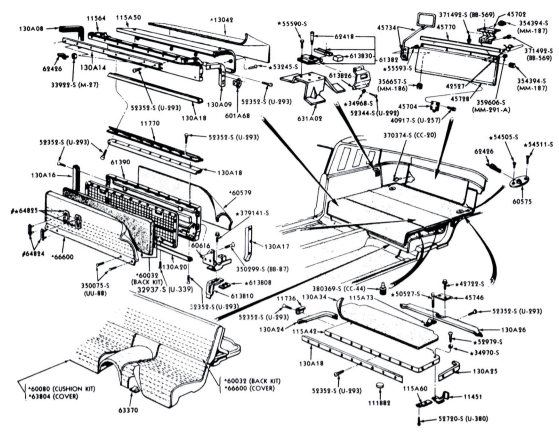

The 1967-1970 Mustang SportsRoof fold-down rear seat assembly.

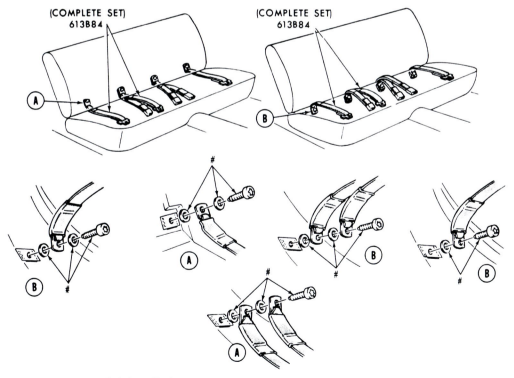

Typical 1970 Mustang rear seat belt installation.

Mustang Console Panel Application Chart

Colors & Applicable Part Number Suffixes

Body Type	Part Number Less Suffix	White	Black	Blue	Aqua	Ivy Gold	Nugget Gold	Red	Ginger
1965									
65,76 w/o A/C Before 12/1/64	C5OZ-65045A36	CAF	—	—	—	—	—	—	—
65,76 w/A/C Before 8/20/64	C5ZZ-65045A36	CAF	—	—	—	—	—	—	—
63,65,76 w/A/C From 12/1/64	C5ZZ-65045A36	CAF	CAB	—	—	—	—	—	—
1966	C5ZZ-65045A36	—	CAB	—	—	—	—	—	—
1967	C7ZZ-65045A36	—	A1A	A1B	—	—	—	—	—
1968	C8ZZ-65045A36	—	A1A	A1B	—	—	—	—	—
1969	C9ZZ-65045A36	—	C1A	—	C1K	C1G	C1Y	C1D	—
1970	DOZZ-65045A36	—	G	—	—	—	—	—	H

Body Type Codes
63: Fastback
65: Hardtop
76: Convertible

MUSTANG CENTER INSTRUMENT PANEL APPLICATION CHART

YEAR	BODY TYPE	DESCRIPTION	PART NUMBER
67/68	All, Std. Interior	Camera case finish	C7ZZ-6504774-B
68	All	Wood grain finish	C8ZZ-6504774-A
69	Mach 1 & Grandé	Light teakwood finish, w/o radio, Incl. attaching parts	C9ZZ-6504774-C
	Before 1/6/69.	Light teakwood finish, with radio, Incl. attaching parts	C9ZZ-6504774-D
69/70	Mach 1 & Grandé	Dark teakwood finish, w/o radio, Incl. attaching parts	C9ZZ-6504774-E
	From 1/6/69	Dark teakwood finish, with radio, Incl. attaching parts	C9ZZ-6504774-F
69/70	Exc Mach 1 & Grandé	Black cameracase finish, w/o radio, Incl. attach. parts	C9ZZ-6504774-A
69/70	Exc Mach 1 & Grandé	Black Corinthian grain finish - with radio	C9ZZ-6504774-B

MUSTANG INSTRUMENT PANEL GLOVE COMPARTMENT DOOR APPLICATIONS

YEAR	PART NUMBER	DESCRIPTION
65/66	C5ZZ-6506024-D	All Deluxe interiors; Wood grain finish
67/68	C7ZZ-6506024-A	
69/70	C9ZZ-6506024-A	

MUSTANG CONSOLE PANEL GLOVE COMPARTMENT DOOR APPLICATIONS

YEAR	PART NUMBER	DESCRIPTION
65/66	C5ZZ-6506024-B	With Camera Case finish
65/66	C5ZZ-6506024-C	With wood grain finish, From 3/8/65
67/68	C8ZZ-6506024-A	
	379162-S(CC34A)	Bumper
69	C9ZZ-6506024-B1Y	Nugget gold - less hinge - no catch - plain
	C9ZZ-6506024-B1D	Red
69/70	(4) 52720-S8(U380)	No. 8 pan head screws - 18 x 3/8"
69/70	C9ZZ-6506024-B1A	Black, less hinge, no catch, plain, Before 9/2/69
	C9ZZ-6506024-B2B	Blue
70	DOZZ-6506024-C	Red, Before 9/2/69
70	DOZZ-6306024-K	Black, less hinge, magnetic catch, plain, From 9/2/69
	DOZZ-6306024-B	Blue, to 12/1/69
	DOZZ-6306024-F	Ginger
	DOZZ-6306024-A	Green
	DOZZ-6306024-D	Red
	DOZZ-6306024-C	Tobacco
70	DOZZ-6306024-K	Black, less hinge, positive catch, plain, From 12/1/69
	DOZZ-6306024-H	Blue
	DOZZ-6306024-M	Ginger
	DOZZ-6306024-G	Green
	DOZZ-6306024-L	Red

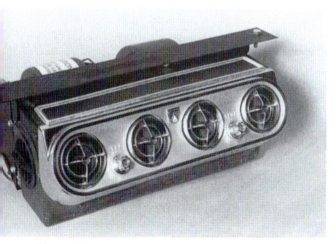

Air conditioning in a Mustang was a bolt-on option (even if it was factory installed) until 1967 when it became an integrated part of the instrument panel. This compact 1965 model air handler contains the evaporator core, a fan, a thermostatic control valve, and the two control switches. Hang-on air conditioning can only recycle air in the passenger compartment because there are no provisions for a fresh-air duct.

The 1966 air conditioning unit has a black camera-case finish and smaller, less intricate vents, and is slightly smaller in size.

A full-length console with front compartment and rear ashtray was and remains a popular Mustang option.

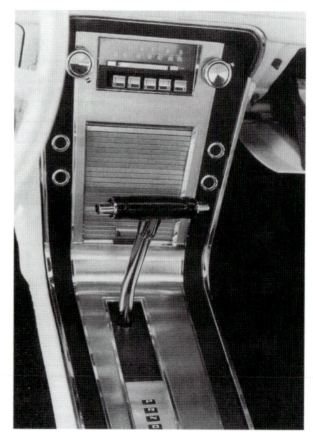

The Convenience Control Panel option, consisting of four warning lights, is located in the console when air conditioning is installed. Otherwise, the lights are positioned in the center of the dash panel just above the radio.

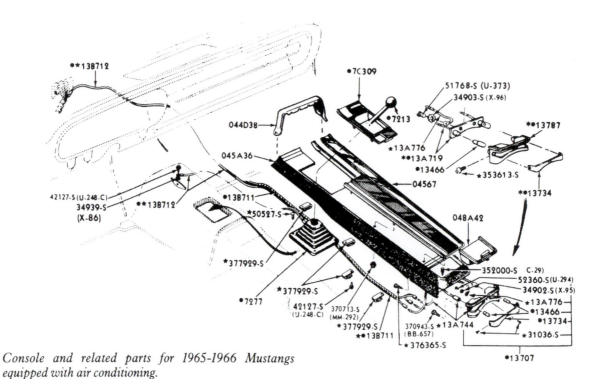

Console and related parts for 1965-1966 Mustangs equipped with air conditioning.

124

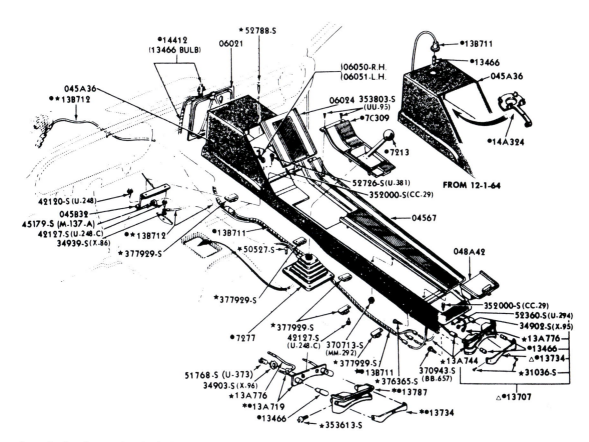

Console and related parts for 1965-1966 Mustangs without air conditioning.

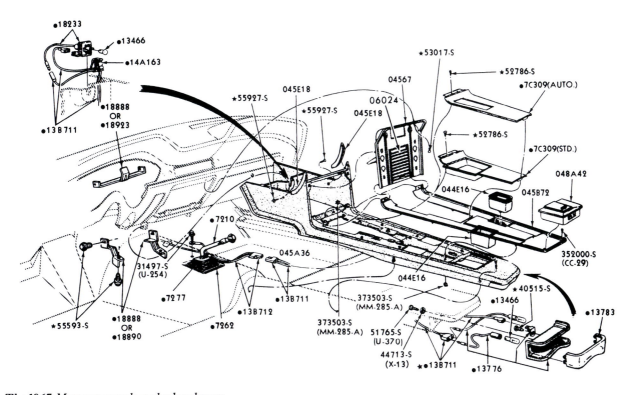

The 1967 Mustang console and related parts.

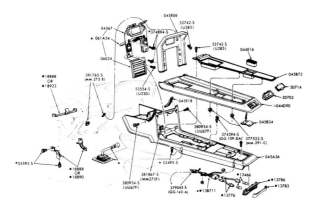

The 1968 Mustang console and related parts.

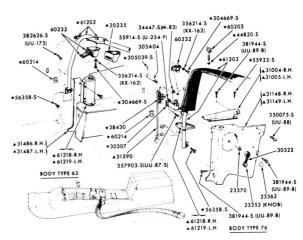

The 1969-1970 Shelby Mustang rollbar and related parts.

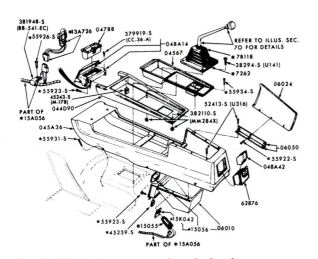

The 1969-1970 Mustang console and related parts.

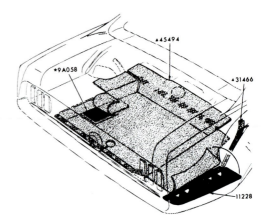

The 1969-1970 Mustang luggage compartment trim.

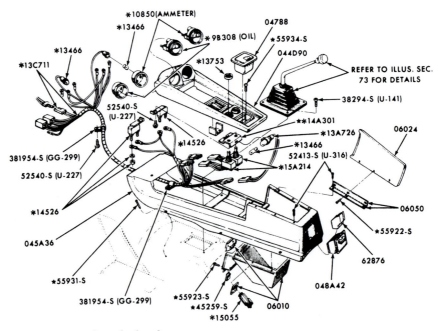

The 1969-1970 Shelby Mustang console and related parts.

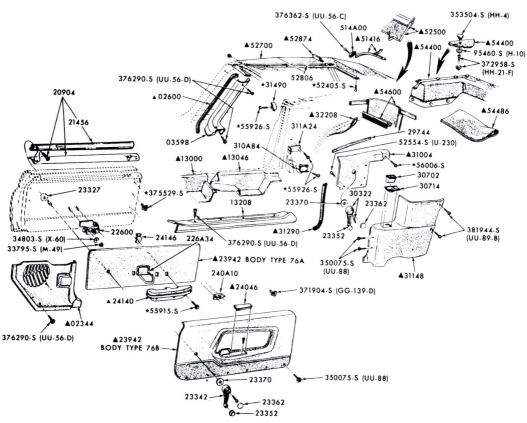

The 1969-1970 Mustang convertible door and quarter trim
panels and related parts.

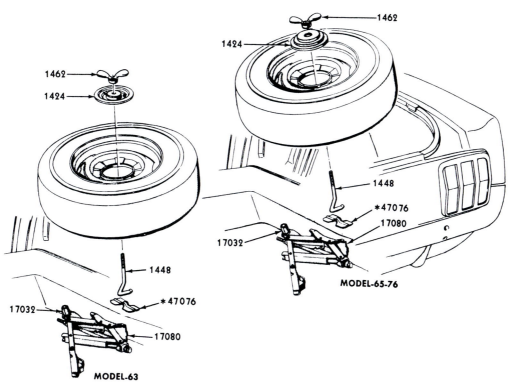

The 1965-1966 Mustang spare wheel, jack, and related
parts.

127

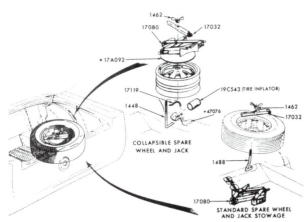

Both a standard and an optional collapsible spare were offered in 1969 and 1970 Mustangs.

A full-sized spare tire in a 1968 Mustang hardtop model.

The Boss 429 battery was placed on the passenger side of the trunk floor for better distribution of weight. The spare tire was moved to the driver's side of the car.

Correct placement of a Space Saver spare tire in a 1969 Mustang SportsRoof.

The correct storage for a full-size spare tire in a 1970 Mustang SportsRoof.

128

Chapter 4

Engine

From 1964 through 1970 surprisingly few engines powered the Ford Mustangs. Several shared exterior componentry, but applications of accessories varied according to the weight of the car, the options included (especially air conditioning), and performance packages. Included in this chapter will be not only the engines and their internal components, but assemblies and subassemblies either located in the engine compartment or in the category of engine-driven accessories, most notably air conditioning.

From the base 170ci six-cylinder engine to the 429ci NASCAR engine in the special edition 1969 and 1970 Boss 429s, the sources of power evolved along with the Mustang itself. Due in part to the popularity of the Mustang and the nature of auto sales competition, especially with GM, in the 1960s, Ford involved itself in remarkable levels of research and development of performance engines. This pleased not only the potential Mustang buyer, but the performance enthusiast in general; the appreciation of the more powerful Ford V-8 engines of that era continues into the 1990s. It is remarkable that today's 5.0 liter engines are based on the 302ci introduced in 1968—which, in turn, derived from the 260ci V-8 and 221ci V-8 of the early 1960s.

Today, enthusiasts are deeply involved in a quest to authenticate many engines, accessories, and subassemblies, but especially the more uncommon "muscle" parts of the past. Many original components, especially equipment related to emissions controls, were discarded or swapped with no regard for their future value, rarity, or difficulty in identification and replacement. In this chapter we will attempt to provide guidelines for identification based upon production dates, original dimensions, tie-ins to related componentry, and cross-references to various applications and options.

Much of this material is drawn from vintage Ford references, though the reader should note that Ford always has made running changes in its supply system and there is no guarantee that all part numbers will relate directly to the original factory-installed equipment. The reason for this is that Ford, as time passed, tended to consolidate applications of many parts in order to reduce inventories and costs. A replacement part may be less specialized than the original piece, but will work satisfactorily, according to Ford. That doesn't necessarily help the concours restorer in search of assembly-line perfection.

But the part numbers themselves are not the goal here; the value of this document lies in the description, dimension, and application of Ford replacement componentry. Those facts can help anyone to a better understanding of what was original equipment or what was accepted in the past as original equipment.

The 289 HiPo Engine

A K-Code High Performance 289, nicknamed HiPo, is an A-Code 289 4-V that has been modified and strengthened to handle high-rpm operation. The engine block is basically unchanged. It is necessary to shift the torque and horsepower curve to a higher-rpm level when, as in this case, cubic inches are in limited supply. As stresses on internal components increase dramatically with higher rpm, it is necessary to beef up pieces and areas that are known to fail. An engine will not make more high-rpm power just by making some internal components stronger. Other modifications, such as free-flowing induction and exhaust systems and a radical camshaft profile are needed to successfully shift the powerband upward.

K-Code 289 High Performance Nomenclature

To better contain the forces generated by the HiPo crankshaft, special heavy-duty main bearing caps were installed. All 289 HiPo engines used a two-bolt block, meaning the main bearing caps are held in place with just two bolts. The oil passages

continued on next page

supplying the lifter, cam, and main bores are sealed with screw-in pipe plugs instead of pressed-in caps for increased durability. The 4-V flat-tappet hydraulic camshaft is replaced with a solid-lifter cam, which promotes durability and enables the engine to breathe at higher rpm. The cylinder heads were exclusive HiPo pieces.

Specifications

Gross brake horsepower	271 @ 6000rpm
Gross torque	312 @ 3400rpm
Bore	4.00in
Stroke	2.87in
Compression ratio	10.5:1 (1964-1968)
Combustion chamber volume (cc)	47.7-50.7cc
Bore spacing	4.38in
Crankshaft material	Nodular iron
Main journal diameter	2.2486in
Rod journal diameter	2.1232in
Block deck height	8.206in
Deck height clearance	0.016in
Compression height	1.60in
Connecting rod length, center to center	5.155in
Intake valve head diameter	1.665in (1964) 1.778in (1965-1968)
Exhaust valve head diameter	1.450in
Valve spring pressure (closed)	83.5-92.5lb @ 1.77in
Valve spring pressure (open)	234.5-259.5lb @ 1.32in
Valve lash (mechanical)	0.020in (hot)
Rocker arm ratio	1.60:1
Firing order	15426378

280 HiPo Part Numbers

Part number	Description
C4OZ-6010-C	Engine Block (5-bolt bellhousing) 1964-1965
C5OZ-6010-C	Engine Block (6-bolt bellhousing) 1966-1968
C5OZ-12127-E	Distributor (dual point, mechanical advance)
C3OZ-6250-C	Camshaft (solid lifter) Marked #VE
C9ZZ-6200-C	Connecting Rod (5.155in long)
C3OZ-6500-A	Lifter (solid, 0.8742in O.D. 2in long)
C3OZ-6A527-A	Rocker Arm Stud (2 1/2in long, 3/8x24 top, 7/16x14 bottom)
C4OZ-6A574-A	Valve Cover Kit (COBRA, aluminum)
C3OZ-6211-M	Rod Bearings (std.)
C3AZ-6333-A	Upper Main Bearings (std. red 0.0956in) 1963-1965
C3AZ-6333-B	Upper Main Bearings (std. blue 0.0960in) 1963-1965
C3AZ-6333-P	Upper Main Bearings (std. 0.0959in) 1966
C3AZ-6333-H	Lower Main Bearings (std. red 0.0956in) 1963-1965
C3AZ-6333-J	Lower Main Bearings (std. blue 0.0960in) 1963-1965
C3AZ-6333-AA	Lower Main Bearings (std. 0.0959in) 1966
C3AZ-6337-A	Upper Main Thrust Bearing (std. 0.0956in) 1963-1965
C3AZ-6337-B	Upper Main Thrust Bearing (std. 0.0960in) 1963-1965
C3AZ-6337-P	Upper Main Thrust Bearing (std. 0.0959in) 1966
C3AZ-6337-H	Lower Main Thrust Bearing (std. 0.0956in) 1963-1965
C3AZ-6337-J	Lower Main Thrust Bearing (std. 0.0960in) 1963-1965
C3AZ-6337-AA	Lower Main Thrust Bearing (std. 0.0959in) 1966
C3OZ-6303-B	Crankshaft (nodular iron)
C5OZ-6049-A	Cylinder Head
C3AZ-6051-C	Cylinder Head Gasket
C3OZ-6505-A	Valve (exhaust)
C4OZ-6507-A	Valve (intake)
C3OZ-6A511-A	Spring (valve)
C3OZ-6514-A	Valve Spring Retainer
7HA-6518-A	Valve Stem Lock
C3OZ-6571-B	Valve Stem Seals
C2OZ-6065-A	Head Bolts (short)
C2OZ-6065-B	Head Bolts (long)
C3OZ-6108-L	Piston (includes pin)
C2OZ-6261-A	Bearing Camshaft (front)
C2OZ-6267-A	Bearing Camshaft (#2 journal)
C2OZ-6262-A	Bearing Camshaft (#3 journal)
C2OZ-6270-A	Bearing Camshaft (#4 journal)
C2OZ-6263-A	Bearing Camshaft (#5 journal)
C3OZ-6265-A	Spacer (camshaft sprocket)
C2OZ-6266-A	Plug (camshaft rear bearing)
C3OZ-6268-A	Timing Chain (58 links)
C5OZ-6269-A	Plate (camshaft thrust)
C3OZ-6306-A	Camshaft Sprocket (21 teeth)
C2OZ-6600-A	Oil Pump
C5AZ-6312-B	Crankshaft Pulley (marked #C5AE-A single sheave 6 23/64in diameter 3/8in belt)
C5OZ-6316-A	Crankshaft Damper
C3OZ-6375-C	Flywheel (3- or 4-speed, marked #C3OE-6380-B, used before 7/1/66)
C3OZ-6375-D	Flywheel (3- or 4-speed, marked #A, 160 tooth ring gear, used after 7/1/66)
C4OZ-6375-C	Flywheel (C-4 automatic trans)
C4OZ-6980-A Consists Of:	Engine Dress Up Kit (chrome) C2OZ-2162-A Master Cylinder Cap C4OZ-6A547-A Valve Covers C4GE-6750-A Dip Stick C3DE-6766-C Oil Filler Cap C2SZ-8100-A Radiator Cap C4DZ-9600-C Air Cleaner

The 428ci Engines

The first 428ci engine was engineered for and installed in 1966 Thunderbirds. It is the last and youngest member of Ford's FE engine family. Thunderbird 428s were comparatively docile engines incorporating a mild hydraulic cam profile that generated more than enough low-end torque to get the heavy car away from a stoplight.

The 428ci engine became part of Mustang's option list on April 1, 1968. Capitalizing on years of high-performance development and experience, Ford engineers made numerous modifications that transformed the slow-pulling Thunderbird engine into a tire-smoking brute. The Medium Riser 427/390 Police Interceptor hybrid was thereafter called Cobra Jet, or CJ for short.

Later improvements to the engine's bottom end identified the big block as a Super Cobra Jet, abbreviated as Super CJ or simply SCJ.

Drag Pack was a race option available with most big-block high-performance engine packages.

Cobra Jet

The 428ci is the only FE engine identified as a Cobra Jet or Super Cobra Jet. As compared to other FEs, it closely resembles a bored and stroked 390 GT or PI (Police Interceptor) engine.

The internal features that distinguish a Cobra Jet from a Thunderbird 428ci engine include a high-strength, nodular-cast-iron crankshaft, forged-steel Police Interceptor-type connecting rods with larger $^{13}/_{32}$in nut and bolt, and 427-type low-riser cylinder heads. A Thunderbird 428-4V combustion chamber measures from 68.1cc to 71.1cc as compared to the larger-chambered CJ head which measures from 72.8cc to 75.8cc.

Stock intake runners were 1.34in wide and 1.93in tall. CJ runners measured 1.34in by 2.34in. CJ 2.085in intake valves were 0.060in larger than stock while the 1.658in exhaust valves were 0.100in larger.

The hydraulic CJ cam profile is hotter than the stock 428 version and the 735cfm carburetor is 135cfm larger.

The 428 is the only FE engine that is externally balanced. All other FEs are internally balanced.

Super Cobra Jet

A Super Cobra Jet is a Cobra Jet with some stronger reciprocating pieces added. CJ connecting rods are replaced with forged 427 rods, which use stronger cap screws instead of bolts and nuts to secure the bearing caps.

SCJ engines built before December 26, 1968, were equipped with pistons weighing 692 grams. SCJs built after that date were outfitted with heavier 712 gram pistons.

Each assembly had its own unique crankshaft, flywheel, harmonic balancer, and spacer counterweight balanced to suit the individual application. A heavy-duty oil cooler positioned directly behind the

continued on next page

This special oil filter adapter bolted to the SCJ block, and directed oil to the oil cooler. A system relief valve and pressure gauge port were part of the factory engineered adapter.

The 428ci Cobra Jet engine could be ordered with a little known option called Drag Pack. Among the numerous internal and external drivetrain components included with the Drag Pack option was this heavy-duty engine oil cooler. A 428ci engine equipped with Drag Pack had a stronger lower end and was known as a Super Cobra Jet (SCJ).

grille is also part of the Super CJ equipment package. The air-to-oil heat exchanger is attached to the radiator-core support with factory brackets and plumbed with high-pressure hose from a special oil filter adapter.

Drag Pack

Drag Pack adds an optional V-Code 3.91:1 or W-Code 4.30:1 rear-axle ratio to a 428 SCJ performance package. Low ratio gear sets are available only with Traction-Loc, Ford's own positive-locking differential. In some years, an aftermarket Detroit Locker differential was an available option.

The 351 Engines

A few facts about 351 engines installed in 1969 and 1970 Mustangs:

- Cleveland engines are part of the 335 Series of Ford engines which include the 351C, the 351M (Modified), and the 400ci. The 351M and 400 were never installed in a Mustang. These engines were manufactured at the Cleveland, Ohio, plant, hence the C designation.
- Windsor engines, manufactured at the Windsor plant in Ontario, Canada, include the 221, 260, 289, 302, and 351W versions. Windsor engines are not identified by a commonly known series number.
- In 1969, all 351ci engines with two- or four-barrel induction were Windsor engines.
- In 1970, both Cleveland and Windsor engines were installed in Mustangs.
- Only the Cleveland was available with both two- and four-barrel induction in 1970.
- The 351 Windsor engine was not available with a four-barrel carburetor in 1970.
- The engine code for the two-barrel 351 was H and the code for the four-barrel was M.
- The codes were the same for both engines in 1969 and 1970 regardless of engine type.
- Both engines utilized a 4.00in bore and 3.50in stroke.
- Both engines used ten headbolts to secure each cylinder head.
- Cylinder heads were unique to each engine and are not interchangeable although the patterns for the headbolts were the same.
- Windsor and Cleveland intake manifolds, camshafts, and crankshafts were not interchangeable.
- Stock Windsor connecting rods are longer than Cleveland rods.
- Coolant passes through the intake manifold of a Windsor engine, but not in a Cleveland.
- The thermostat housing attaches to the engine block on a Cleveland with two vertical bolts, and to the intake manifold on a Windsor with two bolts positioned horizontally.
- The Cleveland has wide cylinder heads incorporating canted valves and open-type combustion chambers. The Windsor uses narrower cylinder heads with in-line valves and wedge-shaped combustion chambers.
- The two bolts holding the fuel pump on a Cleveland engine are vertical in relationship to each other; on a Windsor, they are horizontal.
- Rocker arms are unique to each engine.
- The Boss 302 is a Windsor engine that uses Cleveland-type cylinder heads.
- Cleveland and Boss 302 engines use eight bolts to secure each valve cover. All other Windsor engines, including the standard 302, use six bolts per valve cover.
- Cleveland four-barrel heads differ from the two-barrel heads. Four-barrel heads have large intake and exhaust runners and quench-type combustion chambers. Two-barrel heads have small intake and exhaust runners and open combustion chambers.
- Two-barrel and four-barrel 351 Windsor heads are basically the same.
- Cleveland engines have round intake and exhaust ports; Windsor engines have rectangular-shaped ports.
- The intake manifold bolts on a Windsor engine are all vertical. Only four intake bolts, two on each side of the carburetor, on a Cleveland are vertical. The rest are angled toward each cylinder head.
- The Boss 351, which is a Cleveland engine, did not appear until 1971.

Mustang Data Plate Engine Codes, 1964-1970

Code	Years	Engine	Remarks
A	'65-'67	289-4V	
C	'65-'68	289-2V	
D	'64½	289-4V	
F	'64½	260-2V	
	'68-'73	302-2V	
G	'69-'70	Boss 302 (4V)	
H	'69-'70	351-2V	
J	'68	302-4V	The '71 Mustang had a 429-4V Ram Air engine.
K	'65-'67	289-4V (HP)	The solid lifter High Performance, or Hi-Po engine.
L	'69-'73	250-1V	
M	'69-'71	351-4V	A Windsor in '69 & '70; a Cleveland in '70 & '71.
Q	'69-'70	428-4V	The '71-'73 Mustangs had a Q-code 351-4V engine.

Code	Years	Engine	Remarks
R	'68-'70	428-4V	Ram Air Cobra Jet
S	'67-'69	390-4V	
T	'65-'69	200-1V	
U	'64½	170-1V	
W	'68	427-4V	Yes, one is known to exist. A former drag car.
X	'68	302-2V	Uncommon.
Z	'69-'70	Boss 429 (4V)	

Years of Production, Mustang Engines

6-Cylinder Engines

CID	1965	1966	1967	1968	1969	1970
170	x					
200	x	x	x	x	x	x
250					x	x

8-Cylinder Engines

CID	1965	1966	1967	1968	1969	1970
260	x					
289	x	x	x	x		
302				x	x	x
351					x	x
390			x	x	x	
427				x		
428				x	x	x
429					x	x

Note: The 170 cid and 260 cid engines were primarily 1964-1/2 production.

The Falcon's largest contribution to the Mustang was its drivetrain. Base engine for the 1964½ Mustang was the 170ci inline six-cylinder, which was designed for and made its debut in the first production Falcon. Generating 101hp, this economical engine offered reasonably good performance while delivering over 22mpg of regular grade gasoline. Transmission and rear-end components were also Falcon carryovers on the first Mustang. Baseline 170ci engines and three-speed manual transmissions had their drawbacks which led Ford to upgrade the pair. Early 170ci engines incorporated a solid-lifter camshaft and constant-mesh, helical-cut cam gears, which made the little engine noisy. Three-speed transmissions were considered inconvenient because first gear was not synchronized. The car had to be brought to a complete stop before first gear could be engaged without grinding. The code for the 1964½ vintage 170ci engine is U.

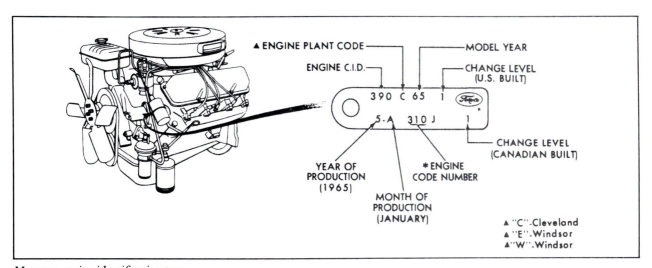

Mustang engine identification tags.

Mustang Engine I.D. Tag Code Identifier Chart, Part One.

Tag Code	Cyl.	CID	Carb.	Data Code
5	6	170	F-1	U
6	6	170	F-1	U
7	6	170	F-1	U
8	6	170	F-1	U
11	6	170	F-1	U
12	6	170	F-1	U
16	6	170	F-1	U
17	6	170	F-1	U
21	6	200	F-1	T
23	6	200	F-1	T
24	6	200	F-1	T
25	6	200	F-1	T
26	6	170	F-1	U
26	6	200	F-1	T
27	6	200	F-1	T
28	6	170	F-1	U
29	6	170	F-1,S/E	U
32	6	200	F-1	T
33	6	200	F-1	T
34	6	200	F-1	T
35	6	200	F-1	T
36	6	200	F-1	T
40	6	200	F-1	T
41	6	200	F-1	T
42	6	200	F-1	T
45	6	250	F-1	L
46	6	250	F-1	L
47	6	250	F-1	L
48	6	250	F-1	L
50	6	250	F-1,S/E	L
200	8	351W	F-2	H
201	8	351W	F-2	H
202	8	351W	F-2	H
203	8	351W	F-2	H
205	8	351W	F-2	H
206	8	351W	F-2	H
207	8	351W	F-2	H
208	8	351W	F-4	M
209	8	351W	F-4	M

Tag Code	Cyl.	CID	Carb.	Data Code
210	8	351W	F-4	M
211	8	351W	F-4	M
212	8	351W	F-4	M
213	8	351W	F-4	M
231	8	289	F-2	C
232	8	289	F-2	C
233	8	289	F-2	C
236	8	289	F-2	C
237	8	289	F-2	C
239	8	289	F-2	C
240	8	289	F-2	C
241	8	289	F-2	C
245	8	289	F-4	K
246	8	289	F-4	K
250	8	289	F-4,P/F	A
252	8	289	F-2	C
253	8	289	F-2	C
257	8	289	F-2	C
271	8	302	F-2	F,G
272	8	302	F-2	F,G
273	8	302	F-2	F,G
274	8	302	F-2	F,G
275	8	302	F-2	F
276	8	302	F-2	F
277	8	302	F-2	F
279	8	302	F-2	F,G
280	8	302	F-2	F,G
281	8	302	F-2	F
282	8	302	F-2	F
283	8	302	F-4	J
284	8	302	F-4	J
285	8	302	F-2	F
287	8	302	F-2	F
288	8	302	F-2	F
296	8	302	F-2	G
299	8	302HP	H-4	G
300	8	302HP	H-4	G
318	8	390GT	F-4	S

Carburetor Identification:

F-1	Ford 1V		F-4	Ford 4V
F-2	Ford 2V		F-4,P/F	Ford 4V, Premium Fuel
F-2,P/F	Ford 2V, Premium Fuel		H-4	Holley 4V

134

Mustang Engine I.D. Tag Code Identifier Chart, Part Two.

Tag Code	Cyl.	CID	Carb.	Data Code
319	8	390GT	F-4	S
321	8	390GT	F-4	S
322	8	390GT	F-4	S
324	8	390GT	F-4	S
341	8	390	F-4	Z
343	8	390	F-4	Z
350	8	427	H-4	W
353	8	427	H-8	R
357	8	390	F-4	Z
359	8	427	F-4	W
360	8	427	H-4	W
361	8	427	H-8	W
364	8	427	H-4	W
382	8	390GT	F-4	S
383	8	390GT	F-4	S
384	8	390GT	F-4	S
385	8	390GT	F-4	S
386	8	390GT	F-4	S
400	8	428	F-4	Q
401	8	428	F-4	Q
407	8	428CJ	H-4	R
408	8	428CJ	H-4	R
410	8	428	F-4	Q
418	8	428CJ	H-4	R
419	8	428CJ	H-4	R
420	8	428CJ	H-4	R
421	8	428CJ	H-4	R
422	8	428SCJ	H-4	R
423	8	428SCJ	H-4	R
424	8	428SCJ	H-4	R
425	8	428SCJ	H-4	R
426	8	428SCJ	H-4	
491	8	260	F-2	F
492	8	260	F-2	F
500	8	260	F-2	F
502	8	260	F-2	F
504	8	260	F-2	F
506	8	260	F-2	F

Tag Code	Cyl.	CID	Carb.	Data Code
534	8	260	F-2	F
536	8	260	F-2	F
538	8	260	F-2	F
540	8	260	F-2	F
548	8	289	F-2	C
549	8	289	F-2	C
550B	8	289	F-4	D
550J	8	289	F-2	C
551B	8	289	F-4	D
551J	8	289	F-2	C
552	8	289	F-4	A
554	8	289	F-4	K
557	8	289	F-2	C
558	8	289	F-2	C
561	8	289	F-2	C
562	8	289	F-2	C
563	8	289	F-4	K
564	8	289	F-4	K
566	8	289	F-4,P/F	A
567	8	289	F-4,P/F	A
600	8	351C	F-2	H
601	8	351C	F-2	H
602	8	351C	F-2	H
604	8	351C	F-2	H
606	8	351C	F-2	H
608	8	351C	F-4	M
609	8	351C	F-4	M
610	8	351C	F-2	H
611	8	351C	F-2	H
612	8	351C	F-4	M
613	8	351C	F-4	M
614	8	351C	F-2	H
615	8	351C	F-2	H
616	8	351C	F-4	M
617	8	351C	F-4	M
630	8	351C	F-4	M
632	8	351C	F-2	H

Carburetor Identification:

F-1	Ford 1V
F-2	Ford 2V
F-2,P/F	Ford 2V, Premium Fuel
F-4	Ford 4V
F-4,P/F	Ford 4V, Premium Fuel
H-4	Holley 4V
H-8	Holley 2-4V

135

The 170ci six-cylinder was replaced with a 200ci version in the fall of 1964. The 30ci and 19hp gains presented no obvious visual changes; it was the internal modifications that made the 200ci more durable. The 170 had four main bearings; the 200 had seven main bearings, which complemented the new improved crankshaft design. All six-cylinder Mustangs produced through the end of the 1970 model year were equipped with four-lug wheels even though drivetrain and suspension components were upgraded over the six-year period. Early six-cylinder engines were painted black except for the long, scalloped valve cover and snorkeled air cleaner lid which were bright red. T is the engine code for the 200.

The earliest first-generation Mustangs could have been equipped with an optional 260ci V-8 engine. These two-barrel low-compression Windsor engines were borrowed from the Fairlane, Ford's only mid-size car for 1964. Sporting 164hp, 260ci base V-8s offered a real boost to the Mustang's performance image. The engine generates lots of low-end torque, which translates into an impressive seat-of-the-pants performance feel. Early V-8 Mustang engines also used a Fairlane air cleaner, which can be identified by its small-diameter lid that fits inside an opening in the top of the housing. Later V-8 air cleaner lids were the same diameter as the lower housing. The earliest V-8s had cast-iron water-pump pulleys and dual generator drivebelts on cars not equipped with power steering. A three-speed Cruise-O-Matic automatic was the only transmission used with the 260ci engine. The engine block and heads were painted black while the valve covers and air cleaner were gold. Color pictures of the very first Mustang (00001) show its 260 engine painted light blue. The total number of 260 engines that were painted light blue is unknown. Production code was F designating a 260ci two-barrel engine.

Mustang Engine Power Comparison Chart

Year	Engine	Data Code	Comment	Brake Horsepower			Torque		
'65-67	289-4V	A		225	@ 4800	in 1965-6-7	305	@	3200
'64-1/2	289-2V	C		195	@ 4400	in 1964	282	@	2400 in 1964
'65-67	289-2V	C		200	@ 4400	in 1965-6-7	282	@	2400
'68	289-2V	C		195	@ 4400	in 1968	288	@	2400 in 1968
'64-1/2	289-4V	D		210	@ 4400		300	@	2400
'64-1/2	260-2V	F		164	@ 4400		285	@	2200
'68-69	302-2V	F		210	@ 4400		300	@	2600
'69-70	Boss 302	G		290	@ 5800		290	@	4300
'69-73	351-2V	H		250	@ 4600		355	@	2600
'68	302-4V	J		230	@ 4800		310	@	2800
'65-68	289-4V	K	HiPo	271	@ 6000		312	@	3400
'69-73	250-1V	L		155	@ 4400		240	@	1600
'69	351-4V	M		290	@ 4800	Windsor, 1969	385	@	3200
'70	351-4V	M		300	@ 5400	Cleveland, 1970	380	@	3400
'69-70	428CJ	Q		335	@ 5200		440	@	3400
'68-70	428CJ	R	Ram Air	335	@ 5200		440	@	3400
'67-69	390-4V	S		320	@ 4800		427	@	3200
'65-70	200-1V	T		120	@ 4400		190	@	2400
'64-1/2	170	U		101	@ 4400		158	@	2400
'69-70	Boss 429	Z		375	@ 5600		450	@	3400

At first introduction, the 289ci two-barrel engine shared the optional spotlight with the 260 but offered an additional 46hp and 29ci. This over-bored version of the 260 generated 210 (gross) horsepower. Early production V-8 engines were equipped with generators instead of alternators and had an oil filler tube protruding from the timing cover. Both features were changed by the end of the calendar year though not at the same time. This engine has a generator but the oil filler opening has been relocated to the driver's side valve cover, a change that became synonymous with all small-block Ford engines. Early V-8 water pumps were made out of aluminum as was the timing cover. The long block was painted black, the valve covers gold. The air cleaner housing and lid were gold but the round snorkel extending toward the right shock tower was gloss black. This engine is in a 1964¹/₂ Mustang equipped with optional power steering. Early power steering pumps, like the example shown, were cast-iron units manufactured by Eaton Corporation and are identified by the small cast-iron pulley and the large oil reservoir perched on top. Production code for the 1964¹/₂ 289ci two barrel engine is C.

The K-code 289ci High Performance engine, or HiPo for short, became available in June 1964 and remained an option until the end of the 1967 production year. It was a popular lightweight performance engine that produced 271 (gross) horsepower with help from a solid-lifter flat-tappet camshaft, 480cfm carburetor, and special free-flowing header-type cast-iron exhaust manifolds. The optional Dress-Up Kit, which includes chromed valve covers and an open-element air cleaner, was standard on HiPo engines. The vacuum-advance diaphragm is deleted from the fixed breaker plate, dual points distributor, and the alternator sports a large-diameter pulley that allows it to survive at high engine rpms.

The D-Code 289ci four-barrel engine could easily be the rarest engine option since it was available only during April through September of 1964. Essentially, it was a four-barrel version of the C-code 289 two-barrel. The only obvious identifying mark was the black, white, and red "289 Cubic Inch 4-V Premium Fuel" decal on the air cleaner lid. Early D-code engines should be equipped with generators and may or may not have the timing cover mounted oil filler tube.

By the beginning of the 1965 model year, the 170ci six-cylinder and the 260ci V-8 had been dropped from the optional engine list. The D-code 289 had evolved into an A-Code 225hp 289ci four-barrel engine. Generators were replaced with alternators when the traditional five-dial instrument cluster took the place of the horizontal speedometer bezel with dual warning lights that was a carryover from the Falcon. Ford installed its own compact power steering pumps in 1965. The small cast-iron pump was surrounded by a tin cover that acted as the reservoir. Over the next few years, the 4in spout mounted on top of the reservoir would be relocated many times to accommodate numerous other engine-driven accessories. The A-Code 289ci engine became the standard engine for the popular GT Equipment Group offered in April of 1965. All V-8 engines produced in 1965 were black with gold valve covers and air cleaners.

The C-code 289 two-barrel remained an option until January 1968 when all 289s were replaced with 302s. Early production C-code 289s were rated 210hp but by the 1965 model year, it was detuned to deliver 200hp. There was no significant difference between the two engines. Changing the compression ratio enabled the factory to vary horsepower figures. The hexagonal snout protruding from the vacuum-advance canister houses the diaphragm return spring. The metal vacuum tube is connected at each end by a threaded fitting. Because the method for connecting the tube changed at some point early in 1966, this threaded tube was used on all 1964½ and 1965 engines. There is no mechanical reason for the vertical loop in the tube that is traditionally formed just in front of the air cleaner.

The Sprint option was a cosmetic package used to enhance the marketability of base-level hardtops. Among the visual effects was an engine dress-up kit consisting of a chrome air cleaner, radiator, oil and master cylinder caps. A "Sports Sprint" or "Sport Sprint 200" garnished the air cleaner top. The T-Code 200ci engine was rated at 120hp in 1966. The Sports Sprint option added nothing to enhance performance.

All engines starting with the 1966 model year were painted a medium shade of blue. A similar color, later referred to as Corporate Blue, became part of Ford's trademark when it was used as the background color for the famous Ford oval. Almost every part sold over dealership counters contained the Ford script printed in Corporate Blue. Engine options for the 1966 model year were simple and easy to remember. There was the base level T-Code 200ci six-cylinder and three optional 289ci V-8s. Pictured is a 1966 Sprint 200 equipped with air conditioning and power steering.

Aside from the blue paint, the base 200ci six-cylinder engine hadn't changed much since 1965. This 1967 model shows the fuel filter canister has disappeared from the top of the fuel pump and the snorkle is missing from the air cleaner lid. The small-diameter metal tube following the route taken by the fuel line is the vacuum advance tube. The fuel filter, which is really just a nylon screen housed in a cylinder, can be seen protruding from under the front edge of the air cleaner.

This C-code 289ci two-barrel could be considered the base-level V-8. Its mild hydraulic-lifter camshaft and dual-plane intake manifold delivered smooth, even power and good gas mileage. The rounded valve covers are another trademark of pre-1967 V-8 engines. The additional tubular firewall-to-fender apron braces were used to strengthen the unibody construction of the convertible. This low-optioned 1966 convertible is common to the era. It has manual brakes, steering, and transmission. The C-code engine was an inexpensive option.

Not a HiPo, this is a 1966 A-code 289 four-barrel engine equipped with an optional Cobra Dress Up Kit. Cobra kits were commonly sold over-the-counter by Ford dealers. Bare aluminum valve covers cast with raised ribs and "Cobra Powered By Ford" on the top surface were part of the kit, which also included a chrome, open-element HiPo air cleaner. This particular engine is in a low-optioned GT as indicated by the large master cylinder with snap-on lid and adjustable proportioning valve used with front disc brakes.

The T-code 1965 200ci six-cylinder was outfitted with the latest accessories. This is a late 1964¹/₂ because it has an oil-pressure switch threaded into the left rear corner of the block indicating the instrument panel is the Falcon-type with low oil-pressure warning light. The later 1965 bezel utilized an oil-pressure gauge, which required a large-diameter gold-anodized sender. It is also equipped with a Ford power steering pump and an alternator. Note the location of the filler tube for the power steering reservoir. The fuel filter is located on top of the inverted fuel pump and the vacuum advance tube is clipped to the fuel line.

An unusual option package by today's standards but common for the no-frills 1960s. A K-code HiPo engine in a stripped down non-GT. It's a late 1964 model because it has an oil-pressure switch needed for the Falcon-styled instrument cluster but instead of a generator, it is equipped with an alternator. It has a heater but no windshield washer.

C-code 289s could have been ordered in any body style or with any other option through 1967 except for the GT Equipment Group, which required an A-code four-barrel. Internally, all 289 A- and C-code engines were the same, except each had its own camshaft profile. The engine's compression ratio was dictated by the size of the combustion chamber in the cylinder heads. Windsor engines built before the middle of 1967 used slotted pushrod holes in the cylinder heads to maintain rocker-to-valve stem alignment. The exact date of the change is unknown. These engines were equipped with conventional, rounded, non-lettered valve covers. The air cleaner snorkel slips over a hot air duct and contains a temperature-controlled trap door. The bottom of the hot air duct wraps around the right side exhaust manifold. To enhance cold weather driveability, the trap door would be held open for the first few minutes after startup. The door would block the open end of the snorkel forcing the engine to draw air, warmed by the exhaust manifold, through the hot air tube and into the carburetor. After the engine achieved normal operating temperature, the door would close allowing the engine to breathe fresh, relatively cool air from the engine compartment.

By the end of the 1966 production year Chevrolet was a distant third in the pony car race. The Camaro was to debut in 1967 with their performance engine, the 295hp 350ci, designed to blow away a 289 HiPo and impress Ford-bound new car buyers. The Camaro performance car would be called—what else?—a Super Sport. But Henry's boys dealt the bow-tie brigade a tough hand in 1967 by introducing the first Mustang powered by a big-block engine. The S-code 390ci is a successor to the first FE Series engine introduced in 1958. This version produced 320hp. Chevrolet was caught off guard and in a last minute effort to meet Ford head on, stuffed a 396ci engine in the Camaro and shoveled it out the gate to do battle with the Mustang. A 1967 390 GT was impressive indeed, but the true potential of a big-block Mustang wouldn't be realized for another year. A 390-powered Mustang was hard to work on and even harder to keep cool but there was no stopping 427lb-ft of torque once the tachometer needle cleared 2800rpm. This heavily optioned GT is equipped with power brakes, power steering, and air conditioning.

In 1967 and 1969, the S-code GT engine was rated 320hp. In 1968 it drew a rating of 325hp. If the owner did not opt for Ram Air, the engine received a chrome air cleaner lid complete with High Performance decal. The LeMans finned aluminum valve covers shown here are not factory installed but were available through Ford Parts Departments.

Ford took a giant leap ahead of the competition when, in the middle of the 1968 production year, it built the first Mustangs equipped with a Cobra Jet 428ci engine. Cobra Jet and Super Cobra Jets were nicknames that stayed with the 428 until its demise at the end of the 1970 production year. This big-block beast, like the 390, is a member of the FE engine family. Early R-code Mustangs, referred to as 68$^{1/2}$ Cobra Jets because they were not introduced until April 1, were conservatively rated at 335hp. Pictured is a 1969 Q-code 428 CJ. The Q signifies non-Ram Air.

Because big-block engines dominated the performance market, small-blocks were considered by many to be economy or passenger-car units, a stigma that prevailed even though in 1967 the popular GT package included any engine as long as it had a four-barrel carburetor. In addition to being offered one year only, those conditions make the 230hp 1968 J-code 302 four-barrel engine somewhat rare. Economy-minded buyers could choose between the T-code 200ci six-cylinder, the C-code 289ci two-barrel V-8, or the F-code 302ci two-barrel V-8, each offering good performance and efficiency. Serious performance buyers, obvi-ously giving no thought to fuel economy, chose either the S-code 390ci or the R-code 428ci V-8 engine. Both were only available with a four-barrel carburetor. The J-code 302 replaced the K-code 289ci HiPo, though that is where the similarity ends. The J-code was a four-barrel version of the F-code 302. It didn't have a special block, head castings, or flat-tappet camshaft. The ignition system was also common to other Windsor engines. Its hydraulic cam profile, 10.0:1 compression ratio, and four-barrel induction system gave it 35 more horsepower than the two-barrel version.

141

The Mustang was a longer, heavier car in 1969. For that reason, an optional L-code 250ci six-cylinder engine was offered as a step up from the base level T-code 200ci six-cylinder. The 250ci was highly refined compared to all other sixes and offered smooth economical performance. Generating 155hp at 4000rpm and 240lb-ft of torque at 1600rpm, the big six-cylinder could perform almost as well as the entry level F-code 302ci V-8. With two-barrel induction, the 302 engine made 220hp at 4600rpm and 300lb-ft of torque at 2600rpm. For $39 a customer could upgrade from a 200ci to a 250ci engine.

A G-code Boss 302 is similar in many respects to the 289 HiPo in that it has special canted valve heads with large intake and exhaust runners, a special block with four-bolt main bearing caps and screw-in core plugs, and a solid-lifter camshaft. Horsepower output was conservatively rated at 290. Boss 302 engines were engineered to compete in Trans-Am racing during the 1969-1970 season. Few Boss 302 components were designed for or will work with standard production 302 Windsor engines. The free-flowing heads and induction system provided extra-quick throttle response and the strong bottom end kept the engine together during sustained high-rpm operation. Boss 302s are still considered one of the most desirable performance engines of the decade.

There were nine different engine options available for Mustang in 1969, more than in any other year. Cubic inch options were: 200, 250, 302, 351, 390, 428, and 429. The 200ci six was standard for a non-performance car. There were two individual 302s, and two 428ci engines that were each given a separate code. The entry level V-8 was this F-code 302ci two-barrel engine.

Except for some necessary external changes that mostly involved the accessory drive assemblies, the 200ci six-cylinder remained mostly unchanged throughout its six-year tenure. It was replaced by the L-code 250ci six-cylinder as the base engine beginning with 1971 production. This basic 200 with optional power steering is in a 1967 convertible.

Even though the 428 Cobra Jet and High Performance 390 are both members of the FE engine family, the 428 shares a closer relationship to the race-bred 427. Cobra Jet engines received harder nodular-iron crankshafts and Police Interceptor rods. Both pieces are stronger and more durable than the stock Thunderbird 428 that was never installed in a Mustang by the factory. All CJs were equipped with dished, cast-aluminum pistons with double valve reliefs. CJ cylinder heads closely resemble 406ci and 427ci four-barrel low-riser pieces, and feature larger-than-stock valve sizes. A 735cfm carburetor replaced the stock 600cfm units used on non-CJ engines. It's unusual to see a 428 equipped with air conditioning, power steering, and power brakes. The R engine code for 1968, 1969, and 1970 indicates the 428ci engine is equipped with a Ram Air hood scoop. In 1968 the fixed scoop was permanently attached to the hood. Ram Air scoops in 1969 and 1970, like the one shown, were bolted to the engine.

Cleveland 351ci engines appeared in 1970. If a two-barrel 351ci engine was ordered in a new 1970 Mustang, there was no way to tell whether it would be delivered with a Cleveland or a Windsor block. Only the Cleveland was offered with a four-barrel induction system in 1970. M-code four-barrel Cleveland engines developed 300hp and 380lb-ft of torque. With an 11.0:1 compression ratio, premium fuel was required and indicated on the air cleaner decal. Ram Air was an option if a 351-4V was installed in a Mach 1 but, because the basic engine specifications did not change, it was not given its own code (as were 428ci Ram Air engines).

The Z-code Boss 429 was the biggest and baddest big-block of them all. It was only installed in 1969 and 1970 Mustangs. Ford had to legitimize the engine so NASCAR would allow it in Grand National racing. To meet the requirement, at least 500 of the Hemi-styled engines had to be installed in passenger cars and sold to the public. Virtually every part of the Boss 429 is special. The spark plug holes in the center of the massive heads required a one-of-a-kind valve cover. The canted valves were activated by two different-length rocker arms. Even the intake and exhaust manifolds were particular to the application. The Z-code 429 incorporates a crescent-shaped combustion chamber, which, according to the Ford engineers, "generates low-end torque commonly associated with wedge engines while combining the high rpm breathing capability of a hemi."

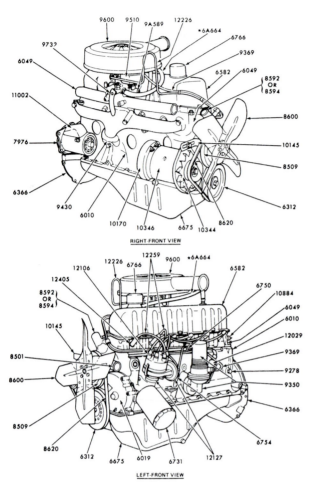

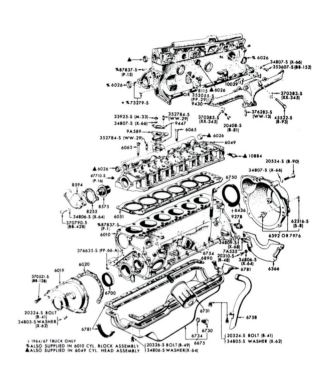

Right and left front views of a typical 170, 200, or 250 engine.

Typical 170, 200, and 250ci engine block and related parts.

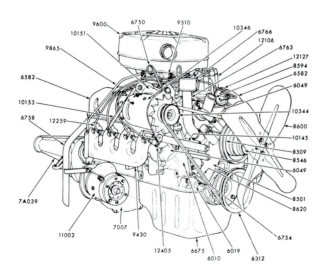

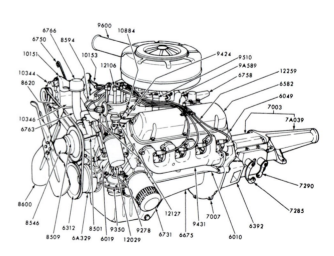

Right and left front views of a typical 260ci engine and transmission assembly.

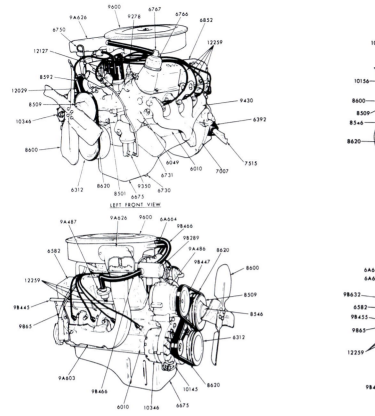

Right front and left front views of 302 and 351 Windsor engines.

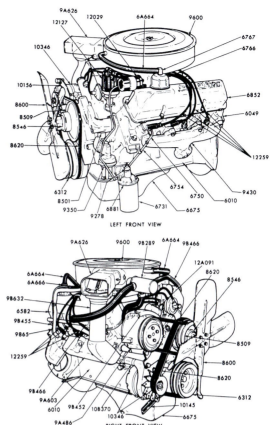

Right front and left front views of 390 and 428 engines.

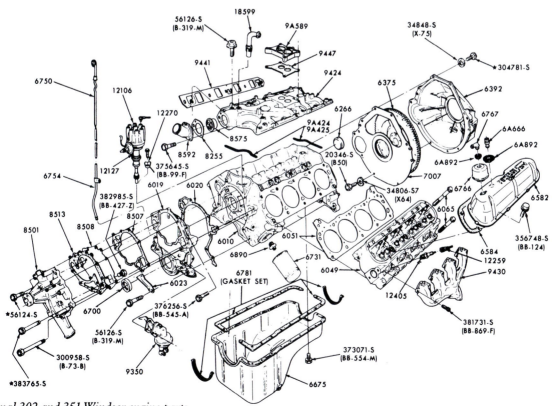

External 302 and 351 Windsor engine parts.

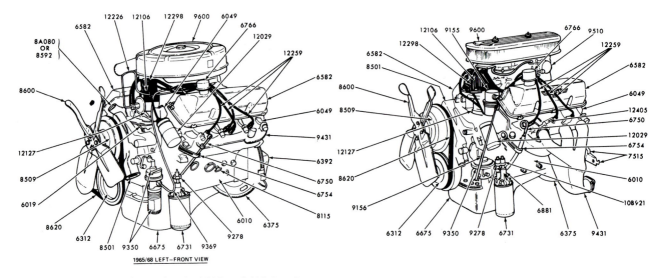

Right and left front views of typical 390 and 428ci engines.

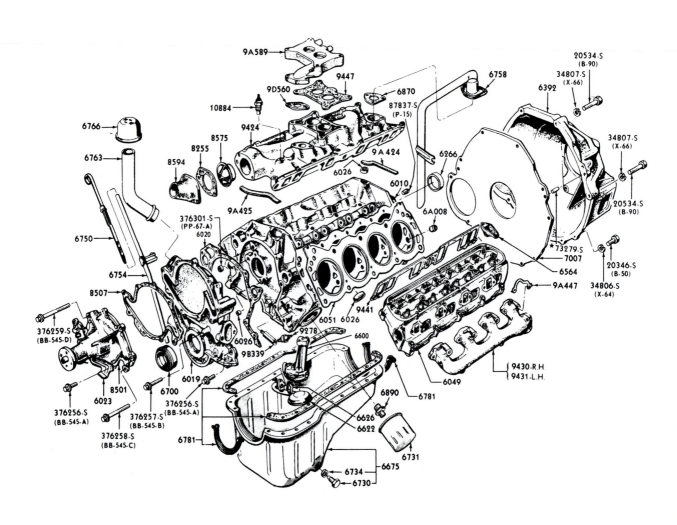

Typical 260 and 289ci engine block and related parts.

Mustang Spark Plug Application Chart, 14MM - 18MM, 8-Cylinder Engines

Year	Model/Description	C.I.D.	LSA	Part Number	NSA	Part Number	HDSA	Part Number
65		260	BF42	B8A-12405-A	BF42	B8A-12405-A	BF42	B8A-12405-A
65/69	2/B,4/B R.F OR P.F	289	BF42	B8A-12405-A	BF42	B8A-12405-A	BTF42	C6TZ-12405-A
65/69	Special (4/B)	289	B432	C0AZ-12405-A	BF32	C0AZ-12405-A	BF32	C0AZ-12405-A
65/68	2/B, 4/B	352,390	BF42	B8A-12405-A	BF-42	B8A-12405-A	BF-42	B8A-12405-A
68/69	4/B	427,428	BF42	B8A-12405-A	BF-42	B8A-12405-A	BF-42	B8A-12405-A
		429						
68/70		302	BF42	B8A-12405-A	BF42	B8A-12405-A	BF42	B8A-12405-A
68/69		427	BF32	C0AZ-12405-A	BF32	C0AZ-12405-A	BF32	C0AZ-12405-A
69/70	Boss	302,429	AF32	C9ZZ-12405-A	AF32	C9ZZ-12405-A	AF32	C9ZZ-12405-A
69/70	Boss	302,429	ARF32	C9PZ-12405-A	ARF32	C9PZ-12405-A	ARF32	C9PZ-12405-A
69/70	Boss	351-2V	BF42	B8A-12405-A	BF42	B8A-12405-A	BF42	B8A-12405-A
69/70		351-4V	BF32	C0AZ-12405-A	BF32	C0AZ-12405-A	BF32	C0AZ-12405-A
		390, 428						
69/70		390	BF42	B8A-12405-A	BF42	B8A-12405-A	BF42	B8A-12405-A
69/70		351	AF42	C9ZZ-12405-B	AF42	C9ZZ-12405-B	ARF42	C9PZ-12405-B
70	Before 11/5/69	351	AF32	C9ZZ-12405-A	AF32	C9ZZ-12405-A	ARF32	C9PZ-12405-A
70	From 11/15/69	351	AF42	C9ZZ-12405-B	AF42	C9ZZ-12405-B	ARF42	C9PZ-12405-A
70	4/B	351	AF42	C9ZZ-12405-B	AF42	C9ZZ-12405-B	AF42	C9ZZ-12405-B

LSA: Light Service Autolite   NSA: Normal Service Autolite   HDSA: Heavy Duty Service Autolite

MUSTANG DISTRIBUTOR APPLICATION AND IDENTIFICATION CHART, Part One.

| | | | | | CALIBRATION CODE | | | | |
| | | | SERV. REPL. | DPHRGM. | CAM | Springs | (12191-2) | | STOP |
YEAR	MODEL	I.D.	DISTRIBUTOR	(12370)	(12210)	PRIM.	SEC.	VAC.	(12202)
6-cylinder 170 CID									
65	C4	C4DF-12127-B C8UF-12127-J	C4DZ-12127-E	302		231	211		
66	S/T	C4ZF-12127-A	C4DZ-12127-D	302		226	331		
66	3/S/T with T/E	C6DF-12127-A C7TF-12127-J,L	C6DZ-12127-A	304 304	110 110	240 237	229 225	2 14	
6-cylinder 200 CID									
65/66	C4 except T/E	C8DF-12127-H	C4OZ-12127-F	302		226	213		
66	C4 with T/E	C6DF-12127-E C6DF-12127-K	C6DZ-12127-K	304 304	110 110	234 234	240 240	218 217	7 3
66	3/4/S/T with T/E	C6DF-12127-C	C6DZ-12127-C	304	110	234	240	217	3
65/67	S/T except T/E	C5DF-12127-E C8DF-12127-G	C4DZ-12127-D	302 302		226 226	215 212		
65/67	C4 with T/E	C5DF-12127-F C5DF-12127-K C8DF-12127-H	C4OZ-12127-F	302 302 302		212 226 226	212 213 213		
67	C4 with T/E	C7DF-12127-D	C7DZ-12127-F	304	111	234	233	217	3
67	3/S/T with T/E	C7DF-12127-C	C7DZ-12127-F	304	111	238	244	217	3
67	C4 with Imco	C6DF-12127-D	C6DZ-12127-D	304	110	234	240	229	2
67	C4 with Imco	C7DF-12127-F	C6DZ-12127-F	304	111	236	242	216	14
68/69	3/S/T with Imco	C8DF-12127-C	C8DZ-12127-C	374	111	238	244	245	16
68/69	C4 with Imco	C8DF-12127-D	C8DZ-12127-D	374	111	237	246	245	11
70	S/T	DODF-12127-J	DODZ-12127-C	304	110	236	235	217	14
70	A/T	DODF-12127-C	DODZ-12127-C	360	110	236	235	241	3

MUSTANG DISTRIBUTOR APPLICATION AND IDENTIFICATION CHART, Part Two.

YEAR	MODEL	I.D.	SERV. REPL. DISTRIBUTOR	CALIBRATION CODE					
				DPHRGM. (12370)	CAM (12210)	Springs (12191-2) PRIM.	SEC.	VAC.	STOP (12202)
6-cylinder 250 CID									
69	S/T	C9OF-12127-R	C9OZ-12127-A	304	111	234	244	217	14
69	A/T	C9OF-12127-U	C9OZ-12127-V	304	110	236	244	248	1
		C9OF-12127-V		304	110	243	240	225	3
70	A/T,S/T,Imco	D0OF-12127-A	D2OZ-12127-P	360	110	243	241	218	13
8-cylinder 260 CID									
65	S/T,C4	C4OF-12127-B	C4OZ-12127-B		103	223	206	218	1
		C4ZF-12127-B,E		301	103	222	230	211	3
		C5ZF-12127-J		303	108	236	240	218	6
		C5JF-12127-B		303	108	237	240	218	1
8-cylinder 289 CID									
65/67	4/B carb. w/ T/E 4/B S/T exc. T/E	C50F-12127-E	C50Z-12127-E		107	236	235		
65	Special 4/B carb.	C3OF-12127-D,F	C50Z-12127-E		104	222	232		
65	4/B S/T exc. Hi-Po	C4ZF-12127-C Z5AF-12127-B	C7ZZ-12127-A	301	103	222	204	216	10
65	Special	C4ZF-12127-D	C5OZ-12127-E						
65	C4 exc. Special	C4GF-12127-B C5GF-12127-C	C7ZZ-12127-A	301 303	103 107	228 241 210	201 233	216 216	10 10
65/66	2/B S/T exc. T/E	C5AF-12127-M	C7ZZ-12127-A	303	107	241	240	216	1
65/66	2/B,C4,C/M exc. T/E	C5AF-12127-N	C7ZZ-12127-A	303	107	234	233	216	11
65/66	4/B exc. T/E	C5GF-12127-A	C7ZZ-12127-A	303	108	234	235	218	1
66	2/B,3/4/S/T,T/E	C6AF-12127-J	C7OZ-12127-D	303	108	243	233	218	11
66	2/B,C/M,C4,T/E	C6AF-12127-AK	C6AZ-12127-S	303	108	236	219	216	11
66	4/B, 3/4/S/T & T/E	C6ZF-12127-A	C7ZZ-12127-C	303	108	243	235	216	6
66	4/B, C4 & T/E	C7ZF-12127-B	C7OZ-12127-E	303					
67	2/B & C4 exc. T/E	C7AF-12127-AE	C7OZ-12127-B	303	107	243	235	216	2
67	2/B & C4 exc. T/E	C7OF-12127-B	C7ZZ-12127-A	303	107	234	244	216	11
67	2/B, C4 & T/E	C7AF-12127-AH	C7AZ-12127-A	303	107	236	244	216	10
67	2/B, C4 & T/E	C7OF-12127-J	C7AZ-12127-A	303	107	236	244	217	9
67	2/B,3/4/S/T exc. T/E	C7OF-12127-A	C7OZ-12127-A	303	107	243	233	216	4
67	2/B, C4 & T/E	C7OF-12127-E	C7OZ-12127-E	303	107	236	244	217	9
67	4/B, C4 exc. T/E	C7ZF-12127-B	C7ZZ-12127-A	303					
67	4/B, 3/4/S/T, T/E	C7ZF-12127-C,E	C7ZZ-12127-C	303	107	243	235	216	11, 2
67	4/B,C4,T/E	C7ZF-12127-D	C7ZZ-12127-C	303	107	234	235	218	2
67	4/B,C4,T/E	C7ZF-12127-G	C7ZZ-12127-H	303	107	241	244	225	2
67	4/B,C4,T/E	C7ZF-12127-H	C7OZ-12127-E	303	107	234	235	216	2
67	Special 4/B,T/E	C7ZF-12127-J	C7ZZ-12127-K		107	236	235		
67 68	2/B,3/4/S/T,T/E 2/B,3/S/T,T/E	C7OF-12127-D	C7AZ-12127-U	303	108	237	240	218	2
67/68	Special 4/B,T/E	C7OF-12127-K	C7ZZ-12127-K		107	236	235		
67/68	4/B, 3/4/S/T exc. T/E	C7ZF-12127-A C7ZF-12127-F	C7ZZ-12127-A	303 303	108 107	234 243	235 234	218 218	1 2
68	2/B,A/T,Imco	C8OF-12127-C	C8OZ-12127-D	35	107	236	233	229	2
8-cylinder 302 CID									
68	2/B,A/T,Imco	C8OF-12127-C	C8OZ-12127-C	35	107	236	233	229	2
68	4/B,A/T,Imco	C8ZF-12127-B	C8ZZ-12127-A	307					
68	4/B,A/T,Imco	C8ZF-12127-D	C8ZZ-12127-D	303	108	238	235	217	11
68	4/B,3/S/T,T/E	C8ZF-12127-A	C8ZZ-12127-A	307	108	236	235	248	2
69	S/T, Imco	C8AF-12127-E	C8AZ-12127-E	356	107	236	233	217	11

MUSTANG DISTRIBUTOR APPLICATION AND IDENTIFICATION CHART, Part Three.

YEAR	MODEL	I.D.	SERV. REPL. DISTRIBUTOR	DPHRGM. (12370)	CAM (12210)	Springs (12191-2) PRIM.	SEC.	VAC.	STOP (12202)
8-cylinder 289 CID continued									
69	2/B,A/T w/A/C, Imco w/o A/C	C9AF-12127-N	C9AZ-12127-M	303	107	234	235	229	2
69	A/T with A/C	C9AF-12127-R	C9AZ-12127-R	356	107	234	235	245	9
69	Boss 4/B,S/T w/ T/E	C9ZF-12127-B	C9ZZ-12127-E	311	112		233	218	16
69/70	Boss 4/B,S/T w/ T/E	C9ZF-12127-E	D1ZZ-12127-A	311	112	238	235	225	15
70	2/B,A/T,Imco	DOAF-12127-T	DOOZ-12127-AL	310	113	236	252	217	3
70	2/B,S/T,Imco	DOAF-12127-Y	DOAZ-12127-Y	356	113	236	235	217	1
70	2/B,A/T,Imco	DOOF-12127-AC	D20Z-12127-H	375	113	236	252	245	7
8-cylinder 351 CID									
69	2/B,A/T,S/T,Imco	C9OF-12127-M	DOOZ-12127-M	303	107	241	233	218	13
69	2/B,A/T,S/T,Imco	DOOF-12127-M	DOOZ-12127-M	303	107	241	233	248	5
69	A/T,4/B	C9OF-12127-T	C9OZ-12127-Z	303	107	236	235	218	6
69	A/T,4/B	C90F-12127-Z	DOOZ-12127-R	303	107	241	244	245	11
69	S/T,4/B,Imco	C90F-12127-N	DOOZ-12127-N	303	107	237	235	220	6
69	S/T,4/B,Imco	DOOF-12127-N	DOOZ-12127-N	303	107	237	235	229	6
69	4/B,A/T,Imco	DOOF-12127-R	DOOZ-12127-R	303	107	241	244	245	11
70	2/B,S/T,Imco	DOAF-12127-H	DOAZ-12127-H	307	107	241	233	248	#7
70	Shelby GT350 w/ S/T								
70	2/B,A/T,Imco	DOAF-12127-V / DOAF-12127-AC	DOAZ-12127-V	354 / 354	107 / 113	241 / 236	233 / 235	248 / 248	#7 / #16
70	Shelby GT350 w/ A/T	DOAF-12127-V / DOAF-12127-AC	DOAZ-12127-V	354 / 354	107 / 113	241 / 236	233 / 235	248 / 248	#7 / #16
70	4/B,S/T,A/T,Imco	DOOF-12127-Z	DOOZ-12127-G	357	107	241	235	217	2
70	2/B,S/T,Imco	DOOF-12127-E / DOOF-12127-T	D2ZZ-12127-A	361 / 355	119 / 107	236 / 251	233 / 240	250 / 245	/ 9
70	2/B,A/T,Imco	DOOF-12127-U	DOOZ-12127-U	303	107	241	233	217	1
70	S/T,4/B,Imco	DOOF-12127-V	DOOZ-12127-V	356	107	238	233	217	5
8-cylinder 390 CID									
67	4/B,3/4/S/T exc. T/E	C7OF-12127-H	C7AZ-12127-U	303	107	243	244	216	11
67	4/B,C6,3/4/S/T,T/E	C7OF-12127-F,G	C7OZ-12127-F	303	108	243	233	216	12
68/69	A/T with T/E								
68	4/B,T/E	C8OF-12127-D	C8OZ-12127-D	357	108	243	233	216	11
68	2/B,C6 with Imco	C8WF-12127-B	C8WY-12127-B	356	107	236	233	216	10
68	2/B,S/T,T/E	C8AF-12127-M	C8AZ-12127-M	355	107	236	233	245	9
68/69	2/B,A/T,Imco	C8AF-12127-N	C7AZ-12127-D	356	107	241	233	216	8
8-cylinder 428 CID									
67/69	CJ A/T, Imco	C7OZ-12127-F	C7OZ-12127-F						
68/69	C6,S/T,T/E	C8OF-12127-D	C8OZ-12127-D	357	108	243	233	216	11
69	A/T,T/E	C8OF-12127-J	C8OZ-12127-J	303	107	243	244	216	12
69	CJ S/T with T/E	C8OF-12127-H	D8OZ-12127-H	357	107	243	244	216	11
70	CJ 4/B,S/T,T/E	DOZF-12127-C	DOZZ-12127-C	322	118	234	244	218	17
70	CJ 4/B,A/T,T/E GT350	DOZF-12127-G	DOZZ-12127-D	303	107	236	233	217	11
8-cylinder 429 CID									
69	Boss 4/B Spec. Before 2/28/69	C9AF-12127-U	C9ZZ-12127-D	311	112	237	244	229	11
69	Boss 4/B Spec. From 2/28/69	C9ZF-12127-D	C9ZZ-12127-D	307	112	238	233	225	10

*   For   Shelby GT350 with A/T, change stop #7 or #16 to #14.

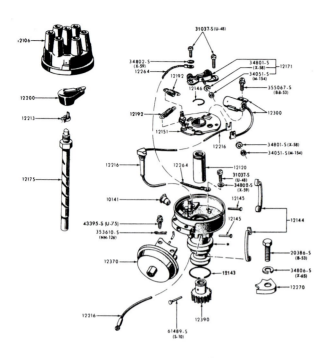

Exploded view of a six-cylinder distributor.

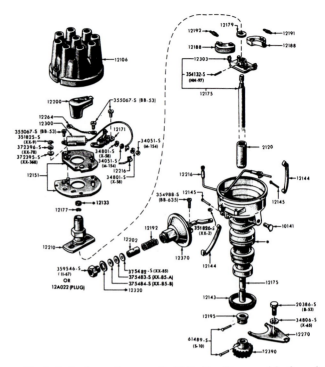

Exploded view of an early V-8 distributor with forged centrifugal weights.

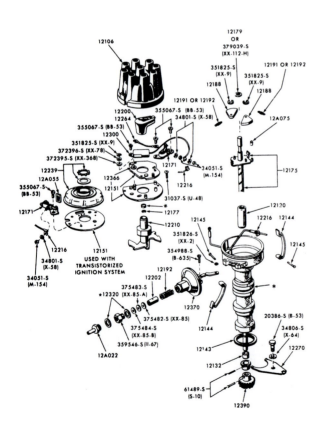

Exploded view of a V-8 distributor with stamped centrifugal weights.

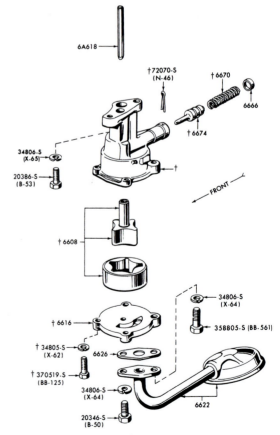

Oil pump and related parts for 170 and 200ci engines.

150

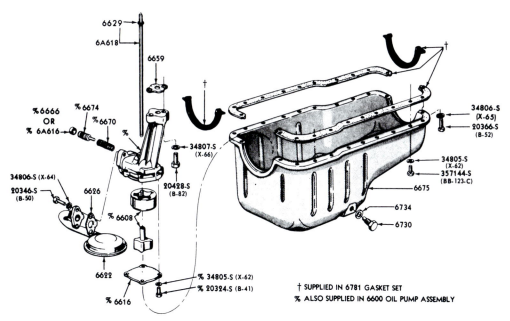

Typical oil pump, pan and related parts for 260, 289, 302, 351, and 429ci engines.

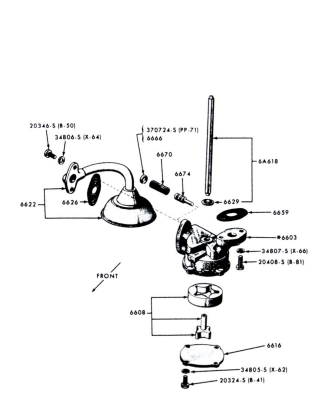

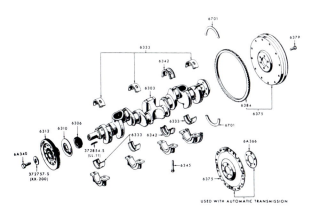

Typical crankshaft, flywheel, main bearings, and related parts for early 1965 model 170ci with four main bearings.

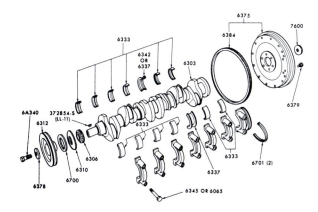

Oil pump and related parts for 390 and 428ci engines.

Typical crankshaft, flywheel, main bearings, and related parts for 200 and 250ci engines with seven main bearings.

151

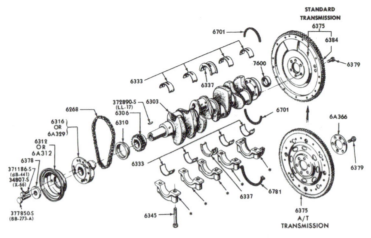

Typical crankshaft, flywheel, main bearings, and related parts for 260, 289, 302, 351, and 429ci engines.

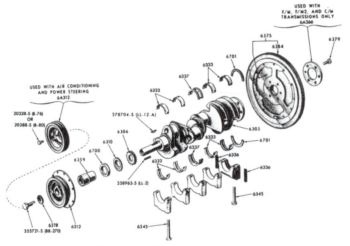

Crankshaft, flywheel, main bearings, and related parts for 390 and 428ci engines.

HiPo engines utilize thicker main bearing caps as compared to a standard 289. The block, however, is virtually unchanged.

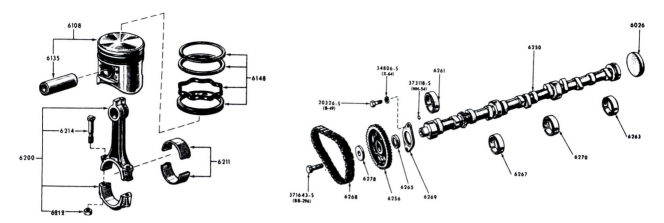

Typical piston, connecting rod, rings, engine camshaft, gear, bearings, and related parts for 170, 200, and 250ci engines.

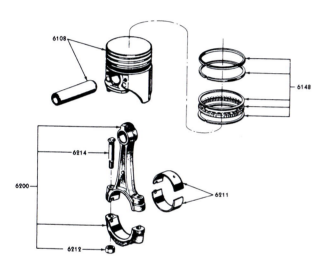

Typical piston, connecting rod, rings, and related parts for 260, 289, 302, 351, 400, and 429ci engines.

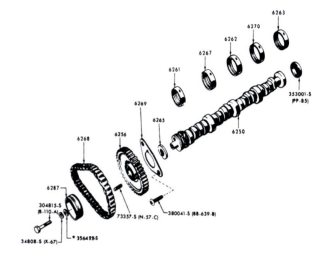

Typical camshaft, gear, bearings, and related parts for 390 and 428ci engines.

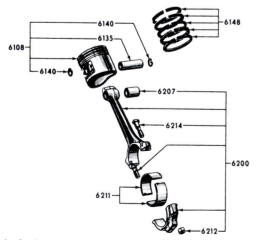

Typical piston, connecting rod, and related parts for 390 and 428ci engines.

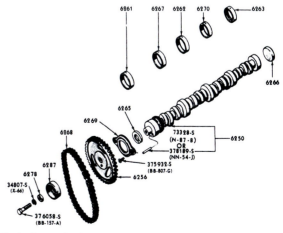

Typical camshaft, gear, bearings, and related parts for 289, 351, and 429ci engines.

Mustang Exhaust Manifold Application Chart, 1965-1970

For six-cylinder applications:

Years	CID	Part Number
65/67	200	C3OZ-9430-A
65/67	170	C3OZ-9430-A
67	200	D3BZ-9430-A
68	200	D3BZ-9430-A
69/70	200	D3BZ-9430-A
69	250	D3BZ-9430-A

For eight-cylinder applications:

Years	CID	Right Hand	Left Hand	Notes
65/67	289 K	C5ZZ-9430-B	C3OZ-9431-B	
65/68	260,289	D4DZ-9430-E	D0OZ-9431-D	
67	390	C6OZ-9430-A	C7OZ-9431-A	
68	390	C6OZ-9430-A	C7OZ-9431-A	Before 2/15/68
68	390	C8OZ-9430-B	C7OZ-9431-A	From 2/15/68
68	427	C6OZ-9430-A	C7OZ-9431-A	
68	428 CJ	C8OZ-9430-C	C8OZ-9431-B	
68/70	302	DOAZ-9430-C	D0OZ-9431-D	
		r/b D4DZ-9430-E &		
		D5DZ-9A603-C(2/75)		
69	351	C9AZ-9430-A	C9OZ-9431-A	
69	390	C9LZ-9430-B	C7OZ-9431-A	
69	428 CJ	C8OZ-9430-C	C8OZ-9431-B	
69/71	Boss 302	C9ZZ-9430-B	C9ZZ-9431-A	
69/70	Boss 429	C9AZ-9430-B	C9AZ-9431-A	
70	351W-2V	C9AZ-9430-A	C9OZ-9431-A	
70	351C-2V	D2OZ-9430-B	D0AZ-9431-A	
70	351	D0AZ-9430-B	D0AZ-9431-B	
70	428 CJ	C9OZ-9430-C	C8OZ-9431-B	
70	428 SCJ	C9OZ-9430-C	C8OZ-9431-B	

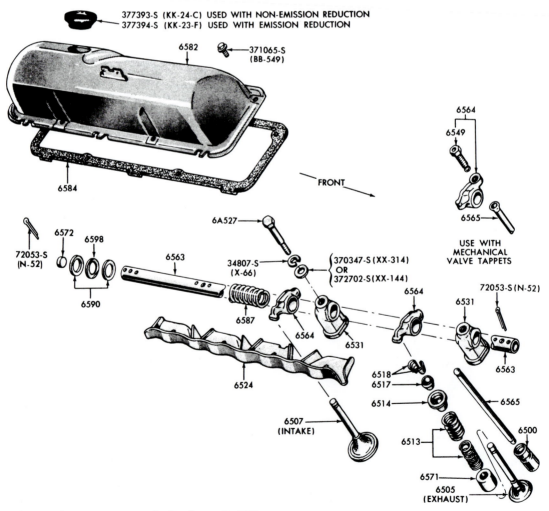

Valves, springs, rocker arms, cover, and related parts for 390 and 428ci engines.

Boss 302 engines were dressed out and finely detailed. A dress-up kit which included either chrome valve covers for 1969 or polished finned aluminum valve covers for 1970 were standard equipment. Here you can see the mangled mess of wires above the coil that incorporates the rev limiter and the 1970 vintage decal proclaiming the engine a Boss 302 built by Ford.

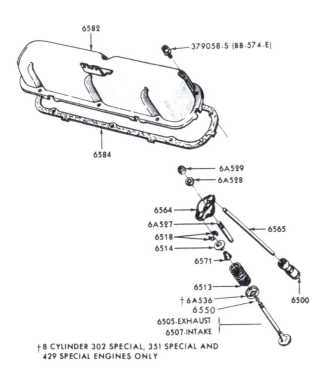

Typical valves, springs, rocker arms, cover, and related parts for all V-8 engines.

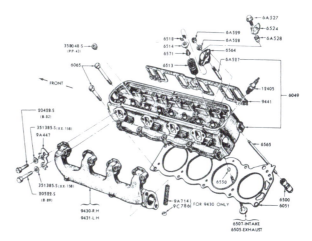

Typical cylinder head, exhaust manifold, gaskets, and related parts for all V-8 engines.

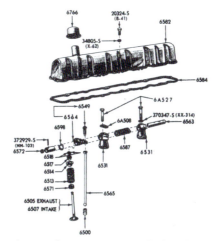

Valves, springs, rocker arms, cover and related parts for 170, 200, and 250ci engines.

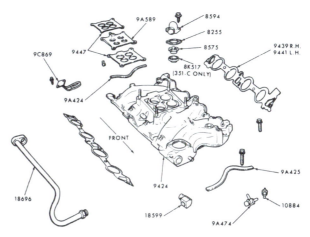

Typical intake manifold and related parts for 1970 351C and 1969-1970 429ci engines. Note: the thermostat and housing are not attached to the intake manifold on 351C engines.

MUSTANG INTAKE MANIFOLD APPLICATIONS CHART

Year	Cyl/CID	Part Number	Description
65	8/260 (Emission Reduction)	C4OZ-9424-E	Pkg. Includes one
			C5AZ-8592-C Connection Assy.
65	8/260 (Exc. w/ Emission Reduction)	C3AZ-9424-G	Pkg. Includes one
			C3AZ-10911-A Adapter
65	8/289 (4/B Carb. & Exc. Emission	C3OZ-9424-C	Pkg. Includes one
	Reduction		C3AZ-10911-A Adapter
			Before 8/20/65
65/67	8/289 (2B Carb)	C4AZ-9424-H	Pkg. Includes one
			C6AZ-8592-C Connection Assy.
66/68	8/289,302 (4B Carb.)	C4OZ-9424-H	
65	8/289 (4/B Carb)	C4OZ-9424-H	
65	8/289 (4/B Carb. & Emis. Reduction)	C4OZ-9424-H	Before 8/20/65
65/69	8/289,302 High-Perf. (4/B Carb)	C9OZ-9424-D	
65/68	8/289,302 (4/B Carb.)	C9OZ-9424-D	
68	8/427 (K, C6, T/E & 4/B Carb.)	C6ZA-9424-H	
66	8/390 High-Perf. (4/B Carb.)	C6AZ-9424-H	
66/67	8/390 (4/B Carb.)	C6AZ-9424-N	
68/70	8/427CJ (4/B Carb.)	C8OZ-9424-B	Cast Iron 1.60" Primary Openings,
			1.70" Secondary
66/70	8/390 High-Perf., 4/B Carb.	C8OZ-9424-B	Cast Iron 1.60" Primary Openings,
			1.70" Secondary
68	8/390 (2/B Carb.)	C9AZ-9424-E	
68	8/390 (4/B Carb.)	C8AZ-9424-C	Pkg Includes one 8A7617-B Plug
68	8/289 (2/B Carb.)	C4AZ-9424-J	
68/70	8/302 (2/B Carb.)	C4AZ-9424-J	
69	8/351 (4/B Carb.)	C9OZ-9424-B	
69	8/390 (4/B Carb.)	C9ZZ-9424-A	
69/70	8/351W High-Perf. (4/B Carb.)	C9OZ-9424-E	Aluminum High-Riser
69/70	8/429 Boss (4/B Carb.)	C9AZ-9424-D	Aluminum
69/70	8/302 Boss (4/B Carb.)	C9ZZ-9424-C	Aluminum
69	8/251 (2/B Carb.)	C9OZ-9424-A	
70	8/351W (2/B Carb.)	C9OZ-9424-A	
69/70	8/302 Boss	D0ZC-9425-A	Aluminum "Cross-Boss" Base Only uses
	Off-Highway Units		D0ZX-9C484-A Cover Gasket
			Inline 4V Carb.
			Use D0ZX-9C483-A Cover
70	8/351C (4/B Carb.)	D0AZ-9424-C	
70	8/351C 2/B Carb.)	D1AZ-9424-D	

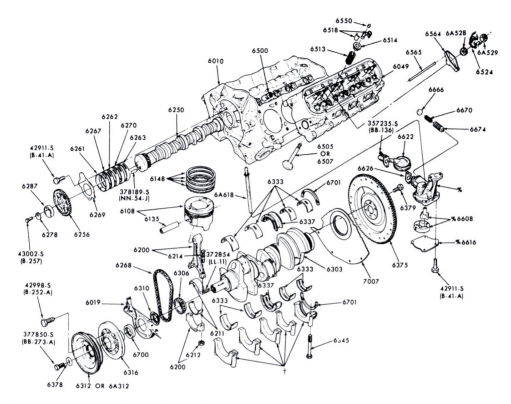

Exploded view of 302 and 351 Windsor internal engine parts.

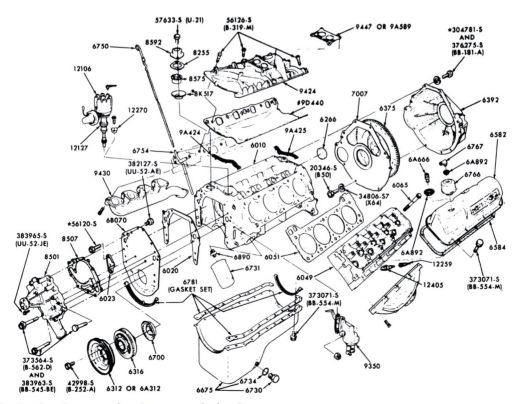

The 351 Cleveland engine external engine parts and related hardware.

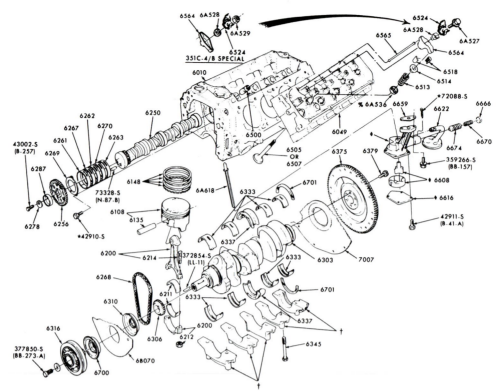

An exploded view of a 351 Cleveland long-block assembly.

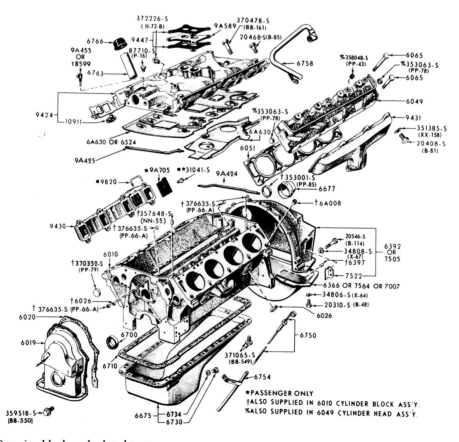

The 390 and 428 engine block and related parts.

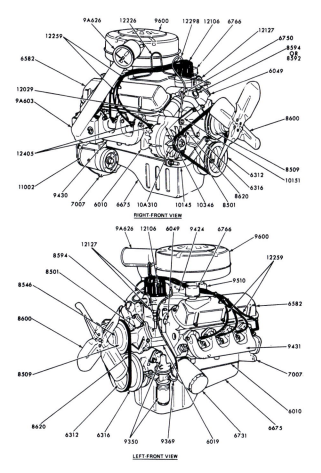

Right and left front views of a typical 1965-1968 289ci engine.

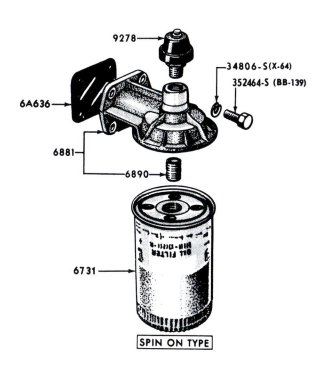

Engine oil filter, adapter, and related parts for 1968-1970 model 390 and 428ci engines.

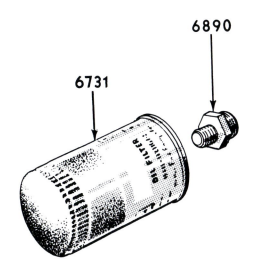

Engine oil filter and adapter fitting for all engines except 390 and 428.

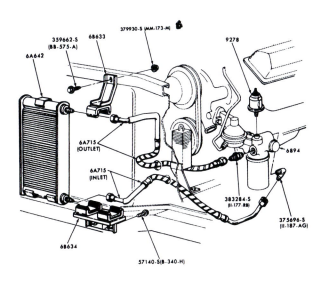

Engine oil cooler assembly and attaching hardware for 1969-1970 Boss 302, Boss 429, and 428 Super Cobra Jet engines.

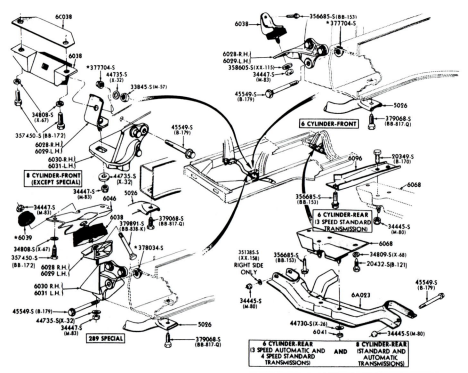

Engine and transmission mounts, accessories, and hardware for 1965-1966 Mustang (all engines and all transmissions).

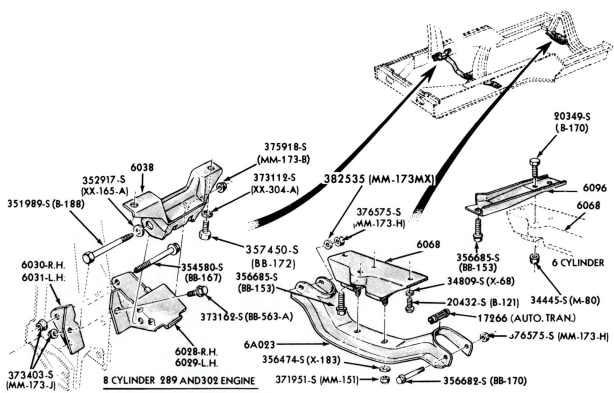

Engine and transmission mounts, accessories, and hardware for 1967-1970 Mustang equipped with six-cylinder or small-block V-8 engines.

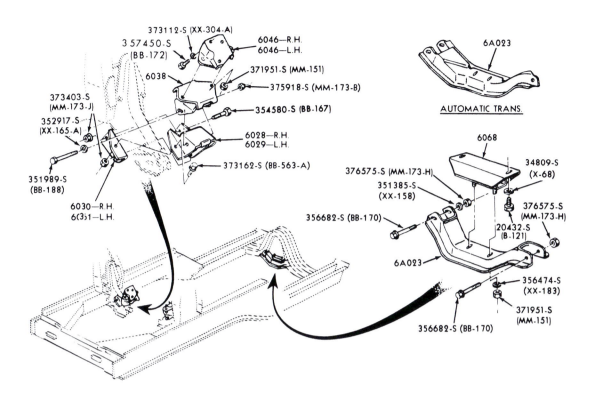

Engine and transmission mounts, accessories, and hardware for 1967-1970 Mustang equipped with 390 or 428ci engines.

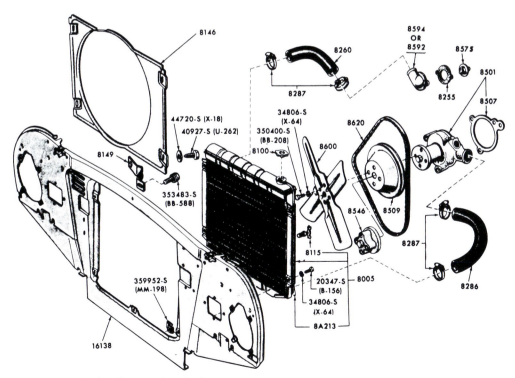

Typical cooling system and related parts for 1965-1970 Mustang equipped with all six-cylinder and V-8 engines except 390 or 428.

MUSTANG WATER PUMP ASSEMBLY APPLICATION CHART

Year	Notes	Engine	Description	Part Number
65		170,200		D4DZ-8501-A
65	2	260,289	Aluminum; uses C4OZ-8512-B &	C5AZ-8501-K
			C4OZ-8530-C	
65	2,5	289		D3UZ-8501-A
65	1	289		C5OZ-8501-A
65	1,4	289		D3UZ-8501-A
66		200		D4DZ-8501-A
66	7	289		D3UZ-8501-A
66	7	289	Aluminum; uses C4OZ-8530-C Bearing	C5AZ-8501-K
			with C4AZ-6019-B	
66	6	289		D3UZ-8501-A
66	1	289		C5OZ-8501-A
67		200		D4DZ-8501-A
67	2	289		D3UZ-8501-A
67	1	289		C5OZ-8501-A
67		390		D0AZ-8501-D
68		200		D4DZ-8501-A
68	1	289		C5OZ-8501-A
68	2,8	289,302		D3UZ-8501-A
68		390		D0AZ-8501-D
69		200		D4DZ-8501-A
69		250		D0DZ-8501-A
69	8	302-2V,351	Except Boss 302	D3UZ-8501-A
69		Boss 302		C9ZZ-8501-A
69		390,428CJ		D0AZ-8501-D
69		Boss 429	Pump incl. C8VZ-8507-A & C8SZ-8513-A	C9VZ-8501-A
70		200		D4DZ-8501-A
70		250		D0DZ-8501-A
70		Boss 302		D0ZZ-8501-B
70		351C	Incl. D0AZ-8513-A gasket; r/b D2SZ-8501-A	D0AZ-8501-E
70		428CJ		D0AZ-8501-D
70		302,351W	Except Boss 302	D0OZ-8501-C

Notes:

1   Used with High Performance 289
2   Except with High Performance 289
3   With generator or alternator
4   With alternator
5   With alternator, with A/C
6   Except with High Performance 289, with Thermactor
7   Except with High Performance 289, without Thermactor
8   Change water bypass tube for 289, 302 when necessary.

MUSTANG RADIATOR SHROUD APPLICATION CHART

Year	Engine	Notes	Description	Part Number
65	200	1	One-piece type	C3DZ-8146-C
65	260,289	1	One-piece type	C3DZ-8146-D
65	289	2	One-piece type	C3DZ-8146-D
66	200	1	One-piece type	C3DZ-8146-C
66	289	1	One-piece type; use w/ C3DZ-8005-K core	C6ZZ-8146-A
66	289	1	One-piece type; use w/ C3DZ-8005-K core	C3DZ-8146-D
66	289	2	One-piece type	C3DZ-8146-D
67	200	1	One-piece type-plastic	C7ZZ-8146-C
67	289	1	One-piece type-plastic, marked C7ZE-B	C9ZZ-8146-B
67	289	2	One-piece type-plastic, marked C7ZE-B	C9ZZ-8146-B
67	390	1,3,5,11	One-piece type-plastic, marked C7ZE-A	C7ZZ-8146-A
68	200	1,3		C7ZZ-8146-C
68	289	1,12	Plastic, marked C9OE-F	C9OZ-8146-A
68	289	4,11	Plastic, marked C9OE-F	C9OZ-8146-A
68	302	1	Plastic, marked C9OE-F	C9OZ-8146-A
68/70	390	1,3,5		C8ZZ-8146-A
68/70	428 CJ			C8ZZ-8146-A
68/70	302 (GT350)			C9OZ-8146-A
69	200	1 or 3		C7ZZ-8146-C
69	250	1 or 3,6,9	Plastic, use on 23-1/4 inch wide radiator	C9ZZ-8146-A
69	250	1 or 3,10	Plastic, use on 20-1/4 inch wide radiator	C9ZZ-8146-C
69	302,351	11	Plastic, marked C9ZE-C, w/ 20-inch radiator	C9ZZ-8146-B
69	302,351	3,6	Plastic, marked C9ZE-C, w/ 20-inch radiator	C9ZZ-8146-B
69	302,351	1,3	Plastic, marked C9OE-F, w/ 24-inch radiator	C9OZ-8146-A
69	302,351	3,6	Plastic, marked C9OE-F, w/ 24-inch radiator	C9OZ-8146-A
69	Boss 302		Plastic, marked C9OE-F, w/ 24-inch radiator	C9OZ-8146-A
70	200			C7ZZ-8146-C
70	250		Plastic	C9ZZ-8146-C
70	302		Plastic, marked D0ZE-B	D0ZZ-8146-B
70	351-2V		Plastic, marked D0ZE-B	D0ZZ-8146-B
70	351-4V		Plastic, marked D0ZE-B	D0ZZ-8146-B
70	302,351		Plastic, marked D0ZE-A or E	D0ZZ-8146-A
70	Boss 302		Plastic, marked D0ZE-A or E	D0ZZ-8146-A
70	351-4V		Plastic, marked D0ZE-A or E	D0ZZ-8146-A
70	428 CJ			C8ZZ-8146-A

Notes:

1   with Air Conditioning
2   High Performance
3   with Extra Cooling
4   with IMCO (Improved Combustion
5   with Thermactor
6   with Hang-on A/C
7   with 3.50:1 rear axle
8   without 3.50:1 rear axle
9   Before 12/16/68
10 From 12/16/68
11 with Standard transmission
12 except w/ High Performance

163

MUSTANG RADIATOR APPLICATION CHART

Year	Engine	Notes	Core Width	Core Height	Core Thickness	Part Number
65/66	170,200	1,2,4	17-1/4	16-1/2	1-1/4	C5ZZ-8005-C
65/66	260,289	1,2,3,4	17-1/4	17-1/2	1-1/4	C3DZ-8005-K
67	200	1,2,4	20-1/4	16-7/16	1-1/4	C9ZZ-8005-A
67	289	1,2,4	20-1/4	16-7/16	1-1/4	C9ZZ-8005-B
67	390	1,2,4	23-1/4	16	2	C7ZZ-8005-C
68	200	1,2,4	20-1/4	16-7/16	1-1/4	C9ZZ-8005-A
68	289-2V	1	20-1/4	16-7/16	1-1/4	C9ZZ-8005-B
68	289-2V	2,4	24-3/16	16	1-1/2	C9ZZ-8005-C
68	289 HiPo	1,2,4	24-3/16	16	1-1/2	C9ZZ-8005-C
68	302	1	20-1/4	16-7/16	1-1/4	C9ZZ-8005-B
68	302	2,4	24-3/16	16	1-1/2	C9ZZ-8005-C
68	390	1,2,4	24-3/16	16	2-1/4	C8ZZ-8005-C
68	428	1,2,4	24-3/16	16	2-1/4	C8ZZ-8005-C
69	200	1,2,4	20-1/4	16-7/16	1-1/4	C9ZZ-8005-A
69	250	1,2,4,5	23-1/4	15-7/16	1-1/4	C9ZZ-8005-D
69	250	1,2,4,6	20-1/4	16-7/16	1-1/4	C9ZZ-8005-E
69	302-2V,351	1	20-1/4	16-7/16	1-1/4	C9ZZ-8005-B
69	351	2,4	24-3/16	16	1-1/2	C9ZZ-8005-C
69	Boss 302	1	24-3/16	16	1-1/2	C9ZZ-8005-C
69	Boss 302	2,4	24-3/16	16	1-1/2	C9ZZ-8005-C
69	390 GT	1,2,4	24-3/16	16	2-1/4	C8ZZ-8005-C
69	428 CJ	1,2,4	24-3/16	16	2-1/4	C8ZZ-8005-C
69	Boss 429	1,2,4	24-3/16	16	2-1/4	C8ZZ-8005-C
70	200	1,4	20-1/4	16-7/16	1-1/4	C9ZZ-8005-A
70	200	2	20-1/4	16-7/16	1-1/4	C9ZZ-8005-E
70	250	1,2,4	20-1/4	16-7/16	1-1/4	C9ZZ-8005-E
70	302	1	20-1/4	16-7/16	1-1/4	C9ZZ-8005-E
70	351-2V	1	20-1/4	16-7/16	1-1/4	C9ZZ-8005-E
70	351-4V	2,7	20-1/4	16-7/16	1-1/4	C9ZZ-8005-E
70	Boss 302	1,2	24-3/16	16	2-1/4	D0ZZ-8005-C
70	428 CJ	1,2,4	24-3/16	16	2-1/4	C8ZZ-8005-C
70	Boss 429	1,2,4	24-3/16	16	2-1/4	C8ZZ-8005-C
70	302	2,4	24-3/16	16	2-1/4	D0ZZ-8005-D
70	351-2V & 4V	2,4	24-3/16	16	2-1/4	D0ZZ-8005-D
70	351-4V	1,2,8	24-3/16	16	2-1/4	D0ZZ-8005-D

Notes:
1. Standard Cooling
2. Extra Cooling
3. Super Extra Cooling
4. With Air Conditioning
5. Before 12/16/68
6. From 12/16/68
7. Without 3.50:1 rear axle
8. With 3.50:1 rear axle

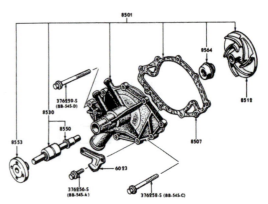

Aluminum water pump (without cover) assembly and attaching hardware for 1965 260 and 289ci engines.

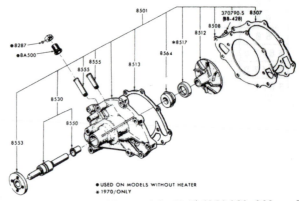

Iron water pump (with cover) for 1965-1970 289, 302, and 351W engines.

An information tag explaining antifreeze warranty and service specifications was attached to the radiator filler neck or overflow hose by the dealer during the standard predelivery check.

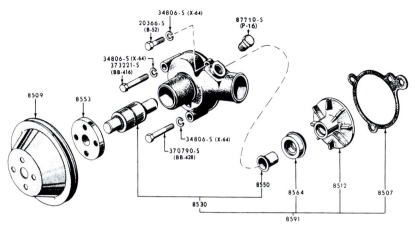

Engine water pump assembly and attaching hardware for 170, 200, and 250ci engines.

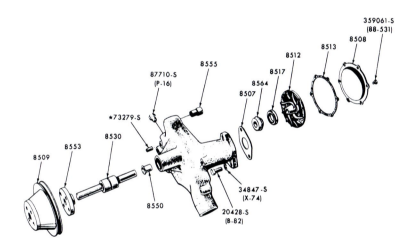

Water pump assembly and attaching hardware for 390 and 428ci engines.

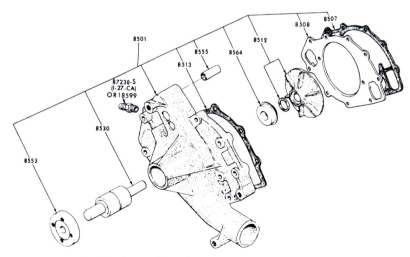

Water pump assembly and attaching hardware for 351 Cleveland and 429ci engines.

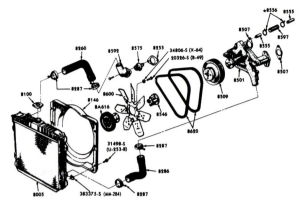

Cooling system and related parts for 1967-1970 Mustang equipped with 390 or 428 engines.

MUSTANG FAN CLUTCH ASSEMBLY APPLICATION CHART

Year	Engine	Notes	Description	Part Number
65	260,289	1		C6OZ-8A616-D
66	289	2,3,5	3-3/16" depth, marked C6ZE-A	C6ZZ-8A616-A
66	289	4,6		C6OZ-8A616-D
66	289	7		C6OZ-8A616-D
67	289,390	8	2.91" depth, marked C7ZE-B	C7OZ-8A616-C
67	289	9	3-3/16" depth, marked C6ZE-A	C6ZZ-8A616-A
67	428		for GT-500, not replaced	
68	390 GT	10	marked C8OE-A	C8OZ-8A616-A
68	200,289 302,428CJ	11	marked C8OE-B or C	C8OZ-8A616-B
68	428		for GT-500	C8ZX-8A616-A
69	250		marked C9DE-A or C9ZE-C	C9DZ-8A616-A
69	390GT	1	marked C8OE-A	C8OZ-8A616-A
69	390GT	12	marked C8OE-B or C	C8OZ-8A616-B
69	428CJ, or SCJ		marked C9ZE-B	C9ZZ-8A616-A
70	250	1	marked C9DE-A or C9ZE-A	C9DZ-8A616-A
70	428CJ	1,13	marked C9ZE-B	C9ZZ-8A616-A
70	428SCJ	13	not used from 9/1/69	C9ZZ-8A616-A
70	428CJ	1,14		D0ZZ-8A616-A

Notes:
1. with factory installed A/C
2. with hang-on A/C, w/ or w/o Thermactor
3. Before 1/5/66
4. From 1/5/66
5. Use with C6ZZ-8805-A, 2-1/4" core.
6. Use with C3DZ-8805-K, 1-1/4" core.
7. Integral A/C, w/ or w/o Thermactor
8. except hang-on A/C
9. with hang-on A/C
10. with Thermactor
11. without A/C
12. Standard cooling package
13. Before 9/1/69
14. From 9/1/69

MUSTANG FAN BLADE ASSEMBLY APPLICATION CHART, PART ONE, 1965-1968

Year	Engine	Notes	Description	Blades	Diam.	Hole	Part Number
65	170,200	1		6	15-1/16	5/8	C9DZ-8600-A
65	170,200	3	Replaces C2DA-A,C2OA-A	4	15-1/2	5/8	C2DZ-8600-D
65	260,289	4,5,6		4	17	5/8	C2OA-8600-B
65	260,289	2,7		5	17-1/4	2-3/8	C3OZ-8600-D
65	260,289	1,11	Aluminum, replaces 6-blade fan	5	17	5/8	C5AZ-8600-A
65	289K	10		4	17-1/8	5/8	C6OZ-8600-D
65	289	2,8		7	17-1/2	2-3/8	C4OZ-8600-D
66	200	3	Replaces C2DA-A,C2OA-A	4	15-1/2	5/8	C2DZ-8600-D
66	200	12		6	15-1/16	5/8	C9DZ-8600-A
66	289K	10	marked C3OA-C	4	17-1/8	5/8	C6OZ-8600-D
66	289	4,9,12	marked C6OE-B,C6AE-E,C1VV-D	4	17-1/2	5/8	C6OZ-8600-A
66	289	5,6,9,13	marked C5AE-B	5	17	5/8	C5AZ-8600-A
66	289	1	marked C6OE-G	7	17-1/2	2-3/8	C4OZ-8600-D
67	200	3,5,14	Replaces C2DA-A,C2OA-A	4	15-1/2	5/8	C2DZ-8600-D
67	200	12		6	15-1/16	5/8	C9DZ-8600-A
67	289K	10	marked C6OE-D	4	17-1/8	5/8	C6OZ-8600-D
67	289	3,9,15,17	marked C6AE-E or C1VV-D	4	17-1/2	5/8	C6OZ-8600-A
67	289	4,9,12	marked C6AE-E or C1VV-D	4	17-1/2	5/8	C6OZ-8600-A
67	289	5,6,9,13,16	marked C5AE-B	5	17	5/8	C5AZ-8600-A
67	289	9,12,13	marked C5AE-B	5	17	5/8	C5AZ-8600-A
67	289	12	marked C6DA-A	5	17-1/2	5/8	C6DZ-8600-B
67	289	12	marked C6OE-G	7	17-1/2	2-3/8	C4OZ-8600-D
67	390	5	marked C6OE-F	7	18-1/4	2-3/8	C6OZ-8600-F
68	200	3,5 or 6 or 12		6	15-1/16	5/8	C9DZ-8600-A
68	289	3,5		4	17-1/8	5/8	C6OZ-8600-D
68	289,302	12		5	17-1/2	5/8	C8SZ-8600-B
68	302	3,5		4	17-1/2	5/8	C6OZ-8600-A
68	351	5,6,17		4	17-1/2	5/8	C6OZ-8600-A
68	390	5,6,12	marked C8OE-B	7	18-1/4	2-3/8	C6OZ-8600-A
68	GT350		marked C6OE-G	7	17-1/2	2-3/8	C4OZ-8600-D

Notes:
1. with Hang-on A/C
2. with factory-installed Hang-on A/C
3. Except with A/C
4. Except Hi-Po
5. Standard Cooling
6. Extra Cooling
7. with factory generator
8. with factory alternator
9. with Thermactor
10. with Hi-Po engine
11. with generator or alternator
12. with A/C
13. with Power Steering
14. includes IMCO
15. with Auto. Transmission
16. before 11/14/66
17. from 11/14/66
18. with Manual Transmission

MUSTANG FAN BLADE ASSEMBLY APPLICATION CHART, PART TWO, 1969-1970

Year	Engine	Notes	Description	Blades	Diam.	Hole	Part Number
69	200	2	marked C9ZE-D	4	16	5/8	C9ZZ-8600-D
69	200	3		6	15-1/16	5/8	C9DZ-8600-A
69	200,250	1,3	marked C5AE-B	5	17	5/8	C5AZ-8600-A
69	250	4		4	17-1/8	5/8	C9OZ-8600-A
69	250	4 or 9	marked C9ZE-C	6	17	2-5/8	C9ZZ-8600-B
69	302-2V,351	4		5	17-1/2	5/8	C8SZ-8600-B
69	302-2V	2,3		5	17-1/2	5/8	C6OZ-8600-A
69	351	2,3	marked C8SE-A	4	17-9/16	5/8	C9OZ-8600-A
69	302-2V,351	1,3		5	18	5/8	C5AZ-8600-K
69	Boss 302		marked C9WE-A	5	17-1/2	2-3/8	C9WZ-8600-A
69	Boss 302			4	17-1/8	5/8	C6OZ-8600-D
69	Boss 302			5	17-1/2	5/8	C8SZ-8600-B
69	390 GT		marked C8OE-B	7	18-1/4	2-3/8	C8OZ-8600-A
69	390	1,3	marked C8AE-D	5	19	5/8	C8AZ-8600-D
69	428CJ,SCJ	2,4	marked C9ZE-E	7	18-1/4	2-5/8	C9ZZ-8600-C
69	428 SCJ	2	marked C9OE-H	6	18	5/8	C9OZ-8600-D
69	Boss 429		marked C9ZE-F	7	18	3/4	C9ZZ-8600-B
70	200	2,10	marked C9ZE-D	4	16	5/8	C9ZZ-8600-A
70	200	3,10		6	15-1/16	5/8	C9DZ-8600-A
70	200	2,3,11	marked C8YE-8600-A	5	16-1/2	5/8	C8YZ-8600-A
70	200,250	1,3,14	marked C5AE-B	5	17	5/8	C5AZ-8600-A
70	250	2,3		4	17-1/8	5/8	C9OZ-8600-A
70	250	4	marked C9ZE-C	6	17	2-5/8	C9ZZ-8600-B
70	302	4		5	17-1/2	5/8	C8SZ-8600-B
70	351	2 or 3,4		5	17-1/2	5/8	C8SZ-8600-B
70	Boss 302			5	17-1/2	5/8	C8SZ-8600-B
70	351	2 or 3	marked C8SE-A	4	17-9/16	5/8	C9OZ-8600-B
70	302-2V	2 or 3		4	17-9/16	5/8	C9OZ-8600-B
70	428CJ	2,12	marked C9ZE-E	7	18-1/4	2-5/8	C9ZZ-8600-C
70	428CJ,SCJ	4		7	18-1/4	2-5/8	C9ZZ-8600-C
70	428 SCJ	2,13		7	18-1/4	2-5/8	C9ZZ-8600-C
70	428 SCJ	12		6	18	5/8	C9OZ-8600-D
70	428 CJ	13		7	18	5/8	D0TZ-8600-B
70	Boss 429		marked D0ZE-A	5	18	1	D0ZZ-8600-A

Notes:
1. with Hang-on A/C
2. Standard Cooling
3. Extra Cooling
4. with A/C
5. with Power Steering
6. includes IMCO
7. with Auto. Transmission
8. with Manual Transmission
9. Economy 1V model
10. Before 8/27/69
11. From 8/27/69
12. Before 9/1/69
13. From 9/1/69
14. Slot existing holes away from center hole (4 places).

166

MUSTANG RADIATOR HOSE APPLICATION CHART, PART ONE, 1965-1967

Year	Engine	Notes	Type	Interior Diameter	Length	Part Number
65	170,200	M	Upper	1-1/4		C5TZ-8260-A
		M	Lower			D2PZ-8286-H
		F	Upper			C9PZ-8260-F
65	260,289	M,1	Upper			C3DZ-8260-J
		M,1	Lower	1-3/4	14-7/8	C3DZ-8286-F
		F,1	Upper			C9PZ-8260-K
65	260,289	M,2	Upper			C5TZ-8260-A
		M,2	Lower	1-3/4	14-7/8	C3DZ-8286-F
65	289	M,3	Upper			D2PZ-8260-H
		M,3	Lower	1-3/4	14-7/8	C3DZ-8286-F
		F,3	Upper			C9PZ-8260-K
65	289	M,4	Upper			C5TZ-8260-A
		M,4	Lower	1-3/4	14-7/8	C3DZ-8286-F
66	200	M	Upper			C2OZ-8260-H
		M	Lower			D2PZ-8286-H
		F	Upper			C9PZ-8260-F
66	289	M,5	Upper			D2PZ-8260-H
		M,5	Lower	1-3/4	14-7/8	C3DZ-8286-F
		F,5	Upper			C9PZ-8260-K
66	289	M,6	Upper			C5TZ-8260-A
		M,6	Lower	1-3/4	14-7/8	C3DZ-8286-F
66	289	M,8	Upper			D2PZ-8260-H
		M,8	Lower	1-3/4	14-7/8	C3DZ-8286-F
		F,8	Upper			C9PZ-8260-F
		F,8	Lower			C9PZ-8286-R
67	200	M	Upper			C2OZ-8260-F
		M	Lower			D2PZ-8286-H
		F	Upper			C9PZ-8260-F
67	289	M,7	Upper			D2PZ-8260-H
		M,7	Lower	1-3/4	14-7/8	C3DZ-8286-F
		F,7	Upper			C9PZ-8260-K
67	289	M,6	Upper			C5TZ-8260-A
		F,6	Lower	1-3/4	14-7/8	C3DZ-8286-F
67	390	M	Upper	1-3/4	14-1/2	C5AZ-8260-G
		M	Lower			D2PZ-8286-J
		F	Upper			C9PZ-8260-R

Notes:
- M   Moulded Hose
- F   Flexible Hose; to be used when moulded hose not available.
- 1   with generators, except with 4 (2V) Carb. Kit.
- 2   with generators & 4 (2V) Carb. Kit.
- 3   with alternators, except with 4 (2V) Carb. Kit.
- 4   with alternators & 4 (2V) Carb. Kit.
- 5   without A/C, except with 4 (2V) Carb. Kit.
- 6   with 4 (2V) Carb. Kit.
- 7   except with 4 (2V) Carb. Kit.
- 8   with A/C

MUSTANG RADIATOR HOSE APPLICATION CHART, PART TWO, 1968-1969

Year	Engine	Notes	Type	Interior Diameter	Length	Part Number
68	200	M	Upper			C2OZ-8260-H
		M	Lower			D2PZ-8286-H
		F	Upper			C9PZ-8260-F
68	289-4V	M,9	Upper	1-1/2		C5AZ-8260-F
		M,9	Lower	1-3/4		C8ZZ-8286-A
		F,9	Upper			C9PZ-8260-L
68	289-2V,302	M,9	Upper	1-1/2	13	C8ZZ-8260-C
		M,9	Lower	1-3/4	14-7/8	C3DZ-8286-F
		F,9	Upper			C9PZ-8286-T
68	289-2V,302	M,10	Upper	1-1/2		C5AZ-8260-F
		M,10	Lower	1-3/4		C8ZZ-8286-A
		F,10	Upper			C9PZ-8260-L
68	390-4V,428CJ	M	Upper	1-3/4	14-1/2	C5AZ-8260-G
		M	Lower			D2PZ-8286-J
		F	Upper			C9PZ-8260-R
69	200	M	Upper			C2OZ-8260-H
		M	Lower			D2PZ-8286-H
		F	Upper			C9PZ-8260-F
69	250	M,11	Upper			C9ZZ-8260-D
		M,11	Lower	1-7/8	18	C9ZZ-8286-A
69	250	M,12	Upper	1-1/2	11	C9ZZ-8260-A
		M,12	Lower	1-7/8	18	C9ZZ-8286-A
		F,12	Upper			C9PZ-8260-N
69	302,351	M,9	Upper			D2PZ-8260-H
		M,9	Lower	1-3/4	14-7/8	C3DZ-8286-F
		F,9	Upper			C9PZ-8260-K
69	351,Boss 302	M,10	Upper			D2PZ-8260-H
		M,10	Lower	1-3/4	14-7/8	C3DZ-8286-F
		F,10	Upper			C9PZ-8260-K
69	390,428CJ	M	Upper	1-3/4	14-1/2	C5AZ-8260-G
		M	Lower			D2PZ-8286-J
		F	Upper			C9PZ-8260-R
69	Boss 429	M	Upper	1-1/2	11-1/4	B9A-8286-D
		M	Lower			C9AZ-8286-D

Notes:
- M   Moulded Hose
- F   Flexible Hose; to be used when moulded hose not available.
- 9   Standard cooling
- 10   Extra Cooling or A/C
- 11   Before 12/16/68
- 12   From 12/16/68

MUSTANG RADIATOR HOSE APPLICATION CHART, PART THREE, 1970

Year	Engine	Notes	Type	Interior Diameter	Length	Part Number
70	200	M	Upper			C2OZ-8260-H
		M	Lower			D2PZ-8286-H
		F	Upper			C9PZ-8260-F
70	250	M	Upper	1-1/2	11	C9ZZ-8260-A
		M	Lower	1-7/8	18	C9ZZ-8286-A
		F	Upper			C9PZ-8260-N
70	351C	M,9,10	Upper			D2PZ-8260-M
		M,9,10	Lower	1-3/4	14-7/8	D0ZZ-8286-A
		F,9,10	Upper			C9PZ-8260-L
		F,9,10	Lower	1-3/4	16-1/2	C9PZ-8286-R
70	302,351W	M,9,10	Upper			D2PZ-8260-H
		M,9,10	Lower	1-3/4	14-7/8	D0ZZ-8286-A
		F,9,10	Upper			C9PZ-8260-T
		F,9,10	Lower	1-3/4	16-1/2	C9PZ-8286-R
70	Boss 302	M	Upper			D2PZ-8260-H
		M	Lower	1-3/4	14-7/8	D0ZZ-8286-A
		F	Upper			C9PZ-8260-T
		F	Lower	1-3/4	16-1/2	C9PZ-8286-R
70	428CJ	M	Upper	1-3/4	14-1/2	C5AZ-8260-G
		M	Lower			D2PZ-8286-J
		F	Upper			C9PZ-8260-R
70	Boss 429	M	Upper	1-1/2	11-1/4	B9A-8286-D
		M	Lower			C9AZ-8286-D

Notes:
- M   Moulded Hose
- F   Flexible Hose; to be used when moulded hose not available.
- 8   with A/C
- 9   Standard cooling
- 10   Extra Cooling or A/C

The Tecumseh cast-iron air conditioning compressor (left) was used primarily from 1965 through 1967, but not always. The York aluminum case compressor (right) was used intermittently through the years 1965 through 1970.

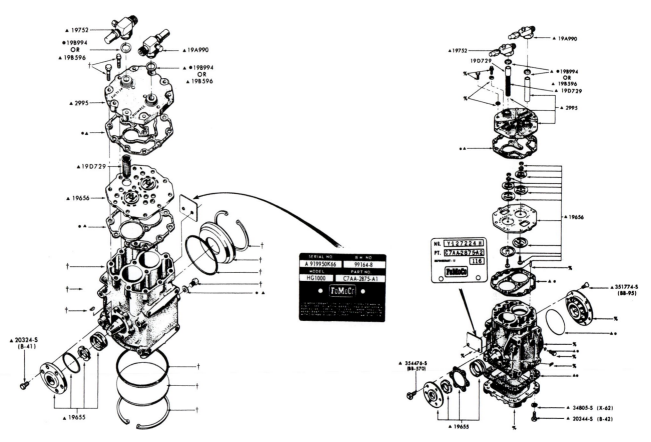

The Tecumseh cast-iron air conditioning compressor used on all 1965-1970 Mustangs.

The York aluminum air conditioning compressor used on all 1965-1970 Mustangs.

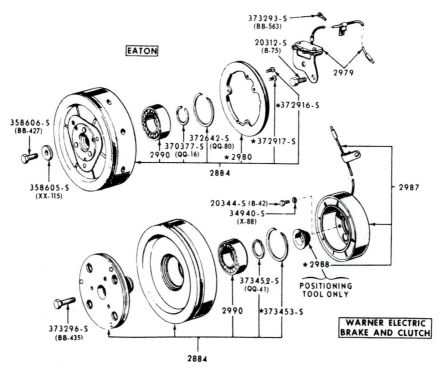

Eaton and Warner air conditioner compressor clutches used on all 1965-1970 Mustangs.

MUSTANG AIR CONDITIONER COMPRESSOR CLUTCH AND PULLEY APPLICATION CHART

YEAR	MODEL	TYPE	IDENTIFICATION	PART NUMBER
65/66	6 cylinder	2C	C4DA-2981-B, B1	C8OZ-2884-G
65/66	6 cylinder	6C	C4DA-2981-B2,	
65/66	6 cylinder	4C	C4DA-2981-C	C5DZ-2884-A
65/66	8 cylinder 260, 289	2B	C3AA-2981-A, A1	C3AZ-2884-A
65/66	8 cylinder 260, 289	6B	C3AA-2981-A2	
65	8 cylinder 260,289	5A	C4OA-2981-A	C3AZ-2884-C
65	8 cylinder 260,289	4A	C3AA-2981-B	C3AZ-2884-C
65/66	8 cylinder 260,289	4A	C2AA-2981-C	C8OZ-2884-G
65/66	8 cylinder 289	2B	C2AA-2981-A, A1	C8OZ-2884-B
65/66	8 cylinder 289	6B	C2AA-2981-A2	
66	8 cylinder 390	5B	C4AA-2981-A	C6AZ-2884-A
67	6 cylinder	2C	C7AA-2981-B	C7AZ-2884-B
67	6 cylinder	6C	C7OA-2981-B	C7OZ-2884-B
67	6 cylinder	2C	C4DA-2981-B, B1	C8OZ-2884-G
67	6 cylinder	6C	C4DA-2981-B2	
67	6 cylinder	4C	C7ZA-2981-C	C7ZZ-2884-B
67	8 cyl. 289 (exc. GT-350)	2C	C7AA-2981-B	C7AZ-2884-B
67	8 cyl. 289 (exc. GT-350)	3B	C7AA-2981-F	C9AZ-2884-A
67	8 cyl. 289 (exc. GT-350)	2B	C2AA-2981-A, A1	C8OZ-2884-B
67	8 cyl. 289 (exc. GT-350)	6B	C2AA-2981-A2	C8OZ-2884-B
67	8 cyl. 289 GT-350	5B	C7SA-2981-B	C7AZ-2884-D
67	8 cylinder 390	6B	C7AA-2981-H,	C9AZ-2884-B
67	8 cylinder 390	6B	C7SA-2981-A,	C9AZ-2884-B
67	8 cylinder 390	6B	C9AA-2981-G	C9AZ-2884-B
67	8 cylinder 390	2B	C2AA-2981-A, A1	C8OZ-2884-B
67	8 cylinder 390	6B	C2AA-2981-A2	C8OZ-2884-B
67	8 cylinder 390	2B	C7AA-2981-C	C7AZ-2884-C
68	6 cylinder	5C	C8OA-2981-A	C8OZ-2884-A
68	8 cylinder 289, 302	3B	C7AA-2981-F	C9AZ-2884-A
68	8 cylinder 289, 302	3B	C9AA-2981-F	C9AZ-2884-A
68	8 cylinder 289, 302	5B	C7AA-2981-G	C9AZ-2884-H
68	8 cylinder 390	6B	C7AA-2981-H,	C9AZ-2884-B
68	8 cylinder 390	6B	C7SA-2981-A,	C9AZ-2884-B
68	8 cylinder 390	6B	C9AA-2981-G	C9AZ-2884-B
68	8 cylinder 390, 428	5B	C7AA-2981-J	C8AZ-2884-F
69	6 cylinder 250	5C	C90A-2981-E	C9OZ-2884-B
69	8 cylinder 302, 351	3B	C7AA-2981-F,	C9AZ-2884-A
69	8 cylinder 302, 351	3B	C9AA-2981-F	C9AZ-2884-A
69	8 cylinder 302, 351	5B	C9AA-2981-D, D1, D2	C9AZ-2884-D
69		6B	C7AA-2981-H,	C9AZ-2884-B
69	8 cylinder 390, 428	6B	C7SA-2981-A,	C9AZ-2884-B
69	8 cylinder 390, 428	6B	C9AA-2981-G	C9AZ-2884-B
69	8 cylinder 390, 428	5B	C7AA-2981-J	C8AZ-2884-F
70		5C	C90A-2981-E	C9OZ-2884-B
70	8 cyl. 302-2B, 351, 428	5B	C9AA-2981-D, D1, D2	C9AZ-2884-D
70	8 cylinder 351	3B	C7AA-2981-F	C9AZ-2884-A
70	8 cylinder 351	3B	C9AA-2981-F	C9AZ-2884-A

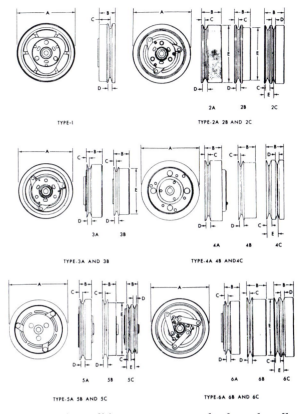

TYPE-1   TYPE-2A 2B AND 2C   2A 2B 2C

TYPE-3A AND 3B   TYPE-4A 4B AND 4C   3A 3B   4A 4B 4C

TYPE-5A 5B AND 5C   TYPE-6A 6B AND 6C   5A 5B 5C   6A 6B 6C

Mustang air-conditioner compressor clutch and pulley reference.

MUSTANG AIR CONDITIONER COMPRESSOR CLUTCH AND PULLEY I.D. CHART

PART NUMBER	TYPE	A	B	C	D	E	*	VENDOR	STAMPED NO.	REMARKS
C3AZ-2884-A	2B	6-3/4	1-7/8	7/16	1/2	6-1/16	1	Eaton	C3AA-2981-A, A1	Has integral field-use w/C8SZ-2979-A.
C3AZ-2884-A	6B	6-3/4	1-7/8	7/16	1/2	6-1/16	1	Eaton	C3AA-2981-A2	Has integral field-use w/C8SZ-2979-A.
C3AZ-2884-C	4A	6-7/8	1	7/16	7/16	1/2		1	Warner	C3AA-2091-B	Less field-use w/C3SZ-2987-A.
C3AZ-2884-C	5A	6-3/4	1-5/8	7/16	1/2		1	Pitts	C4OA-2981-A	Less field-use w/C3SZ-2987-A.
C5DZ-2884-A	4C	6-7/8	2	1/2	3/8	1	2	Warner	C4DA-2981-C	Less field-use w/C3SZ-2987-A.
C6AZ-2884-A	5B	6-11/16	2-1/8	2/8	1/2	6-3/8	1	Pitts	C4AA-2981-A	Less field-use w/C3SZ-2987-A.
C7AZ-2884-B	2C	6-1/4	1-1/2	1/2	1/2	1-3/16	2	Eaton	C7AA-2981-B	Has integral field-use w/C8SZ-2979-A.
C7AZ-2884-C	2B	6-3/4	1 3/4	3/8	1/2	5-5/16	1	Eaton	C7AA-2981-C	Has integral field-use w/C8SZ-2979-A.
C7AZ-2884-D	5B	6-11/16	1-5/8	3/8	1/2	6	1	Pitts	C7SA-2981-B	Less field-use w/C3SZ-2987-A.
C7OZ-2884-B	6C	7	1-1/2	1/2	3/8	1-1/16	2	Eaton	C7OA-2981-B	Has integral field-use w/C8SZ-2979-A.
C7ZZ-2884-B	4C	6-7/8	2-1/16	1/2	3/8	1-1/16	2	Warner	C7ZA-2981-C	Less field-use w/C7AZ-2987-A.
C8AZ-2884-F	5B	6-11/16	1-5/8	3/8	1/2	6	1	Pitts	C7AA-2981-J	Less field-use w/C8AZ-2987-C.
C8OZ-2884-A	5C	6-3/4	1-7/16	3/8	3/8	1-1/8	2	Pitts	C8OA-2981-A	Less field-use w/C8AZ-2987-C.
C8OZ-2884-B	2B	6-3/4	2-1/4	3/8	1/2	6-3/8	1	Eaton	C2AA-2981-A, A1	Used on 1967-has integral field-use with C8SZ-2979-A.
	6B	6-3/4	1-7/8	7/16	1/2	6-1/16	1	Eaton	C3AA-2981-A2	Has integral field-use w/C8SZ-2979-A.
	6B	6-3/4	2-1/4	3/8	1/2	6-3/8	1	Eaton	C7OA-2981-F	Has integral field-use w/C8SZ-2979-A.
C8OZ-2884-G	2C	6-3/4	2-5/16	1/2	3/8	1-1/16	2	Eaton	C4DA-2981-B, B1	Has integral field-use w/C8SZ-2979-A.
	4A	6-7/8	2-1/8	3/8	1/2			1	Warner	C2AA-2981-C	Has wire and field assembly.
	6C	6-3/4	2-5/16	1/2	3/8	1-1/16	2	Eaton	C4DA-2981-B2	Has integral field-use w/C8SZ-2979-A.
C9AZ-2884-A	3B	6-5/16	2-1/16	3/8	1/2	6	1	Eaton	C7AA-2981-F	Has integral field-use w/C8SZ-2979-A.
									C9AA-2981-F	
C9AZ-2884-B	6B	6-3/4	2	5/8	1/2	6	1	Eaton	C7AA-2981-H	Has integral field-use w/C8SZ-2979-A.
	6B	6-3/4	2-1/16	3/8	1/2	6	1	Eaton	C7SA-2981-A	Has integral field-use w/C8SZ-2979-A.
	6B	6-3/4	2-1/16	5/8	1/2	6	1	Eaton	C9AA-2981-F	Has integral field-use w/C8SZ-2979-A.
C9AZ-2884-D	5B	6-11/16	1-5/8	3/8	1/2	5-3/16	1	Pitts	C9AA-2981-D	Less field-use w/C8AZ-2987-D.
	5B	6-5/16	1-1/2	3/8	1/2	5-3/16	1	GPD	C9AA-2981-D1	
	5B	6-5/16	1-1/2	3/8	1/2	5-3/16	1	Pitts	C9AA-2981-D2	
C9AZ-2884-H	5B	6-1/4	5/8	5/16	1/2	6	1	Pitts	D2AA-2981-G	Less field-use w/C8AZ-2987-D.
C9OZ-2884-B	5C	6-1/4	1-7/16	3/8	3/8	1	2	Pitts	C90A-2981-E	Less field-use w/C9AZ-2987-A.

169

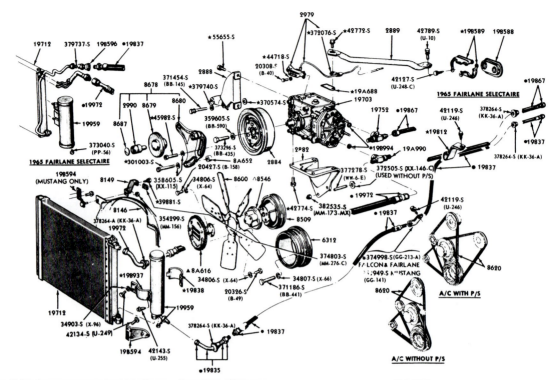

Air-conditioning compressor, condenser, brackets, hoses, and related hardware for 1965-1966 Mustangs equipped with eight-cylinder engines (with alternator).

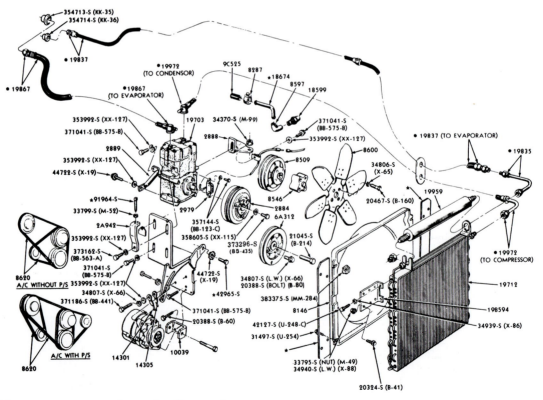

Air-conditioner compressor, condenser, brackets, and related hardware for hang-on system installed on 1967 Mustangs equipped with six-cylinder engines.

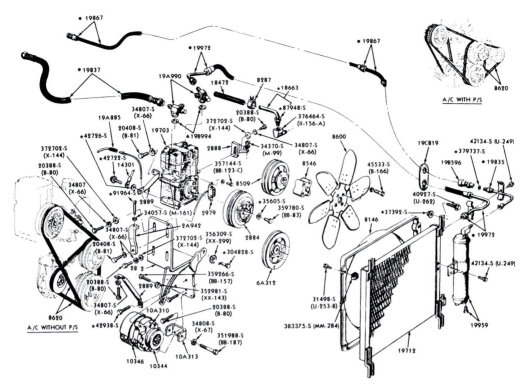

Air-conditioning compressor, condenser, brackets, hoses, and related hardware for 1967 Mustangs equipped with six-cylinder engines and factory-installed integral air conditioning.

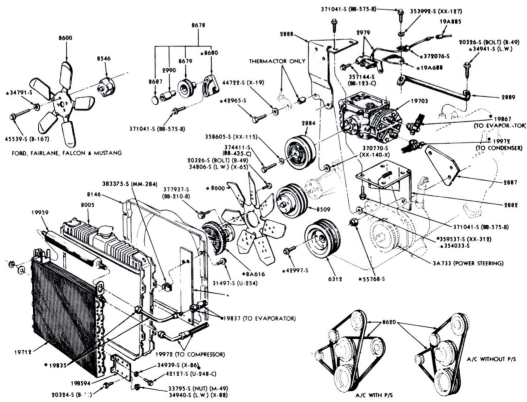

Air-conditioning compressor, condenser, brackets, hoses, and related hardware for 1967 Mustangs equipped with a 298ci engine and hang-on or dealer-installed air conditioning.

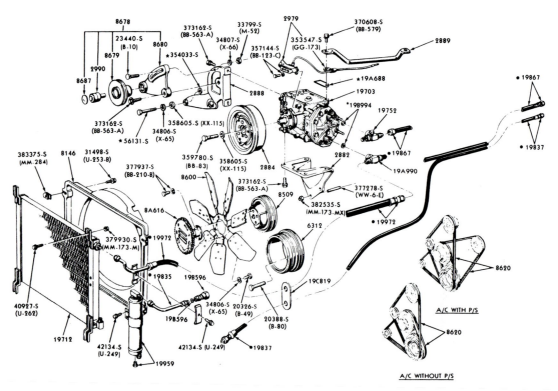

Air-conditioning compressor, condenser, brackets, hoses, and related hardware for 1967 Mustangs equipped with 289ci engines and factory-installed integral air conditioning.

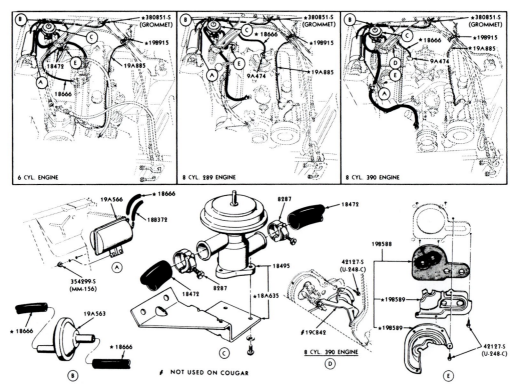

Vacuum reservoir, hose connections, vacuum-operated heater control valve, and heater hoses for 1967 Mustangs equipped with factory-installed integral air conditioning.

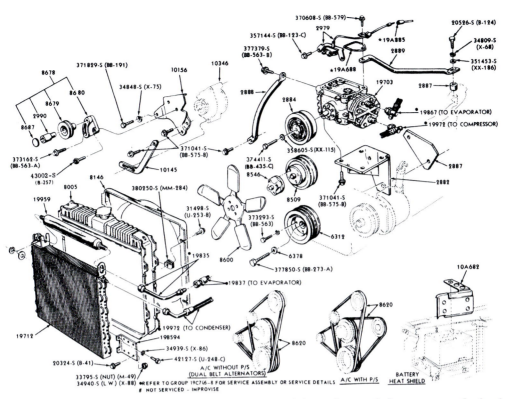

Air-conditioning compressor, condenser, brackets, hoses, and related hardware for 1967 Mustangs equipped with a *390ci engine and hang-on or dealer-installed air conditioning.*

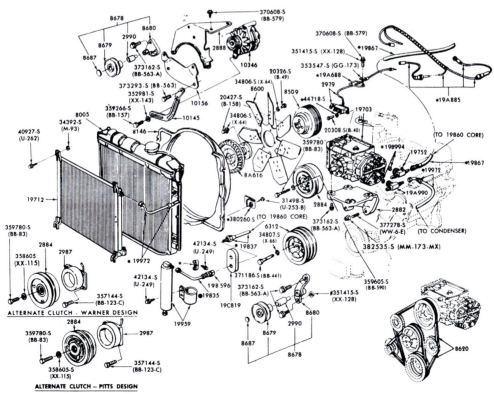

Air-conditioning compressor, condenser, brackets, hoses, and related hardware for 1967-1970 Mustangs equipped *with a 390 or a 428ci engine and factory-installed integral air conditioning.*

173

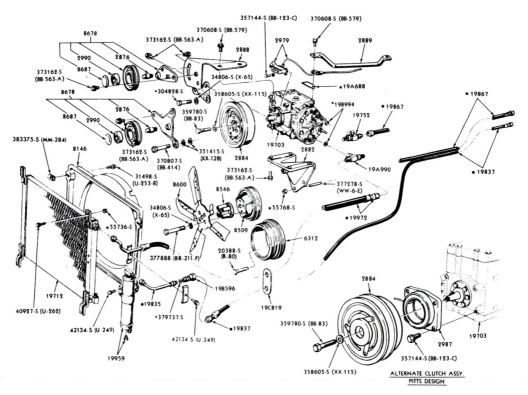

Air-conditioning compressor, condenser, brackets, hoses, and related hardware for 1967-1970 Mustangs equipped *with a 302 or 351ci engine and factory-installed integral air conditioning.*

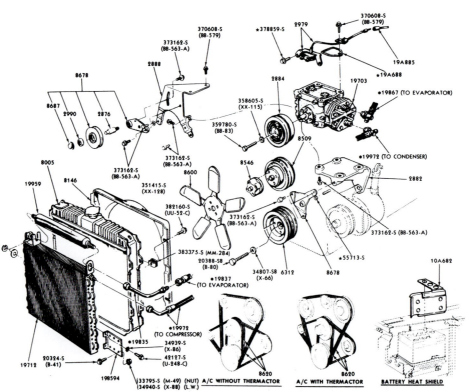

Air-conditioning compressor, condenser, brackets, hoses, and related hardware for 1968 Mustangs equipped with a *390ci engine and hang-on or dealer-installed air conditioning.*

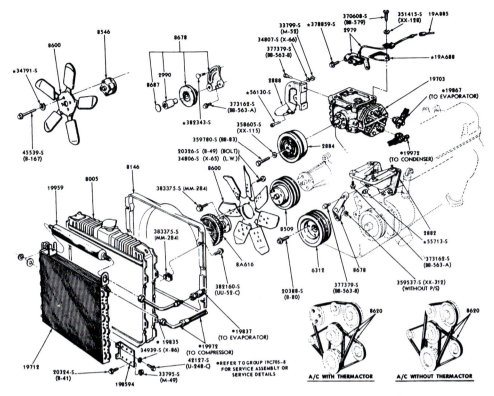

Air-conditioning compressor, condenser, brackets, hoses, and related hardware for 1968 Mustangs equipped with a 289 or a 302ci engine and hang-on or dealer-installed air conditioning.

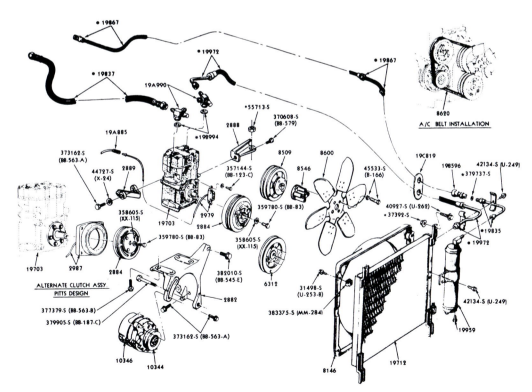

Air-conditioning compressor, condenser, brackets, hoses, and related hardware for 1968-1970 Mustangs equipped with six-cylinder engines and factory-installed integral air conditioning.

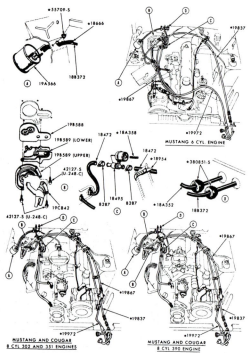

Vacuum reservoir, hose connections, vacuum-operated heater control valve, and heater hoses for 1969-1970 Mustangs equipped with factory-installed integral air conditioning.

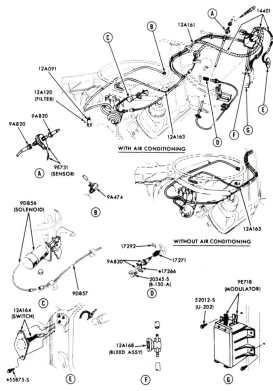

Distributor modulator for 1970 Mustang equipped with a 351ci engine and Ram Air.

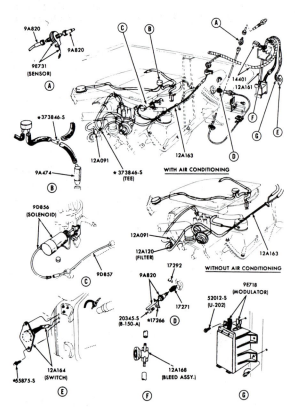

Distributor modulator for 1970 Mustang equipped with a 302ci engine.

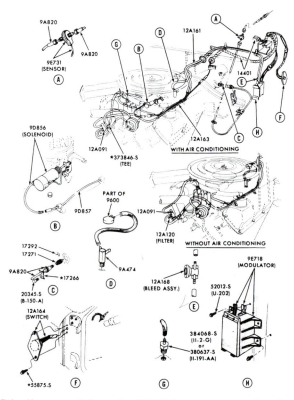

Distributor modulator for 1970 Mustang equipped with a 351ci engine without Ram Air option.

176

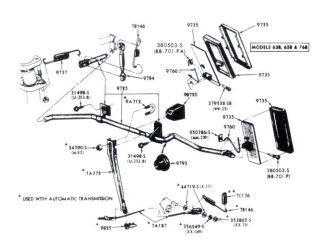

Accelerator linkage for 1965-1968 Mustangs equipped with six-cylinder engines.

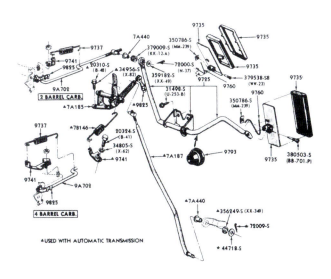

Accelerator linkage for 1965 Mustangs equipped with V-8 engines.

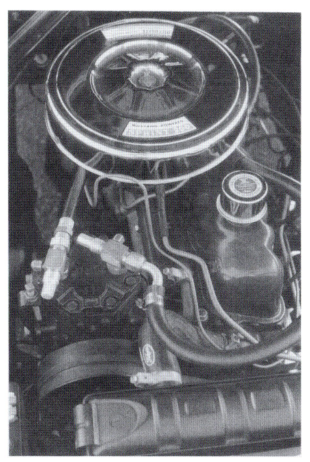

Few sales promotions included or bothered with a particular engine or drivetrain combination. The Sports Sprint package introduced in the spring of 1966 was a cosmetic option designed around the base Mustang hardtop. Besides numerous exterior appearance upgrades, the base 200ci six-cylinder also received a few dress-up items. A chrome air cleaner lid replaced the stock Corporate Blue version. A special decal proclaimed the cubic inch displacement and identified the package as a Sprint. The oil filler cap, radiator cap, and master cylinder cap were also chrome. Internally the engine and drivetrain were identical to the non-Sprint regular production models, though to this day rumors of special cam grinds, unique cylinder heads, and higher output persist.

MUSTANG ACCELERATOR PEDAL to CARB THROTTLE CABLE ASSEMBLY CHART
1969 and 1970

Year	Engine	Notes	Description	Part Number
69	All 8s		22.71" long	C9ZZ-9A758-A
69	All 6s		30.50" long	C9ZZ-9A758-C
70	All 8s	Except Boss 429	22.83" long	C9ZZ-9A758-E
70	All 6s		30.00" long	C9ZZ-9A758-D

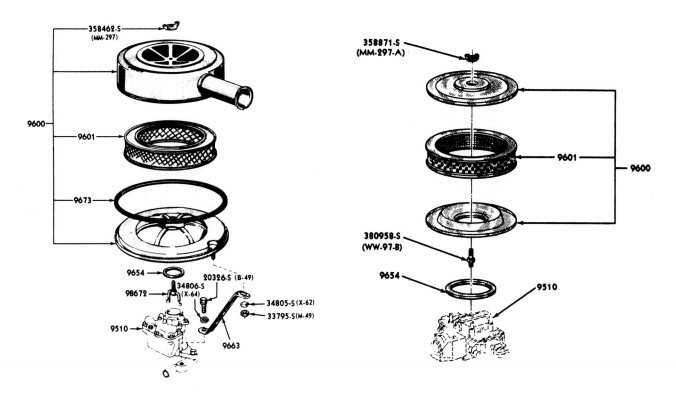

Air cleaner assembly for 1965-1967 Mustangs equipped with a six-cylinder engine.

Air cleaner for 1965-1967 Mustangs equipped with 289 High Performance (HiPo) engine.

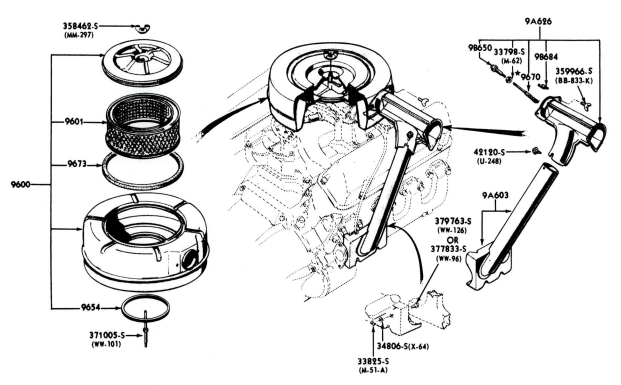

Air cleaner assembly for 1965-1967 Mustangs equipped with a V-8 engine (except 289 HiPo).

MUSTANG CARBURETOR AIR CLEANER ELEMENT APPLICATION CHART

Year	Engine	Model	Description	Part Number
68	289	Except Hi-Po	11.32" I.D.; 13.30" O.D., 2.80" high.	C8AZ-9601-A
68/70	302		Used with Air Cleaner Assemblies C8AF-D,	
68	390	w/ 2V carb.	C8AZ-A,D;C8OZ-A,B;C8SZ-A,B;D0OZ-A;	
69,70	351	w/o Ram Air		
65/67	260,289	Except Hi-Po	7.5" I.D.; 10.04" O.D., 2.38" high.	C5ZZ-9601-B
68	289	2V, open emission	Used with Air Cleaner Assembly C5ZZ-C,D	
68	302	4V, open emission		
67	390		11.32" I.D.; 13.30" O.D., 2.22" high.	B7SZ-9601-A
68	390	4V & Thermactor	Used with Air Cleaner Assemblies C7SZ-A,	
69	390	4V, Exc. GT & Ram Air	C7ZZ-F;C5ZZ-W;C8OZ-C;C8ZZ-B;C9OZ-E,H;	
68,69	428CJ	w/ 4V carb.	C9ZZ-B,F,H,J;D0ZZ-C,F,G,N;	
69	390	GT w/ 4V carb.		
69,70	302	Boss 302 w/ 4V		
69	351,390	w/ Ram Air		
69,70	429	Boss 429 w/ 4V		
65/67	289	High Performance		
68	289	Canada only.		
70	351	w/ 2V, Ram Air		
70	428CJ			
70	302	Boss 302 w/ Ram Air		
70	351	4V, Ram Air	11.32" I.D.; 13.30" O.D., 2.50" high. Used with Air Cleaner Assembly D0OZ-C	D0GY-9601-A
67	428	GT500	w/ 4V or 8V Carb.	EDJ-9601-A
68	302,428	GT350/500 Exc. KR		
65	170		7.96" I.D.; 9.90" O.D., 2.26" high.	C1KE-9601-A
65/67	170,200		Used with Air Cleaner Assemblies C3DZ-C, C6ZZ-M;C7ZZ-A	
69,70	250		9.86" I.D.; 11.75" O.D., 2.00" high. Used with Air Cleaner Assemblies C9ZZ-A; D0DZ-A	C9ZZ-9601-A
70	200		8.94" I.D.; 10.90" O.D., 2.12" high. Used with Air Cleaner Assembly D0DZ-C	C8TZ-9601-A
67/69	200	w/ Imco & C4	8.35" I.D.; 10.28" O.D., 2.25" high. Used with Air Cleaner Assemblies C7DZ-A; C8ZZ-A;C7ZZ-B	C8ZZ-9601-A
67,68	289,302	GT350 w/ P/S	w/ Supercharger, 9" cylindrical	S2MS-9601-A
67,68	289,302	GT350 w/o P/S	w/ Supercharger, 9" cylindrical	S7MS-9601-H

MUSTANG CARBURETOR AIR CLEANER ASSEMBLY APPLICATION CHART, Part One.

Year	Engine	Model	Description	Part Number
65/67	170,200	Except Imco with C4.	Color "Blue."	C3DZ-9600-C
66	200		Chrome.	C6ZZ-9600-M
67	200	With Imco.	12.25" dia., 2.52" high, color "Blue" tray, and Chrome cover; use w/ Carter carb.	C7ZZ-9600-B
67	200	With Imco & C4.	12.25" dia., 2.52" high, color "Blue."	C7DZ-9600-A
67	200	With Thermactor	12.25" dia., 2.52" high, color "Blue" tray, and Chrome cover; use w/ Ford carb.	C7ZZ-9600-A
68	200	w/ Ford carb; US only	Dry type, 12.4" dia., 3.48" high	C8ZZ-9600-A
69	200	w/ Ford carburetor	Dry type, 12.4" dia., 3.48" high	C8ZZ-9600-A
68	200	Open emission	Canada only.	C6DF-9600-F
69	250		14.62" diameter; 3.25" high.	C9ZZ-9600-A
70	200		13.47" diameter; 3.63" high.	D0DZ-9600-C
70	250		14.62" diameter; 3.24" high.	D0DZ-9600-A
65/67	289	High Performance	14.05" diam., 2.61" high	C5ZZ-9600-W
68	289	w/ 4V, open emission.		
66/70	390	with 4V carburetor		
65/67	260,289		17.25 diam., 4.22" high, color "Blue" tray and Chrome cover.	C5ZZ-9600-D
68	289	w/ 2V, open emission.		
68	302	w/ 4V, open emission.		
67	289	Exc. High Peformance	17.25 diam., 4.22" high, color "Blue" tray and Chrome cover.	C5ZZ-9600-C
67	390	Except GT	16.79 diam., 3.66" high, color "Blue" tray and Chrome cover.	C7SZ-9600-A
67	390	GT	16.79 diam., 3.66" high.	C7ZZ-9600-F
68	390	GT, 4V, open emission		
67	428	w/ 8V carb.		S7MS-9600-A
68	302,428	w/ 8V carb.		S7MS-9600-A
67,68	289,302	w/ Supercharger	Cylindrical, 9" long.	S7MS-9600-H
68	390	GT w/ 4V	17" diam., 4.20" high	C8OZ-9600-B
68	390	Exc. GT w/ 4V	17" diam., 4.20" high	C8OZ-9600-A
68	302		17.84" diam., 4.20" high	C8AZ-9600-D
	351			
	289	Exc. High Peformance		
	390	w/ 2V carb.		
69,70	351,428	GT350/500	18" diam., 4.98" high	C9ZZ-9600-B
68	428CJ	w/ 4V & Ram Air		C8ZZ-9600-B
68,69	428CJ*	w/ 4V, w/o Ram Air	16.79" diam., 3.66" high	C8OZ-9600-C
69	390	GT w/ 4V		
69	302	Boss 302		
69	428CJ#	w/ 4V, w/o Ram Air	16.79" diam., 3.66" high, Chrome cover.	C9OZ-9600-H
69	351	w/ Ram Air	18.83 diam., 6.14" high, w/ door in cover	C9ZZ-9600-H
69	390	w/o Ram Air, Exc. GT	(Exc. GT) 16.79" diam., 3.66" high	C9OZ-9600-E
69	390	GT, 4V, Ram Air	18.83 diam., 5.82" high, w/ door in cover	C9ZZ-9600-J
69	428CJ*	w/ 4V & Ram Air	18.83 diam., 5.50" high	D0ZZ-9600-F
70	428CJ	w/ Ram Air		
69	428CJ#	w/ 4V & Ram Air	18.83 diam., 5.50" high, "Cobra Jet"	C9ZZ-9600-F
70	302	Boss 302 w/o Ram Air	16.79" diam., 3.66" high.	D0ZZ-9600-C
70	302	Boss 302 w/ Ram Air	18.83 diameter	D0ZZ-9600-N
70	351C	2V,4V,w/o Ram Air	17" diam., 4.20" high	D0ZZ-9600-M
70	302	2V, w/o Ram Air	17.84" diam., 4.20" high	D0ZZ-9600-B
70	351W			
70	351W	2V, w/ Ram Air	18.83 diam., 6.14" high	D0ZZ-9600-G
70	351C	2V,4V,w/ Ram Air	18.88 diam., 6.25" high	D0ZZ-9600-S
70	390	4V,w/o Ram Air	16.79" diam., 3.66" high.	D0ZZ-9600-D

Notes:
* Before 2/17/69
# From 2/17/69

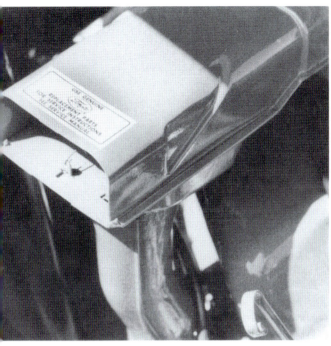

Because cars were being built as fast as the plants could turn them out, Ford became inconsistent with their assembly procedures. This 1967 302ci engine sports a decal promoting Genuine Ford replacement parts on its air cleaner snorkel, though this application was not universal with all cars and/or engines.

Specification and warning decals changed size, type, and location every year. Each engine option came with a different set of decals as well. This exhaust emissions decal, located on the air cleaner snorkel, lists tuning information for a 1970 Cobra Jet engine.

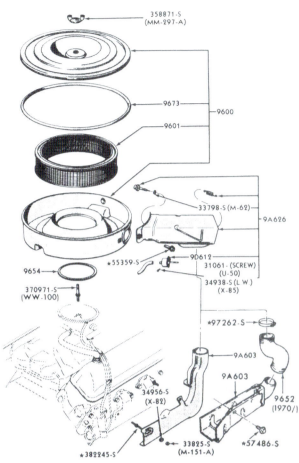

Air cleaner assembly for 1968-1970 Mustangs equipped with 289 or 302ci engines, and 1969 Mustangs equipped with 351ci engine.

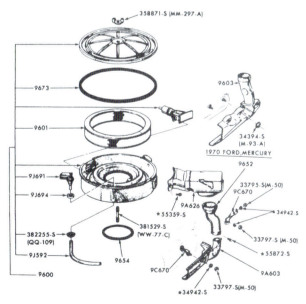

Air cleaner assembly (non-Ram Air) for 1969-1970 Mustangs equipped with 428ci engine.

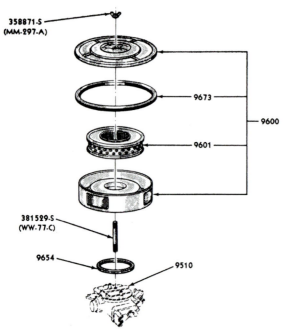

358871-S
(MM-297-A)

9673

9600

9601

381529-S
(WW-77-C)

9654

9510

Air cleaner assembly for 1967 GT Mustangs equipped with 390ci engine.

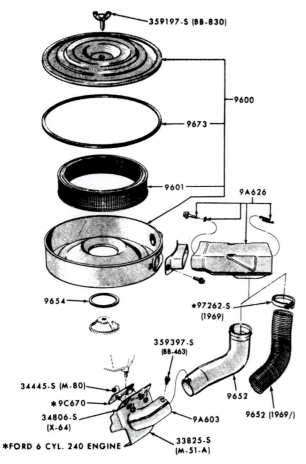

359197-S (BB-830)

9600

9673

9601

9A626

9654

*97262-S
(1969)

359397-S
(BB-463)

9652

34445-S (M-80)

*9C670

34806-S
(X-64)

9A603

9652 (1969/)

*FORD 6 CYL. 240 ENGINE

33825-S
(M-51-A)

Air cleaner assembly for 1968-1970 Mustangs equipped with six-cylinder engines.

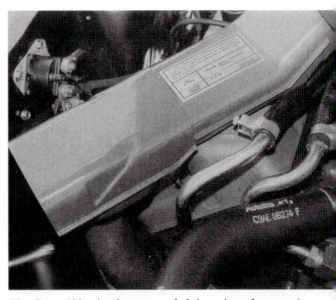

The Boss 429 air cleaner snorkel is unique because it required an extra-long extension to bridge the wide cylinder heads. Even the mighty Boss 429 had a hot air intake tube connecting the exhaust manifold stove to the air cleaner. The stove provided the carburetor a source of warm air to enhance cold-weather operation.

The Ram Air system in 1969 and 1970 consisted of a finned aluminum scoop integrated into the air cleaner lid. The functional scoop, which nearly doubled the height of the stock air cleaner, extended through a hole in the hood. Fresh air flowing over the hood was diverted to the air cleaner by the scoop. A vacuum-operated trap door located between the scoop and the air cleaner opened during wide-open-throttle operation and allowed fresh air to enter the engine. Otherwise the system was non-functional. It was commonly called a Shaker hood scoop because it vibrated or shook with the normal movement of the engine. Ram Air was available only with four-barrel engines.

182

Compare this snorkel attached to a 428ci air cleaner to the Boss 429 cleaner. Both are equipped with Ram Air and both were produced in 1970.

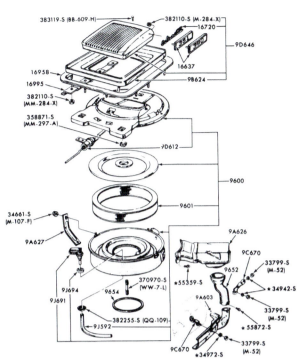

Ram Air (Shaker) scoop and air cleaner assembly for 1969 Mustangs equipped with 351, 390, and 428 engines, and 1970 Mustangs equipped with 428 engines.

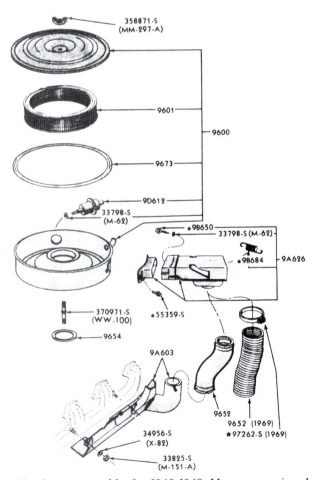

Air cleaner assembly for 1968-1969 Mustangs equipped with 390ci engines.

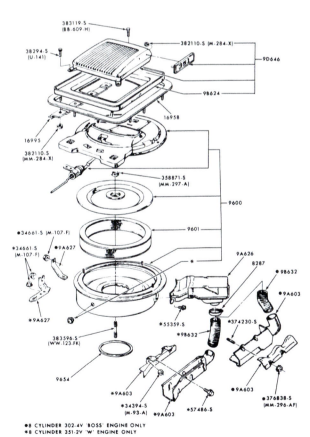

Ram Air (Shaker) scoop and air cleaner assembly for 1970 Mustangs equipped with 302-4V and 351 Windsor engines.

MUSTANG AIR CLEANER HOT AIR TUBE ASSEMBLY APPLICATION CHART

Year	Engine	Model	Description	Part Number
68	200		Steel, 2.51" diam. on (1) end & 2.74" dia.	C8ZZ-9652-A
69	200,250	before 10/15/68	Paper & Aluminum, 2.02" I.D., 18" long, cut.	C9UZ-9652-A
69	390	w/ 4V Carb.		
69,70	302	Boss		
70	429CJ			
70	200,250	All		
70	302,390	w/ 2V Carb.		
70	351W	w/ 2V Carb.		
70	302	Boss, w/ 4V		
70	351C			D0OZ-9652-A
68	390		Upper (steel) 2.03" dia. on (1) end &	C8AZ-9652-A
68,69	428CJ	w/ 4V Carb.	2.85" diameter on the other.	
69	390	w/ 4V & Ram Air	8.36" formed length.	
70	428CJ		Use w/o transistor ignition.	
70	351	W/ 2V & Ram Air		

MUSTANG CARBURETOR AIR CLEANER SCOOP & SEAL ASSEMBLY APPLICATION CHART

Year	Engine	Model	Description	Part Number
69/70	428CJ	w/ 4V & Ram Air	Marked "Cobra Jet"	C9ZZ-9D646-A
69	351,390	w/ Ram Air	Replace Cobra Jet name plates w/	C9ZZ-9D646-A
			(2) C9ZZ-16637-C for 351	
			(2) C9ZZ-16637-D for 390	
70	351	W/ 4V Carb.		C9ZZ-9D646-A
70	351	w/ 2V,4V & Ram Air	w/ White Hood Stripes	D0ZZ-9D646-A
70	302	Boss, w/ 4V	w/ White Hood Stripes	D0ZZ-9D646-A
70	351	w/ 2V,4V & Ram Air	w/ Black Hood Stripes	D0ZZ-9D646-B
70	302	Boss, w/ 4V	w/ Black Hood Stripes	D0ZZ-9D646-B

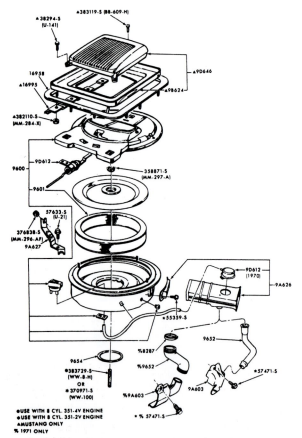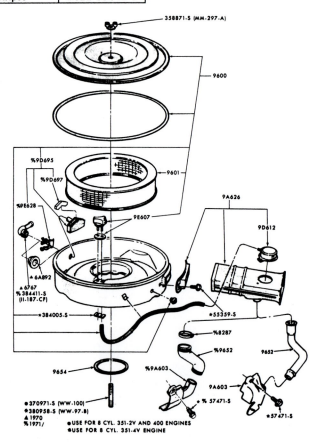

Ram Air (Shaker) scoop and air cleaner assembly for 1970 Mustangs equipped with 351 Cleveland engines.

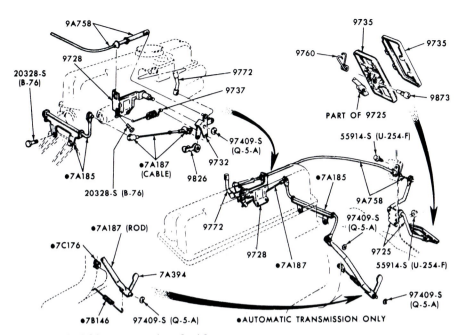

Accelerator linkage for 1969-1970 Mustangs equipped with six-cylinder engines.

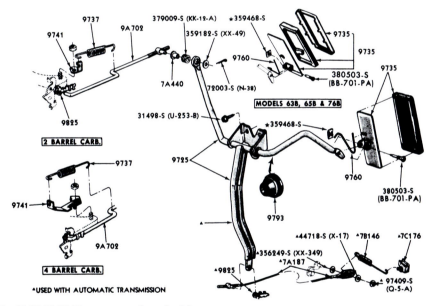

Accelerator linkage for 1967-1968 Mustangs equipped with V-8 engines.

MUSTANG ACCELERATOR PEDAL to CARB THROTTLE CABLE ASSEMBLY CHART

1969 and 1970

Year	Engine	Notes	Description	Part Number
6 9	All 8s		22.71" long	C9ZZ-9A758-A
6 9	All 6s		30.50" long	C9ZZ-9A758-C
7 0	All 8s	Except Boss 429	22.83" long	C9ZZ-9A758-E
7 0	All 6s		30.00" long	C9ZZ-9A758-D

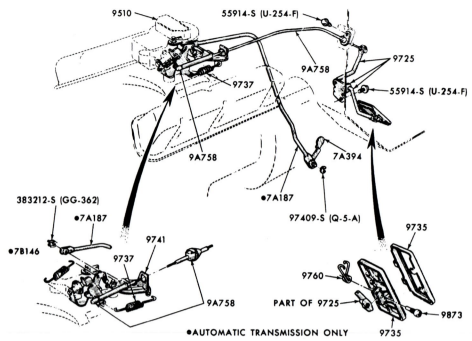

*Accelerator linkage for 1969-1970 Mustangs equipped with
V-8 engines.*

MUSTANG CARBURETOR CHOKE CONTROL ASS'Y APPLICATION CHART, 1965.

Year	Engine	Description	Part Number
65/67	289 High Peformance	58.00" long, 7/16" -14 Thread	C5OZ-9700-A
69/70	Boss 302	57.62" long, 7/16" -14 Thread	C5ZZ-9700-C
70	Shelby GT350/500	44.00" long, 6 1/2" -20 Thread	C9ZZ-9700-C
70	Boss 429	41" long	C9ZZ-9700-B

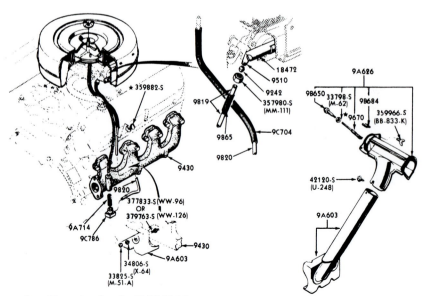

*Thermostatic choke control and hot air tubes for 1965-1966
Mustang equipped with 260 or 289ci engines.*

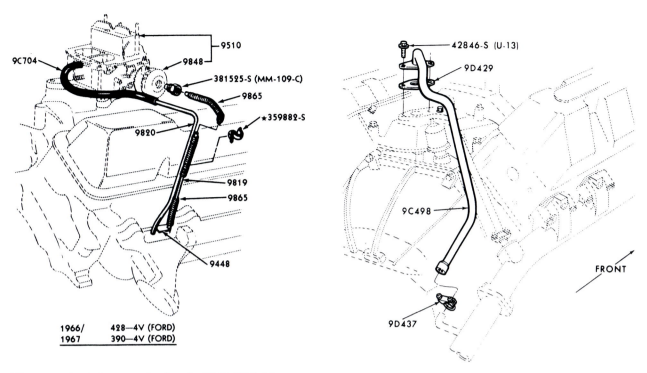

9510
9848
9C704
381525-S (MM-109-C)
9865
★359882-S
9820
9819
9865
9448

1966/   428—4V (FORD)
1967   390—4V (FORD)

42846-S (U-13)
9D429
9C498
9D437

FRONT

Thermostatic choke control tubes for 1967-1970 Mustang equipped with 390 or 428ci engines.

Boss 429 exhaust manifold heat tube assembly.

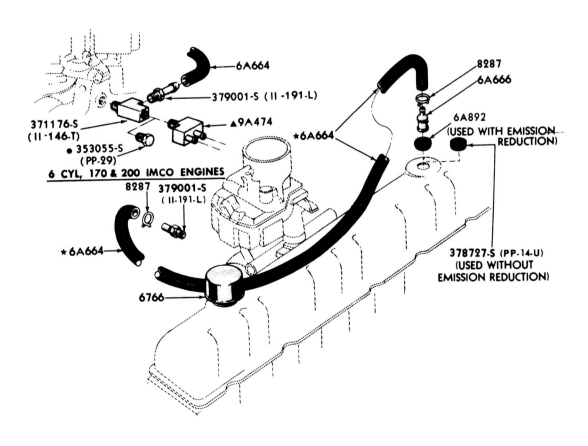

6A664
379001-S (11-191-L)
371176-S (11-146-T)
▲9A474
● 353055-S (PP-29)

8287
6A666
6A892 (USED WITH EMISSION REDUCTION)
★6A664

6 CYL, 170 & 200 IMCO ENGINES

8287   379001-S (11-191-L)
★6A664
6766

378727-S (PP-14-U) (USED WITHOUT EMISSION REDUCTION)

Crankcase emissions (open) evacuation system for 170 and 200ci engines.

Mustang Engine Emission Control Systems Application Chart

Year	Engine	Data Code	Emissions Equipment
'65-67	289-4V	A	Positive (Closed) Crancase Ventilation (PCV) - All 50 States Thermactor System in California
'65-68	289-2V	C	Positive (Closed) Crancase Ventilation (PCV) - All 50 States Thermactor System in California Improved Combustion Exhaust Emissions Control System (ICS) - With Automatic Transmission - Beginning in 1968
'64-1/2	289-4V	D	Positive (Closed) Crancase Ventilation (PCV) - All 50 States
'64-1/2	260-2V	F	Positive (Closed) Crancase Ventilation (PCV) - All 50 States
'68-73	302-2V	F	Positive (Closed) Crancase Ventilation (PCV) - All 50 States Thermactor System in California Improved Combustion Exhaust Emissions Control System (ICS) - with Automatic Transmission
'69-70	Boss 302	G	Positive (Closed) Crancase Ventilation (PCV) Thermactor System - All 50 States
'69-73	351-2V	H	Positive (Closed) Crancase Ventilation (PCV) - All 50 States Thermactor System in California Improved Combustion Exhaust Emissions Control System (ICS) - with Automatic Transmission
'68	302-4V	J	Positive (Closed) Crancase Ventilation (PCV) - All 50 States Thermactor System in California Improved Combustion Exhaust Emissions Control System (ICS) - with Automatic Transmission
'65-68	289-4V	K	Positive (Closed) Crancase Ventilation (PCV) - All 50 States Thermactor System in California Improved Combustion Exhaust Emissions Control System (ICS) - with Automatic Transmission Beginning In 1968
'69-73	250-1V	L	Positive (Closed) Crancase Ventilation (PCV) - All 50 States Thermactor System in California
'69-71	351-4V	M	Positive (Closed) Crancase Ventilation (PCV) Thermactor System in California Improved Combustion Exhaust Emissions Control System (ICS) -
'69-70	428CJ	Q	Positive (Closed) Crancase Ventilation (PCV) Thermactor System Improved Combustion Exhaust Emissions Control System (ICS) -
'68-70	428 CJ	R	Positive (Closed) Crancase Ventilation (PCV) Thermactor System Improved Combustion Exhaust Emissions Control System (ICS) -
'67-69	390-4V	S	Positive (Closed) Crancase Ventilation (PCV) - All 50 States Thermactor System In California
'65-70	200-1V	T	Positive (Closed) Crancase Ventilation (PCV) - All 50 States Thermactor System In California Improved Combustion Exhaust Emissions Control System (ICS) - with Automatic Transmission Beginning In 1968
'64-1/2	170	U	Positive (Closed) Crancase Ventilation (PCV)
'69-70	Boss 429	Z	Positive (Closed) Crancase Ventilation (PCV) Thermactor System

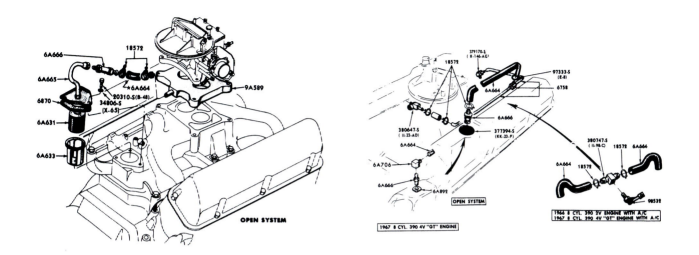

Intake manifold type crankcase evacuation (open) system for 1965 model 260 and 289 engines.

Open emissions reduction hot idle compensator and related parts for 1967 model 390ci engines.

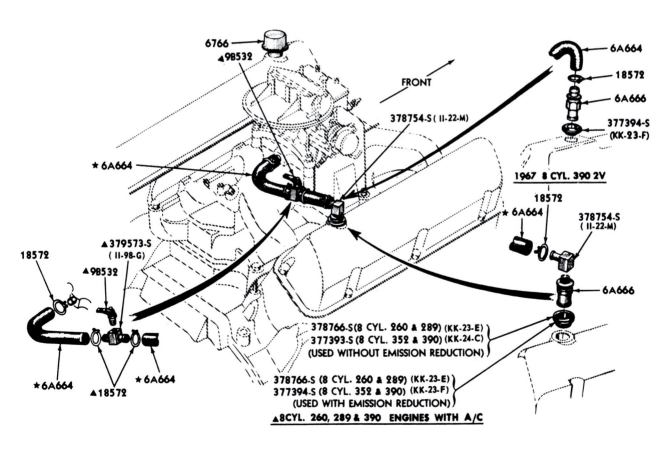

Engine emissions reduction, crankcase evacuation, hot idle compensator, and related parts for 1965-1970 260, 289, and 351W engines.

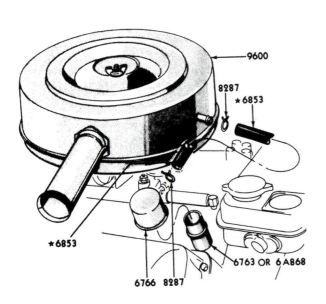

Closed emissions reduction air cleaner oil breather cap and related parts for all engines.

An engine equipped with a PCV (positive crankcase ventilation) system used a vented oil cap. Air entered the vented cap as the induction pulled crankcase fumes from the engine. Engines equipped with CCV (closed crankcase ventilation) systems had sealed oil caps. Venting the lower air cleaner housing was the factory's attempt to provide more air to a non-Ram Air-equipped big-block.

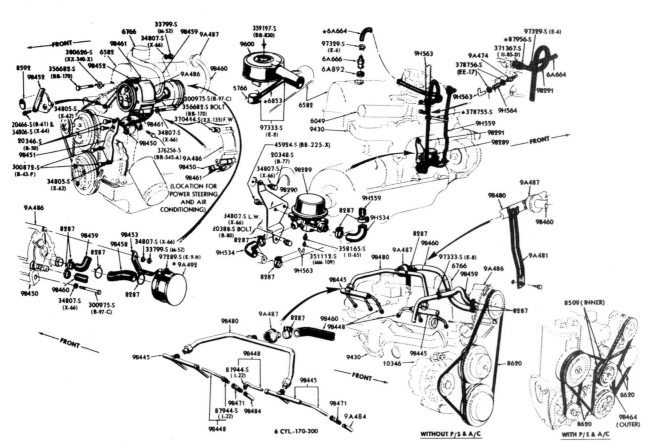

Intake manifold type Thermactor emissions control system for 1966 Mustang equipped with 200ci engine (California only).

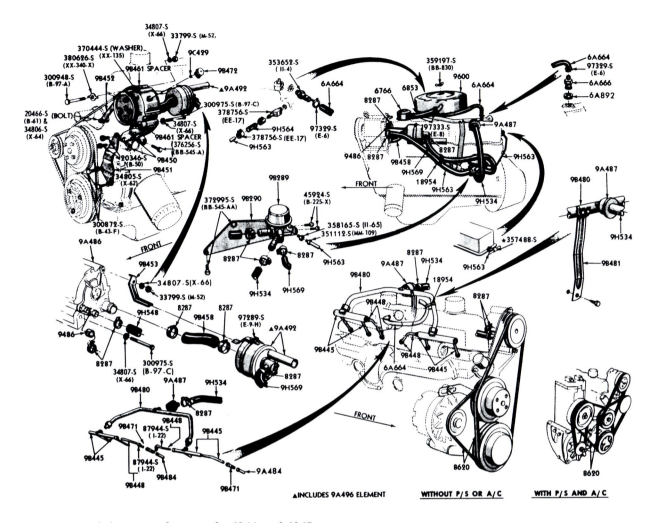

Thermactor emissions control system for 1966 and 1967 Mustang equipped with 200ci engine (California only).

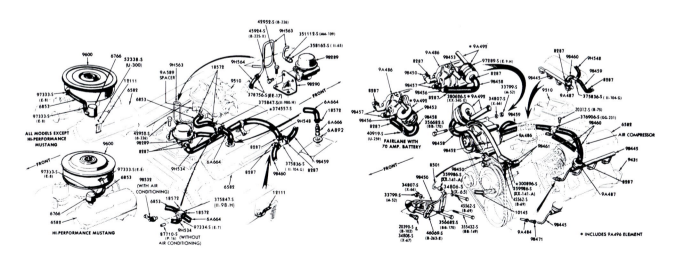

Intake manifold type Thermactor emissions control system for 1966 Mustang equipped with 289ci engine.

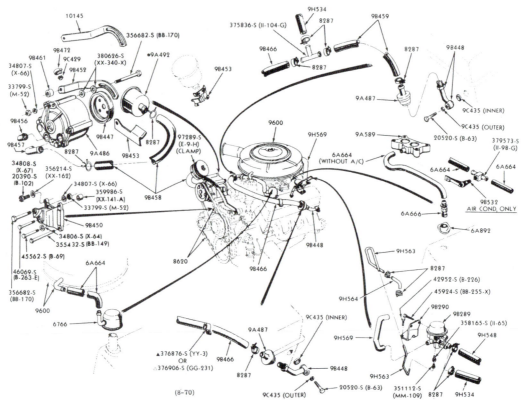

Thermactor emissions control system for 1967 Mustang equipped with a 289ci engine (except 289 HiPo).

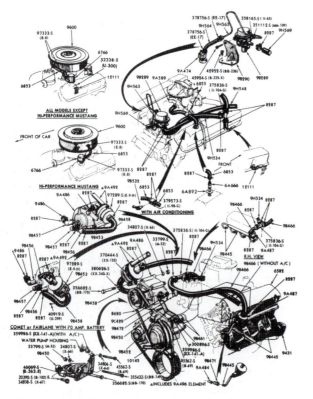

Thermactor emissions control system for 1966 and 1967 Mustang equipped with 289 HiPo engine.

By 1968 all Ford engines utilized some vacuum and/or electrical controls that greatly improved cold-weather startup and exhaust emission ratings. This was accomplished mostly by regulating the ignition timing based on the engine's operating temperature. The "vacuum tree," threaded into the thermostat housing, is really a temperature-activated vacuum switch that controls the dual-diaphragm vacuum advance canister attached to the distributor.

192

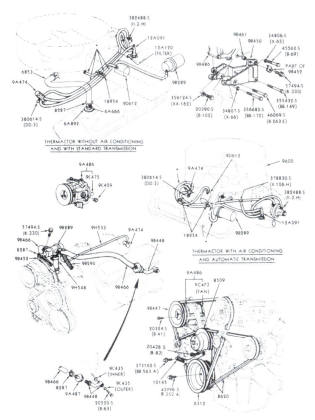

Thermactor emission control system used on 1968 Mustangs equipped with 289 engines.

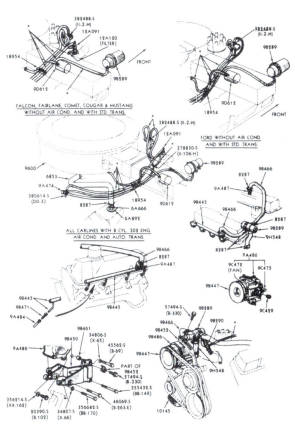

Thermactor emissions control system for 1968 Mustang equipped with 289 and 302ci engines.

In 1966, all Mustangs sold in California were equipped with Thermactor emissions reduction equipment designed to inject fresh air into the exhaust ports in an effort to promote more complete burning of the spent gasses.

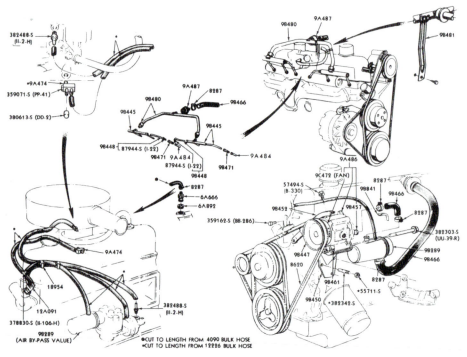

Thermactor emissions control system for 1968 Mustang equipped with 200ci engine.

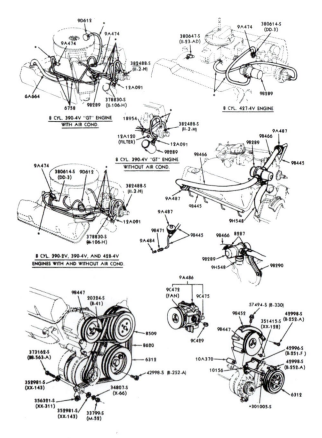

Thermactor emissions control system for 1968 through 1970 Mustang equipped with 390 and 428ci engines.

By 1968, most big-block Ford engines were equipped with some type of emissions device. The Thermactor system on this 428ci engine consists of a belt-driven air pump, several check valves, and a network of hoses needed to service the two air distribution manifolds connected to each set of exhaust ports. Simply put, the pump forces fresh air into the exhaust ports just above the valve. The presence of oxygen and moisture in the air combined with the hot exhaust temperatures promotes complete burning of any unused fuel. The air pump can be seen under the top radiator hose and the air bypass valve, identified with 424S. The two fresh air hoses leading to the manifolds can be seen above the thermostat housing.

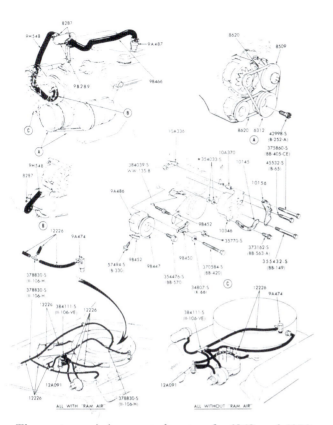

Thermactor emissions control system for 1969 and 1970 Boss 302 Mustangs.

Beginning in 1969, power steering filler necks were much smaller in diameter and the cap contained a little dipstick. This compact neck was located at the back of the pump and angled rearward. Other than rotating the canister which angled the neck from side to side, no other variation was necessary.

MUSTANG EXHAUST AIR SUPPLY MANIFOLD ASSEMBLY APPLICATION CHART

Years	Cyl/CID	Part Number	Description
66/68	6/200	C6DZ-9B445-A	FRONT
66/68	6/200	C6DZ-9B445-B	REAR
66/67	8/289	C6OZ-9B445-A	R.H.
67	8/289K	C6OZ-9B445-A	FROM 4/17/67
66/67	8/289	C6OZ-9B445-B	L.H.
67	8/289K (T/E)	C6OZ-9B445-B	L.H. FROM 4/17/67
68	8/289-2V/302	C8AZ-9B445-A	R.H. & L.H.
67	8/390 (T/E)	C6AZ-9B445-C	R.H. BEFORE 9/1/66
67/68	8/390 (T/E)	C9ZZ-9B445-A	R.H.
68	8/427 (T/E)	C9ZZ-9B445-A	R.H.
68/69	8/428CJ (T/E &4/B CARB)	C9ZZ-9B445-A	R.H.
70	8/428CJ (4/B CARB)	C9ZZ-9B445-A	
68/69	8/428CJ (4/BCARB) (T/E)	C9ZZ-9B445-B	L.H.
70	8/428CJ (4/B CARB)	C9ZZ-9B445-B	
67/68	8/390 (T/E)	C9ZZ-9B445-B	L.H.
68	8/427K (T/E)	C9ZZ-9B445-B	L.H.
69	8/429 BOSS (T/E)	C9AZ-9B445-B	R.H. & L.H. ID: C9AE-9B466-A
70	8/429 BOSS (T/E)	D0AZ-9B445-A	R.H. & L.H.

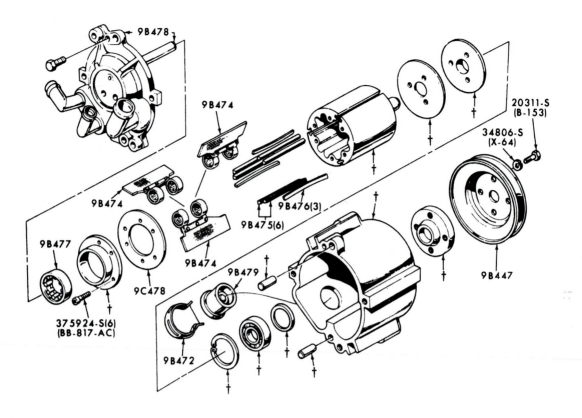

*Thermactor exhaust air supply pump used on 1966 and
1967 Mustangs.*

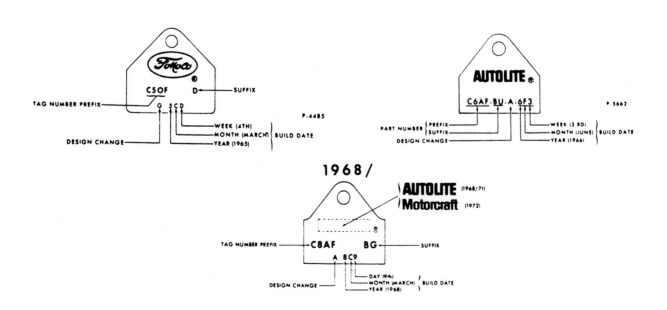

Mustang carburetor identification tags.

EXHAUST AIR SUPPLY PUMP PULLEY APPLICATION CHART

Years	Cyl/CID	Part Number	Notes	Description
66/67	6/170, 200	C6TZ-9B447-B	1	4.74" O.D.-Ident. C6TE-9B447-B
66/67	6/170, 200	C6DZ-9B447-B	2	4.58" O.D.-Ident. C6DE-9B447-B
67	8/390 (T/E)	C6AZ-9B447-E		5.95" O.D.-Ident. C6AE-9B447-E
67	8/289 (w/ T/E & A/C)	C6AZ-9B447-E	3	5.95" O.D.-Ident. C6AE-9B447-E
67	8/289	C6AZ-9B447-E	4	5.95" O.D.-Ident. C6AE-9B447-E
67	8/289	C6AZ-9B447-D	5	5.65" O.D.-Ident. C6AE-9B447-D
66/67	8/289 (w/ T/E, except A/C)	C6OZ-9B447-A	6	4.07" O.D.-Ident. C6OE-9B447-B
67	8-289 (4/B carb. & T/E, except A/C)	C6OZ-9B447-A	7	4.07" O.D.-Ident. C6OE-9B447-B
67	8/289 (2/B carb., S/T, & T/E, except A/C)	C6OZ-9B447-A	7	4.07" O.D.-Ident. C6OE-9B447-B
66	8/289 (A/C) (T/E)	C6AZ-9B447-C		4.93" O.D.-Ident. C6AE-9B447-C
66/67	6/170,200	C6TZ-9B447-A		5.33" O.D.-Ident. C6TE-9B447-A
67	8/289 (T/E) (except A/C)	C7AZ-9B447-A	8	3.97" O.D.-Ident. C7ZE-9B447-A
67	8/289 (S/T & T/E, exc. A/C)	C7AZ-9B447-A	9	3.97" O.D.-Ident. C7ZE-9B447-A
67	8/289	C7AZ-9B447-E		4.75" Diam., ident. C7OE-9B447-B
67	8/289K, 4/B carb. & T/E	C7AZ-9B447-D	10	4.31" O.D. ident. C6AE-9B447-F
68	8/289,302 (AC &/OR P/S) (T/E)	C8ZA-9B447-D		5.89" Diam., ident. C8AE-9C480-B
68	8/390 (4/B carb.) T/E A/C	C8OZ-9B447-B		4.981" Diam.-ident. C8OE-9C480-B
68	8/390 (P/S & 55 AMP.ALT.) (T/E)	C8AZ-9B447-E		5.68" Diam.-ident. C8AE-9C480-D
69	8/302 BOSS (T/E)	C8AZ-9B447-E		5.68" Diam.-ident. C8AE-9C480-D
68	6 & 8/200, 289, 302, 390 (except A/C) (T/E)	C8AZ-9B447-B		4.75" Diam.-ident. C8AE-9C480-A
68	8/390 (GT 4/B carb..) T/E except A/C	C8AZ-9B447-B		4.75" Diam.-ident. C8AE-9C480-A
68/69	8/428 (except A/C) (T/E)	C8AZ9B447-B		4.75" Diam.-ident. C8AE-9C480-A
70	8/428 CJ	C8AZ-9B447-B		4.75" Diam.-ident. C8AE-9C480-A
68	8/427 (4B & T/E)	C8OZ-9B447-A	11	5.49" Diam.-ident. C8OE-9C480-A
69	8/428 CJ (A/C) (T/E)	C9OZ-9B447-A		5.10" O.D.-ident. C9OE-9C480-A
70	8/428 CJ	C9OZ-9B447-A		5.10" O.D.-ident. C9OE-9C480-A
69/70	8/429 (T/E)	C9AZ-9B447-A		6.251" Dia.-Ident. C9AE-9C480-A
70	8/302 BOSS (T/E)	D0ZZ-9B447-A		Ident. D0ZE-9C480-A

Notes:

1	Except w/ P/S and A/C; except Imco w/ C4		
2	With P/S, except A/C; with T/E	7	From 11/14/66
3	Before 8/29/66	8	From 9/23/66 to 11/14/66
4	With T/E and A/C,from 9/23/66	9	From 9/23/66
5	With T/E and A/C,from 8/29/66 to 9/23/66	10	With Super Extra Cooling
6	Before 11/14/66	11	With or Without Power Steering

Carburetor Application Chart
Mustang 170 & 200 6-Cylinder Engines, 1965-1970

Year	CID	Model	Type	Identification	Part Number	Replaced By:
65 (64)	170		F-1	C6PF-J; C8OF-F	C5OZ-9510-A	D0PZ-9510-A
65 (64)	170	1	F-1	C4ZF-J,L	C5ZZ-9510-E	D0PZ-9510-A
65 (64)	170	2	F-1	C4ZF-K,M	C5ZZ-9510-F	D0PZ-9510-A
65 (64)	170		F-1	C5DF-H,K,L,M	C5DZ-9510-C	D0PZ-9510-A
				C6DF-R,S		
65/67	200		F-1	C6PF-J; C8OF-F	C5OZ-9510-H	D0PZ-9510-A
65/67	200		H-1	D0PF-K	D0PZ-9510-A	
65	200		F-1	C5OF-E	C5OZ-9510-A	D0PZ-9510-A
65	200		F-1	C5OF-F	C5ZZ-9510-B	D0PZ-9510-A
65	200		F-1	C5OF-N	C5DZ-9510-E	D0PZ-9510-A
65/67	200		F-1	C5OF-R,Z,Y	C5DZ-9510-C	D0PZ-9510-A
				C6OF-AC,AD		
66	200		F-1	C6DF-C	C6DZ-9510-A	D0PZ-9510-G
66	200		F-1	C6OF-G	C6OZ-9510-D	D0PZ-9510-G
66/67	200		F-1	C7DF-J	C6DZ-9510-E	D0PZ-9510-G
66/67	200		F-1	C7DF-K	C6OZ-9510-M	D0PZ-9510-G
66/69	200		F-1	C8PF-L	C6DZ-9510-F	D0PZ-9510-G
67	200		F-1	C7OF-N	C7OZ-9510-J	D0PZ-9510-G
67	200		F-1	C7OF-R	C7OZ-9510-K	D0PZ-9510-G
67	200		C-1	C7DF-T	C7DZ-9510-T	D0PZ-9510-G
68	200		F-1	C8OF-A	C8OZ-9510-A	D0PZ-9510-G
68/69	200		F-1	C8OF-B	C8OZ-9510-B	D0PZ-9510-G
68	200		F-1	C6PF-J	C5OZ-9510-H	D0PZ-9510-A
				C8OF-E,F		
68	200		H-1	D0PF-K	D0PZ-9510-A	
69	200		F-1	C9DF-B	C9DZ-9510-B	D0PZ-9510-G
66/69	200		F-1	C9DF-B	C9DZ-9510-C	D0PZ-9510-G
66/69	200		H-1	D0PF-L	D0PZ-9510-G	
70	200		C-1	D0DF-C,M	D0DZ-9510-C	D2DZ-9510-G
70	200		C-1	D0DF-D,L	D0DZ-9510-D	D2DZ-9510-G
70	200		C-1	D0DF-G,T	D0DZ-9510-G	D2DZ-9510-G
70	200		C-1	D0DF-H,V	D0DZ-9510-H	D2DZ-9510-G
70	200		C-1	D0PF-AD	D0DZ-9510-J	D2DZ-9510-G

Model:

1	with Manual Transmission
2	with C4 Transmission
C-1	Carter 1V
F-1	Ford 1V
H-1	Holley 1V

Carburetor Application Chart
Mustang 250 cid 6-Cylinder Engines, 1969-1970

Year	CID	Model	Type	Identification	Part Number	Replaced By:
69	250	1	F-1	C9OF-A	C9OZ-9510-A	D0PZ-9510-T
69	250	2	F-1	C9OF-B	C9OZ-9510-B	
69	250	3	F-1	C9OF-J	C9OZ-9510-J	D0PZ-9510-T
69	250	4	F-1	C9OF-K	C9OZ-9510-K	D0PZ-9510-T
69	250	5	F-1	C9OF-M	C9OZ-9510-M	D0PZ-9510-T
69	250	6	F-1	C9OF-B	C9OZ-9510-L	D0PZ-9510-T
69	250		H-1	D0PF-D	D0PZ-9510-T	
70	250		C-1	D0PF-AB	D0ZZ-9510-AA	
70	250	7	C-1	D0ZF-C	D0ZZ-9510-C	D0ZZ-9510-AA
70	250	8	C-1	D0ZF-D	D0ZZ-9510-D	D0ZZ-9510-AA
70	250	9	C-1	D0ZF-E	D0ZZ-9510-E	D0ZZ-9510-C
70	250		C-1	D0ZF-F	D0ZZ-9510-F	D0ZZ-9510-AA

Model:

1	with C4 and IMCO, without A/C
2	with Manual Transmission and IMCO, without A/C
3	with Manual Transmission and IMCO, with A/C
4	with C4 and IMCO, with A/C
5	Economy model, with C4, M/T, and IMCO
6	with C4, M/T, and IMCO
7	with Manual Transmission and IMCO, cfm 215
8	with C4, IMCO, and A/C; cfm 215
9	with Manual Transmission and IMCO, without A/C, cfm 215

C-1	Carter 1V
F-1	Ford 1V
H-1	Holley 1V

Carburetor Application Chart
Mustang 260 cid 8-Cylinder Engines, 1965 (1964-1/2)

CID	Note:	Type	Identification	Part Number	Replaced By:
260	1	F-2	C4ZF-R,N;C4DF-AB	C5ZZ-9510-K	D2AZ-9510-D
			C4OF-BR,BS;C4DF-AC		
260	2	F-2	C9OF-B	C5ZZ-9510-L	D2AZ-9510-D
260	1	F-2	C9OF-J	C2AZ-9510-J	D2AZ-9510-D
260	1	F-2	C9OF-K	C5ZZ-9510-C	D2AZ-9510-D
260	1	F-2	C9OF-M	C2AZ-9510-K	D2AZ-9510-D
260	1	F-2	C9OF-B	C8ZZ-9510-H	D2AZ-9510-D
260		F-2	D0PF-D	D0AZ-9510-AC	D2AZ-9510-D

Notes:

1	Stamping identification located on edge of carburetor mounting flange.
2	Stamped identification on carburetor mounting flange is main body identification only. Carburetor identification appears on identification tag.

F-2 Ford 2V

Carburetor Application Chart, Part One
Mustang 289 cid 8-Cylinder Engines, 1965-1968

Year	Note:	Type	Identification	Part Number	Replaced By:
65/66	1	H-4	D0PF-U	C9AZ-9510-AE	
65/66	2	F-2	C6PF-F	C2AZ-9510-J	
65/67	2	F-2	C6PF-F	C2AZ-9510-K	D2AZ-9510-D
66	2,3	F-2	C6DF-E	C6DZ-9510-C	D2AZ-9510-D
66	2,4	F-2	C6DF-F	C6DZ-9510-D	D2AZ-9510-D
67	2,5	F-2	C7DF-E,S	C7DZ-9510-E	D2AZ-9510-D
67	2,3	F-2	C7DF-G	C7DZ-9510-G	D2AZ-9510-D
67	2,6	F-2	C7DF-F,R	C7DZ-9510-F	D2AZ-9510-D
67	2,4	F-2	C7DF-H,N,V	C7DZ-9510-H	D2AZ-9510-D
68	2,3	F-2	C8AF-AK	C8ZZ-9510-F	D2AZ-9510-D
68	2,7	F-2	C8ZF-G	C8ZZ-9510-G	D2AZ-9510-D
68	2,7	F-2	C8AF-L	C8AZ-9510-AR	D2AZ-9510-D
68	8	F-2	C8DF-E	C8DF-9510-E	D2AZ-9510-D
68	8	F-2	C8AF-AF;C8ZF-H	C8ZF-9510-H	D2AZ-9510-D
68	9	F-2	C8OF-S;C8ZF-E	C8OF-9510-S	D2AZ-9510-D
68	9	F-2	C8DF-F	C8DF-9510-F	D2AZ-9510-D
68	2,10	F-4	C6ZF-C,F	C4OZ-9510-F	C4OZ-9510-G
68	2,3	F-2	C8AF-BD;C8PF-T	C8ZZ-9510-H	D2AZ-9510-D
67	2,11	F-2	C8AF-BD;C8PF-T	C8ZZ-9510-H	D2AZ-9510-D
65	2,12	F-4	C4OF-AL,AT,BU,BT	C4OZ-9510-F	C4OZ-9510-G
65	2	F-2	C5ZF-A,B	C5ZZ-9510-H	D2AZ-9510-D
65	14	F-2	C5ZF-G,H;C6DF-A,B	C5ZZ-9510-L	D2AZ-9510-D
66	13,14	F-2	C5ZF-G,H;C6DF-A,B	C5ZZ-9510-L	D2AZ-9510-D
65	1,2	F-4	C5ZF-C,D,E,F	C5ZZ-9510-J	C9AZ-9510-AE
65	1,2	F-4	C5ZF-J,K,L,M	C5ZZ-9510-M	C9AZ-9510-AE
			C6ZF-A,B		
66	1,2	F-4	C5ZF-J,K,L,M	C5ZZ-9510-M	C9AZ-9510-AE
			C6ZF-A,B		
65	1	F-4	C6PF-H	C3AZ-9510-AU	C9AZ-9510-AE
66	1,13	F-4	C6PF-H	C3AZ-9510-AU	C9AZ-9510-AE

Notes:

1. Except High-Performance
2. Stamping identification located on edge of carburetor mounting flange.
3. With manual transmission and Thermactor.
4. With C4 transmission and Thermactor.
5. With manual transmission, except Thermactor.
6. With C4 transmission, except Thermactor.
7. With C4 transmission and Imco.
8. Canada only. Manual transmission; open emission.
9. Canada only. Automatic transmission, open emission.
10. Canada only. Open emission.
11. With Thermactor.
12. High Performance.
13. Except Thermactor.
14. Stamped identification on carb mounting flange is main body identifcation only. Carburetor identification appears on identification tag.

Carburetor Application Chart, Part Two
Mustang 289 cid 8-Cylinder Engines, 1965-1968

Year	Note:	Type	Identification	Part Number	Replaced By:
65/67	2,12	F-4	C5OF-L,M,T,U	C4OZ-9510-F	C4OZ-9510-G
65/67	12	F-4	D0PF-V	C4OZ-9510-G	
68	10	H-4	C6PF-F	C4OZ-9510-G	
65	1,2	F-4	C4GF-AE,AF,AZ,BA	C5ZZ-9510-D	C9AZ-9510-AE
			C4ZF-C		
65	1	H-4	D0PF-U	C9AZ-9510-AE	
65/68	8	H-4	D0PF-AN	D0PF-9510-U	not replaced
65/68	9	H-4	C9OF-R	C9OZ-9510-N	
66	1,2,3	F-4	C6ZF-D	C6ZZ-9510-A	C9AZ-9510-AE
66	1,2,4	F-4	C6ZF-E	C6ZZ-9510-B	C9AZ-9510-AE
67	1,2,5	F-4	C7DF-A	C7DZ-9510-A	D2AZ-9510-M
67	1,2,5	F-4	C7DF-L,AE	C7DZ-9510-L	D2AZ-9510-M
67	1,2,11,13	F-4	C8PF-V	C7AZ-9510-AT	D2AZ-9510-M
67	1,2,14	F-4	C7DF-C,AG	C7DZ-9510-C	D2AZ-9510-M
67	1,2,6	F-4	C7DF-B	C7DZ-9510-B	D2AZ-9510-M
67	1,2,6	F-4	C7DF-M,AF	C7DZ-9510-M	D2AZ-9510-M
67	1,2,4	F-4	C7DF-D,AH	C7DZ-9510-D	D2AZ-9510-M
67	2,3,12,15	F-4	C8ZF-K	C7DZ-9510-E	C7DZ-9510-C
67	1	F-4	D2PF-SA	D2AZ-9510-M	

Notes:

1. Except High-Performance
2. Stamping identification located on edge of carburetor mounting flange.
3. With manual transmission and Thermactor.
4. With C4 transmission and Thermactor.
5. With manual transmission, except Thermactor.
6. With C4 transmission, except Thermactor.
7. With C4 transmission and Imco.
8. 600 cfm
9. 600 cfm, center pivot.
10. Canada only. Open emission.
11. With or without Thermactor.
12. High Performance.
13. Manual or Automatic transmission.
14. With Thermactor.
15. 4-barrel carburetor with manual choke.

F-2   Ford 2V
F-4   Ford 4V
H-4   Holley 4V

Carburetor Application Chart
Mustang 302 cid 8-Cylinder Engines, 1968-1970

Year	Note:	Type	Identification	Part Number	Replaced By:
68	1,2	F-2	C8AF-BD;C8PF-T	C8ZZ-9510-H	D2AZ-9510-D
69	1,2	F-2	C8AF-BD;C8PF-T	C2AZ-9510-J	D2AZ-9510-D
68	1,8	F-4	C8AF-AS;C8PF-V	C2AZ-9510-K	D2AZ-9510-M
69	1,14	F-2	C9AF-A,T	C9AZ-9510-T	D2AZ-9510-D
69	Boss	F-4	C9ZF-G	C9ZZ-9510-G	D2AZ-9510-M
68/69	10	F-4	C8ZF-M	C8ZF-9510-M	D2AZ-9510-M
68/71	11	F-4	C8ZF-L	C8ZF-9510-L	D2AZ-9510-M
68/71	12	F-4	C8ZF-A,B	C8ZF-9510-A	D2AZ-9510-M
68	1,3	F-4	C8ZF-D	C8ZZ-9510-D	D2AZ-9510-M
68	1,4	F-4	C8ZF-C	C8ZZ-9510-C	D2AZ-9510-M
68/71	6	H-4	D0PF-AN	D0PZ-9510-U	
68/71	7	H-4	C9OF-R	C9OZ-9510-N	
69	4,5,8	H-4	C9ZF-J	C9ZZ-9510-J	D0ZZ-9510-Z
69/71	5,15	F-4		D0ZX-9510-A	
69/71	5,16	F-4		D0ZX-9510-B	
70	2	F-2	D0AF-C	D0AZ-9510-C	D2AZ-9510-D
68/70	9	F-2	D0AF-U	D0AZ-9510-U	D2AZ-9510-D
70	9	F-2	D0AF-D	D0AZ-9510-D	D2AZ-9510-D
69/70		F-2	D0AF-D	D0AZ-9510-AC	D2AZ-9510-D
68/71	12	F-4	D2PF-SA	D2AZ-9510-M	
70		H-4	D0ZF-Z	D0ZZ-9510-Z	

Notes:

1. Stamping identification located on edge of carburetor mounting flange.
2. With manual transmission and Imco.
3. With C4 transmission and Imco.
4. With manual transmission and Thermactor.
5. Boss.
6. 600 cfm
7. 600 cfm, center pivot.
8. 4-barrel carburetor with manual choke.
9. Automatic transmission, IMCO, and A/C.
10. Canada only. Manual transmission; open emission.
11. Canada only. Automatic transmission, open emission.
12. Canada only. Open emission.
13. With C4 or FMX transmissions, and Imco.
14. With C6 or FMX transmissions, and Imco.
15. Off Highway vehicles, in-line carb, 1-11/16" dia. throat, 875 cfm.
16. Off Highway vehicles, in-line carb, 2-1/4" dia. throat, 1425 cfm.

F-2   Ford 2V
F-4   Ford 4V
H-4   Holley 4V

Carburetor Application Chart
Mustang 351 cid 8-Cylinder Engines, 1969-1970

Year	Note:	Type	Identification	Part Number	Replaced By:
69	1,2	F-2	C9ZF-A	C9ZZ-9510-A	D2AZ-9510-D
69	2	F-4	C9ZF-C	C9ZZ-9510-C	D2AZ-9510-M
69	1,3	F-2	C9ZF-B	C9ZZ-9510-B	D0AZ-9510-AB
69	3	F-4	C9ZF-D	C9ZZ-9510-D	D2AZ-9510-M
69	4	F-2	C9AF-J,Z; C9ZF-L	C9AZ-9510-AD	D2AZ-9510-D
			C9ZF-M		
69	1,3	F-4	C9ZF-D	C9AZ-9510-AC	D2AZ-9510-M
69	5	F-4	D0PF-AG; D1OF-AAA	D0OZ-9510-U	D2AZ-9510-M
70		F-4	D0PF-AG; D1OF-AAA	D0OZ-9510-U	D2AZ-9510-M
69/71	1,6	H-4	D0PF-AN (Windsor)	D0PZ-9510-U	
69/71	7	H-4	C9OF-R (Windsor)	C9OZ-9510-N	
70	8	F-4	D0OF-C,Y,AC	D0OZ-9510-C	D2AZ-9510-M
70	9	F-4	D0OF-D,Z,AB	D0OZ-9510-C	D2AZ-9510-M
70	10	F-4	D0OF-G	D0OZ-9510-G	D2AZ-9510-M
70	11	F-4	D0OF-H,AA,AD	D0OZ-9510-H	D2AZ-9510-M
70	12	F-2	D0AF-E	D0AZ-9510-E	D2AZ-9510-D
70	13	F-2	D0AF-F	D0AZ-9510-F	D2AZ-9510-D
70	14	F-2	D0AF-V	D0AZ-9510-V	D2AZ-9510-D
69/70	3	F-2	D0AF-J,AR,AS,AT,AU,AV	D0AZ-9510-AB	D2AZ-9510-D
70		F-2	D2AF-FB,FC,FD,GB,GC,GD	D2AZ-9510-D	D2AZ-9510-P
			D2PF-GA,GB; D4PE-FA		

Notes:

1 Stamping identification located on edge of carburetor mounting flange.
2 With manual transmission and Imco, w/ or w/o Ram Air.
3 With FMX transmission and Imco, w/ or w/o Ram Air.
4 With manual transmission or FMX, and Imco.
5 With Imco.
6 Manual, C4 or FMX transmission, 600 cfm.
7 Center pivot, 600 cfm.
8 With C4, FMX & Imco., w/o A/C, 605 cfm.
9 With manual transmission and Imco, w/o A/C, 605 cfm.
10 With manual transmission, Imco, and A/C, 605 cfm.
11 With C4, FMX, Imco, & A/C, 605 cfm.
12 With manual transmission and Imco, 351 cfm.
13 With FMX transmission and Imco, 351 cfm.
14 With FMX transmission, A/C, and Imco, 351 cfm.

F-2 Ford 2V
F-4 Ford 4V
H-4 Holley 4V

Carburetor Application Chart
Mustang 390 cid 8-Cylinder Engines, 1967-1969

Year	Model	Notes	Type	Identification	Part No.	Replaced By
67	w/ M/T exc. T/E	1,2	H-4	C7OF-A	C7OZ 9510-L	C9AZ 9510-U
67	w/ C/6 exc. T/E	1,2	H-4	C7OF-B	C7OZ 9510-M	C9AZ 9510-U
67	w/ M/T & T/E	1,2	H-4	C7OF-C	C7OZ 9510-N	C9AZ-9510-U
67	w/ C6 & T/E	1,2	H-4	C7OF-D	C7OZ 9510-P	C8OZ 9510-D
68	GT w/ M/T	1,2	H-4	C7OF-A	C7OZ 9510-L	
	open emission					
68	GT, w/ A/T	1,2	H-4	C7OF-B	C7OZ 9510-M	C9AZ 9510-U
	open emission					
68	w/ A/T	1,4	F-2	C8AF-AZ,BA,BB	C8AZ 9510-AP	D2AZ 9510-D
				C8OF-AE,AF		
				C8PF-U,C8WF-A		
68	w/ C6 &	1,2	F-2	C8OF-K	C8OZ 9510-K	D2AZ 9510-D
	Imco w/ P.F.					
67		2,3	H-4	C8OF C	C8OZ 9510-C	C9AZ 9510-U
68	GT w/ M/T & T/E	2,3	H-4	C8OF C	C8OZ 9510-C	
68	GT w/ C6 & M/T	2,3	H-4	C8OF-D	C8OZ 9510-D	
67	w/ C6 & T/E	2,3	H-4	C8OF-D	C8OZ 9510-D	
69	w/ M/T & Imco	2	F-4	C9ZF-E	C9ZZ 9510-E	D2AZ 9510-M
	w/ or w/o Ram Air					
69	GT W/ C6 & Imco	2	F-4	C9ZF-F	C9ZZ 9510-F	D2AZ 9510-M
	w/ or w/o Ram Air					
69	GT W/ C6 & Imco	5	F-4	D0PF-AG	C0OZ 9510-U	D2AZ 9510-M
	w/ or w/o Ram Air					
68		6	F-2	D0AF-J, AF, AS, AT, AU, AV	D0AZ 9510-AB	D2AZ 9510-D

Notes:

1 Stamping identification is located on edge of carburetor mounting flange
2 Service package includes mounting gasket
3 Stamping identification is located on choke plate flange
4 Package includes gasket, limiter, cap gasket, adaptor, screw
5 Package includes C8SZ 9447-A, gasket, limiter, spacer, plug & screw
6 Package includes gasket, limiter, cap, gasket, hose, washer, adaptor, screw

F-2 Ford Two-barrel
F-4 Ford Four-barrel
H-4 Holley Four-barrel

Carburetor Application Chart
Mustang 428 cid 8-Cylinder Engines, 1968-1970

Year	Model	Notes:	Type	Identification	Part Number	Replaced By:
68/69		1,2	H-4	C8OF-AB	C8OZ-9510-AB	C9AZ-9510-U
68	CJ w/ C6 & T/E	1,2	H-4	C8OF-AB	C8OZ-9510-AB	C9AZ-9510-U
68	CJ w/ M/T & T/E	1,2	H-4	C9AF-U	C8OZ-9510-AA	C9AZ-9510-U
68/70	CJ w/ C6 & T/E	2	H-4		C9AZ-9510-U	
68	GT500 w/ T/E		H-4	C9AF-N,ED	C9ZX-9510-A	
70	GT500	2	H-4	D0ZF-G,H,U,T,	C9AZ-9510-N	C9AZ-9510-U
70	M/T & T/E	2	H-4	AA,AB,AC,AD	D0ZZ-9510-H	

Notes:

1 Stamping identification located on edge of carburetor mounting flange.
2 Service package includes mounting gasket

H-4 Holley 4V

Carburetor Application Chart
Mustang 429 cid 8-Cylinder Engines, 1969-1970

Year	Model	Notes	Type	Identification	Part No.	Replaced By
6 9	Boss w/ M/T	1,2,5	H-4	C9AF-S	C9AZ 9510-S	
	& Thermactor				(CA-708)	
7 0	CJ w/ M/T, C6	2,3	R-4	D0OF-B	D0OZ 9510-B	
	& IMCO				(CA-771)	
	w/ or w/o A/C					
7 0	Boss w/ M/T	1,2,4	H-4	D0OF-S	D0OZ 9510-S	D0ZZ 9510-H
	& Thermactor				(CA-776)	(CA-781)
7 0	Boss w/ M/T	2,4	H-4	D0ZF-G,H,U,T	D0ZZ 9510-H	
	& Thermactor			AA,AB,AC,AD	(CA-781)	

Notes:

1 w/ manual choke
2 Service package includes mounting gasket
3 715 cfm
4 735 cfm
5 750 cfm
H-4 Holley four-barrel
R-4 Rochester Quadra-jet

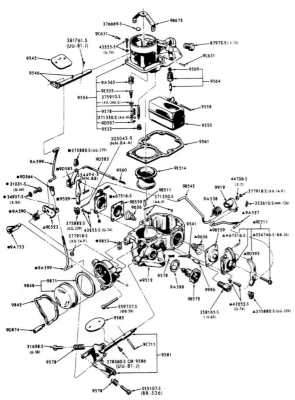

Exploded view of Ford 1V carburetor for 1965 model 170 and 1966-1970 model 200ci engines. See chart for application.

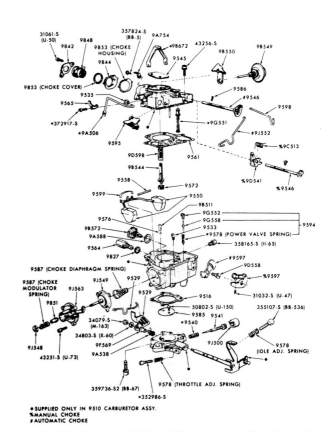

Exploded view of a Holley 1V carburetor. See chart for application.

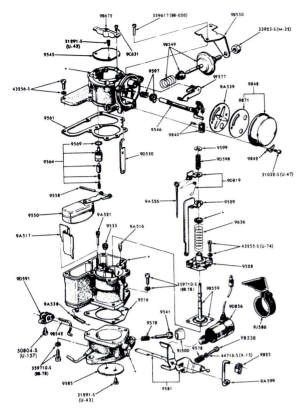

Exploded view of Ford 1V carburetor used on 1969-1970 250ci engines. See chart for application.

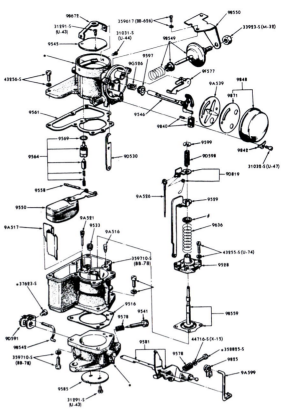

Exploded view of a Carter 1V carburetor used on 1967 200ci engines with IMCO. See chart for application.

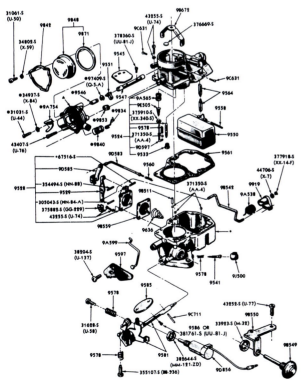

Exploded view of Carter 1V carburetor used on some 1970 model 200ci engines. See chart for application.

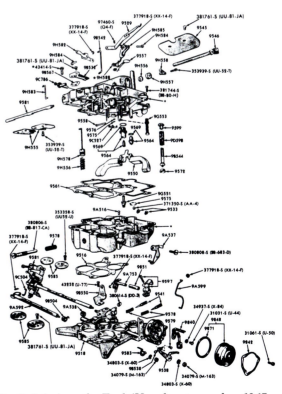

Exploded view of a Ford 4V carburetor used on 1967 and later engines. See chart for application.

203

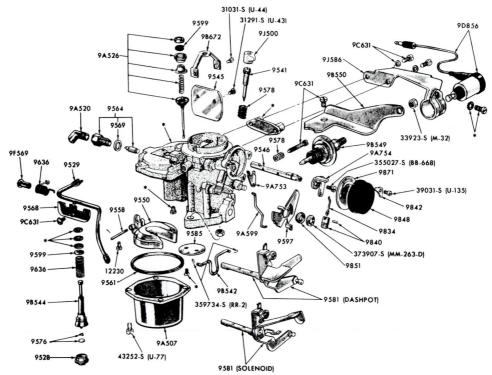

Exploded view of Carter 1V carburetor used on 1970 250ci engines. See chart for application.

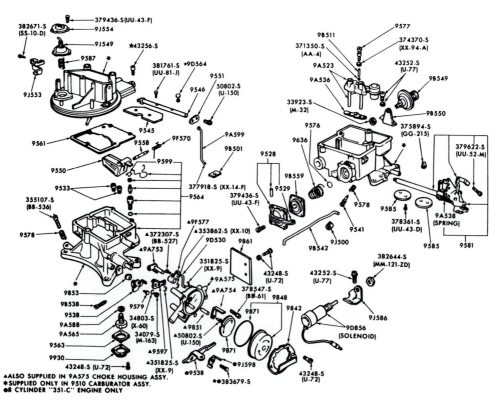

▲ALSO SUPPLIED IN 9A575 CHOKE HOUSING ASSY.
★SUPPLIED ONLY IN 9510 CARBURATOR ASSY.
●8 CYLINDER "351-C" ENGINE ONLY

Exploded view of Ford 2V carburetor used on 1970 Mustangs equipped with V-8 engines. See chart for application.

204

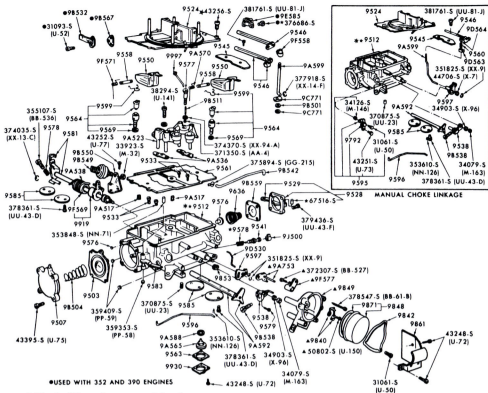

Exploded view of Ford 4V carburetor with piston-type choke and accelerator pump check valve. See chart for application.

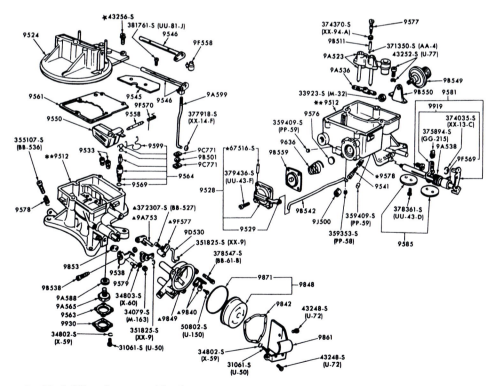

Exploded view of a Ford 2V carburetor with piston-type choke and accelerator pump check valve. See chart for application.

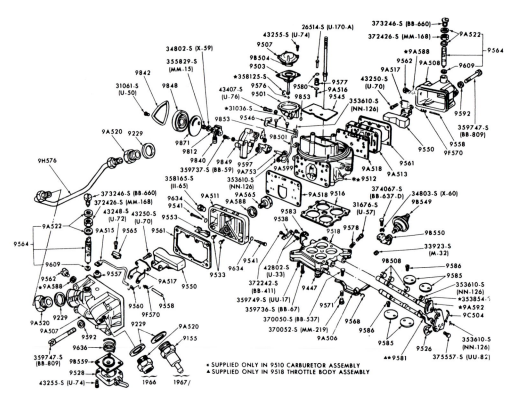

Exploded view of Holley 4V carburetor used on Boss 302, 429 CJ and SCJ, and Boss 429 engines. See chart for application.

FUEL PUMP ASSEMBLY CHART, for Six-Cylinder Mustangs

Year	Cyl/CID	Part Number	Description
65	6/170	C3DZ-9350-A	ident. by 6803 stamped
		r/b C3AZ-9350-Y	on pump mounting flange
65	6/170-200	C3AZ-9350-T	ident. by 0227 stamped
		r/b C3AZ-9350-Y	on fuel pump mounting flange
65	6/170-200	C3AZ-9350-V	ident. by 0485 stamped ON
		r/b C3AZ-9350-Y	on mounting flange
65	6/170, 200	C3AZ-9350-Y	CARTER - ident. by 3938-S
			stamped on mounting flange
65	6/170, 200	C5DE-99350-B	CARTER - ident. by 3913 stamped
		OR D2TE-9350-RA	on mounting flange
		r/b C3AZ-9350-Y	
66/67	6/200	C5UZ-9350-A	ident. by 0290 stamped on
		r/b C5UZ-9350-C	mounting flange
66/67	6/200	C5UZ-9350-C	CARTER - ident. by 4092 stamped
			on mounting flange
68/70	6/200	C8DZ-9350-A	CARTER - ident. by 4532-S or
		r/b D3TZ-9350-A	4531-S stamped on mounting flange
69	6/250	C8DZ-9350-A	CARTER - ident. by 4532-S or
		r/b D3TZ-9350-A	4531-S stamped on mounting flange
68/70	6/200	D3TZ-9350-A	identified D3TE-AA and also 6399-S
			on mounting flange - CARTER
69	6/250	D3TZ-9350-A	identified D3TE-AA and also 6399-S
			on mounting flange - CARTER

FUEL PUMP ASSEMBLY CHART, for Eight-Cylinder Mustangs

Year	Cyl./CID	Part Number	Description
65	8/260, 289	C3AZ-9350-M	CARTER-18 deg. inlet angle & 3/8"
			inlet tube, ident. by 3734-S
			Stamp on Mount. Flange
			used w/ oil pressure gauge
65	8/260, 289	C3AZ-9350-S	CARTER - ident. by 3911-S
		r/b C5OZ-9350-A	Stamp on Mount. Flange
65	8/289 (Exc. K)	C3AZ-9350-S	CARTER - ident. by 3911-S
		r/b C5OZ-9350-A	Stamp on Mount. Flange
65	8/289-4V K	C5OZ-9350-A	CARTER - ident. by 3939-S
			Stamp on Mount. Flange
67/68	8/390 (GT)	C6AZ-9350-B	CARTER - ident. by 4194-S
			Stamp on Mount. Flange
67/68	8/289, 302 (GT350) 4/B CARB)	S7MK-9350-B	Supercharger
66/67	8/289 (Exc. K)	C5AZ-9350-B	CARTER - ident. by 4193
			Stamp on Mount. Flange
66/67	8/289K (4/B Carb)	C6ZZ-9350-A	CARTER - ident. by 4201
			Stamp on Mount. Flange
68	8/289 (2/B Carb)	C8OZ-9350-A	CARTER - ident. by 4567
		r/b D0AZ-9350-B	Stamp on Mount. Flange
68/69	8/302	C8OZ-9350-A	CARTER - ident. by 4567
		r/b D0AZ-9350-B	Stamp on Mount. Flange
69	8/351	C8OZ-9350-A	CARTER - ident. by 4567
		r/b D0AZ-9350-B	Stamp on Mount. Flange
69/70	302-4V Boss	C9ZZ-9350-A	CARTER = ident. by 4910-S
			Stamp on Mount. Flange
68	8/427K	C7AZ-9350-A	CARTER = ident. by 4441-S
68/70	8/428CJ	C7AZ-9350-A	Stamp on Mount. Flange
68	8/390 (2/B Carb)	C7SZ-9350-A	CARTER - ident. by 4385
		r/b D4TZ-9350-A	Stamp on Mount. Flange
69	8/390	C7SZ-9350-A	CARTER - ident. by 4385
		r/b D4TZ-9350-A	Stamp on Mount. Flange
69/70	429 BOSS (4/B Carb)	C9AZ-9350-A	CARTER - ident. by 4842-S
			Stamp on Mount. Flange
70	8/351C	D0AZ-9350-A	CARTER - ident. by D0AE-E &
			also 4861-S
			Stamp on Mount. Flange
70	8/302 (2/B Carb)	D0AZ-9350-B	CARTER - ident. by 4896-S
		r/b D3OZ-9350-B	OR SA Stamp on Mount. Flange
70	8/302 (2/B Carb)	D3OZ-9350-B	CARTER - ident. by MS-6477-S
			Stamp on Mount. Flange
70	8/351W	D0AZ-9350-C	CARTER - ident. by 4888-S OR
			SA Stamp on Mount. Flange

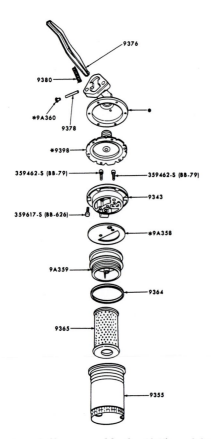

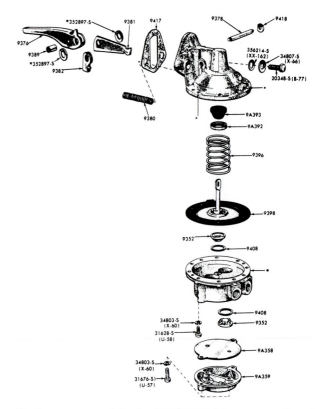

Fuel pump and filter assembly for 1965 model 260 and 289ci engines.

Fuel pump assembly for 1967-1970 Mustangs equipped with 390ci engine, and 1968-1970 Mustangs equipped with 428ci engine.

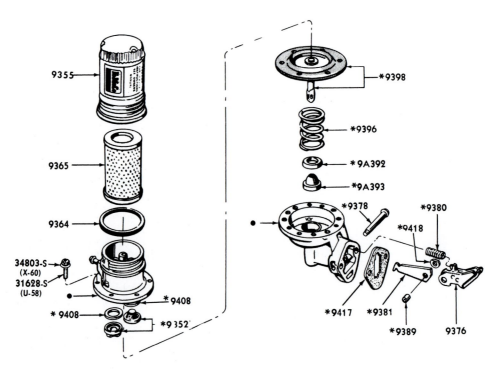

Fuel pump and filter assembly for 1965 model 170 and 200ci engines.

Mustang Fuel Tank Applications

Year	Model	Part Number	Description
65/68		C5ZZ-9002-D	16 GAL. CAPACITY
69		C9ZZ-9002-A	20 GAL. CAPACITY
70	WITHOUT EV/EM	D0ZZ-9002-A	22 GAL. CAPACITY
70	WITH EV/EM	D0ZZ-9002-B	20 GAL. CAPACITY

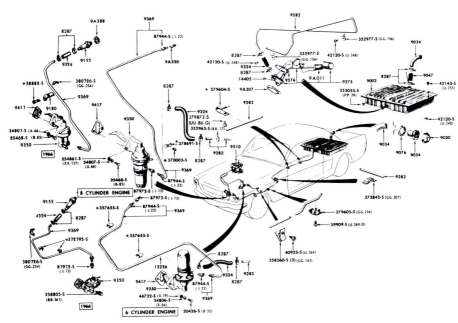

1965-1968 Mustang complete fuel delivery system and mounting hardware.

MUSTANG FUEL TANK FILLER CAP APPLICATION CHART

Year	Model	Part Number	Description
66/67	GT	C7ZZ-9030-C	Ident. by letters "GT"
68	GT/CS	C8ZZ-9030-C	Pop-Off type cap assy. -
			Ident. by Mustang Emblem
67	Exc. GT	C8ZZ-9030-C	Pop-Off type cap assy. -
			Ident. by Mustang Emblem
67	GT	C8ZZ-9030-D	Pop-Off type cap assy. -
			Ident. by letters "GT"
68	GT Exc. GT/CS	C8ZZ-9030-3	Pop-Off type cap assy. -
			Ident. by letters "GT"
69	GT	C9ZZ-9030-B	Pop-Off type cap assy. -
			Ident. by letters "GT"
69	Mach 1	C9ZZ-9030-C	Pop-Off type cap assy. -
			Ident. by Mustang Emblem
65		C9ZZ-9030-A	Ident. by Mustang Emblem
66/68		C9ZZ-9030-A	Ident. by Mustang Emblem
69	Exc. GT AND Mach 1	C9ZZ-9030-A	Ident. by Mustang Emblem
70	Exc. Mach 1 w/o EV/EM	C9ZZ-9030-A	Ident. by Mustang Emblem
70	Exc. Mach 1, w/ EV/EM	C0ZZ-9030-A	Ident. by Mustang Emblem
70	Mach 1 w/ EV/EM	D0ZZ-9030-D	Pop-Off type cap assy. -
			Ident. by Mustang Emblem
70	Mach 1 w/o EV/EM	D0ZZ-9030-E	Pop-Off type cap assy. -
			Ident. by Mustang Emblem

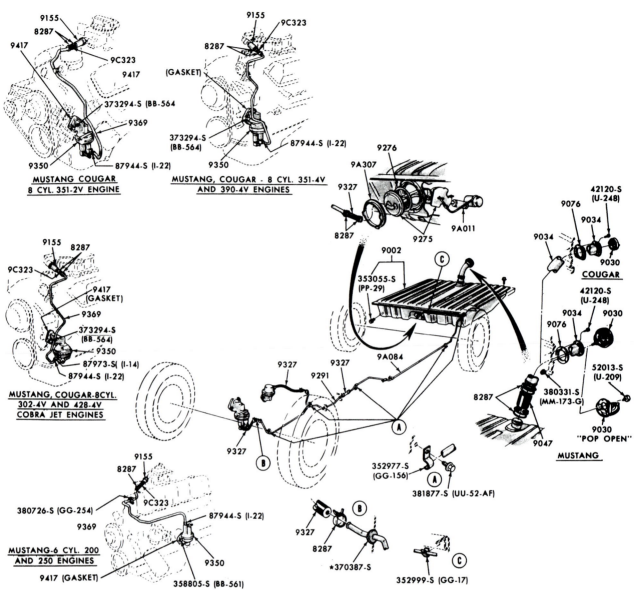

*1969 Mustang fuel system and related parts. All models
except Boss 429.*

MUSTANG FUEL TANK UNIT GAUGE ASSEMBLY CHART

Year	Model	Part Number	Description
65/68	w/o low fuel warn system	C8ZZ-9275-C	includes C8ZZ-9275-B gauge assy.,
			C0AF-9276-A gasket, C8AF-9327-A
67/68	with low fuel warn system	C8ZZ-9275-D	includes C8ZZ-9275-B gauge assy.,
			C0AF-9276-A gasket, C8AF-9327-A
69	w/o low fuel warn system	C9WY-9275-A	gauge & outlet tube assy. - identified
			C9WF-9275-A 3/8" line-service pkg.
			includes C0AF-9276-A
70	with low fuel warn system	D0WY-9275-A	includes gauge assy. C0AF-9276-A
			gasket identified D0WF-9275-A

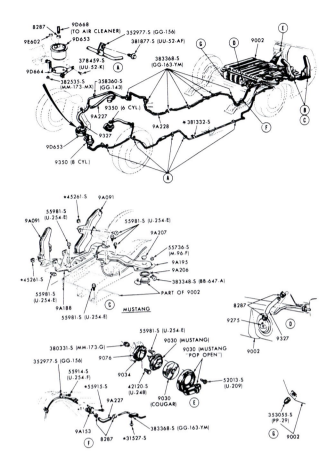

8287
9D668
(TO AIR CLEANER)
9E602
9D653
352977-S (GG-156)
381877-S (UU-52-AF)
378459-S (UU-52-K)
9002
9D664
383368-S (GG-163-YM)
382535-S (MM-173-MX)
358360-S (GG-143)
9350 (6 CYL)
9A227
9327
9A228
*381332-S
9D653
9350 (8 CYL.)

*45261-S
9A091
9A091
55981-S (U-254-E)
55981-S (U-254-E)
9A207
55736-S (M-96-F)
9A195
9A206
*45261-S
383348-S (BB-647-A)
55981-S (U-254-E)
PART OF 9002
9A188
55981-S (U-254-E)
MUSTANG
8287
9275

380331-S (MM-173-G)
55981-S (U-254-E)
9030 (MUSTANG)
9030 (MUSTANG "POP OPEN")
352977-S (GG-156)
9076
9034
55914-S (U-254-F)
*55915-S
42120-S (U-248)
9030 (COUGAR)
52013-S (U-209)
9A227
9A153
8287
*31527-S
383368-S (GG-163-YM)
9002
353055-S (PP-29)
9002

1970 Mustang fuel system without evaporative emission controls.

8287
55981-S (U-254-E)
9327
353055-S (PP-29)
9275
9002
9350 (6 CYL.)
9327
*370387-S
9350 (8 CYL.)
9327
352977-S (GG-156)
381877-S (UU-52-AF)
380331-S (MM-173-G)
9076
55981-S (U-254-E)
9034
9030 COUGAR
42120-S (U-248)
52013-S (U-209)
9030 (MUSTANG)
9030 (MUSTANG "POP OPEN")

1970 Mustang fuel system with evaporative emission controls.

Chapter 5

Drivetrain

A Mustang is made up of hundreds of subassemblies. The steering wheel, the radio, and most of the various wiring harnesses and electrical pigtails are subassemblies that are composed of numerous smaller parts. Most minor subassemblies, such as the rearview mirrors, door panels, and window regulators, are manufactured and assembled by independent companies under contract to Ford Motor Company. Major subassemblies, such as the engine, transmission, and rear axle, are manufactured by Ford and built at different divisions within the company.

Each plant has its own internal systems and production procedures. To categorize components and to keep track of running changes that affect parts procurement, each subassembly is equipped with a small metal tag. Each tag is attached in the same place and in a similar manner. The coded information on the tag tells where the assembly was manufactured, what car line it was manufactured for (Ford, Torino, Mustang, and so on), the date it was assembled, the number of changes that have been implemented since its conception, and other miscellaneous facts that help describe the component in greater detail.

It may be that the exploded views of Mustang drivetrains in this chapter will save the restorer weeks of headaches and mysteries. Even the weekend mechanic will find that the disassemblies and reassemblies necessary for repairs and maintenance are made easier with a map. For that reason, suspension, brakes, steering, wheels, and exhaust are presented as a general running gear and underchassis chapter. Because most of the components in these subsystems are not in general day-to-day view of the average car owner, they tend to be more of a mystery to the novice than, say, interior parts or exterior trim.

Fortunately, the complications inherent in the mix-and-match nature of drivetrain components do not apply here. Through this chapter the reader will find that certain applications are quite narrow, and the possibilities for swaps are reduced by safety considerations or lack of interchangeability.

The real value of this chapter can be found in the exploded views, where the differences in model years and body styles become more evident. Someone rebuilding a steering system, for instance, can be more assured that the replacement components are compatible; that person also can take advantage of correlated part numbers when dealing with Ford or other vendors for such replacement parts.

Many Mustangers wish to upgrade their braking and steering systems to power assist, and the information herein will provide an exacting guide to necessary parts. But hobbyists are reminded that any work on the steering or braking systems requires a dedication to safety. Ford's original specifications for parts of those systems still apply as minimum requirements. If there are any questions as to brake parts or steering linkage compatibility, the advice of experts should be obtained.

Mustang Transmission Applications, 1964-1970

Three-Speed Manual Transmissions

Ford 2.77
Ford 3.03

Four-Speed Manual Transmissions

Dagenham
Ford Heavy Duty
Borg Warner T-10
Ford Close Ratio HD

Automatic Transmissions

	C-4	Cruise-O-Matic
C-4	Select-Shift	Cruise-O-Matic
C-6	Select-Shift	Cruise-O-Matic
	FMX	Select-Shift

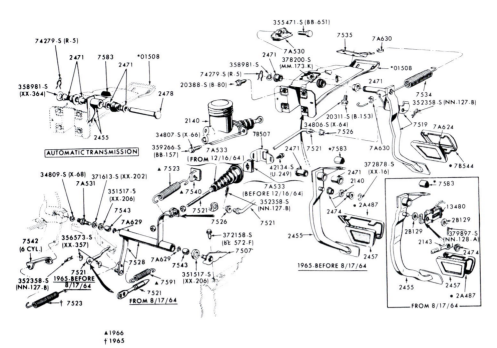

All first-generation Mustangs used a ridged mechanical linkage between the pedal and the clutch-release bearing. A rod (7521) connected to the pedal activates a lever (7528) called a bellcrank. The crank pushes an adjustable rod (also 7521) that pushes a clutch fork (7515) that is actually a lever. At the end of the fork is a sealed bearing (7580). The bearing presses the clutch fingers (part of pressure plate 7563) and disengages the clutch disc (7550). The size of the clutch disc and pressure plate and the configuration of the bellcrank differ between six- and eight-cylinder Mustangs. In later years, high-performance engines were outfitted with extra-heavy-duty clutches and bellcranks. Interestingly, the factory service manual provides instructions for lubricating the hood hinges but never addresses the clutch pedal bushings (2471), a high-wear item.

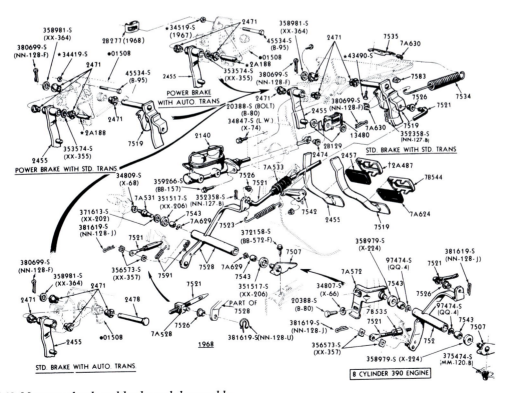

The 1967-1969 Mustang clutch and brake pedal assembly.

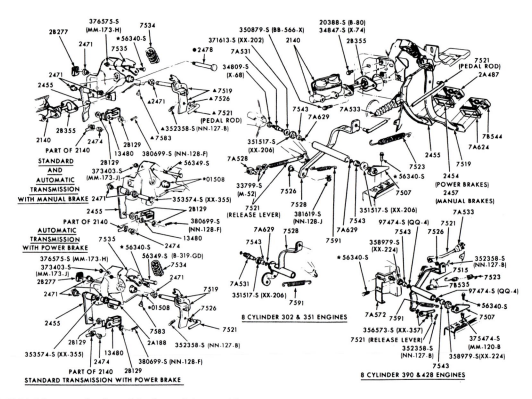

The 1969-1970 Mustang clutch and brake pedal assembly.

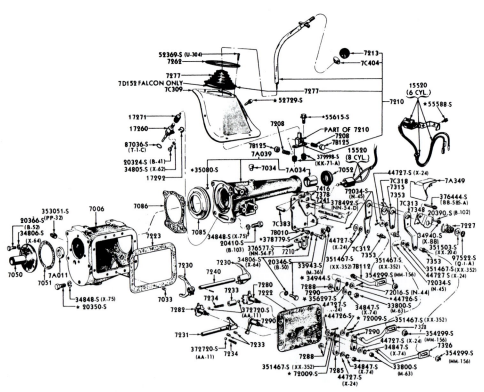

The Ford shifter for the Ford 4-speed transmission, 1965-1967. Factory shifters incorporate a long throw, in reference to the distance the lever must travel between gear selections. Long-throw shifters require less effort compared to short- *throw shifters, and that accomplished one of Ford's primary goals: to make Mustangs equipped with manual transmissions fun and easy to drive.*

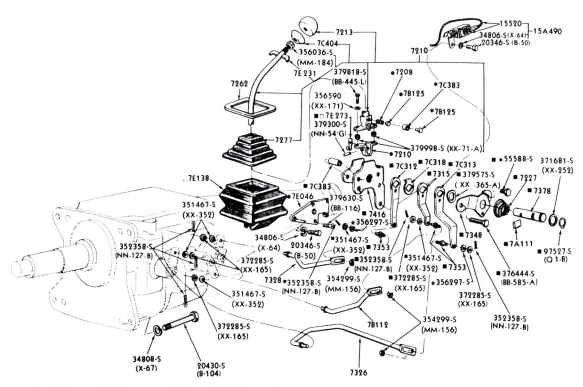

Four-speed shifter and linkage used from 1965 through 1968 on Ford-built Toploader transmissions installed in Mustangs.

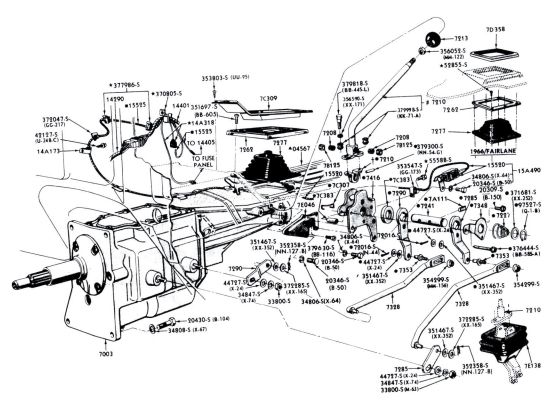

Three-speed shifter and linkage used with Ford-built transmissions between 1965 and 1968.

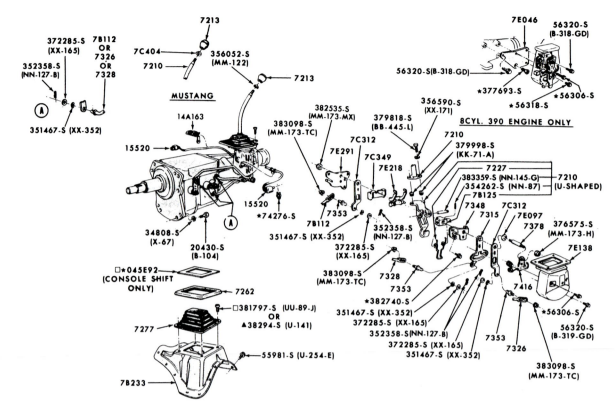

A typical view of a shifter and linkage installed in 1969 Mustangs equipped with Ford-built Toploader four-speed transmissions.

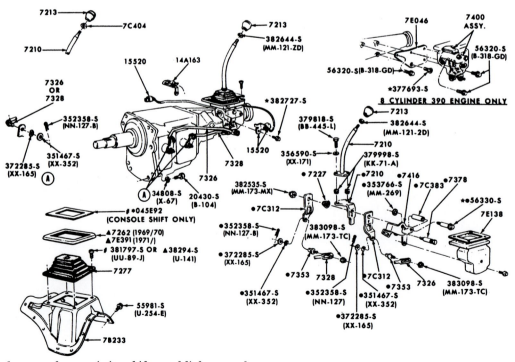

Mustang three-speed transmission shifter and linkage used with 1969-1970 Ford-built transmissions.

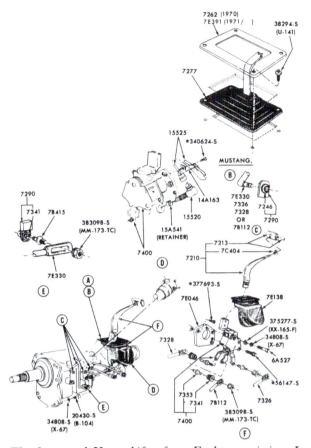

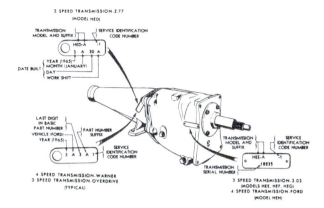

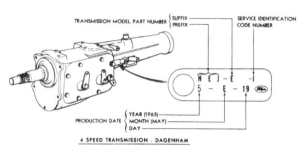

Manual transmission identification for 1965.

The four-speed Hurst shifter for a Ford transmission. In 1970, Ford began installing Hurst™ four-speed shift handles in Mustangs equipped with high-performance engines. The rectangular-shaped chrome handles are embossed with the letters H-U-R-S-T on each side. Using Hurst shift handles was a ploy by Ford's marketing experts to improve the company's image among high-performance enthusiasts. Aftermarket short-throw Hurst shifters are well known for their quick-shift engagement. But Ford installed only the Hurst shift handle and levers, not the entire assembly. The remainder of the linkage connecting the shifter to the transmission was Ford's own. The result is an improved Ford shifter that compromises Hurst's original performance standards.

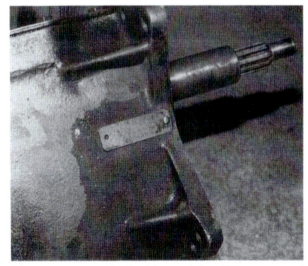

Mustangs were outfitted with one of five different manual transmissions: a 2.77 three-speed, a 3.03 three-speed, a Dagenham four-speed, a Ford four-speed, or a Warner built four-speed. The 2.77 and 3.03 are commonly thought to represent gear ratios but actually are the measurement (in inches) between the countershaft and the mainshaft. In other words, a transmission with a 3.03 designation indicates the center of the countershaft is 3.03in from the center of the mainshaft. A tag affixed to the gear housing or tailshaft extension contains coded information indicating the transmission's model number, service identification code number, and the date of manufacture.

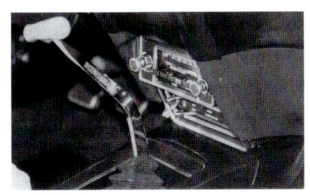

The 1970 Hurst shifter.

Mustang Transmission Tag Codes By Year and Drivetrain, 1965 and 1966.

Year	Tag Code	Engine	Trans Type	Notes
1965	HED-AV	170	2.77	
	CHED-AV, C4Z,3,A	170	2.77	
	HEJ-B	170	D/4/S	
	HED-BD	200	2.77	
	CHED-BD, C5Z,3,A	200	2.77	
	HEJ-D	200	D/4/S	Before 7/1/65
	HEJ-E	200	D/4/S	After 7/1/65
	HEF-BB	260	3.03	
	HEF-BK	289	3.03	
	HEF-CS	289	3.03	
	HEF-CV	289	3.03	
	HEH-G	260, 289	F/4/S	Before 8/20/64
	HEH-P	260, 289	F/4/S	From 8/20/64 to 12/30/64
	HEH-BR	260, 289	F/4/S	From 12/30/64 to 2/1/65
	HEH-BT	289	F/4/S	From 2/1/65
	HEH-S	289 HiPo	F/4/S	Before 8/20/64
	HEH-T	289 HiPo	F/4/S	From 8/20/64 to 10/1/64
	HEH-BX	289 HiPo	F/4/S	After 10/1/64
	HEK-M	289	W/4/S	Before 11/23/64
	HEK-V	289	W/4/S	After 11/23/64
	HEK-R	289	W/4/S	
1966	HEJ-E	200	D/4/S	
	HED-BG	200	2.77	
	RED-B	200	2.77	
	HEF-CV	289	3.03	Before 11/1/65
	HEF-CW	289	3.03	After 11/1/65
	HEK-AD	289	W/4/S	
	HEH-BW	289	F/4/S	
	HEH-BX	289 HiPo	F/4/S	

KEY:
F - Ford-built transmission
W - Borg Warner-built transmission
D - Dagenham (English-built) transmission
3/S - Three forward gears (speeds)
4/S - Four forward gears (speeds)

Mustang Transmission Tag Codes By Year and Drivetrain, 1967 to 1969.

Year	Tag Code	Engine	Trans Type	Notes
1967	RAN-S	200	3.03	
	RAN-S1	200	3.03	
	RUG-E	289	F/4/S	
	RUG-E1	289	F/4/S	
	RUG-E2	289	F/4/S	
	RUG-N	289 HiPo	F/4/S	
	RUG-N1	289 HiPo	F/4/S	
	RUG-N2	289 HiPo	F/4/S	
	RAT-N	390	3.03	
	RAT-N1	390	3.03	
	RUG-M	390	F/4/S	
	RUG-M1	390	F/4/S	
	RUG-M2	390	F/4/S	
1968	RAN-S1	200	3.03	
	RAN-D1	289	3.03	
	RUG-E2	289-302	F/4/S	
	RAT-U	302	3.03	
	RAT-N1	390 GT	3.03	
	RUG-M2	390 GT	F/4/S	w/ 2.78 low gear
	RUG-AD	390 GT	F/4/S	w/ 2.32 low gear
	RUG-S	428	F/4/S	
	RUG-AE	428	F/4/S	
	RUG-AE1	428	F/4/S	
1969	RAN-AM	200-250	3.03	
	RAT-U1	302	3.03	
	RAT-AM	351	3.03	
	RUG-AG	302-351	F/4/S	w/ 2.32 low gear
	RUG-E3	302-351	F/4/S	w/ 2.78 low gear
	RUG-AD1	390	F/4/S	w/ 2.32 low gear
	RUG-M3	390	F/4/S	w/ 2.78 low gear
	RUG-AE2	428-429	F/4/S	

KEY:
F - Ford-built transmission
W - Borg Warner-built transmission
D - Dagenham (English-built) transmission
3/S - Three forward gears (speeds)
4/S - Four forward gears (speeds)

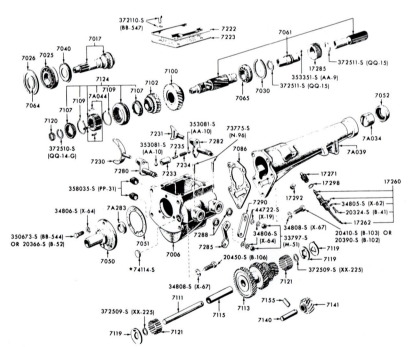

The shift levers extend through the side of the main case of a Ford transmission, and there are no shift rails. Once the mainshaft is assembled, it is lowered into the case through an opening in the top, hence the term Toploader. A stamped-tin cover is used to seal the opening. Ford-built 2.77 three-speed transmissions have a non-synchronized first gear, which means first gear cannot be engaged while the car is moving. These light-duty gearboxes were installed behind six-cylinder engines in 1965 and 1966 Mustangs. By 1967, the fully synchronized 3.03 three-speed transmission had replaced the 2.77.

218

Mustang Transmission Tag Codes By Year and Drivetrain, 1970.

Year	Tag Code	Engine	Trans Type	Notes
1970	RAN-AV	200-250	3.03	
	RAN-AV1	200-250	3.03	
	RAT-BA	302	3.03	
	RAT-BA1	302	3.03	
	RAT-BB	351	3.03	
	RAT-BB1	251	3.03	
	RAT-BB2	351	3.03	
	RUG-AV	302-351	F/4/S	w/ 2.78 low gear
	RUG-AV1	302-351	F/4/S	w/ 2.78 low gear
	RUG-AW	302-351	F/4/S	w/ 2.32 low gear
	RUG-AW1	302-351	F/4/S	w/ 2.32 low gear
	RUG-AZ	428-429	F/4/S	
	RUG-AZ1	428-429	F/4/S	

KEY:

F - Ford-built transmission
W - Borg Warner-built transmission
D - Dagenham (English-built) transmission
3/S - Three forward gears (speeds)
4/S - Four forward gears (speeds)

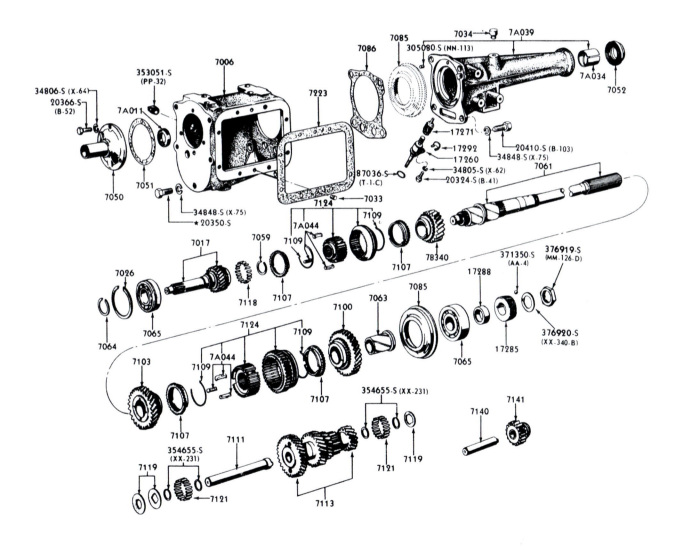

English-built Dagenham transmissions were lightweight units designed to offer the six-cylinder Mustang buyer an optional fourth gear. The transmission's durability was questionable at best, and they were quickly phased out early in 1966.

219

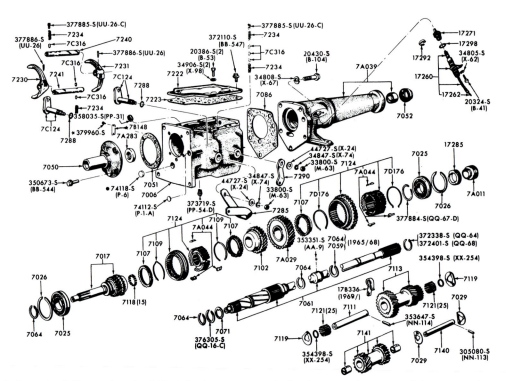

An exploded view of a fully synchronized Ford-built 3.03 transmission. The engineering term "3.03" is the distance in inches between the center of the countershaft and the center of the mainshaft.

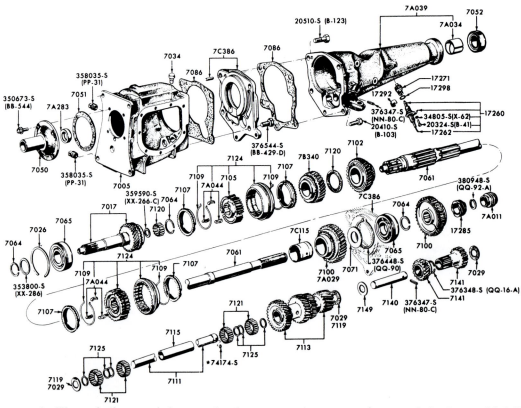

The side cover of a Warner-built transmission contains the shift rails, forks, and a shift rail interlock mechanism. A shift rail interlock will not allow two gears to be engaged at the same time. The side cover provides the only access to the main case once the transmission is assembled. Warner three-speed transmissions are fully synchronized, and were installed in some 1965 and 1966 V-8-powered Mustangs.

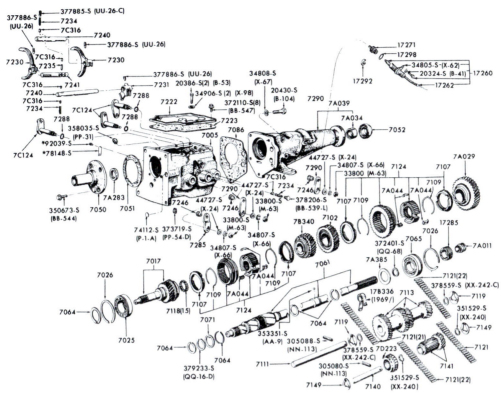

Exploded view of the Ford Toploader four-speed transmission.

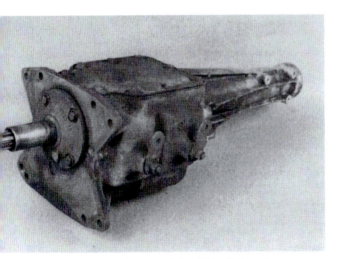

Ford's Toploader four-speed is still hailed as the strongest, most reliable manual transmission ever built. Numerous high-performance versions were built beginning in 1967 when Ford began installing big-block engines in Mustangs. Designed at a time when total vehicle weight and maximum fuel mileage were not major issues, more was better, or in this case, stronger. The Toploader's gear case and tailhousing were made of heavy cast iron, and each gear and shaft on average, 15 percent larger than necessary. Some rare race-bred Toploaders installed behind 428 Cobra Jet engines were outfitted with cast-aluminum tailhousings in an effort to save weight.

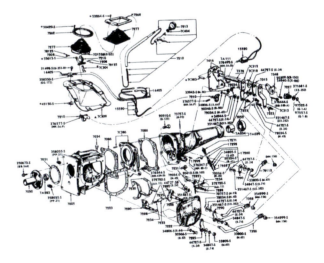

The four-speed Warner transmission shifter. Though they looked similar from inside the passenger compartment, Ford-built shifters were unique to a particular type and manufacturer of transmission. A four-speed lever designed to fit a Warner-built transmission would not fit a Toploader Ford unit, for example. All Ford-type four-speed shifters incorporate a manual release reverse lock-out lever or trigger located near the knob. Ford typically used slotted shift rods as a means for adjustment, a system designed for quick, efficient assembly at the factory. Aftermarket performance shifters normally use stronger, threaded rods.

MUSTANG CLUTCH DISC AND PRESSURE PLATE CHART

YEAR	MODEL AND DESCRIPTION	CID	TRANS.	*SPRINGS	DIAM.	DISC MATCHING DISC	PLATE
6 5	6 Cyl.	1 7 0	All	6	8-1/2"	@C5DZ-7550-A	@C2OZ-7563-C
		2 0 0	All	6	8-1/2"	^@C5DZ-7550-A	@C5OZ-7563-B
	8 Cyl.	2 6 0	3.03	6L-Pink	10"	@C6OZ-7550-G	@C2OZ-7563-D
				6S-Orange			
	8 Cyl. exc. K	2 8 9	All	6L-4S	10-1/2"	@C5AZ-7550-F	@C2OZ-7563-D
	6 Cyl.	2 0 0	2.77	6	8-1/2"	~@C5DZ-7550-B	#@C5OZ-7563-B
6 6	6 Cyl.	2 0 0	D/4/S	6	8-1/2"		
6 5/6 6	8 Cyl., K-Code	2 8 9	All 4/S	8 Gray	10-1/2"	@C7ZZ-7550-B	@C7ZZ-7563-B
6 6	6 Cyl.	2 0 0	2.77	6 Alum.	9"	@C6OZ-7550-E	@C6DZ-7563-C
6 6/6 7	8 Cyl. exc. K	2 8 9	All	6L-6S	10"	@C6DZ-7550-C	@C2OZ-7563-D
	Before 5/1/67						
6 7	8 Cyl. exc. K	2 8 9	All	6L-6S	10"	@C6DZ-7550-C	@C2OZ-7563-F
	From 5/1/67						

* L=Large, S=Small   ~ From 6/8/65

@ Supplied only as a remanufactured item   # From 2/4/65

^ Before 5/8/65

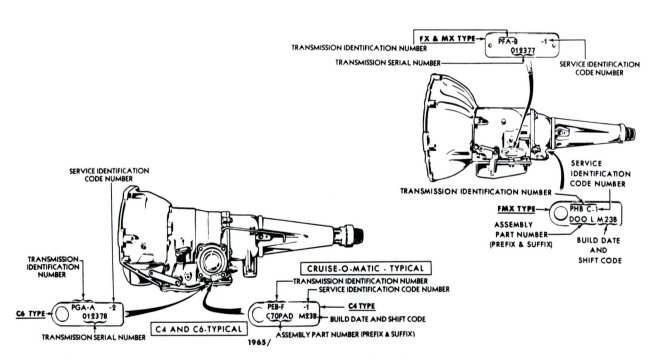

Three different automatic transmissions were installed in Mustangs from 1965 through 1970. All were designed, engineered, and built by Ford, and each has three forward speeds. All six-cylinder engines and 302ci and smaller V-8 engines received C4 transmissions. All Mustangs equipped with 351ci engines were outfitted with FMX transmissions, and all big-block engines were mated with a C6. The C4 transmissions are better known by their trade name, Cruise-O-Matic. A metal tag bolted to the driver's side servo cover on C4 and C6 transmissions or to the extension housing on FMX transmissions is used to identify each unit. The tag is stamped with the transmission's identification number as well as its service code number. Tags affixed to C6 transmissions list the unit's serial number. C4 and FMX tags show the prefix and suffix of the transmission's assembly part number in addition to the build date and shift code.

Mustang Automatic Transmissions by Year, Code, Engine Size and Type.

Production Year	Transmission Code	Engine CID	Transmission Type
1965	PCS-C	170	C4
	PCS-F	200	C4
	PCW-G	260	C4
	PCW-H	289	C4
	PCW-J	289	C4
1966	PCS-Y	200	C4
	PCW-AS	289	C4
	PCW-BA	289 HiPo	C4
1967	PEB-B	200	C4
	PEE-C	289	C4
	PEE-K	289 HiPo	C4
	PGA-P, P1	390GT	C6
1968	PEB-B1	200	C4
	PEE-C1	289	C4
	PEE-S	302	C4
	PGA-S	390-2V	C6
	PGA-P2	390-GT	C6
	PGB-AF	427/428CJ*	C6
1969	PEB-B1	200	C4
	PEA-AA	250 Economy	C4
	PEE-AD	250	C4
	PEE-AC	302	C4
	PHB-E	351-2V	FMX
	PHB-H	351-4V	FMX
	PGA-Y, AE	390	C6
	PGB-AF1	427/428CJ*	C6
1970	PEB-B3	200	C4
	PEE-AD1	250	C4
	PEE-AC1	302	C4
	PHB-E1	351-2V	FMX
	PHB-P	351-4V	FMX
	PGB-AF2	428CJ	C6

* A Regular Production Mustang equipped with a 427cid engine was proposed but never built.

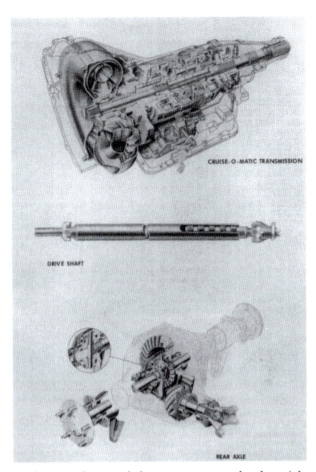

Ford automatic transmissions are programmed to the weight of the vehicle, torque output of the engine, and the rear-end gear ratio. Shift points are controlled by a combination of throttle position and load. Cruise-O-Matic C4 transmissions installed in 1965 Mustangs have a five-position shift selector. Placing the selector handle in the position marked with a red dot inside a black circle allows the transmission to upshift and downshift through all three forward gears automatically. Selecting the position marked with a black dot inside a black circle eliminates first gear from the automatic sequence. The factory believed starting out in second gear would limit tire spin during slippery driving conditions. The idea was abandoned in 1966.

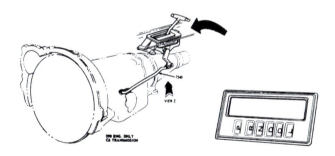

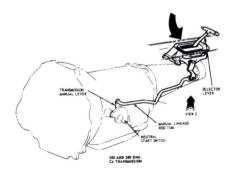

C4 and C6 transmission console linkages.

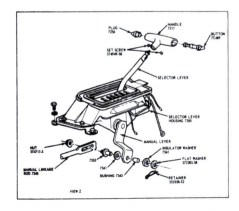

223

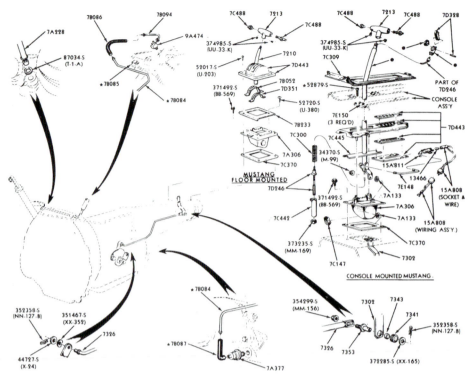

Automatic transmission floor shift control selector mechanisms for 1967-1968 Mustangs.

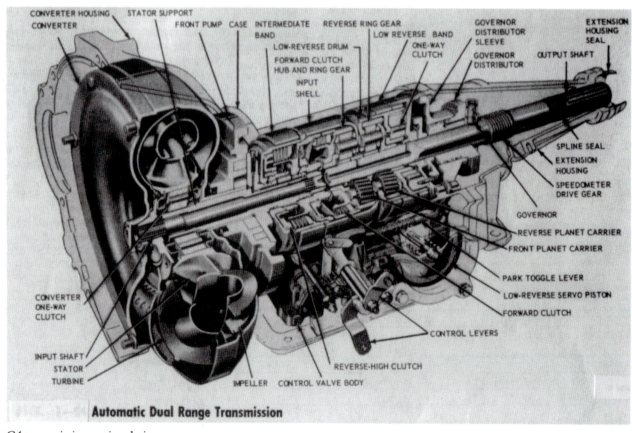

Automatic Dual Range Transmission

C4 transmission sectional view.

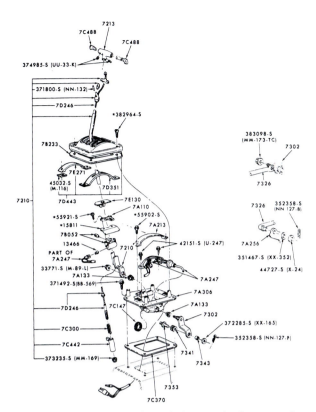

Automatic transmission floor shift control selector mechanisms for 1969-1970 Mustangs.

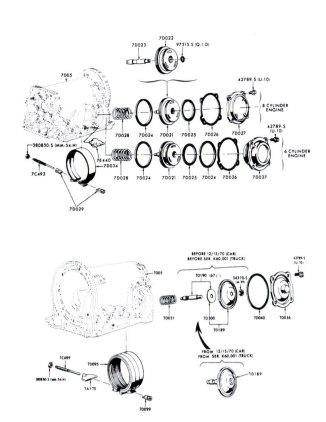

C4 automatic transmission front and rear servos and bands for 1965-1970 Mustangs.

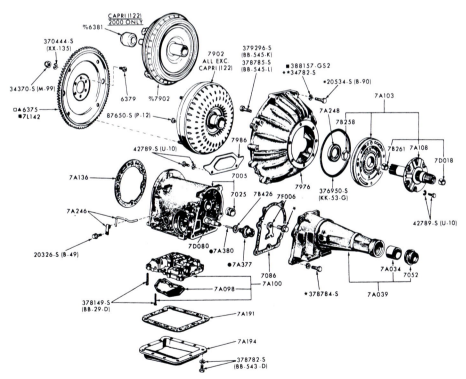

C4 automatic transmissions are lightweight and dependable. The bellhousing, main case, and extension housing are aluminum. All automatic-equipped Mustangs built in 1965 and 1966 were equipped with C4 transmissions. Different

bellhousings (7976) were used to adapt the transmission to various six- and eight-cylinder engines. Different extension housings (7A039) were used to adapt the units to various body styles.

225

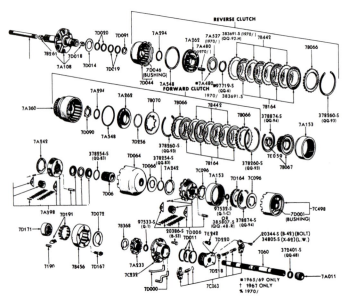

In an automatic transmission, different gear ratios are achieved by directing power through a series of compact planetary gear sets. The forward clutch is applied while the planet one-way clutch or low-reverse band prevents the low-reverse drum and reverse planet carrier from turning. The power flow is through the input shaft, the forward clutch, the ring gear, the planet gears, and the sun gears.

Counterclockwise rotation of the sun gear turns the reverse planet gear clockwise. With the reverse planet carrier held stationary, the clockwise rotation of the reverse planet gears rotates the reverse ring gear and hub clockwise. The hub of the reverse ring gear is splined to the output shaft which rotates clockwise at reduced speed, but with increased torque.

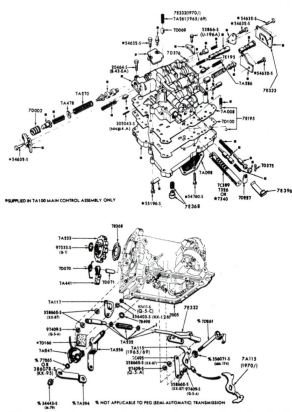

C4 automatic transmission main control valve body, parking pawl, throttle, and manual control linkage for 1965-1970 Mustangs.

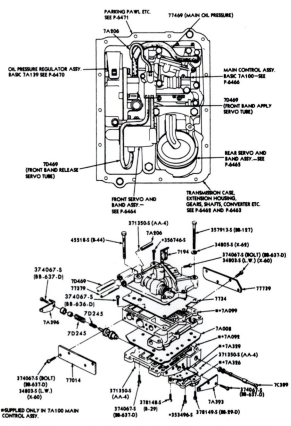

The FMX transmission valve body is completely different in operation compared to the C4 and C6 valve bodies.

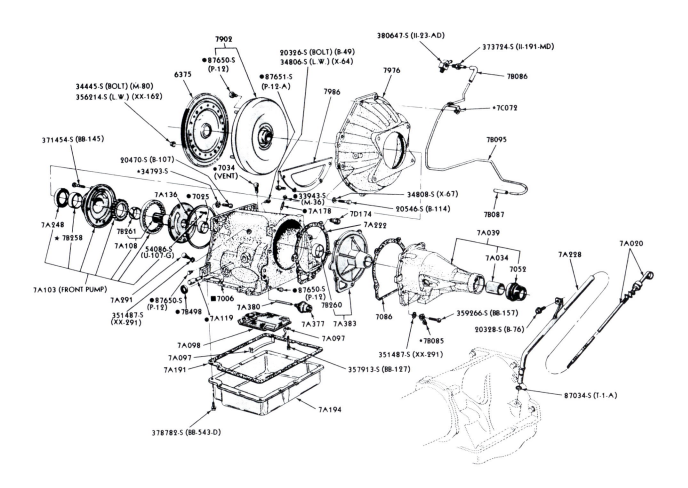

FMX transmissions were used behind mid-range torque engines such as the 351 Windsor in 1969-1970 and the 351 Cleveland in 1970; Cleveland engines were not installed in Mustangs in 1969. FMX transmissions have a cast-iron main case (7006), and an aluminum bellhousing (7976) and extension housing (7A039). The vacuum line (7B095) attaches to the intake manifold at fitting 380647-S and to the modulator valve, 7A337.

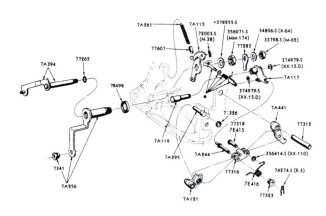

The FMX parking pawl, 1969-1970.

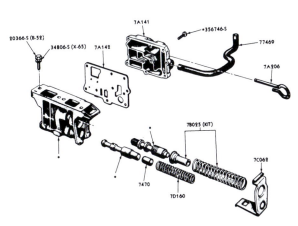

The FMX oil pressure regulator assembly, 1969-1970.

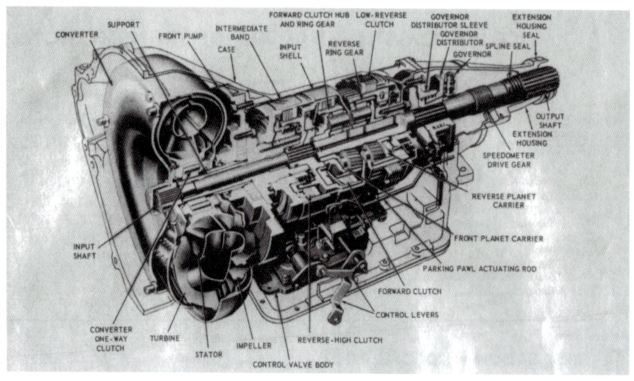

C6 transmission sectional view.

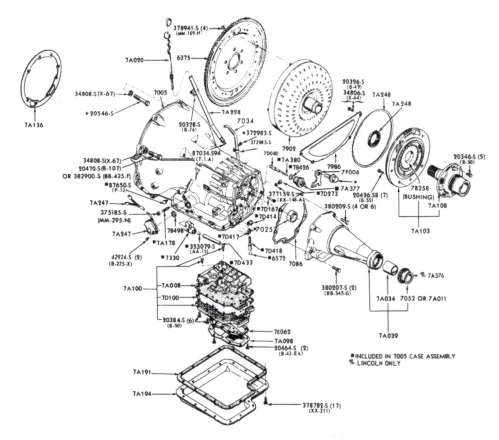

The C6 automatic transmission case and related parts.

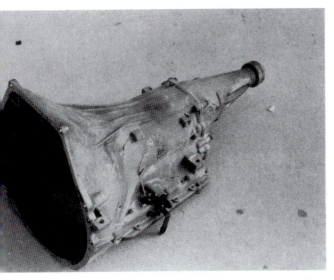
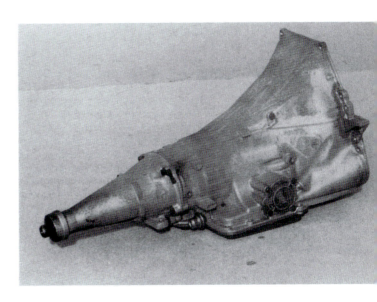

Ford's C6 is the brute of all automatic transmissions. Millions of C6 transmissions were installed in trucks and full-size Ford cars.

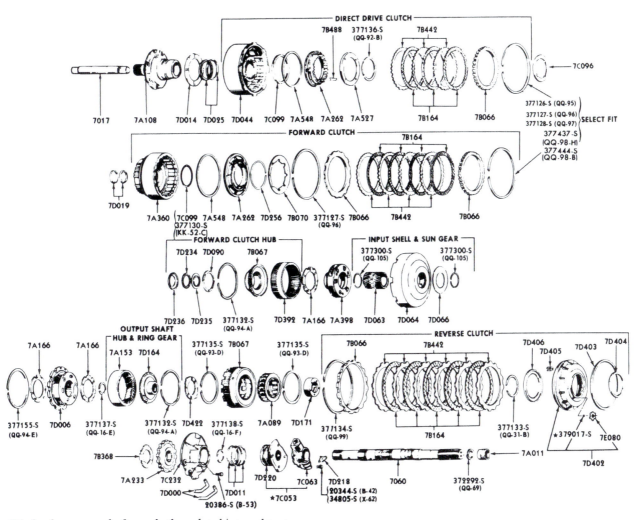

C6 clutches, gears, shafts, and other related internal parts.

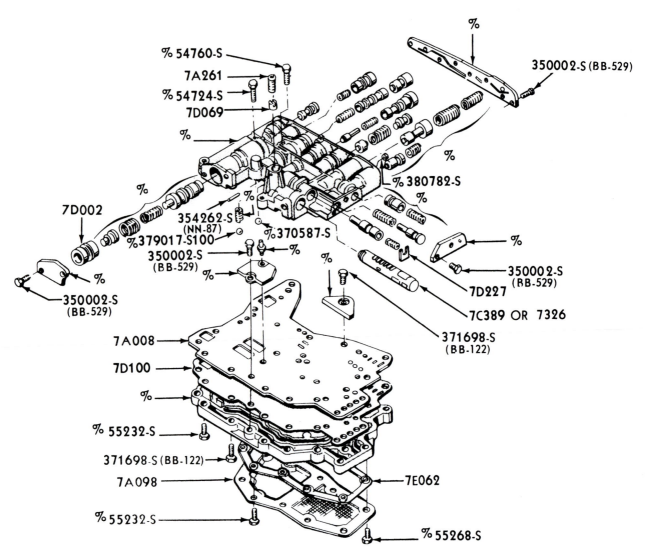

C6 automatic transmission main control valve body, parking pawl, throttle, and manual control linkage for 1967-1970 Mustangs.

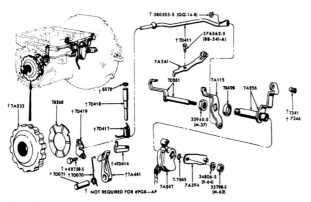

The C6 parking pawl, throttle, and manual control linkage, 1965-1970.

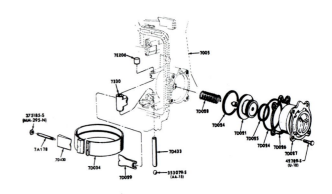

The C6 intermediate servo and band, 1965-1970.

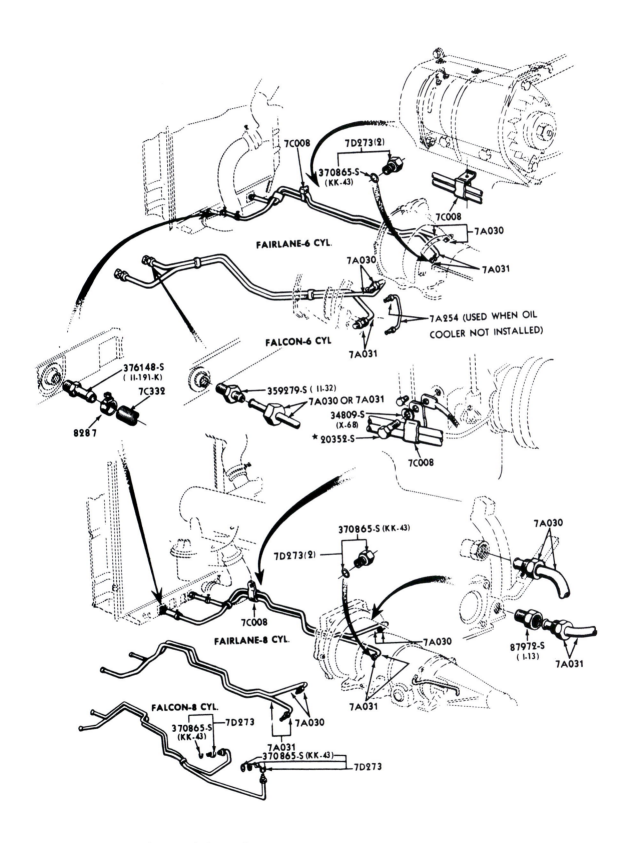

The 1965 Mustang automatic transmission cooling system.

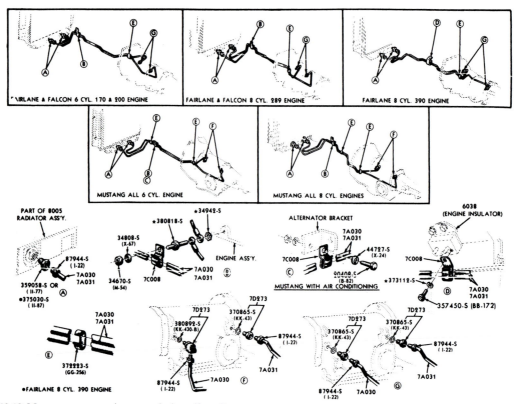

The 1966-1968 Mustang automatic transmission oil cooling system.

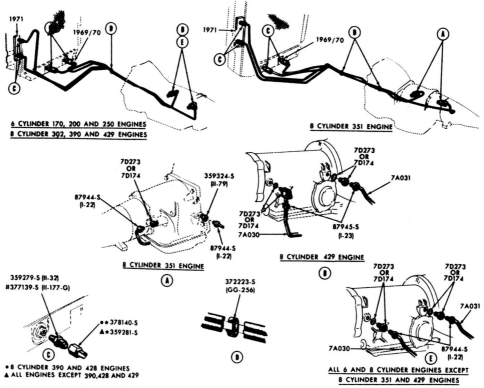

The 1969-1970 Mustang transmission oil cooling system (all engines).

232

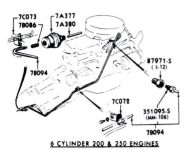

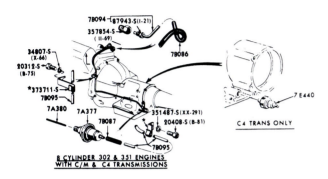

Automatic transmission vacuum throttle valve, lines, and fittings for 1965-1970 Mustangs.

Year	Model	Trans.	Speed Control Modulator or NOX Emission		Length	Remarks	Part Number
65/66		3/M/T	Yes	No	48-11/16		C5ZZ-17260-E
65/66	6 Cyl.	4/M/T			58-13/16		C5DZ-17260-A
65/66		C4			58-13/16		C5DZ-17260-A
65/66	8 Cyl.	4/M/T			64-15/16		C5OZ-17260-A
67		ALL	X		42-3/4	Pump to Speedo	C7ZZ-17260-H
67		ALL	X		36-7/16	Pump to Speedo	C7ZZ-17260-F
67		3/M/T, C4		X	63-1/16		C7ZZ-17260-D
67		C6		X	66-9/16		C7ZZ-17260-C
68		C4, C6		X	66-9/16	w/o 3.91 or 4.30 Axle	C7ZZ-17260-J
67/68		4/M/T		X	77-1/16		C7ZZ-17260-J
68	390	3/M/T		X	77-1/16		C7ZZ-17260-J
68	Exc.390	3/M/T		X	58-13/16		C7DZ-17260-C
68		C6		X	62-3/4	w/ 3.91 or 4.30 Axle	C8ZZ-17260-F
						Adapter C8ZZ-17294-A	
						also required	
68		ALL	X		57-13/16	Pump to Speedo	C8ZZ-17260-E
69		ALL	X		56	Pump to Speedo	C8ZZ-17260-D
69		C6		X	63-1/2	w/o 3.91 or 4.30 Axle	C9ZZ-17260-B
69		Exc.4/M/T		X	56		C9ZZ-17260-C
69/70		4/M/T		X	66-1/2	w/o 3.91 or 4.30 Axle	C9ZZ-17260-A
69	428	4/M/T		X	66-1/2	w/ 3.91 or 4.30 Axle	C9ZZ-17260-A
69		4/M/T		X	70	w/ 3.91 or 4.30 Axle	C9ZZ-17260-F
						Adapter C9ZZ-17294-A	
						also Required	
						From 1/31/69	
69	Exc. 428	4/M/T/		X	70	w/ 3.91 or 4.30 Axle	C9ZZ-17260-F
						Adapter C9ZZ-17294-A	
						also Required	
						Before 1/31/69	
70		4/M/T/		X	70	w/ 3.91 or 4.30 Axle	C9ZZ-17260-F
						Adapter C9ZZ-17294-A	
						also Required	
						From 1/31/69	
69/70		C6		X	58	w/ 3.91 or 4.30 Axle	C9ZZ-17260-G
						Adapter C8ZZ-17294-1	
						also Required	
70		C4		X	56		D0OZ-17260-C
70		C/M		X	56		D0OZ-17260-C
70		C/M		X	61-13/16		D0OZ-17260-D
70		C/6		X	61-13/16	w/o 3.91 or 4.30 Axle	D0OZ-17260-D
70		3/M/T		X	53-13/16		D0OZ-17260-A

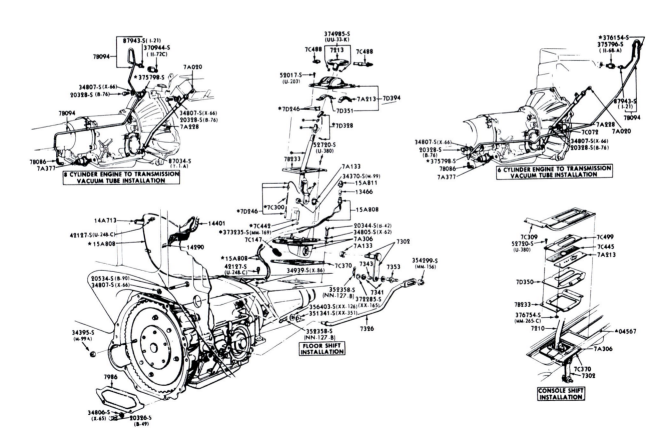

Automatic transmission floor shift control selector mechanisms for 1965-1966 Mustangs.

MUSTANG SPEEDOMETER DRIVEN GEAR IDENTIFICATION CHART
All years and models, 1965-1970.

DRIVEN GEAR	TYPE	MATERIAL	COLOR	TEETH
C0DD-17271-A	3a	Nylon	Wine	16
C0DD-17271-B	3a	Nylon	Gold or Yellow	18
C0DD-17271-C	3a	Nylon	Pink	19
C1DD-17271-A	3a	Nylon	Black	20
C2DZ-17271-F	3a	Nylon	Green or White	18
C2DZ-17271-G	3a	Nylon	Purple	17
C2DZ-17271-H	3a	Nylon	Blue	20
C2DZ-17271-J	3a	Nylon	Orange	16
C3DZ-17271-B	3a	Nylon	Green or White	17
C4DZ-17271-A	3a	Nylon	Pink-end only	19
C4OZ-17271-A	3a	Nylon	Red	21
C7SZ-17271-A	3	Nylon	Green	17
C7SZ-17271-B	3	Nylon	Gray	18
C7VY-17271-A	3	Nylon	Tan	19
C8SZ-17271-B	3	Nylon	Orange	20
D0OZ-17271-A	3	Nylon	Purple	21

MUSTANG SPEEDOMETER DRIVE GEAR IDENTIFICATION CHART
All years and models, 1965-1970.

DIMENSIONS:

TYPE	MATERIAL	COLOR	TEETH	I.D.	O.D.	Length	PART NUMBER
1	Steel	None	7	1-13/64"	2-3/16"	31/32"	C2DZ-17285-A
2	Nylon	None	6	1-5/32"	2-1/64"	11/16"	C0DR-17285-A
2a	Steel	None	6	1-3/8"	2"	11/16"	C2OZ-17285-C
2a	Nylon	Blue	7	1"	1-17/32"	1-1/8"	D0RY-17285-A
2a	Steel	None	7	1-1/32"	1-25/32"	7/16"	D1RY-17285-A
2a	Steel	None	8	1-1/8"	1-7/8"	7/16"	D1RY-17285-A
2b	Nylon	Yellow	7	1-3/8'	2"	11/16"	C3OZ-17285-C
3	Steel	None	6	1-3/32"	1-29/32"	35/64"	D1FZ-17285-A
3	Steel	None	6	1-19/64"	2"	39/64"	C3OZ-17285-A
3	Steel	None	7	1-3/8"	2"	11/16"	C8OZ-17285-B
3	Steel	None	8	1-19/64"	2"	39/64"	C5DZ-17285-C
3	Steel	None	8	1-19/64"	2-1/64"	39/64"	C5OZ-17285-B
4	Nylon	Green	6	1-3/8"	1-13/16"	11/16"	B7C-17285-A
4	Nylon	Black	7	1-1/4"	2"	11/16"	C6ZZ-17285-A
4	Nylon	Gray	8	1-3/8"	2-1/64"	11/16"	C5DZ-17285-B
4a	Nylon	Pink	6	1-3/8"	1-13/16"	11/16"	C5ZZ-17285-A
4a	Nylon	Black	7	1-3/8'	1-13/16"	11/16"	C4DZ-17285-A
4a	Nylon	Yellow	7	1-3/8'	2-1/64"	11/16"	C8AZ-17285-A
4a	Nylon	Brown	8	1-3/8'	2-1/64"	11/16"	C8OZ-17285-B
4b	Nylon	None	7	1-5/32"	2"	11/16"	C2OZ-17285-B
4b	Nylon	Pink or Yellow	7	1-3/8'	2"	11/16"	C3OZ-17285-C
4b	Steel	None	7	1-3/8'	2"	11/16"	C3OZ-17285-C

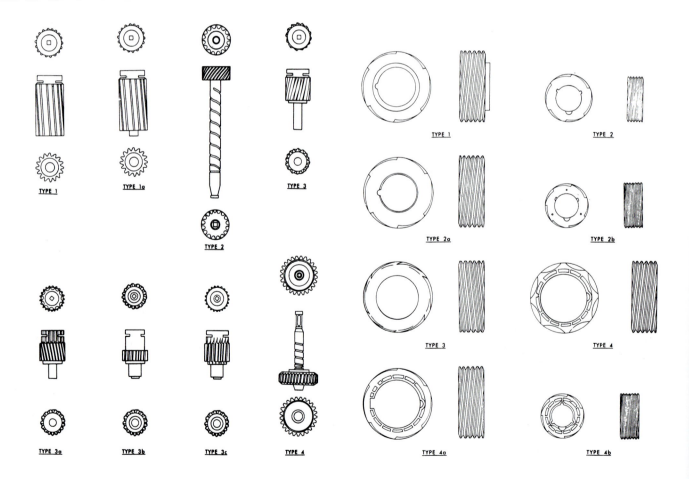

Speedometer drive gears, 1965.

MUSTANG SPEEDOMETER DRIVE GEAR APPLICATION CHART, 1965, Part One.

ENGINE CYL.	C.I.D.	TRANS.	TIRE SIZE	DRIVE GEAR	DRIVEN GEAR
			2.80 REAR AXLE RATIO		
6	200	C4	6.95x14	$	CODD-17271-A
8	289				
8	289	C4	6.50x13	$	CODD-17271-A
8	289	3/M/T	6.50x13		
	(Before 12/1/64)			C3OZ-17285-C	CODD-17271-A
	(From 12/1/64)			C8OZ-17285-B	C0DD-17271-B
8	289	3/M/T	6.95x14		
	(Before 12/1/64)			C3OZ-17285-C	CODD-17271-A
	(From 12/1/64)			C8OZ-17285-B	C0DD-17271-B
8	289	W/4/S	6.95x14		
	(HEK-L,R,V-Before 11/23/64)			*C5DZ-17285-C	C2DZ-17271-J
	(HEK-L,P,R,U,V-From 11/23/64)			C5DZ-17285-C	C2DZ-17271-F
8	289	W/4/S	6.50x13		
	(HEK-P,R,U,V)			C5DZ-17284-C	C4DZ-17271-A
8	289	W/4/S	6.95x14		
	(HEK-J Before 11/23/64)			*C5DZ-17285-B	C0DD-17271-A
	(HEK-J,S From 11/23/64)			C5OZ-17285-B	C0DD-17271-B
			2.83 REAR AXLE RATIO		
6	170,200	C4	6.50x13	$	CODD-17271-A
6	170,200	C4	6.95x14	$	CODD-17271-A
6	170	3/M/T	6.95x14	C2OZ-17285-B	CODD-17271-A
			3.00 REAR AXLE RATIO		
6	200	C4	6.95x14	$	C3DZ-17271-B
8	289				
8	289	C4	6.50x13	$	C3DZ-17271-B
8	289	3/M/T	6.50x13		
	(Before 12/1/64)			C3OZ-17285-C	C3DZ-17271-B
	(From 12/1/64)			C3OZ-17285-B	C1DZ-17271-A
8	289	3/M/T	6.95x14		
	(Before 12/1/64)			C3OZ-17285-C	C3DZ-17271-B
8	289	W/4/S	6.95x14		
	(HEK-L,M Before 11/23/64)			*C5DZ-17285-C	C2DZ-17271-G
	(HEK-L,M,P,R,U,V From 11/23/64)			C5DZ-17285-C	C4DZ-17271-A
8	289	W/4/S	6.50x13		
	(HEK-M Before 11/23/64)			*C5DZ-17285-C	C2DZ-17271-J
	(HEK-M From 11/23/64)			C5DZ-17285-C	C4DZ-17271-A
			3.20 REAR AXLE RATIO		
8	289	W/4/S	6.95x14		
	HEK-J Before 11/23/64			*C5OZ-17285-B	C3DZ-17271-B
	HEK-J,S From 11/23/64			C5OZ-17285-B	CODD-17271-C

*If drive gear is replaced, driven gear must also be replaced
$ Part of transmission output shaft

MUSTANG SPEEDOMETER DRIVE GEAR APPLICATION CHART, 1965, Part Two.

ENGINE CYL.	C.I.D.	TRANS.	TIRE SIZE	DRIVE GEAR	DRIVEN GEAR
			3.20 REAR AXLE RATIO		
6	170,200	C4	6.50x13	$	CODD-17271-B
6	170,200	C4	6.95x14	$	CODD-17271-B
6	170,200	3/M/T	6.50x13	C2OZ-17285-B	CODD-17271-B
6	170,200	3/M/T	6.95x14	C2OZ-17285-B	CODD-17271-B
			3.25 REAR AXLE RATIO		
6	200	C4	6.95x14	$	CODD-17271-B
8	289	C/M	7.75x15	$	C3DZ-17271-B
6	200	3/M/T	6.95x14	C2OZ-17285-B	CODD-17271-B
8	289	3/M/T	6.95x14	C8OZ-17285-B	C4OZ-17271-A
8	289	W/4/S	6.95x14		
	Before 11/23/64			*C5DZ-17285-C	C2DZ-17271-F
	From 11/23/64			C5DZ-17285-C	C2DZ-17271-H
			3.50 REAR AXLE RATIO		
6	170	C4	6.50x13	$	C1DD-17271-A
8	289				
6	170,200	C4	6.95x14	$	C1DD-17271-A
8	289				
6	170,200	3/M/T	6.50x13	C2OZ-17285-B	C1DD-17271-A
6	170,200	3/M/T	6.95x14	C2OZ-17285-B	C1DD-17271-A
8	289	W/4/S	6.95x14		
	(HEK-L)			C5DZ-17285-C	C2DZ-17271-H
8	289	W/4/S	6.95x14		
	(HEK-J)			C5OZ-17285-B	C1DD-17271-A
8	289	W/4/S	6.95x14		
	(HEK-K)			C3OZ-17285-A	C3DZ-17271-B
			3.89 REAR AXLE RATIO		
8	289	C4	6.95x14	$	C4OZ-17271-A
8	289	C4	6.95x14	$	C4OZ-17271-A
8	289	W/4/S	6.95x14	C3OZ-17285-A	CODD-17271-A
8	289	F/4/S	6.95x14	C5ZZ-17285-A	C4DZ-17271-A
			4.11 REAR AXLE RATIO		
8	289	W/4/S	6.95x14	C3OZ-17285-A	C1DD-17271-A
8	289	F/4/S	6.95x14	C5ZZ-17285-A	C2DZ-17271-H

*If drive gear is replaced, driven gear must also be replaced
$ Part of transmission output shaft

MUSTANG SPEEDOMETER DRIVE GEAR APPLICATION CHART, 1966.

ENGINE CYL.	C.I.D.	TRANS.	TIRE SIZE	DRIVE GEAR	DRIVEN GEAR
			2.80 REAR AXLE RATIO		
6	170,200	C4	6.95x14	$	CODD-17271-A
8	289				
8	289	3/M/T	6.95x14	C8OZ-17285-B	CODD-17271-B
8	289	F/4/S	6.95x14	C4DZ-17285-A	C2DZ-17271-J
8	289	W/4/S	6.95x14	C6ZZ-17285-A	C2DZ-17271-J
			2.83 REAR AXLE RATIO		
6	170,200	C4	6.95x14	$	CODD-17271-A
8	289				
6	170,200	3/M/T	6.95x14	C2OZ-17285-B	CODD-17271-A
			3.00 REAR AXLE RATIO		
6	170,200	C4	6.95x14	$	C3DZ-17271-B
8	289				
8	289	3/M/T	6.95x14	C8OZ-17285-B	CODD-17271-C
8	289	W/4/S	6.95x14	C6ZZ-17285-A	C20Z-17271-B
8	289	F/4/S	6.95x14	C4DZ-17285-A	C2DZ-17271-G
			3.20 REAR AXLE RATIO		
6	170,200	C4	6.95x14	$	C3DZ-17271-B
8	289				
6	170,200	3/M/T	6.95x14	C2OZ-17285-B	CODD-17271-B
6	170,200	D/4/S	6.95x14	C5ZZ-17285-B	C2DZ-17271-F
			3.25 REAR AXLE RATIO		
8	289	C4	6.95x14	$	C3DZ-17271-B
6	170,200	C4	6.95x14	$	CODD-17271-B
8	289				
6	170,200	3/M/T	6.95x14	C2OZ-17285-B	CODD-17271-B
8	289	3/M/T	6.95x14	C8OZ-17285-B	C4OZ-17271-A
8	289	F/4/S	6.95x14	C4DZ-17285-A	C2DZ-17271-F
			3.50 REAR AXLE RATIO		
6	170,200	C4	6.95x14	$	C1DD-17271-A
8	289				
6	170,200	3/M/T	6.95x14	C2OZ-17285-B	C1DD-17271-A
			3.89 REAR AXLE RATIO		
6	170,200	C4	6.95x14	$	C40Z-17271-A
8	289				
8	289	F/4/S	6.95x14	C5ZZ-17285-A	C4DZ-17271-A

$ Part of transmission output shaft

MUSTANG SPEEDOMETER DRIVE GEAR APPLICATION CHART, 1967, Part One.

ENGINE CYL.	C.I.D.	TRANS.	TIRE SIZE	DRIVE GEAR	DRIVEN GEAR
			2.75 REAR AXLE RATIO		
8	390	C6	F70x14	$	C3DZ-17271-B
			2.79 REAR AXLE RATIO		
8	289	C4	6.95x14,7.35x14	$	C7SZ-17271-B
8	390	C4	F70x14	$	C7SZ-17271-A
8	289	3/M/T	6.95x14,7.35x14	C8OZ-17285-B	CODD-17271-B
8	289	3/M/T	F70x14	C8OZ-17285-B	C3DZ-17271-B
8	289	4/M/T	6.95x14,7.35x14	C4DZ-17285-A	C2DZ-17271-J
			2.80 REAR AXLE RATIO		
6	200	C4	7.35x14	$	CODD-17271-A
8	289	C4	6.95x14	$	C7SZ-17271-B
8	289	C4	F70x14	$	CODD-17271-A
8	289	3/M/T	6.95x14,7.35x14	C8OZ-17285-B	CODD-17271-B
8	289	3/M/T	F70x14	C8OZ-17285-B	CODD-17271-B
8	289	4/M/T	6.95x14,7.35x14	C4DZ-17285-A	C2DZ-17271-J
			2.83 REAR AXLE RATIO		
6	170,200	C4	6.95x14,7.35x14	$	CODD-17271-A
6	170,200	3/M/T(RED)	6.95x14,7.35x14	C2OZ-17285-B	CODD-17271-A
6	170,200	3/M/T(RAN)	6.95x14,7.35x14	C3OZ-17285-C	CODD-17271-A
			3.00 REAR AXLE RATIO		
6	200	C4	7.35x14	$	C3DZ-12721-B
8	289	C4	6.95x14	$	C7VY-17271-A
8	289	C4	7.35x14,F70x14	$	C7VY-17271-A
8	289,390	C6	7.35x14,F70x14	$	CODD-17271-C
8	289,390	3/M/T(RAN)	7.35x14,F70x14	C8OZ-17285-B	CODD-17271-B
8	289,390	3/M/T(RAN)	6.95x14	C8OZ-17285-B	CODD-17271-B
8	289,390	3/M/T(RAT)	6.95x14, 7.35x14	C8OZ-17285-B	CODD-17271-C
8	289,390	4/M/T			
8	289,390	3/M/T(RAT) 4/M/T	F70x14	C4DZ-17285-A	C2DZ-17271-J
			3.20 REAR AXLE RATIO		
6	170,200	C4	6.95x14,7.35x14	C2OZ-17285-B	CODD-17271-B
6	170,200	3/M/T(RED)	6.95x14,7.35x14	C3OZ-17285-C	CODD-17271-B
			3.20 REAR AXLE RATIO		
6	170,200	3/M/T(RAN)	6.95x14,7.35x14	C3OZ-17285-C	CODD-17271-B
			3.25 REAR AXLE RATIO		
6	170,200	C4	7.35x14	$	CODD-17271-B
8	390	C6	F70x14	$	C1DD-17271-A
6	170,200	3/M/T(RAN)	7.35x14	C3OZ-17285-C	CODD-17271-B
8	289,390	3/M/T(RAT) 4/M/T	7.35x14	C8OZ-17285-B	C4OZ-17271-A
8	289,390	3/M/T(RAN)	F70x14	C4DZ-17285-A	C2DZ-17271-G

MUSTANG SPEEDOMETER DRIVE GEAR APPLICATION CHART, 1967, Part Two.

ENGINE CYL.	C.I.D.	TRANS.	TIRE SIZE	DRIVE GEAR	DRIVEN GEAR
			3.50 REAR AXLE RATIO		
6	170,200	C4	7.35x14	$	CODD-17271-C
8	289		F70x14	$	CODD-17271-C
6	200	3/M/T(RAN)	7.35x14	C3OZ-17285-C	CODD-17271-C
8	289	4/M/T	F70x14	C5ZZ-17285-A	C2DZ-17271-J
			3.89 REAR AXLE RATIO		
8	289	C4	F70x14	$	C4OZ-17271-A
8	289	4/M/T	F70x14	C5ZZ-17285-A	C2DZ-17271-F

$ Part of transmission output shaft

235

64) CYL.	C.I.D.	TRANS.	TIRE SIZE	DRIVE GEAR	DRIVEN GEAR
			2.75 REAR AXLE RATIO		
8	390	C6	F70x14	$ - 8 teeth	C3DZ-17271-B
8	390	C6	7.35x14,E70x14, FR70x14	$ - 8 teeth	C3DZ-17271-B
8	390	C6	185Rx14	$ - 8 teeth	C0DD-17271-B
			2.79 REAR AXLE RATIO		
8	289,302	C4	6.95x14,185Rx14,E70x14	$	C7SZ-17271-B
8	289,302	C4	F70x14	$	C7SZ-17271-B
8	289,302	C4	7.35x14,FR70x14	$	C7SZ-17271-A
8	289,302	3/M/T	6.95x14,185Rx14,E70x14	C8OZ-17285-B	C0DD-17271-B
8	289,302	3/M/T	F70x14	C8OZ-17285-B	C3DZ-17271-B
8	289,302	3/M/T	FR70x14	C8OZ-17285-B	C3DZ-17271-B
8	289,302	4/M/T	6.95x14,185Rx14,7.35x14, E70x14,F70x14,FR70x14	C4DZ-17285-A	C2DZ-17271-J
			2.83 REAR AXLE RATIO		
6	170,200	C4	6.95x14,7.35x14	$	C7SZ-17271-B
6	170,200	3/M/T	6.95x14	C3OZ-17285-C	C0DD-17271-A
			3.00 REAR AXLE RATIO		
6	200	C4	6.95x14	$	C7VY-17171-A
8	289,302	C4	7.35x14,E70x14, F70x14,FR70x14,185Rx14	$ - 8 teeth	C0DD-17271-C
6	200	3/M/T	7.35x14	C3OZ-17285-C	C3DZ-17271-B
8	289,302	3/M/T	6.95x14	C8OZ-17285-B	C0DD-17271-C
8	289,302	3/M/T	7.35x14,E70x14, F70x14,FR70x14,185Rx14	C8OZ-17285-B	C0DD-17271-C
8	390	3/M/T	7.35x14,185Rx14,E70x14	C4DZ-17285-A	C2DZ-17271-G
			3.00 REAR AXLE RATIO		
8	289,302 390	4/M/T	6.95x14,E70x14,185Rx14	C4DZ-17285-A	C2DZ-17271-G
8	390	3/M/T	F70x14	C4DZ-17285-A	C2DZ-17271-J
8	289,302 390	4/M/T	F70x14	C4DZ-17285-A	C2DZ-17271-J
8	390	3/M/T	FR70x14	C4DZ-17285-A	C2DZ-17271-J
8	289,302 390	4/M/T	FR70x14,7.35x14	C4DZ-17285-A	C2DZ-17271-J
			3.20 REAR AXLE RATIO		
6	170,200	C4	6.95x14	$	C8SZ-17271-B
6	170,200	3/M/T	6.95x14	C3OZ-17285-C	C0DD-17271-B
6	200	3/M/T	7.35x14	C3OZ-17285-C	C3DZ-17271-B

CYL	C.I.D.	TRANS.	TIRE SIZE	DRIVE GEAR	DRIVEN GEAR
			3.25 REAR AXLE RATIO		
8	302	C4	F70x14,FR70x14	$	C8SZ-17271-B
8	170,200	C4	7.35x14	$	D0OZ-17271-A
8	289,302	C4	7.35x14	$	C8SZ-17271-B
8	289,302	C4	C70 x 14	$	D0OZ-17271-A
8	390	C6	7.35x14	$ - 8 teeth	C1DD-17271-A
8	390	C6	F70x14,FR70x14	$ - 8 teeth	C1DD-17271-A
8	390	C6	E70x14,185Rx14	$ - 8 teeth	C4OZ-17271-A
6	170,200	3/M/T	7.35x14,E70x14	C3OZ-17285-C	C0DD-17271-B
8	289	3/M/T	7.35x14	C8OZ-17285-B	C1DD-17271-A
8	289	3/M/T	F70x14	C8OZ-17285-B	C1DD-17271-A
8	289	3/M/T	6.95x14,185Rx14, E70x14,FR70x14	C8OZ-17285-B	C4OZ-17271-A
8	390	3/M/T	7.35x14,F70x14, FR70x14,E70x14,185Rx14	C4DZ-12785-A	C2DZ-17271-F
8	289,302 390	4/M/T	7.35x14,F70x14, FR70x14,E70x14,185Rx14	C4DZ-12785-A	C2DZ-17271-F
8	289,302	4/M/T	6.95x14	C4DZ-12785-A	C2DZ-17271-F

$ Part of transmission output shaft

ENGINE CYL	C.I.D.	TRANS.	TIRE SIZE	DRIVE GEAR	DRIVEN GEAR
			2.33 REAR AXLE RATIO		
6	250	C4	E78x14	$	C0DD-17271-A
			2.79 REAR AXLE RATIO		
6 8	250 302	C4	C78x14	$	C7SZ-17271-B
8	302	C4	F70x14	$	C7SZ-17271-A
6 8	250 302	C4	E78x14	$	C7SZ-17271-A
6 8	250 302	3/M/T	C78x14	C8OZ-17285-B	C0DD-17271-B
6 8	250 302	3/M/T	E78x14	C8OZ-17285-B	C3DZ-17271-B
8	302	4/M/T	F70x14,C78x14,E78x14	C4DZ-17285-A	C2DZ-17271-J
			2.83 REAR AXLE RATIO		
6	200	C4	E78x14	$	C7SZ-17271-B
6	200	C4	C78x14	$	C7SZ-17271-B
			3.00 REAR AXLE RATIO		
6 8	200,250 302	C4,C6	F70x14 FR70x14 E78x14	$ - 8 teeth	C7VY-17271-A
6 8	200,250 302	C4	C78x14	$ - 8 teeth	C8SZ-17271-B
6 8	250 302,351	3/M/T	F70x14,FR70x14,E78x14	C8OZ-17285-B	C0DD-17271-C
6 8	250 302,351	3/M/T	C78x14	C8OZ-17285-B	C1DD-17271-A
8	390	3/M/T	FR70x14,E78x 14	C4DZ-17285-A	C2DZ-17271-J
8	390	3/M/T	F70x14	C4DZ-17285-A	C2DZ-17271-J
8	302,351 390	4/M/T	E78x14 FR70x14	C4DZ-17285-A	C2DZ-17271-J
8	302,351	4/M/T	F70x14	C4DZ-17285-A	C2DZ-17271-G
			3.08 REAR AXLE RATIO		
6	200	C4	C78x14	$	C8SZ-17271-B
6	200	C4	E78x14	$	C7VY-17271-A
6	200	3/M/T	C78x14	C8OZ-17285-B	C1DD-17271-A
6	200	3/M/T	E78x14	C8OZ-17285-B	C0DD-17271-C
			3.25 REAR AXLE RATIO		
6 8	250 302,351	C4	E78x14	$ - 8 teeth	C8SZ-17271-B
6 8	250 302,351 390,429	C4	F70x14 FR70x14	$ - 8 teeth	C8SZ-17271-B
6 8	250 302,351	C4	E70x14 C78x14	$ - 8 teeth	D0OZ-17271-A

ENGINE CYL	C.I.D.	TRANS.	TIRE SIZE	DRIVE GEAR	DRIVEN GEAR
			3.25 REAR AXLE RATIO (Continued)		
6 8	250 302,351	3/M/T	E78x14	$ - 8 teeth	C1DD-17271-A
8	302,351	3/M/T	F70x14,FR70x14	C8OZ-17285-B	C1DD-17271-A
6 8	250 302,351	3/M/T	C78x14	C8OZ-17285-B	C4OZ-17271-A
8	390	3/M/T	F70x14,FR70x14,E78x14	C4DZ-17285-A	C2DZ-17271-F
8	428	4/M/T	F70x14,FR70x14	C5ZZ-17285-A	C2DZ-17271-J
			3.50 REAR AXLE RATIO		
8	390,428	C6	F70x14,FR70x14,E78x14	$ - 8 teeth	D0OZ-17271-A
8	351,428	4/M/T	FR70x14	C5ZZ-17285-A	C2DZ-17271-J
8	351,428	4/M/T	F70x14	C5ZZ-17285-A	C2DZ-17271-J
8	302,351 390	4/M/T	F70x14,FR70x14,E78x14	C4DZ-17285-A	C4DZ-17271-A
			3.91 REAR AXLE RATIO		
8	390,428	C6	F70x14,FR70x14	$ - 8 teeth	C7SZ-17271-B
8	302,390	4/M/T	F70x14,FR70x14	C4DZ-17285-A	C2DZ-17271-J
8	351,428	4/M/T	F70x14,FR70x14	C5ZZ-17285-A	C2DZ-17271-F
			4.30 REAR AXLE RATIO		
8	428	C6	F70x14,FR70x14	$ - 8 teeth	C7SZ-17271-B
8	302,390	4/M/T	F70x14,FR70x14	C4DZ-17285-A	C2DZ-17271-G
8	351,428	4/M/T	F70x14,FR70x14	C5ZZ-17285-A	C2DZ-17271-H

$ Part of transmission output shaft

ENGINE CYL	C.I.D.	TRANS.	TIRE SIZE	DRIVE GEAR	DRIVEN GEAR
2.75 REAR AXLE RATIO					
8	351	C4	E78x14	$	C7SZ-17271-A
8	351	C4	F70x14	$	C7SZ-17271-A
8	351	3/M/T	E78x14	C8OZ-17285-B	C3DZ-17271-B
8	351	3/M/T	F70x14	C8OZ-17285-B	C3DZ-17271-B
2.79 REAR AXLE RATIO					
6 8	250 302	C4	E78x14	$	C7SZ-17271-A
6 8	250 302	3/M/T	E78x14	C8OZ-17285-B	C3DZ-17271-B
8	302	3/M/T	F70x14	C8OZ-17285-B	C3DZ-17271-B
3.00 REAR AXLE RATIO					
6 8	200,250 302,351	C4	F70x14,E78x14	$ - 8 teeth	C7VY-17271-A
6 8	250 302,351	3/M/T	F70x14,E78x14	C8OZ-17285-B	CODD-17271-C
8	302,351	4/M/T	E78x14	C4DZ-17285-A	C2DZ-17271-G
8	302,351	4/M/T	F70x14	C4DZ-17285-A	C2DZ-17271-J
3.08 REAR AXLE RATIO					
6	170,200	3/M/T	E78x14	C8OZ-17285-B	CODD-17271-C
3.25 REAR AXLE RATIO					
6 8	250 302,351	C4	E78x14	$ - 8 teeth	C8SZ-17271-B
6 8	250 302,351	3/M/T	E78x14	C8OZ-17285-B	C1DD-17271-A
6 8	200,250 302,351	3/M/T	F70x14	C8OZ-17285-B	C1DD-17271-A
8	302,351 428	4/M/T	F70x14	C4DZ-17285-A	C2DZ-17271-F
3.50 REAR AXLE RATIO					
8	351,428	C6	F70x14	$ - 8 teeth	DOOZ-17271-A
8	302,351 428,429	4/M/T	F70x14	C4DZ-17285-A	C2DZ-17271-H
3.91 REAR AXLE RATIO					
8	302,429	4/M/T	F60x15	C4DZ-17285-A	C2DZ-17271-J

$ Part of transmission output shaft

Mustang Rear Axle Tag Code Identification Chart, Part One.

Axle Code	Model Year	Axle Ratio	Ring Gear Diameter	Carrier Type	Axle Splines
WCY-E	65-70	3.20:1	7-1/4	Integral	24 Spline
WCY-F	65	3.50:1	7-1/4	Integral	24 Spline
WCY-L	65-66	3.20:1	7-1/4	Integral	24 Spline
WCY-R	65-70	2.83:1	7-1/4	Integral	24 Spline
WCY-AA	65-66	2.83:1	7-1/4	Integral	24 Spline
WCY-AJ	66-68	3.20:1	7-1/4	Integral	24 Spline
WCY-AJ1	66-68	3.20:1	7-1/4	Integral	24 Spline
WCY-AJ2	69-70	3.08:1	7-1/4	Integral	24 Spline
WCZ-E	65-67	2.80:1	8	Removable	28 Spline
WCZ-F	65-70	3.00:1	8	Removable	28 Spline
WCZ-F1	65-70	3.00:1	8	Removable	28 Spline
WCZ-G	65	3.50:1	8	Removable	28 Spline
WCZ-H	65	3.89:1	9	Removable	28 Spline
WCZ-J	65	4.11:1	9	Removable	28 Spline
WCZ-P	65	3.50:1	9	Removable	28 Spline
WCZ-R	66	3.89:1	9	Removable	28 Spline
WCZ-S	66	3.50:1	9	Removable	28 Spline
WCZ-T	66	3.50:1	9	Removable	28 Spline
WCZ-V1	67-70	2.79:1	8	Removable	28 Spline
WCZ-W	68	3.25:1	8	Removable	28 Spline
WES-F	67-70	3.00:1	9	Removable	28 Spline
WES-G	67	3.25:1	9	Removable	28 Spline
WES-H	67-68	3.50:1	9	Removable	28 Spline
WES-J	67	3.89:1	9	Removable	28 Spline
WES-K	67	3.50:1	9	Removable	28 Spline
WES-M	68-70	3.25:1	9	Removable	28 Spline

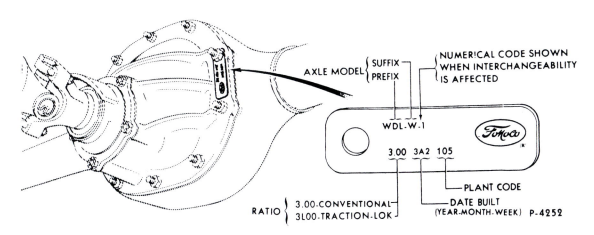

A typical rear axle identification tag contains numerous bits of information that are essential for cataloging and locating repair parts.

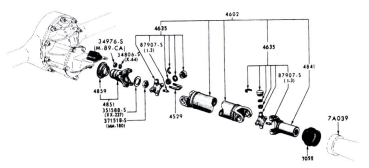

Driveshaft assembly for 1965-1972 Mustangs. The length, diameter, type of slip yoke (4841), and type of rear U-joint flange (4851) as well as the size of the universal joints (4635) depend on the displacement of the engine and the type of transmission used.

Mustang Rear Axle Tag Code Identification Chart, Part Two.

Axle Code	Model Year	Axle Ratio	Ring Gear Diameter	Carrier Type	Axle Splines
WES-N	6 8	3.00:1	9	Removable	28 Spline
WES-P	6 8	3.25:1	9	Removable	28 Spline
WES-R	6 8	3.25:1	9	Removable	28 Spline
WES-T	69-70	2.75:1	9	Removable	28 Spline
WES-T1	70-72	2.75:1	9	Removable	28 Spline
WES-U	6 8	3.50:1	9	Removable	31 Spline
WES-V	6 8	3.00:1	9	Removavle	28 Spline
WES-Y	6 8	3.50:1	9	Removable	31 Spline
WES-Z	6 8	3.00:1	9	Removable	28 Spline
WES-AA	69-70	3.00:1	9	Removable	28 Spline
WES-AB	69-70	3.25:1	9	Removable	28 Spline
WES-AC	69-70	3.00:1	9	Removable	28 Spline
WES-AD	69-70	3.25:1	9	Removable	28 Spline
WES-AE	69-70	3.50:1	9	Removable	31 Spline
WES-AG	69-70	2.75:1	9	Removable	28 Spline
WES-AH	69-70	3.00:1	9	Removable	31 Spline
WES-AJ	69-70	3.25:1	9	Removable	31 Spline
WFB-A	69-70	3.25:1	9	Removable	28 Spline
WFB-C	69-70	3.25:1	9	Removable	28 Spline
WFB-D	69-70	3.00:1	9	Removable	28 Spline
WFD-A	69-70	3.50:1	9	Removable	31 Spline
WFD-B	68-70	3.91:1	9	Removable	31 Spline
WFD-C	68-70	4.30:1	9	Removable	31 Spline
WFD-D	68-70	3.91:1	9	Removable	31 Spline
WFD-E	69-70	4.30:1	9	Removable	31 Spline
WFD-F	69-70	3.50:1	9	Removable	31 Spline
WFD-J	6 9	3.25:1	9	Removable	31 Spline
WFD-K	69-70	3.00:1	9	Removable	31 Spline
WFD-L	69-70	3.00:1	9	Removable	31 Spline
WFD-M	7 0	3.25:1	9	Removable	31 Spline
WFL-A	7 0	3.00:1	8	Removable	28 Spline
WFU-E	7 0	4.30:1	9	Removable	31 Spline
WDJ-B	65-66	2.80:1	8	Removable	28 Spline
WDJ-C	65-69	3.00:1	8	Removable	28 Spline
WDJ-C1	65-69	3.00:1	8	Removable	28 Spline
WDJ-C2	6 9	3.00:1	8	Removable	28 Spline

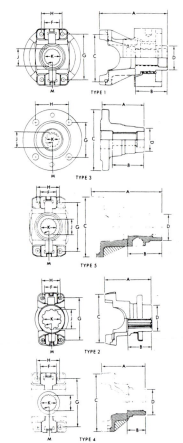

Rear axle universal joint flange assembly.

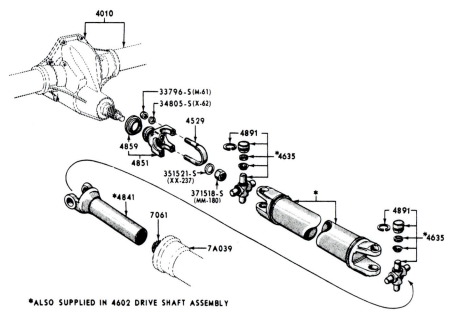

*ALSO SUPPLIED IN 4602 DRIVE SHAFT ASSEMBLY

Power is transmitted from the transmission to the rear axle via a cylindrical steel propeller shaft or driveshaft. Because the rear axle is part of the suspension system, a universal joint at each end of the driveshaft allows for misalignment between the two units as the tires follow the contour of the road. The six-cylinder-equipped Mustang had a smaller-diameter driveshaft compared to a V-8-powered car. The front slip yoke is keyed to the transmission family. The rear yoke or pinion flange is keyed to the rear axle assembly.

238

MUSTANG DRIVESHAFT/REAR AXLE UNIVERSAL JOINT FLANGE DIMENSION CHART

Part Number	A	B	C	D	F	G	H	J	K	Splines
C2DZ-4851-A	2-15/16"	1-15/64"		1-21/32"	1"	2-7/32"	1-23/64"	1-1/64"	1-5/16"	23
D2ZF-4851-A	2-15/16"	1-15/64"		1-21/32"	1"	2-7/32"	1-23/64"	1-1/64"	1-5/16"	23
C3OZ-4851-A	4-13/32"	2-5/8"	3-7/32"	1-13/16"	1-1/8"	2-31/32"	1-37/64"	1-7/64"	1-1/64"	25
C3AZ-4851-L	5-1/16"	2-27/64"	3-7/32"	1-13/16"	1-1/8"	2-31/32"	1-37/64"	1-15/64"	1-9/64"	28
D2SZ-4851-A	5-1/16"			3-5/8"	1-13/16"	3-5/16"	1-37/64"	1-15/64"	1-9/64"	28
D2OZ-4851-A	4-25/32"	2-9/64"	3-5/8"	1-23/64"	1-1/8"	3-5/16"	1-37/64"	1-15/64"	1-9/64"	28

Note: Use with illustration labled: Flange Assy.- Rear Axle Universal Joint.

MUSTANG DRIVESHAFT/REAR AXLE UNIVERSAL JOINT FLANGE ASSEMBLY APPLICATION CHART

Year	Ring Gear	Identification	Part Number	Type
65/68	7-1/4	WCY	C2DZ-4851-A	2
		(exc. R,AA,AJ)		
65/70	7-1/4	WCY-R,AA,AJ	D2ZF-4851-A	2
65/70	8	WCZ,WDJ	C3OZ-4851-A	2
65/70	9		C3AZ-4851-L	2
67/71	9	28 spline axles	D2SZ-4851-A	5
68/71	9	31 spline axles	D2OZ-4851-A	4

Note: Use with illustration labled: Flange Assy.- Rear Axle Universal Joint.

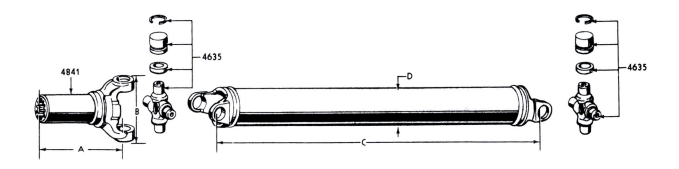

Typical 1965-1970 Mustang driveshaft, slip yoke, and universal joints.

Year	Engine	Transmission Type	Yoke Code	Yoke Type	Yoke Part Number	Notes	Driveshaft Diam.	Driveshaft Length	U-Joint Front	U-Joint Rear
65	170,200	3-S, 4-S	5	2	C1UZ-4841-A		2-1/2	51	J	J
65	170,200	C4	14	1	C5ZZ-4841-B		2-1/2	51	J	J
65	200	C4	6	2	C5DZ-4841-A		2-3/4	50-25/32	M	L
65	289	3-S, 4-S	6	2	C5DZ-4841-A	1	2-3/4	50-25/32	M	L
65	289	3-S, 4-S	7	2	C5DZ-4841-B	2	2-3/4	50-25/32	M	L
65	260,289	C4	6	2	C5DZ-4841-A	3	2-3/4	51-1/16	M	L
65	289 HiPo	4-S	7	2	C5DZ-4841-B	4	2-3/4	49-23/64	M	L
65	289 HiPo	4-S	3	2	C3AZ-4841-D	5	2-3/4	49-23/64	C	D
66	200	3-S	5	2	C1UZ-4841-A		2-1/2	49-63/64	J	J
66	200	4-S	5	2	C1UZ-4841-A		2-1/2	51	J	J
66	200	C4	6	2	C5DZ-4841-A		2-3/4	50-25/32	M	L
66	289	3-S, 4-S	6	2	C5DZ-4841-A	6	2-3/4	50-25/32	M	L
66	289	C4	6	2	C5DZ-4841-A	6	2-3/4	51-1/16	M	L
66	289	3-S, 4-S	6	2	C5DZ-4841-A	7	2-3/4	49-23/64	M	L
67	200	3-S	14	2	C5ZZ-4841-B		2-1/2	51	J	J
67	200	C4	3	4	C3AZ-4841-D		2-3/4	50-31/32	E	F
67	289	C4, 3-S, 4-S	3	4	C3AZ-4841-D	6	3	50-31/32	E	F
67	289	C4	4	2	C3AZ-4841-G	7	3	50-1/64	G	H
67	390	3-S, 4-S	4	2	C3AZ-4841-G	8	3	50-1/64	G	H
67	390	C6	16	2	C7SZ-4841-A	8	3-1/2	46-19/32	G	H
67	289,428	4-S	16	2	C7SZ-4841-A	9	3	50-1/64	G	H
68	289	C4, 4-S	4	2	C3AZ-4841-G	8	3	50-1/64	G	H
68	390	3-S, 4-S	4	2	C3AZ-4841-G	8	3	50-1/64	G	H
68	390,428CJ	C6	16	2	C7SZ-4841-A		3-1/2	46-19/32	G	H
68	200	3-S	14	2	C5ZZ-4841-B		2-1/2	51	J	J
68	200	C4	3	4	C3AZ-4841-D		3	50-31/32	E	F
68	289-2V,302	C4, 3-S, 4-S	3	4	C3AZ-4841-D	10	3	50-31/32	E	F
68	289-2V,302	C4, 3-S, 4-S	3	4	C3AZ-4841-D	11	3	50-7/32	E	F
68	428 CJ	4-S	3	2	C3AZ-4841-D		3	50	G	H

Notes:
1 From 12/15/64. Except HiPo
2 Before 12/15/64. Except HiPo
3 Mechanics Type. Except HiPo
4 From 10/5/64
5 Before 10/5/64
6 2V & 4V Except HiPo
7 HiPo
8 4V
9 Shelby GT-350, GT-500
10 Except GT
11 GT

Note: The drive shaft and slip yoke illustrations must be included with this chart

Year	Engine	Transmission Type	Yoke Code	Yoke Type	Yoke Part Number	Notes	Driveshaft Diam.	Driveshaft Length	U-Joint Front	U-Joint Rear
69	200	3-S	14	2	C5ZZ-4841-B		2-1/2	51	J	J
69	200	C4	3	4	C3AZ-4841-D	1	3	50-31/32	E	F
69	200,302	C4, 3-S, 4-S	3	4	C3AZ-4841-D	2	3	50-31/32	E	F
69	250	C4, 3-S	3	4	C3AZ-4841-D		3	50-11/16	E	F
69	302	C4, 3-S, 4-S	3	4	C3AZ-4841-D	3	3	50-7/32	E	F
69	250	C4	3	4	C3AZ-4841-D		3	50-7/32	E	F
69	351	3-S, 4-S	3	4	C3AZ-4841-D		3	50-7/32	E	F
69	351	FMX	2	4	C3AZ-4841-A		3	50-5/8	E	F
69	390	3-S, 4-S	4	2	C3AZ-4841-G	4	3	50-1/64	G	H
69	Boss 302	3-S, 4-S	4	2	C3AZ-4841-G	4	3	50-1/64	G	H
69	390,428	C6	16	2	C7SZ-4841-A		3-1/2	46-1932	G	H
69	428	4-S	16	2	C7SZ-4841-A		3	50	G	H
69	Boss 429	4-S	16	2	C7SZ-4841-A		3	50-7/8	G	H
70	200,250	C4, 3-S	3	4	C3AZ-4841-D		3	50-11/16	E	F
70	200,302	C4, 3-S, 4-S	3	4	C3AZ-4841-D	1	3	50-31/32	E	F
70	351	C4, 3-S, 4-S	3	4	C3AZ-4841-D	5	3	50-7/32	E	F
70	351	FMX	2	4	C3AZ-4841-A	5	3	50-5/8	E	F
70	Boss 302	4-S	4	2	C3AZ-4841-G	6	3	50-1/64	G	H
70	351-4V	4-S	4	2	C3AZ-4841-G	6	3	50-1/64	G	H
70	351	FMX	16	2	C7SZ-4841-A	6	3	50-5/8	G	H
70	428	C6	16	2	C7SZ-4841-A		3-1/2	46-19/32	G	H
70	428	4-S	16	2	C7SZ-4841-A		3	50	G	H
70	Boss 429	4-S	16	2	C7SZ-4841-A		3	50-7/8	G	H

Notes:
1 7-1/4" Ring Gear
2 7-1/4" Ring Gear, Except Boss
3 8-3/4" Ring Gear, Except Boss
4 Boss 4-Speed only
5 w/ 28 spline axles
6 w/ 31 spline axles

Note: The drive shaft and slip yoke illustrations must be included with this chart

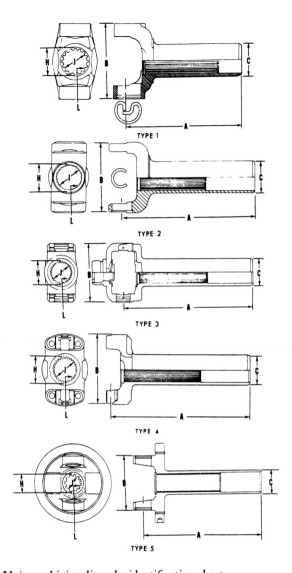

TYPE 1

TYPE 2

TYPE 3

TYPE 4

TYPE 5

Universal joint slip yoke identification chart.

MUSTANG UNIVERSAL JOINT CODES AND DESCRIPTIONS CHART

Part Number	U-Joint Code	Type
C3AZ-4635-E	C	Dana (Spicer) or Ford-1260, 3-15/16" span
C3AZ-4635-F	D	Dana (Spicer) or Ford-1260, 3-15/16" span
C3AZ-4635-E	E	Cleveland Steel-1310, 3-1/4" span
C3AZ-4635-F	F	Cleveland Steel-1310, 3-1/4" span
C3AZ-4635-G	G	Cleveland Steel-1330, 3-5/8" span
C3AZ-4635-H	H	Cleveland Steel-1330, 3-5/8" span
C3UZ-4635-B	J	Dana (Spicer)-1100, 2-21/32" span
C5DZ-4635-A	L	Mechanics-1260, 3-15/32" span
C5DZ-4635-B	M	Mechanics-1260, 3-15/32" span

This chart correlates with the Universal Joint Slip Yoke Identification Chart,
the Universal Joint Identification Illustration,
and the Mustang Driveshaft Assembly Application Chart.

MUSTANG UNIVERSAL JOINT IDENTIFICATION CHART

Part Number	U-Joint Code	Industry Designation	A	B	C	D	E	F	G	H	Type
C3AZ-4635-E	C	1260	3-15/32"	3-15/32"	2-31/32"	2-31/32"	1-1/16"	1-1/16"	19/32"	9/16"	D
C3AZ-4635-F	D	1260	3-15/32"	3-15/32"	2-31/32"	2-31/32"	1-1/16"	1-1/8"	19/32"	9/16"	D
C3AZ-4635-E	E	1310	3-1/4"	3-1/4"	3"	3"	1-1/16"	1-1/16"	11/16"	17/32"	C
C3AZ-4635-F	F	1310	3-1/4"	3-1/4"	3"	3"	1-1/16"	1-1/8"	11/16"	17/32"	C
C3AZ-4635-G	G	1330	3-5/8"	3-5/8"	3-13/32"	3-13/32"	1-1/16"	1-1/16"	11/16"	19/32"	C
C3AZ-4635-H	H	1330	3-5/8"	3-5/8"	3-13/32"	3-13/32"	1-1/16"	1-1/8"	11/16"	19/32"	C
C3UZ-4635-B	J	1100	2-21/32"	2-21/32"	2-13/64"	2-1/2"	1"	1"	35/64"	17/32"	D
C5DZ-4635-A	L	1260	3-15/32"	3-15/32"	2-31/32"	2-31/32"	1"	1-1/8"	19/32"	29/64"	M
C5DZ-4635-B	M	1260	3-15/32"	3-15/32"	2-31/32"	2-31/32"	1"	1"	19/32"	29/64"	M

Types:
D   Dana (Spicer) or Ford
C   Cleveland
M   Mechanics

This chart correlates with the Universal Joint Slip Yoke Identification Chart,
the Universal Joint Identification Illustration,
and the Mustang Driveshaft Assembly Application Chart.

MUSTANG DRIVESHAFT SLIP YOKE SPECIFICATIONS CHART

Part Number	Slip Yoke Code	A	B	C	H	J	Splines	Type
C3AZ-4841-A	2	8-7/32"	3-1/2"	1-11/16"	1-3/8"	1-17/64"	31	1
C3AZ-4841-D	3	8-3/32"	3-1/2"	1-1/2"	1-7/32"	1-3/32"	28	1
C3AZ-4841-G	4	8-7/32"	3-7/8"	1-1/2"	1-7/32"	1-3/32"	28	1
C1UZ-4841-A	5	5-29/32"	2-15/32"	1-3/8"	1-7/64"	63/64"	25	2
C5DZ-4841-A	6	8-3/32"	3-3/16"	1-1/2"	1-7/32"	1-3/32"	28	2
C5DZ-4841-B	7	8-1/4"	3-3/16"	1-1/2"	1-7/64"	63/64"	25	2
C5ZZ-4841-B	14	5-29/32"		1-1/2"	1-7/32"	1-3/32"	28	2
C7SZ-4841-A	16	8-5/32"	3-29/32"	1-11/16"	1-3/8"	1-17/64"	31	1

This chart correlates with the Universal Joint Slip Yoke Identification Chart,
the Universal Joint Identification Illustration,
and the Mustang Driveshaft Assembly Application Chart.

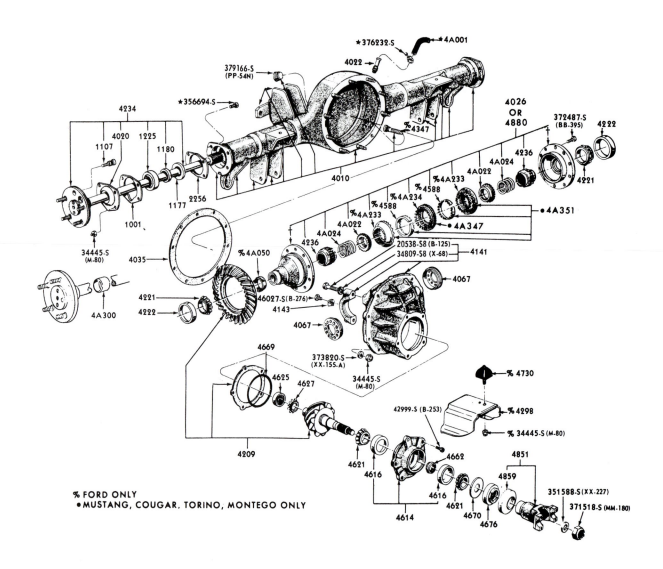

★376232-S
4A001
4022
379166-S (PP-54N)
4026 OR 4880
372487-S (BB-395)
4222
★356694-S
4234
4020 1225
1107 1180
4347
4236
4A024
4A022
4221
4010
%4A233
%4A234
4588
4A022
%4A233
%4A234
4588
4A024
4A022
4236
4A351
4A347
20538-S8 (B-125)
34809-S8 (X-68)
4141
4067
1177 2256
1001
34445-S (M-80)
4035
%4A050
46027-S (B-276)
4143
373820-S (XX-155-A)
34445-S (M-80)
4067
4A300
4221
4222
4669
4625 4627
4730
4298
42999-S (B-253)
34445-S (M-80)
4209
4621
4616
4662
4851
4859
4616
4621
4614
4670
4676
351588-S (XX-227)
371518-S (MM-180)

% FORD ONLY
• MUSTANG, COUGAR, TORINO, MONTEGO ONLY

All V-8-powered Mustangs were equipped with axle housings with a removable gear carrier. That means the cast-iron center housing containing the ring and pinion gears can be removed from the rear axle as an assembly. Unlike the integral rear axle, the ring and pinion gears, the pinion carrier, and the associated bearings remain in adjustment or "set up" within the portable center housing. Besides having a removable or integral housing, all Ford rear axles are categorized by the diameter of the ring gear. The ring gear in an integral housing will measure $6^3/4$, $7^1/4$, or $7^3/4$in. Only the $7^1/4$in integral rear axle was installed under a Mustang.

Rear axles having a removable carrier were manufactured in two sizes. The smallest was equipped with an 8in diameter ring gear and the larger a 9in gear. The 8 and 9in axles are similar in appearance, assembly, and fundamental operation, but share few interchangeable components. Virtually each piece of a 9in rear axle is larger and stronger compared to its little brother. The steel "banjo" housing, so called because of its shape, is the basic component of an 8 or 9in rear axle. The transfer of power through the differential is exactly the same as the integral rear axle housing.

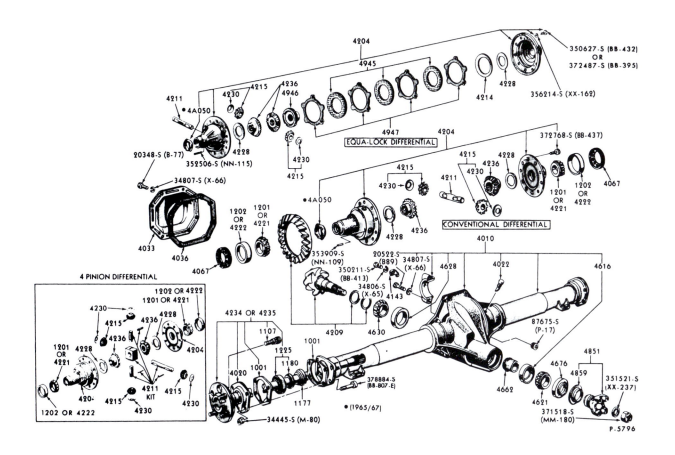

4204
4945
4204
350627-S (BB-432)
OR
372487-S (BB-395)
4228
4214
356214-S (XX-162)
4211
4230
4215
4236
4946
4947
4204
372768-S (BB-437)
• 4A050
EQUA-LOCK DIFFERENTIAL
4215
4228
20348-S (B-77)
4228
4230
4215
4230
4211
4236
1202
OR
4222
4067
352506-S (NN-115)
4215
1201
OR
4221
34807-S (X-66)
• 4A050
CONVENTIONAL DIFFERENTIAL
4230
4228
4236
1202
OR
4222
1201
OR
4221
4010
4033
353909-S
(NN-109)
4228
4236
4628
4022
4616
4036
20522-S
(B89)
34807-S
(X-66)
4067
350211-S
(BB-413)
34806-S
(X-65)
4143
4 PINION DIFFERENTIAL
87675-S
(P-17)
1202 OR 4222
4230
1201 OR 4221
4228
4234 OR 4235
4209
4630
4851
4215
4236
4204
1107
4676
4859
4236
1225
1001
4662
4621
351521-S
(XX-237)
1201
OR
4221
4228
4020
1001
1180
378884-S
(BB-807-E)
371518-S
(MM-180)
420-
4211
KIT
4215
4215
4230
• (1965/67)
1202 OR 4222
4230
1177
34445-S (M-80)
P-5796

Ford manufactured two types of rear axle housings between 1965 and 1970. The type used under lightweight economy cars powered by six-cylinder engines like the Falcon, the Mustang, and the Fairlane housed the ring and pinion gears within the rear axle assembly, and was appropriately called an integral rear axle. It is a lightweight unit consisting of a one-piece cast-iron differential center housing outfitted with steel axle tubes that are pressed into place and tack welded. The center housing is machined to support the ring gear carrier and pinion gear. The outboard ends of the axle tubes are designed to accept a bearing, which supports the outer end of each axle. A four bolt flange, welded to the outer end of each tube, accommodates the brake backing plate and a bearing retainer. As with all modern-day differentials, power is transmitted from the pinion gear to the ring gear

(4209), which rotates the carrier housing (4204). Each axle is attached to the carrier housing via an internally splined "side gear" (4236). The side gears mesh with the spider gears (4215), which are pinned to the carrier housing with a case-hardened steel rod (4211). The axles in a non-locking rear axle or conventional differential, rotate independently from each other. Power delivered by the driveshaft will be transmitted to the wheel with the least rolling resistance. An EquaLock differential incorporates a locking system that consists of three double-faced clutch discs, four friction discs, and a spring-steel bevel washer that, when assembled in the special ring gear carrier, locks both axles together as power is applied. Under light load conditions the clutches will slip, thus allowing each axle to rotate independently.

243

Mustang Differential Case Assembly Application Chart

Year	Axle Ident.	Notes	Part Number	Description
65	WCL & WCZ		D0OZ-4204-A	w/ 8" R/G, medium differential bearing, 2 pinion, non-Locking
65/69	WDJ		C4OZ-4204-B	w/ 8" R/G, medium differential bearing, 2 pinion Equalock
69/70	WFL		C9OZ-4204-F	w/ 8" R/G, medium differential bearing, 2 pinion Traction-Lok
65/70	WCZ & WES	1	D0OZ-4204-D	w/ 9" R/G, medium differential bearing, 2 pinion non-Locking
67/70	WES	1	C2AZ-4204-K	w/ 9" R/G, large differential bearing,
				2 or 4 pinion non-Locking, w/ 28 spline axles
69/70	WES	1	C9OZ-4204-B	w/ 9" R/G, large differential bearing,
				4 pinion non-Locking w/ 31 spline axles
67/68	WES		C4AZ-4204-F	w/ 9" R/G, large differential bearing,
				2 or 4 pinion Equalock w/ 28 spline axles
				7/16" or 1/2" diameter bolt holes optional.
69/70	WFB	1	C0OZ-4204-C	w/ 9" R/G, large differential bearing,
				4 pinion Traction-Lok w/ 28 spline axles
69/70	WFD	1	C0OZ-4204-C	w/ 9" R/G, large differential bearing,
				4 pinion Traction-Lok w/ 31 spline axles
70/72	All	2	D0OZ-2404-D	w/ 9" R/G, slim line differential bearing, 4 pinion non-Locking
				w/ 31 spline axles. Includes C9AZ-4221-A bearing,
				C9AZ-4222-A cup, (2) C9AZ-4228-A washers.
		2	D2AZ-4204-D	w/ 9" R/G, slim line differential bearing,
				2 pinion non-Locking w/ 28 spline axles.
		2	D0OZ-4204-C	w/ 9" R/G, slim line differential bearing,
				2 or 4 pinion Traction-Lok w/ 28 or 31 spline axles.
				Includes C9AZ-4221-A bearing, C9AZ-4222-A cup.
		2	D0O0Z-4204-E	w/ 9" R/G, slim line differential bearing,
				no-spin 2 pinion w/ 31 spline axles.
				Includes C9AZ-4221-A bearing, C9AZ-4222-A cup.
70	WFU-E	1	D0OZ-4204-B	w/ 9" R/G, large differential bearing,
				no-spin differential w/ 31 spline axles.
70	WFU-E	2	D0OZ-4204-E	w/ 9" R/G, slim line differential bearing,
				no-spin Locker w/ 31 spline axles.
65/68	WCY		C4DZ-4204-A	w/ 7-1/4" R/G, small differential bearing, 2 pinion Equalock
66	WCZ		C4DZ-4204-E	w/ 9" R/G, medium differential bearing,
				2 pinion Equalock w/ 28 spline axles.
68	WES-R		C4DZ-4204-E	w/ 9" R/G, medium differential bearing,
				2 pinion Equalock w/ 28 spline axles.
65/70	WCY		C1DW-4204-B	w/ 7-1/4" R/G, small differential bearing,
				2 or 4 pinion non-Locking.

Notes:

1 Used before 5/13/70
2 Used after 5/13/70

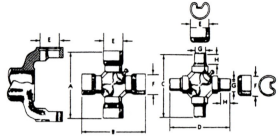

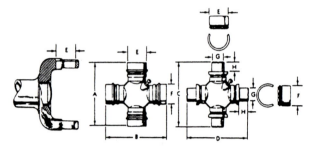

DANA (SPICER) OR FORD DESIGN

MECHANICS, CLEVELAND STEEL OR SACO DESIGN

Universal joint identification chart.

Mustang Rear Axle Differential Side Gear Kit Chart

YEAR	MODEL	AXLE IDENT.	PART NUMBER	DESCRIPTION
65/68	8", 9" R/G		C9AZ-4236-B	28 splines- 4 omitted- with hub.
				Consists of (2) C2AW-4236-A gears
				(Use 1 piece for locking axle) and
				(2) C9OZZ-4228-A washers.
70	8 cylinder 427	WFU-D, E	C4AZ-4236-A	31 splines- 4 omitted- with hub.
	Exc. locking axle			Consists of (2) C2AW-4236-A gears and
				(2) C9OZZ-4228-A washers.
69/70	8", 9" R/G		C9AZ-4236-A	With locking differential- 28 spline incl.
				(1) C9OW-4236-A gear- 21/32" long,
				(1) C9OW-4236-B gear- 1 3/16" long,
				(2) C9OZ-4228-A washers.
			C9AZ-4236-B	With std. differential- 28 spline includes
				(2) C9OW-4236-B gears 1 3/16" long,
				(2) C9OZ-4228-A washers.
65/70	6-3/4", 7", 7-1/4" R/G		C1DZ-4236-C	24 splines- consists of:
				(2) DODZ 4236-A gears and
				(2) CODW 4228-A washers.

Mustang Rear Axle Differential Assembly Application Chart

YEAR	AXLE TAG I.D.	PART NUMBER	RATIO	GEAR SIZE	LOCKING	DESCRIPTION
67	WCZ-V,V2	C7OW-4200-F	2.79	8	NO	
67	WCZ-F,F2	C7OW-4200-G	3.00	8	NO	
68	WCZ-W	C7OW-4200-H	3.25	8	NO	
68	WFD-B,D,D2	C8OW-4200-C	3.91	9	YES	
69/70	WES-AC	C9OW-4200-D	3.00	9	NO	
69	WES-T,T1,T2	C9OW-4200-H	2.75	9	NO	
69	WES-AA	C9OW-4200-G	3.00	9	NO	
69	WES-AD,AD2	C9OW-4200-K	3.25	9		
69	WFB-C,C2	C9OW-4200-V	3.25	9	YES	TRACTION-LOK
70	WFL-A,A2	C0OW-4200-A	3.00	8	YES	TRACTION-LOK

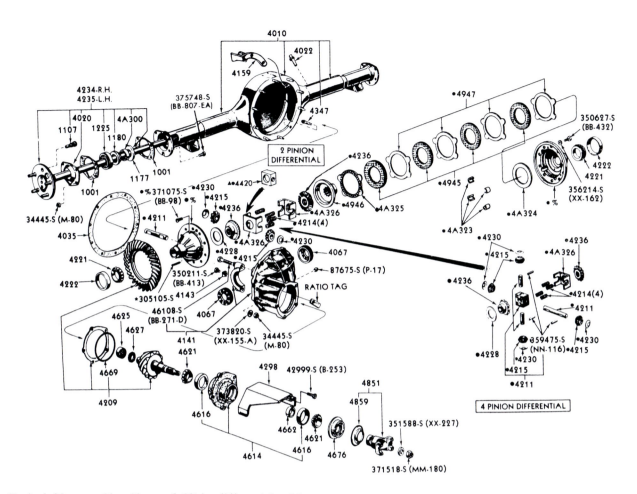

Typical Mustang 8in, 9in, and 9³/8in differential with Traction-Lok.

MUSTANG REAR AXLE SEAL ASSEMBLY CHART

YEAR	MODEL	AXLE IDENT.	PART NUMBER	DESCRIPTION
65/67	9", 9 3/8" R/G	Exc. WER	D1UZ-4676-A	1 13/16" I.D.- 3 5/16"" flange dia.,
				3" seal dia.- 1/2" thick-double lip seal
68/70	9", 9 3/8" R/G	Exc. WER	D1UZ-4676-A	1 13/16" I.D.- 3 5/16"" flange dia.,
				3" seal dia.- 1/2" thick
65/67	7 1/4", 8" R/G		C2OZ-4676-B	1 13/16" I.D.- 2 15/16" flange dia.,
				2 5/8" seal dia. - 29/64" thick
68	7", 8" R/G		C2OZ-4676-B	1 13/16" I.D.- 2 15/16" flange dia.,
				2 5/8" seal dia. - 29/64" thick
65/69	7 1/4" R/G		C1UZ-4676-C	1 21/32" I.D.- 2 5/8" O.D.- 29/64"
				thick- use with 1100 univ. joints only
68/70	9", 9 3/8" R/G	Exc. WER	C2AZ-4676-B	
	7", 8" R/G		C2OZ-4676-B	

MUSTANG REAR AXLE PINION BEARING RETAINER ASSEMBLY CHART

YEAR	MODEL APPLICATION	RETAINER AND CUP ASSEMBLY	CUPS	BEARINGS
65/70	7 1/4" R/G--	None required	CODW-4616-A	CODW-4621-A
	integral carrier		TBAA-4616-A	C1DZ-4630-A
65/67	8" R/G	C6OZ-4614-B	CODW-4616-A	CODW-4621-A
68/70	8" R/G	C6OZ-4614-A	CODW-4616-A	CODW-4621-A
65/70	9" R/G- 28 spline shaft	D2SZ-4614-A	B7A-4616-A	B7A-4621-A
67/70	9" R/G- 31 spline shaft	C3AZ-4614-B	B7A-4616-A	B7A-4621-A
			TBAA-4616-A	TBAA-4621-A

MUSTANG REAR AXLE DIFFERENTIAL BEARING CONE CHART - ROLLER and CUP

YEAR	MODEL	CONE-ROLLER	CUP	DESCRIPTION
65/70	7 1/4" R/G	C1UW-4221-A	C1UW-4222-A	S - small size
	7 3/4", 8" R/G	B7A-4221-A	B7A-4222-A	M - medium size
	9" R/G Before 5/13/70	B7A-4221-A	B7A-4222-A	M - medium size
	From 5/13/70	B7A-4221-B	B7A-4222-B	L - large size
70	9" R/G From 5/13/70	C9AZ-4221-A	C9AZ-4222-A	SL - slim-line size

MUSTANG REAR AXLE DIFFERENTIAL PINION KIT CHART

YEAR	MODEL	AXLE IDENTIFICATION	PART NUMBER	DESCRIPTION
65/69	8", 9" R/G		C8OZ-4215-A	(2) C1AW-4215-C pinions
	with equalock axles			(2) B7A-4230-A washers
65/72	8", 9" R/G	WER-F, G, H	C9AZ-4215-A	(2) DOAW-4215-A pinions
	with conventional axles			(2) DOAZ-4230-A washers
68/70	8" and 9" R/G		C8OZ-4215-A	(4) C9OW-4215-A gears
	with traction lok axles			(4) C9OZ-4230-A washers
65/70	7 1/4" R/G		CODZ-4215-C	(2) CODW-4215-C pinions
				(2) CODW-4230-C washers

MUSTANG REAR AXLE SHAFT ASSEMBLY APPLICATION CHART

YEAR	MODEL	AXLE IDENTIFICATION	PART NUMBER	DESCRIPTION
65/66 (U.S. only)	7 1/4" R/G	WCY	#C4DZ-4234-A	24 splines-R.H. 29-15/16"
			#C4DZ-4234-B	L.H. 26 7/16"
65/66 (Can. only)	7 1/4" R/G	WCY	#C4DZ-4234-A	24 splines-R.H. 29-15/16"
			C4DW-4275-A	L.H. 26-7/16"
65/66	8" R/G	WCZ, WDJ	*C2OZ-4234-A	28 splines-R.H. 30-1/8"
			*C2OZ-4235-B	L.H. 26-5/64"
65/66	9" R/G	WCZ	*C5OZ-4234-B	28 splines-R.H. 30-1/8"
			*C5OZ-4234-A	L.H. 26-5/64"
67/69	8", 9" R/G	WCZ, WDJ, WES, WFB	*C6OZ-4234-F	28 splines-R.H. 31-1/8"
	Before 3/15/69		*C9OZ-4234-B	L.H. 27-1/16"
69/70	8", 9" R/G		*C9OZ-4234-A	28 splines-R.H. 31 1/8"
	From 3/15/69		#C6DZ-4234-C	L.H. 27-1/16"
67/70	7 1/4" R/G	WCY	#C6DZ-4234-D	24 splines-R.H. 30-15/16"
			*C9OZ-4234-B	L.H. 27-7/16"
67/70	9" R/G		*C9OZ-4234-D	31 splines-R.H. 31-1/8"
				L.H. 27-1/16"

\# Includes CODZ-1225-C bearing (small).

* Includes DOAZ-1225-A bearing (medium).

MUSTANG REAR AXLE HOUSING ASSEMBLY APPLICATION CHART

YEAR	MODEL	AXLE IDENTIFICATION	PART NUMBER	DESCRIPTION
65/66	7 1/4" R/G	WCY	C4DZ-4010-G	integral carrier
67/69	7 1/4" R/G	WCY	C7ZZ-4010-A	integral carrier
70	7 1/4" R/G	WCY	DOZZ-4010-B	integral carrier
65/66	8" R/G	WCZ,WDJ	C4DZ-4010-F	incl. (1) 378511-S clamp
67/69	8" R/G	WCZ, WDJ	C7ZZ-4010-E	
70	8" R/G	WCZ,WFL	C9ZZ-4010-B	
67/68	9" R/G Before 4/01/68	WES,WFD	DOZZ-4010-C	
68/70	9" R/G From 4/01/68 To 6/01/70	WES,WFB,WFD,WFU	DOZZ-4010-D	
70	9" R/G From 6/01/70 To 9/25/70	WES,WFB,WFD,WFU	DOZZ-4010-E	
70	9" R/G From 9/25/70	WES,WFB,WFD,WFU	D1ZZ-4010-B	

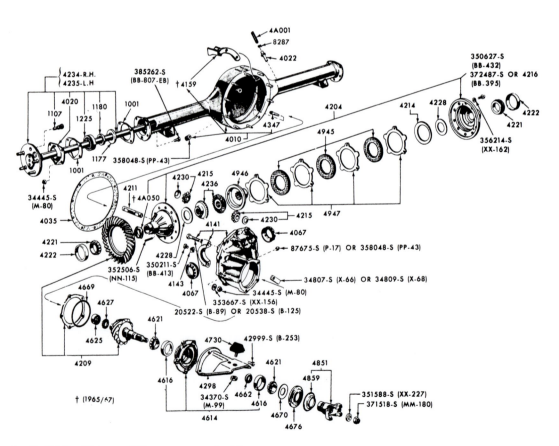

An example of a 7³/₄in, 8³/₄in, and 9in open or non-locking rear axle with removable carrier used in 1965-1970 Mustangs.

246

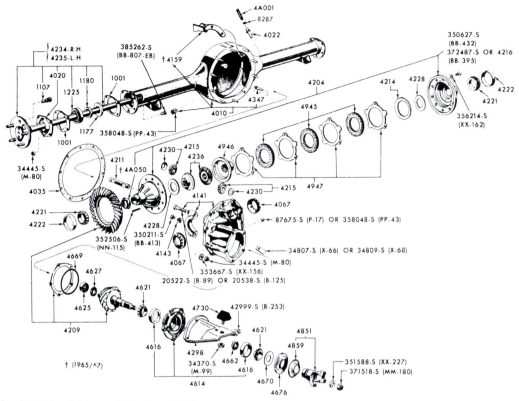

An example of a 7³/₄in, 8³/₄in, and 9in Equa Lock rear axle with removable carrier used in 1965-1970 Mustangs.

MUSTANG RING GEAR and PINION SETS APPLICATION CHART

Year	Ring Gear Diameter	Ratio	Part Number	Number of Teeth Gear	Pinion
65	7-1/4	2.83	C5DZ-4209-C	34	12
65	7-1/4	3.50	C1DZ-4209-Z	35	10
66/70	7-1/4	2.83	C5DZ-4209-C	34	12
69/70	7-1/4	3.08	C9ZZ-4209-A	37	12
65/70	8	2.80/2.79	C4OZ-4209-K	39	14
65/70	8	3.00	C4OZ-4209-H	39	13
65/70	8	3.50	C4OZ-4209-J	35	12
68	8	3.25	C4DZ-4209-D	39	12
65	9	4.11	B7AZ-4209-K	37	9
65/70	9	3.50	C9OZ-4209-A	35	10
65/67	9	3.89	B7AZ-4209-N	35	9
67/70	9	3.00	C0AZ-4209-E	39	13
67/70	9	3.25	B8AZ-4209-C	39	12
68/70	9	2.75	C7AZ-4209-J	44	16
68/70	9	3.91	C8OZ-4209-A	43	11
68/70	9	4.30	C8OZ-4209-B	43	10

Mustang Locking Differential Conversion and Replacment Kits.

1965/69   Part Number: C9OZ-4026-B

Items:	Part Number:	Description
1	B9A-4159-A	Lubricator
1	C4AZ-4204-F	Case
1	C2AW-4236-A	Side Gear
1	C4AZ-4946-A	Hub
1	352506-S	Pin
1	C4AZ-4214-A	Spring
3	B9A2-4945-A	Clutch Plate
1	C2AZ-4236-B	Side Gear
4	B9AZ-4947-A	Clutch Plate
10	350627-S	Bolt-7/16x20
5.5 pints		Lubricant

1965/70   Part Number: C4DZ-4880-B
Notes: (7 & 7-3/4 inch ring gear) Use with integral carrier.

Items:	Part Number:	Description
1	B9A-4159-A	Lubricator
1	C4DZ-4204-A	Case
1	C4DZ-4236-A	Side Gear
1	C4DZ-4946-A	Hub
1	305086-S	Pin
1	C4DZ-4214-A	Spring
3	B9AZ-4945-A	Clutch Plate
1	C4DZ-4236-B	Side Gear
4	C4DZ-4947-A	Clutch Plate
8	379237-S	Bolt-3/8" 24 X 11/64"

Chapter 6

Suspension, Brakes, Steering, Wheels, and Exhaust

The groupings of topics throughout this book are primarily based on Ford's system of categorization within their original parts catalogs. For 1964 to 1970, an enormous variety of drivetrain assemblies and components were utilized in the quest of such myriad goals as ultra economy and rocket-like acceleration. The 1969 Mustang E, a plain six-cylinder SportsRoof, was manufactured with fuel mileage in mind; the 1969 Mach 1 428ci Cobra Jet with the Drag Pack option was intended to spin the shortest time imaginable in quarter-mile competition. Ironically, because weight always remained a strong factor in Ford's drivetrain development programs, the CJ and the E were not that far apart in concept and material.

In between the two extremes, millions of Mustangs were made that represented complete compromise between economy and power. Each of those could have had any number of different drivetrain component combinations depending on engine sizes, handling options, owner preferences, and ease of driveability.

The drivetrain is almost wholly out of sight of the average show judge or auto admirer. But many Mustangs, when restored, are forced to accommodate replacement assemblies, and compatibility of these assemblies or subassemblies is an absolute necessity to the car owner. While compatibility is obviously important in situations of engine swaps, for instance, the replacement of worn slip yokes and U-joints or damaged driveshafts requires exactitude even in "unmodified" cars. That is

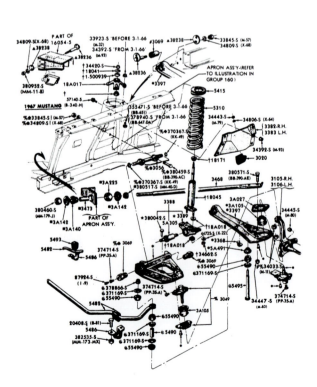

The 1965 Mustang front suspension system.

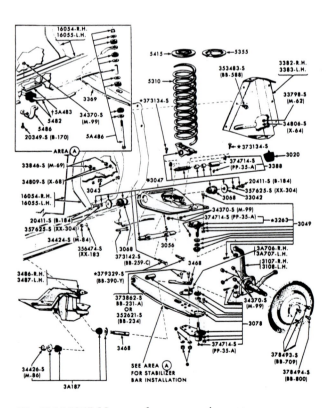

The 1966-1967 Mustang front suspension system.

where the charts and drawings of this chapter will benefit all.

In the realm of the drivetrain, Ford has managed over the years to maintain a surprisingly broad and complete stock of parts. Its decision to keep such parts in the supply system is based upon supply and demand and, obviously, over the years, owners have been interested in keeping a significant number of Mustangs on the road. Hence, the reader may find, in this chapter, part numbers that still apply and that will be, if not perfectly accurate, genuine guidelines for Ford service department personnel in locating needed items.

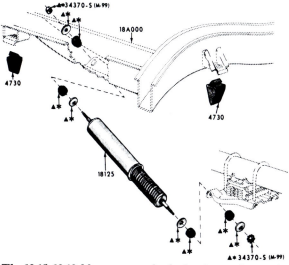

The 1965-1969 Mustang front shock absorber and mounting hardware.

The 1965-1968 Mustang rear shock absorber and mounting hardware.

1964-1/2 Front Spring Application Chart, Hardtops before 8/20/64

CYL/CID	Load	Transmission	Steering	A/C	Marking Stripes	Part Number
6/170	1304	3/S, 4/S, C4	M	N	1 Pink	C5ZZ-5310-A
						r/b C5ZZ-5310-B
6/170	1304	3/S	P	N	1 Pink	C5ZZ-5310-A
						r/b C5ZZ-5310-B
6/170	1369	4/S, C4	P	N	1 Green	C5ZZ-5310-B
6/170	1369	3/S		A	1 Green	C5ZZ-5310-B
6/170	1438	3/S, 4/S, C4	P	A	1 Violet	C5ZZ-5310-D
						r/b C5ZZ-5310-C
6/170	1438	4/S, C4	M	A	1 Violet	C5ZZ-5310-D
						r/b C5ZZ-5310-C
6/200	1279	4/S	M	N	1 Pink	C5ZZ-5310-A
						r/b C5ZZ-5310-B
8/260	1438	3/S, C4	M	N	1 Violet	C5ZZ-5310-D
						r/b C5ZZ-5310-C
8/260	1438	3/S	P	N	1 Violet	C5ZZ-5310-D
						r/b C5ZZ-5310-C
8/260	1438	3/S, 4/S, C4	M	N	1 Red	C5ZZ-5310-F
						r/b C5ZZ-5310-E
8/260	1516	C4	P	N	1 Gray	C5ZZ-5310-C
8/260	1516	3/S, C4	M	A	1 Gray	C5ZZ-5310-C
8/260	1516	3/S, 4/S, C4	M/P	N	1 Brown	C5ZZ-5310-E
8/260	1516	3/S, 4/S, C4	M/P	A	1 Brown	C5ZZ-5310-E
8/260	1516	3/S, C4	P	A	1 Gray	C5ZZ-5310-C
8/289-4V	1438	4/S, C4	M	N	1 Violet	C5ZZ-5310-D
						r/b C5ZZ-5310-C
8/289-4V	1516	4/S, C4	P	N	1 Gray	C5ZZ-5310-C
8/289-4V	1516	4/S, C4	M	A	1 Gray	C5ZZ-5310-C
8/289-4V	1516	4/S, C4	P	A	1 Gray	C5ZZ-5310-C
8/289-4V	1438	4/S	M	N	1 Red	C5ZZ-5310-F
						r/b C5ZZ-5310-E
8/289-4V	1516	4/S	P	N	1 Brown	C5ZZ-5310-E
8/289-4V	1516	4/S	M	A	1 Brown	C5ZZ-5310-E
8/289-4V	1516	4/S	P	A	1 Brown	C5ZZ-5310-E

1964-1/2 Front Spring Application Chart, Convertibles before 8/20/64

CYL/CID	Load	Transmission Types	Steering	A/C	Marking Stripes	Part Number
6/170	1304	3/S, 4/S, C4	M	N	1 Pink	C5ZZ-5310-A
						r/b C5ZZ-5310-B
6/170	1369	3/S, 4/S	P	N	1 Green	C5ZZ-5310-B
6/170	1438	3/S	P	A	1 Violet	C5ZZ-5310-D
						r/b C5ZZ-5310-C
6/170	1438	C4	P	N	1 Violet	C5ZZ-5310-D
						r/b C5ZZ-5310-C
6/170	1438	3/S, 4/S, C4	M	A	1 Violet	C5ZZ-5310-D
						r/b C5ZZ-5310-C
6/170	1516	4/S, C4	P	A	1 Gray	C5ZZ-5310-C
8/260	1516	3/S, C4	M/P	N	1 Gray	C5ZZ-5310-C
8/260	1516	3/S, 4/S, C4	M/P	N	1 Brown	C5ZZ-5310-E
8/260	1516	3/S, 4/S, C4	M/P	A	1 Brown	C5ZZ-5310-E
8/260	1516	3/S, C4	M/P	A	1 Gray	C5ZZ-5310-C
8/289-4V	1516	3/S, C4	M/P	A	1 Gray	C5ZZ-5310-C
8/289-4V	1516	4/S, C4	M/P	N	1 Brown	C5ZZ-5310-E
8/289-4V	1516	3/S, 4/S	M/P	N	1 Gray	C5ZZ-5310-C
8/289-4V	1516	4/S, C4	M/P	A	1 Brown	C5ZZ-5310-E

1965 Mustang Front Spring Application Chart, 8/20/64-4/1/65
Hardtop and Fastback models.

CYL/CID	Model	Load	Transmission	Steering	A/C	Marking Stripes	Part Number
6/200	HT/FB	1279	3/S	M	N	1 Pink	C5ZZ-5310-A
							r/b C5ZZ-5310-B
6/200	HT	1279	4/S	M	N	1 Pink	C5ZZ-5310-A
							r/b C5ZZ-5310-B
6/200	HT/FB	1344	3/S, 4/S, C4	P	N	1 Green	C5ZZ-5310-B
6/200	HT/FB	1344	3/S	M	A	1 Green	C5ZZ-5310-B
6/200		1344	4/S, C4	M	N	1 Green	C5ZZ-5310-B
6/200	HT	1344	4/S	M	A	1 Green	C5ZZ-5310-B
6/200	HT	1344	C4	M	N	1 Green	C5ZZ-5310-B
6/200	HT/FB	1413	3/S, 4/S, C4	P	A	1 Violet	C5ZZ-5310-D
							r/b C5ZZ-5310-C
6/200	HT/FB	1413	C4	M	A	1 Violet	C5ZZ-5310-D
							r/b C5ZZ-5310-C
6/200	FB	1413	4/S	M	A	1 Violet	C5ZZ-5310-D
							r/b C5ZZ-5310-C
8/289	HT/FB	1413	3/S	M	N	1 Violet	C5ZZ-5310-D
							r/b C5ZZ-5310-C
8/289	HT/FB	1490	3/S	P	N	1 Gray	C5ZZ-5310-C
8/289	HT/FB	1490	3/S	M	A	1 Gray	C5ZZ-5310-C
8/289	HT/FB	1490	4/S, C4	M/P	N	1 Gray	C5ZZ-5310-C
8/289	HT/FB	1490	3/S, 4/S, C4	P	A	1 Gray	C5ZZ-5310-E
8/289	HT/FB	1490	4/S, C4	M	A	1 Gray	C5ZZ-5310-E
8/289-4V	HT/FB	1413	3/S, 4/S	M	N	1 Red	C5ZZ-5310-F
							r/b C5ZZ-5310-E
8/289-4V	HT/FB	1491	3/S, 4/S	P	N	1 Brown	C5ZZ-5310-E
8/289-4V	HT/FB	1491	3/S, 4/S	M	A	1 Brown	C5ZZ-5310-E
8/289-4V	HT/FB	1491	3/S, 4/S	P	A	1 Brown	C5ZZ-5310-E

1965 Mustang Front Spring Application Chart, from 4/1/65

CYL/CID	Model	Load	Transmission	Steering	A/C	Marking Stripes	Part Number
6/200	HT/FB	1279	3/S, 4/S, C4	M	N	1 Pink	C5ZZ-5310-A
							r/b C5ZZ-5310-B
6/200	HT/FB	1344	3/S, 4/S, C4	M/P	A	1 Green	C5ZZ-5310-B
6/200	HT/FB	1344	3/S, 4/S, C4	P	N	1 Green	C5ZZ-5310-B
8/289	HT/FB	1413	3/S, 4/S, C4	M/P	N	1 Violet	C5ZZ-5310-D
							r/b C5ZZ-5310-C
8/289	HT/FB	1491	3/S, 4/S, C4	M/P	A	1 Gray	C5ZZ-5310-C
8/289 K	HT/FB	1413	3/S, 4/S	M	N	1 Red	C5ZZ-5310-E
							r/b C5ZZ-5310-E
8/289 GT	HT/FB	1413	C4	M/P	N	1 Red	C5ZZ-5310-F
							r/b C5ZZ-5310-E
8/289 GT	HT/FB	1491	3/S, 4/S, C4	M/P	A	1 Brown	C5ZZ-5310-E
6/200	Conv	1279	3/S	M	N	1 Pink	C5ZZ-5310-A
							r/b C5ZZ-5310-B
6/200	Conv	1344	4/S, C4	M/P	N	1 Green	C5ZZ-5310-B
6/200	Conv	1344	3/S	P	N	1 Green	C5ZZ-5310-B
6/200	Conv	1413	3/S, 4/S, C4	M/P	A	1 Violet	C5ZZ-5310-D
							r/b C5ZZ-5310-C
8/289	Conv	1491	3/S, 4/S, C4	M	N	1 Gray	C5ZZ-5310-C
8/289	Conv	1491	3/S, 4/S, C4	M	A	1 Gray	C5ZZ-5310-C
8/289	Conv	1491	4/S, C4	P	N	1 Gray	C5ZZ-5310-C
8/289	Conv	1491	3/S, 4/S, C4	P	A	1 Gray	C5ZZ-5310-C
8/289 K	Conv	1491	3/S, 4/S	M	N	1 Brown	C5ZZ-5310-E
8/289 GT	Conv	1491	3/S, 4/S, C4	M	N	1 Brown	C5ZZ-5310-E

1965 Mustang Front Spring Application Chart, 8/20/64-4/1/65
Convertibles.

CYL/CID	Model	Load	Transmission	Steering	A/C	Marking Stripes	Part Number
6/200	Conv	1344	3/S	M/P	N	1 Green	C5ZZ-5310-B
6/200	Conv	1344	4/S	M	N	1 Green	C5ZZ-5310-B
6/200	Conv	1344	C4	M	N	1 Green	C5ZZ-5310-B
6/200	Conv	1490	4/S	M	N	1 Gray	C5ZZ-5310-C
6/200	Conv	1490	C4	P	A	1 Gray	C5ZZ-5310-C
6/200	Conv	1413	3/S	M/P	A	1 Violet	C5ZZ-5310-D
							r/b C5ZZ-5310-C
6/200	Conv	1413	4/S	P	N	1 Violet	C5ZZ-5310-D
							r/b C5ZZ-5310-C
6/200	Conv	1413	4/S	M	A	1 Violet	C5ZZ-5310-D
							r/b C5ZZ-5310-C
6/200	Conv	1413	C4	P	N	1 Violet	C5ZZ-5310-D
							r/b C5ZZ-5310-C
6/200	Conv	1413	C4	M	A	1 Violet	C5ZZ-5310-D
							r/b C5ZZ-5310-C
8/289	Conv	1490	3/S, 4/S, C4	M	N	1 Gray	C5ZZ-5310-C
8/289	Conv	1490	3/S	P	N	1 Gray	C5ZZ-5310-C
8/289	Conv	1490	3/S, 4/S	M	A	1 Gray	C5ZZ-5310-C
8/289	Conv	1490	3/S, 4/S, C4	P	A	1 Gray	C5ZZ-5310-C
8/289	Conv	1490	4/S, C4	P	N	1 Gray	C5ZZ-5310-C
8/289-4V	Conv	1516	3/S, 4/S	M/P	A	1 Brown	C5ZZ-5310-E
8/289-4V	Conv	1491	3/S, 4/S	M/P	N	1 Brown	C5ZZ-5310-E

1966 Mustang Front Spring Application Chart, from 2/14/66
(Hardtops and Fastbacks, Without Thermactor)

CYL/CID	Model	Load	Transmission	Steering	A/C	Marking Stripes	Part Number
6/200	HT/FB	1279	3/S, 4/S, C4	M/P	N	1 Pink	C5ZZ-5310-A
							r/b C5ZZ-5310-B
6/200	HT/FB	1279	3/S	M	A	1 Pink	C5ZZ-5310-B
							r/b C5ZZ-5310-B
6/200	HT/FB	1344	4/S, C4	M	A	1 Green	C5ZZ-5310-B
6/200	HT/FB	1344	3/S, 4/S, C4	P	A	1 Green	C5ZZ-5310-B
8/289	HT/FB	1413	3/S, 4/S, C4	M/P	N	1 Violet	C5ZZ-5310-D
							r/b C5ZZ-5310-C
8/289	HT/FB	1490	3/S, 4/S, C4	M/P	A	1 Gray	C5ZZ-5310-C
8/289-2V HD	HT/FB	1413	3/S, 4/S, C4	M/P	N	1 Red	C5ZZ-5310-F
							r/b C5ZZ-5310-E
8/289-2V HD	HT/FB	1413	3/S, 4/S, C4	M	A	1 Brown	C5ZZ-5310-E
8/289-4V	HT/FB	1413	3/S, 4/S, C4	M/P	N	1 Violet	C5ZZ-5310-D
							r/b C5ZZ-5310-C
8/289-4V	HT/FB	1490	3/S, 4/S, C4	M/P	A	1 Gray	C5ZZ-5310-C
8/289-4V HD	HT/FB	1413	3/S, 4/S, C4	M/P	N	1 Red	C5ZZ-5310-F
							r/b C5ZZ-5310-E
8/289-4V HD	HT/FB	1491	3/S, 4/S, C4	M/P	A	1 Brown	C5ZZ-5310-E
8/289-4V K	HT/FB	1413	3/S, 4/S	M/P	N	1 Red	C5ZZ-5310-F
							r/b C5ZZ-5310-E
8/289-4V K	HT/FB	1491	3/S, 4/S	M/P	A	1 Brown	C5ZZ-5310-E
8/289-4V GT	HT/FB	1413	3/S, 4/S, C4	M/P	N	1 Red	C5ZZ-5310-F
							r/b C5ZZ-5310-E
8/289-4V GT	HT/FB	1491	3/S, 4/S, C4	M/P	A	1 Brown	C5ZZ-5310-E

1966 Mustang Front Spring Application Chart, before 2/14/66
(All models, Without Thermactor)

CYL/CID	Model	Load	Transmission	Steering	A/C	Marking Stripes	Part Number
6/200	HT/FB	1279	3/S, 4/S, C4	M/P	N	1 Pink	C5ZZ-5310-A
							r/b C5ZZ-5310-B
6/200	HT/FB	1279	3/S	M	A	1 Pink	C5ZZ-5310-A
							r/b C5ZZ-5310-B
6/200	HT/FB	1344	4/S, C4	M	A	1 Green	C5ZZ-5310-B
6/200	HT/FB	1344	3/S, 4/S, C4	P	A	1 Green	C5ZZ-5310-B
8/289	HT/FB	1413	3/S, 4/S, C4	M/P	N	1 Violet	C5ZZ-5310-D
							r/b C5ZZ-5310-C
8/289	HT/FB	1491	3/S, 4/S, C4	M/P	A	1 Gray	C5ZZ-5310-C
8/289 HD	HT/FB	1413	3/S, 4/S, C4	M/P	N	1 Red	C5ZZ-5310-E
							r/b C5ZZ-5310-E
8/289 HD	HT/FB	1413	3/S, 4/S, C4	M/P	A	1 Brown	C5ZZ-5310-E
6/200	Conv	1279	3/S	M	N	1 Pink	C5ZZ-5310-A
							r/b C5ZZ-5310-B
6/200	Conv	1344	4/S, C4	M	N	1 Green	C5ZZ-5310-B
6/200	Conv	1344	3/S, 4/S, C4	P	N	1 Green	C5ZZ-5310-B
6/200	Conv	1344	3/S	M	A	1 Green	C5ZZ-5310-B
6/200	Conv	1413	4/S, C4	M	A	1 Violet	C5ZZ-5310-D
							r/b C5ZZ-5310-C
6/200	Conv	1413	3/S, 4/S, C4	P	A	1 Violet	C5ZZ-5310-D
							r/b C5ZZ-5310-C
8/289	Conv	1491	3/S, 4/S, C4	M/P	N	1 Gray	C5ZZ-5310-C
8/289	Conv	1491	3/S, 4/S, C4	M/P	A	1 Gray	C5ZZ-5310-C
8/289 HD	Conv	1491	3/S, 4/S, C4	M/P	N	1 Brown	C5ZZ-5310-E
8/289 HD	Conv	1491	3/S, 4/S, C4	M/P	A	1 Brown	C5ZZ-5310-E

1966 Mustang Front Spring Application Chart, from 2/14/66
(Convertibles, Without Thermactor)

CYL/CID	Load	Transmission	Steering	A/C	Marking Stripes	Part Number
6/200	1279	3/S	M	N	1 Pink	C5ZZ-5310-A
						r/b C5ZZ-5310-B
6/200	1344	4/S, C4	M	N	1 Green	C5ZZ-5310-B
6/200	1344	3/S, 4/S, C4	P	N	1 Green	C5ZZ-5310-B
6/200	1344	3/S	M	A	1 Green	C5ZZ-5310-B
6/200	1413	3/S	P	A	1 Violet	C5ZZ-5310-D
						r/b C5ZZ-5310-C
6/200	1413	4/S, C4	M/P	A	1 Violet	C5ZZ-5310-D
						r/b C5ZZ-5310-C
8/289-2V	1490	3/S, 4/S, C4	M/P	N	1 Gray	C5ZZ-5310-C
8/289-2V	1490	3/S, 4/S, C4	M/P	A	1 Gray	C5ZZ-5310-C
8/289-2V HD	1491	3/S, 4/S, C4	M/P	N	1 Brown	C5ZZ-5310-E
8/289-2V HD	1491	3/S, 4/S, C4	M/P	A	1 Brown	C5ZZ-5310-E
8/289-4V	1490	3/S, 4/S, C4	M/P	N	1 Gray	C5ZZ-5310-C
8/289-4V	1490	3/S, 4/S, C4	M/P	A	1 Gray	C5ZZ-5310-C
8/289-4V HD	1491	3/S, 4/S, C4	M/P	N	1 Brown	C5ZZ-5310-E
8/289-4V HD	1491	3/S, 4/S, C4	M/P	A	1 Brown	C5ZZ-5310-E
8/289-4V K	1491	3/S, 4/S	M/P	N	1 Brown	C5ZZ-5310-E
8/289-4V K	1491	3/S, 4/S	M/P	A	1 Brown	C5ZZ-5310-E
8/289-4V GT	1491	3/S, 4/S, C4	M/P	N	1 Brown	C5ZZ-5310-E
8/289-4V GT	1491	3/S, 4/S, C4	M/P	A	1 Brown	C5ZZ-5310-E

1966 Mustang Front Spring Application Chart, before 2/14/66
(Hardtops and Fastbacks, With Thermactor)

CYL/CID	Model	Load	Transmission	Steering	A/C	Marking Stripes	Part Number
6/200	HT/FB	1279	3/S, 4/S, C4	M/P	N	1 Pink	C5ZZ-5310-A
							r/b C5ZZ-5310-B
6/200	HT/FB	1344	3/S, 4/S, C4	M	A	1 Green	C5ZZ-5310-B
6/200	HT/FB	1344	3/S, 4/S, C4	P	A	1 Green	C5ZZ-5310-B
6/200	FB	1344	4/S, C4	P	A	1 Green	C5ZZ-5310-B
6/200	HT	1413	C4	P	A	1 Violet	C5ZZ-5310-D
							r/b C5ZZ-5310-C
8/289-2V	HT/FB	1413	3/S, 4/S, C4	M	N	1 Violet	C5ZZ-5310-D
							r/b C5ZZ-5310-C
8/289-2V	FB	1413	3/S, 4/S, C4	P	N	1 Violet	C5ZZ-5310-D
							r/b C5ZZ-5310-C
8/289-2V	HT	1413	3/S, C4	P	N	1 Violet	C5ZZ-5310-D
							r/b C5ZZ-5310-C
8/289-2V	HT	1491	4/S	P	N	1 Gray	C5ZZ-5310-C
8/289-2V	HT/FB	1491	4/S	M/P	A	1 Gray	C5ZZ-5310-C
8/289-2V HD	HT/FB	1413	3/S, 4/S, C4	M	N	1 Red	C5ZZ-5310-F
							r/b C5ZZ-5310-E
8/289-2V HD	FB	1413	3/S, 4/S, C4	P	N	1 Red	C5ZZ-5310-F
							r/b C5ZZ-5310-E
8/289-2V HD	HT	1413	3/S, C4	P	N	1 Red	C5ZZ-5310-F
							r/b C5ZZ-5310-E
8/289-2V HD	HT	1491	4/S	P	N	1 Brown	C5ZZ-5310-E
8/289-2V HD	HT/FB	1491	4/S, C4	M/P	A	1 Brown	C5ZZ-5310-E
8/289-4V	HT/FB	1413	3/S, 4/S, C4	M	N	1 Violet	C5ZZ-5310-D
							r/b C5ZZ-5310-C
8/289-4V	HT/FB	1413	3/S	P	N	1 Violet	C5ZZ-5310-D
							r/b C5ZZ-5310-C
8/289-4V	HT/FB	1491	4/S, C4	P	N	1 Gray	C5ZZ-5310-C
8/289-4V	HT/FB	1491	3/S, 4/S, C4	M/P	A	1 Gray	C5ZZ-5310-C
8/289-4V HD	HT/FB	1413	3/S, 4/S, C4	M	N	1 Red	C5ZZ-5310-F
							r/b C5ZZ-5310-E
8/289-4V HD	HT/FB	1413	3/S	P	N	1 Red	C5ZZ-5310-F
							r/b C5ZZ-5310-E
8/289-4V HD	HT/FB	1491	4/S, C4	P	N	1 Brown	C5ZZ-5310-E
8/289-4V HD	HT/FB	1491	3/S, 4/S, C4	M/P	A	1 Brown	C5ZZ-5310-E
8/289-4V K	HT/FB	1413	3/S, 4/S	M	N	1 Red	C5ZZ-5310-F
							r/b C5ZZ-5310-E
8/289-4V K	FB	1413	3/S	P	N	1 Red	C5ZZ-5310-F
							r/b C5ZZ-5310-E
8/289-4V K	HT	1491	3/S	P	N	1 Brown	C5ZZ-5310-E
8/289-4V K	HT/FB	1491	4/S	P	N	1 Brown	C5ZZ-5310-E
8/289-4V K	HT/FB	1491	3/S	M/P	A	1 Brown	C5ZZ-5310-E
8/289-4V K	FB	1491	4/S	M/P	A	1 Brown	C5ZZ-5310-E
8/289-4V K	HT	1491	4/S	M	A	1 Brown	C5ZZ-5310-E
8/289-4V K	HT	1491	3/S, 4/S, C4	M/P	A	1 Brown	C5ZZ-5310-E

1966 Mustang Front Spring Application Chart, Convertibles, before 2/14/66
(With Thermactor)

CYL/CID	Model	Load	Transmission	Steering	A/C	Marking Stripes	Part Number
6/200	Conv	1344	3/S, 4/S, C4	M	N	1 Green	C5ZZ-5310-B
6/200	Conv	1344	4/S, C4	P	N	1 Green	C5ZZ-5310-B
6/200	Conv	1413	C4	P	N	1 Violet	C5ZZ-5310-D
							r/b C5ZZ-5310-C
6/200	Conv	1413	3/S, 4/S, C4	M/P	A	1 Violet	C5ZZ-5310-D
							r/b C5ZZ-5310-C
8/289	Conv	1491	3/S, 4/S, C4	M/P	N	1 Gray	C5ZZ-5310-C
8/289	Conv	1491	3/S, 4/S, C4	M/P	A	1 Gray	C5ZZ-5310-C
8/289	Conv	1491	3/S, 4/S, C4	M/P	N	1 Brown	C5ZZ-5310-E
8/289	Conv	1491	3/S, 4/S, C4	M/P	A	1 Brown	C5ZZ-5310-E
							r/b C5ZZ-5310-C

1966 Mustang Front Spring Application Chart, from 2/14/66
(With Thermactor)

CYL/CID	Model	Load	Transmission	Steering	A/C	Marking Stripes	Part Number
6/200	HT/FB	1279	3/S, 4/S, C4	M	N	1 Pink	C5ZZ-5310-A
							r/b C5ZZ-5310-B
6/200	HT/FB	1279	3/S, 4/S	P	N	1 Pink	C5ZZ-5310-A
							r/b C5ZZ-5310-B
6/200	FB	1279	C4	P	N	1 Pink	C5ZZ-5310-A
							r/b C5ZZ-5310-B
6/200	HT	1344	C4	P	N	1 Green	C5ZZ-5310-B
6/200	HT/FB	1344	3/S, 4/S	M/P	A	1 Green	C5ZZ-5310-B
6/200	HT/FB	1344	C4	M	A	1 Green	C5ZZ-5310-B
6/200	FB	1344	C4	P	A	1 Green	C5ZZ-5310-B
6/200	HT	1413	C4	P	A	1 Violet	C5ZZ-5310-D
							r/b C5ZZ-5310-C
8/289 2V	HT/FB	1413	3/S, 4/S, C4	M	N	1 Violet	C5ZZ-5310-D
							r/b C5ZZ-5310-C
8/289 2V	HT/FB	1413	3/S, C4	P	N	1 Violet	C5ZZ-5310-D
							r/b C5ZZ-5310-C
8/289 2V	FB	1413	4/S	P	N	1 Violet	C5ZZ-5310-D
							r/b C5ZZ-5310-C
8/289 2V	HT	1490	4/S	P	N	1 Gray	C5ZZ-5310-C
8/289 2V	HT/FB	1490	3/S, 4/S, C4	M/P	A	1 Gray	C5ZZ-5310-C
8/289 2V HD	HT/FB	1413	3/S, 4/S, C4	M	N	1 Red	C5ZZ-5310-F
							r/b C5ZZ-5310-E
8/289 2V HD	HT/FB	1413	3/S, C4	P	N	1 Red	C5ZZ-5310-F
							r/b C5ZZ-5310-E
8/289 2V HD	FB	1413	4/S	P	N	1 Red	C5ZZ-5310-F
							r/b C5ZZ-5310-E
8/289 2V HD	HT	1491	4/S	P	N	1 Brown	C5ZZ-5310-E
8/289 2V HD	HT/FB	1491	3/S, 4/S, C4	M/P	A	1 Brown	C5ZZ-5310-E
8/289 4V	HT/FB	1413	3/S, 4/S, C4	M	N	1 Violet	C5ZZ-5310-D
8/289 4V	HT/FB	1413	3/S	P	N	1 Violet	C5ZZ-5310-D
							r/b C5ZZ-5310-C
8/289 4V	HT/FB	1490	4/S, C4	P	N	1 Gray	C5ZZ-5310-C
8/289 4V	HT/FB	1490	3/S, 4/S, C4	M/P	A	1 Gray	C5ZZ-5310-C
8/289 4V HD	HT/FB	1413	3/S, 4/S, C4	M	N	1 Red	C5ZZ-5310-F
							r/b C5ZZ-5310-E
8/289 4V HD	HT/FB	1413	3/S	P	N	1 Red	C5ZZ-5310-F
							r/b C5ZZ-5310-E
8/289 4V HD	HT/FB	1491	4/S, C4	P	N	1 Brown	C5ZZ-5310-E
8/289 4V HD	HT/FB	1491	3/S, 4/S, C4	M/P	A	1 Brown	C5ZZ-5310-E
8/289 4V K	HT/FB	1413	3/S, 4/S	M	N	1 Red	C5ZZ-5310-F
							r/b C5ZZ-5310-E
8/289 4V K	FB	1413	3/S	P	N	1 Red	C5ZZ-5310-F
							r/b C5ZZ-5310-E
8/289 4V K	HT	1491	3/S	P	N	1 Brown	C5ZZ-5310-E
8/289 4V K	HT/FB	1491	4/S	P	N	1 Brown	C5ZZ-5310-E
8/289 4V K	HT/FB	1491	3/S, 4/S	P	A	1 Brown	C5ZZ-5310-E
8/289 4V GT	HT/FB	1413	3/S, 4/S, C4	M	N	1 Red	C5ZZ-5310-F
							r/b C5ZZ-5310-E
8/289 4V GT	HT/FB	1413	3/S	P	N	1 Red	C5ZZ-5310-F
							r/b C5ZZ-5310-E
8/289 4V GT	HT/FB	1491	4/S, C4	P	N	1 Brown	C5ZZ-5310-E
8/289 4V GT	HT/FB	1491	3/S, 4/S, C4	M/P	A	1 Brown	C5ZZ-5310-E
6/200	Conv	1344	3/S, 4/S, C4	M	N	1 Green	C5ZZ-5310-B
6/200	Conv	1344	3/S, 4/S	P	N	1 Green	C5ZZ-5310-B
6/200	Conv	1413	C4	P	N	1 Violet	C5ZZ-5310-D
							r/b C5ZZ-5310-C
6/200	Conv	1413	3/S, 4/S, C4	M/P	A	1 Violet	C5ZZ-5310-D
							r/b C5ZZ-5310-C
8/289 2V	Conv	1490	3/S, 4/S, C4	M/P	N	1 Gray	C5ZZ-5310-C
8/289 2V	Conv	1490	3/S, 4/S, C4	M/P	A	1 Gray	C5ZZ-5310-C
8/289 2V HD	Conv	1491	3/S, 4/S, C4	M/P	N	1 Brown	C5ZZ-5310-E
8/289 2V HD	Conv	1491	3/S, 4/S, C4	M/P	A	1 Brown	C5ZZ-5310-E
8/289 4V	Conv	1490	3/S, 4/S, C4	M/P	N	1 Gray	C5ZZ-5310-C
8/289 4V	Conv	1490	3/S, 4/S, C4	M/P	A	1 Gray	C5ZZ-5310-C
8/289 4V HD	Conv	1491	3/S, 4/S, C4	M/P	N	1 Brown	C5ZZ-5310-E
8/289 4V HD	Conv	1491	3/S, 4/S, C4	M/P	A	1 Brown	C5ZZ-5310-E
8/289 4V K	Conv	1491	3/S, 4/S	M/P	N	1 Brown	C5ZZ-5310-E
8/289 4V K	Conv	1491	3/S, 4/S	M/P	A	1 Brown	C5ZZ-5310-E
8/289 4V GT	Conv	1491	3/S, 4/S, C4	M/P	N	1 Brown	C5ZZ-5310-E
8/289 4V GT	Conv	1491	3/S, 4/S, C4	M/P	A	1 Brown	C5ZZ-5310-E

1967 Mustang Front Spring Application Chart
(Manual Transmissions, Without Thermactor)
Note: Refer to chart for spring code identification.

Engine	Model	Note	Three-Speed Options: None	A/C	P/S	A/C & P/S	Four-Speed Options: None	A/C	P/S	A/C & P/S
200	F/B		4T	4G	4T	4W	4T	4W	4G	4W
289-2V	F/B		4H	4J	4J	4V	4J	4V	4J	4V
289-4V	F/B		4H	4V	4J	4V	4J	4V	4J	4V
390	F/B		4F	4E	4E	4U	4F	4E	4E	4U
390	F/B	1	4S	4R	4R	4R	4S	4R	4R	4R
390	F/B	2	4K	4L	4L	4L	4K	4L	4L	4L
200	H/T		4T	4G	4G	4W	4T	4W	4G	4W
289-2V	H/T		4H	4V	4J	4V	4J	4V	4J	4V
289-4V	H/T		4J	4V	4J	4V	4J	4V	4J	25
390	H/T		4F	4E	4E	4U	4F	4E	4E	4U
390	H/T	1	4S	4R	4R	4P	4S	4R	4R	4P
390	H/T	2	4K	4L	4L	4L	4K	4L	4L	4L
200	Conv	3	4G	4W	4W	68	4W	68	4W	68
200	Conv	4	4G	4W	4W	4J	4W	4J	4W	4J
289-2V	Conv	3	4J	25	4V	25	4V	25	4V	25
289-2V	Conv	4	4J	4F	4T	4F	4T	4F	4T	4F
289-4V	Conv	3	4V	25	4V	25	4V	25	4V	25
289-4V	Conv	4	4T	4F	4T	4F	4T	4F	4T	4F
390	Conv		4E	4U	4U	4D	4E	4U	4U	4D
390	Conv	1	4R	4P	4R	4P	4R	4P	4P	4P
390	Conv	2	4L	4M	4L	4M	4L	4M	4L	4M

Notes:
1 Improved Handling Package
2 Racing only
3 Before 9/1/66
4 From 9/1/66

1967 Mustang Front Spring Application Chart
(Manual Transmissions, With Thermactor)
Note: Refer to chart for spring code identification.

Engine	Model	Note	Three-Speed Options: None	A/C	P/S	A/C & P/S	Four-Speed Options: None	A/C	P/S	A/C & P/S
200	F/B	3	4T	4G	4G	4W	4G	4W	4G	68
200	F/B	4	4T	4G	4G	4W	4G	4W	4G	4J
289-2V	F/B	3	4J	4V	4J	4V	4J	4V	4V	25
289-2V		4	4J	4T	4J	4T	4J	4T	4T	4F
289-4V	F/B	3	4J	4V	4J	25	4J	4V	4J	25
289-4V		4	4J	4T	4J	4F	4J	4T	4T	4F
390	F/B		4F	4E	4E	4U	4F	4E	4E	4U
390	F/B	1	4S	4R	4R	4P	4S	4R	4R	4P
390	F/B	2	4K	4L	4L	4M	4K	4L	4L	4M
200	H/T	3	4T	4W	4G	4W	4G	4W	4W	68
200	H/T	4	4T	4W	4G	4W	4G	4W	4W	4J
289-2V	H/T	3	4J	4V	4J	25	4J	4V	4V	25
289-2V	H/T	4	4J	4T	4J	4F	4J	4T	4T	4F
289-4V	H/T	3	4J	4V	4V	25	4J	4V	4V	25
289-4V	H/T	4	4J	4T	4T	4F	4J	4T	4T	4F
390	H/T		4E	4U	4E	4U	4E	4U	4E	4U
390	H/T	1	4R	4R	4R	4P	4R	4R	4R	4P
390	H/T	2	4L	4L	4L	4M	4L	4L	4L	4M
200	Conv	3	4G	68	4W	68	4W	68	68	4V
200	Conv	4	4G	4J	4W	4J	4W	4J	4J	4T
289-2V	Conv	3	4V	25	4V	4E	4V	25	25	4E
289-2V	Conv	4	4T	4F	4T	4E	4T	4F	4F	4E
289-4V	Conv	3	4V	25	25	4E	4V	25	25	4E
289-4V	Conv	4	4T	4F	4F	4E	4T	4F	4F	4E
390	Conv		4E	4U	4U	4D	4E	4U	4U	4D
390	Conv	1	4R	4P	4P	4N	4R	4P	4P	4N
390	Conv	2	4L	4M	4M	4M	4L	4M	4M	4M

Notes:
1 Improved Handling Package
2 Racing only
3 Before 9/1/66
4 From 9/1/66

1967 Mustang Front Spring Application Chart
(Automatic Transmissions, Without Thermactor)
Note: Refer to chart for spring code identification.

Engine	Model	Note	C4 None	A/C	P/S	A/C & P/S	C6 None	A/C	P/S	A/C & P/S
200	F/B		4T	4G	4G	4W				
289-2V	F/B		4H	4J	4J	4V				
289-4V	F/B		4J	4V	4J	4V				
390	F/B						4F	4E	4E	4U
390	F/B	1					4S	4R	4R	4P
390	F/B	2					4K	4L	4L	4L
200	H/T		4T	4W	4G	4W				
289-2V	H/T		4J	4V	4J	4V				
289-4V	H/T		4J	4V	4J	4V				
390	H/T						4F	4E	4E	4U
390	H/T	1					4S	4R	4R	4P
390	H/T	2					4K	4L	4L	4M
200	Conv	3	4G	4W	4W	68				
200	Conv	4	4G	4W	4W	4J				
289-2V	Conv	3	4V	25	4V	25				
289-2V	Conv	4	4T	4F	4T	4F				
289-4V	Conv	3	4V	25	4V	25				
289-4V	Conv	4	4T	4F	4T	4F				
390	Conv						4E	4U	4U	4D
390	Conv	1					4R	4P	4P	4P
390	Conv	2					4L	4M	4L	4M

Notes:
1 Improved Handling Package
2 Racing only
3 Before 9/1/66
4 From 9/1/66

1967 Mustang Front Spring Application Chart
(Automatic Transmissions, With Thermactor)
Note: Refer to chart for spring code identification.

Engine	Model	Note	C4 None	A/C	P/S	A/C & P/S	C6 None	A/C	P/S	A/C & P/S
200	F/B	3	4G	4W	4G	4W				
200	F/B	4	4G	4W	4G	4W				
289-2V	F/B	3	4J	4V	4J	4V				
289-2V	F/B	4	4J	4T	4J	4T				
289-4V	F/B	3	4J	4V	4V	25				
289-4V	F/B	4	4J	4T	4T	4F				
390	F/B						4E	4U	4E	4U
390	F/B	1					4R	4R	4R	4P
390	F/B	2					4L	4L	4L	4M
200	H/T	3	4G	4W	4G	68				
200	H/T	4	4G	4W	4G	4J				
289-2V	H/T	3	4J	4V	4V	25				
289-2V	H/T	4	4J	4T	4T	4F				
289-4V	H/T	3	4J	4V	4V	25				
289-4V	H/T	4	4J	4J	4T	4F				
390	H/T		4E	4U	4E	4U				
390	H/T	1	4R	4P	4R	4P				
390	H/T	2	4L	4L	4L	4M				
200	Conv	3	4W	68	4W	4V				
200	Conv	4	4W	4J	4W	4T				
289-2V	Conv	3	4V	25	25	4E				
289-2V	Conv	4	4T	4F	4F	4E				
289-4V	Conv	3	4V	25	25	4E				
289-4V	Conv	4	4T	4F	4F	4E				
390	Conv						4U	4U	4U	4D
390	Conv	1					4R	4P	4P	4N
390	Conv	2					4L	4M	4M	4M

Notes:
1 Improved Handling Package
2 Racing only
3 Before 9/1/66
4 From 9/1/66

1968 MUSTANG Front Spring Application Chart
(Automatic Transmissions, Standard Springs)
Note: Refer to chart for spring code identification.

Engine	Model	Note	C4 None	A/C	P/S	A/C & P/S	C6 None	A/C	P/S	A/C & P/S
200	F/B	1	4G	4W	4W	4J				
200	F/B	2	4W	4J	4J	4V				
289-2V	F/B		4J	4F	4V	4F				
289-4V	F/B		4V	4F	4V	4E				
302	F/B		4V	4F	4V	4F				
390-2	F/B						4U	4D	4D	4Y
390-4	F/B	1,3					4L	4M	4M	4M
390-4	F/B	2,3					4L	4M	4M	4M
390-4	F/B						4U	4D	4U	4D
427	F/B	3					4M	4M	4M	1Q
200	H/T	1	4G	4J	4W	4J				
200	H/T	2	4W	4J	4J	4V				
289-2V	H/T		4V	4F	4V	4F				
289-4V	H/T		4V	4F	4F	4E				
302	H/T		4V	4F	4V	4F				
390-2	H/T						4U	4D	4D	4Y
390-4	H/T	1,3					4M	4M	4M	6D
390-4	H/T	2,3					4M	4M	4M	1Q
390-4	H/T						4U	4D	4U	4D
427	H/T	3					4M	1Q	4M	1Q
200	Conv	1	4W	4J	4J	4V				
200	Conv	2	4J	4V	4J	4V				
289-2V	Conv		4V	4F	4F	4E				
289-4V	Conv		4F	4E	4F	4E				
302	Conv		4F	4E	4F	4E				
390-2	Conv						4D	4Y	4D	4Y
390-4	Conv	1,3					4M	6D	4M	6D
390-4	Conv	2,3					4M	1Q	4M	1Q
390-4	Conv						4D	4Y	4D	4Y
427	Conv	3					4M	1Q	1Q	1Q

Notes:
1 Before 12/11/67
2 From 12/11/67
3 Improved Handling Package

1968 MUSTANG Front Spring Application Chart
(Manual Transmissions, Standard Springs)
Note: Refer to chart for spring code identification.

Engine	Model	Note	Three-Speed None	A/C	P/S	A/C & P/S	Four-Speed None	A/C	P/S	A/C & P/S
200	F/B	1	4G	4W	4G	4J				
200	F/B	2	4W	4J	4W	4J				
289-2V	F/B		4V	4F	4V	4F	4V	4F	4V	4F
289-4V	F/B						4V	4F	4F	4E
302	F/B		4F	4F	4F	4E	4V	4F	4F	4E
390-2	F/B		4U	4D	4U	4D	4U	4D	4U	4D
390-4	F/B	1,3	4L	4M	4M	4M	4M	4M	4M	6D
390-4	F/B	2,3	4L	4M	4M	4M	4M	4M	4M	1Q
390-4	F/B		4U	4D	4U	4D	4U	4D	4D	4D
427	F/B	3	4M	4M	4M	1Q	4M	1Q	4M	1Q
200	H/T	1	4G	4W	4W	4J				
200	H/T	2	4W	4J	4W	4J				
289-2V	H/T		4V	4F	4V	4F	4V	4F	4F	4E
289-4V	H/T						4V	4F	4F	4E
302	H/T		4F	4F	4F	4E	4V	4F	4F	4E
390-2	H/T		4U	4D	4U	4D	4U	4D	4D	4D
390-4	H/T	1,3	4L	4M	4M	6D	4M	4M	4M	6D
390-4	H/T	2,3	4L	4M	4M	1Q	4M	4M	4M	1Q
390-4	H/T		4U	4D	4U	4D	4U	4D	4D	4Y
427	H/T	3	4M	1Q	4M	1Q	4M	1Q	4M	1Q
200	Conv	1	4W	4J	4W	4J				
200	Conv	2	4J	4V	4J	4V				
289-2V	Conv		4F	4E	4F	4E	4F	4E	4F	4E
289-4V	Conv						4F	4E	4F	4E
302	Conv		4F	4E	4F	4E	4F	4E	4E	4E
390-2	Conv		4U	4D	4D	4D	4D	4D	4D	4Y
390-4	Conv	1,3	4M	6D	4M	6D	4M	6D	6D	6D
390-4	Conv	2,3	4M	1Q	4M	1Q	4M	1Q	1Q	1Q
390-4	Conv		4D	4D	4D	4Y	4D	4Y	4D	4Y
427	Conv	3	4M	1Q	1Q	1Q	4M	1Q	1Q	1Q

Notes:
1 Before 12/11/67
2 From 12/11/67
3 Improved Handling Package

1968 MUSTANG Front Spring Application Chart
(Automatic Transmissions, Heavy Duty Suspension)
Note: Refer to chart for spring code identification.

Engine	Model	C4 None	C4 A/C	C4 P/S	C4 A/C & P/S	C6 None	C6 A/C	C6 P/S	C6 A/C & P/S
289-2V	F/B	4X	4S	4X	4S				
289-4V	F/B	4X	4S	4S	4R				
302	F/B	4X	4S	4S	4S				
390-2V	F/B					4P	4N	4N	4N
390-4V	F/B					4P	4N	4P	4N
428	F/B					4P	4N	4N	4C
289-2V	H/T	4X	4S	4S	4S				
289-4V	H/T	4S	4S	4S	4R				
302	H/T	4X	4S	4S	4R				
390-2V	H/T					4P	4N	4N	4N
390-4V	H/T					4P	4N	4P	4N
428	H/T					4N	4C	4N	4C
289-2V	Conv	4S	4R	4S	4R				
289-4V	Conv	4S	4R	4S	4R				
302	Conv	4S	4R	4S	4R				
390-2V	Conv					4N	4N	4N	4C
390-4V	Conv					4N	4N	4N	4C
428	Conv					4N	4C	4C	4C

1968 MUSTANG Front Spring Application Chart
(Manual Transmissions, Heavy Duty Suspension)
Note: Refer to chart for spring code identification.

Engine	Model	Three-Speed None	A/C	P/S	A/C & P/S	Four-Speed None	A/C	P/S	A/C & P/S
289-2V	F/B	4X	4S	4S	4S	4S	4S	4S	4R
289-4V	F/B					4S	4S	4S	4R
302	F/B	4S	4S	4S	4R	4S	4S	4S	4R
390-2V	F/B	4P	4N	4P	4N	4P	4N	4P	4N
390-4V	F/B	4P	4N	4P	4N	4P	4N	4P	4N
428	F/B	4P	4N	4N	4N	4P	4N	4N	4C
289-2V	H/T	4X	4S	4S	4R	4S	4S	4S	4R
289-4V	H/T					4S	4R	4S	4R
302	H/T	4S	4S	4S	4R	4S	4R	4S	4R
390-2V	H/T	4P	4N	4P	4N	4P	4N	4P	4N
390-4V	H/T	4P	4N	4P	4N	4P	4N	4P	4N
428	H/T	4P	4N	4N	4N	4N	4N	4N	4C
289-2V	Conv	4S	4R	4S	4R	4S	4R	4S	4R
289-4V	Conv					4S	4R	4R	4R
302	Conv	4S	4R	4R	4R	4S	4R	4R	4R
390-2V	Conv	4P	4N	4N	4C	4P	4N	4N	4C
390-4V	Conv	4P	4N	4N	4C	4N	4C	4N	4C
428	Conv	4N	4C	4N	4C	4N	4C	4N	4C

1969 MUSTANG Front Spring Application Chart
Hardtop models.
(Manual Transmissions, Standard Suspension.)
Note: Refer to chart for spring code identification.

Engine	Notes	Three-Speed None	A/C	P/S	A/C & P/S	Four-Speed None	A/C	P/S	A/C & P/S
200	1,2,5	4W	4W	4W	4J				
200	1,2,6	4G	4G	4G	4W				
250	1,2,5	4J	4J	4J	4V				
250	1,2,6	4G	4J	4W	4J				
302	1,2,5	4V	4F	4V	4F	4V	4F	4F	4E
302	1,2,6	4J	4V	4J	4V	4J	4V	4J	4F
351-2V	1,2,5	4F	4E	4F	4E	4F	4E	4F	4E
351-2V	1,2,6	4V	4F	4V	4E	4V	4F	4F	4E
351-4V	1,2,5	4F	4E	4F	4E	4F	4E	4E	4E
351-4V	1,2,6	4V	4F	4F	4E	4V	4F	4F	4E
390	1,2,7	4E	4U	4E	4U				
390	1,2,8	4F	4E	4E	4U	4F	4E	4E	4U
428	1,2,9	4M	4M	4M	1Q	4M	4M	4M	1Q
428	1,2,10	4M	4M	4M	1Q	4M	4M	4M	1Q
200	3,4,5	4W	4J	4W	4J				
200	3,4,6	4G	4G	4G	4W				
250	3,4,5	4J	4V	4J	4V				
250	3,4,6	4G	4J	4W	4J				
302	3,4,5	4V	4F	4V	4E	4V	4F	4F	4E
302	3,4,6	4J	4V	4J	4F	4J	4V	4J	4F
351-2V	3,4,5	4F	4E	4F	4E	4F	4E	4E	4E
351-2V	3,4,6	4V	4F	4V	4E	4V	4F	4F	4E
351-4V	3,4,5	4F	4E	4E	4E	4F	4E	4E	4U
351-4V	3,4,6	4V	4F	4F	4E	4V	4F	4F	4E
390	3,4,7	4E	4U	4E	4U	4E	4U	4U	4U
390	3,4,8	4F	4E	4E	4U	4F	4E	4E	4U
428	3,4,9	4M	4M	4M	1Q	4M	4M	4M	1Q
428	3,4,10	4M	4M	4M	1Q	4M	4M	4M	1Q

Notes:

1	Std. Interior, Bucket Seats
2	Deluxe Interior, Bucket Seats
3	Std. Interior, Bench Seat
4	Deluxe Interior, Bench Seat
5	Before 9/11/68, with .69" Dia. Stabilizer Bar
6	From 9/11/68, with .69" Dia. Stabilizer Bar
7	Before 9/11/68, with .72" Dia. Stabilizer Bar
8	From 9/11/68, with .72" Dia. Stabilizer Bar
9	Before 9/11/68, with .95" Dia. Stabilizer Bar, Competition Suspension
10	From 9/11/68, with .95" Dia. Stabilizer Bar, Competition Suspension

1969 MUSTANG Front Spring Application Chart
SportsRoof and Mach 1 models.
(Manual Transmissions, Standard Suspension.)
Note: Refer to chart for spring code identification.

Engine	Model	Three-Speed Options: None	A/C	P/S	A/C & P/S	Four-Speed Options: None	A/C	P/S	A/C & P/S
200	1,2,4	4W	4W	4W	4J				
200	1,2,5	4G	4G	4G	4W				
250	1,2,4	4W	4J	4J	4V				
250	1,2,5	4G	4W	4W	4J				
302	1,2,4	4J	4F	4V	4F	4V	4F	4V	4E
302	1,2,5	4W	4J	4J	4V	4J	4V	4J	4V
351-2V	1,2,4	4V	4E	4F	4E	4F	4E	4F	4E
351-2V	1,2,5	4J	4F	4V	4F	4J	4F	4V	4E
351-4V	1,2,4	4F	4E	4F	4E	4F	4E	4F	4E
351-4V	1,2,5	4J	4F	4V	4E	4J	4F	4V	4E
390	1,2,6	4E	4U	4E	4U	4E	4U	4E	4U
390	1,2,7	4F	4E	4E	4U	4F	4E	4E	4U
428	1,2,8	4L	4M	4M	1Q	4M	4M	4M	1Q
428	1,2,9	4L	4M	4M	1Q	4M	4M	4M	1Q
429	1,2								6L
351-2V	3,4	4F	4E	4F	4E	4F	4E	4E	4E
351-2V	3,5	4J	4F	4J	4E	4V	4F	4F	4E
351-4V	3,4	4F	4E	4E	4E	4F	4E	4E	4U
351-4V	3,5	4V	4F	4F	4E	4V	4F	4F	4E
390	3,6	4E	4U	4E	4U	4E	4U	4U	4U
390	3,7	4F	4E	4E	4U	4F	4E	4E	4U
428	3,8	4M	4M	4M	1Q	4M	4M	4M	1Q
428	3,9	4M	4M	4M	1Q	4M	4M	4M	1Q
429	3								6L

Notes:
1. Std. Interior, Bucket Seats
2. Deluxe Interior, Bucket Seats
3. Mach 1
4. Before 9/11/68, with .69" Dia. Stabilizer Bar
5. From 9/11/68, with .69" Dia. Stabilizer Bar
6. Before 9/11/68, with .72" Dia. Stabilizer Bar
7. From 9/11/68, with .72" Dia. Stabilizer Bar
8. Before 9/11/68, with .95" Dia. Stabilizer Bar, Competition Suspension
9. From 9/11/68, with .95" Dia. Stabilizer Bar, Competition Suspension

1969 MUSTANG Front Spring Application Chart
Grande models.
(Manual Transmissions, Standard Suspension.)
Note: Refer to chart for spring code identification.

Engine	Notes.	Three-Speed Options: None	A/C	P/S	A/C & P/S	Four-Speed Options: None	A/C	P/S	A/C & P/S
200	1	4W	4J	4W	4J				
200	2	4G	4W	4G	4W				
250	1	4J	4V	4J	4F				
250	2	4W	4J	4W	4J				
302	1	4V	4F	4F	4E	4V	4F	4F	4E
302	2	4J	4V	4J	4F	4J	4V	4V	4F
351-2V	1	4F	4E	4E	4U	4F	4E	4E	4U
351-2V	2	4V	4F	4F	4E	4V	4F	4F	4E
351-4V	1	4F	4E	4E	4U	4F	4E	4E	4U
351-4V	2	4V	4F	4F	4E	4V	4E	4F	4E
390	3	4E	4U	4U	4D	4E	4U	4U	4D
390	4	4F	4U	4E	4U	4E	4U	4E	4U
428	5	4M	1Q	4M	1Q	4M	1Q	4M	1Q
428	6	4M	1Q	4M	1Q	4M	1Q	4M	1Q

Notes:
1. Before 9/11/68, with .69" Dia. Stabilizer Bar
2. From 9/11/68, with .69" Dia. Stabilizer Bar
3. Before 9/11/68, with .72" Dia. Stabilizer Bar
4. From 9/11/68, with .72" Dia. Stabilizer Bar
5. Before 9/11/68, with .95" Dia. Stabilizer Bar, Competition Suspension
6. From 9/11/68, with .95" Dia. Stabilizer Bar, Competition Suspension

1969 MUSTANG Front Spring Application Chart
Convertible models.
(Manual Transmissions, Standard Suspension.)
Note: Refer to chart for spring code identification.

Engine	Notes	Three-Speed Options: None	A/C	P/S	A/C & P/S	Four-Speed Options: None	A/C	P/S	A/C & P/S
200	1	4W	4J	4J	4V				
200	2	4G	4W	4G	4J				
250	1	4J	4V	4V	4F				
250	2	4W	4J	4J	4V				
302	1	4V	4F	4F	4E	4V	4F	4F	4E
302	2	4J	4V	4V	4F	4J	4V	4V	4F
351-2V	1	4F	4E	4E	4U	4F	4E	4E	4U
351-2V	2	4V	4E	4F	4E	4V	4E	4F	4E
351-4V	1	4F	4E	4E	4U	4F	4E	4E	4U
351-4V	2	4V	4E	4F	4E	4V	4E	4F	4E
390	3	4E	4U	4U	4D	4E	4U	4U	4D
390	4	4E	4U	4E	4D	4E	4U	4E	4D
428	5	4M	1Q	4M	1Q	4M	1Q	4M	1Q
428	6	4M	1Q	4M	1Q	4M	1Q	4M	1Q

Notes:
1. Before 9/11/68, with .69" Dia. Stabilizer Bar
2. From 9/11/68, with .69" Dia. Stabilizer Bar
3. Before 9/11/68, with .72" Dia. Stabilizer Bar
4. From 9/11/68, with .72" Dia. Stabilizer Bar
5. Before 9/11/68, with .95" Dia. Stabilizer Bar, Competition Suspension
6. From 9/11/68, with .95" Dia. Stabilizer Bar, Competition Suspension

1969 MUSTANG Front Spring Application Chart
SportsRoof and Mach 1 models.
(Automatic Transmissions, Standard Suspension.)
Note: Refer to chart for spring code identification.

Engine	Note	FMX Options: None	A/C	P/S	A/C & P/S	C4 Options: None	A/C	P/S	A/C & P/S	C6 Options: None	A/C	P/S	A/C & P/S
200	1,2,4					4W	4W	4W	4J				
200	1,2,5					4G	4G	4G	4G				
250	1,2,4					4W	4J	4J	4V				
250	1,2,5					4G	4W	4W	4J				
302	1,2,4					4J	4V	4V	4F				
302	1,2,5					4W	4J	4J	4V				
351-2V	1,2,4	4F	4E	4F	4E								
351-2V	1,2,5	4J	4F	4V	4E								
351-4V	1,2,4	4F	4E	4F	4E								
351-4V	1,2,5	4J	4F	4V	4E								
390	1,2,6									4E	4U	4E	4U
390	1,2,7									4F	4E	4E	4U
428	1,2,8									4M	4M	4M	1Q
428	1,2,9									4M	4M	4M	1Q
351-2V	3,4	4F	4E	4E	4E								
351-2V	3,5	4V	4F	4F	4E								
351-4V	3,4	4F	4E	4E	4U								
351-4V	3,5	4V	4F	4F	4E								
390	3,6									4E	4U	4U	4D
390	3,7									4F	4U	4E	4U
428	3,8									4M	1Q	4M	1Q
428	3,9									4M	1Q	4M	1Q

Notes:
1. Std. Interior, Bucket Seats
2. Deluxe Interior, Bucket Seats
3. Mach 1
4. Before 9/11/68, with .69" Dia. Stabilizer Bar
5. From 9/11/68, with .69" Dia. Stabilizer Bar
6. Before 9/11/68, with .72" Dia. Stabilizer Bar
7. From 9/11/68, with .72" Dia. Stabilizer Bar
8. Before 9/11/68, with .95" Dia. Stabilizer Bar, Competition Suspension
9. From 9/11/68, with .95" Dia. Stabilizer Bar, Competition Suspension

1969 MUSTANG Front Spring Application Chart
Hardtop models.
(Automatic Transmissions, Standard Suspension.)
Note: Refer to chart for spring code identification.

Engine	Notes	FMX None	A/C	P/S	A/C & P/S	C4 None	A/C	P/S	A/C & P/S	C6 None	A/C	P/S	A/C & P/S
200	1,2,5					4W	4W	4W	4J				
200	1,2,6					4G	4G	4G	4W				
250	1,2,5					4W	4J	4J	4V				
250	1,2,6					4G	4J	4W	4W				
302	1,2,5					4V	4F	4V	4F				
302	1,2,6					4J	4J	4J	4V				
351-2V	1,2,5	4F	4E	4F	4E								
351-2V	1,2,6	4V	4F	4F	4E								
351-4V	1,2,5	4F	4E	4E	4E								
351-4V	1,2,6	4V	4F	4F	4E								
390	1,2,7									4E	4U	4U	4D
390	1,2,8									4F	4U	4E	4U
428	1,2,9									4M	1Q	4M	1Q
428	1,2,10									4M	1Q	4M	1Q
200	3,4,5					4W	4W	4W	4J				
200	3,4,6					4G	4G	4G	4W				
250	3,4,5					4J	4J	4J	4V				
250	3,4,6					4G	4W	4W	4J				
302	3,4,5					4V	4F	4V	4F				
302	3,4,6					4J	4V	4J	4V				
351-2V	3,4,5	4F	4E	4E	4E								
351-2V	3,4,6	4V	4F	4F	4E								
351-4V	3,4,5	4F	4E	4E	4U								
351-4V	3,4,6	4V	4F	4F	4E								
390	3,4,7									4E	4U	4U	4D
390	3,4,8									4F	4U	4E	4U
428	3,4,9									4M	1Q	4M	1Q
428	3,4,10									4M	1Q	4M	1Q

Notes:
1 Std. Interior, Bucket Seats
2 Deluxe Interior, Bucket Seats
3 Std. Interior, Bench Seat
4 Deluxe Interior, Bench Seat
5 Before 9/11/68, with .69" Dia. Stabilizer Bar
6 From 9/11/68, with .69" Dia. Stabilizer Bar
7 Before 9/11/68, with .72" Dia. Stabilizer Bar
8 From 9/11/68, with .72" Dia. Stabilizer Bar
9 Before 9/11/68, with .95" Dia. Stabilizer Bar, Competition Suspension
10 From 9/11/68, with .95" Dia. Stabilizer Bar, Competition Suspension

1969 MUSTANG Front Spring Application Chart
Grande models.
(Automatic Transmissions, Standard Suspension.)
Note: Refer to chart for spring code identification.

Engine	Notes	FMX None	A/C	P/S	A/C & P/S	C4 None	A/C	P/S	A/C & P/S	C6 None	A/C	P/S	A/C & P/S
200	1					4W	4W	4W	4J				
200	2					4G	4G	4G	4W				
250	1					4J	4V	4J	4V				
250	2					4G	4J	4W	4J				
302	1					4V	4F	4F	4F				
302	2					4J	4V	4J	4F				
351-2V	1	4F	4E	4E	4U								
351-2V	2	4V	4F	4F	4E								
351-4V	1	4F	4E	4E	4U								
351-4V	2	4V	4E	4F	4E								
390	3									4E	4U	4U	4D
390	4									4E	4U	4E	4D
428	5									4M	1Q	1Q	1Q
428	6									4M	1Q	1Q	1Q

Notes:
1 Before 9/11/68, with .69" Dia. Stabilizer Bar
2 From 9/11/68, with .69" Dia. Stabilizer Bar
3 Before 9/11/68, with .72" Dia. Stabilizer Bar
4 From 9/11/68, with .72" Dia. Stabilizer Bar
5 Before 9/11/68, with .95" Dia. Stabilizer Bar, Competition Suspension
6 From 9/11/68, with .95" Dia. Stabilizer Bar, Competition Suspension

1969 MUSTANG Front Spring Application Chart
Convertible models.
(Automatic Transmissions, Standard Suspension.)
Note: Refer to chart for spring code identification.

Engine	Notes	FMX None	A/C	P/S	A/C & P/S	C4 None	A/C	P/S	A/C & P/S	C6 None	A/C	P/S	A/C & P/S
200	1					4W	4J	4W	4J				
200	2					4G	4W	4G	4W				
250	1					4J	4V	4J	4F				
250	2					4W	4J	4W	4J				
302	1					4V	4F	4F	4E				
302	2					4J	4V	4V	4F				
351-2V	1	4F	4E	4E	4U								
351-2V	2	4V	4F	4F	4E								
351-4V	1	4F	4E	4E	4U								
351-4V	2	4V	4E	4F	4E								
390	3									4U	4U	4U	4D
390	4									4E	4U	4U	4D
428	5									4M	1Q	1Q	1Q
428	6									4M	1Q	1Q	1Q

Notes:
1 Before 9/11/68, with .69" Dia. Stabilizer Bar
2 From 9/11/68, with .69" Dia. Stabilizer Bar
3 Before 9/11/68, with .72" Dia. Stabilizer Bar
4 From 9/11/68, with .72" Dia. Stabilizer Bar
5 Before 9/11/68, with .95" Dia. Stabilizer Bar, Competition Suspension
6 From 9/11/68, with .95" Dia. Stabilizer Bar, Competition Suspension

1969 MUSTANG Front Spring Application Chart
SportsRoof and Mach 1 models.
(Manual Transmissions, Heavy Duty Suspension.)
Note: Refer to chart for spring code identification.

Engine	Model	Three-Speed None	A/C	P/S	A/C & P/S	Four-Speed None	A/C	P/S	A/C & P/S
302	1,2,4	4V	4S	4V	4S	4V	4S	4S	4S
302	1,2,5	4X	4S	4X	4S	4X	4S	4S	4S
351	1,2,5	4S	4R	4S	4R	4S	4R	4S	4R
351-2V	1,2,5	4S	4R	4S	4R	4S	4R	4R	4R
351-4V	1,2,5	4S	4R	4S	4R	4S	4R	4R	4R
390	1,2,4	4R	4R	4R	4P	4R	4R	4R	4P
390	1,2,5	4R	4R	4R	4P	4R	4R	4R	4P
302	3,4	4V	4S	4S	4R	4V	4S	4S	4R
302	3,5	4X	4S	4S	4R	4X	4S	4S	4R
351-2V	3,4	4S	4R	4S	4R	4S	4R	4R	4R
351-2V	3,5	4S	4R	4S	4R	4S	4R	4R	4R
351-4V	3,4	4S	4R	4R	4R	4S	4R	4R	4R
351-4V	3,5	4S	4R	4R	4R	4S	4R	4R	4R
390	3,4	4R	4P	4R	4P	4R	4P	4R	4P
390	3,5	4R	4P	4R	4P	4R	4P	4R	4P

Notes:
1 Std. Interior, Bucket Seats
2 Deluxe Interior, Bucket Seats
3 Mach 1
4 Before 9/11/68, with .85" Dia. Stabilizer Bar With GT or Handling Suspension Option
5 From 9/11/68, with .85" Dia. Stabilizer Bar With GT or Handling Suspension Option

1969 MUSTANG Front Spring Application Chart
Hardtop and Grande models.
(Manual Transmissions, Heavy Duty Suspension.)
Note: Refer to chart for spring code identification.

Engine	Model	Three-Speed Options: None	A/C	P/S	A/C & P/S	Four-Speed Options: None	A/C	P/S	A/C & P/S
302	1,2,6	4V	4S	4S	4S	4S	4V	4S	4R
302	1,2,7	4X	4S	4S	4S	4X	4S	4S	4R
351-2V	1,2,6	4S	4R	4S	4R	4S	4R	4S	4R
351-2V	1,2,7	4S	4R	4S	4R	4S	4R	4S	4R
351-4V	1,2,6	4S	4R	4S	4R	4S	4R	4S	4R
351-4V	1,2,7	4S	4R	4S	4R	4S	4R	4R	4R
390	1,2,6	4R	4P	4R	4P	4R	4P	4R	4P
390	1,2,7	4R	4P	4R	4P	4R	4P	4R	4P
302	3,4,6	4V	4S	4S	4R	4V	4S	4S	4R
302	3,4,7	4X	4S	4S	4R	4X	4S	4S	4R
351-2V	3,4,6	4S	4R	4S	4R	4S	4R	4R	4R
351-2V	3,4,7	4S	4R	4S	4R	4S	4R	4R	4R
351-4V	3,4,6	4S	4R	4R	4R	4S	4R	4R	4R
351-4V	3,4,7	4S	4R	4R	4R	4S	4R	4R	4R
390	3,4,6	4R	4P	4R	4P	4R	4P	4R	4P
390	3,4,7	4R	4P	4R	4P	4R	4P	4R	4P
302	5,6	4V	4S	4S	4R	4V	4S	4S	4R
302	5,7	4X	4S	4S	4R	4X	4S	4S	4R
351-2V	5,6	4S	4R	4R	4R	4S	4R	4R	4P
351-2V	5,7	4S	4R	4R	4R	4S	4R	4R	4R
351-4V	5,6	4S	4R	4R	4P	4S	4R	4R	4P
351-4V	5,7	4S	4R	4R	4P	4S	4R	4R	4P
390	5,6	4R	4P	4R	4P	4R	4P	4P	4P
390	5,7	4R	4P	4R	4P	4R	4P	4P	4P

Notes:
1 Std. Interior, Bucket Seats
2 Deluxe Interior, Bucket Seats
3 Std. Interior, Bench Seats
4 Deluxe Interior, Bench Seats
5 Grande model.
6 Before 9/11/68, with .85" Dia. Stabilizer Bar With GT or Handling Suspension Option
7 From 9/11/68, with .85" Dia. Stabilizer Bar With GT or Handling Suspension Option

1969 MUSTANG Front Spring Application Chart
Convertible models.
(Manual Transmissions, Heavy Duty Suspension.)
Note: Refer to chart for spring code identification.

Engine	Model	Three-Speed Options: None	A/C	P/S	A/C & P/S	Four-Speed Options: None	A/C	P/S	A/C & P/S
302	1	4S	4S	4S	4R	4S	4S	4S	4R
302	2	4S	4S	4S	4R	4S	4S	4S	4R
351	1	4S	4R	4R	4P	4S	4R	4R	4P
351-2V	2	4S	4R	4R	4P	4S	4R	4R	4P
351-4V	2	4S	4R	4R	4P	4S	4R	4R	4P
390	1	4R	4P	4P	4P	4R	4P	4P	4N
390	2	4R	4P	4P	4P	4R	4P	4P	4N

Notes:
1 Before 9/11/68, with .85" Dia. Stabilizer Bar With GT or Handling Suspension Option
2 From 9/11/68, with .85" Dia. Stabilizer Bar With GT or Handling Suspension Option

1969 MUSTANG Front Spring Application Chart
SportsRoof and Mach 1 models.
(Automatic Transmissions, Heavy Duty Suspension.)
Note: Refer to chart for spring code identification.

Engine	Model	FMX None	A/C	P/S	A/C & P/S	C4 None	A/C	P/S	A/C & P/S	C6 None	A/C	P/S	A/C & P/S
302	1,2,4					4V	4S	4V	4S				
302	1,2,5					4X	4S	4X	4S				
351	1,2,4	4S	4R	4S	4R								
351-2V	1,2,5	4S	4R	4S	4R								
351-4V	1,2,5	4S	4R	4S	4R								
390	1,2,4									4R	4P	4R	4P
390	1,2,5									4R	4P	4R	4P
390	3,4					4V	4S	4S	4S				
390	3,5					4X	4S	4S	4S				
351-2V	3,4	4S	4R	4R	4R								
351-2V	3,5	4S	4R	4R	4R								
351-4V	3,4	4S	4R	4R	4R								
351-4V	3,5	4S	4R	4R	4R								
390	3,4									4R	4P	4P	4P
390	3,5									4R	4P	4P	4P

Notes:
1 Std. Interior, Bucket Seats
2 Deluxe Interior, Bucket Seats
3 Mach 1
4 Before 9/11/68, with .85" Dia. Stabilizer Bar With GT or Handling Suspension Option.
5 From 9/11/68, with .85" Dia. Stabilizer Bar With GT or Handling Suspension Option.

1969 MUSTANG Front Spring Application Chart
Hardtop and Grande models.
(Automatic Transmissions, Heavy Duty Suspension.)
Note: Refer to chart for spring code identification.

Engine	Notes.	FMX None	A/C	P/S	A/C & P/S	C4 None	A/C	P/S	A/C & P/S	C6 None	A/C	P/S	A/C & P/S
302	1,2,6					4V	4S	4S	4S				
302	1,2,7					4X	4S	4S	4S				
351-2V	1,2,6	4S	4R	4S	4R								
351-2V	1,2,7	4S	4R	4S	4R								
351-4V	1,2,6	4S	4R	4R	4R								
351-4V	1,2,7	4S	4R	4R	4R								
390	1,2,6									4R	4P	4P	4P
390	1,2,7									4R	4P	4P	4P
302	3,4,6					4V	4S	4S	4S				
302	3,4,7					4X	4S	4S	4S				
351-2V	3,4,6	4S	4R	4R	4R								
351-2V	3,4,7	4S	4R	4R	4R								
351-4V	3,4,6	4S	4R	4R	4R								
351-4V	3,4,7	4S	4R	4R	4R								
390	3,4,6									4R	4P	4P	4P
390	3,4,7									4R	4P	4P	4P
302	5,6					4V	4S	4S	4R				
302	5,7					4X	4S	4S	4R				
351-2V	5,6	4S	4R	4R	4R								
351-2V	5,7	4S	4R	4R	4R								
351-4V	5,6	4S	4R	4R	4P								
351-4V	5,7	4S	4R	4R	4P								
390	5,6									4R	4P	4P	4N
390	5,7									4R	4P	4P	4N

Notes:
1 Std. Interior, Bucket Seats
2 Deluxe Interior, Bucket Seats
3 Std. Interior, Bench Seat
4 Deluxe Interior, Bench Seat
5 Grande model.
6 Before 9/11/68, with .85" Dia. Stabilizer Bar With GT or Handling Suspension Option.
7 From 9/11/68, with .85" Dia. Stabilizer Bar

1969 MUSTANG Front Spring Application Chart
Convertible models.
(Automatic Transmissions, Heavy Duty Suspension.)
Note: Refer to chart for spring code identification.

FMX

Engine	Notes	None	A/C	P/S	A/C & P/S
302	1				
302	2				
351	1	4S	4R	4R	4P
351-2V	2	4S	4R	4R	4P
351-4V	2	4S	4R	4R	4P
390	1				
390	2				

C4

None	A/C	P/S	A/C & P/S
4V	4S	4S	4R
4X	4S	4S	4R

C6

None	A/C	P/S	A/C & P/S
4R	4P	4P	4N
4R	4P	4P	4N

Notes:
1   Before 9/11/68, with .85" Dia. Stabilizer Bar With GT or Handling Suspension Option.
2   From 9/11/68, with .85" Dia. Stabilizer Bar With GT or Handling Suspension Option.

1970 MUSTANG Front Spring Application Chart
SportsRoof and Mach 1 models.
(Manual Transmissions, Standard Suspension.)
Note: Refer to chart for spring code identification.

Engine	Model	Three-Speed Options: None	A/C	P/S	A/C & P/S	Four-Speed Options: None	A/C	P/S	A/C & P/S
200	1,2,4	4G	4J	4W	4J				
200	1,2,5	4G	4G	4G	4W				
250	1,2,4	4W	4V	4J	4V				
250	1,2,5	4G	4J	4W	4J				
302-2V	1,2,4	4J	4F	4V	4F	4V	4F	4V	4E
302-2V	1,2,5	4W	4V	4J	4V	4J	4V	4J	4F
302-4V	1,2					6Y	6Y	6Y	4K
351-2V	1,2,4	4V	4E	4F	4E	4F	4E	4F	4E
351-2V	1,2,5	4J	4F	4V	4E	4J	4F	4V	4E
351-4V	1,2,4	4F	4E	4F	4E	4F	4E	4F	4E
351-4V	1,2,5	4J	4F	4V	4E	4J	4F	4V	4E
428	1,2					4L	4M	4M	1Q
429	1,2								6L
428	3					4M	1Q	4M	1Q
429	3								6L

Notes:
1   Std. Interior, Bucket Seats
2   Deluxe Interior, Bucket Seats
3   Mach 1
4   Before 8/28/69
5   From 8/28/69

1970 MUSTANG Front Spring Application Chart
Hardtop and Grande models.
(Manual Transmissions, Standard Suspension.)
Note: Refer to chart for spring code identification.

Engine	Model	Three-Speed Options: None	A/C	P/S	A/C & P/S	Four-Speed Options: None	A/C	P/S	A/C & P/S
200	1,2,4	4G	4J	4W	4J				
200	1,2,5	4G	4W	4G	4W				
250	1,2,4	4W	4V	4J	4V				
250	1,2,5	4G	4J	4W	4J				
302	1,2,4	4V	4F	4V	4E	4V	4F	4V	4E
302	1,2,5	4J	4V	4J	4F	4J	4V	4J	4F
351-2V	1,2,4	4F	4E	4F	4E	4F	4E	4F	4U
351-2V	1,2,5	4J	4V	4J	4E	4V	4F	4V	4E
351-4V	1,2,4	4F	4E	4F	4U	4F	4E	4F	4U
351-4V	1,2,5	4V	4F	4V	4E	4V	4E	4V	4E
428	1,2					4M	1Q	4M	1Q
200	3,4	4W	4J	4W	4V				
200	3,5	4G	4W	4G	4W				
250	3,4	4J	4V	4J	4F				
250	3,5	4W	4J	4W	4J				
302	3,4	4V	4F	4V	4E	4V	4E	4F	4E
302	3,5	4J	4V	4J	4F	4J	4V	4J	4F
351-2V	3,4	4F	4E	4F	4U	4F	4E	4E	4U
351-2V	3,5	4V	4E	4F	4E	4V	4E	4F	4E
351-4V	3,4	4F	4E	4E	4U	4F	4E	4E	4U
351-4V	3,5	4V	4E	4F	4E	4V	4E	4F	4E
428	3					4M	1Q	4M	1Q

Notes:
1   Std. Interior, Bucket Seats
2   Deluxe Interior, Bucket Seats
3   Grande
4   Before 8/28/69
5   From 8/28/69

1970 MUSTANG Front Spring Application Chart
SportsRoof and Mach 1 models.
(Automatic Transmissions, Standard Suspension.)
Note: Refer to chart for spring code identification.

Engine	Model	FMX (or C6; see note.) Options: None	A/C	P/S	A/C & P/S	C4 Options: None	A/C	P/S	A/C & P/S
200	1,2,4					4G	4W	4G	4J
200	1,2,5					4G	4G	4G	4W
250	1,2,4					4W	4J	4J	4V
250	1,2,5					4G	4W	4G	4J
302-2V	1,2,4					4J	4F	4V	4F
302-2V	1,2,5					4W	4V	4J	4V
351-2V	1,2,4	4F	4E	4F	4E				
351-2V	1,2,5	4J	4F	4V	4E				
351-4V	1,2,4	4F	4E	4F	4E				
351-4V	1,2,5	4J	4F	4V	4E				
428	1,2,6	4M	1Q	4M	1Q				
428	3,6	4M	1Q	4M	1Q				

Notes:
1   Std. Interior, Bucket Seats
2   Deluxe Interior, Bucket Seats
3   Mach 1
4   Before 8/28/69
5   From 8/28/69
6   C6 Trasmission; not FMX.

1970 MUSTANG Front Spring Application Chart
Convertible models.
(Manual Transmissions, Standard Suspension.)
Note: Refer to chart for spring code identification.

Engine	Model	Three-Speed Options: None	A/C	P/S	A/C & P/S	Four-Speed Options: None	A/C	P/S	A/C & P/S
200	1,2,3	4W	4J	4W	4V				
200	1,2,4	4G	4W	4G	4J				
250	1,2,3	4J		4J	4F				
250	1,2,4	4W	4J	4W	4V				
302	1,2,3	4V	4E	4F	4E	4V	4E	4F	4E
302	1,2,4	4J	4F	4J	4F	4J	4F	4V	4E
351-2V	1,2,3	4F	4E	4E	4U	4F	4U	4E	4U
351-2V	1,2,4	4V	4E	4F	4E	4V	4E	4F	4U
351-4V	1,2,3	4F	4U	4E	4U	4F	4U	4E	4U
351-4V	1,2,4	4V	4E	4F	4U	4V	4E	4F	4U
428	1,2					4M	1Q	4M	1Q

Notes:
1   Std. Interior, Bucket Seats
2   Deluxe Interior, Bucket Seats
3   Before 8/28/69
4   From 8/28/69

1970 MUSTANG Front Spring Application Chart
Convertible models.
(Automatic Transmissions, Standard Suspension.)
Note: Refer to chart for spring code identification.

Engine	Model	FMX (or C6; see note.) Options: None	A/C	P/S	A/C & P/S	C4 Options: None	A/C	P/S	A/C & P/S
200	1,2,3					4G	4J	4W	4J
200	1,2,4					4G	4W	4G	4W
250	1,2,3					4J	4V	4J	4F
250	1,2,4					4W	4J	4W	4J
302	1,2,3					4V	4F	4F	4E
302	1,2,4					4J	4F	4J	4F
351-2V	1,2,3	4F	4U	4E	4U				
351-2V	1,2,4	4V	4E	4F	4U				
351-4V	1,2,3	4F	4U	4E	4U				
351-4V	1,2,4	4V	4E	4F	4U				
428	1,2,5	4M	1Q	4M	1Q				

Notes:
1   Std. Interior, Bucket Seats
2   Deluxe Interior, Bucket Seats
3   Before 8/28/69
4   From 8/28/69
5   C6 Transmission; not FMX.

1970 MUSTANG Front Spring Application Chart
Hardtop and Grande models.
(Automatic Transmissions, Standard Suspension.)
Note: Refer to chart for spring code identification.

Engine	Model	FMX (or C6; see note.) Options: None	A/C	P/S	A/C & P/S	C4 Options: None	A/C	P/S	A/C & P/S
200	1,2,4					4G	4W	4G	4J
200	1,2,5					4G	4G	4G	4W
250	1,2,4					4W	4V	4J	4V
250	1,2,5					4G	4J	4W	4J
302	1,2,4					4V	4F	4V	4F
302	1,2,5					4J	4V	4J	4F
351-2V	1,2,4	4F	4E	4F	4U				
351-2V	1,2,5	4V	4F	4V	4E				
351-4V	1,2,4	4F	4E	4F	4U				
351-4V	1,2,5	4V	4E	4V	4E				
428	1,2,6	4M	1Q	4M	1Q				
200	3,4					4G	4J	4W	4J
200	3,5					4G	4W	4G	4W
250	3,4					4J	4V	4J	4V
250	3,5					4G	4J	4W	4J
302	3,4					4V	4F	4V	4E
302	3,5					4J	4V	4J	4F
351-2V	3,4	4F	4E	4F	4U				
351-2V	3,5	4V	4E	4F	4E				
351-4V	3,4	4F	4E	4E	4U				
351-4V	3,5	4V	4E	4F	4E				
428	3,6	4M	1Q	4M	1Q				

Notes:
1   Std. Interior, Bucket Seats
2   Deluxe Interior, Bucket Seats
3   Grande
4   Before 8/28/69
5   From 8/28/69
6   C6 Transmission; not FMX.

1970 MUSTANG Front Spring Application Chart
Heavy Duty Suspension, All Models with Manual Transmissions.
Note: Refer to chart for spring code identification.

Engine	Notes	Three-Speed Options: None	A/C	P/S	A/C & P/S	Four-Speed Options: None	A/C	P/S	A/C & P/S
302-2V	1	4X	4S	4X	4S	4X	4S	4X	4S
351	1	4K	4L	4K	4L	4K	4L	4K	4L
351	2	4K	4L	4K	4L	4K	4L	4K	4L
302	3	4X	4S	4X	4R	4X	4S	4X	4R
351	3	4K	4L	4K	4L	4K	4L	4K	4L
302	4	4X	4S	4S	4R	4X	4S	4S	4R
351	4	4K	4L	4K	4L	4K	4L	4K	4L
302	5	4X	4R	4S	4R	4S	4R	4S	4R
351	5	4K	4L	4L	4M	4K	4L	4L	4M

Notes:
1   SportsRoof, Standard or Deluxe Interior
2   Mach 1
3   Hardtop, Standard or Deluxe Interior
4   Hardtop, Grande model
5   Convertible, Standard or Deluxe Interior

1970 MUSTANG Front Spring Application Chart
Heavy Duty Suspension, All Models with Automatic Transmissions.
Note: Refer to chart for spring code identification.

Engine	Notes	FMX Options: None	A/C	P/S	A/C & P/S	C4 Options: None	A/C	P/S	A/C & P/S
302-2V	1					4X	4S	4X	4S
351	1	4K	4L	4K	4L				
351	2	4K	4L	4K	4L				
302	3					4X	4S	4X	4S
351	3	4K	4L	4K	4L				
302	4					4X	4S	4S	4R
351	4	4K	4L	4K	4L				
302	5					4S	4R	4S	4R
351	5	4K	4L	4L	4M				

Notes:
1   SportsRoof, Standard or Deluxe Interior
2   Mach 1
3   Hardtop, Standard or Deluxe Interior
4   Hardtop, Grande model
5   Convertible, Standard or Deluxe Interior

Spring Code	Part Number	Color Stripe	Normal Load Lbs.	No. of Coils	Wire Dia. Inches	Free Length
25	C7ZZ-5310-AJ	1 Orange	1610	9-3/4	.675	18-1/2
	r/b C7ZZ-5310-C (4F)					
68	C7ZZ-5310-AL	1 Brown	1454	9-3/16	.575	16-5/8
	r/b C7ZZ-5310-Z (4J)					
82	C5ZZ-5310-A	1 Pink	1279	8-1/2	.570	15-1/8
	r/b C5ZZ-5310-B					
84	C5ZZ-5310-B	1 Green	1344	8-1/2	.570	15-3/8
86	C5ZZ-5310-C	1 Gray	1490	8-1/2	.585	15-1/2
88	C5ZZ-5310-D	1 Violet	1413	8-1/2	.585	15-1/4
	r/b C5ZZ-5310-C (86)					
89	C5ZZ-5310-E	1 Brown	1491	8	.600	14-1/8
90	C5ZZ-5310-F	1 Red	1413	8	.600	13-7/8
	r/b C5ZZ-5310-E (89)					
1Q	C7ZZ-5310-AR	Gold/Gray	1850	8-3/4	.650	15-1/8
4A	C7ZZ-5310-H	Gray/Green	2130	8-1/2	.760	15 1/8
	r/b C9AZ-5310-Z (4J)					
4C	C7ZZ-5310-BB	Gray/Yellow	1900	9	.635	16
4D	C7ZZ-5310-A	Pink/Violet	1790	9-1/2	.610	16-7/8
4E	C7ZZ-5310-B	Tan/Violet	1650	9	.600	16-3/8
4F	C7ZZ-5310-C	Orange/Violet	1580	9	.600	16-1/8
4G	C7ZZ-5310-F	1 Green	1342	9-1/4	.575	16-1/8
4H	C7ZZ-5310-Y	Orange/Red	1400	8-3/4	.585	15-3/4
	r/b C7ZZ-5310-Z (4J)					
4J	C7ZZ-5310-Z	Gold/Red	1460	8-3/4	.585	16
4K	C7ZZ-5310-AA	Gold/Orange	1580	8	.635	14-3/8
4L	C7ZZ-5310-AB	Gold/Tan	1670	8-3/4	.650	14-5/8
4M	C7ZZ-5310-AC	Gold/Pink	1760	8-3/4	.650	14-7/8
4N	C7ZZ-5310-AD	Green/Yellow	1820	9	.635	15-3/4
4P	C7ZZ-5310-AD	Gold/Yellow	1740	9	.635	15-1/2
4R	C7ZZ-5310-AF	Tan/Yellow	1660	8-3/4	.625	15-1/4
4S	C7ZZ-5310-AG	Orange/Yellow	1580	8-3/4	.625	15
4T	C7ZZ-5310-AH	1 Pink	1286	9-1/4	.575	15-7/8
	r/b C7ZZ-5310-F (4G)					
4U	C7ZZ-5310-AK	Gold/Violet	1720	9-1/2	.610	16-5/8
4V	C7ZZ-5310-AN	Red/Yellow	1520	9 1/2	.600	16-1/4
4W	C7ZZ-5310-AP	Brown/Gray	1398	9-1/4	.575	16-3/8
	r/b C7ZZ-5310-Z (4J)					
4X	C7ZZ-5310-AZ	Violet/Yellow	1500	8-3/4	.625	14-3/4
4Y	C7ZZ-5310-BA	Gray/Violet	1860	9-1/2	.610	17-1/8
6D	C8ZZ-5310-A	Gray/Gold	1850	8-3/4	.650	15-1/8
6L	C9ZZ-5310-B	Data not provided in Master Parts Chart				
6Y	D0ZZ-5310-A	2 Gold/Violet	1490	8-1/8	.629	14-5/16
	r/b C7ZZ-5310-AA (4K)					

MUSTANG FRONT STABILIZER BAR ASSEMBLY CHART #1, 1965-1968

Year	Cyl/CID	Model	Type	Dia.	Identification	Part Number
65	6/170		S			C5ZZ-5482-B
65	6/200		S			C5ZZ-5482-B
65	8/260		S			C5ZZ-5482-B
65	8/289	EXC. GT350 K	S			C5ZZ-5482-B
65	8/289	GT350	S			S1MS-5482-A
65	8/289	K	S	13/16	NONE	C5ZZ-5482-A
66	6/200		S			C5ZZ-5482-B
66	8/289	EXC. GT350 K	S			C5ZZ-5482-B
66	8/289	GT350	S			S1MS-5482-A
66	8/289	K	S	13/16	NONE	C5ZZ-5482-A
67	6/200		S	'3/4		C7WY-5482-A
67	8/289	EXC. GT350, GT K	S	'3/4		C7WY-5482-A
67	8/289	GT350	S			C9ZZ-5482-E
67	8/289	GT w/ IMPROVED HANDLING PKG	S	'7/8	1G	C7ZZ-5482-C
67	8/289	w/ MAXIMUM HANDLING PKG	S			C9ZZ-5482-E
67	8/289	K	S			C9ZZ-5482-E
67	8/390		S	'3/4	1Y-1B	C7ZZ-5482-B
67	8/390	GT w/ IMPROVED HANDLING PKG	S	'7/8	1G	C7ZZ-5482-C
67	8/390	GT500	S			C9ZZ-5482-E
68	6/200		S	'3/4		C7WY-5482-A
68	8/289	EXC. GT 350, GT	S	'3/4		C7WY-5482-A
68	8/289	GT350	S			C9ZZ-5482-E
68	8/289	GT w/ IMPROVED HANDLING PKG	S	'7/8	1G	C7ZZ-5482-C
68	8/289	GT w/ MAXIMUM HANDLING PKG	S			C9ZZ-5482-E
68	8/302	EXC. GT350,GT	S	'3/4		C7WY-5482-A
68	8/302	GT350	S	.		C9ZZ-5482-E
68	8/302	GT w/ IMPROVED HANDLING PKG	S	'7/8	1G	C7ZZ-5482-C
68	8/302	GT w/ MAXIMUM HANDLING PKG	S			C9ZZ-5482-E
68	8/390	EXC. GT	S	'3/4	1Y-1B	C7ZZ-5482-B
68	8/390	GT w/ IMPROVED HANDLING PKG.	S	'7/8	1G`	C7ZZ-5482-C
68	8/390	GT w/ MAXIMUM HANDLING PKG	S			C9ZZ-5482-E
68	8/428	GT w/ MAXIMUM HANDLING PKG	S			C9ZZ-5482-E
68	8/428	GT350/500	S			C9ZZ-5482-E
68	8/428	GT350/500	S			C9ZZ-5482-E

MUSTANG FRONT STABILIZER BAR ASSEMBLY CHART #2, 1969 and 1970

Year	Cyl/CID	Model	Type	Dia.	Ident.	Part Number
69	6/200		S	11/16	1P-1GO	C9ZZ-5482-B
69	6/250		S	11/16	1P-1GO	C9ZZ-5482-B
69	8/302-2B		S	11/16	1P-1GO	C9ZZ-5482-B
69	8/302-2B	GT w/ IMPROVED HANDLING PKG	S	7/8	1G	C7ZZ-5482-C
69	8/302-4B	BOSS (Note 1)	S	7/8	1G	C9ZZ-5482-D
69	8/302-4B	BOSS (Note 2)	S	3/4	1Y-1B	C9ZZ-5482-C
69	8/302-4B	GT w/ IMPROVED HANDLING PKG	S	7/8	1G	C7ZZ-5482-C
69	8/351	All, non-Mach 1	S	11/16	1P-2GO	C9ZZ-5482-B
69	8/351	MACH 1	S	7/8	1G	C9ZZ-5482-D
69	8/390	All, non-Mach 1 w/o SPECIAL HANDLING PKG	S	3/4	1Y-1B	C9ZZ-5482-C
69	8/390	w/ SPECIAL HANDLING PKG	S	7/8	1G	C9ZZ-5482-D
69	8/390	GT w/ IMPROVED HANDLING PKG	S	7/8	1G	C7ZZ-5482-C
69	8/428		S	15/16	1G-1Y	C9ZZ-5482-E
69	8/429	BOSS	S	15/16	1G-1Y	C9ZZ-5482-E
70	6/200		S			D0ZZ-5482-A
70	6/250		S			D0ZZ-5482-A
70	8/302-2/B		S			D0ZZ-5482-A
70	8/302-2/B		H/D	11/16	1P-2GO	C9ZZ-5482-B
70	8/302-2/B	W/ COMPETITION HANDLING PKG	S	7/8	1G	C9ZZ-5482-D
70	8/302-4/B	BOSS	S	15/16	1G-1Y	C9ZZ-5482-E
70	8/351		S			D0ZZ-5482-A
70	8/351		H/D	15/16	1G-1Y	C9ZZ-5482-E
70	8/428			15/16	1G-1Y	C9ZZ-5482-E

Notes:
1 Before 4/14/69
2 From 4/14/69

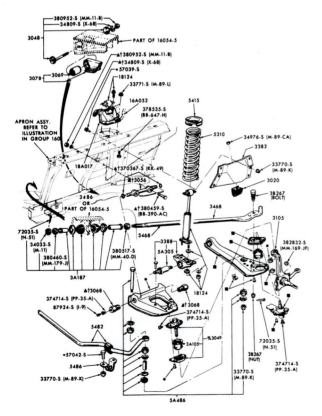

Typical 1968-1970 Mustang front suspension system.

Year	Model	Description	Part Number
65/66	Exc. GT-350		C3DZ-5486-A
65/66	GT-350		C0DD-5486-A
67	6 & 8 Cyl		C6OZ-5486-B
	Exc. 289-4V		
67	8 Cyl 289 4V		C7ZZ-5486-A
68	6 & 8 Cyl.		C6OZ-5486-B
	Exc. 390 w/ Competition		
	Handling Package		
	or GT Equipment Group		
68	8 Cyl 390 w/ Competition		C7ZZ-5486-A
	Handling Package		
	or GT Equipment Group		
69	6/8 Cyl. Exc. 390 w/ Comp.		C6OZ-5486-B
	Handling Pkg, 428, Boss		
69	8 Cyl 390 w/ Competition		C7ZZ-5486-A
	Handling Package		
	w/ GT Equipment Group		
69	8 Cyl 428 W/GT & Comp.		C7ZZ-5486-A
	Handling Pkg.		
69	Boss 302	Before 4/14/69	C6OZ-5486-B
69	Boss 302	From 4/14/69	C7ZZ-5486-A
69	Boss 429	R.H., for Front Stab. Bar	C9ZZ-5486-A
69	Boss 429	L.H., for Front Stab. Bar	C9ZZ-5486-B
69	Boss 429	for Rear Stab. Bar	C9ZZ-5486-C
70	6 & 8 Cyl 302	for Front Stab. Bar	C6OZ-5486-B
70	8 Cyl 351 Exc. Mach 1 &	for Front Stab. Bar	C6OZ-5486-B
	all Comp. Handling Pkg		
70	Boss 302 8 Cyl, 428	for Rear Stab. Bar	D0OZ-5486-A
	Competition Handling Pkg		
70	8 Cyl 351, Exc. Mach 1,	for Front Stab. Bar	C7ZZ-5486-A
	w/ GT & Comp. Hand. Pkgs		
70	Mach 1, 8 Cyl 351	for Front Stab. Bar	C7ZZ-5486-A
70	8 Cyl. 428	for Front Stab. Bar	C7ZZ-5486-A
70	Boss 429	R.H., for Front Stab. Bar	C9ZZ-5486-A
70	Boss 429	L.H., for Front Stab. Bar	C9ZZ-5486-B
70	Boss 429	for Rear Stab. Bar	D0OZ-5486-A

Year	Model	Description	Part Number
65/66	F/B & Conv., 6 cyl. & 8 cyl. 260,	4 leaf-650 lb. load rate	C5ZZ-5560-D
	289-2V, 289-4V Premium Fuel	C4ZA-5556-B,D,F,N,U	
65/66	Hardtop, 6 Cyl., & 8 cyl., 260,	4 leaf-610 lb. load rate	C5ZZ-5560-C
	289-2V, 289-4V Premium Fuel	C4ZA-5556-C,E,M,T	
65/66	F/B & Conv., 8 cyl. 289-4V Hi-Po	4 leaf-650 lb. load rate	C5ZZ-5560-E
		C4ZA-5556-K,L,S,Y	
		r/b C7ZZ-5560-M	
65/66	Hardtop, 8 cyl. 289-4V Hi-Po	4 leaf-610 lb. load rate	C5ZZ-5560-F
		C4ZA-5556-H,J,R,V	
67	Hardtop, 6 Cyl. & 8 cyl. 289	4 leaf-650 lb. load rate	C4DZ-5560-J
	Before 9/20/66	C4DA-5556-U	
67	F/B, 6 cyl. & 8 cyl., 289-2V &	4 leaf-650 lb. load rate	C4DZ-5560-J
	289-4V (P.F.) from 9/20/66	C4DA-5556-U	
67	Hardtop, 6 cyl., 8 cyl. 289-2V,	4 leaf-650 lb. load rate	C4DZ-5560-J
	289-4V & 390 from 9/20/66	C4DA-5556-U	
67	F/B, 6 cyl. & 8 cyl.,	4 leaf-650 lb. load rate	C7ZZ-5560-A
	Before 9/20/66	C7ZA-5556-J,AB	
		r/b C4DZ-5560-J	
67	F/B, 8 Cyl. 390, from 9/20/66	4 leaf-650 lb. load rate	C7ZZ-5560-A
		C7ZA-5556-J,AB	
		r/b C4DZ-5560-J	
67	Conv. 6 cyl, 8 cyl. 289-2V,	4 leaf-650 lb. load rate	C7ZZ-5560-A
	289-4V (P.F.), 390 from 9/20/66	C7ZA-5556-J,AB	
		r/b C4DZ-5560-J	
67	F/B, Conv. 8 cyl. 390	4 leaf-665 lb. load rate	C7ZZ-5560-C
	Before 10/26/66	C7ZA-5556-N,AD	
		r/b C7ZZ-5560-M	
67	Hardtop 8 cyl. 390	4 leaf-625 lb. load rate	C7ZZ-5560-D
	Before 10/26/66	C7ZA-5556-S,AF	
		r/b C7ZZ-5560-M	
67	F/B, 8 cyl. 289, 390, from	4 leaf-665 lb. load rate	C7ZZ-5560-M
	10/26/66, Handling Package	C7ZA-5556-AS,AT,AU,AV	
67	H/T, Conv. 8 cyl., from	4 leaf-665 lb. load rate	C7ZZ-5560-M
	10/26/66, Handling Package	C7ZA-5556-AS,AT,AU,AV	
67	F/B, Conv. 8 cyl. 289, 390, before	4 leaf-665 lb. load rate	C7ZZ-5560-J
	11/15/66, Comp. Handling GT only	C7ZA-5556-AG	
		r/b C7ZZ-5560-M	
67	Hardtop, 8 cyl. 289, 390, before	4 leaf-625 lb. load rate	C7ZZ-5560-K
	11/15/66, Comp. Handling GT only	C7ZA-5556-AJ	
		r/b C7ZZ-5560-T	

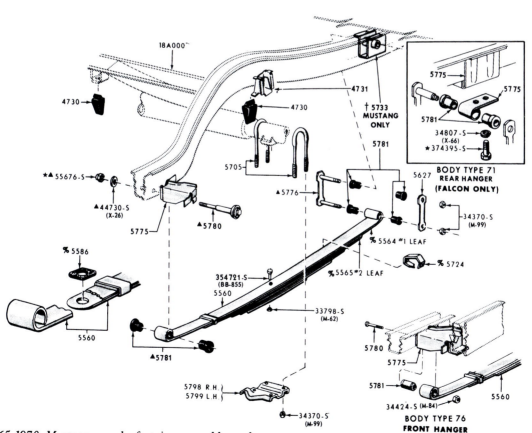

The 1965-1970 Mustang rear leaf spring assembly and attaching hardware.

Year	Model	Description	Part Number
67/68	F/B 8 cyl. 289 for competition	4 leaf-625 lb. load rate	C7ZZ-5560-U
	handling GT only, before 11/15/66	C7ZA-5556-AN,AR	
		r/b C7ZZ-5560-T	
67/68	H/T 8 cyl. 289, 390 for comp.	4 leaf-625 lb. load rate	C7ZZ-5560-U
	handling GT only, before 11/15/66	C7ZA-5556-AN,AR	
		r/b C7ZZ-5560-T	
67/68	GT-350; GT-500	4 leaf-625 lb. load rate	C7ZZ-5560-U
		C7ZA-5556-AN,AR	
		r/b C7ZZ-5560-T	
67/68	F/B 8 cyl. 390 for competition	4 leaf-665 lb. load rate	C7ZZ-5560-T
	handling GT only, before 11/15/66	C7ZA-5556-AL,AM	
67/68	Conv. 8 cyl. 289, 390 for comp	4 leaf-665 lb. load rate	C7ZZ-5560-T
	handling GT only, before 11/15/66	C7ZA-5556-AL,AM	
67/68	GT-350; GT-500	4 leaf-665 lb. load rate	C7ZZ-5560-T
		C7ZA-5556-AL,AM	
68	F/B, 6 cyl., 8 cyl., 289-2V	4 leaf-650 lb. load rate	C4DZ-5560-J
	& 302-4V except GT-350	C4DA-5556-U	
68	Hardtop	4 leaf-650 lb. load rate	C4DZ-5560-J
		C4DA-5556-U	
68	F/B 8 cyl. 289,302-4V	4 leaf-625 lb. load rate	C7ZZ-5560-D
	Except GT-350	C7ZA-5556-S, AF	
		r/b C7ZZ-5560-M	
68	H/T 8 cyl. 289,302-4V	4 leaf-625 lb. load rate	C7ZZ-5560-D
	Except GT-350	C7ZA-5556-S, AF	
		r/b C7ZZ-5560-M	
68	F/B 8 cyl. 289,302,390-4V	4 leaf-625 lb. load rate	C7ZZ-5560-M
	Except GT-350	C7ZA-5556-AS,AT,AU,AV	
68	H/T, Conv. 8 cyl. 289, 302-4V	4 leaf-625 lb. load rate	C7ZZ-5560-M
	& 390-4V, except GT-350	C7ZA-5556-AS,AT,AU,AV	
68	F/B, Conv. 8 cyl. 390-2VPF & 4V	4 leaf-650 lb. load rate	C7ZZ-5560-A
		C7ZA-5556-J,AB	
		r/b C7ZZ-5560-J	
68	Conv. 6 cyl., 8 cyl. 289-2V,	4 leaf-650 lb. load rate	C7ZZ-5560-A
	& 302-4V, except GT-350	C7ZA-5556-J,AB	
		r/b C7ZZ-5560-J	
68	F/B, Conv. 8 cyl. 390-4V	4 leaf-665 lb. load rate	C7ZZ-5560-C
		C7ZA-5556-N,AD	
		r/b C7ZZ-5560-M	
68	Conv. 8 cyl. 289-2V,	4 leaf-665 lb. load rate	C7ZZ-5560-C
	& 302-4V, except GT-350	C7ZA-5556-N,AD	
		r/b C7ZZ-5560-M	
68	F/B,H/T,Conv. 8 cyl. 390-2V(P.F.),	4 leaf-665 lb. load rate	C7ZZ-5560-C
	428CJ-4V w/ impr. handling	C7ZA-5556-N,AD	
	package, except GT-500	r/b C7ZZ-5560-M	

Year	Model	Description	Part Number
69	F/B 8 Cyl. 302, Before 9/10/68	4 leaf-700 lb. load rate	C9ZZ-5560-A
		C9ZA-5556-B	
69	F/B 351, 390-4V; exc. GT-350;	4 leaf-700 lb. load rate	C9ZZ-5560-A
	Exc. Mach 1; Before 9/10/68	C9ZA-5556-B	
69	Conv. 6 Cyl.; 8 Cyl. 302, 351,	4 leaf-700 lb. load rate	C9ZZ-5560-A
	390-4V; exc. GT-350	C9ZA-5556-B	
69	F/B 8 Cyl. 302 w/ Improved	4 leaf-665 lb. load rate	C7ZZ-5560-M
	Handling Package	C7ZA-5556-AS,AT,AU,AV	
69	Hardtop, 8 Cyl. 302, 351, 390-4V	4 leaf-665 lb. load rate	C7ZZ-5560-M
	w/ Improved Handling Package	C7ZA-5556-AS,AT,AU,AV	
69	F/B 8 Cyl. 390 for Competition	4 leaf-665 lb. load rate	C7ZZ-5560-T
	Handling GT only.	C7ZA-5556-AL,AM	
69	Conv. 8 Cyl. 289, 390 for	4 leaf-665 lb. load rate	C7ZZ-5560-T
	Competition Handling GT only.	C7ZA-5556-AL,AM	
69	Hardtop, exc. Grandé, 6 Cyl.,	4 leaf-650 lb. load rate	C4DZ-5560-J
	8 Cyl. 302,351,390	C4DA-5556-U	
69	Hardtop, Grandé from 9/10/68	4 leaf-650 lb. load rate	C4DZ-5560-J
		C4DA-5556-U	
69	F/B 8 Cyl. 289 for Competition	4 leaf-625 lb. load rate	C7ZZ-5560-U
	Handling GT only.	C7ZA-5556-AN,AR	
		r/b C7ZZ-5560-T	
69	H/T 8 Cyl. 289, 390 for Comp.	4 leaf-625 lb. load rate	C7ZZ-5560-U
	Handling GT only.	C7ZA-5556-AN,AR	
		C7ZA-5556-AN,AR	
69	Hardtop, Grandé , all 6 Cyl., 8 Cyl.	4 leaf-665 lb. load rate	C9ZZ-5560-E
	302, 351,390-4V Before 9/10/68	C9ZA-5556-K,M	
		r/b C4DZ-5560-J	
69	Conv. 6 Cyl., 8 Cyl. 302,351,390	4 leaf-650 lb. load rate	C7ZZ-5560-A
		C7ZA-5556-J,AB	
		r/b C4DZ-5560-J	
69	F/B 6 Cyl., 8 Cyl. 351,390, Exc.	4 leaf-595 lb. load rate	C9ZZ-5560-H
	GT-350, Mach 1, From 9/10/68	C9ZA-5556-R	
69	F/B, 8 cyl. 302, Exc. Boss 302	4 leaf-595 lb. load rate	C9ZZ-5560-H
	From 9/10/68	C9ZA-5556-R	
69	F/B, H/T, 428 Exc. GT-500 &	4 leaf-690 lb. load rate	C9ZZ-5560-D
	Grandé; w/o trunk battery	C9ZA-5556-H	
		2 Gold, 1 Violet Stripes	
69	F/B, H/T, 428 Exc. GT-500 &	4 leaf-730 lb. load rate	C9ZZ-5560-C
	Grandé; with trunk battery	C9ZA-5556-F	
		2 Yellow, 2 Brown Stripes	
69	Conv., 428 Exc. GT-500;	4 leaf-730 lb. load rate	C9ZZ-5560-C
	with or without trunk battery	C9ZA-5556-F	
		2 Yellow, 2 Brown Stripes	

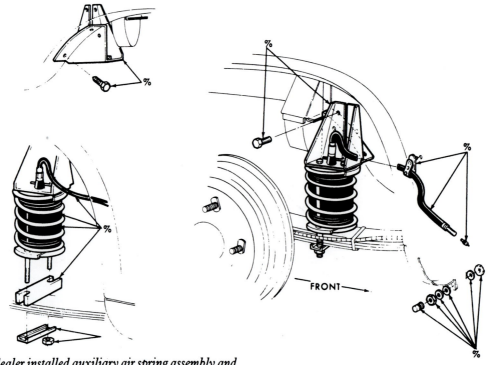

Optional dealer installed auxiliary air spring assembly and mounting hardware for all 1965-1970 Mustangs.

Year	Model	Right Hand	Left Hand	Notes
'65'66		C5DZ-5796-A	C5DZ-5796-B	
'67	Exc. 428-CJ	C6DZ-5796-A	C6DZ-5796-B	
'68	Exc. 428-CJ	C6DZ-5796-A	C6DZ-5796-B	
'68	8 Cyl. 428-CJ	C8ZZ-5796-A	C8ZZ-5796-B	
'69	Exc. Grandé, Boss 302, 428-CJ	C6DZ-5796-A	C6DZ-5796-B	
'69	Grandé	C9OZ-5796-C	C9OZ-5796-B	Before 9/10/68
'69	Grandé	C6DZ-5796-A	C6DZ-5796-B	From 9/10/68
'69	8 Cyl 428-CJ	C8ZZ-5796-A	C8ZZ-5796-B	
'69	Boss 302	C8ZZ-5796-A	C8ZZ-5796-B	
'70	6 Cyl., 8 Cyl. 302-2V, 351	C6DZ-5796-A	C6DZ-5796-B	
'70	8 Cyl. 428-CJ, 429-CJ A/T	C6DZ-5796-A	C6DZ-5796-B	
'70	8 Cyl. 428-CJ, 429-CJ M/T	C8ZZ-5796-A	C8ZZ-5796-B	
'70	Boss 302	C8ZZ-5796-A	C8ZZ-5796-B	

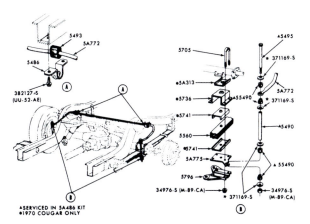

Rear sway bar and attaching hardware for 1970 Mustangs equipped with optional handling package.

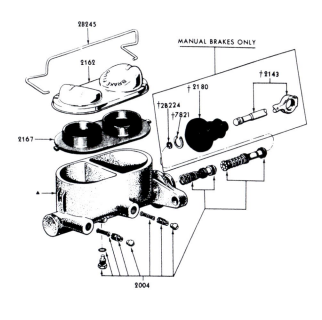

The 1967-1970 Mustang brake master cylinder with dual reservoir.

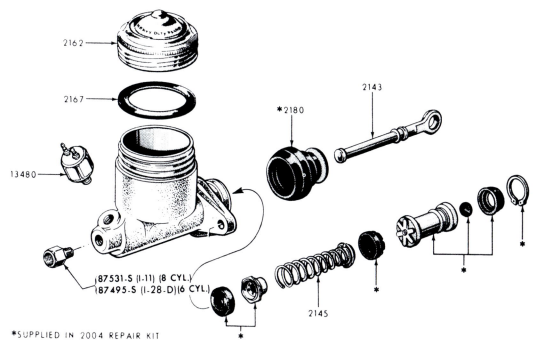

The 1965-1966 Mustang brake master cylinder with single reservoir.

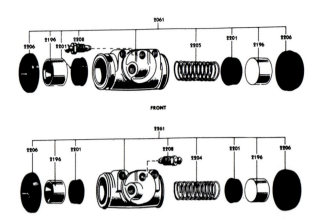

The 1966-1970 Mustang front and rear wheel cylinder assemblies.

MUSTANG FRONT BRAKE CYLINDER ASSEMBLY APPLICATION CHART

YEAR	MODEL	LOCATION	DIAMETER	PART NUMBER	NOTES
65/69	9" x 2-1/4" brakes	R.H.	1-1/16"	C5DZ-2061-A	
		L.H.		C5DZ-2061-A	
65/69	10" x 2-1/4" brakes	R.H.	1-1/8"	C3OZ-2061-B	
		L.H.		C3OZ-2062-B	
66/69	10" x 2-1/2" brakes	R.H.	1-3/32"	C6OZ-2061-A	1
				C9TZ-2062-B	2
		L.H.	7/8"	C6OZ-2062-A	1
				C9TZ-2062-B	2
70	9" x 2-1/4" brakes	R.H.	1-1/16"	C5DZ-2061-A	
		L.H.		C5DZ-2062-A	
70	10" x 2-1/4", or	R.H.	1-1/8"	C3OZ-2061-B	
	10" x 2-1/2" brakes	L.H.		C3OZ-2062-B	

NOTES:
1. Original
2. Service Replacement

MUSTANG REAR BRAKE CYLINDER ASSEMBLY APPLICATION CHART

YEAR	MODEL	LOCATION	DIAMETER	PART NUMBER	NOTES
65		R.H.	13/16"	C3DZ-2261-A	
		L.H.		C3DZ-2261-A	
65	6 cylinder	R.H.	29/32"	C5DZ-2261-B	
		L.H.		C5DZ-2261-B	
65/66	6 cylinder	R.H.	27/32"	C5DZ-2261-A	
		L.H.		C5DZ-2261-A	
66		R.H.	7/8"	C6OZ-2261-A	1
				D2ZZ-2261-A	2
		L.H.		C6OZ-2262-A	1
				D2ZZ-2261-A	2
65/66	8 cylinder	R.H.	29/32"	C3OZ-2261-B	
		L.H.		C3OZ-2261-B	1
				D2ZZ-2262-B	2
67/68	8 cylinder 390-4/B	R.H.	13/16"	C7ZZ-2262-A	
		L.H.		C7ZZ-2262-A	
67/69	6 cylinder	R.H.	27/32"	C5DZ-2261-A	
		L.H.		C5DZ-2261-A	
67/69	8 cyl. 289-4/B-GT	R.H.	7/8"	C6OZ-2262-A	1
				D2ZZ-2262-A	2
		L.H.		C6OZ-2262-A	1
				D2ZZ-2262-A	2
67/69		R.H.	7/8"	C6OZ-2261-A	1
				D2ZZ-2261-A	2
		L.H.		C6OZ-2262-A	1
				D2ZZ-2262-A	2
70	6 cylinder 200	R.H.	27/32"	C5DZ-2261-A	
		L.H.		C5DZ-2261-A	
70	6 cyl. 250, 8 cyl. 302	R.H.	7/8"	C6OZ-2261-A	1
				D2ZZ-2261-A	2
		L.H.		C6OZ-2262-A	1
				D2ZZ-2262-A	2
70	8 cylinder 351, 428	R.H.	29/32"	C3OZ-2262-B	1
				D2ZZ-2262-B	2
		L.H.		C3OZ-2262-B	1
				D2ZZ-2262-B	2

NOTES:
1. * Original
2. ^ Service replacement

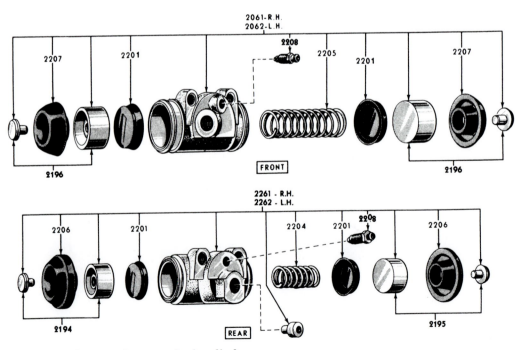

The 1965 Mustang front and rear wheel cylinder assemblies.

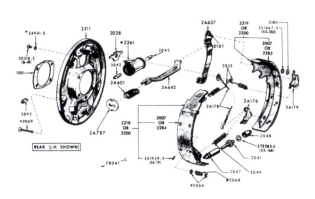

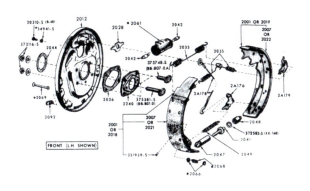

The 1965-1970 Mustang front and rear drum brake assemblies.

By 1967 the chassis had been redesigned and the new body was designed to accept a common brake booster and new dual reservoir master cylinder. The brake system was split to separate the front brakes from the rear brakes hence the reason for the two-chamber master cylinder. The split system provided two wheel brakes if either the front or the rear circuits failed.

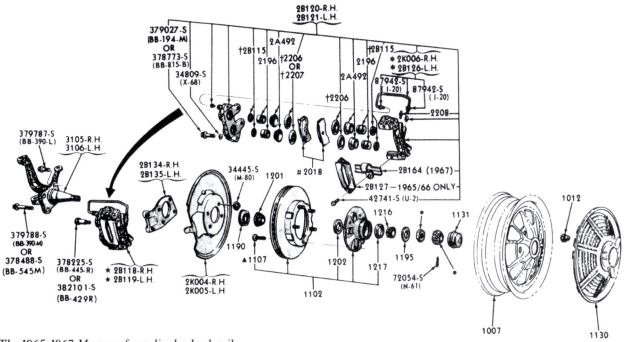

The 1965-1967 Mustang front disc brake details.

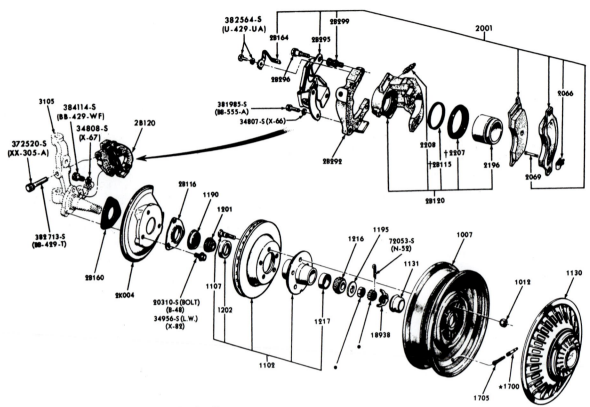

The 1968-1970 Mustang front disc brake details.

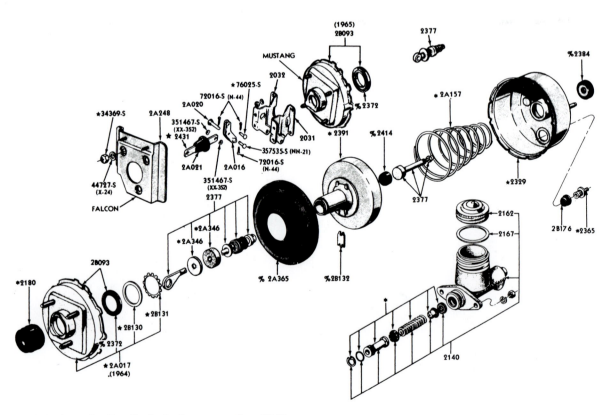

Exploded view of a Bendix brake booster used on 1965-1966 Mustangs.

As we mentioned earlier, the first Mustang was adapted from the Falcon. Neither car was engineered for power brakes because there was not enough distance provided between the left shock tower and the firewall for a brake booster and master cylinder. So, in an effort to retrofit the old chassis, an elaborate bracket and lever assembly was used to adapt a compact Bendix booster and single piston master cylinder. To clear the shock tower, the bracket positioned the assembly higher than stock and angled it slightly upward. The linkage connected the remote booster to the brake pedal. At $42.29, power brakes was not a popular option in 1966.

POWER BRAKE BOOSTER INSTALLATION KIT
Retrofit for Mustangs

YEAR	MODEL						
65/66	Drum brakes						C6ZZ-2A091-A
	Consists of:						
	C6ZA-2A040-C	Tube	C6ZA-2420-A	Tube	(2) 376428-S8	Clamp	
	B9SS-2A047-A	Hose	C6AZ-9A474-A	Fitting	(2) 376977-S2	Screw, washer	
	C6ZA-2B195-A	Booster, M. cyl.	C6AZ-9A474-B	Fitting	380613-S	Cap	
	C6OA-2420-D	Tube			380614-S	Cap	
67	Drum brakes without collapsible steering column						C7ZZ-2A091-A
	Consists of:						
	C7ZA-2A040-F	Tube	C7ZZ-2455-B	Pedal (M/T)	(4) 55748-S	Locknut	
	C1AA-2A047-D	Hose	C7ZZ-2455-K	Pedal (A/T)	351053-S	Strap	
	C7ZA-2A188-A	Spacer	(2) B7AZ-2471-A	Bushing	353574-S7	Washer	
	C7WA-2B195-E	Booster, M. cyl.	C7OA-7B086-A	Connector	(2) 376428-S8	Clamp	
	C7ZA-2B253-E	Tube	C6AZ-9A474-A	Fitting	376977-S2	Screw, washer	
	C6OA-2420-D	Tube	C6AZ-9A474-B	Fitting	380613-S	Cap	
	C70A-2420-A	Tube	34419 - S2	Locknut	380614-S	Cap	
	C7ZA-2420-A	Tube	(4) 44728-S	Washer		Installation sketch	
	C7ZA-2420-B	Tube	45534-S2	Bolt			
68	Drum brakes						C8ZZ-2A091-A
	Consists of:						
	C8WY-2O05-A	Booster	C8AA-2420-G	Tube	45534-S2	Bolt	
	C8ZA-2A040-E	Tube	C8ZZ-2455-A	Pedal (A/T)	(4) 55748-S	Locknut	
	C8AA-2A040-A	Hose	C8ZZ-2455-C	Pedal (M/T)	351053-S	Strap	
	C8ZA-2169-A	Piston	(2) 33799-S	Nut	353574-S7	Washer	
	C7ZA-2A188-A	Spacer	34419-S2	Locknut	353777-S	Connector	
	C8ZA-2B253-E	Tube	(2) 34807-S2	Lockwasher	(2) 376428-S8	Clamp	
			(4) 44728-S	Washer	376977-S2	Screw, washer	
69	Drum brakes		With manual transmission use C9ZZ-2455-D in place of kit pedal.				C9ZZ-2A091-A
	Consists of:						
	C9ZJ-2005-B	Booster	C8ZA-2B253-E	Tube	353777-S	Connector	
	C9ZJ-2B022-A	Gasket	C8AA-2420-G	Tube	(2) 376428-S8	Clamp	
	C8ZA-2A040-E	Tube	C9ZZ-2455-E	Pedal (A/T)	376977-S2	Screw, washer	
	C8ZZ-2A047-A	Hose	56349-S4	Bolt	(6) 377706-S	Locknut	
	C9AZ-2169-F	Piston	351053-S	Strap	380699-S100	Pin	
	C7ZA-2A188-A	Spacer	35374-S7	Washer	382802-S100	Locknut	
70	Drum brakes		With man. trans., use D1ZZ-2455-A in place of kit pedal. Not replaced.				DOZZ-2A091-A
	Consists of:						
	C9ZJ-2005-B	Booster	C7ZA-2A188-A	Spacer	353574-S7	Washer	
	C9ZJ-2B022-A	Gasket	DOZJ-2B253-A	Tube	(2) 376428-S8	Clamp	
	DOZJ-2A040-A	Tube	C9ZZ-2455-A	Pedal (A/T)	376977-S2	Screw, washer	
	B9SS-2A047-A	Hose	DOZA-3A762-A	Clamp	(6) 377706-S	Locknut	
	C9AZ-2169-F	Piston	56349-S4	Bolt	380699-S100	Pin	
					382802-S100	Locknut	

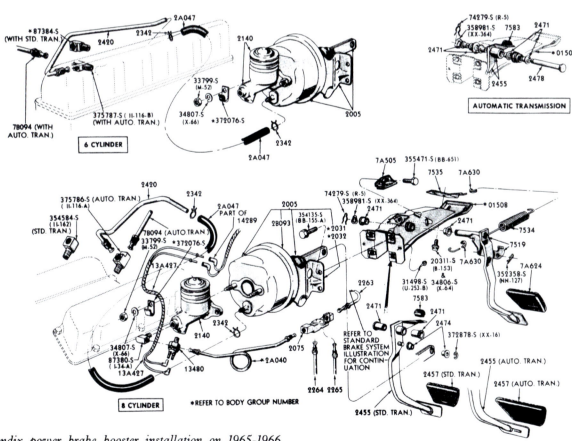

Bendix power brake booster installation on 1965-1966 Mustangs.

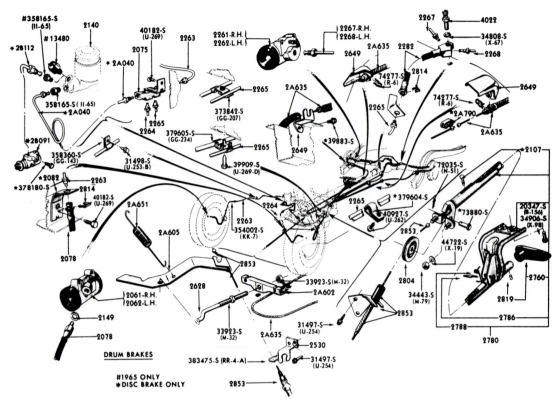

Exploded view of 1965-1966 Mustang disc and drum brake systems.

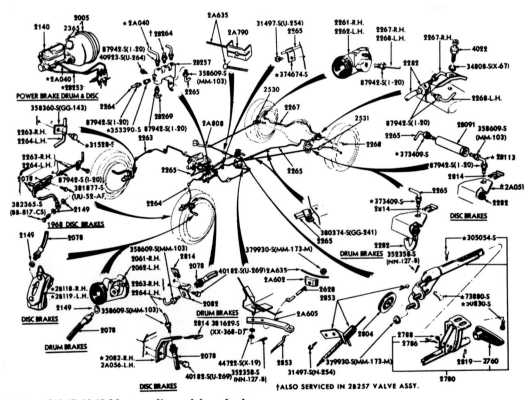

Exploded view of 1967-1968 Mustang disc and drum brake systems.

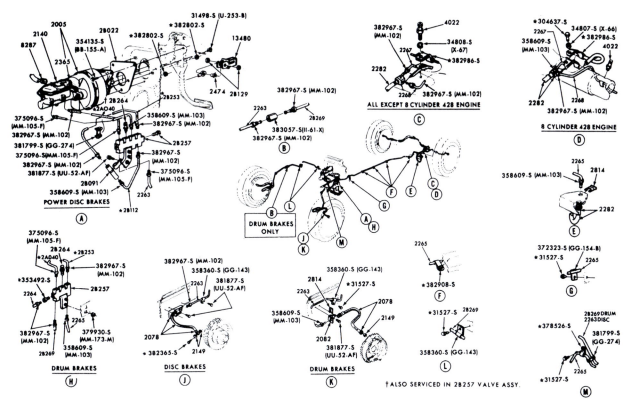

Exploded view of 1969-1970 Mustang disc and drum brake systems.

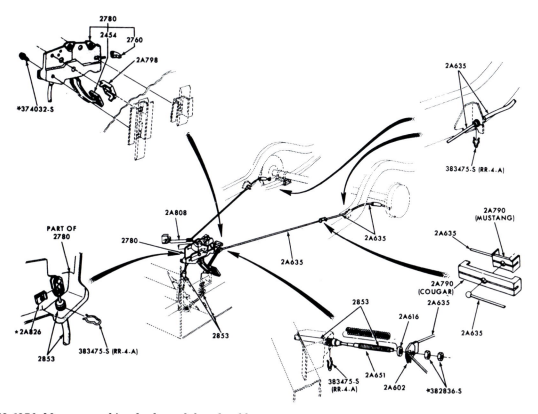

The 1969-1970 Mustang parking brake pedal and cable assembly.

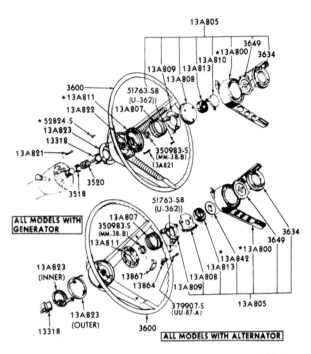

The 1965-1966 Mustang standard steering wheel, horn button, and related parts.

A bulbous crash pad, part of the new government-imposed safety standards, adorns the steering wheel horn ring in 1967.

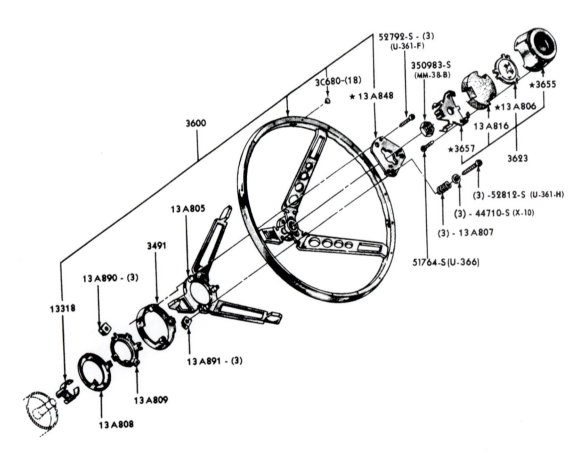

The 1965-1966 Mustang woodgrain steering wheel, horn button, and related parts.

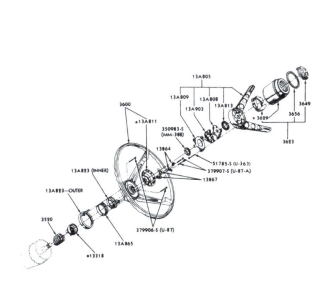

The 1967 Mustang standard three-spoke steering wheel, horn button, and related parts.

A Rim Blow steering wheel was a Mustang option in 1969 and 1970. The horn would sound when a rubber strip, encircling the inside diameter of the wheel, was pressed. This three-spoke center pad is part of the standard interior package.

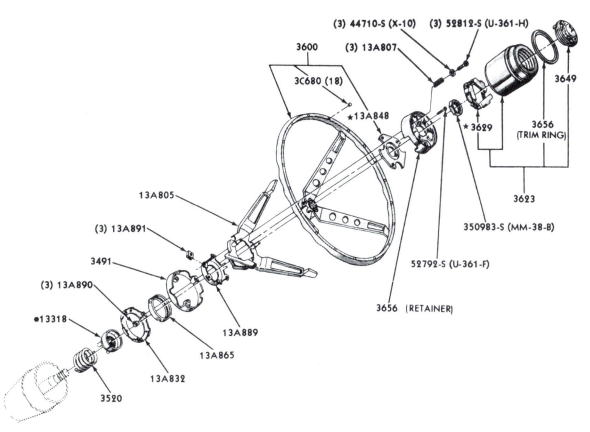

The 1967 Mustang woodgrain steering wheel, horn button, and related parts.

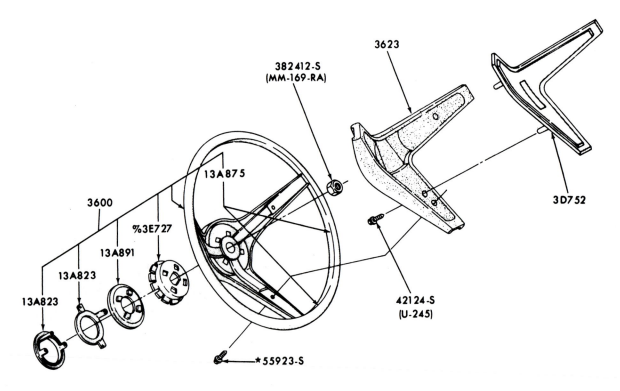

*The 1969-1970 Shelby Mustang three-spoke steering wheel
with Rim Blow horn.*

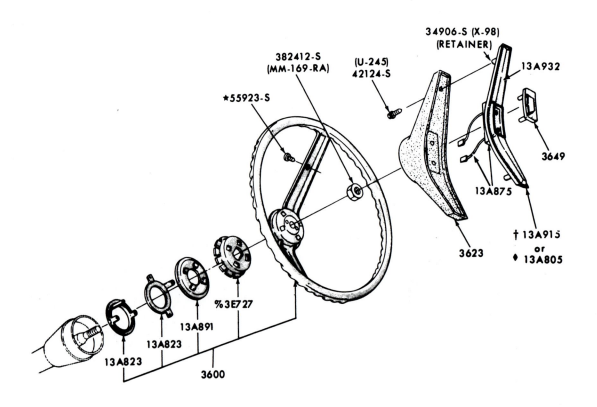

*The 1969-1970 Mustang standard two-spoke steering
wheel.*

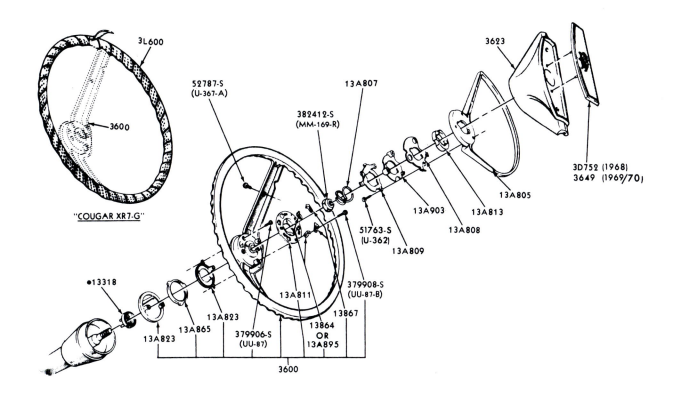

The 1968 Mustang two-spoke steering wheel, horn ring, and related parts.

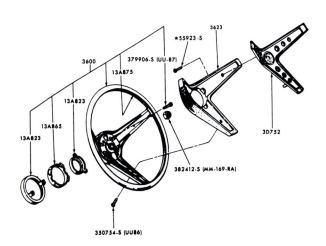

The 1969 Mustang three-spoke steering wheel with Rim Blow horn.

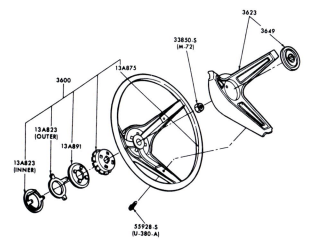

The 1969-1970 Mustang three-spoke steering wheel with Rim Blow horn.

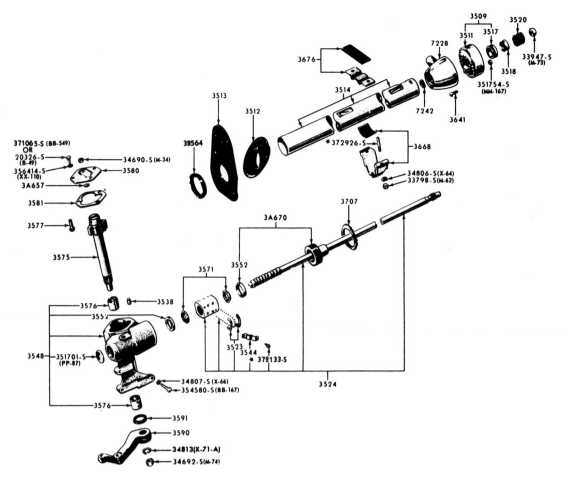

An exploded view of a typical 1965 Mustang steering column and gearbox. Note the steering shaft (3524) extends the length of the steering column. The steering wheel attaches to the splined upper end. When installed, the wheel, column, and gearbox become a complete assembly.

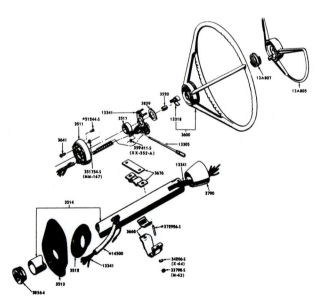

Steering column and wheel for 1965 and 1966 Mustangs with standard interior.

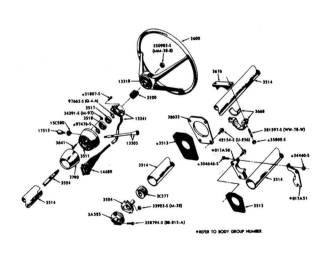

Steering column assembly and related parts for 1967 Mustangs with fixed wheel (as opposed to tilt wheel).

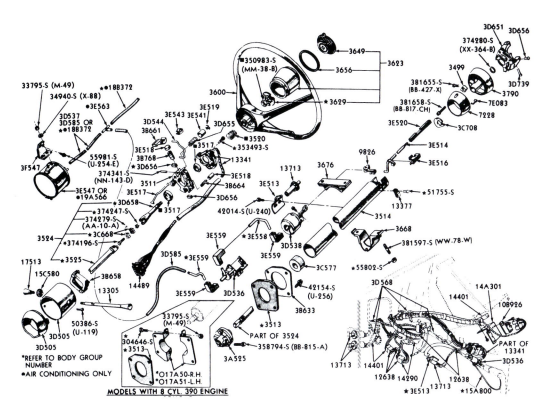

Steering column assembly and related parts for 1967 Mustangs with tilt wheel.

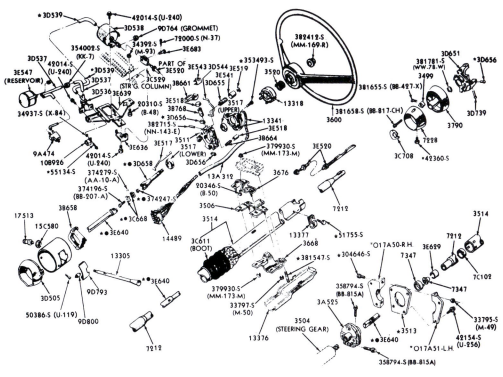

Steering column assembly and related parts for 1968 Mustangs with tilt wheel.

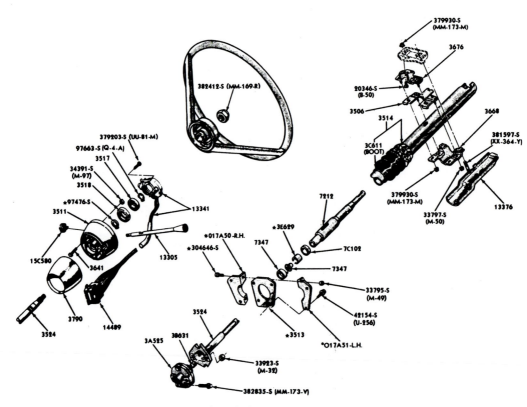

*Steering column assembly and related parts for 1968
Mustangs with fixed wheel (as opposed to tilt wheel).*

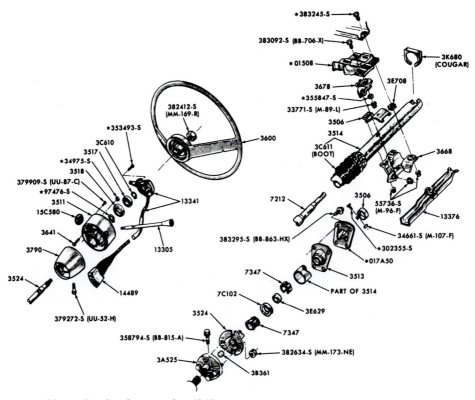

*Steering column assembly and related parts for 1969
Mustangs with fixed wheel (as opposed to tilt wheel).*

276

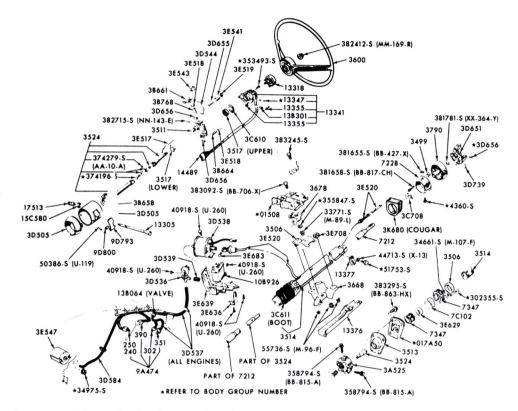

*Steering column assembly and related parts for 1969
Mustangs with tilt wheel.*

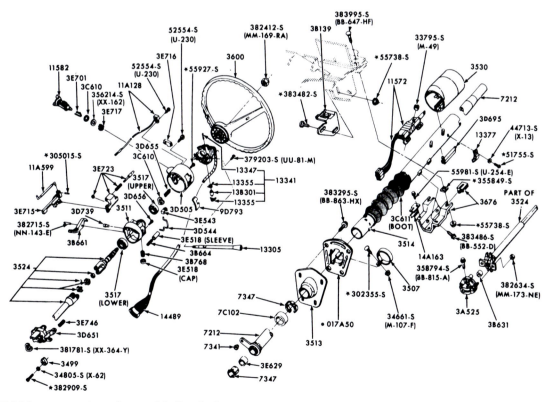

The 1970 Mustang steering column with tilt wheel.

277

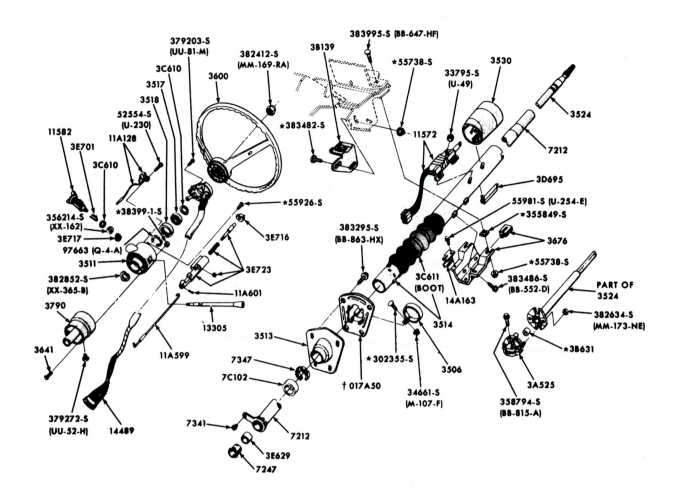

Steering column assembly and related parts for 1970 Mustangs with fixed wheel (as opposed to tilt wheel).

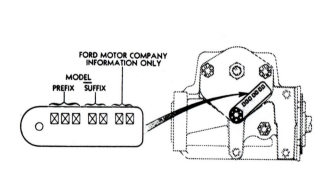

The model prefix and suffix are listed on the stamped identification tag attached to the steering gearbox. The information can be used to validate a unit's correct application and date of manufacture.

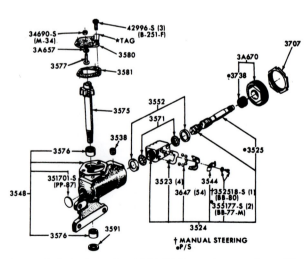

An exploded view of a 1965-1970 steering gearbox. The only difference betwen a power and non-power steering box is the gear ratio.

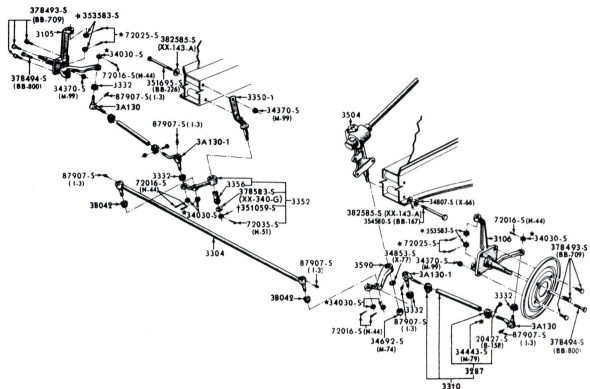

*Typical manual steering system for 1965 and 1966 Mustangs
equipped with six-cylinder engines.*

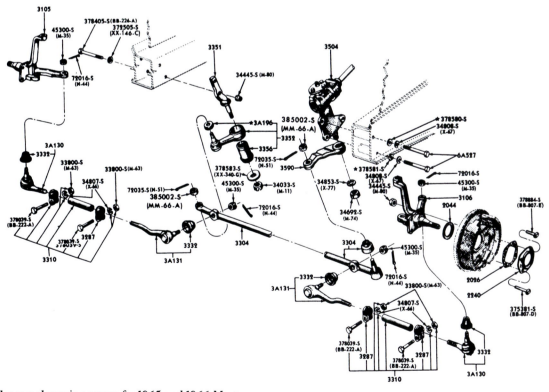

*Typical manual steering system for 1965 and 1966 Mustangs
equipped with V-8 engines.*

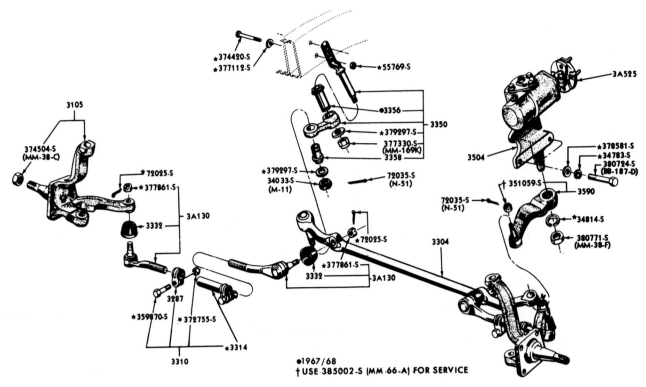

Typical manual steering system for 1966-1970 Mustangs.

MUSTANG POWER STEERING INSTALLATION KIT APPLICATION CHART

Year	Model	Notes	Cyl/CID	Linkage Kit	Pump Kit	Air Conditioner Adapter Kit
65	w/ alternator	1,3,5	8/289	C5ZZ-3A634-D	C5ZZ-3A635-F	C5PZ-3A635-H
	w/ alternator, Before 4/22/65	4,6	8/289	C5ZZ-3A634-D	C5ZZ-3A635-K	C5PZ-3A635-G
	w/ alternator, From 4/22/65	2,4	8/289	C5ZZ-3A634-D	C5ZZ-3A635-K	C5ZZ-3A635-L
66			6/200	C5ZZ-3A634-F	C6ZZ-3A635-C	C5DZ-3A635-C
		2,4	8/289	C5ZZ-3A634-G	C5ZZ-3A635-K	C5ZZ-3A635-L
67			6/200	C6ZZ-3A634-A	C7OZ-3A635-C	C7DZ-3A635-B
	w/ alternator, Before 5/01/67	8,9	8/289	C5ZZ-3A634-B	C7OZ-3A635-C	C7ZZ-3A635-E
	w/ alternator, From 5/01/67	7,9	8/289	C7ZZ-3A634-B	C7OZ-3A635-C	C7ZZ-3A635-E
	w/ alternator, Before 5/01/67	10	8/390	C7ZZ-3A634-A	C7ZZ-3A635-C	C7OZ-3A635-E
	w/ alternator, From 5/01/67	10	8/390	C7ZZ-3A634-B	C7ZZ-3A635-C	C7OZ-3A635-E
68			6/200	C8ZZ-3A634-A	C8OZ-3A635-A	None required
			289,302	C8ZZ-3A634-A	C8OZ-3A635-C	C8OZ-3A635-E
			8/390	C8ZZ-3A634-A	C8ZZ-3A635-A	C8OZ-3A635-E
69			6/200	C8ZZ-3A634-A	C9ZZ-3A635-A	None required
			6/250	C8ZZ-3A634-B	C9OZ-3A635-A	None required
			8/302	C8ZZ-3A634-A	C9ZZ-3A635-B	C9ZZ-3A635-E
			8/351	C8ZZ-3A634-B	C9ZZ-3A635-C	C9ZZ-3A635-F
			8/390	C8ZZ-3A634-A	C9ZZ-3A635-C	C9ZZ-3A635-E
			8/428	Not available	Not available	Not available
70		11	6/200	DOZZ-3A634-A	DOZZ-3A635-G	None required
			6/250	DOZZ-3A634-A	DOZZ-3A635-F	None required
		11	8/302	DOZZ-3A634-A	DOZZ-3A635-C	None required
		11	351(W)	DOZZ-3A634-A	DOZZ-3A635-D	None required
		11	351(C)	DOZZ-3A634-A	DOZZ-3A635-E	None required
			8/428	Not available	Not available	Not available

Notes:

1 For units with Eaton P.S. pump. Not for units with cast iron water pump.
2 Use with pumps ident. w/ tag number HBA-AC2, HBA-AC3, HBA-AC4, HBA-AD2, HBA-AD3.
3 Includes Eaton Pump.
4 Includes Ford Pump.
5 Use with pumps ident. w/ tag number HBA-A32, HBA-AE3, HBA-AE4, HBA-AF2, HBA-AF3.
6 Use with pumps ident. w/ tag number HBA-A3, HBA-AE1, HBA-AF, HBA-AAF1, HBA-AR.
7 Use C5ZZ-3590-A with this kit for models w/o special handling package (Before 5/01/67).
8 Use C7ZZ-3590-C with this kit for models with special handling package.
9 Not for use on High Performance engines.
10 Includes Ford gear and Ford pump.
11 Not to be used with C78 x 14 tires.

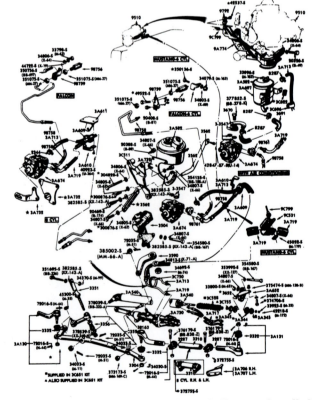

Power steering system with an Eaton-built pump installed on early 1965 Mustangs.

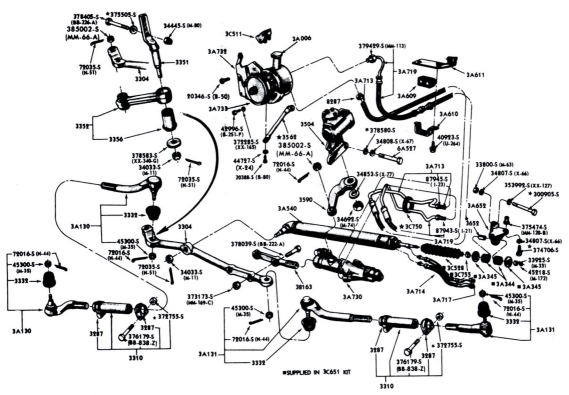

Power steering system with Ford-built pump as installed on 1965 and 1966 Mustangs equipped with a six-cylinder engine.

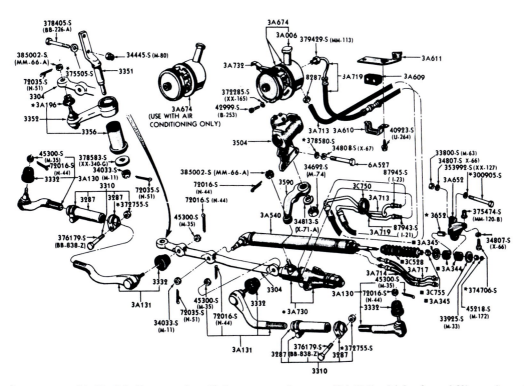

Power steering system with Ford-built pump installed on 1965 and 1966 Mustangs equipped with V-8 engines. Note

the pump (3A674) with its slanted filler neck needed for cars equipped with optional air conditioning.

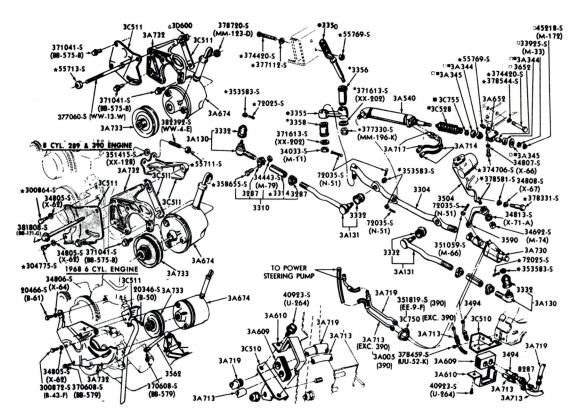

Variations of the power steering system installed on 1967 and 1968 Mustangs based on engine type and size.

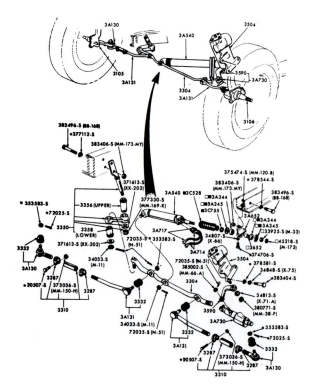

Typical power steering linkage and hardware available as an option on all 1965-1970 Mustangs.

YEAR	MODEL	DESCRIPTION	APPROX. DEV. LENGTH (INCHES)	PART NUMBER
65	170, 200, w/ Eaton pump	Control valve to pump-return	43-1/2	C5DZ-3A713-C
	Before 3/2/64	Control valve to cylinder	9	C3DZ-4A714-A
	From 3/2/64	Control valve to cylinder	9-1/4	C5DZ-3A714-A
	Before 3/2/64	Cylinder to valve	9-1/2	C3DZ-3A717-A
	From 3/2/64	Cylinder to valve	10	C5DZ-3A717-A
		Pump to control valve-pressure	34	C5DZ-3A719-D
	6 cyl. 170 with Ford pump	Control valve to pump-return	32	C5ZZ-3A713-E
		Control valve to cylinder	9	C3DZ-3A714-A
		Cylinder to valve	9-1/2	C3DZ-3A717-A
		Pump to control valve-pressure	31	C5ZZ-3A719-C
	6 cyl. 200 with Ford pump	Control valve to pump-return	45	C5DZ-3A713-A
		Control valve to cylinder	9-1/2	C5DZ-3A714-A
		Cylinder to valve	10	C5DZ-3A717-A
		Pump to control valve-pressure	70	C5DZ-3A719-A
	260, 289 with Eaton pump	Control valve to pump-return	32	C5ZZ-3A713-E
		Control valve to cylinder	9	C3DZ-3A714-A
		Cylinder to valve	9-1/2	C3DZ-3A717-A
		Pump to control valve-pressure	41	C5ZZ-3A719-E
	8 cyl. 260 with Ford pump	Con. valve to pump-return (w/o A/C)	29-3/4	C5ZZ-3A713-A
		Con. valve to pump-return (with A/C)	34-1/2	C5ZZ-3A713-B
		Control valve to cylinder	9	C3DZ-3A714-A
		Cylinder to valve	9-1/2	C3DZ-3A717-A
		Pump to control valve-pressure	29-3/4	C5ZZ-3A719-A
	8 cyl. 289 with Ford pump	Control valve to pump-return	35	C5ZZ-3A713-D
		Control valve to cylinder	9	C3DZ-3A714-A
		Cylinder to valve	9-1/2	C3DZ-3A717-A
		Pump to control valve-pressure	42-1/2	C5ZZ-3A719-D
66	6 cylinder 200	Control valve to pump-return	45	C5DZ-3A713-A
		Control valve to cylinder	9-1/2	C5DZ-3A714-A
		Cylinder to valve	10	C5DZ-3A717-A
		Pump to control valve-pressure	70	C5DZ-3A719-A
	8 cylinder 289	Control valve to pump-return	35	C5ZZ-3A713-D
		Control valve to cylinder	9	C3DZ-3A714-A
		Cylinder to valve	9-1/2	C3DZ-3A717-A
		Pump to control valve-pressure	42-1/2	C5ZZ-3A719-D

MUSTANG POWER STEERING HOSE ASSEMBLY APPLICATION CHART, 1965-1966

YEAR	MODEL	DESCRIPTION	APPROX. DEV. LENGTH (INCHES)	PART NUMBER
67	6 cylinder	Control valve to pump-return	32-1/2	C7OZ-3A713-A
		Control valve to cylinder	9-1/2	C6OZ-34714-A
		Cylinder to valve	9-3/4	C6OZ-3A717-A
		Pump to control valve-pressure	31	C7OZ-3A719-A
	8 cylinder 289	Control valve to pump-return	30	C7OZ-3A713-D
		Control valve to cylinder	9-1/2	C6OZ-3A714-A
		Cylinder to valve	9-3/4	C6OZ-3A717-A
	(exc. GT350)	Pump to control valve-pressure	41	C7OZ-3A719-C
	(GT350)	Pump to control valve-pressure		C7ZX-3A719-A
	8 cylinder 390	Pump outlet to insulator-return	15-1/2	C7ZZ-3A713-A
		From insulator to valve-return		C7ZZ-3A713-B
		Control valve to cylinder	9-1/2	C6OZ-3A714-A
		Cylinder to valve	9-3/4	C6OZ-3A717-A
		Pump to valve outlet tube-pressure		C7ZZ-3A719-B
		Valve outlet tube to pressure hose	17-3/4	C7ZZ-3494-A
68	6 cylinder 200	Control valve to pump-return	32-1/2	C7OZ-3A713-A
		Control valve to cylinder	9-1/2	C6OZ-3A714-A
		Cylinder to valve	9-3/4	C6OZ-3A717-A
		Pump to control valve-pressure	30	C8OZ-3A719-B
	8 cyl. 289, 302	Control valve to pump-return	30	C7OZ-317A3-C
		Control valve to cylinder	9-1/2	C6OZ-3A714-A
		Cylinder to valve	9-3/4	C6OZ-3A717-A
		Pump to control valve-pressure	51	C8OZ-3A719-C
	390, 428CJ (w/o A/C)	Pump outlet tube to insulator-return	15-1/2	C7ZZ-3A713-C
		From insulator to valve-return	21	C8ZZ-3A713-A
		Control valve to cylinder	9-1/2	C6OZ-3A714-A
		Cylinder to valve	9-3/4	C6OZ-3A717-A
	(exc. GT 350/500)	From pump to valve outlet tube-pressure	16	C9ZZ-3A719-B
	(GT 350/500)	From pump to valve outlet tube-pressure		C7ZX-3A719-A
		Valve outlet tube to pressure hose	17-1/2	C7ZZ-3494-B
	8 cyl. 428CJ with A/C	From valve to insulator-return	21	C8ZZ-3A713-A
		From insulator to cooler-return	15-1/2	C7ZZ-3A713-C
		From cooler to pump-return	AR	● 3A005
		Control valve to cylinder	9-1/2	C6OZ-3A714-A
		Cylinder to valve	9-3/4	C6OZ-3A717-A
	(exc. GT 350/500)	From pump to valve outlet tube-pressure	16	C9ZZ-3A717-B
	(GT 350/500)	From pump to valve outlet tube-pressure		C7ZX-3A719-A
		Valve outlet tube to pressure hose	17-1/2	C7ZZ-3494-B

● Cut to appropriate length from C7AZ-3A005-A (3/8" I.D. - 5/8" O.D.) bulk hose, and use (2) B5A-2344-A clamps

MODEL	DESCRIPTION	APPROX. DEV. LENGTH (INCHES)	PART NUMBER
6 cylinder 200	Control valve to pump-return	32-1/2	C7OZ-3A713-A
	Control valve to cylinder		C6OZ-3A714-A
	Cylinder to valve	9-3/4	C6OZ-3A717-A
	Pump to control valve-pressure	30	C8PZ-31719-B
6 cylinder 250	Control valve to pump-return		C7OZ-3A713-A
	Control valve to cylinder	9-1/2	C6OZ-3A714-A
	Cylinder to valve	9-3/4	C6OZ-3A717-A
	Pump to control valve-pressure	32-1/2	C9OZ-3A719-B
302 (w/o oil cooler), 351	Control valve to pump-return		C8ZZ-3A713-A
	Control valve to cylinder	9-1/2	C6OZ-3A714-A
	Cylinder to valve	9-3/4	C6OZ-3A717-A
	Pump to valve outlet tube-pressure	27	C9ZZ-3A719-A
	Valve outlet tube to pressure hose	17-1/2	C7ZZ-3494-B
302 (with oil cooler)	Control valve to cooler-return		C8ZZ-3A713-A
	From cooler to pump-return		● 3A005
	Insulator for return line		* 3A609
	Control valve to cylinder-inner	9-1/2	C6OZ-3A714-A
	Cylinder to valve-outer	9-3/4	C6OZ-3A717-A
	Pump to valve outlet tube-pressure		C9ZZ-3A719-C
	Valve outlet tube to pressure hose	17-1/2	C7ZZ-3494-B
390, 428 CJ, 429 Boss	From valve to insulator-return	21	C8ZZ-3A713-A
	From insulator to cooler-return	15-1/2	C7ZZ-3A713-C
	From cooler to pump-return		● 3A005
	Insulator for return line	AR	* 3A609
	Control valve to cylinder	9-1/2	C6OZ-3A714-A
	Cylinder to valve	9-3/4	C6OZ-3A717-A
(exc. Boss)	Pump to valve outlet tube-pressure		C9ZZ-3A719-B
Boss 429	From pump to valve outlet-pressure		C9ZZ-3A719-D
	Valve outlet tube to pressure hose	17-1/2	C7ZZ-3494-B

● Cut to appropriate length from C7AZ-3A005-A (3/8" I.D. - 5/8" O.D.) bulk hose, and use (2) B5A-2344-A clamps
* Cut to appropriate length from C7AZ-3A609-A bulk stock.

MODEL	DESCRIPTION	APPROX. DEV. LENGTH (INCHES)	PART NUMBER
6 cylinder 200	Control valve to pump-return	29	DOZZ-3A713-A
	Control valve to cylinder	9-1/2	C6OZ-3A714-A
	Cylinder to valve	9-3/4	C6OZ-3A717-A
	Pump to control valve-pressure	30	DOZZ-3A719-F
6 cylinder 250	Control valve to pump-return	29	DOZZ-3A713-A
	Control valve to cylinder	9-1/2	D6OZ-3A714-A
	Cylinder to valve	9-3/4	C6OZ-3A717-A
	Pump to control valve-pressure	32-1/2	DOZZ-3A719-F
302 (w.o oil cooler), 351	Control valve to pump-return	21	C8ZZ-3A713-A
	Control valve to cylinder	9-1/2	C6OZ-3A7114-A
	Cylinder to valve	9-3/4	C6OZ-3A717-A
Before 1/26/70	From pump to valve outlet tube-pressure	22-1/2	DOZZ-3A719-H
From 1/26/70	From pump to valve outlet tube-pressure	25	DOZZ-3A719-E
	Valve outlet tube to pressure hose	17-1/2	C7ZZ-3494-B
	From cooler to pump-return		● 3A005
	Insulator for above return line		* 3A609
302 (with oil cooler)	Control valve to cooler-return	21	C8ZZ-3A7113-A
	From cooler to pump-return		● 3A005
	Insulator for above return line		* 3A609
	Control valve to cylinder-inner	9-1/2	C6OZ-3A714-A
	Cylinder to valve-outer	9-3/4	C6OZ-3A717-A
	From pump to valve outlet tube-pressure	24-1/2	DOZZ-3A719-G
	Valve outlet tube to pressure hose	17-1/2	C7ZZ-3494-B
8 cyl. 428CJ, 429 Boss	From valve to insulator-return	21	C8ZZ-3A713-A
	From insulator to cooler-return	AR	● 3A005
	From cooler to pump-return	AR	● 3A005
	Insulator for return line	AR	* 3A609
	Control valve to cylinder	9-1/2	C6OZ-3A714-A
	Cylinder to valve	9-3/4	C6OZ-31717-A
428 CJ	From pump to valve outlet tube-pressure		C9ZZ-3A719-B
429 Boss	From pump to valve outlet tube-pressure		C9ZZ-3A719-D

● Cut to appropriate length from C7AZ-3A005-A (3/8" I.D. - 5/8" O.D.) bulk hose, and use (2) B5A-2344-A clamps
* Cut to appropriate length from C7AZ-3A609-A bulk stock.

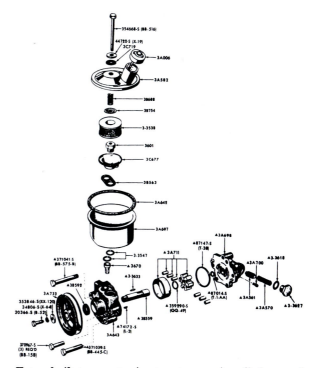

Eaton-built power steering pumps were installed on early 1965 Mustangs. The oil reservoir (3A697) is mounted on the left fender apron to make room for the compressor on air-conditioned cars.

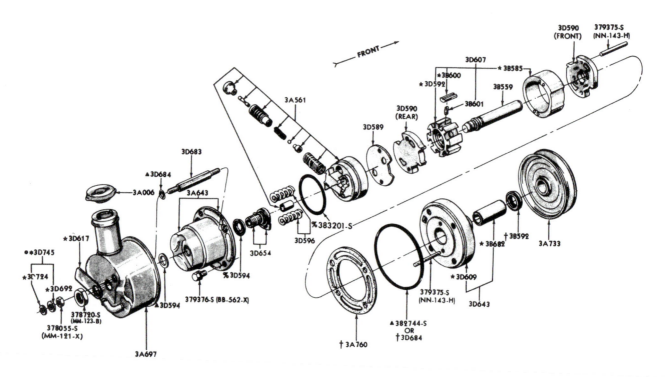

FRONT

3D590 (FRONT)   379375-S (NN-143-H)

3D607   *3B585

*3B600   3B559

*3D592   3B601

3A561   3D590 (REAR)   3B589

3D683

▲3D684   *3A006

3A643

%383201-S

*3D617

**3D745   3D596   3D654

*3D724   %3D594   3A733

*3D692   †3B592   *3B682

378720-S (MM-123-B)   ▲3D594   *3D609

378055-S (MM-121-X)   379376-S (BB-562-X)   3D643

3A697   379375-S (NN-143-H)

▲382744-S OR †3D684

† 3A760

A Ford-built power steering pump with large diameter filler cap (3A006) was installed on all late 1965 and all 1966   *Mustangs. The filler neck was canted rearward to make room for the compressor on air-conditioned cars.*

The power steering filler neck changed places many times over the years. Pre-1969 power steering pumps (shown) had a large-diameter filler neck. If installed on a six-cylinder engine, the neck entered straight up from the center of the cannister. The air-conditioning compressor, if equipped, did not interfere with neck because it was located on the opposite side of the engine. V-8 engines used the same pump although the bracketry slanted the neck slightly to the driver's side. The filler neck was located to the back of the cannister and angled rearward (shown) in order to clear the compressor if the same V-8 engine was equipped with air conditioning.

Early 1965 Mustangs were equipped with Eaton-manufactured power steering pumps. Eaton pumps are easily identified by their separate reservoirs. This pump is on a non-air-conditioned car, however, when air conditioning is added, the reservoir is located on the left inner fender apron and connected to the pump by hoses.

MUSTANG POWER STEERING PUMP ASSEMBLY APPLICATION CHART

YEAR	MODEL	DESCRIPTION/IDENTIFICATION MARKING	PART NUMBER
65	6 cyl. 170 without A/C	Eaton pump	C2AZ-3A674-B
	8 cyl. 260 without A/C	Eaton pump	C5OZ-3A764-B
	8 cyl. 260 with A/C	Eaton pump	C5AZ-3A674-D
65/66	6 cyl. 200	HBA-AN,AN1,AN2,AN3,AN4 (Ford pump)	C5DZ-3A674-BRM
	8 cyl. 289 without A/C	HBA-AC,AC1,AC2,AC3,AC4 (Ford pump)	C5DZ-3A674-ARM
	8 cyl. 289 with A/C	HBA-AD,AD1,AD2,AD3,AD4 (Ford pump)	C5DZ-3A674-CRM
67/68	Exc. GT 350/500	HBA-BF,BF1	C7OZ-3A674-A
	GT350/500	HBA-BH,BH1	C7TZ-3A674-A
69	Exc. Boss 429	HBA-BF,BF1	C7OZ-3A674-A
	Boss 429	HBA-BZ,CD	DOZZ-3A674-A
70	8 cyl. 302,351	HBA-CC	DOZZ-3A674-B
	6 cyl. & 8 cyl. 428	HBA-BR	DOZZ-3A674-B
	Boss 429	HBA-BZ,CD	DOZZ-3A674-C

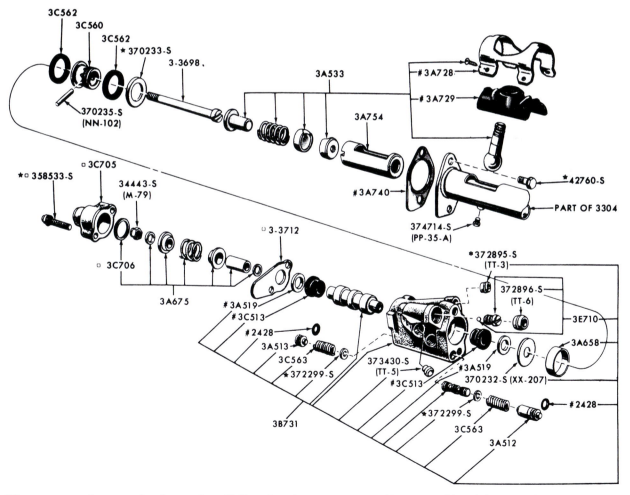

The power steering control valve used on 1965 and early 1966 Mustangs. Unlike the removable valve used on late 1966 and later cars, this unit is part of the drag link (3304). (See view of steering linkage.)

285

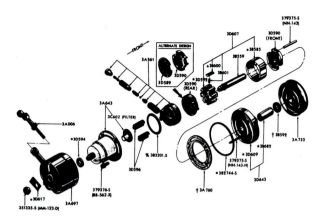

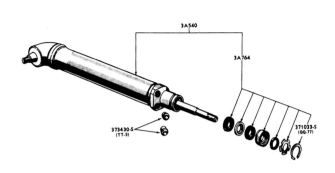

Typical Ford-built power steering pump used on all 1967-1970 Mustangs. Note the small-diameter dipstick (3A006) and tube.

The power steering cylinder (3A540) is a welded unit and cannot be rebuilt. The rod packing (3A764) and the hose seats (373430-S) are common service items.

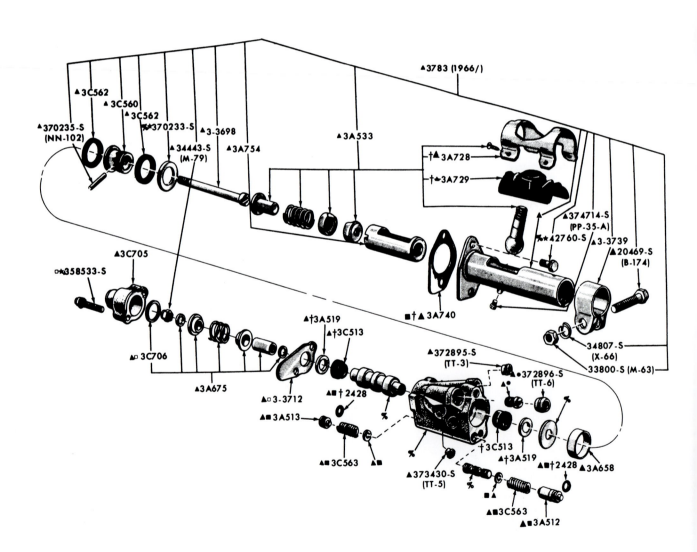

An exploded view of the power steering control valve used on all 1966-1970 Mustangs.

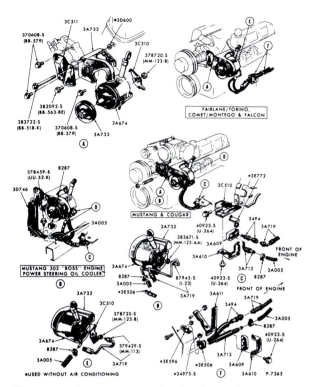

Power steering pump mounting hardware for 1970 Mustangs equipped with 302 or 351ci engines.

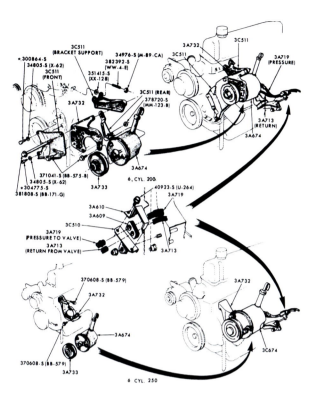

Power steering pump mounting hardware for 1969 and 1970 Mustangs equipped with a 250ci six-cylinder engine.

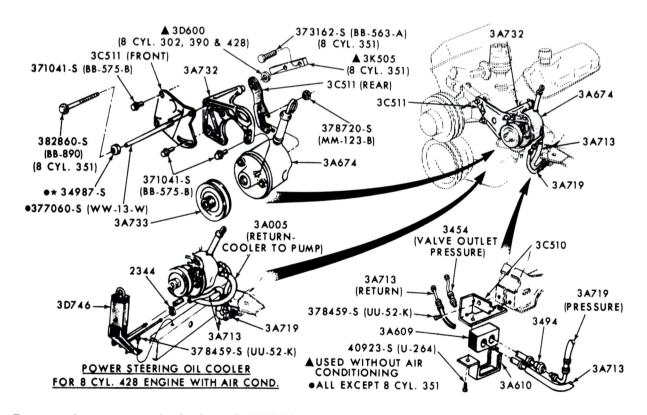

Power steering pump mounting hardware for 1970 Mustangs equipped with 428ci engines.

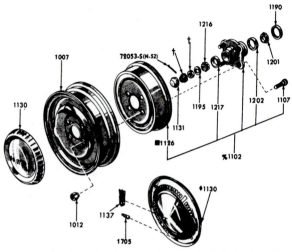

Typical 1965-1970 Mustang front wheel hub, bearings, rim, and cover assembly.

MUSTANG HUB CAP OR WHEEL COVER APPLICATION CHART, 1965 and 1966

1965

PART NUMBER	IDENTIFICATION	DIAM.	DESCRIPTION
C5ZZ-1130-W	C5ZA-1130-J	2-1/2"	Imprinted "Ford Mustang" - Incl. attaching parts (exc. GT350)
C5ZZ-1130-A	C4ZA-1130-F	13"	Imprinted "Mustang" - Black center (exc. GT350)
C5ZZ-1130-H	C4ZA-1130-H	13"	Imprinted "Mustang" - Black center - Incl. spinner (exc. GT350)
C5ZZ-1130-K	C4ZA-1130-K	13"	Imprinted "Mustang" - Black center (exc. GT350)
C5ZZ-1130-P	C5ZA-1130-D	13"	Imprinted "Mustang" - Black center (exc. GT350)
C5ZZ-1130-J	C4ZA-1130-M	13"	Imprinted "Mustang" - Black center - Incl. spinner (exc. GT350)
C5ZZ-1130-S	C5ZA-1130-F	13"	Imprinted "Mustang" - Black center - Incl. spinner (exc. GT350)
C40Z-1130-H		13"	Wire (except GT350)
C5ZZ-1130-C	C4ZA-1130-E	14"	Imprinted "Mustang" - Black center (exc. GT350)
C5ZZ-1130-J	C4ZA-1130-J	14"	Imprinted "Mustang" - Black center (exc. GT350)
C5ZZ-1130-N	C5ZA-1130-C	14"	Imprinted "Mustang" - Black center (exc. GT350)
C5ZZ-1130-L	C4ZA-1130-L	14"	Imprinted "Mustang" - Black center - Incl. spinner (exc. GT350)
C5ZZ-1130-R	C5ZA-1130-E	14"	Imprinted "Mustang" - Black center - Incl. spinner (exc. GT350)
C4AZ-1130-H	C4AA-1130-F	14"	Wire (except GT350)
C4AZ-1130-L	C4AA-1130-R	14"	Simulated wire, Incl. spinner, R/W/B center (exc. GT350)
C3AZ-1130-Z	C3AA-1130-Z,AF	15"	Includes spinner - Stainless steel (exc. GT350)
S1MS-1130-A		3"	Cap assembly - Use with Cragar 15" wheel (GT350)
S2MS-1130-B	Consists of:	2-3/4"	Cap assembly - Use with S2MS-1007-B & C (GT350)
	S2MS-1131-B		Bracket
	S2MS-1132-A		Emblem (GT350)
	S2MS-1133-A		Plastic cap
	(2) S2MS-1135-A		Nut
S2MS-1130-C	Consists of:	2-1/2"	Cap assembly - Use with S2MS-1007-A (GT350)
	S2MS-1130-A		Cap - Die cast imprinted "CS"
	S7MS-1131-B		Bracket
			Hex bolt 1/4"-20 x 5/8"

1966

PART NUMBER	IDENTIFICATION	DIAM.	DESCRIPTION
C5ZZ-1130-W	C5ZA-1130-J	2-1/2"	Imprinted "Ford Mustang" - Includes attaching parts
C6DZ-1130-A	C6DA-1130-A	9-1/2"	Imprinted "Ford" - 36 depressions
C6ZZ-1130-A	C6ZA-1130-A	14"	Black center
C6ZZ-1130-A	C6ZA-1130-B	14"	Black center - Includes spinner
C6OZ-1130-N	C80A-1130-M	14"	Simulated mag - Plain chrome center
C6OZ-1130-F	C6OA-1130-E	14"	Simulated mag, Chrome center, Also serviced in C6OZ-1130-J kit
S2MS-1130-B	Consists of:	2-3/4"	Cap assembly - Use with S2MS-1007-B & C kit
	S2MS-1131-B		Bracket
	S2MS-1132-A		Emblem (GT350)
	S2MS-1133-A		Plastic cap
	S2MS-1135-A		Nut
S2MS-1130-C	Consists of:	2-1/2"	Cap assembly - Use with S2MS-1007-A
	S2MS-1130-A		Cap - Die cast imprinted "CS"
	S7MS-1131-B		Bracket
			Hex bolt 1/4"-20 x 5/8"

MUSTANG HUB CAP OR WHEEL COVER APPLICATION CHART, 1967 and 1968

1967

PART NUMBER	IDENTIFICATION	DIAM.	DESCRIPTION
C5ZZ-1130-W	C5ZA-1130-J	2-1/2"	Imprinted "Ford Mustang" - Includes attaching parts (exc. GT350)
C7OZ-1130-C	C7OA-1130-C	2-1/2"	Push-in type - Includes crest - Red center (exc. GT350)
C7ZZ-1130-A	C7ZA-1130-E	3-3/4"	Push-in type (exc. GT350)
C7DZ-1130-A	C7DA-1130-D	9-5/8"	Black center - Ford emblem (exc. GT350)
C7AZ-1130-A	C7AA-1130-A	10-1/2"	Black center - Ford emblem (exc. GT350)
C6OZ-1130-K	C6OA-1130-E	14"	Simul. mag, Chrome center (exc. GT350)
C7OZ-1130-D	C7OA-1130-D	14"	Wire - Includes spinner - Blue center (exc. GT350)
C6OZ-1130-N	C8OA-1130-M	14"	Simulated mag - Chrome center (exc. GT350)
C7ZZ-1130-H	C7ZA-1130-H	14"	Imprinted "Mustang" - 21 openings - Red center (exc. GT350)
C7ZZ-1130-E	C7ZA-1130-G	14"	Simulated wire - Red center (exc. GT350)
C7ZZ-1130-B	C7ZA-1130-B	14-1/8"	Imprinted "Mustang" - 21 openings - Red center (exc. GT350)
C6AZ-1130-C	C6AA-1130-E	16-1/4"	Simul. steel wheel, incl. crest - Red center (exc. GT350)
C7AZ-1130-H	C7AA-1130-E	15"	Wire - Includes spinner - Blue center (exc. GT350)
S7MS-1130-B	Consists of:	2-1/2"	Cap assembly - Use with S7MS-1007-D (GT350)
	S7MS-1131-B		Bracket
	S7MS-1132-A		Emblem (Shelby Cobra)
	S7MS-1133-B		Cap
			Hex bolt 1/4"-20 x 5/8"
S7MS-1130-C	Consists of:	2-3/4"	Cap assembly - Use with S7MS-1007-C (GT350)
	S7MS-1131-A		Bracket
	S2MS-1132-B		Emblem (Shelby Cobra)
	S7MS-1133-A		Cap
	(2) 42127-S		Screws
S7MS-1130-A		16-1/4"	Cover-styled (GT350)

1968

PART NUMBER	IDENTIFICATION	DIAM.	DESCRIPTION
C8OZ-1130-C	C8OA-1130-C,D	7-1/2"	Includes GT emblem
C8OZ-1130-G	C8OA-1130-H,J	7-1/2"	Plain center
C8ZZ-1130-F	C8ZA-1130-D	10-1/2"	Black center - Includes Mustang emblem
C6OZ-1130-K	C6OA-1130-E	14"	Simulated mag - Chrome center - Also svcd in C6OZ-1130-J kit
C6OZ-1130-N	C8OA-1130-M	14"	Simulated mag - Chrome center
C8ZZ-1130-A	C8ZA-1130-A	14"	Imprinted "Mustang" - 16 openings
C7ZZ-1130-E	C7ZA-1130-G	14"	Simulated wire - Red center
C8ZZ-1130-E	C8ZA-1130-E	14"	Includes Mustang emblem - 16 openings - Red center
C6AZ-1130-K	C6AA-1130-J	15"	Simulated mag wheel
	C8AA-1130-H,L		
C8OZ-1130-J	C8OA-1130-N	14"	Simulated wire - Plain center
C8OZ-1130-C	C6AA-1130-E	16-1/4"	Simul. steel wheel - Bolt-on type crest - Red center
S8MS-1130-A		16-1/4"	Die-cast cover

MUSTANG HUB CAP OR WHEEL COVER APPLICATION CHART, 1969 and 1970

1969

PART NUMBER	IDENTIFICATION	DIAM.	DESCRIPTION
C9ZZ-1130-F		2-3/16"	Use with C9ZZ-1007-H wheel - Mustang emblem in center
C9ZZ-1130-E		2-3/4"	Black center - Use with styled steel wheels - Mustang emblem
C9ZZ-1130-D	S9MS-1130-B	2-3/4"	Black center - Use with snap-on type styled steel wheels
C8OZ-1130-C	C8OA-1130-C,D	7-1/2"	Includes GT emblem
C8OZ-1130-G		7-1/2"	Plain center
C8AZ-1130-D	C8AA-1130-D	10-1/2"	Black center - Includes Ford crest
C9ZZ-1130-A	C9ZA-1130-B	14"	Imprinted "Mustang," Plain center, Also svcd in C9ZZ-1130-B kit
C7ZZ-1130-E	C7ZA-1130-G	14"	Simulated wire - Red center
C7AZ-1130-C		16-1/4"	Simul. bolt-on type steel wheel - Includes crest - Red center

1970

PART NUMBER	IDENTIFICATION	DIAM.	DESCRIPTION
C9ZZ-1130-E	NONE	2-3/4"	Use w/ styled steel wheels, Mustang emblem, Black ctr (Boss)
C9ZZ-1130-D	S9MS-1130-B	2-3/4"	Use w/ snap-on type style steel wheels - Black ctr (GT350/500)
C8OZ-1130-G	C8OA-1130-H,J	7-1/2"	Use w/ styled steel wheels - Plain ctr (except Boss, GT350/500)
D0AZ-1130-E	D0ZA-1130-H	10-1/4"	Imprint "Ford Motor Company," Chrome finish, Circ. black stripes (except Boss, GT350/500) - Before 12/24/69
D0AZ-1130-H	D0AA-1130-G	10-1/4"	Imprint "Ford Motor Company," Chrome finish, Circ. black stripes (except Boss, GT350/500) - From 12/24/69
	D2AA-1130-AA		
D5DZ-1130-B	D0OA-1130-K	10-1/4"	Imprint "Ford Motor Company" - Brushed chrome finish - Circular black stripes, Use w/ 1210 trim ring (exc. Boss, GT350/500)
	D0ZA-1130-J		
C6OZ-1130-N	D8OA-1130-M	14"	Simulated mag - Plain chrome center (exc. Boss, GT350/500)
D0ZZ-1130-A	D0ZA-1130-K	14-1/8"	Imprint "Mustang,"Chrome bkgrd, 16 depressions Exc. Boss, GT350, GT500.
D0ZZ-1130-D	D0ZA-1130-E,L	15-1/4"	Simul. styled steel, Mustang embl., Black bkgrnd. - Use w/14x7 wheels (except Boss, GT350/500)
D0ZZ-1130-E	D0ZA-1130-F,M	15-1/4"	Simul. styled steel, Mustang emblem, Black bkgrnd. - Use w/14x6 wheels (except Boss, GT350/500)
C8OZ-1130-J	C8OA-1130-N	14"	Simulated wire - Plain center hub (exc. Boss, GT350/500)
D0ZZ-1130-F	D0ZA-1130-G,N	16-1/4"	Simul. styled steel, Mustang emblem, Black bkgrnd., Use w/15x7 wheels. (except Boss, GT350/500)

This wire cover with spinner with the vintage Ford crest in the center was used on early 1964¹/₂ Mustangs.

Mustangs built between April and September 1964 were outfitted with 13in wheels as standard equipment. Cars optioned with a V-8 engine and Special Handling Package received 14in wheels. This standard full disc wheelcover was manufactured in both 13in and 14in sizes through September 1965.

The standard wheelcover became optional when a three-prong spinner was added. It too was available in 13 and 14in sizes.

The vintage Ford crest center emblem in the wire wheelcover spinner was replaced by what would be later known as the emblem signifying Ford's new luxury full-size car, the LTD. This wire cover with spinner was introduced in the fall of 1964.

Styled Steel wheels were available only in 14in size. In 1965 Styled Steels featured a one-piece stamped center and chrome rim.

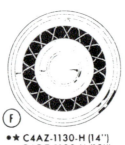

Ⓕ
- ●★ C4AZ-1130-H (14'')
- ●C4OZ-1130-H (13'')
MUSTANG

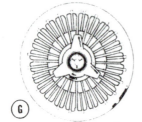

Ⓖ
%★ C4AZ-1130-L (14'')
(RED, WHITE AND BLUE CENTER)
MUSTANG

Ⓙ
★ S1MS-1130-A (3'')
(GT-350)
MUSTANG-HUB CAP

Ⓚ
S2MS-1130-B (2 3/4'')
(GT-350)
MUSTANG-HUB CAP

Ⓛ
★S2MS-1130-C (2 1/2'')
(GT-350)
MUSTANG-HUB CAP

Standard and optional 1965 Mustang wheelcovers.

In 1966, the Styled Steel wheel rim was painted, then fitted
with a polished stainless-steel trim ring.

Only 14in tires and wheels were offered in 1966 and spinner
wheelcovers were the in thing. This design, less the spinner,
was the standard wheel cover for 1966. It too became an
option when the spinner was added.

Ⓚ
▲C5ZZ-1130-A (13'')
▲C5ZZ-1130-K (13'')
●C5ZZ-1130-P (13'')
▲C5ZZ-1130-C (14'')
▲C5ZZ-1130-J (14'')
●C5ZZ-1130-N (14'')
(BLACK CENTER)
MUSTANG

Ⓛ
#▲★ C5ZZ-1130-B (13'')
#▲★C5ZZ-1130-M (13'')
#●C5ZZ-1130-S (13'')
#▲★C5ZZ-1130-L (14'')
#★C5ZZ-1130-R (14'')
(BLACK CENTER)
MUSTANG

Ⓜ
C5ZZ-1130-W (2 1/2'')
(HUB CAP)
MUSTANG

● CHROME
▲ RUSTLESS STEEL
SPINNER IN CENTER
% SIMULATED WIRE
   WITH SPINNER

*Standard and optional 1965 Mustang wheelcovers
(continued).*

290

E

C5AZ-1130-A (10 1/2")
C6DZ-1130-A (9 1/2)
(HUB CAP)
MUSTANG

K

C5ZZ-1130-W (2 1/2")
("MUSTANG" EMBLEM)
MUSTANG-HUB CAP

L

S2MS-1130-B (2 3/4")
(GT-350)
MUSTANG-HUB CAP

M

S2MS-1130-C (2 1/2")
(GT-350)
MUSTANG-HUB CAP

Standard and optional 1966 Mustang wheelcovers.

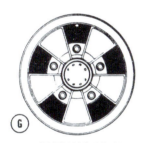

G

*C6OZ-1130-K (14")
#C6OZ-1130-N (14")
FAIRLANE, FALCON, MUSTANG

*Standard and optional 1966 Mustang wheelcovers
(continued).*

*By 1967 the spinner had been labeled unsafe by our overly
protective government and was therefore banned from all
factory production wheels and wheelcovers. This smooth
centered wire cover was offered as a Mustang option from
1967 through 1970.*

*1967 Styled Steel wheels took on a slightly different shape
which became unique to the year. The center cap was
scalloped and the polished trim ring was wider than in
1966.*

C

C5ZZ-1130-W (2 1/2")
("MUSTANG" EMBLEM)
MUSTANG-HUB CAP

D

S7MS-1130-A (16 1/4")
(GT-350/500)
MUSTANG

E

S7MS-1130-B (2 1/2")
GT-350/500
MUSTANG

F

S7MS-1130-C (2 3/4")
GT-350/500
MUSTANG

G

C6AZ-1130-C (16 1/4")
(RED CENTER)
FORD, MUSTANG

Standard and optional 1967 Mustang wheelcovers.

E
C6ZZ-1130-A (14'')
(BLACK CENTER)
MUSTANG

F
#★C6ZZ-1130-B (14'')
(BLACK CENTER)
MUSTANG

Standard and optional 1966 Mustang wheelcovers (continued).

A
C7OZ-1130-C (2 1/2'')
(RED CENTER)
FAIRLANE, MUSTANG

F
C7ZZ-1130-A (3 3/4'')
(MUSTANG CENTER)
MUSTANG-HUBCAP

G
●C7ZZ-1130-B (14'')
▲C7ZZ-1130-G (14'')
MUSTANG (RED CENTER)

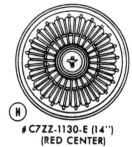

H
#C7ZZ-1130-E (14'')
(RED CENTER)
MUSTANG

Standard and optional 1967 Mustang wheelcovers (continued).

B
●C6OZ-1130-K (14'')
#C6OZ 1130-N (14'')
FAIRLANE, FALCON, MUSTANG

G
%C7AZ-1130-H (15'')
★%C7OZ-1130-F (14'')
(BLUE CENTER)
FORD, FAIRLANE, FALCON, MUSTANG

D
C7AZ-1130-A (10 1/2'')
C7DZ-1130-A (9 5/8'')
(BLACK CENTER)
FORD, FAIRLANE, FALCON, MUSTANG

Standard and optional 1967 Mustang wheelcovers (continued).

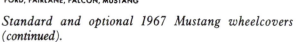

Styled Steel wheels changed completely in 1968 and remained a separate option for all V-8-equipped body styles. The wheel was argent in color (pictured) or chromed. The polished stainless-steel trim ring and round center cap were the same in either case.

The letters GT graced the center of the cap when the Sport Handling Package was included. These wheels were available through the 1969 model year.

1968 was the first year a wheel nut cover replaced the full disc as standard equipment. This "poverty cap" differed from the corporate wheel nut cover only because it had a Mustang running horse emblem in its center instead of a Ford crest.

The base full disc cover for 1968 had the Mustang name stamped in block letters twice around its center.

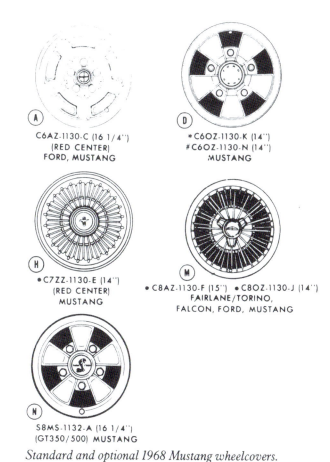

Ⓐ C6AZ-1130-C (16 1/4")
(RED CENTER)
FORD, MUSTANG

Ⓓ *C6OZ-1130-K (14")
#C6OZ-1130-N (14")
MUSTANG

Ⓗ •C7ZZ-1130-E (14")
(RED CENTER)
MUSTANG

Ⓜ •C8AZ-1130-F (15") •C8OZ-1130-J (14")
FAIRLANE/TORINO,
FALCON, FORD, MUSTANG

Ⓝ S8MS-1132-A (16 1/4")
(GT350/500) MUSTANG

Standard and optional 1968 Mustang wheelcovers.

Deluxe wheelcovers for 1968 are similar to the base full disc cover except they have a bright plastic center disc encasing a running horse emblem.

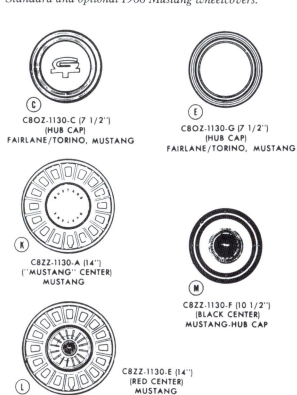

Ⓒ C8OZ-1130-C (7 1/2")
(HUB CAP)
FAIRLANE/TORINO, MUSTANG

Ⓔ C8OZ-1130-G (7 1/2")
(HUB CAP)
FAIRLANE/TORINO, MUSTANG

Ⓚ C8ZZ-1130-A (14")
("MUSTANG" CENTER)
MUSTANG

Ⓜ C8ZZ-1130-F (10 1/2")
(BLACK CENTER)
MUSTANG-HUB CAP

Ⓛ C8ZZ-1130-E (14")
(RED CENTER)
MUSTANG

Standard and optional 1968 Mustang wheelcovers (continued).

293

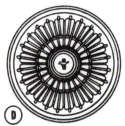

A — C6AZ-1130-C (16 1/4'')
(RED CENTER)
MUSTANG

D — ●C7ZZ-1130-E (14'')
(RED CENTER)
MUSTANG

G — C8AZ-1130-D (10 1/2'')
(BLACK CENTER)
FAIRLANE/TORINO,
FALCON, FORD, MUSTANG

H — C80Z-1130-C (7 1/2'')
(HUB CAP)
FAIRLANE/TORINO, MUSTANG

Standard and optional 1969 Mustang wheelcovers.

These argent five-spoke wheels, exclusive to 1969 Boss 302 Mustangs, were the forerunners of the popular Magnum 500 wheel. This early Magnum features a bright trim ring and argent-colored wheel center.

A — C80Z-1130-G (7 1/2'')
(HUB CAP)
FAIRLANE/TORINO, MUSTANG

The base full disc wheelcover for 1969 was this heavy-looking five-spoke version.

H — C9ZZ-1130-A (14'')
(PLAIN CENTER-BLACK LETTERS)
MUSTANG

J — C9ZZ-1130-E (2 3/4'')
(BLACK CENTER)
MUSTANG

K — C9ZZ-1130-D (2 3/4'')
GT-350/500 (BLACK CENTER)
MUSTANG

Standard and optional 1969 Mustang wheelcovers (continued).

The chrome 1968 Styled Steel wheel with smooth center cap was the standard wheel for all 1969 Mach 1 Mustangs. Unfortunately, this wheel was not offered in 15in sizes.

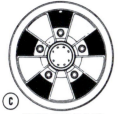

C
C6OZ-1130-N (14'')
(PLAIN CENTER)
FAIRLANE/TORINO, MUSTANG

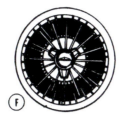

F
C8AZ-1130-F (15'')
C8OZ-1130-J (14'')
MUSTANG

G
C8OZ-1130-G (7 1/2'')
(HUB CAP)
FAIRLANE/TORINO, MUSTANG

K
C9ZZ-1130-D (2 3/4'')
GT-350/500 (BLACK CENTER)
MUSTANG

L
C9ZZ-1130-E 2 3/4''
(BLACK CENTER)
MUSTANG

Standard and optional 1970 Mustang wheelcovers.

C
* D0AZ-1130-E (10 1/4'')
* D0AZ-1130-H (10 1/4'')
(CHROME FINISH-BLACK LETTERS)
★ D0AZ-1130-G (10 1/4'')
* D5DZ-1130-B (10 1/4'')
FAIRLANE/TORINO, FORD,
MAVERICK, MUSTANG-HUB CAP

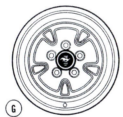

G
▼ % D0OZ-1130-G (16 1/4'')
▼ □ D0OZ-1130-D (15 1/4'')
(RED CENTER)
FAIRLANE/TORINO
% D0ZZ-1130-F (16 1/4'')
□ D0ZZ-1130-D (15 1/4'')
■ D0ZZ-1130-E (15 1/4'')
(BLACK CENTER)
MUSTANG

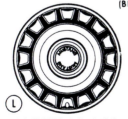

L
D0ZZ-1130-A (14 1/8'')
(''MUSTANG'' CENTER)
MUSTANG

Standard and optional 1970 Mustang wheelcovers (continued).

The Styled Steel wheel changed again in 1970. The rim was painted dark argent and the bright trim ring changed slightly.

More 1970 Mustangs were outfitted with this base full disc cover than the standard 10$\frac{1}{2}$in lug nut cover introduced in 1968. This attractive cover has sixteen radial spokes and a large brightmetal center disc.

A new simulated alloy wheelcover with five lug bolts and bright trim ring became standard equipment for the Mach 1 in 1970.

295

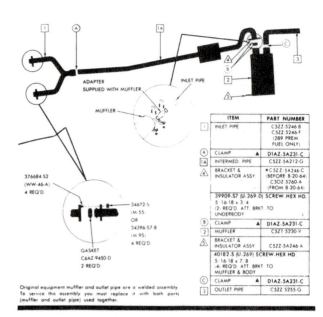

ITEM		PART NUMBER
1	INLET PIPE	C5ZZ-5246-B / C5ZZ-5246-F (289 PREM FUEL ONLY)
A	CLAMP	D1AZ-5A231-C
1A	INTERMED. PIPE	C5ZZ-5A212-G
△	BRACKET & INSULATOR ASSY.	*C5ZZ-5A246-C (BEFORE 8-20-64) C3OZ-5260-A (FROM 8-20-64)
	39909-S7 (U-269-D) SCREW-HEX HD. 5/16-18 x 3/4 (2) REQ'D. ATT. BRKT. TO UNDERBODY	
B	CLAMP	D1AZ-5A231-C
2	MUFFLER	C5ZZ-5230-V
△	BRACKET & INSULATOR ASSY.	C5ZZ-5A246-A
	40182-S (U-269) SCREW-HEX HD. 5/16-18 x 7/8 (4) REQ'D. ATT. BRKT. TO MUFFLER & BODY	
C	CLAMP	D1AZ-5A231-C
3	OUTLET PIPE	C5ZZ-5255-G

Original equipment muffler and outlet pipe are a welded assembly. To service this assembly you must replace it with both parts (muffler and outlet pipe) used together.

ORIGINAL SERVICE SYSTEM (REPLACED BY CONSOLIDATED SYSTEM ABOVE)

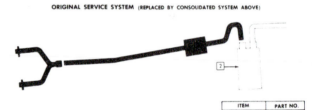

	ITEM	PART NO.
2	MUFFLER	*C5ZZ-5230-D

Complete exhaust system and related hardware for 1965 Mustangs equipped with 289 4-V premium-fuel engines and 260 and 289 2-V regular-fuel engines.

1965 MUSTANG—8 CYL. 289-4B SPECIAL (BEFORE 10-15-64)—INLINE MUFFLER

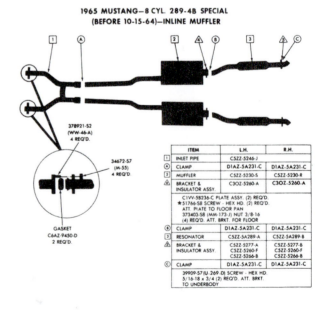

	ITEM	L.H.	R.H.
1	INLET PIPE	C5ZZ-5246-J	
A	CLAMP	D1AZ-5A231-C	D1AZ-5A231-C
2	MUFFLER	C5ZZ-5230-S	C5ZZ-5230-R
△	BRACKET & INSULATOR ASSY.	C3OZ-5260-A	C3OZ-5260-A
	C1VV-5B236-C PLATE ASSY. (2) REQ'D. *51766-S8 SCREW-HEX HD. (2) REQ'D. ATT. PLATE TO FLOOR PAN 373403-S8 (MM-173-J) NUT 3/8-16 (4) REQ'D. ATT. BRKT. FOR FLOOR		
B	CLAMP	D1AZ-5A231-C	D1AZ-5A231-C
3	RESONATOR	C5ZZ-5A289-A	C5ZZ-5A289-B
△	BRACKET & INSULATOR ASSY.	C5ZZ-5277-A C5ZZ-5260-F C5ZZ-5266-B	C5ZZ-5277-B C5ZZ-5260-F C5ZZ-5266-B
C	CLAMP	D1AZ-5A231-C	D1AZ-5A231-C
	39909-S7 (U-269-D) SCREW-HEX HD. 5/16-18 x 3/4 (2) REQ'D. ATT. TO UNDERBODY		

Complete exhaust system and related hardware for 1965 Mustangs equipped with 289 High Performance engines built before 10/15/64.

The black-centered Mangum 500 was the standard wheel for all Boss 429 Mustangs and an optional wheel for the 1970 Boss 302.

CONSOLIDATED SERVICE REPLACEMENT (REPLACES ORIGINAL SERVICE SYSTEM BELOW)

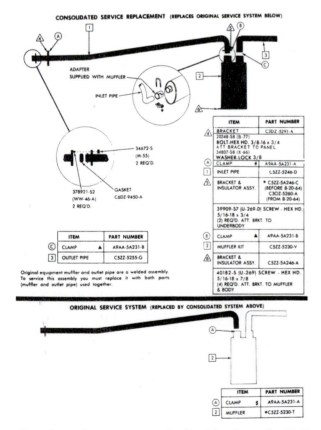

	ITEM	PART NUMBER
△	BRACKET	C3DZ-5291-A
	20348-S8 (B-77) BOLT-HEX HD. 3/8-16 x 3/4 ATT BRACKET TO PANEL 34807-S8 (X-66) WASHER-LOCK 3/8	
A	CLAMP #	A9AA-5A231-A
1	INLET PIPE	C5ZZ-5246-D
△	BRACKET & INSULATOR ASSY.	*C5ZZ-5A246-C (BEFORE 8-20-64) C3OZ-5260-A (FROM 8-20-64)
	39909-S7 (U-269-D) SCREW-HEX HD. 5/16-18 x 3/4 (2) REQ'D. ATT. BRKT. TO UNDERBODY	
B	CLAMP △	A9AA-5A231-B
2	MUFFLER KIT	C5ZZ-5230-V
△	BRACKET & INSULATOR ASSY.	C5ZZ-5A246-A
	40182-S (U-269) SCREW-HEX HD. 5/16-18 x 7/8 (4) REQ'D. ATT. BRKT. TO MUFFLER & BODY	
C	CLAMP △	A9AA-5A231-B
	OUTLET PIPE	C5ZZ-5255-G

Original equipment muffler and outlet pipe are a welded assembly. To service this assembly you must replace it with both parts (muffler and outlet pipe) used together.

ORIGINAL SERVICE SYSTEM (REPLACED BY CONSOLIDATED SYSTEM ABOVE)

	ITEM	PART NUMBER
A	CLAMP $	A9AA-5A231-A
2	MUFFLER	*C5ZZ-5230-T

Complete exhaust system and related hardware for 1965 Mustangs equipped with 170 and 200ci engines.

Exhaust tips or trumpets were more cosmetic than functional, and were a standard feature on all GT and Mach 1 Mustangs. The 1965-1966 GT exhaust trumpets protrude through a chrome-trimmed hole in the rear valance. Backup or reverse lights were optional in 1965 and standard equipment in 1966 on GT models.

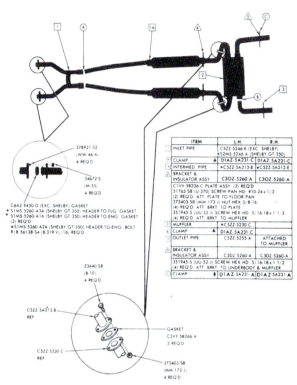

378921-S2
(WW-46-A)
4 REQ'D

34672-S
(M-55)
4 REQ'D

C6AZ-9450-D (EXC SHELBY) GASKET
* S1MS-5260-A3A (SHELBY GT-350) HEADER-TO-FLG. GASKET
* S1MS-5260-A1A (SHELBY GT-350) HEADER-TO-ENG. GASKET
(2) REQ'D
* S1MS-5260-A2A (SHELBY GT-350) HEADER-TO-ENG. BOLT
R/B 56138-S4 (B-319-V) (16) REQ'D

23440-S8
(B-10)
4 REQ'D

C5ZZ-5A213-B
REF

GASKET
C3VY-5B266-A
2 REQ'D

C5ZZ-5230-C
REF

373403-S8
(MM-173-J)
4 REQ'D

ITEM	L.H.	R.H.
1 INLET PIPE	C5ZZ-5246-K (EXC SHELBY) *S2MS-5246-A (SHELBY GT 350)	
A CLAMP	D1AZ-5A231-C	D1AZ-5A231-C
2 INTERMED PIPE	*C5ZZ-5A213-B	*C5ZZ-5A212-E
BRACKET & INSULATOR ASSY	C3OZ-5260-A	C3OZ-5260-A
C1VV-5B236-C PLATE ASSY (2) REQ'D 51765-SB (U-370) SCREW-PAN HD #10-24 x 1/2 (2) REQ'D ATT PLATE TO FLOOR PAN 373403-S8 (MM-173-J) NUT-HEX 3/8-16 (4) REQ'D ATT BRKT TO PLATE 351945-S (UU-52-J) SCREW HEX HD 5/16-18 x 1-1/2 (4) REQ'D ATT BRKT TO MUFFLER		
MUFFLER		*C5ZZ-5230-C
A CLAMP	D1AZ-5A231-C	ATTACHED TO MUFFLER
OUTLET PIPE	C5ZZ-5255-A	ATTACHED TO MUFFLER
BRACKET & INSULATOR ASSY	C3DZ-5260-A	C3DZ-5260-A
351945-S (UU-52-J) SCREW-HEX HD. 5/16-18 x 1 1/2 (4) REQ'D ATT. BRKT. TO UNDERBODY & MUFFLER		
CLAMP	D1AZ-5A231-A	D1AZ-5A231-A

Complete exhaust system and related hardware for 1965 Mustangs and GT-350 Shelby Mustangs (built before 10/15/64) equipped with 289 4-V engines.

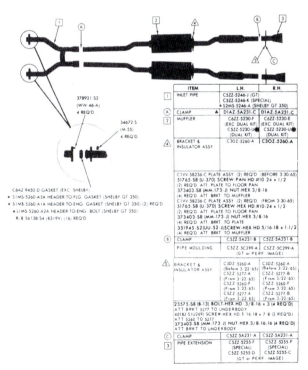

378921-S2
(WW-46-A)
4 REQ'D

34672-S
(M-55)
4 REQ'D

C6AZ-9450-D GASKET (EXC. SHELBY)
* S1MS-5260-A3A HEADER-TO-FLG. GASKET (SHELBY GT 350)
* S1MS-5260-A1A HEADER-TO-ENG. GASKET (SHELBY GT 350) (2) REQ'D
* S1MS-5260-A2A HEADER-TO-ENG. BOLT (SHELBY GT 350)
R/B 56138-S4 (B319V) (16) REQ'D

ITEM	L.H.	R.H.
1 INLET PIPE	C5ZZ-5246-J (GT) C5ZZ-5246-K (SPECIAL) *S2MS-5246-A (SHELBY GT 350)	
A CLAMP	D1AZ-5A231-C	D1AZ-5A231-C
2 MUFFLER	C6ZZ-5230-F (EXC DUAL KIT) C5ZZ-5230-U (DUAL KIT)	C6ZZ-5230-E (EXC DUAL KIT) C5ZZ-5230-U (DUAL KIT)
BRACKET & INSULATOR ASSY	C3OZ-5260-A	C3OZ-5260-A
C1VV-5B236-C PLATE ASSY (2) REQ'D (BEFORE 3-30-65) 51765-SB (U-370) SCREW-PAN HD #10-24 x 1/2 (2) REQ'D ATT. PLATE TO FLOOR PAN 373403-S8 (MM-173-J) NUT-HEX 3/8-16 (4) REQ'D ATT BRKT TO MUFFLER		
C1VV-5B236-C PLATE ASSY (2) REQ'D (FROM 3-30-65) 51765-SB (U-370) SCREW-HEX HD #10-24 x 1/2 (2) REQ'D ATT. PLATE TO FLOOR PAN 373403-S8 (MM-173-J) NUT-HEX 3/8-16 (4) REQ'D ATT. PLATE TO PLATE 351945-S2 (UU-52-J) SCREW-HEX HD 5/16-18 x 1-1/2 (4) REQ'D ATT BRKT TO MUFFLER		
B CLAMP	C5ZZ-5A231-B	C5ZZ-5A231-B
PIPE MOULDING	C5ZZ-5C299-A (GT or PERF. IMAGE)	C5ZZ-5C299-A (GT or PERF. IMAGE)
BRACKET & INSULATOR ASSY	C3OZ-5260-A (Before 3-22-65) C5ZZ-5277-A (From 3-22-65) C5ZZ-5260-F (From 3-22-65) C5ZZ-5277-A (From 3-22-65)	C3OZ-5260-A (Before 3-22-65) C5ZZ-5277-B (From 3-22-65) C5ZZ-5260-F (From 3-22-65) C5ZZ-5277-B (From 3-22-65)
23575-S8 (B-13) BOLT-HEX HD 3/8-16 x 3 (4 REQ'D) ATT BRKT 5277 TO UNDERBODY 40182-S (U-269) SCREW-HEX HD 5 16 18 x 7 8 (2 REQ'D) ATT 5260 TO 5277 373403-S8 (MM-173-J) NUT-HEX 3/8-16-16 (4 REQ'D) ATT-BRKT TO UNDERBODY		
C CLAMP	C5ZZ-5A231-A	C5ZZ-5A231-A
3 PIPE EXTENSION	C5ZZ-5255-F (SPECIAL) C5ZZ-5255-D (GT or PERF. IMAGE)	C5ZZ-5255-F (SPECIAL) C5ZZ-5255-C

Complete exhaust system and related hardware for 1965 GT Mustangs equipped with 289 4-V engines, non-GT Mustangs equipped with 289 High Performance engines, and GT-350 Shelby Mustangs (all built from 10/15/64).

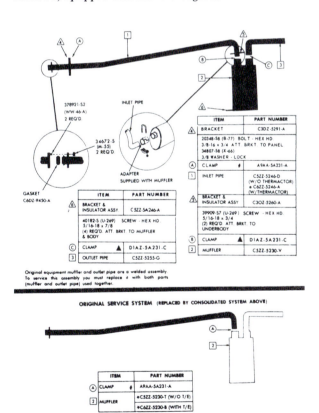

378921-S2
(WW-46-A)
2 REQ'D

INLET PIPE

34672-S
(M-55)
2 REQ'D

ADAPTER
SUPPLIED WITH MUFFLER

GASKET
C6DZ-9450-A

ITEM	PART NUMBER
BRACKET & INSULATOR ASSY	C5ZZ-5A246-A
40182-S (U-269) SCREW - HEX HD. 5/16-18 x 7/8 (4) REQ'D ATT. BRKT. TO MUFFLER & BODY	
C CLAMP	D1AZ-5A231-C
3 OUTLET PIPE	C5ZZ-5255-G

ITEM	PART NUMBER
BRACKET	C3DZ-5291-A
20348-S8 (B-77) BOLT - HEX HD 3/8-16 x 3/4 ATT BRKT TO PANEL 34807-S8 (X-66) 3/8 WASHER - LOCK	
CLAMP	A9AA-5A231-A
1 INLET PIPE	C5ZZ-5246-D (W/O THERMACTOR) *C6ZZ-5246-A (W/THERMACTOR)
BRACKET & INSULATOR ASSY	C3OZ-5260-A
39909-S7 (U-269) SCREW - HEX HD. 5/16-18 x 3/4 (2) REQ'D ATT. BRKT. TO UNDERBODY	
2 CLAMP	D1AZ-5A231-C
3 MUFFLER	C5ZZ-5230-V

Original equipment muffler and outlet pipe are a welded assembly. To service this assembly you must replace it with both parts (muffler and outlet pipe) used together.

ORIGINAL SERVICE SYSTEM (REPLACED BY CONSOLIDATED SYSTEM ABOVE)

ITEM	PART NUMBER
A CLAMP	A9AA-5A231-A
2 MUFFLER	*C5ZZ-5230-T (W/O T/E) *C6ZZ-5230-B (WITH T/E)

Complete exhaust system and related hardware for 1966 Mustangs equipped with 200ci engines.

1966 MUSTANG—8 CYL. 289-2B & 4B
CONSOLIDATED SERVICE REPLACEMENT (REPLACES ORIGINAL SERVICE SYSTEM BELOW)

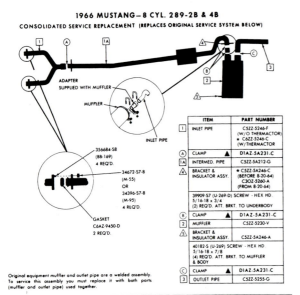

ITEM		PART NUMBER
1	INLET PIPE	C5ZZ-5246-F (W/O THERMACTOR)
		★ C6ZZ-5246-C (W/THERMACTOR)
A	CLAMP	▲ D1AZ-5A231-C
1A	INTERMED. PIPE	C5ZZ-5A212-G
⚠	BRACKET & INSULATOR ASSY.	★ C5ZZ-5A246-C (BEFORE 8-20-64) C3OZ-5260-A (FROM 8-20-64)
		39909-S7 (U-269-D) SCREW - HEX HD. 5/16-18 x 3/4 (2) REQ'D. ATT. BRKT. TO UNDERBODY
B	CLAMP	▲ D1AZ-5A231-C
2	MUFFLER	C5ZZ-5230-V
⚠	BRACKET & INSULATOR ASSY.	C5ZZ-5A246-A
		40182-S (U-269) SCREW - HEX HD. 5/16-18 x 7/8 (4) REQ'D. ATT. BRKT. TO MUFFLER & BODY
C	CLAMP	▲ D1AZ-5A231-C
3	OUTLET PIPE	C5ZZ-5255-G

Original equipment muffler and outlet pipe are a welded assembly. To service this assembly you must replace it with both parts (muffler and outlet pipe) used together.

ORIGINAL SERVICE SYSTEM (REPLACED BY CONSOLIDATED SYSTEM ABOVE)

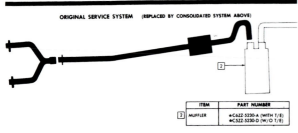

ITEM		PART NUMBER
2	MUFFLER	★C6ZZ-5230-A (WITH T/E) ★C5ZZ-5230-D (W/O T/E)

Complete exhaust system and related hardware for 1966 Mustangs equipped with 289 2-V and 4-V engines.

1966 MUSTANG—8 CYL. 289-4B PREM. FUEL - WITH STD. PIPE EXTENSIONS
(INCLUDES MODELS W/289-2B & DUAL EXHAUST KIT - ●)

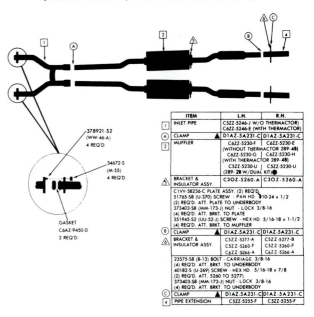

ITEM		L.H.	R.H.
1	INLET PIPE	C5ZZ-5246-J W/O THERMACTOR) C6ZZ-5246-E (WITH THERMACTOR)	
A	CLAMP	▲ D1AZ-5A231-C	D1AZ-5A231-C
2	MUFFLER	C6ZZ-5230-F (WITHOUT THERMACTOR 289-4B) C6ZZ-5230-G (WITH THERMACTOR 289-4B) C5ZZ-5230-U (289-2B W/DUAL KIT)●	C6ZZ-5230-E C6ZZ-5230-H C5ZZ-5230-U
⚠	BRACKET & INSULATOR ASSY.	C3OZ-5260-A	C3OZ-5260-A
		C1VV-5B236-C PLATE ASSY. (2) REQ'D 51765-S8 (U-370) SCREW - PAN HD. #10-24 x 1/2 (2) REQ'D. ATT. PLATE TO UNDERBODY 373403-S8 (MM-173-J) NUT - LOCK 3/8-16 (4) REQ'D. ATT. BRKT. TO PLATE 351945-S2 (UU-52-J) SCREW - HEX HD. 5/16-18 x 1-1/2 (4) REQ'D. ATT. BRKT. TO MUFFLER		
B	CLAMP	▲ D1AZ-5A231-C	D1AZ-5A231-C
⚠	BRACKET & INSULATOR ASSY.	C5ZZ-5277-A C5ZZ-5260-F C6ZZ-5266-A	C5ZZ-5277-B C5ZZ-5260-F C6ZZ-5266-A
		23575-S8 (B-13) BOLT - CARRIAGE 3/8-16 (4) REQ'D. ATT. BRKT. TO UNDERBODY 40182-S (U-269) SCREW - HEX HD. 5/16-18 x 7/8 (2) REQ'D. ATT. 5260 TO 5277 373403-S8 (MM-173-J) NUT - LOCK 3/8-16 (4) REQ'D. ATT. BRKT. TO UNDERBODY		
C	CLAMP	▲ D1AZ-5A231-C	D1AZ-5A231-C
4	PIPE EXTENSION	C5ZZ-5255-F	C5ZZ-5255-F

Complete exhaust system and related hardware for 1966 Mustangs equipped with 289 4-V premium-fuel engines with standard pipe extensions and 298 V-2 engines with dual exhaust kit.

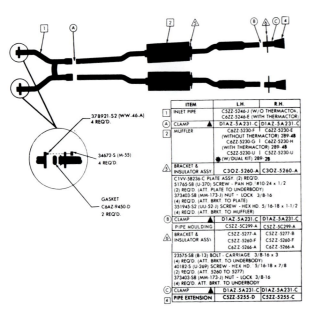

ITEM		L.H.	R.H.
1	INLET PIPE	C5ZZ-5246-J (W/O THERMACTOR) C6ZZ-5246-E (WITH THERMACTOR)	
A	CLAMP	▲ D1AZ-5A231-C	D1AZ-5A231-C
2	MUFFLER	C6ZZ-5230-F (WITHOUT THERMACTOR) 289-4B C6ZZ-5230-G (WITH THERMACTOR) 289-4B C5ZZ-5230-U (W/DUAL KIT) 289-2B	C6ZZ-5230-E C6ZZ-5230-H C5ZZ-5230-U
⚠	BRACKET & INSULATOR ASSY.	C3OZ-5260-A	C3OZ-5260-A
		C1VV-5B236-C PLATE ASSY. (2) REQ'D 51765-S8 (U-370) SCREW - PAN HD. #10-24 x 1/2 (2) REQ'D. ATT. PLATE TO UNDERBODY 373403-S8 (MM-173-J) NUT - LOCK 3/8-16 (4) REQ'D. ATT. BRKT. TO PLATE 351945-S2 (UU-52-J) SCREW - HEX HD. 5/16-18 x 1-1/2 (4) REQ'D. ATT. BRKT. TO MUFFLER		
B	CLAMP	▲ D1AZ-5A231-C	D1AZ-5A231-C
	PIPE MOULDING	C5ZZ-5C299-A	C5ZZ-5C299-A
⚠	BRACKET & INSULATOR ASSY.	C5ZZ-5277-A C5ZZ-5260-F C6ZZ-5266-A	C5ZZ-5277-B C5ZZ-5260-F C6ZZ-5266-A
		23575-S8 (B-13) BOLT - CARRIAGE 3/8-16 x 3 (4) REQ'D. ATT. BRKT. TO UNDERBODY 40182-S (U-269) SCREW - HEX HD. 5/16-18 x 7/8 (2) REQ'D. ATT. 5260 TO 5277 373403-S8 (MM-173-J) NUT - LOCK 3/8-16 (4) REQ'D. ATT. BRKT TO UNDERBODY		
C	CLAMP	▲ D1AZ-5A231-C	D1AZ-5A231-C
4	PIPE EXTENSION	C5ZZ-5255-D	C5ZZ-5255-C

Complete exhaust system and related hardware for 1966 GT Mustangs equipped with 289 4-V engines, Mustangs equipped with optional performance image dual exhaust, and 298 V-2 engines with dual exhaust kit.

1966 MUSTANG—8 CYL. 289-4B SPECIAL—INCLUDES SHELBY GT 350
1966 MUSTANG—8 CYL. 289 W/DUAL EXHAUST KIT - ●

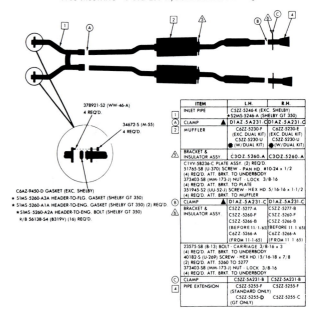

ITEM		L.H.	R.H.
1	INLET PIPE	C5ZZ-5246-K (EXC. SHELBY) ★S2MS-5246-A (SHELBY GT 350)	
A	CLAMP	▲ D1AZ-5A231-C	D1AZ-5A231-C
2	MUFFLER	C5ZZ-5230-F (EXC. DUAL KIT) C5ZZ-5230-U (W/DUAL KIT)	C6ZZ-5230-E (EXC. DUAL KIT) C5ZZ-5230-U (W/DUAL KIT)
⚠	BRACKET & INSULATOR ASSY.	C3OZ-5260-A	C3OZ-5260-A
		C1VV-5B236-C PLATE ASSY. (2) REQ'D. 51765-S8 (U-370) SCREW - PAN HD. #10-24 x 1/2 (4) REQ'D. ATT. BRKT. TO UNDERBODY 373403-S8 (MM-173-J) NUT - LOCK 3/8-16 (4) REQ'D. ATT. BRKT. TO PLATE 351945-S2 (UU-52-J) SCREW - HEX HD. 5/16-16 x 1-1/2 (4) REQ'D. ATT. BRKT. TO MUFFLER		
B	CLAMP	▲ D1AZ-5A231-C	D1AZ-5A231-C
⚠	BRACKET & INSULATOR ASSY.	C5ZZ-5277-A C5ZZ-5260-F C6ZZ-5266-B (BEFORE 11 1 65) C6ZZ-5266-A (FROM 11-1-65)	C5ZZ-5277-B C5ZZ-5260-F C6ZZ-5266-B (BEFORE 11 1 65) C6ZZ-5266-A (FROM 11-1-65)
		23575-S8 (B-13) BOLT - CARRIAGE 3/8-16 x 3 (4) REQ'D. ATT. BRKT. TO UNDERBODY 40182-S (U-269) SCREW - HEX HD 15/16-18 x 7/8 (2) REQ'D. ATT. 5260 TO 5277 373403-S8 (MM-173-J) NUT - LOCK 3/8-16 (4) REQ'D. ATT. BRKT. TO UNDERBODY		
C	CLAMP	C5ZZ-5A231-B	C5ZZ-5A231-B
4	PIPE EXTENSION	C5ZZ-5255-F (STANDARD ONLY) C5ZZ-5255-D (GT ONLY)	C5ZZ-5255-F C5ZZ-5255-C

★ SIMS-5260-A3A HEADER-TO-FLG. GASKET (SHELBY GT 350)
★ SIMS-5260-A1A HEADER-TO-ENG. GASKET (SHELBY GT 350) (2) REQ'D
★ SIMS-5260-A2A HEADER-TO-ENG. BOLT (SHELBY GT 350) R/B 5613B-S4 (B319V) (16) REQ'D.

Complete exhaust system and related hardware for 1966 Mustangs equipped with 289 High Performance engines, Shelby GT-350 Mustangs, and 289 engines equipped with dual exhaust kit.

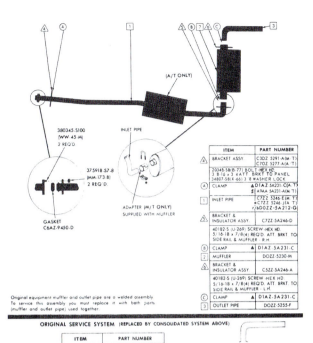

Table (top left diagram)

ITEM	PART NUMBER
△ BRACKET ASSY.	C3DZ-5291-A (M-T) C7OZ-5277-A (A-T)
20348-S8 (B-77) BOLT-HEX HD. 3/8-16 x 3/4 ATT BRKT TO PANEL 34807-S8 (X-66) 3/8 WASHER LOCK	
Ⓐ CLAMP	▲ D1AZ-5A231-C (A-T) ⱥ A9AA-5A231-A (M-T)
1 INLET PIPE	▲ C7ZZ-5246-E (M-T) ⱥ C7ZZ-5246-J (A-T) r/b DOZZ-5A212-G
△ BRACKET & INSULATOR ASSY.	C7ZZ-5A246-D
40182-S (U-269) SCREW-HEX HD 5/16-18 x 7/8(4) REQ'D ATT. BRKT. TO SIDE RAIL & MUFFLER - R.H.	
Ⓑ CLAMP	▲ D1AZ-5A231-C
2 MUFFLER	DOZZ-5230-M
△ BRACKET & INSULATOR ASSY.	C5ZZ-5A246-A
40182-S (U-269) SCREW-HEX HD 5/16-18 x 7/8(4) REQ'D ATT. BRKT. TO SIDE RAIL & MUFFLER - L.H.	
Ⓒ CLAMP	▲ D1AZ-5A231-C
3 OUTLET PIPE	DOZZ-5255-F

Original equipment muffler and outlet pipe are a welded assembly.
To service this assembly you must replace it with both parts
(muffler and outlet pipe) used together.

ORIGINAL SERVICE SYSTEM (REPLACED BY CONSOLIDATED SYSTEM ABOVE)

ITEM	PART NUMBER
2 MUFFLER	★ C7ZZ-5230-C (M-T) ★ C7ZZ-5230-F (A-T)

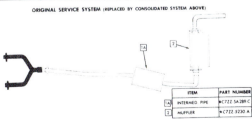

*Complete exhaust system and related hardware for 1967
Mustangs equipped with 200ci engines.*

*These quad tips split each tailpipe into two smaller-
diameter chrome tubes with angle-cut openings. This style
exhaust outlet was standard equipment on 1967-1969
Mustang GTs and the 1969 Mach 1.*

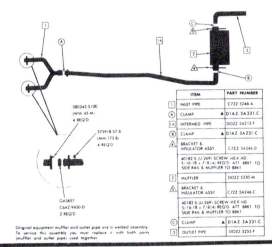

Table (lower left diagram)

ITEM	PART NUMBER
1 INLET PIPE	C7ZZ-5246-A
Ⓐ CLAMP	▲ D1AZ-5A231-C
1A INTERMED. PIPE	DOZZ-5A212-F
Ⓑ CLAMP	▲ D1AZ-5A231-C
△ BRACKET & INSULATOR ASSY.	C7ZZ-5A246-D
40182-S (U-269) SCREW-HEX HD. 5/16-18 x 7/8(4) REQ'D ATT BRKT TO SIDE RAIL & MUFFLER TO BRKT.	
2 MUFFLER	DOZZ-5230-M
△ BRACKET & INSULATOR ASSY.	C7ZZ-5A246-C
40182-S (U-269) SCREW-HEX HD. 5/16-18 x 7/8(4) REQ'D ATT BRKT TO SIDE RAIL & MUFFLER TO BRKT.	
Ⓒ CLAMP	▲ D1AZ-5A231-C
3 OUTLET PIPE	DOZZ-5255-F

Original equipment muffler and outlet pipe are a welded assembly.
To service this assembly you must replace it with both parts
(muffler and outlet pipe) used together.

ORIGINAL SERVICE SYSTEM (REPLACED BY CONSOLIDATED SYSTEM ABOVE)

ITEM	PART NUMBER
1A INTERMED. PIPE	★ C7ZZ-5A289-C
2 MUFFLER	★ C7ZZ-5230-A

*Complete exhaust system and related hardware for 1967
Mustangs equipped with 289 2-V and 4-V premium-fuel
engines.*

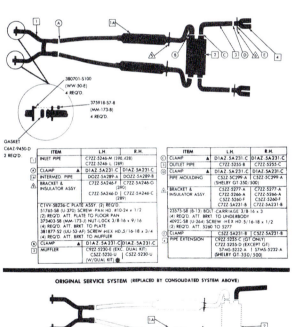

Table (right diagram)

ITEM	L.H.	R.H.
1 INLET PIPE	C7ZZ-5246-M (390,428) C7ZZ-5246-L (289)	
Ⓐ CLAMP ▲	D1AZ-5A231-C	D1AZ-5A231-C
1A INTERMED. PIPE	DOZZ-5A289-A	DOZZ-5A289-B
△ BRACKET & INSULATOR ASSY.	C7ZZ-5A246-F (390) C7ZZ-5A246-D (289)	C7ZZ-5A246-G C7ZZ-5A246-C (289)
C1VV-5B236-C PLATE ASSY. (2) REQ'D. 51765-S8 (U-370) SCREW-PAN HD. #10-24 x 1/2 (2) REQ'D. ATT. PLATE TO FLOOR PAN 373403-S8 (MM-173-J) NUT-LOCK 3/8-16 x 9/16 (2) REQ'D. ATT. BRKT. TO PLATE 381877-S2 (UU-52-AF) SCREW-HEX HD. 5/16-18 x 3/4 (4) REQ'D. ATT. BRKT. TO MUFFLER		
Ⓑ CLAMP ▲	D1AZ-5A231-C	D1AZ-5A231-C
2 MUFFLER	C9ZZ-5230-E (EXC. DUAL KIT) C5ZZ-5230-U (W/DUAL KIT)	C5ZZ-5230-U

ITEM	L.H.	R.H.
Ⓒ CLAMP	D1AZ-5A231-C	D1AZ-5A231-C
3 OUTLET PIPE	C7ZZ-5255-B	C7ZZ-5255-C
1A CLAMP	D1AZ-5A231-C	D1AZ-5A231-C
△ PIPE MOULDING	C5ZZ-5C299-A (SHELBY GT-350/500)	C5ZZ-5C299-A
△ BRACKET & INSULATOR ASSY.	C5ZZ-5277-A C7ZZ-5260-A C7ZZ-5A231-B	C7ZZ-5277-A C7ZZ-5266-A C5ZZ-5260-F
23575-S8 (B-13) BOLT-CARRIAGE 3/8-16 x 3 (4) REQ'D. ATT. BRKT. TO UNDERBODY 40925-S8 (U-264) SCREW-HEX HD.5/16-18 x 1/2 (2) REQ'D. ATT. 5260 TO 5277		
Ⓒ CLAMP	C5ZZ-5A231-B	C5ZZ-5A231-B
4 PIPE EXTENSION	C9ZZ-5255-C (GT ONLY) C7ZZ-5255-D (EXCEPT GT) S7MS-5232-A | S7MS-5232-A (SHELBY GT-350/500)	

ORIGINAL SERVICE SYSTEM (REPLACED BY CONSOLIDATED SYSTEM ABOVE)

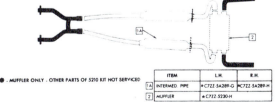

✿ - MUFFLER ONLY - OTHER PARTS OF 5210 KIT NOT SERVICED

ITEM	L.H.	R.H.
1A INTERMED. PIPE	★ C7ZZ-5A289-G	★ C7ZZ-5A289-H
2 MUFFLER	★ C7ZZ-5230-H	

*Complete exhaust system and related hardware for 1967
GT Mustangs equipped with 289 and 390 4-V engines,
standard Mustangs equipped with 390 4-V engines, and
GT-350 and GT-500 Shelby Mustangs.*

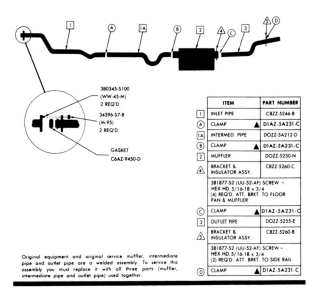

ITEM		PART NUMBER
1	INLET PIPE	C8ZZ-5246-B
A	CLAMP ▲	D1AZ-5A231-C
1A	INTERMED. PIPE	DOZZ-5A212-D
B	CLAMP ▲	D1AZ-5A231-C
2	MUFFLER	DOZZ-5230-N
⚠	BRACKET & INSULATOR ASSY.	C8ZZ-5260-C
	381877-S2 (UU-52-AF) SCREW - HEX HD. 5/16-18 x 3/4 (4) REQ'D. ATT. BRKT. TO FLOOR PAN & MUFFLER	
C	CLAMP	D1AZ-5A231-C
3	OUTLET PIPE	DOZZ-5255-E
⚠	BRACKET & INSULATOR ASSY.	C8ZZ-5260-B
	381877-S2 (UU-52-AF) SCREW - HEX HD. 5/16-18 x 3/4 (2) REQ'D. ATT. BRKT. TO SIDE RAIL	
D	CLAMP ▲	D1AZ-5A231-C

380345-S100 (WW-45-M) 2 REQ'D.
34396-S7-8 (M-95) 2 REQ'D.
GASKET C6AZ-9450-D

Original equipment and original service muffler, intermediate pipe and outlet pipe are a welded assembly. To service this assembly you must replace it with all three parts (muffler, intermediate pipe and outlet pipe) used together.

ORIGINAL SERVICE SYSTEM (REPLACED BY CONSOLIDATED SYSTEM ABOVE)

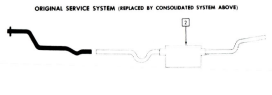

ITEM		PART NUMBER
2	MUFFLER	*C8ZZ-5230-A

Complete exhaust system and related hardware for a 1968 Mustang equipped with a 200ci engine.

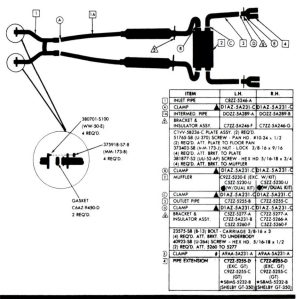

ITEM		L.H.	R.H.
1	INLET PIPE	C8ZZ-5246-A	
A	CLAMP	D1AZ-5A231-C	D1AZ-5A231-C
1A	INTERMED. PIPE	DOZZ-5A289-A	DOZZ-5A289-B
⚠	BRACKET & INSULATOR ASSY.	C7ZZ-5A246-F	C7ZZ-5A246-G
	C1VV-5B236-C PLATE ASSY. (2) REQ'D.		
	51765-S8 (U-370) SCREW - PAN HD. #10-24 x 1/2 (2) REQ'D. ATT. PLATE TO FLOOR PAN		
	373403-S8 (M-M-173-J) NUT - LOCK 3/8-16 x 9/16 (4) REQ'D. ATT. BRKT. TO PLATE		
	381877-S2 (UU-52-AF) SCREW - HEX HD. 5/16-18 x 3/4 (4) REQ'D. ATT. BRKT. TO MUFFLER		
S	CLAMP	D1AZ-5A231-C	D1AZ-5A231-C
2	MUFFLER	C9ZZ-5230-E (EXC. W/KIT) C5ZZ-5230-U (W/DUAL KIT)	C5ZZ-5230-U (W/DUAL KIT)
C	CLAMP	D1AZ-5A231-C	D1AZ-5A231-C
3	OUTLET PIPE	C7ZZ-5255-B	C7ZZ-5255-C
D	CLAMP	D1AZ-5A231-C	D1AZ-5A231-C
⚠	BRACKET & INSULATOR ASSY.	C5ZZ-5277-A C7ZZ-5A231-B C5ZZ-5260-F	C7ZZ-5277-A C7ZZ-5266-A C5ZZ-5260-F
	23575-S8 (B-13) BOLT - CARRIAGE 3/8-16 x 3 (4) REQ'D. ATT. BRKT. TO UNDERBODY		
	40923-S8 (U-264) SCREW - HEX HD. 5/16-18 x 1/2 (2) REQ'D. ATT. 5260 TO 5277		
S	CLAMP ♦	A9AA-5A231-A	A9AA-5A231-A
4	PIPE EXTENSION	C7ZZ-5255-D (EXC. GT) C9ZZ-5255-C (GT) *SBMS-5232-B (SHELBY GT-350)	C7ZZ-5255-D (EXC. GT) C9ZZ-5255-C (GT) *SBMS-5232-B (SHELBY GT-350)

380701-S100 (WW-50-E) 4 REQ'D.
375918-S7-8 (MM-173-B) 4 REQ'D.
GASKET C6AZ-9450-D 2 REQ'D.

ORIGINAL SERVICE SYSTEM (REPLACED BY CONSOLIDATED SYSTEM ABOVE)

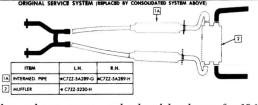

ITEM		L.H.	R.H.
1A	INTERMED. PIPE	*C7ZZ-5A289-G	*C7ZZ-5A289-H
2	MUFFLER	* C7ZZ-5230-H	

Complete exhaust system and related hardware for 1968 GT Mustangs equipped with 289 2-V and 302 4-V engines and Shelby GT-350 Mustangs.

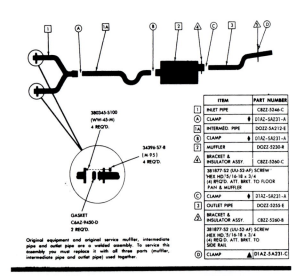

ITEM		PART NUMBER
1	INLET PIPE	C8ZZ-5246-C
A	CLAMP ♦	D1AZ-5A231-A
1A	INTERMED. PIPE	DOZZ-5A212-E
B	CLAMP	D1AZ-5A231-A
2	MUFFLER	DOZZ-5230-R
⚠	BRACKET & INSULATOR ASSY.	C8ZZ-5260-C
	381877-S2 (UU-52-AF) SCREW - HEX HD. 5/16-18 x 3/4 (4) REQ'D. ATT. BRKT. TO FLOOR PAN & MUFFLER	
C	CLAMP	D1AZ-5A231-A
3	OUTLET PIPE	DOZZ-5255-E
⚠	BRACKET & INSULATOR ASSY.	C8ZZ-5260-B
	381877-S2 (UU-52-AF) SCREW - HEX HD. 5/16-18 x 3/4 (4) REQ'D. ATT. BRKT. TO SIDE RAIL	
D	CLAMP ▲	D1AZ-5A231-C

380345-S100 (WW-45-M) 4 REQ'D.
34396-S7-8 (M-95) 4 REQ'D.
GASKET C6AZ-9450-D 2 REQ'D.

Original equipment and original service muffler, intermediate pipe and outlet pipe are a welded assembly. To service this assembly you must replace it with all three parts (muffler, intermediate pipe and outlet pipe) used together.

ORIGINAL SERVICE SYSTEM (REPLACED BY CONSOLIDATED SYSTEM ABOVE)

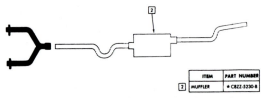

ITEM		PART NUMBER
2	MUFFLER	* C8ZZ-5230-B

Complete exhaust system and related hardware for 1968 Mustangs equipped with 289 2-V and 302 4-V engines.

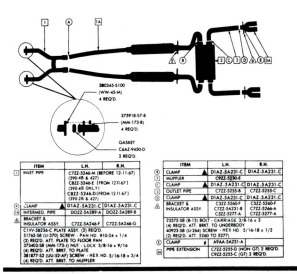

ITEM		L.H.	R.H.
1	INLET PIPE	C7ZZ-5246-M (BEFORE 12-11-67) (390-4B & 427) D1AZ-5A231-C (FROM 12-11-67) (390-4B ONLY) C8ZZ-5246-D (FROM 12-11-67) (390-2B & 427)	
A	CLAMP ▲	D1AZ-5A231-C	D1AZ-5A231-C
1A	INTERMED. PIPE	DOZZ-5A289-A	DOZZ-5A289-B
⚠	BRACKET & INSULATOR ASSY.	C7ZZ-5A246-F	C7ZZ-5A246-G
	C1VV-5B236-C PLATE ASSY. (2) REQ'D.		
	51765-S8 (U-370) SCREW - PAN HD. #10-24 x 1/4 (2) REQ'D. ATT. PLATE TO FLOOR PAN		
	373403-S8 (M-M-173-J) NUT - LOCK 3/8-16 x 9/16 (4) REQ'D. ATT. BRKT. TO PLATE		
	381877-S2 (UU-52-AF) SCREW - HEX HD. 5/16-18 x 3/4 (4) REQ'D. ATT. BRKT. TO MUFFLER		

ITEM		L.H.	R.H.
B	CLAMP ▲	D1AZ-5A231-C	D1AZ-5A231-C
2	MUFFLER	C9ZZ-5230-E	
C	CLAMP	D1AZ-5A231-C	D1AZ-5A231-C
3	OUTLET PIPE	C7ZZ-5255-B	C7ZZ-5255-C
D	CLAMP	D1AZ-5A231-C	D1AZ-5A231-C
⚠	BRACKET & INSULATOR ASSY.	C5ZZ-5260-F C7ZZ-5A231-B C5ZZ-5277-A	C5ZZ-5260-F C7ZZ-5266-A C7ZZ-5277-A
	23575-S8 (B-13) BOLT - CARRIAGE 3/8-16 x 3 (4) REQ'D. ATT. BRKT. TO UNDERBODY		
	40923-S8 (U-264) SCREW - HEX HD. 5/16-18 x 1/2 (2) REQ'D. ATT. 5260 TO 5277)		
E	CLAMP ♦	A9AA-5A231-A	
3A	PIPE EXTENSION	C7ZZ-5255-D (NON GT) 2 REQ'D. C9ZZ-5255-C (GT) 2 REQ'D.	

ORIGINAL SERVICE SYSTEM (REPLACED BY CONSOLIDATED SYSTEM ABOVE)

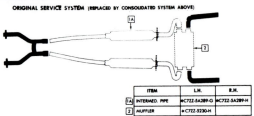

ITEM		L.H.	R.H.
1A	INTERMED. PIPE	*C7ZZ-5A289-G	*C7ZZ-5A289-H
2	MUFFLER	*C7ZZ-5230-H	

Complete exhaust system and related hardware for 1968 Mustangs equipped with 390 2-V and 4-V engines.

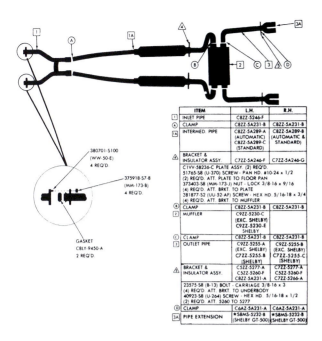

ITEM		L.H.	R.H.
[1]	INLET PIPE	C8ZZ-5246-F	
[A]	CLAMP	C8ZZ-5A231-B	C8ZZ-5A231-B
[1A]	INTERMED. PIPE	C8ZZ-5A289-A (AUTOMATIC) C8ZZ-5A289-C (STANDARD)	C8ZZ-5A289-B (AUTOMATIC & STANDARD)
△	BRACKET & INSULATOR ASSY.	C7ZZ-5A246-F	C7ZZ-5A246-G
	C1VV-5B236-C PLATE ASSY. (2) REQ'D. 51765-S8 (U-370) SCREW - PAN HD. #10-24 x 1/2 (2) REQ'D. ATT. PLATE TO FLOOR PAN 373403-S8 (MM-173-J) NUT - LOCK 3/8-16 x 9/16 (4) REQ'D. ATT. BRKT. TO PLATE 381877-S2 (UU-52-AF) SCREW - HEX HD. 5/16-18 x 3/4 (4) REQ'D. ATT. BRKT. TO MUFFLER		
[B]	CLAMP	C8ZZ-5A231-B	C8ZZ-5A231-B
[2]	MUFFLER	C9ZZ-5230-C (EXC. SHELBY) C9ZZ-5230-E SHELBY	
[C]	CLAMP	C8ZZ-5A231-B	C8ZZ-5A231-B
[3]	OUTLET PIPE	C9ZZ-5255-A (EXC. SHELBY) C7ZZ-5255-B (SHELBY)	C9ZZ-5255-B (EXC. SHELBY) C7ZZ-5255-C (SHELBY)
△	BRACKET & INSULATOR ASSY.	C5ZZ-5277-A C5ZZ-5260-F C8ZZ-5A231-A	C7ZZ-5277-A C5ZZ-5260-F C7ZZ-5266-A
	23575-S8 (B-13) BOLT - CARRIAGE 3/8-16 x 3 (4) REQ'D. ATT. BRKT. TO UNDERBODY 40923-S8 (U-264) SCREW - HEX HD. 5/16-18 x 1/2 (2) REQ'D. ATT. 5260 TO 5277		
[D]	CLAMP	C6AZ-5A231-A	C6AZ-5A231-A
[3A]	PIPE EXTENSION	*S8MS-5232-B (SHELBY GT-500)	*S8MS-5232-B (SHELBY GT-500)

380701-S100 (WW-50-E) 4 REQ'D.

375918-S7-8 (MM-173-B) 4 REQ'D.

GASKET C8LY-9450-A 2 REQ'D.

Complete exhaust system and related hardware for 1968 GT Mustangs equipped with 428 4-V engines and Shelby GT-500 Mustangs.

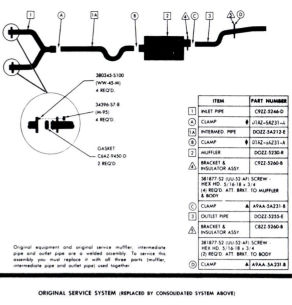

380345-S100 (WW-45-M) 4 REQ'D.

34396-S7-8 (M-95) 4 REQ'D.

GASKET C6AZ-9450-D 2 REQ'D.

ITEM		PART NUMBER
[1]	INLET PIPE	C9ZZ-5246-D
[A]	CLAMP	D1AZ-5A231-A
[1A]	INTERMED. PIPE	DOZZ-5A212-E
[B]	CLAMP	D1AZ-5A231-A
[2]	MUFFLER	DOZZ-5230-R
△	BRACKET & INSULATOR ASSY.	C9ZZ-5260-B
	381877-S2 (UU-52-AF) SCREW - HEX HD. 5/16-18 x 3/4 (4) REQ'D. ATT. BRKT. TO MUFFLER & BODY	
[C]	CLAMP	A9AA-5A231-B
[3]	OUTLET PIPE	DOZZ-5255-E
△	BRACKET & INSULATOR ASSY.	C8ZZ-5260-B
	381877-S2 (UU-52-AF) SCREW - HEX HD. 5/16-18 x 3/4 (4) REQ'D. ATT. BRKT. TO BODY	
[D]	CLAMP	A9AA-5A231-B

Original equipment and original service muffler, intermediate pipe and outlet pipe are a welded assembly. To service this assembly you must replace it with all three parts (muffler, intermediate pipe and outlet pipe) used together.

ORIGINAL SERVICE SYSTEM (REPLACED BY CONSOLIDATED SYSTEM ABOVE)

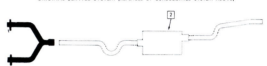

ITEM		PART NUMBER
[2]	MUFFLER	*C9ZZ-5230-F

Complete exhaust system and related hardware for a 1969 Mustang equipped with a 302 2-V engine.

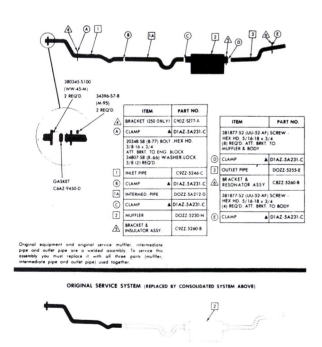

380345-S100 (WW-45-M) 2 REQ'D.

34396-S7-8 (M-95) 2 REQ'D.

GASKET C6AZ-9450-D

ITEM		PART NO.
△	BRACKET (250 ONLY)	C90Z-5277-A
[A]	CLAMP	D1AZ-5A231-C
	20348-S8 (B-77) BOLT - HEX HD. 3/8-16 x 3/4 ATT. BRKT. TO ENG. BLOCK 34807-S8 (X-66) WASHER-LOCK 3/8 (2) REQ'D.	
[1]	INLET PIPE	C9ZZ-5246-C
[B]	CLAMP	D1AZ-5A231-C
[1A]	INTERMED. PIPE	DOZZ-5A212-D
[C]	CLAMP	D1AZ-5A231-C
[2]	MUFFLER	DOZZ-5230-N
△	BRACKET & INSULATOR ASSY.	C9ZZ-5260-B

ITEM		PART NO.
△	381877-S2 (UU-52-AF) SCREW - HEX HD. 5/16-18 x 3/4 (8) REQ'D. ATT. BRKT. TO MUFFLER & BODY	
[D]	CLAMP	D1AZ-5A231-C
[3]	OUTLET PIPE	DOZZ-5255-E
△	BRACKET & RESONATOR ASSY	C8ZZ-5260-B
	381877-S2 (UU-52-AF) SCREW - HEX HD. 5/16-18 x 3/4 (4) REQ'D. ATT. BRKT. TO BODY	
[E]	CLAMP	D1AZ-5A231-C

Original equipment and original service muffler, intermediate pipe and outlet pipe are a welded assembly. To service this assembly you must replace it with all three parts (muffler, intermediate pipe and outlet pipe) used together.

ORIGINAL SERVICE SYSTEM (REPLACED BY CONSOLIDATED SYSTEM ABOVE)

ITEM		PART NO.
[2]	MUFFLER	*C9ZZ-5230-D

Complete exhaust system and related hardware for a 1969 Mustang equipped with a 200 or 250ci engine.

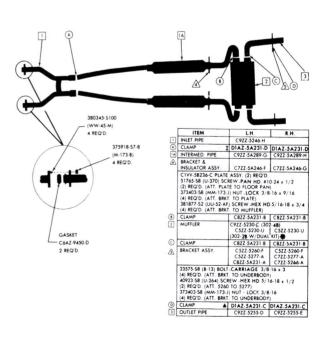

380345-S100 (WW-45-M) 4 REQ'D.

375918-S7-8 (M-173-B) 4 REQ'D.

GASKET C6AZ-9450-D 2 REQ'D.

ITEM		L.H.	R.H.
[1]	INLET PIPE	C9ZZ-5246-H	
[A]	CLAMP	D1AZ-5A231-D	D1AZ-5A231-D
[1A]	INTERMED. PIPE	C9ZZ-5A289-G	C9ZZ-5A289-H
△	BRACKET & INSULATOR ASSY.	C7ZZ-5A246-F	C7ZZ-5A246-G
	C1VV-5B236-C PLATE ASSY. (2) REQ'D. 51765-S8 (U-370) SCREW-PAN HD. #10-24 x 1/2 (2) REQ'D. (ATT. PLATE TO FLOOR PAN) 373403-S8 (MM-173-J) NUT-LOCK 3/8-16 x 9/16 (4) REQ'D. (ATT. BRKT. TO PLATE) 381877-S2 (UU-52-AF) SCREW-HEX HD 5/16-18 x 3/4 (4) REQ'D. (ATT. BRKT. TO MUFFLER)		
[B]	CLAMP	C8ZZ-5A231-B	C8ZZ-5A231-B
[2]	MUFFLER	C9ZZ-5230-C (302-4B) C5ZZ-5230-U (302-2B W/DUAL KIT)	C5ZZ-5230-U
[C]	CLAMP	C8ZZ-5A231-B	C8ZZ-5A231-B
△	BRACKET ASSY.	C5ZZ-5260-F C5ZZ-5277-A C8ZZ-5A231-A	C5ZZ-5260-F C7ZZ-5277-A C7ZZ-5266-A
	23575-S8 (B-13) BOLT-CARRIAGE 3/8-16 x 3 (4) REQ'D. (ATT. BRKT. TO UNDERBODY) 40923-S8 (U-264) SCREW-HEX HD 5/16-18 x 1/2 (2) REQ'D. (ATT. 5260 TO 5277) 373403-S8 (MM-173-J) NUT-LOCK 3/8-16 (4) REQ'D. (ATT. BRKT. TO UNDERBODY)		
[D]	CLAMP	D1AZ-5A231-C	D1AZ-5A231-C
[3]	OUTLET PIPE	C9ZZ-5255-D	C9ZZ-5255-E

Complete exhaust system and related hardware for a 1969 Boss 302 Mustang and models equipped with a 302 2-V engine and dual exhausts.

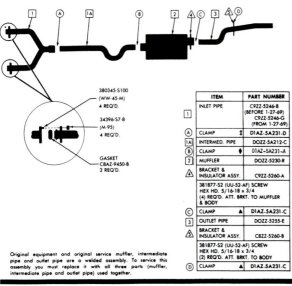

ITEM		PART NUMBER
1	INLET PIPE	C9ZZ-5246-B (BEFORE 1-27-69) C9ZZ-5246-G (FROM 1-27-69)
A	CLAMP	D1AZ-5A231-D
1A	INTERMED. PIPE	DOZZ-5A212-C
B	CLAMP	D1AZ-5A231-A
2	MUFFLER	DOZZ-5230-R
⚠	BRACKET & INSULATOR ASSY.	C9ZZ-5260-A
	381877-S2 (UU-52-AF) SCREW HEX HD. 5/16-18 x 3/4 (4) REQ'D. ATT. BRKT. TO MUFFLER & BODY	
C	CLAMP	D1AZ-5A231-C
3	OUTLET PIPE	DOZZ-5255-E
⚠	BRACKET & INSULATOR ASSY.	C8ZZ-5260-B
	381877-S2 (UU-52-AF) SCREW HEX HD. 5/16-18 x 3/4 (2) REQ'D. ATT. BRKT. TO BODY	
D	CLAMP	D1AZ-5A231-C

380345-S100 (WW-45-M) 4 REQ'D.

34396-S7-8 (M-95) 4 REQ'D.

GASKET C8AZ-9450-B 2 REQ'D.

Original equipment and original service muffler, intermediate pipe and outlet pipe are a welded assembly. To service this assembly you must replace it with all three parts (muffler, intermediate pipe and outlet pipe) used together.

ORIGINAL SERVICE SYSTEM (REPLACED BY CONSOLIDATED SYSTEM ABOVE)

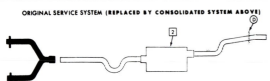

ITEM		PART NUMBER
2	MUFFLER	*C9ZZ-5230-A
D	CLAMP	D1AZ-5A231-A

Complete exhaust system and related hardware for a 1969 Mustang equipped with a 351 2-V engine.

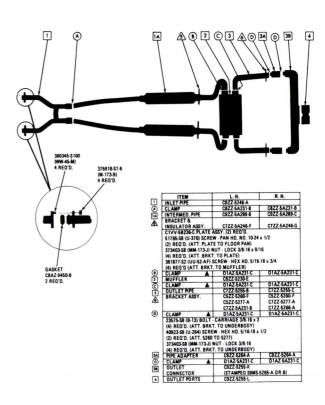

380345-S100 (WW-45-M) 4 REQ'D.

375918-S7-8 (M-173-B) 4 REQ'D.

GASKET C8AZ-9450-B 2 REQ'D.

ITEM		L. H.	R. H.
1	INLET PIPE	C8ZZ-5246-A	
A	CLAMP	C8ZZ-5A231-B	C8ZZ-5A231-B
1A	INTERMED. PIPE	C9ZZ-5A289-B	C9ZZ-5A289-C
⚠	BRACKET & INSULATOR ASSY.	C7ZZ-5A246-F	C7ZZ-5A246-G
	C1VV-5823G-C PLATE ASSY. (2) REQ'D.		
	51765-S8 (U-370) SCREW - PAN HD. NO. 10-24 x 1/2 (2) REQ'D. (ATT. PLATE TO FLOOR PAN)		
	373403-S8 (MM-173-J) NUT - LOCK 3/8-16 x 9/16 (4) REQ'D. (ATT. BRKT. TO PLATE)		
	381877-S2 (UU-52-AF) SO SCREW - HEX HD. 5/16-18 x 3/4 (4) REQ'D. (ATT. BRKT. TO MUFFLER)		
B	CLAMP	D1AZ-5A231-C	D1AZ-5A231-C
2	MUFFLER	C9ZZ-5230-E	
C	CLAMP	D1AZ-5A231-C	D1AZ-5A231-C
3	OUTLET PIPE	C7ZZ-5255-B	C7ZZ-5255-C
⚠	BRACKET ASSY.	C7ZZ-5260-F C5ZZ-5277-A C7ZZ-5A231-B	C7ZZ-5260-F C7ZZ-5277-A C7ZZ-5266-A
D	CLAMP	D1AZ-5A231-C	D1AZ-5A231-C
	23575-S8 (B-13) BOLT - CARRIAGE 3/8-16 x 3 (4) REQ'D. (ATT. BRKT. TO UNDERBODY)		
	40923-S8 (U-264) SCREW - HEX HD. 5/16-18 x 1/2 (2) REQ'D. (ATT. 5260 TO 5277)		
	373403-S8 (MM-173-J) NUT - LOCK 3/8-16 (4) REQ'D. (ATT. BRKT. TO UNDERBODY)		
3A	PIPE ADAPTER	C5ZZ-5264-A	C9ZZ-5264-A
D	CLAMP	D1AZ-5A231-C	D1AZ-5A231-C
3B	OUTLET CONNECTOR	C5ZZ-5260-E (STAMPED SBMS-5265-A OR B)	
4	OUTLET PORTS	C5ZZ-5255-L	

Complete exhaust system and related hardware for a 1969 Shelby GT-350 Mustang.

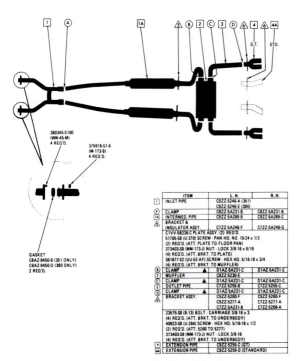

380345-S100 (WW-45-M) 4 REQ'D.

375918-S7-8 (M-173-B) 4 REQ'D.

GASKET C8AZ-9450-B (351 ONLY) C6AZ-9450-D (390 ONLY) 2 REQ'D.

ITEM		L. H.	R. H.
1	INLET PIPE	C5ZZ-5246-A (351) C9ZZ-5246-E (390)	
A	CLAMP	C8ZZ-5A231-B	C8ZZ-5A231-B
1A	INTERMED. PIPE	C9ZZ-5A289-B	C9ZZ-5A289-C
⚠	BRACKET & INSULATOR ASSY.	C7ZZ-5A246-F	C7ZZ-5A246-G
	C1VV-5823G-C PLATE ASSY. (2) REQ'D.		
	51765-S8 (U-370) SCREW - PAN HD. NO. 10-24 x 1/2 (2) REQ'D. (ATT. PLATE TO FLOOR PAN)		
	373403-S8 (MM-173-J) NUT - LOCK 3/8-16 x 9/16 (4) REQ'D. (ATT. BRKT. TO PLATE)		
	381877-S2 (UU-52-AF) SCREW - HEX HD. 5/16-18 x 3/4 (4) REQ'D. (ATT. BRKT. TO MUFFLER)		
B	CLAMP	D1AZ-5A231-C	D1AZ-5A231-C
2	MUFFLER	C9ZZ-5230-E	
C	CLAMP	D1AZ-5A231-C	D1AZ-5A231-C
3	OUTLET PIPE	C7ZZ-5255-B	C7ZZ-5255-C
D	CLAMP	D1AZ-5A231-C	D1AZ-5A231-C
⚠	BRACKET ASSY.	C5ZZ-5260-F C7ZZ-5277-A C7ZZ-5A231-B	C5ZZ-5260-F C7ZZ-5277-A C7ZZ-5266-A
	23575-S8 (B-13) BOLT - CARRIAGE 3/8-16 x 3 (4) REQ'D. (ATT. BRKT. TO UNDERBODY)		
	40923-S8 (U-264) SCREW - HEX HD. 5/16-18 x 1/2 (2) REQ'D. (ATT. 5260 TO 5277)		
	373403-S8 (MM-173-J) NUT - LOCK 3/8-16 (4) REQ'D. (ATT. BRKT. TO UNDERBODY)		
4	EXTENSION PIPE	C9ZZ-5255-C (GT)	
4A	EXTENSION PIPE	C9ZZ-5255-D (STANDARD)	

Complete exhaust system and related hardware for 1969 Standard and GT Mustangs equipped with either 351 4-V or 390 4-V engines.

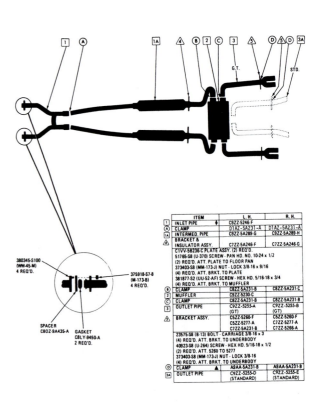

380345-S100 (WW-45-M) 4 REQ'D.

375918-S7-8 (M-173-B) 4 REQ'D.

SPACER C8OZ-9A435-A   GASKET C8LY-9450-A 2 REQ'D.

ITEM		L. H.	R. H.
1	INLET PIPE	C9ZZ-5246-F	D1AZ-5A231-A
A	CLAMP	D1AZ-5A231-A	D1AZ-5A231-A
1A	INTERMED. PIPE	C9ZZ-5A289-G	C9ZZ-5A289-H
⚠	BRACKET & INSULATOR ASSY.	C7ZZ-5A246-F	C7ZZ-5A246-G
	C1VV-5823G-C PLATE ASSY. (2) REQ'D.		
	51765-S8 (U-370) SCREW - PAN HD. NO. 10-24 x 1/2 (2) REQ'D. ATT. PLATE TO FLOOR PAN		
	373403-S8 (MM-173-J) NUT - LOCK 3/8-16 x 9/16 (4) REQ'D. ATT. BRKT. TO PLATE		
	381877-S2 (UU-52-AF) SCREW - HEX HD. 5/16-18 x 3/4 (4) REQ'D. ATT. BRKT. TO MUFFLER		
B	CLAMP	C8ZZ-5A231-B	C8ZZ-5A231-C
2	MUFFLER	C9ZZ-5230-C	
C	CLAMP	C8ZZ-5A231-B	C9ZZ-5A255-B
3	OUTLET PIPE	C9ZZ-5255-A (GT)	C9ZZ-5255-B (GT)
⚠	BRACKET ASSY.	C5ZZ-5260-F C7ZZ-5277-A C7ZZ-5A231-B	C5ZZ-5260-F C7ZZ-5277-A C7ZZ-5266-A
	23575-S8 (B-13) BOLT - CARRIAGE 3/8-16 x 3 (4) REQ'D. ATT. BRKT. TO UNDERBODY		
	40923-S8 (U-264) SCREW - HEX HD. 5/16-18 x 1/2 (2) REQ'D. ATT. BRKT. 5260 TO 5277		
	373403-S8 (MM-173-J) NUT - LOCK 3/8-16 (4) REQ'D. ATT. BRKT. TO UNDERBODY		
D	CLAMP	A9AA-5A231-B	A9AA-5A231-B
3A	OUTLET PIPE	C9ZZ-5255-D (STANDARD)	C9ZZ-5255-E (STANDARD)

Complete exhaust system and related hardware for 1969 standard and GT Mustangs equipped with a 428 4-V engine.

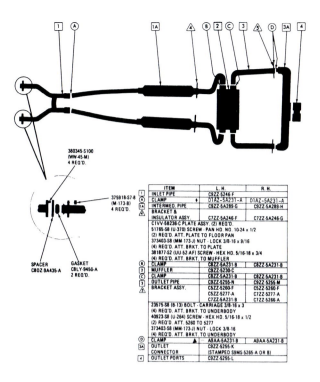

ITEM		L.H.	R.H.
1	INLET PIPE	C9ZZ-5246-F	
A	CLAMP	D1AZ-5A231-A	D1AZ-5A231-A
1A	INTERMED. PIPE	C9ZZ-5A289-G	C9ZZ-5A289-H
△	BRACKET & INSULATOR ASSY.	C7ZZ-5A246-F	C7ZZ-5A246-G
	C1VV-5B236-C PLATE ASSY. (2) REQ'D.		
	51765-S8 (U-370) SCREW - PAN HD. NO. 10-24 x 1/2 (2) REQ'D. ATT. PLATE TO FLOOR PAN		
	373403-S8 (MM-173-J) NUT - LOCK 3/8-16 x 9/16 (4) REQ'D. ATT. BRKT. TO PLATE		
	381877-S2 (UU-52-AF) SCREW - HEX HD. 5/16-18 x 3/4 (4) REQ'D. ATT. BRKT. TO MUFFLER		
B	CLAMP	C8ZZ-5A231-B	C8ZZ-5A231-B
2	MUFFLER	C9ZZ-5230-C	
C	CLAMP	C8ZZ-5A231-B	C8ZZ-5A231-B
3	OUTLET PIPE	C9ZZ-5255-N	C9ZZ-5255-M
△	BRACKET ASSY.	C5ZZ-5260-F C5ZZ-5277-A C7ZZ-5A231-B	C5ZZ-5260-F C5ZZ-5277-A C7ZZ-5266-A
	23575-S8 (B-13) BOLT - CARRIAGE 3/8-16 x 3 (4) REQ'D. ATT. BRKT. TO UNDERBODY		
	40923-S8 (U-264) SCREW - HEX HD. 5/16-18 x 1/2 (2) REQ'D. ATT. 5260 TO 5277		
	373403-S8 (MM-173-J) NUT - LOCK 3/8-16 (4) REQ'D. ATT. BRKT. TO UNDERBODY		
D	CLAMP	A9AA-5A231-B	A9AA-5A231-B
3A	OUTLET CONNECTOR	C8ZZ-5255-K (STAMPED S9MS-5265-A OR B)	
4	OUTLET PORTS	C9ZZ-5255-L	

Complete exhaust system and related hardware for a 1969 Shelby GT-500 Mustang.

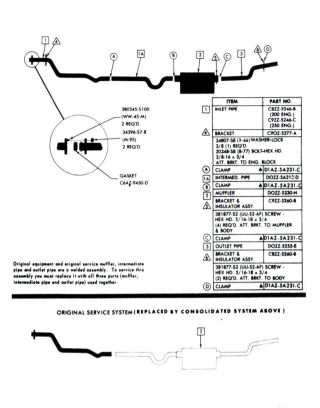

	ITEM	PART NO.
1	INLET PIPE	C8ZZ-5246-B (200 ENG.) C9ZZ-5246-C (250 ENG.)
△	BRACKET	C9OZ-5277-A
		34807-S8 (X-66) WASHER-LOCK 3/8 (1) REQ'D. 20348-S8 (B-77) BOLT-HEX HD. 3/8-16 x 3/4 ATT. BRKT. TO ENG. BLOCK
A	CLAMP	D1AZ-5A231-C
1A	INTERMED. PIPE	DOZZ-5A212-D
B	CLAMP	D1AZ-5A231-C
2	MUFFLER	DOZZ-5230-N
△	BRACKET & INSULATOR ASSY.	C9ZZ-5260-B
		381877-S2 (UU-52-AF) SCREW- HEX HD. 5/16-18 x 3/4 (4) REQ'D. ATT. BRKT. TO MUFFLER & BODY
C	CLAMP	D1AZ-5A231-C
3	OUTLET PIPE	DOZZ-5255-E
△	BRACKET & INSULATOR ASSY.	C9ZZ-5260-B
		381877-S2 (UU-52-AF) SCREW- HEX HD. 5/16-18 x 3/4 (2) REQ'D. ATT. BRKT. TO BODY
D	CLAMP	D1AZ-5A231-C

Original equipment and original service muffler, intermediate pipe and outlet pipe are a welded assembly. To service this assembly you must replace it with all three parts (muffler, intermediate pipe and outlet pipe) used together.

ORIGINAL SERVICE SYSTEM (REPLACED BY CONSOLIDATED SYSTEM ABOVE)

	ITEM	PART NO.
2	MUFFLER	DOZZ-5230-L

Complete exhaust system and related hardware for a 1970 Mustang equipped with a 200 or 250ci engine.

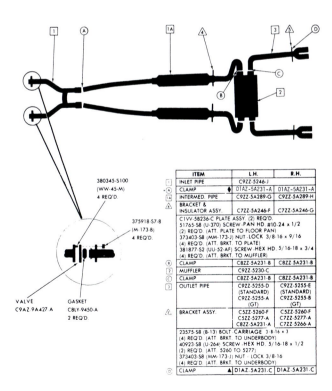

ITEM		L.H.	R.H.
1	INLET PIPE	C9ZZ-5246-J	
A	CLAMP	D1AZ-5A231-A	D1AZ-5A231-A
1A	INTERMED. PIPE	C9ZZ-5A289-G	C9ZZ-5A289-H
△	BRACKET & INSULATOR ASSY.	C7ZZ-5A246-F	C7ZZ-5A246-G
	C1VV-5B236-C PLATE ASSY (2) REQ'D.		
	51765-S8 (U-370) SCREW-PAN HD. #10-24 x 1/2 (2) REQ'D. (ATT. PLATE TO FLOOR PAN)		
	373403-S8 (MM-173-J) NUT-LOCK 3/8-16 x 9/16 (4) REQ'D. (ATT. BRKT. TO PLATE)		
	381877-S2 (UU-52-AF) SCREW-HEX HD. 5/16-18 x 3/4 (4) REQ'D. (ATT. BRKT. TO MUFFLER)		
B	CLAMP	C8ZZ-5A231-B	C8ZZ-5A231-B
2	MUFFLER	C9ZZ-5230-C	
C	CLAMP	C8ZZ-5A231-B	C8ZZ-5A231-B
3	OUTLET PIPE	C9ZZ-5255-D (STANDARD) C9ZZ-5255-A (GT)	C9ZZ-5255-E (STANDARD) C9ZZ-5255-B (GT)
△	BRACKET ASSY.	C5ZZ-5260-F C5ZZ-5277-A C8ZZ-5A231-A	C5ZZ-5260-F C7ZZ-5277-A C7ZZ-5266-A
	23575-S8 (B-13) BOLT-CARRIAGE 3/8-16 x 3 (4) REQ'D (ATT. BRKT. TO UNDERBODY)		
	40923-S8 (U-264) SCREW-HEX HD. 5/16-18 x 1/2 (2) REQ'D (ATT. 5260 TO 5277)		
	373403-S8 (MM-173-J) NUT-LOCK 3/8-16 (4) REQ'D (ATT. BRKT. TO UNDERBODY)		
D	CLAMP	D1AZ-5A231-C	D1AZ-5A231-C

Complete exhaust system and related hardware for a 1969 Boss 429 Mustang.

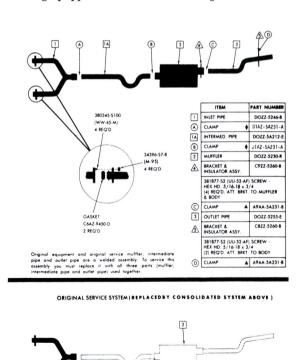

	ITEM	PART NUMBER
1	INLET PIPE	DOZZ-5246-B
A	CLAMP	D1AZ-5A231-A
1A	INTERMED. PIPE	DOZZ-5A212-E
B	CLAMP	D1AZ-5A231-A
2	MUFFLER	DOZZ-5230-R
△	BRACKET & INSULATOR ASSY.	C9ZZ-5260-B
		381877-S2 (UU-52-AF) SCREW - HEX HD. 5/16-18 x 3/4 (4) REQ'D. ATT. BRKT. TO MUFFLER & BODY
C	CLAMP	A9AA-5A231-B
3	OUTLET PIPE	DOZZ-5255-E
△	BRACKET & INSULATOR ASSY.	C8ZZ-5260-B
		381877-S2 (UU-52-AF) SCREW - HEX HD. 5/16-18 x 3/4 (2) REQ'D. ATT. BRKT. TO BODY
D	CLAMP	A9AA-5A231-B

Original equipment and original service muffler, intermediate pipe and outlet pipe are a welded assembly. To service this assembly you must replace it with all three parts (muffler, intermediate pipe and outlet pipe) used together.

ORIGINAL SERVICE SYSTEM (REPLACED BY CONSOLIDATED SYSTEM ABOVE)

	ITEM	PART NUMBER
2	MUFFLER	DOZZ-5230-K

Complete exhaust system and related hardware for a 1970 Mustang equipped with a 302ci engine.

Mustang's leaner, meaner high-performance breeds, the Boss 302 and Boss 429, were designed to be more functional than visual. Both were outfitted with the base Mustang rear valance and ordinary turn downs at the end of their dual tailpipes.

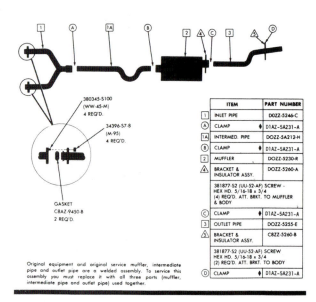

ITEM		PART NUMBER
1	INLET PIPE	D0ZZ-5246-C
A	CLAMP	D1AZ-5A231-A
1A	INTERMED. PIPE	D0ZZ-5A212-H
B	CLAMP	D1AZ-5A231-A
2	MUFFLER	D0ZZ-5230-R
△	BRACKET & INSULATOR ASSY.	D0ZZ-5260-A
	381877-S2 (UU-52-AF) SCREW - HEX HD. 5/16-18 x 3/4 (4) REQ'D. ATT. BRKT. TO MUFFLER & BODY	
C	CLAMP	D1AZ-5A231-A
3	OUTLET PIPE	D0ZZ-5255-E
△	BRACKET & INSULATOR ASSY.	C8ZZ-5260-B
	381877-S2 (UU-52-AF) SCREW HEX HD. 5/16-18 x 3/4 (2) REQ'D. ATT. BRKT. TO BODY	
D	CLAMP	D1AZ-5A231-A

380345-S100 (WW-45-M) 4 REQ'D.
34396-S7-8 (M-95) 4 REQ'D.
GASKET CBAZ-9450-B 2 REQ'D.

Original equipment and original service muffler, intermediate pipe and outlet pipe are a welded assembly. To service this assembly you must replace it with all three parts (muffler, intermediate pipe and outlet pipe) used together.

ORIGINAL SERVICE SYSTEM (REPLACED BY CONSOLIDATED SYSTEM ABOVE)

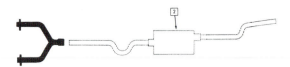

Complete exhaust system and related hardware for a 1970 Mustang equipped with a 351 2-V Cleveland engine.

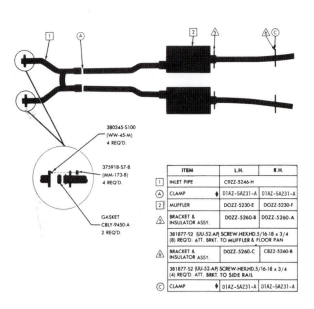

380345-S100 (WW-45-M) 4 REQ'D.
37591B-S7-8 (MM-173-B) 4 REQ'D.
GASKET CBLY-9450-A 2 REQ'D.

ITEM		L.H.	R.H.
1	INLET PIPE	C9ZZ-5246-H	
A	CLAMP	D1AZ-5A231-A	D1AZ-5A231-A
2	MUFFLER	D0ZZ-5230-E	D0ZZ-5230-F
△	BRACKET & INSULATOR ASSY.	D0ZZ-5260-B	D0ZZ-5260-A
	381877-S2 (UU-52-AF) SCREW. HEX HD. 5/16-18 x 3/4 (8) REQ'D. ATT. BRKT. TO MUFFLER & FLOOR PAN		
△	BRACKET & INSULATOR ASSY.	D0ZZ-5260-C	C8ZZ-5260-B
	381877-S2 (UU-52-AF) SCREW. HEX HD. 5/16-18 x 3/4 (4) REQ'D. ATT. BRKT. TO SIDE RAIL		
C	CLAMP	D1AZ-5A231-A	D1AZ-5A231-A

Complete exhaust system and related hardware for a 1970 Boss 302 Mustang.

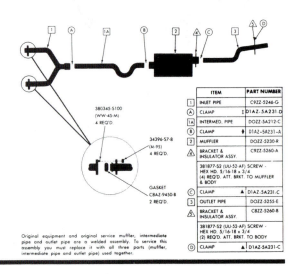

380345-S100 (WW-45-M) 4 REQ'D.
34396-S7-8 (M-95) 4 REQ'D.
GASKET CBAZ-9450-B 2 REQ'D.

ITEM		PART NUMBER
1	INLET PIPE	C9ZZ-5246-G
A	CLAMP	D1AZ-5A231-D
1A	INTERMED. PIPE	D0ZZ-5A212-C
B	CLAMP	D1AZ-5A231-A
2	MUFFLER	D0ZZ-5230-R
△	BRACKET & INSULATOR ASSY.	C9ZZ-5260-A
	381877-S2 (UU-52-AF) SCREW - HEX HD. 5/16-18 x 3/4 (4) REQ'D. ATT. BRKT. TO MUFFLER & BODY	
C	CLAMP	D1AZ-5A231-C
3	OUTLET PIPE	D0ZZ-5255-E
△	BRACKET & INSULATOR ASSY.	C8ZZ-5260-B
	381877-S2 (UU-52-AF) SCREW - HEX HD. 5/16-18 x 3/4 (2) REQ'D. ATT. BRKT. TO BODY	
D	CLAMP	D1AZ-5A231-C

Original equipment and original service muffler, intermediate pipe and outlet pipe are a welded assembly. To service this assembly you must replace it with all three parts (muffler, intermediate pipe and outlet pipe) used together.

ORIGINAL SERVICE SYSTEM (REPLACED BY CONSOLIDATED SYSTEM ABOVE)

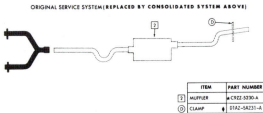

ITEM		PART NUMBER
2	MUFFLER	C9ZZ-5230-A
D	CLAMP	D1AZ-5A231-A

Complete exhaust system and related hardware for a 1970 Mustang equipped with a 351 2-V Windsor engine.

The split exhaust tips were replaced with this flat trumpet with an oval, angular-cut opening for 1970.

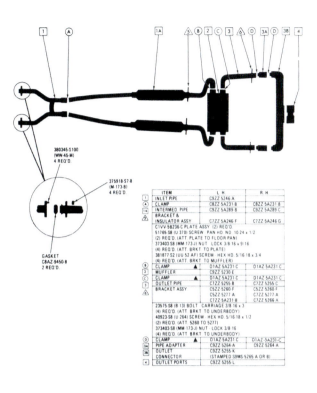

380345-S100 (WW-45-M) 4 REQ'D.

37591B-S7-8 (M-173-B) 4 REQ'D

GASKET C8AZ-9450-B 2 REQ'D.

ITEM	L.H.	R.H.
1 INLET PIPE	C9ZZ 5246-A	
A CLAMP	C8ZZ 5A231-B	C8ZZ 5A231-B
1A INTERMED. PIPE	C9ZZ 5A289-B	C9ZZ 5A289-C
⚠ BRACKET & INSULATOR ASSY	C7ZZ 5A246 F	C7ZZ 5A246 G
C1VV 58236 C PLATE ASSY (2) REQ'D.		
51765-S8 (U 370) SCREW - PAN HD. NO 10-24 x 1/2 (2) REQ'D (ATT. PLATE TO FLOOR PAN)		
373403-S8 (MM-173-J) NUT - LOCK 3/8-16 x 9/16 (4) REQ'D (ATT BRKT TO PLATE)		
381877-S2 (UU-52-AF) SCREW - HEX HD. 5/16-18 x 3/4 (4) REQ'D. (ATT. BRKT. TO MUFFLER)		
B CLAMP	D1AZ 5A231-C	D1AZ 5A231-C
2 MUFFLER	C9ZZ 5230 E	
C CLAMP	D1AZ 5A231-C	D1AZ 5A231-C
3 OUTLET PIPE	C5ZZ 5255-B	C7ZZ 5255-C
⚠ BRACKET ASSY	C5ZZ 5260-F	C5ZZ 5260-F
	C5ZZ 5277 A	C7ZZ 5277 A
	C7ZZ 5A231-B	C7ZZ 5266-A
23575-S8 (B 13) BOLT CARRIAGE 3/8-16 x 3 (4) REQ'D (ATT. BRKT TO UNDERBODY)		
40923-S8 (U 264) SCREW - HEX HD. 5/16-18 x 1/2 (2) REQ'D (ATT 5260 TO 5277)		
373403-S8 (MM-173-J) NUT - LOCK 3/8-16 (4) REQ'D (ATT BRKT TO UNDERBODY)		
D CLAMP	D1AZ 5A231-C	D1AZ-5A231-C
3A PIPE ADAPTER	C9ZZ 5264 A	C9ZZ 5264-A
3B OUTLET CONNECTOR	(STAMPED S9MS 5265 A OR B)	
4 OUTLET PORTS	C9ZZ 5255 L	

Complete exhaust system and related hardware for a 1970 Shelby GT-350 Mustang equipped with a 351 4-V engine.

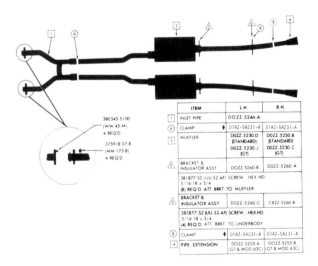

380345-S100 (WW-45-M) 4 REQ'D

37591B-S7-8 (MM-173-B) 4 REQ'D

ITEM	L.H.	R.H.
1 INLET PIPE	DOZZ-5246-A	
A CLAMP	D1AZ-5A231-A	D1AZ-5A231-A
2 MUFFLER	DOZZ-5230-D (STANDARD) DOZZ-5230-J (GT)	DOZZ-5230-B (STANDARD) DOZZ-5230-C (GT)
⚠ BRACKET & INSULATOR ASSY	DOZZ-5260-D	DOZZ-5260-A
381877-S2 (UU-52-AF) SCREW - HEX HD 5/16-18 x 3/4 (8) REQ'D. ATT. BRKT. TO MUFFLER		
⚠ BRACKET & INSULATOR ASSY	DOZZ-5260-C	C8ZZ 5260 B
381877-S2 (UU-52-AF) SCREW - HEX HD. 5/16-18 x 3/4 (4) REQ'D. ATT. BRKT. TO UNDERBODY		
B CLAMP	D1AZ-5A231-A	D1AZ-5A231-A
4 PIPE EXTENSION	DOZZ-5255-A (GT & MOD 63C)	DOZZ-5255-B (GT & MOD 63C)

Complete exhaust system and related hardware for a 1970 standard and GT Mustang equipped with a 351 4-V engine.

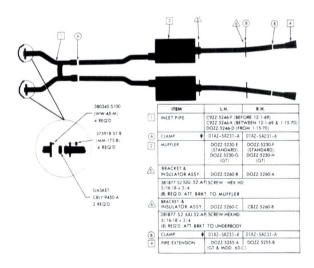

380345-S100 (WW-45-M) 4 REQ'D

37591B-S7-8 (MM-173-B) 4 REQ'D

GASKET C8LY-9450-A 2 REQ'D

ITEM	L.H.	R.H.
1 INLET PIPE	C9ZZ-5246-F (BEFORE 12-1-69) C9ZZ-5246-K (BETWEEN 12-1-69 & 1-15-70) DOZZ-5246-D (FROM 1-15-70)	
A CLAMP	D1AZ-5A231-A	D1AZ-5A231-A
2 MUFFLER	DOZZ-5230-E (STANDARD) DOZZ-5230-G (GT)	DOZZ-5230-F (STANDARD) DOZZ-5230-H (GT)
⚠ BRACKET & INSULATOR ASSY	DOZZ-5260-D	DOZZ-5260-A
381877-S2 (UU-52-AF) SCREW - HEX HD 5/16-18 x 3/4 (8) REQ'D ATT. BRKT. TO MUFFLER		
⚠ BRACKET & INSULATOR ASSY.	DOZZ-5260-C	C8ZZ-5260-B
381877-S2 (UU-52-AF) SCREW.HEX.HD. 5/16-18 x 3/4 (8) REQ'D ATT BRKT TO UNDERBODY		
B CLAMP	D1AZ-5A231-A	D1AZ-5A231-A
4 PIPE EXTENSION	DOZZ-5255-A (GT & MOD 63-C)	DOZZ-5255-B

Complete exhaust system and related hardware for a 1970 standard and GT Mustang equipped with a 428 4-V engine.

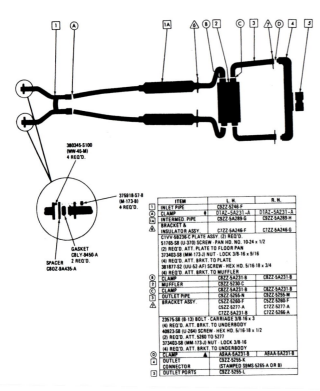

ITEM		L.H.	R.H.
1	INLET PIPE	C9ZZ-5246-F	
A	CLAMP ◆	D1AZ-5A231-A	D1AZ-5A231-A
1A	INTERMED. PIPE	C9ZZ-5A289-G	C9ZZ-5A289-H
△	BRACKET & INSULATOR ASSY.	C7ZZ-5A246-F	C7ZZ-5A246-G
	C1VV-5B236-C PLATE ASSY. (2) REQ'D.		
	51765-S8 (U-370) SCREW - PAN HD. NO. 10-24 x 1/2		
	(2) REQ'D. ATT. PLATE TO FLOOR PAN		
	373403-S8 (MM-173-J) NUT - LOCK 3/8-16 x 9/16		
	(4) REQ'D. ATT. BRKT. TO PLATE		
	381877-S2 (UU-52-AF) SCREW - HEX HD. 5/16-18 x 3/4		
	(4) REQ'D. ATT. BRKT. TO MUFFLER		
B	CLAMP	C8ZZ-5A231-B	C8ZZ-5A231-B
2	MUFFLER	C9ZZ-5230-C	
C	CLAMP	C8ZZ-5A231-B	C8ZZ-5A231-B
3	OUTLET PIPE	C9ZZ-5255-N	C9ZZ-5255-M
△	BRACKET ASSY.	C5ZZ-5260-F	C5ZZ-5260-F
		C5ZZ-5277-A	C7ZZ-5277-A
		C7ZZ-5231-B	C7ZZ-5266-A
	23575-S8 (B-13) BOLT - CARRIAGE 3/8-16 x 3		
	(4) REQ'D. ATT. BRKT. TO UNDERBODY		
	40923-S8 (U-264) SCREW - HEX HD. 5/16-18 x 1/2		
	(2) REQ'D. ATT. 5260 TO 5277		
	373403-S8 (MM-173-J) NUT - LOCK 3/8-16		
	(4) REQ'D. ATT. BRKT. TO UNDERBODY		
D	CLAMP ▲	A9AA-5A231-B	A9AA-5A231-B
4	OUTLET CONNECTOR	C9ZZ-5255-K	
		(STAMPED S9MS-5265-A OR B)	
5	OUTLET PORTS	C9ZZ-5255-L	

Complete exhaust system and related hardware for a 1970 Shelby GT-500 Mustang equipped with a 428 4-V engine.

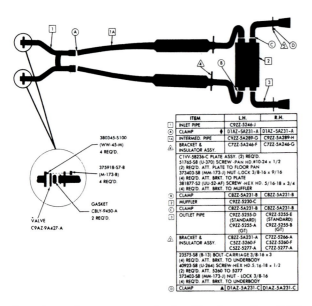

ITEM		L.H.	R.H.
1	INLET PIPE	C9ZZ-5246-J	
A	CLAMP ◆	D1AZ-5A231-A	D1AZ-5A231-A
1A	INTERMED. PIPE	C9ZZ-5A289-G	C9ZZ-5A289-H
△	BRACKET & INSULATOR ASSY.	C7ZZ-5A246-F	C7ZZ-5A246-G
	C1VV-5B236-C PLATE ASSY. (2) REQ'D.		
	51765-S8 (U-370) SCREW - PAN HD. #10-24 x 1/2		
	(2) REQ'D. ATT. PLATE TO FLOOR PAN		
	373403-S8 (MM-173-J) NUT-LOCK 3/8-16 x 9/16		
	(4) REQ'D. ATT. BRKT. TO PLATE		
	381877-S2 (UU-52-AF) SCREW -HEX HD. 5/16-18 x 3/4		
	(4) REQ'D. ATT. BRKT. TO MUFFLER		
B	CLAMP	C8ZZ-5A231-B	C8ZZ-5A231-B
2	MUFFLER	C9ZZ-5230-C	
C	CLAMP	C8ZZ-5A231-B	C8ZZ-5A231-B
3	OUTLET PIPE	C9ZZ-5255-D (STANDARD)	C9ZZ-5255-E (STANDARD)
		C9ZZ-5255-A (GT)	C9ZZ-5255-B (GT)
△	BRACKET & INSULATOR ASSY.	C8ZZ-5A231-A	C7ZZ-5266-A
		C5ZZ-5260-F	C5ZZ-5260-F
		C5ZZ-5277-A	C7ZZ-5277-A
	23575-S8 (B-13) BOLT - CARRIAGE 3/8-16 x 3		
	(4) REQ'D. ATT. BRKT. TO UNDERBODY		
	40923-S8 (U-264) SCREW-HEX HD. 5/16-18 x 1/2		
	(2) REQ'D. ATT. 5260 TO 5277		
	373403-S8 (MM-173-J) NUT - LOCK 3/8-16		
	(4) REQ'D. ATT. BRKT. TO UNDERBODY		
D	CLAMP ▲	D1AZ-5A231-C	D1AZ-5A231-C

Complete exhaust system and related hardware for a 1970 Boss 429 Mustang.

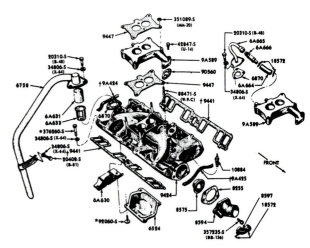

Intake manifold, gaskets, and related parts for 260, 289, 302, and 351W engines.

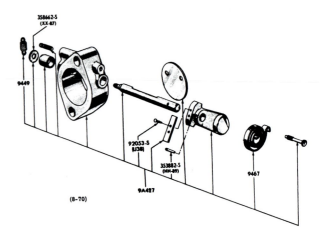

(8-70)

Typical thermostatically controlled exhaust valve (heat riser).

Chapter 7

Wiring and Electrical Systems

Major wiring harnesses were basically similar for all body styles. But pigtails and supplementary harnesses, especially in the realm of factory-installed air conditioning, were added where needed to adapt accessories. Early four-way flashers, Rally-Pacs, convertible tops, and foglamps all had their own pigtail harnesses. An owner upgrading to the use of an in-dash tachometer in a 1969 or 1970 Mach 1, for instance, must replace the entire underdash harness to rewire the gauges and lights as well as the added instrument.

One of the great frustrations in restoring Mustangs is an owner's discovery after a car is assembled that incorrect harness routings or incomplete harnesses are costing either safety or concours points. Add to those problems the possibilities of fire or poor engine performance, and one realizes the importance of getting it right the first time.

This chapter provides cutaway drawings to demonstrate proper placement of the several harnesses needed to wire any Mustang or Shelby. As a supplement, the reader may wish to obtain model-specific wiring diagrams to assist in a complete rewiring. A good source for such reproduction diagrams is Jim Osborn Reproductions in Lawrenceville, Georgia (404-962-7556).

Also included in this area are drawings of correct light buckets, guides to proper lenses, bulbs, and fuses, and a basis for the restorer to plan and establish priorities in budgeting for rebuilding a Mustang.

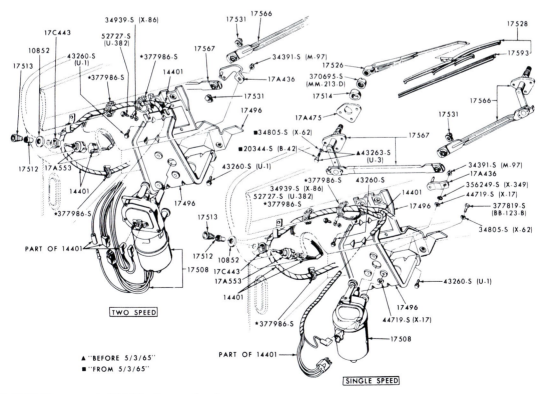

The 1965-1968 Mustang windshield wiper mechanism.

MUSTANG WINDSHIELD WIPER MOTOR ASSEMBLY APPLICATION CHART

YEAR	PART NUMBER	DESCRIPTION
65/66	C3UZ-17508-C	Single speed electric - less drive
65	C3DZ-17508-A	2-speed electric - less drive
66	C6ZZ-17508-A	Used with 2-speed wipers - Includes bracket & drive
67/68	C6OZ-17508-D	Used with 2-speed wipers
69/70	DOZZ-17508-A	Used with 2-speed or intermittent wipers

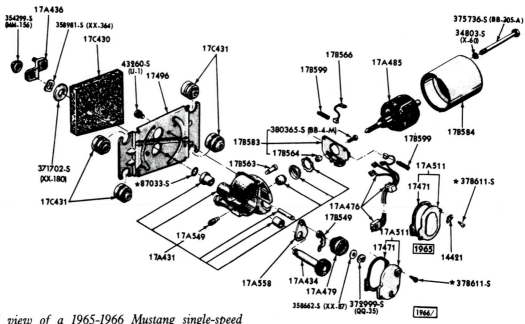

Exploded view of a 1965-1966 Mustang single-speed windshield wiper motor.

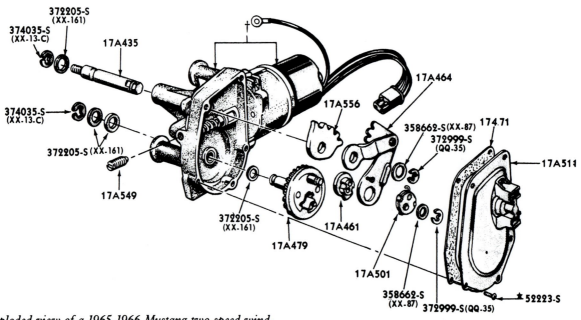

Exploded view of a 1965-1966 Mustang two-speed windshield wiper motor.

308

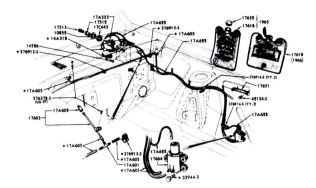

The 1965-1966 Mustang windshield washer system.

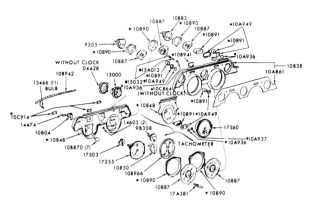

The 1967-1968 Mustang instrument cluster and related parts.

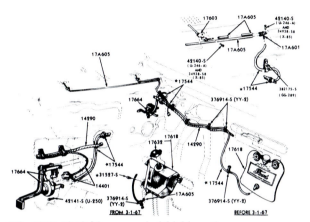

The 1967-1968 Mustang windshield washer system.

MUSTANG SPEEDOMETER ASSEMBLY APPLICATION CHART

Year	Model	Description	Part Number
65		w/o Camera Case Cluster	C5DZ-17255-A
		Rectangular, 120 mph	
65/66		Woodgrain & Camera Case	C5DZ-17255-A
		Cluster, Round, 140 mph	
67/68	Exc. Shelby	Miles-w/o Tripodometer	C7ZZ-17255-E
67/68	Exc. Shelby	Miles-w/ Tripodometer	C7ZZ-17255-F
67/68	All Shelby	140 mph w/ Tripodometer	C8AF-17282-E
69	Exc. Mach 1 & Shelby	Miles-w/ Tripodometer	C9ZZ-17255-B
69/70	All Shelby	140 mph w/ Tripodometer	C9ZZ-17255-N
69/70	Exc. Grandé & Shelby	w/o Tripodometer, 10-mile	D0ZZ-17255-A
		Graduations-Black Dial	
69/70	Grandé	w/o Tripodometer, 5-mile	D0ZZ-17255-B
		Graduations-Gray Blue Dial	
70	Exc. Mach 1	Miles w/o Tripodometer	D0ZZ-17255-C
69/70	Mach 1	Miles-w/ Tripodometer	D0ZZ-17255-D

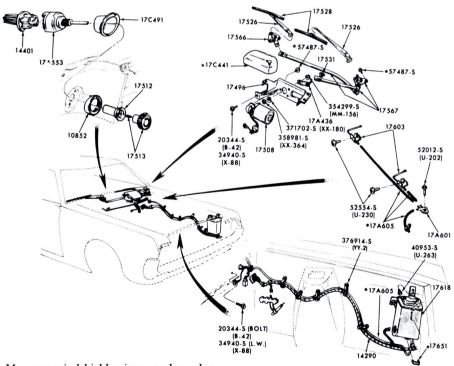

The 1969-1970 Mustang windshield wipers and washer system.

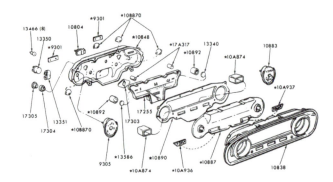

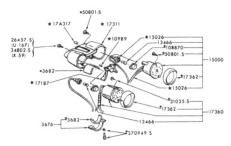

The 1965 Mustang instrument cluster, like this example in a convertible with standard black interior, positions the round fuel and temperature gauges at opposite ends of the horizontal speedometer. Generator charge and oil-pressure warning lights are on either side of the odometer.

The 1965 Mustang instrument cluster (with warning lights) and Rally-Pac.

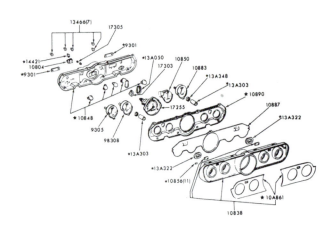

A low-profile Rally-Pac was introduced for 1966. Its case could either be black or color-keyed to the steering column.

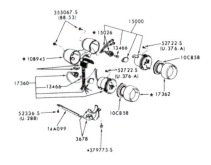

The 1965-1966 Mustang instrument cluster (with gauges) and Rally-Pac.

A tachometer was part of the Rally-Pac option. The standard tachometer stopped at 6000rpm. An 8000rpm tach was mated with the 271hp 289ci HiPo engine.

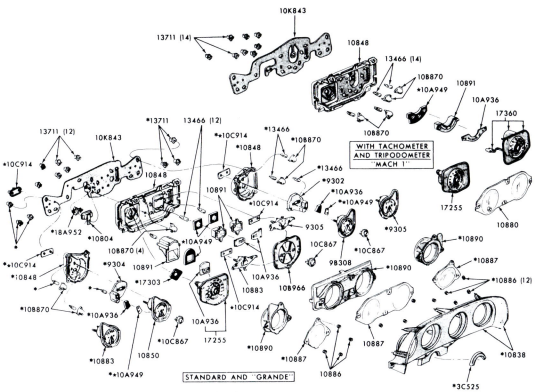

The 1969-1970 Mustang instrument cluster and related parts.

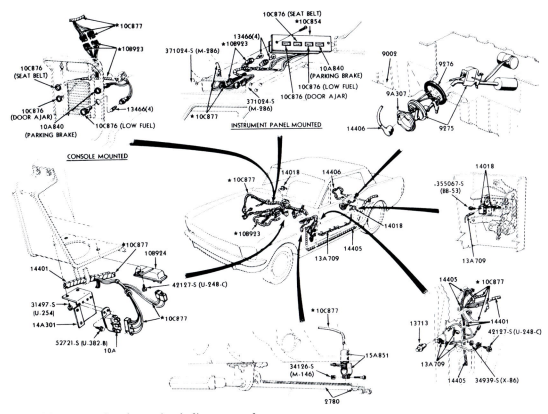

The 1967-1968 Mustang optional warning indicator panel assembly, wiring, and related hardware.

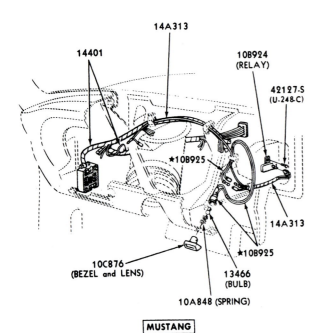

MUSTANG

The 1966-1969 Mustang seat belt warning lamp, wiring, and related hardware.

Amperage	Length	Industry Number	Part Number
1	.62"	AGA-1	B6AZ-14526-D
2	.62"	1AG-2	D4AZ-14526-C
2.5	.62"	1AG-2 1/2	C4GY-14526-A
3	.62"	AGA-3	A6AZ-14526-A
3	1.00"	8AG-3	D4AZ-14526-E
4	.62"	SFE-4	C9SZ-14526-C
4	.84"	AGW-4	C0LY-14526-B
5	.62"	AGA-5	B6AZ-14526-B
6	.75"	SFE-6	C1VY-14526-A
7.5	.88"	SFE-7 1/2	B6AZ-14526-A
9	.88"	SFE-9	A6AZ-14526-B
10	1.25"	AGC-10	B8TZ-14526-A
14	1.06"	SFE-14	A0AZ-14526-A
15	1.25	AGC-15	A2AZ-14526-A
15	.88"	AGW-15	C4SZ-14526-B
20	.62"	AGA-20	8HC-14526
20	1.62"	AGX-20	C5AZ-14526-B
20	1.25"	SGE-20	A0AZ-14526-B
25	1.25"	3AG-25	C6TZ-14526-AB
30	1.25"	AGC-30	A9AZ-14526-A
30	1"	AGX-30	C8OZ-14526-A

FUSIBLE LINK WIRE TYPE FUSE BREAKER CHART

Year	Model	Description	Part Number
'68	Conv. top control	6.00" long - #C8ZB-14A094-A	C8ZZ-14526-C
		16-Gauge Wire	
'69	w/55, 61 OR 65 amp	9" long - 14 Gauge wire	C9AZ-14526-D
	Ford Alternator	r/b D3AZ-14526-D (4-74)	
'69	w/ 38, 42 OR 45 amp	9" long, 16 Gauge wire Fuse Link	C9AZ-14526-A
	Ford Alternator	(Alternator Protection)	

MUSTANG ELECTRICAL CIRCUIT BREAKER ASSEMBLY APPLICATION CHART

Year	Model	Amp	Length	Width	Ident.	Diam.	Part Number
65/67	Fog Lamp	10	1.25"	.78"	White	9/32"	C5ZZ-14526-A
'68	with Fog Lamps	10	1.25"	.79"	White	13/64"	C8ZZ-14526-B
69/70	GT-350/500 Stop Lamp, Fog Lamp	15					C9ZZ-14526-A
'70	w/ automatic seat back hatch	20	1.07"	.40"	Red		C4DZ-14526-C
'65	Conv. Top Control	20	1.07"	.40"	Red		C4DZ-14526-C
'69	GT-350/500 Fog Lamp	20	1.25"	.75"			C9ZZ-14526-B
'67	with A/C	25	1.07"	.40"	Red, Yellow		C5AZ-14526-C
'67	with A/C	25	1.26"	.79"	Red, Yellow		C7AZ-14526-A
'68	6 Cyl. 200, 8 Cyl. 289 with A/C	25	1.25	.79"	Red, Green	13/64"	C8ZZ-14526-A
'69	GT-350/500 w/ Fog Lamp	25	1.25	.79"	Red, Green	13/64"	C8ZZ-14526-A

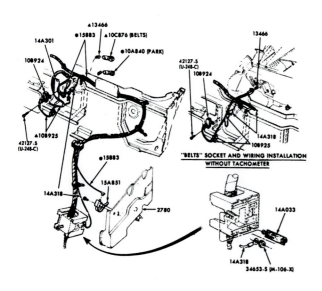

The 1969-1970 Mustang seat belt and parking lamp warning lamp wiring assembly.

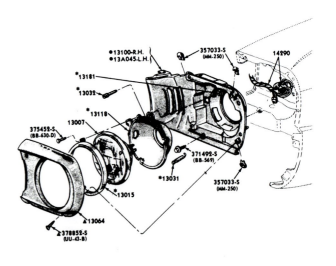

The 1965-1966 Mustang headlamp assembly and attaching hardware.

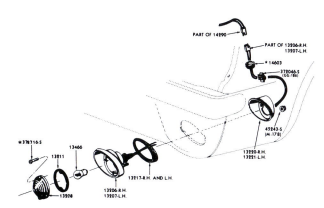

The 1965-1966 Mustang parking lamp, wiring, and attaching hardware.

Industry Number	Contact Base	Candle Power	Part Number
53	Single	1	C4SZ-13466-C
90	Double	6	C6SZ-13466-A
97	Single	4	C3AZ-13466-G
105	Single	12	D0AZ-13466-A
161	Wedge	1	C3AZ-13466-D
194	Wedge	2	C2AZ-13466-C
194A	Wedge	2	C9DZ-13466-A
212-1	Double End	6	C6VY-13466-A
256	Single	1.6	C4SZ-13466-A
257	Single	2	C0AZ-13466-A
562	Single	6	D0ZZ-13466-A
631	Single	6	C3VY-13466-A
1003	Single	15	B6AZ-13466-A
1004	Double	15	C3SZ-13466-A
1142	Double	21	C5ZZ-13466-A
1156	Single	32	C3DZ-13466-A
1157	Double	32.3	C8TZ-13466-A
1157A	Double	32.3	C9AZ-13466-A
1157NA	Double	32.3	C9MY-13466-A
1178A	Double	4	C8ZZ-13466-A
1232	Double	4	C5TZ-13466-A
1445	Single	1	B6A-13466-B
1891	Single	1.9	B9SZ-13466-A
1892	Single	1.3	B9MY-13466-A
1895 (57)	Single	2	C3AZ-13466-B
1895	Single	2	C4SZ-13466-B

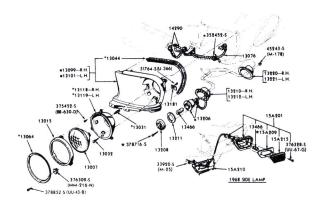

The 1967-1968 Mustang front lighting, wiring, and attaching hardware.

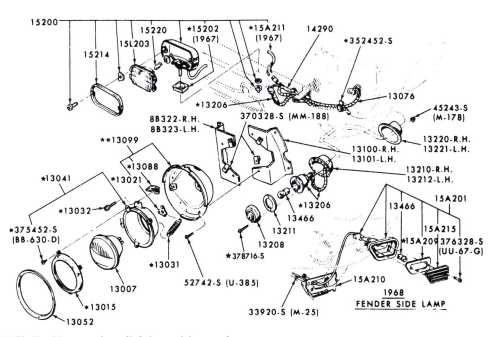

The 1967-1968 Shelby Mustang front lighting, wiring, and attaching hardware.

313

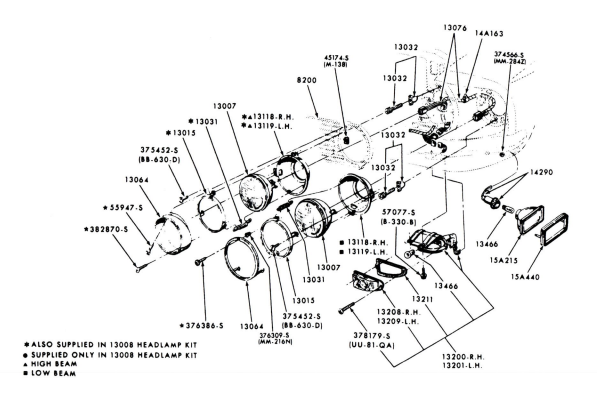

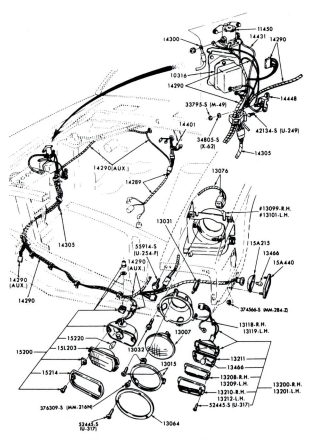

★ ALSO SUPPLIED IN 13008 HEADLAMP KIT
● SUPPLIED ONLY IN 13008 HEADLAMP KIT
▲ HIGH BEAM
■ LOW BEAM

The 1969 Mustang front lighting and attaching hardware.

The 1969-1970 Shelby Mustang front lighting, wiring, and attaching hardware.

Mustang Dash Panel to Headlamp Junction Wire Assembly Application Chart

Year	Model	Description	Part Number
65	With generator		C5ZZ-14290-B
65	With Standard Interior;		C5ZZ-14290-C
	alternator & charge or oil indicator		
	warning lamps		
65	With Deluxe Interior		C5ZZ-14290-D
65	Standard Interior 8 cyl. w/		C5ZZ-14290-D
	ammeter & oil pressure gauges		
66	Before 11/15/65		C6ZZ-14290-A
66	From 11/15/65		C6ZZ-14290-B
67	Exc. GT and Exc. w/tachometer		C7ZZ-14290-AG
67	Exc. GT, w/tachometer		C7ZZ-14290-AD
67	(GT-350/500)	Not replaced	S7MS-14290-A
67	GT w/o tachometer	Not replaced	C7ZZ-14290-AJ
67	GT w/ tachometer		C7ZZ-14290-AF
68	Exc. GT, w/o tachometer		C8ZZ-14290-A
68	Exc. GT, with tachometer	Not replaced	C8ZZ-14290-B
68	GT & GT/CS w/o tachometer		C8ZZ-14290-C
68	GT & GT/CS w/ tachometer		C8ZZ-14290-D
69	Without tachometer		C9ZZ-14290-S
69	With tachometer		C9ZZ-14290-R
69	(GT-350/500)	Instrument panel	C9ZZ-14290-E
		to fog lamp	
70	Exc. Mach 1		D0ZZ-14290-A
70	Mach 1, Before 10/15/69		D0ZZ-14290-K
70	Mach 1, From 10/15/69		D0ZZ-14290-N

314

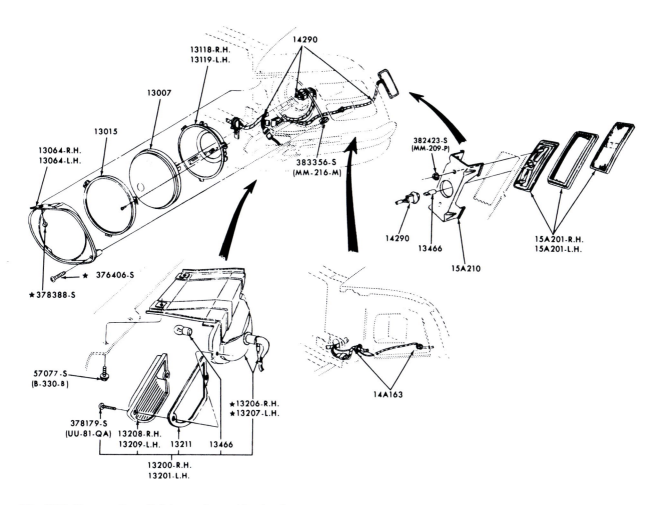

The 1970 Mustang front lighting and attaching hardware.

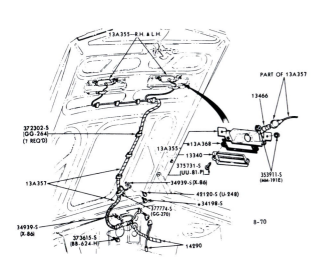

The 1967-1968 Mustang hood-mounted turn indicator lamps, wiring, and attaching hardware.

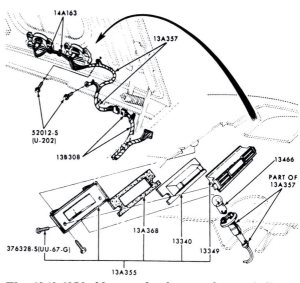

The 1969-1970 Mustang hood-mounted turn indicator lamps, wiring, and attaching hardware.

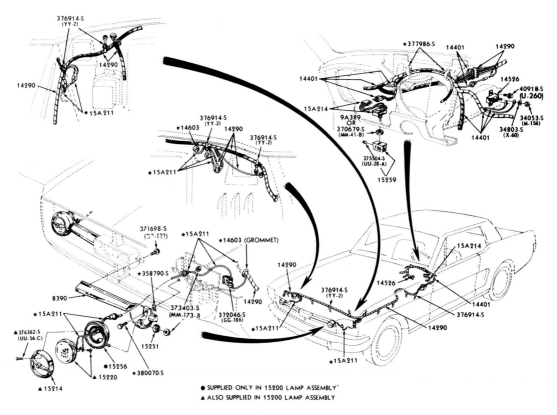

The 1965 Mustang foglamp, wiring, and related parts.

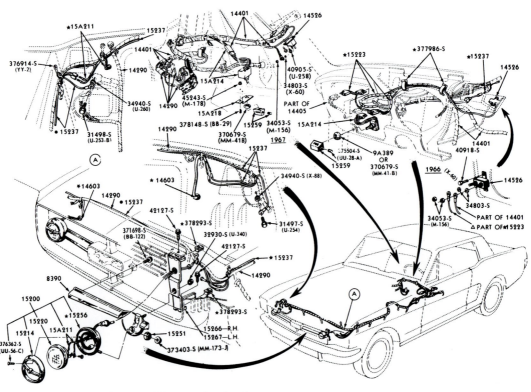

The 1966-1968 Mustang foglamp, wiring, and related parts.

316

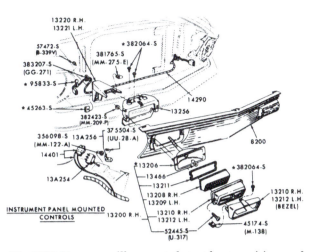

The 1970 Mustang grille-mounted sport lamps, wiring, and mounting hardware.

The 1965-1966 Mustang taillamp.

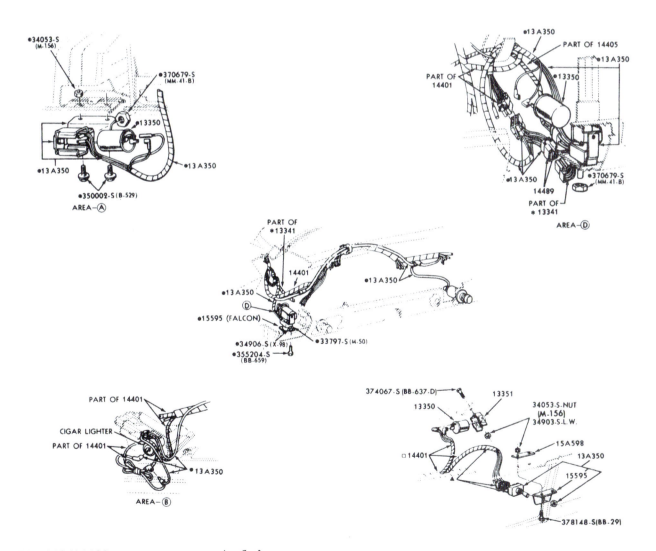

The 1965-1966 Mustang emergency warning flasher system, related wiring, and mounting hardware.

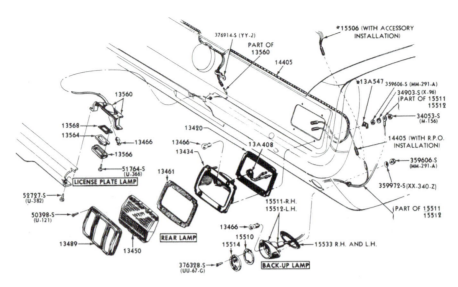

The 1965-1966 Mustang rear light fixtures and related hardware.

The 1967 taillamps on a fastback. The same taillamps were used in 1968, but the surrounding inner groove of the individual chrome bezels was painted black.

The 1967 Mustang tail panel with rear grille option.

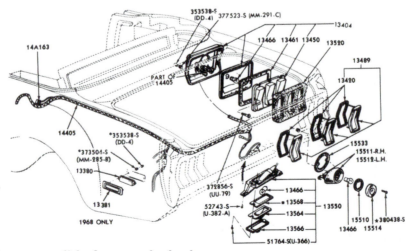

The 1967-1968 Mustang rear light fixtures and related hardware.

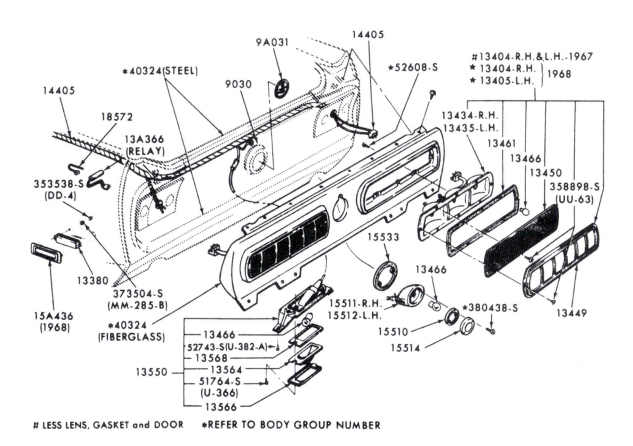

LESS LENS, GASKET and DOOR   *REFER TO BODY GROUP NUMBER

The 1967-1968 Shelby Mustang rear light fixtures and related hardware.

Side marker lights were mandatory on all cars built after 1967, so 1968 Mustangs (shown) are easily distinguished from their third-year cousins. The Mustang's marker lights were unique to each year through 1970.

While the front marker light remained the same throughout the entire 1968 model year, the rear lights changed in January. Early 1968 rear-quarter markers were flush mounted and bordered within a body-colored frame.

Late 1968 rear-quarter marker lights were surface mounted and bordered with chrome trim.

The 1969 Mustang's rectangular front marker lights were installed in the front valance below the front bumper.

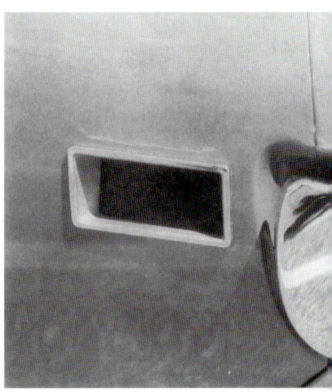

Mustang rear marker lights were recessed using a chrome frame in 1970. The lens is perpendicular in contrast to the contour of the sheet metal.

Mustang rear markers were the same size and shape as the front markers in 1969. Front marker lights have a clear lens and an amber tinted bulb. The rear lights have a red lens and clear bulb.

The 1969 Mustang taillamps.

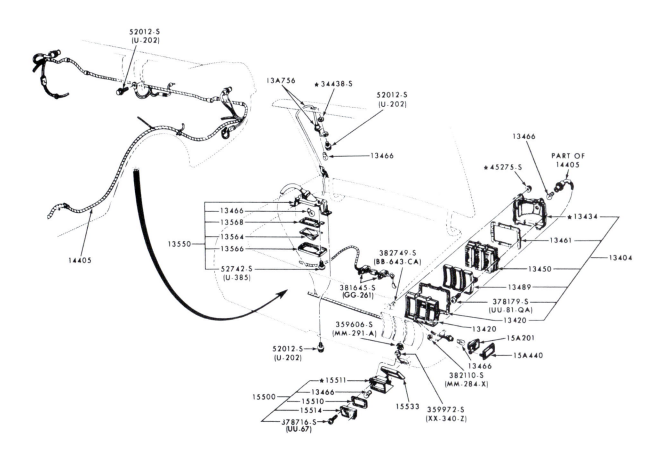

The 1969 Mustang rear light fixtures and related hardware.

The 1970 Mustang taillamp.

The 1970 Boss 302 tail panel.

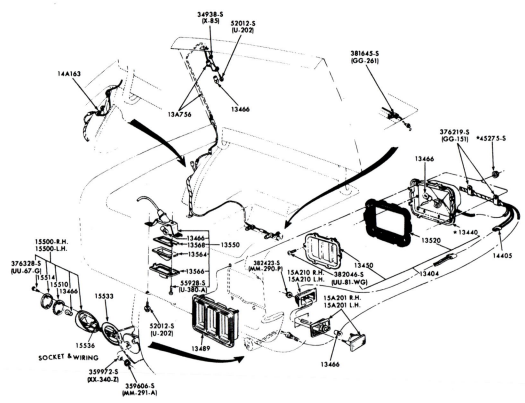

The 1970 Mustang rear light fixtures and related hardware.

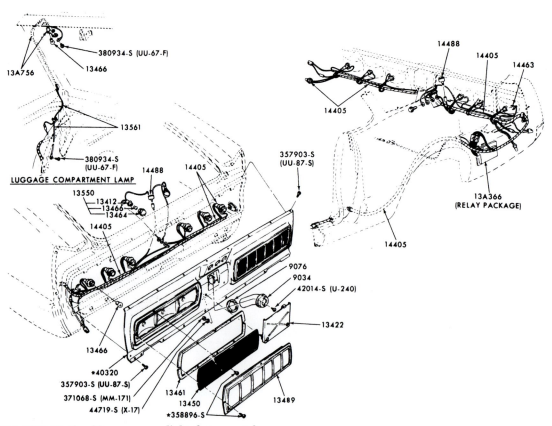

The 1969-1970 Shelby Mustang rear light fixtures and related hardware.

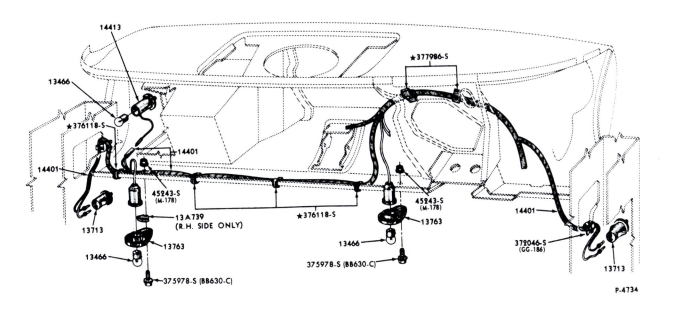

The 1965-1966 Mustang instrument panel mounted courtesy lamps and wiring.

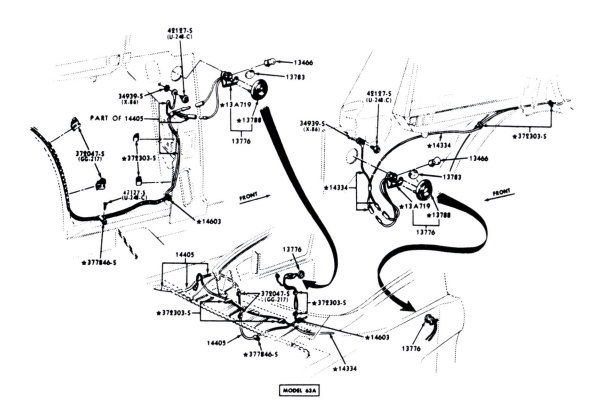

The 1965-1970 Mustang fastback or SportsRoof interior quarter panel courtesy lamps and wiring.

323

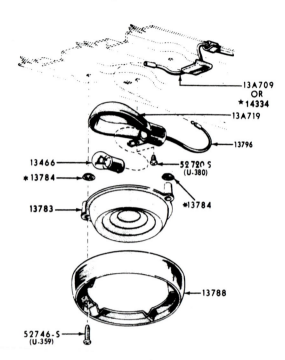

The 1967-1969 Mustang dome lamp.

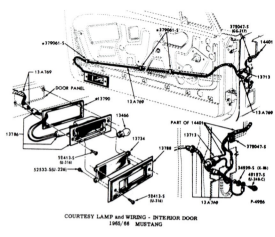

COURTESY LAMP and WIRING - INTERIOR DOOR
1965/66 MUSTANG

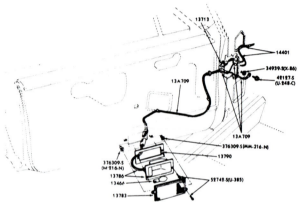

Interior door courtesy lamp and wiring for 1965-1966 Mustang (top) and 1967-1968 Mustang (bottom).

Mustang Rear Lamp Wiring Harness Application Chart

Year	Model	Description	Part Number
68	Except overhead console	Courtesy lamp to switch	C8ZZ-14405-A
	Before 11/1/67	fuel gauge to sender	
68	Except overhead console or safety	Courtesy lamp to switch	C8ZZ-14405-E
	convenience panel from 11/1/67	fuel gauge to sender	
63	With overhead console and/or	Courtest lamp to switch	C8ZZ-14405-F
	safety convenience panel	to fuse panel-fuel gauge	
		sender to gauge to warning	
		relay-defogger	
		switch to defogger motor	
68	(63A, C, 65A, C) Rear window	Courtest lamp to switch	C8ZZ-14405-F
	defogger, and/or safety convenience	to fuse panel-fuel gauge	
		relay-defogger	
		switch to defogger motor	
68	(65) GT - CS		C8ZZ-14405-C
69	Except safety convenience package		C9ZZ-14405-A
69	With safety convenience package		C9ZZ-14405-B
67	(GT350/500)	R.H. & L.H.	S7MS-14405-A
69	(GT350/500) ground		C9ZZ-14405-J
69	(GT350/500)		C9WY-14405-B
70	'6 & 8 cyl. 302-4V Boss 351-390-4V		D0ZZ-14405-B
	'428 CJ with visibility light group		
	Before 12/15/69		
70	From 12/15/69		D0ZZ-14405-B

BULB CHART, Part One, for '65-'70 MUSTANG

Year	Function	Industry Number	Part Number	Notes
65/70	Alternator Charge Indicator	1894	C3AZ-13466-B	
70	Ash Tray Console	1892	B7MY-13466-A	
70	Ash Tray Inst. Panel	1445	B6A-13466-B	
65/68	Back Up Lamp	1142	C5ZZ-13466-A	
69	Back Up Lamp	1156	C3DZ-13466-A	
69	Body Side Lamp - Rear	194A	C9DZ-13466-A	
70	Body Side Lamp - Rear	161	C3AZ-13466-D	
66	Cigar Lighter	1895	C3AZ-13466-B	
65/70	Clock Lamp	1895	C3AZ-13466-B	
66/70	Clock Lamp	1816	B8AZ-13466-B	Rally Pak
65/69	Courtesy Lamp (Instr. Panel)	631	C3VY-13466-A	
65/70	(Console Panel)	1816	B8AZ-13466-A	
65/70	(Quarter Panel)	1003	B6AZ-13466-A	
65/66	(Door Mount)	1004	C3SZ-13466-A	
67/68	(Door Mount)	1004	C3SZ-13466-A	Exc. California
70	(Door Mount)	212	C6VY-13466-A	
70	(Instrument Panel	562	D0ZZ-13466-A	
67/68	Courtesy Lamp (Door Mount)	90	C6SZ-13466-A	California
70	Courtesy Lamp (Pillar)	105	D0AZ-13466-A	
67/69	Dome Lamp	1003	B6AZ-13466-A	Before 6/1/71
70	Dome Lamp	105	D0AZ-13466-A	Before 6/1/71
67/70	Door Ajar	256	C4SZ-13466-A	
68	Front Fender Side Lamp	1178A	C8ZZ-13466-A	
69/70	Front Fender Side Lamp	194A	C9DZ-13466-A	
65	Fuel Indicator	1895	C3AZ-13466-B	
65	Generator Warning Lamp	1895	C3AZ-13466-B	
65	Glove Compt. Instru. Panel	1895	C3AZ-13466-B	
65	Glove Compt. Console Panel	1445	B6A-13466-B	
65/70	Glove Compt. Console Panel	1895	C3AZ-13466-B	
65/70	High Beam Indicator	1895	C3AZ-13466-B	
66	Illuminated Emblem	1003	B6AZ-13466-A	
67/68	Illuminated Emblem	631	C3VY-13466-A	
65/68	Instrument Panel	1895	C3AZ-13466-B	
69/70	Instrument Panel	194	C2AZ-13466-C	
70	Instrument Panel	212-1	C6VY-13466-A	
66/68	Interior Lamp (Mounts on Lower	97	C3AZ-13466-G	
	Quarter Trim Panel 65 Models			

Year	Function	Industry Number	Part Number	Notes
'70	Lights on Lamp	1895	C3AZ-13466-B	
'67	Low Fuel Warning	1891	B9SZ-13466-A	Before 9/6/66
'67/69	Low Fuel Warning	1445	B6A-13466-B	From 9/6/66
'70	Low Fuel Warning	1895	C3AZ-13466-B	
'69	Map Lamp Instrument Panel	1004	C3SZ-13466-A	
'67/70	Map Lamp Roof Console	631	C3VY-13466-A	
'69/70	Marker Lamp-Front	194A	C9DZ-13466-A	
'65/70	Oil Pressure Warning	1895	C3AZ-13466-B	
'65/69	Parking Brake Warning on Safety Convenience Pkg.	257	C0AZ-13466-A	
'67	Parking Brake Warning on Safety Convenience Pkg.	256	C4SZ-13466-A	
'65/66	Parking Lamp	1157	C8TZ-13466-A	
'67/70	Parking Lamp	1157NA Amber	C9MY-13466-A	
'67	Portable Trunk Lamp	1003	B6AZ-13466-A	
'65/66	Radio Dial Lamp	1891	B9SZ-13466-A	
'67/70	Radio Dial Lamp	1893	C1VY-13466-A	
'65	Rear Lamp	1157	C8TZ-13466-A	
'65	Rear License Plate	97	C3AZ-13466-A	
'69	GT350/500	1232	C5TZ-13466-A	
'67/70	Safety Package Lamps	1895	C3AZ-13466-B	
'66/68	Seat Belt Warning (On Safety Convenience Panel)	1895	C3AZ-13466-B	Before 9/6/66
'67	Seat Belt Warning (On Safety Convenience Panel)	1891	B9SZ-13466-A	Before 9/6/66
'67	Seat Belt Warning (On Safety Convenience Panel)	1445	B6A-13466-B	From 9/6/66
'65/70	Speedometer	1895	C3AZ-13466-B	
'70	Sport Lamp	1157A	C9AZ-13466-A	
'70	Stereo Tape Deck	1893	C1VY-13466-A	
'65	Tachometer	1895	C3AZ-13466-B	
'65/70	Temperature Indicator	1895	C3AZ-13466-B	
'65	Transmission Control Selector Dial	1445	B6A-13466-B	
'65/69	Transmission Control Selector Dial	1893	C1VY-13466-A	
'65/71	Turn Signal Indicator	1895	C3AZ-13466-B	
'67/68	Turn Signal Indicator (Hood Mount)	53	C4SZ-13466-C	
'69	Turn Signal Indicator (Hood Mount)	1895	C3AZ-13466-B	
'70	Transmission Control	1445	B6A-13466-B	

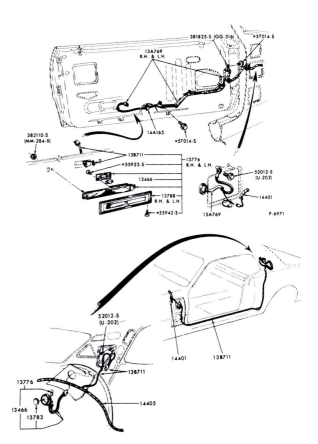

The 1969-1970 Mustang interior door courtesy lamp and wiring (top) and rear pillar-mounted courtesy lamp and wiring (bottom).

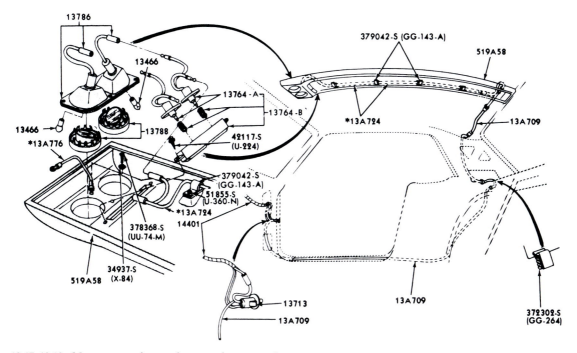

The 1967-1968 Mustang roof console map lamps and wiring.

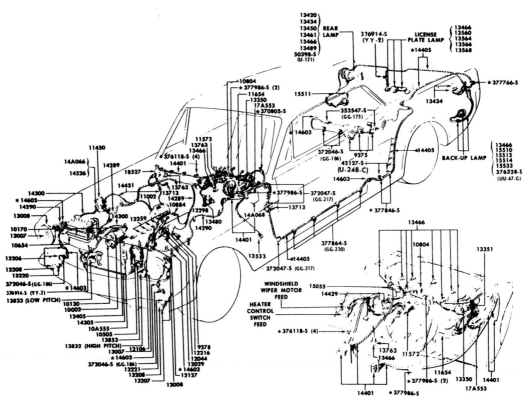

The 1965-1966 Mustang typical electrical connections and wiring.

Mustang Generator/Alternator to Voltage Regulator Wiring Ass'y Application Chart

Year	Model	Description	Part Number
65	6 cyl., with generator		C5ZZ-14305-A
65	8 cyl., with generator		C5ZZ-14305-B
65	6 cyl., with alternator - except		C5DZ-14305-A
	luxury trim		
65	8 cyl., with alternator - except		C5DZ-14305-B
	luxury trim		
65	6 & 8 cyl., with luxury trim		C5GY-14305-B
66	6 cylinder		C6ZZ-14305-A
66	8 cylinder	Heavy duty wiring	C6ZZ-14305-B
67/68	6 cylinder		C7ZZ-14305-A
67	8 cyl. 289, with tachometer		C7ZZ-14305-B
68	289, 302, without tachometer		C7ZZ-14305-B
67	8 cyl. 289, with tachometer		C7ZZ-14305-E
68	289, 302, with tachometer		C7ZZ-14305-E
67/68	8 cyl., 390, 428		C7ZZ-14305-H
	without tachometer		
67/68	8 cyl. 390, 428		C7ZZ-14305-J
	with tachometer		
69	8 cyl. 302, 351, 390, 428		C9WY-14305-G
	with tachometer		
69	6 cyl., or Boss 429		C9WY-14305-G
	with tachometer		
69	8 cyl. 302, 351, 390, 428		C9ZZ-14305-S
	without tachometer		
69	Boss 429 without tachometer		C9ZZ-14305-S
70	8 cyl. 302-2V, 351-2V, 4V,	With tachometer	D0WY-14305-A
	428CJ Before 5/15/70		
70	8 cyl. 302-2V, 351-2V, 4V,	With tachometer	D0WY-14305-C
	428CJ From 5/15/70		
70	6 & 8 cylinder	Without tachometer	D0ZZ-14305-C

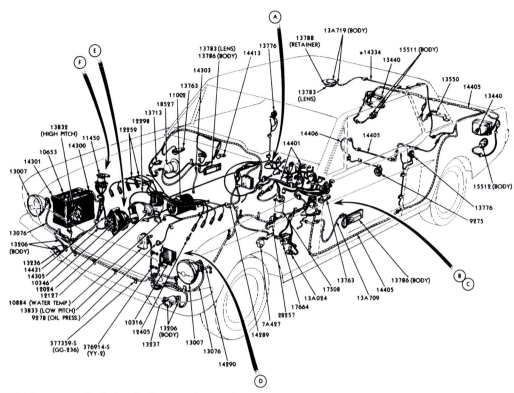

The 1967-1968 Mustang typical electrical connections and
wiring.

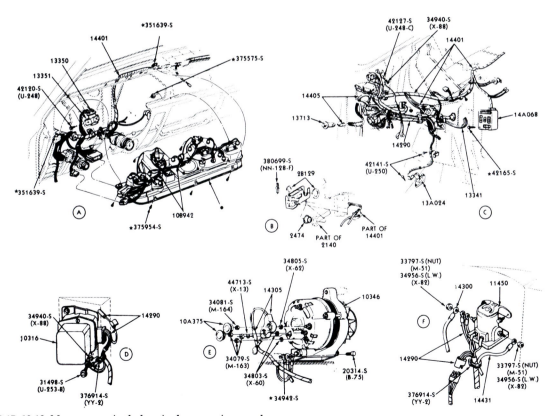

The 1967-1968 Mustang typical electrical connections and
wiring (continued).

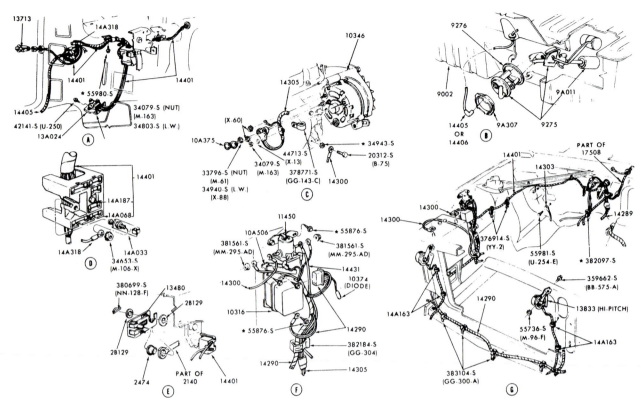

The 1969-1970 Mustang typical electrical connections and wiring.

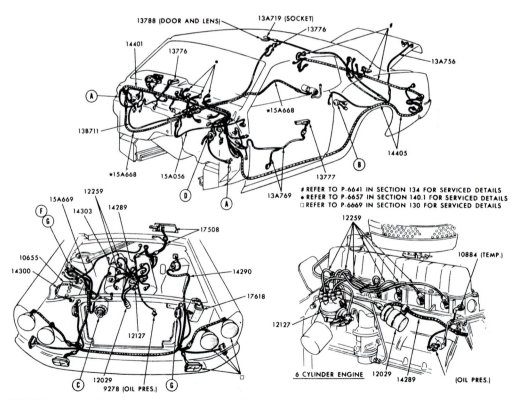

The 1969-1970 Mustang typical electrical connections and wiring (continued).

328

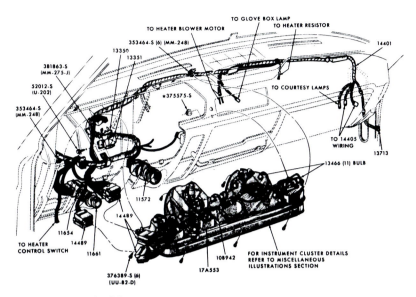

The 1967-1968 Mustang instrument panel wiring.

Mustang Dash to Engine Gauge Feed Wire Assembly Application Chart

Year	Model	Part Number
65	Hardtop, Conv., Std. Interior, 6 cyl.	C5ZZ-14289-J
65	8 cyl. with generator	C5ZZ-14289-J
65	Standard Interior, 8 cyl.	C5ZZ-14289-A
	with alternator	
65	Deluxe Interior, 8 cyl.	C5DZ-14289-B
65	Standard Interior, 8 cyl. with	C5DZ-14289-B
	ammeter & oil pressure gauges	
66	6 cyl.	C6ZZ-14289-A
66	8 cyl. with heavy duty wiring	C6ZZ-14289-B
67	8 cyl. 289	C6ZZ-14289-B
68	8 cyl. 289, 302 before 4/8/68	C6DZ-14289-B
68	8 cyl. 289, 302 from 4/8/68	C8DZ-14289-A
67 / 68	6 cyl.	C7DZ-14289-A
67 / 68	8 cyl. 390, 428	C7ZZ-14289-A
69	8 cyl. 390, 428	D0AZ-14289-A
70	8 cyl. 428CJ	D0AZ-14289-A
69	8 cyl. 429	D0AZ-14289-A
69	8 cyl. 302 Boss	D0ZZ-14289-E
70	Hardtop, 8 cyl. 302-4V w/tachometer	D0ZZ-14289-E
70	SportsRoof, 8 cyl. 302-4V Boss	D0ZZ-14289-E
69	6 cyl.	C9ZZ-14289-A
70/71	6 cyl.	D0DZ-14289-C
69/70	8 cyl. 351-2V (Windsor)	D0OZ-14289-A
69/70	8 cyl. 302-2V	D0OZ-14289-A
70	8 cyl. 351-4V	D0ZZ-14289-A
70	8 cyl. 351-2V (Cleveland)	D0ZZ-14289-A

Mustang Instrument Panel to Dash Panel Wiring Assembly Application Chart

Year	Model	Part Number
69	(GT-350/500)	C5ZZ-5560-D
70	non-Mach 1 w/o A/C or tachometer	C5ZZ-5560-C
70	non-Mach 1 w/o A/C with tachometer	C5ZZ-5560-E
	Before 11/1/69	
70	non-Mach 1 w/o A/C w/tachometer	C5ZZ-5560-F
	From 11/1/69	
70	non-Mach 1 w/o tachometer	C4DZ-5560-J
	Before 11/1/69	
70	non-Mach 1 w/ A/C, w/o tachometer	C4DZ-5560-J
	From 11/1/69	
70	Mach 1 w/o tachometer	C4DZ-5560-J
	Before 11/1/69	
70	Mach 1, w/o tachometer, From 11/1/69	C7ZZ-5560-A
70	Mach 1 w/ tachometer, Before 11/1/69	C7ZZ-5560-A
70	Mach 1, w/ tachometer, From 11/1/69	C7ZZ-5560-A

Mustang Instrument Panel to Dash Panel Wiring Assembly Application Chart

Year	Model	Description	Part Number
65	With single speed wipers	Not replaced	C5ZZ-14401-E
	with generator		
65	With 2 speed wipers w/generator	Not replaced	C5ZZ-14401-F
65	Ecx. Deluxe interior, with single	Must be used w/basic	C5ZZ-14401-M
	or 2 speed wipers Before 4/1/65	17B587 wiring-not used	
		w/fog lamp	
65	Exc. Deluxe interior, with single	Must be used w/basic	C5ZZ-14401-N
	or 2 speed wipers From 4/1/65	17B587 wiring-not used	
		w/fog lamp	
65	Deluxe interior	When used on units w/	C5ZZ-14401-G
		2 speed heater blower	
		motor, basic 18A336	
		is required	
66			C6ZZ-14401-F
67	Exc. GT, Exc. w/tachometer		C7ZZ-14401-AK
67	Exc. GT w/tachometer		C7ZZ-14401-AL
67	GT, Exc. w/ tach., Before 1/3/67	Not replaced	C7ZZ-14401-G
67	GT, Exc. w/ tachometer	Not replaced	C7ZZ-14401-AC
	From 1/3/67 to 4/15/67		
67	GT, Exc. w/ tach., From 4/15/67	Not replaced	C7ZZ-14401-AM
67	GT w/ tachometer Before 1/3/67	Replaced 2/74 by	C7ZZ-14401-H
		C7ZZ-14401-AD	
67	GT, w/ tachometer, From 1/3/67	Not replaced	C7ZZ-14401-AD
	to 4/15/67		
67	GT, w/ tachometer, From 4/15/67	Not replaced	C7ZZ-14401-AN
68	GT/CS, w/ tachometer		C7ZZ-14401-AN
68	With or without fog lamps		C8ZZ-14401-C
	less tachometer		
68	GT/CS, w/o tachometer		C8ZZ-14401-C
68	With or without fog lamps		C8ZZ-14401-D
	with tachometer		
69	Exc. A/C or tach. Before 4/15/69	Except 302-4V Boss	C9ZZ-14401-A
69	Exc. A/C or tach. From 4/15/69	Except 302-4V Boss	C9ZZ-14401-AL
69	Less tachometer, From 4/15/69	With 302-4V Boss	C9ZZ-14401-BC
	to 5/19/69		
69	Less tachometer From 5/19/69	With 302-4V Boss	C9ZZ-14401-BE
69	With tachometer, w/ or w/o A/C	Except 302-4V Boss	C9ZZ-14401-B
	Before 4/15/69		
69	With tachometer, w/ or w/o A/C	Except 302-4V Boss	C9ZZ-14401-AM
	From 4/15/69	not replaced	
69	W/ A/C, w/o tach. Before 4/15/69	Except 302-4V Boss	C9ZZ-14401-C
69	W/ A/C, w/o tach. From 4/15/69	Except 302-4V Boss	C9ZZ-14401-AN
69	W/ Tach. From 4/15/69 to 5/19/69	With 302-4V Boss	C9ZZ-14401-BB
69	W/ tachometer, From 5/19/69	With 302-4V Boss	C9ZZ-14401-BD

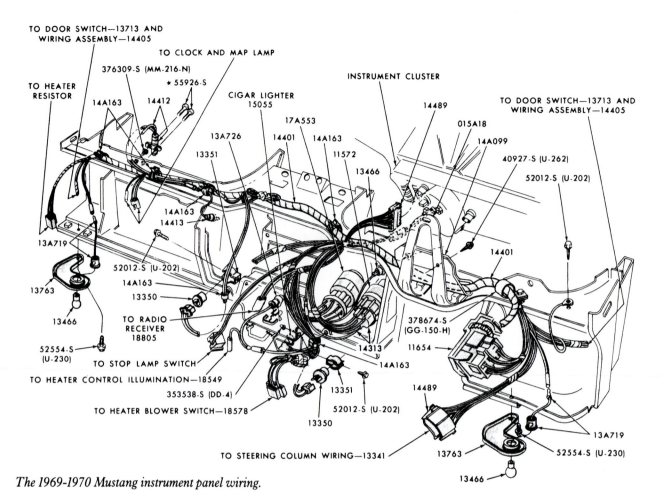

The 1969-1970 Mustang instrument panel wiring.

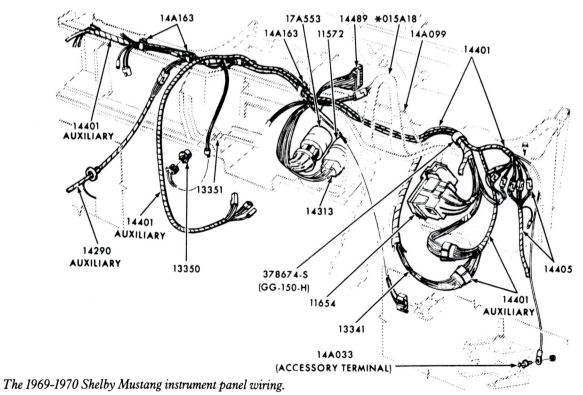

The 1969-1970 Shelby Mustang instrument panel wiring.

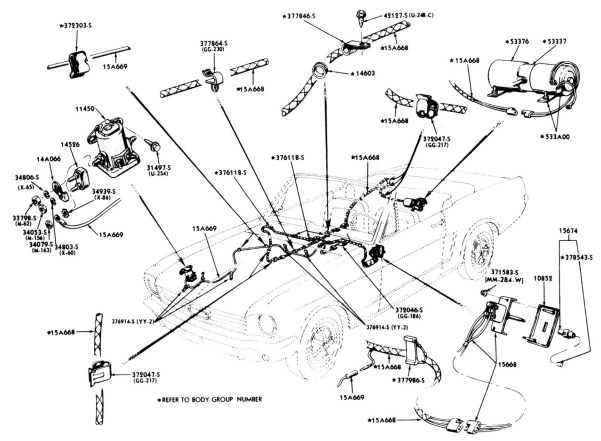

The 1965-1966 Mustang convertible top electrical system.

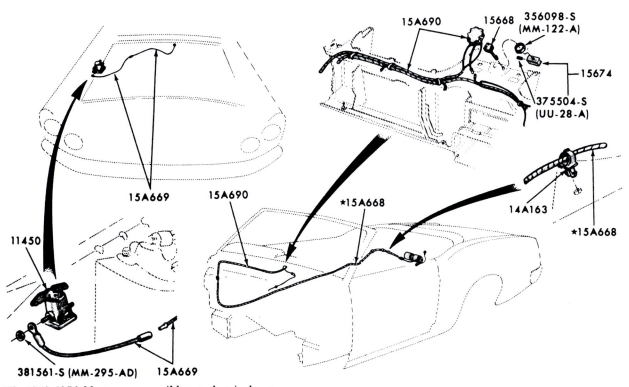

The 1969-1970 Mustang convertible-top electrical system.

MUSTANG GENERATOR I.D. and APPLICATION CHART, 1965.

Engine	Amp.	Notes	Identification	Service Generator	Voltage Regulator	Pulley
170	25	Exc. A/C	C3DF-10000-A	C1DZ-10002-A	C3DZ-10505-A	C2OZ-10130-C
170	30	w/ A/C	C2OF-10000-J	C1DZ-10002-A	C3TZ-10505-B	C2OZ-10130-C
			C3DF-10000-D			
260,289	30		C2OF-10000-G,H	C1TZ-10002-A	C3TZ-10505-B	C2OF-10130-A
			C3OF-10000-B			
			C4OF-10000-A,B,C			

MUSTANG GENERATOR BRACKET APPLICATION CHART, 1965.

Engine	Amp.	Notes	Adjustment Arm	Side Bracket
170	25	Exc. A/C	C2DZ-10145-B	C1DE-10039-A
170	30	w/ A/C	C4DZ-2882-A	C1DE-10039-A
260,289	30	Exc. A/C	C4OZ-10145-A	C2OZ-10151-A
260,289	30	w/ A/C	C3OZ-10145-C	C2OZ-10151-A

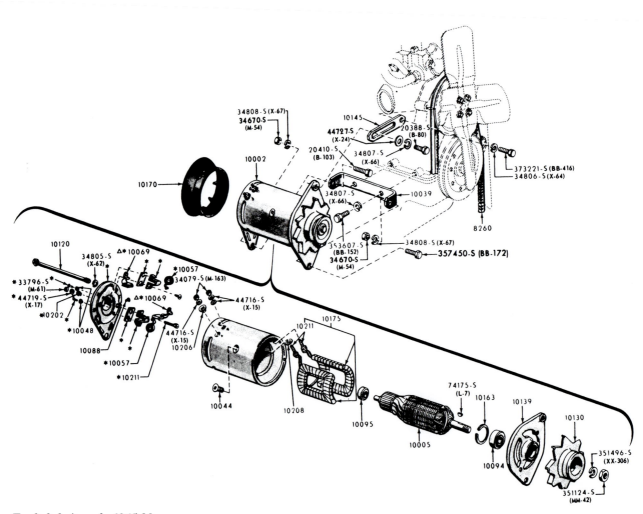

Exploded view of a 1965 Mustang generator.

MUSTANG GENERATOR PULLEY APPLICATION CHART, 1965.

Engine	Amp.	Notes	Identification	Type	Dimensions: A	B	C	D	E	F	Part Number
170	25		C20F-10130-G	1	2.67	.670	.38	5.57	1.62		C2OZ-10130-C
260,289	30	1	C20F-10130-A	1	2.67	.669	.38	5.57	1.92		C2OF-10130-A
260,289	30	2	C20F-10130-B	2	2.67	.670	.38	5.57	2.22	.64	C2OZ-10130-B
260,289	30	3	C30F-10130-B	1	4.32	.670	.38	5.57	1.94		C3OZ-10130-B

Notes

1   Except A/C & Premium Fuel

2   A/C except Premium Fuel

3   Premium Fuel

Note: This chart to accompany Illustrations of Pulley Type 1 and Pulley Type 2, Section 100, Page 3.

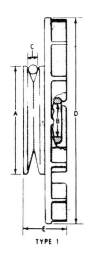
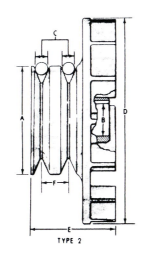

Generator mounting parts.

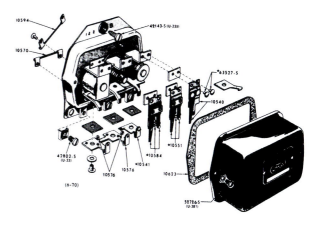

Exploded view of a 1965 Mustang voltage regulator used with a generator.

MUSTANG GENERATOR REGULATOR APPLICATION CHART

Year	Model	Description	Make	Part Number
65	6-cyl. 170 cid	15 volt, 25 amp., 3 terminals Identified C2DF-10505-A Use with generator C1DZ-10002-A	Ford	C3DZ-10505-A
65	All 6-cyl.,8-cyl.	15 volts, 30 amp., 3 terminals Identified C2AF-10505-A; C2TF-10505-B Use with generator C1DZ-10002-A; or C1TZ-10002-A	Ford	C9ZZ-10505-B

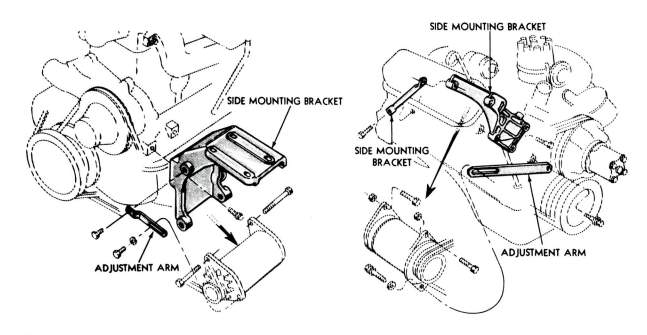

The generator mounting brackets for V-8 and six-cylinder engines of the 1964^1/$_2$ model year.

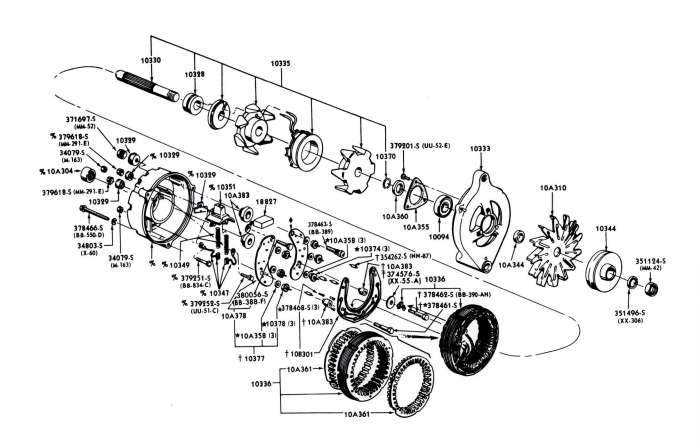

Exploded view of a 1965-1970 Mustang alternator.

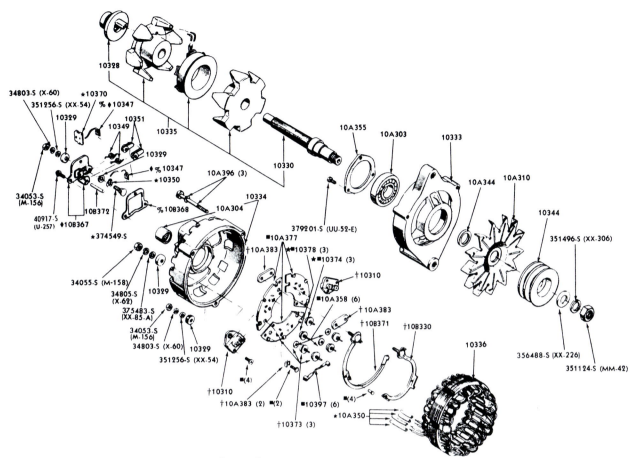

Exploded view of a 1967-1970 Mustang 65 amp alternator.

MUSTANG ALTERNATOR APPLICATION CHART

Year	Engine	Amp. Hrs.	Make	Service Alternator	Voltage Regulator
65	All 6&8	38 42 45	Motorcraft	D2AZ-10346-C	C3SZ-10316-B r/b D4TZ-10316-A
66	All 6&8	38 42	Motorcraft	D2AZ-10346-C	C3SZ-10316-B r/b D4TZ-10316-A
67	All 6&8	38 42 45	Motorcraft	D2AZ-10346-C	C3SZ-10316-B r/b D4TZ-10316-A
67	200,289, 390	55	Motorcraft	D0AZ-10346-F	C3SZ-10316-B r/b D4TZ-10316-A
68	All 6&8	38 42	Motorcraft	D2AZ-10346-C	C3SZ-10316-B r/b D4TZ-10316-A
68	All 6&8	55	Motorcraft	D0AZ-10346-F	C3SZ-10316-B r/b D4TZ-10316-A
69	All 6&8	38 42	Motorcraft	D2AZ-10346-C	C3SZ-10316-B r/b D4TZ-10316-A
69	All 8	55	Motorcraft	D0AZ-10346-F	C3SZ-10316-B r/b D4TZ-10316-A
69	428CJ Boss 429	55	Motorcraft	D0ZZ-10346-B	C3SZ-10316-B r/b D4TZ-10316-A
69	All 8	70	Motorcraft	D1AZ-10346-F	C3SZ-10316-B r/b D4TZ-10316-A
70	All 6&8	38 42	Motorcraft	D2AZ-10346-C	C3SZ-10316-B r/b D4TZ-10316-A
70	428CJ Boss 302	55	Motorcraft	D0ZZ-10346-B	C3SZ-10316-B r/b D4TZ-10316-A
70	6 w/ A/C All 6&8	55	Motorcraft	D0AZ-10346-F	C3SZ-10316-B r/b D4TZ-10316-A

MUSTANG ALTERNATOR PULLEY APPLICATION CHART, Part One, 1965-1967

Year	Engine	Identification	Type	A	B	C	E	F	Amp.	Part Number
65	170,200	C5AF-10A352-B,G,K C9AF-10A352-A,B	3	2.84	.670	.38	1.015		38,42,45	C5AZ-10344-K
65	289, w/o A/C	C5AF-10A352-B,G,K C9AF-10A352-A,B	3	2.84	.670	.38	1.015		38,42,45	C5AZ-10344-K
65	289, w/ A/C	C5AF-10A352-D,J C5TF-10A352-B,K C9AF-10A352-C	6	2.84	.670	.38	1.40	.64	All	C5AZ-10344-L
66	200	C5AF-10A352-B,F, G,K,L C9AF-10A352-A,B	3	2.84	.670	.38	1.015		38,42,55	C5AZ-10344-K
66	289	C5AF-10A352-B,F, G,K,L C9AF-10A352-A,B	3	2.84	.670	.38	1.015		38,42,55	C5AZ-10344-K
66	289	C5AF-10A352-D,J C5TF-10A352-B,K C9AF-10A352-C	6	2.84	.670	.38	1.40	.64	38,42,45	C5AZ-10344-L
66	289	C5AF-10A352-H D1ZF-10A352-A	5	3.05	.670	.38	.91		38,42,55	D1ZZ-10344-A
67	200	C5AF-10A352-B,F, G,K,L C9AF-10A352-A,B	3	2.84	.670	.38	1.02		38,42,55	C5AZ-10344-K
67	289	C5AF-10A352-D,J C5TF-10A352-B,K C9AF-10A352-C	6	2.84	.670	.38	1.40	.64	38,45	C5AZ-10344-L
67	289	C5AF-10A352-B,G,K C9AF-10A352-A,B	3	2.84	.670	.38	1.015		38,45	C5AZ-10344-K
67	390	C5AF-10A352-B,F, G,K,L C9AF-10A352-A,B	3	2.84	.670	.38	1.015		38,55	C5AZ-10344-K
67	390 w/ T/E	C5AF-10A352-D,J C5TF-10A352-B,K C9AF-10A352-C	6	2.84	.670	.38	1.40	.64	38,55	C5AZ-10344-L

MUSTANG ALTERNATOR PULLEY APPLICATION CHART, Part Two, 1968-1969

Year	Engine	Identification	Type	A	B	C	E	F	Amp.	Part Number
68	200	C5AF-10A352-D,J C5TF-10A352-B,K C9AF-10A352-C	6	2.84	.670	.38	1.40	.64	55	C5AZ-10344-L
68	200	C5AF-10A352-B,F, G,K,L C9AF-10A352-A,B	3	2.84	.670	.38	1.015		38	C5AZ-10344-K
68	289	C5AF-10A352-B,J,K C9AF-10A352-A,B	3	2.84	.670	.38	1.015		38 55 w/ P/S	C5AZ-10344-K
68	289	D1ZF-10A352-A	5	3.05	.670	.38	.91		42,55	D1ZZ-10344-A
68	289	C5AF-10A352-D,J C5TF-10A352-B,K C9AF-10A352-C	6	2.84	.670	.38	1.40	.64	55	C5AZ-10344-L
68	302 A/C exc. P/S	C5AF-10A352-D,J C5TF-10A352-B,K C9AF-10A352-C	6	2.84	.670	.38	1.40	.64	55	C5AZ-10344-L
68	302	C5AF-10A352-B,G,K C9AF-10A352-A,B	3	2.84	.670	.38	1.015		38 55 w/ P/S	C5AZ-10344-K
68	390 GT, A/C w/ P/S	C5AF-10A352-B,F, G,K,L C9AF-10A352-A,B	5	2.84	.670	.38	1.015		55	C5AZ-10344-K
68	390 GT	C5AF-10A352-D,J C5TF-10A352-B,K C9AF-10A352-C	6	2.84	.670	.38	1.40	.64	38	C5AZ-10344-L
68	390 A/C exc. P/S	C5AF-10A352-D,J C5TF-10A352-B,K C9AF-10A352-C	6	2.84	.670	.38	1.40	.64	55 w/ P/S	C5AZ-10344-L
68	428CJ	C5AF-10A352-D,J C5TF-10A352-B,K C9AF-10A352-C	6	2.84	.670	.38	1.40	.64	55	C5AZ-10344-L
69	200	C5AF-10A352-B,F, G,K,L C9AF-10A352-A,B	3	2.84	.670	.38	1.015		38,42	C5AZ-10344-K
69	250	C5AF-10A352-B,G,K C9AF-10A352-A,B	3	2.84	.670	.38	1.015		38	C5AZ-10344-K
69	302	C5AF-10A352-B,G,K C9AF-10A352-A,B	3	2.84	.670	.38	1.015		38 42 w/ P/S	C5AZ-10344-K
69	351	C5AF-10A352-B,G,K C9AF-10A352-A,B	3	2.84	.670	.38	1.015		42	C5AZ-10344-K
69	390GT	C5AF-10A352-B,G,K C9AF-10A352-A,B	3	2.84	.670	.38	1.015		38,55	C5AZ-10344-K
69	390GT	C5TF-10A352-B,K C9AF-10A352-C	6	2.84	.670	.38	1.40	.64	55	C5AZ-10344-L
69	428CJ	C5AF-10A352-D,J C5TF-10A352-B,K C9AF-10A352-C	6	2.84	.670	.38	1.40	.64	55	C5AZ-10344-L
69	Boss 429	C5AF-10A352-B,F, G,K,L C9AF-10A352-A,B	3	2.84	.670	.38	1.015		55	C5AZ-10344-K

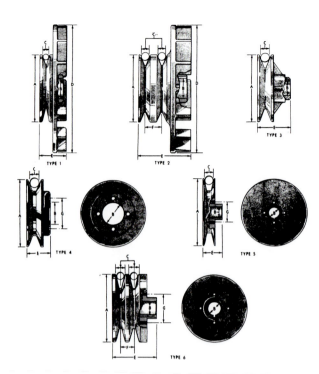

Exploded view of a 1967-1970 Mustang 65 amp alternator.

MUSTANG ALTERNATOR PULLEY APPLICATION CHART, Part Three, 1970

Year	Engine	Identification	Type	A	B	C	E	F	Amp.	Part Number
70	200	C5AF-10A352-B,F, G,K,L C9AF-10A352-A,B	3	2.84	.670	.38	1.015		42	C5AZ-10344-K
70	250	C5AF-10A352-B,G,K C9AF-10A352-A,B	3	2.84	.670	.38	1.015		38	C5AZ-10344-K
70	250 w/ A/C	C5AF-10A352-D,J C5TF-10A352-B,K C9AF-10A352-C	6	2.84	.670	.38	1.40	.64	55	C5AZ-10344-L
70	302	C5AF-10A352-B,F, G,K,L C9AF-10A352-A,B	3	2.84	.670	.38	1.015		38,42 55 w/ A/C	C5AZ-10344-K
70	Boss 302	D1ZF-10A352-A	5	3.05	.670	.38	.91		55	D1ZZ-10344-A
70	351	C5AF-10A352-B,G,K C9AF-10A352-A,B	3	2.84	.670	.38	1.015		38,42,55	C5AZ-10344-K
70	428CJ	C5AF-10A352-D,J C5TF-10A352-B,K C9AF-10A352-C	6	2.84	.670	.38	1.40	.64	55	C5AZ-10344-L
70	429	D1ZF-10A352-A	5	3.05	.670	.38	.91		55	D1ZZ-10344-A

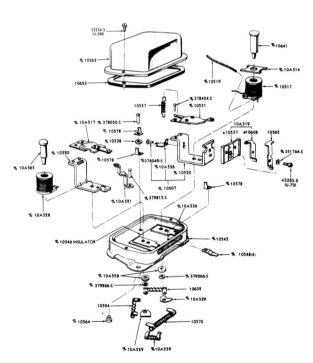

Exploded view of a 1965-1970 Mustang voltage regulator used with an alternator.

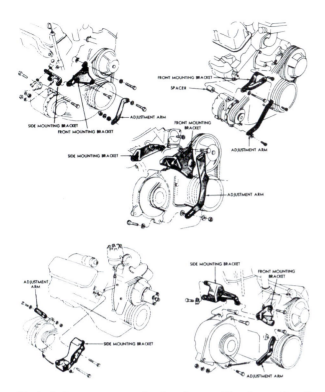

Typical alternator mounting brackets and hardware for all 1965-1970 Ford V-8 engines.

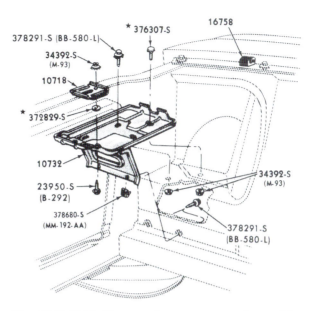

The 1965-1968 Mustang battery tray and attaching hardware.

MUSTANG BATTERY APPLICATION CHART
All engines, 1965-1970.

Motorcraft Group No.	Case Width	Case Length	Case Height	Type	Amperes	Plates
22FC	6-13/16"	9-27/64"	8-5/16"	Premium, dry	49	54
				Standard, dry	42	54
22HF	6-3/4"	9"	8	Premium, dry	45	54
				Premium, dry	54	66
24F	6-13/16"	10-3/4"	8-61/64"	Premium, H/D, dry	81	78
				Premium, dry	55	66
				Standard, dry	41	42
27F	6-13/16"	12-1/2"	9-9/64"	Premium, dry	70	78
				Premium, H/D, dry	94	90
				Premium, dry	77	78

MUSTANG BATTERY MOUNTING PARTS CHART

Year	Amp. Hrs.	Hold Down Clamp Part Number	Carrier or Tray Part Number	Clamp Bolt Part Number	Brace or Bracket Part Number
65	40,45	C2DZ-10718-A	C5ZZ-10732-C		
65	55,65	C5DZ-10718-A	C5ZZ-10732-C		
66	45	C2DZ-10718-A	C5ZZ-10732-C		
66	55	C5DZ-10718-A	C5ZZ-10732-C		
67	45	C5AZ-10718-A	C7ZZ-10732-C	D0AZ-10756-A	C7ZZ-10753-A
67	55	C5AZ-10718-A	C7ZZ-10732-D	D0AZ-10756-A	C7ZZ-10753-A
68	45	C5AZ-10718-A	C7ZZ-10732-C	D0AZ-10756-A	C7ZZ-10753-A
68	55	C5AZ-10718-A	C7ZZ-10732-D	D0AZ-10756-A	C7ZZ-10753-A
69	45	C5AZ-10718-A	C7ZZ-10732-C	D0AZ-10756-A	C7ZZ-10753-A
69	55	C5AZ-10718-A	C7ZZ-10732-D	D0AZ-10756-A	C7ZZ-10753-A
69	85 (note 1)	C5AZ-10718-A	C9ZZ-10732-B	D0AZ-10756-A	C9ZZ-10679-B
70	45 (note 2)	D0OZ-10718-A	C7ZZ-10732-C	D0AZ-10756-A	C9ZZ-10A705-A
70	55 (note 2)	D0OZ-10718-A	C7ZZ-10732-D	D0AZ-10756-A	C9ZZ-10A705-A
70	70 (note 2)	D0OZ-10718-A	C9ZZ-10732-A	D0AZ-10756-A	C9ZZ-10A705-A
70	All (note 3)	D0OZ-10718-A	C9ZZ-10732-B	D0AZ-10756-A	C9ZZ-10679-B
70	All (note 3)	D0OZ-10718-A	C9ZZ-10732-B	D0AZ-10756-A	C9ZZ-10A674-B
70	All (note 3)	D0OZ-10718-A	C9ZZ-10732-B	D0AZ-10756-A	C9ZZ-10A710-B

Notes:
1   Trunk-mounted battery
2   Except Boss
3   Boss

A heavy-duty battery and charging system was an option for every Mustang. Additional optional equipment was required in some cases. The maximum output varied from 55 to 70 amps depending on the year and whether the car was equipped with factory-installed air conditioning. Mustangs built through the 1971 model year were equipped with Autolite batteries. With the 1972 model year, Ford dropped the Autolite name and began equipping Mustangs with Motorcraft batteries.

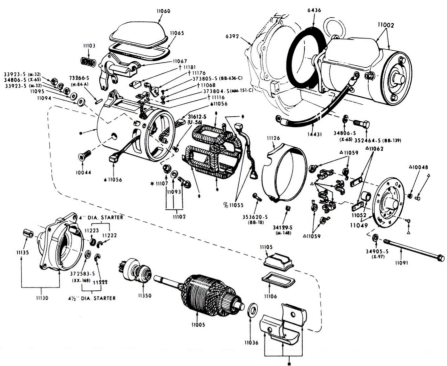

Exploded view of a typical 1965-1970 Mustang starter assembly.

MUSTANG STARTER APPLICATION CHART, 1965-1968

Year	Cyls.	CID	Ident. No.	Serv. Starter Ass'y
1965	6 & 8	260/289	C4OF-11001-A	C2OZ-11002-B
1965	6	200	C5AF-11001-A	C3OZ-11002-C
1965	6	170	C4DF-11001-A,B	C2DZ-11002-A
1966	8	289	C5TF-11001-A	C5TZ-11002-D
1966	8	289	C4ZF-11001-A	C2OZ-11002-B
1966	6	200	C5AF-11001-A	C3OZ-11002-C
1966	6	200	C6VF-11001-A	C6VY-11002-A
1966	6	200	C6OF-11001-A	C6OZ011002-A
1967	6	200	C6OF-11001-A	C6OZ-11002-A
1967	6	200	C7ZF-11001-A	C6OZ-11002-A
1967	6	200	C5AF-11001-A	C3OZ-11002-C
1967	8	289	C4OF-11001-A	C2OZ-11002-B
1967	8	289	C7AF-11001-B	C2OZ-11002-B
1967	8	390	C7AF-11001-A,C	C3OZ-11002-C
1968	6	200	C7ZF-11001-A,B	C6OZ-11002-A
1968	8	289	C7AF-11001-B	C2OZ-11002-B
1968	8	302	C7AF-11001-B	C2OZ-11002-B
1968	8	289	C7AF-11001-D	C5TZ-11002-A
1968	8	302	C7AF-11001-F	C5TZ-11002-D
1968	8	390	C7AF-11001-C	C3OZ-11002-C
1968	8	427	C7AF-11001-C	C3OZ-11002-C
1968	6	200	C7OF-11001-A	C3OZ-11002-C
1968	8	390	C7OF-11001-A	C3OZ-11002-C
1968	8	390	C7AF-1001-E	C6AZ-11002-A
1968	8	427/428	C8AF-11001-A	C8AZ-11002-A

MUSTANG STARTER APPLICATION CHART, 1969-1970

Year	Cyls.	CID	Ident. No.	Serv. Starter Ass'y
1969	6	200	C7ZF-11001-A	C6OZ-11002-A
1969	6	200	C7OF-11001-A	C3OZ-11002-C
1969	6	250	C9ZF-11001-A	C2OZ-11002-B
				r/b D4OZ-11002-A
1969	8	302/351	C9ZF-11001-A	C2OZ-11002-B
				r/b D4OZ-11002-A
1969	8 (s/t)	302/351	C7AF-11001-F	C5TZ-11002-D
1969	8	390	C7AF-11001-C	C3OZ-11002-C
1969	8	390	C7OF-11001-A	C3OZ-11002-C
1969	8	390	C9AF-11001-B	C3OZ-11002-C
1969	8	428/428CJ	C8AF-11001-A	C8AZ-11002-A
				r/b C4TZ-11002-B
1969	8	Boss 429	C9AF-11001-A	C8VY-11002-C
1970	6	200	C7ZF-11001-A	C6OZ-11002-A
1970	6	200	C7DF-11001-A	C2DZ-11002-A
				r/b C3OZ-11002-C
1970	6	200	C7OF-11001-A	C3OZ-11002-C
1970	6	200	C7AF-11001-B	C2OZ-11002-B
				r/b D4OZ-11002-A
1970	6	200	D0OF-11001-A	C3OZ-11002-C
1970	6	200	D0ZF-11001-B	C6OZ-11002-A
1970	6	250	D0ZF-11001-A	C2OZ-11002-B
				r/b D4OZ-11002-A
1970	6	250	C9ZF-11001-A	C2OZ-11002-B
				r/b D4OZ-11002-A
1970	8	302 (a/t)	C7AF-11001-B	C2OZ-11002-B
				r/b D4OZ-11002-A
1970	8	351 (a/t)	C7AF-11001-B	C2OZ-11002-B
				r/b D4OZ-11002-A
1970	8	302 (s/t)	C7AF-11001-F	C5TZ-11002-D
1970	8	351 (s/t)	C7AF-11001-F	C5TZ-11002-D
1970	8	302351	D0AF-11001-B	C2OZ-11002-B
				r/b D4OZ-11002-A
1970	8	302/351	D0AF-11001-C	C5TZ-11002-D
1970	8	428CJ	C8AF-11001-A	C8AZ-11002-A
				r/b C4TZ-11002-B
1970	8	428CJ	D0TF-11001-A	C4TZ-11002-B

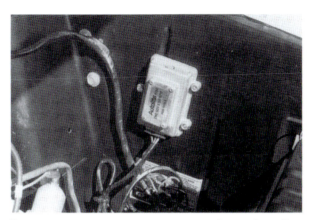

In an attempt to prevent premature destruction, Boss engines were equipped with an electronic rpm-limiting device. The mandatory accessory prevented the engine from exceeding a safe rpm range. This 1970 model interrupts the ignition system at a predetermined 6150rpm as noted on the cover.

At a preset rpm, the Boss 302 rev limiter intercepts the signal to and from the stock ignition coil.

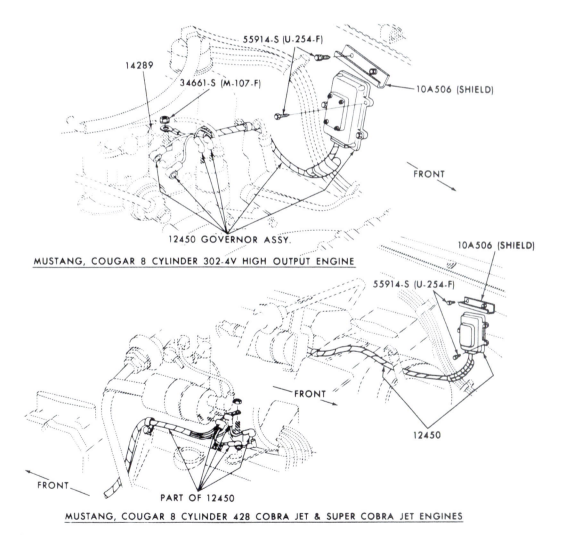

MUSTANG, COUGAR 8 CYLINDER 302-4V HIGH OUTPUT ENGINE

MUSTANG, COUGAR 8 CYLINDER 428 COBRA JET & SUPER COBRA JET ENGINES

Transistorized engine governor for 1969-1970 Mustang equipped with a Boss 302, 428, or 429 engine.

Chapter 8

Options

The Mustang and Shelby restorer is constantly taunted by the possibilities of adding options to the cars. From the introduction of the Mustang in April 1964, Ford attempted to offer as many options as possible in order that the owner or prospective owner might "customize" his or her purchase. For that reason, today's owners are tempted to locate and install certain extras in search of added luxury, convenience, or, as before, personality. It has been said that the early Mustang offered more individual options than any other vehicle in the Ford product line. The reader should note that this chapter does not cover many options that are covered in previous chapters; radios, brakes, upholstery, exterior trim, air conditioning, and steering are good examples of this.

Of course, to the concours camp, there is the ever-present danger of "over restoration," the addition of so many after-the-fact options that a restored Mustang or Shelby bears no resemblance to any car that ever left the Metuchen, Dearborn, or San Jose assembly plants. In the 1960s, the norm was simplicity, and few Mustangs were heavily optioned. In fact, there existed a school of thought that promoted the "sleeper," a car optioned for performance with no regard for chrome and convenience extras.

The majority of the components depicted and described here are no longer available through standard Ford parts channels, and must be located through specialized vendors, reproduction sources, or swap meets. Many vendors advertise original and reproduction parts in periodicals, and many also travel the Mustang show circuit from late spring to early fall. Often, finding an exotic option can be a matter of luck; just as often, the purchase of that item is a matter of expense. A good example would be the discovery of an NOS

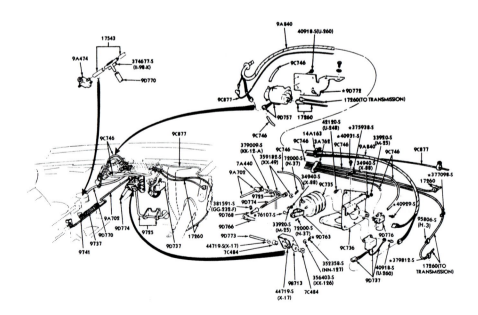

Optional cruise control system (engine compartment) for 1967 Mustang.

hang-on air-conditioning system, complete with both engine compartment and interior brackets, bolts, hoses, belts, and additional hardware. They exist, but it takes a clever researcher to find and buy them.

The drawings in this chapter should allow the restorer to comprehend the choices available, the accuracy needed, and the tasks necessary to upgrade a plain Mustang or to replace damaged original option pieces.

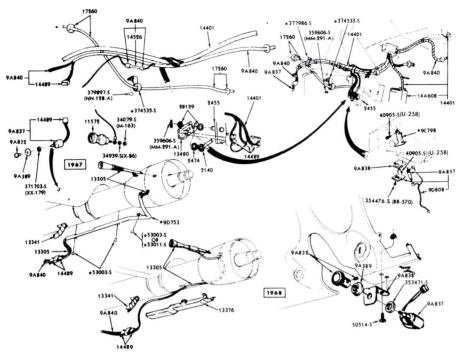

Optional cruise control system (passenger compartment) for 1967-1968 Mustang.

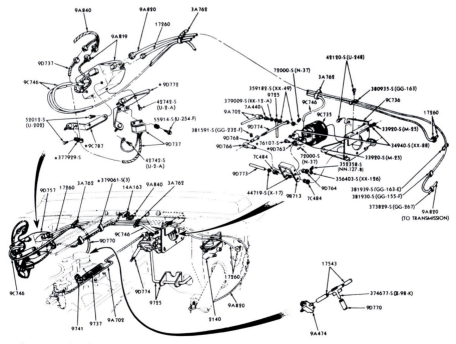

Optional cruise control system (engine compartment) for 1968 Mustang.

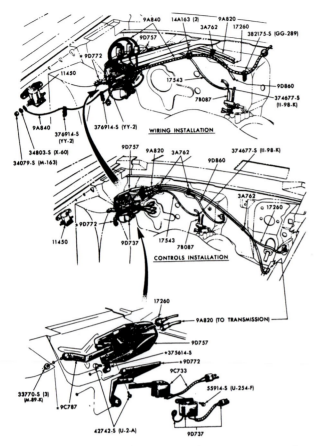

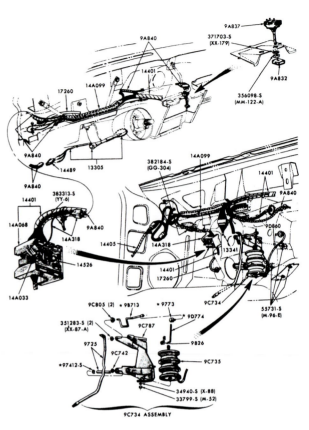

Optional cruise control system (engine compartment) for 1969 Mustang.

Optional cruise control system (passenger compartment) for 1969 Mustang.

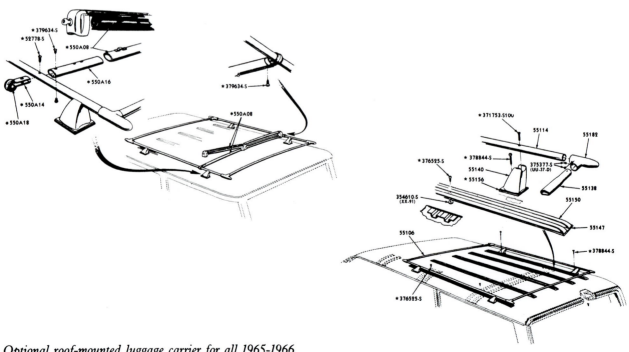

Optional roof-mounted luggage carrier for all 1965-1966 Mustangs.

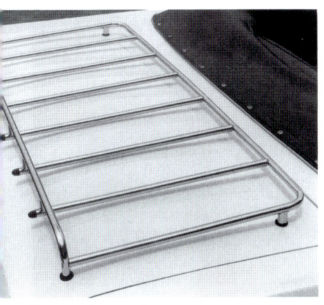

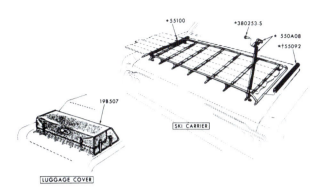

Chrome trunk-mounted luggage carriers were options for all years, but only for hardtops and convertibles. Roof-mounted carriers were available for Mustang fastbacks.

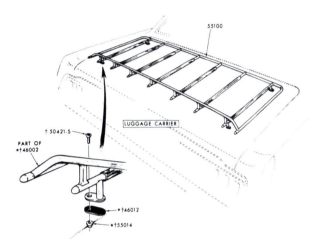

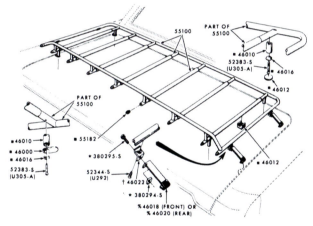

Optional removable rear-deck-mounted luggage carrier for 1969-1970 Mustang.

Optional fixed (non-removable) rear-deck-mounted luggage carrier, ski rack, and luggage cover for 1970 Mustang.

Factory-installed rear window louvers were a popular option on 1969-1970 Mustang SportsRoofs.

343

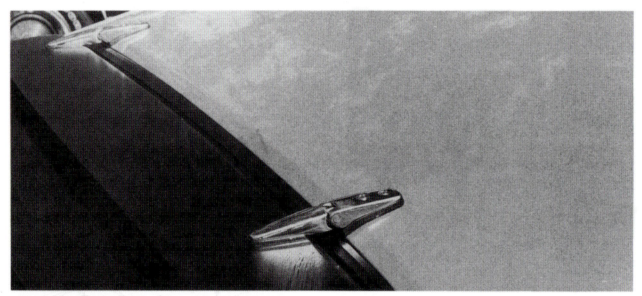

*High-quality OEM louvers featured heavy chrome hinges
and spring-loaded latches.*

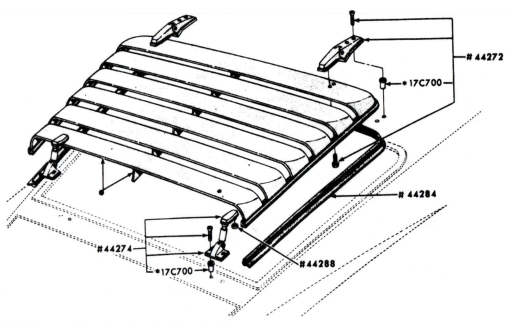

*The 1969-1970 Mustang SportsRoof rear window louvers
and attaching hardware.*

MUSTANG RADIO ANTENNA KIT APPLICATION CHART

YEAR	PART NUMBER	DESCRIPTION
65/68	C5ZZ-18813-B	Manual - front
67	C1SZ-17696-B	F/B, H/T - Univ. electric type - rear qtr. mounted
69/70	C2OZ-17696-A	R.H. - manual - front
69/70	D3AZ-18813-C	(Shelby GT350/500) - Rear antenna

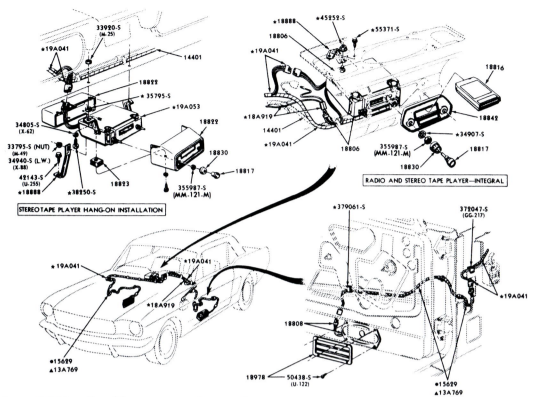

Optional integral AM radio with stereo tape player and hang-on stereo tape deck for 1965-1966 Mustang.

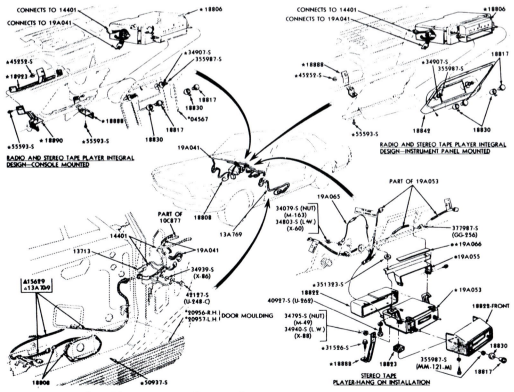

Optional integral AM radio with stereo tape player and hang-on tape deck for 1967 Mustang.

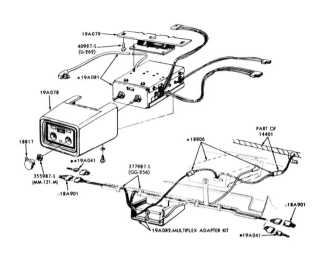

Optional AM/FM radio multiplex adapter for 1967 Mustang.

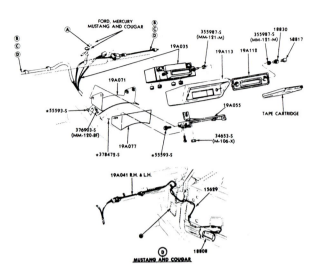

Optional hang-on stereo tape deck, speakers, and wiring for 1968-1970 Mustangs.

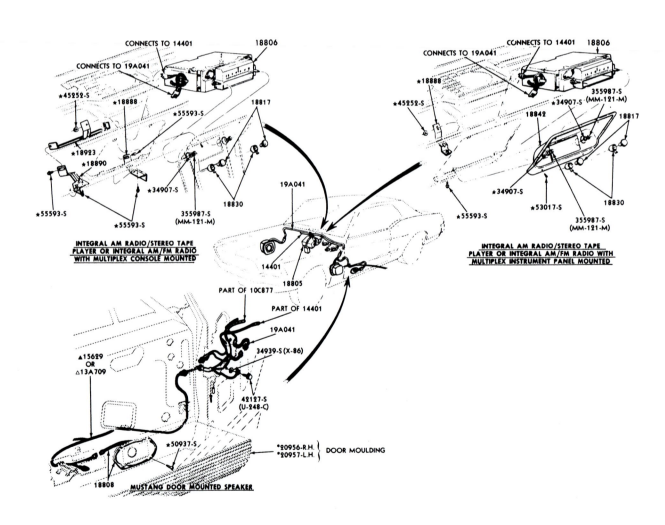

Optional integral AM stereo tape player and AM/FM multiplex radio for 1968 Mustang.

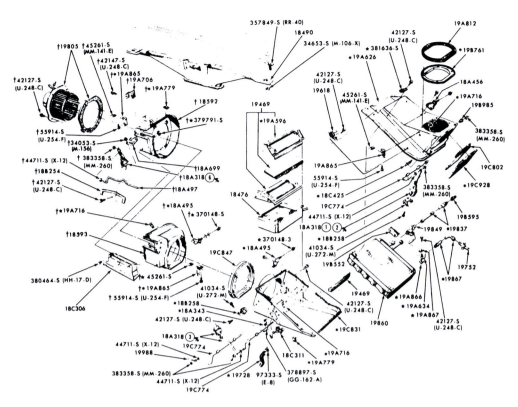

Factory-installed integral air-conditioning evaporator, plenum, blower, and related parts for 1969-1970 Mustangs.

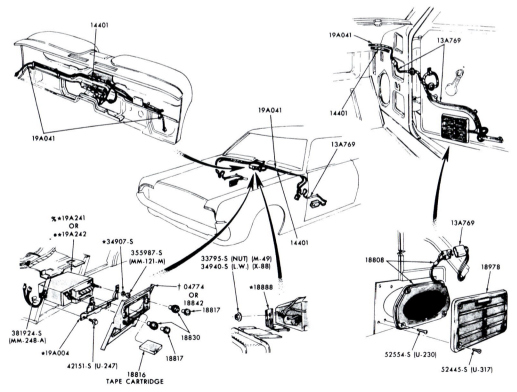

Optional integral AM stereo tape player and/or AM/FM multiplex radio for 1969-1970 Mustangs.

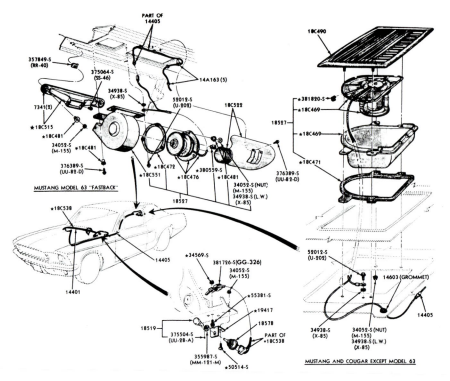

Optional rear window defogger and related parts for 1967 Mustang hardtops and fastbacks.

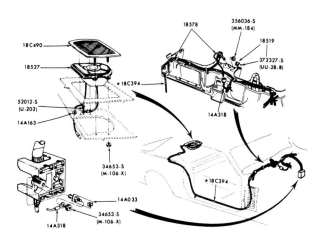

Optional rear window defogger for 1969-1970 Mustang hardtops.

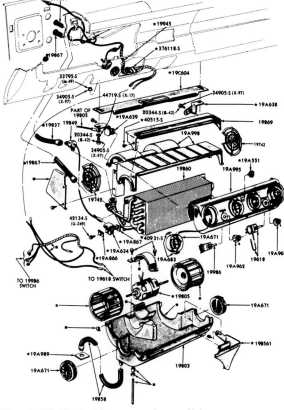

The 1965-1966 Mustang air-conditioner evaporator, blower housing, wiring, and related components.

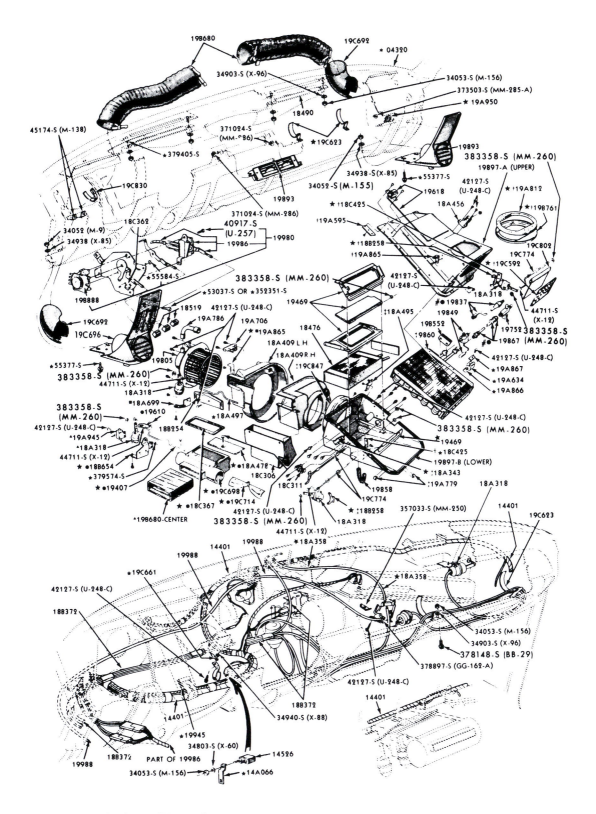

Factory-installed integral air conditioner for 1967-1968 Mustangs.

349

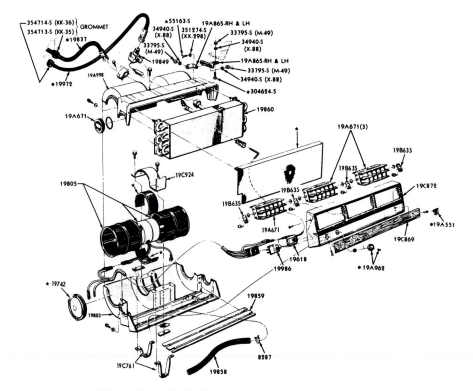

*Optional economy hang-on air conditioner for 1967-1968
Mustangs.*

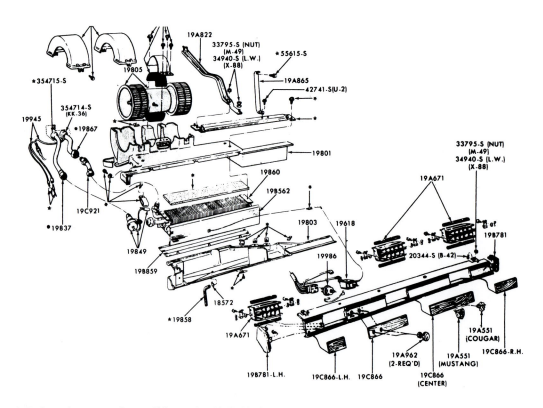

*Optional Deluxe hang-on air conditioner for 1967-1968
Mustangs.*

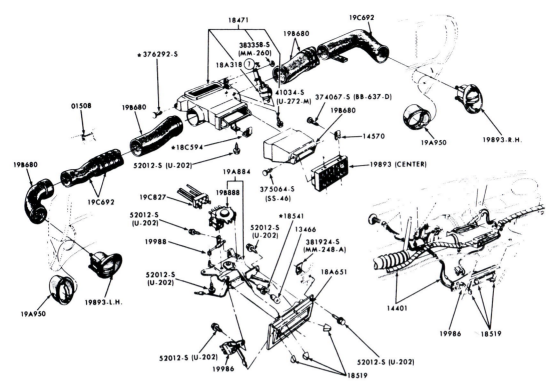

Factory-installed integral air conditioning controls, ducting, wiring, and related parts for 1969-1970 Mustangs.

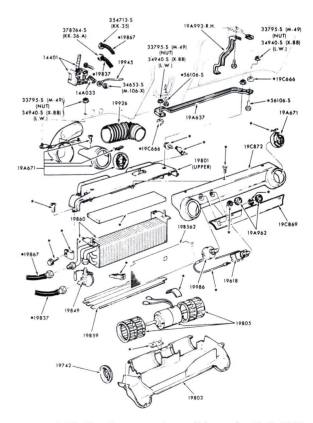

Optional Slimline hang-on air conditioner for 1969-1970 Mustangs.

Chapter 9

1971–1973 Mustangs

SAFETY STANDARD CERTIFICATION LABELS

Vehicle Identification Numbers and Vehicle Data Codes

The Ford system for encoding Vehicle Identification Numbers (VINs) remained the same throughout the first generation of Mustangs (1964 1/2-1973). In 1970 the driver's door-mounted Mustang Warranty Plate was replaced by a Safety Standard Certification Decal which was placed inside the driver's side door jamb. As explained in Chapter 1, page 6, the 11-position alpha-numeric code imprinted on each Safety Standard Certification Label denoted the model year (position one, where a 1 indicates 1971, a 2 indicates 1972, and a 3 means 1973), the assembly plant letter code (position two), the two-digit body series code, the single-letter engine code, and the six-digit sequential build number for that model year (and plant).

Also on the same label are separate codes for the following: body type (two digits and one letter), exterior color code (letter or number), two-position interior trim code, single-letter axle code, single-position (letter or number) transmission code, and two-digit District Sales Office (or DSO) code. The interior trim scheme codes are located in Section 3 of this chapter.

1971-1973 Assembly Plant Codes

Code	Location
F	Dearborn, Michigan
R	San Jose, California
T	Metuchen, New Jersey

1971-1973 Body Series and Style Codes

Serial Code	Style Code	Body Style
01	65D	Hardtop
02	63D	SportsRoof
03	76D	Convertible
04	65F	Hardtop/Grandé model
05	63R	SportsRoof/Mach 1

1971 Exterior Color Codes

Data Code	Name of Color
A	Raven Black
B	Maroon Metallic
C	Dark Green Metallic
D	Grabber Yellow
E	Medium Yellow Gold
I	Grabber Lime
J	Grabber Blue
M	Wimbledon White
N	Pastel Blue
P	Medium Green Metallic
V	Light Pewter Metallic
Z	Grabber Green
3	Bright Red
5	Medium Brown Metallic
6	Bright Blue Metallic
8	Light Gold

1972 Exterior Color Codes

Data Code	Name of Color
2B	Bright Red
2J	Maroon
3B	Light Blue
3F	Grabber Blue
3J	Bright Blue Metallic
4C	Ivy Glow
4E	Bright Lime
4F	Medium Lime Metallic
4P	Medium Green Metallic
4Q	Dark Green Metallic
5A	Light Pewter Metallic
5H	Medium Brown Metallic
6C	Medium Yellow Gold
6E	Medium Bright Yellow
6F	Gold Glow
9A	White

1973 Exterior Color Codes

Data Code	Name of Color
2B	Bright Red
3B	Light Blue
3D	Medium Blue Metallic
3K	Blue Glow
4B	Bright Green Gold
4C	Ivy Glow
4N	Medium Aqua
4P	Medium Green Metallic
4Q	Dark Green Metallic
5A	Light Pewter Metallic
5H	Medium Brown Metallic
5M	Medium Copper Metallic
5T	Saddle Bronze
6B	Light Yellow Gold
6C	Medium Yellow Gold
6E	Medium Bright Yellow
6F	Gold Glow
9A	White

1971 Engine Codes

Code	Engine
C	429-4V Cobra Jet (CJ)
F	302-2V
H	351-2V
J	429-4V CJ or Super CJ Ram Air
L	250-1V (6 cylinder)
M	351-4V
Q	351-4V Ram Air
R	Boss 351

1972 Engine Codes

Code	Engine
F	302-2V
H	351-2V
L	250-1V (6 cylinder)
Q	351-4V
R	351-4V H.O.

1973 Engine Codes

Code	Engine
F	302-2V
H	351-2V
L	250-1V (6 cylinder)
Q	351-4V

1971-1973 Transmission Codes

Code	Transmission Type
1	Three-speed Manual
5	Four-speed Manual (2.78:1)
6	Four-speed Manual (2.32:1)
U	C6 Automatic
W	C4 Automatic
X	FMX Automatic

1971-1973 Rear Axle Codes

Code	Axle Ratio
2	2.75:1
3	2.79:1
4	2.80:1
6	3.00:1
9	3.25:1
A	3.50:1
B	3.07:1
K	2.75:1 Traction-Lok
M	2.80:1 Traction-Lok
O	3.00:1 Traction-Lok
R	3.25:1 Traction-Lok
S	3.50:1 Traction-Lok
V	3.91:1 Traction-Lok
Y	4.11:1 Traction-Lok

1971-1973 District Sales Office Codes

Code	Location
11	Boston
12	Buffalo (1972-1973)
13	New York
14	Pittsburgh (1972-1973)
15	Newark
16	Philadelphia
17	Washington, D.C.
21	Atlanta
22	Charlotte
23	Memphis (1972-1973)
24	Jacksonville
25	Richmond
26	New Orleans (1972-1973)
28	Louisville
32	Cleveland (1965-1971)
33	Detroit (1965-1971)
35	Lansing (1965-1971)
37	Buffalo (1967-1971)
38	Pittsburgh (1967-1971)
41	Chicago
42	Cleveland (1972-1973)
43	Milwaukee

44	Twin Cities
45	Lansing (1972-1973)
46	Indianapolis
47	Cincinnati
48	Detroit (1972-1973)
51	Denver (1965-1971)
52	Dallas (1972-1973)
53	Kansas City
54	Omaha
55	St. Louis
56	Davenport
57	Houston (1972-1973)
58	Twin Cities (1972-1973)
61	Dallas (1965-1971)
62	Houston (1965-1971)
63	Memphis (1965-1971)
64	New Orleans (1965-1971)
65	Oklahoma City (1965-1971)
71	Los Angeles
72	San Jose
73	Salt Lake City
74	Seattle
75	Phoenix
76	Denver (1972-1973)
83	Government
84	Home Office Reserve
85	American Red Cross
87	Body Company
89	Transportation Services
90-99	Export

Note: Refer to Chapter 1, pages 7 and 8, for additional information.

Vehicle Build Date Codes

The first two digits are the day of the month, and the letter code indicates the month a car was built.

Month	First Year Code	Second Year Code
January	A	N
February	B	P
March	C	Q
April	D	R
May	E	S
June	F	T
July	G	U
August	H	V
September	J	W
October	K	X
November	L	Y
December	M	Z

The 1971 Mustang 250ci Air Cleaner decal (white/blue) (DF0172).

The 1971 Mustang 302-2V Regular Fuel Air Cleaner decal (black/red) (DF0182).

The 1971 Mustang 351-2V Regular Fuel Air Cleaner decal (black/red) (DF0184).

The 1971 Mustang 351-4V Premium Fuel Air Cleaner decal (black/red) (DF0185).

The 1971 Mustang 429-4V Premium Fuel Air Cleaner decal
(black/red) (DF0451).

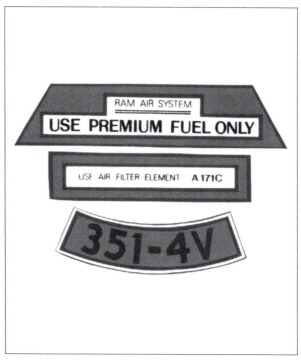

The 1971 Mustang 429 Cobra Air Cleaner decal (yellow/black)
(DF0451).

The 1971 Mustang Boss 351 Ram Air Air Cleaner decal set (three
decals) (DF0260).

The 1971 Mustang 429 Cobra Jet Air Cleaner decal (lime/black)
(DF0395).

The 1971 Mustang Boss 351 Autolite Replacement Parts Air
Cleaner decal (DF0922).

The 1971-1972 Mustang Autolite Replacement Parts Air Cleaner
decal (DF0325).

The 1971-1973 Mustang Air Cleaner front decal (DF0150).

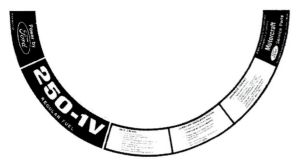

The 1972 Mustang 250-1V Air Cleaner decal (white/blue) (DF1338).

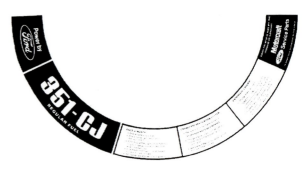

The 1972 Mustang 351-CJ Cobra Jet Air Cleaner decal (white/blue) (DF0365).

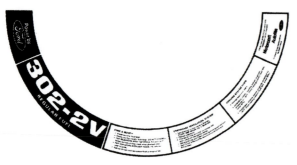

The 1972-1973 302-2V Regular Fuel Air Cleaner decal (white/blue) (DF0584).

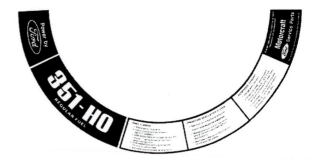

The 1972 Mustang 351-H.O. Air Cleaner decal (yellow/black) (DF0553).

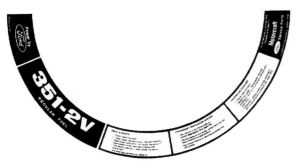

The 1972 Mustang 351-2V Regular Fuel Air Cleaner decal (white/blue) (DF1341).

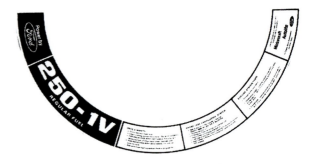

The 1973 Mustang 250-1V Air Cleaner decal (white/blue) (DF0643).

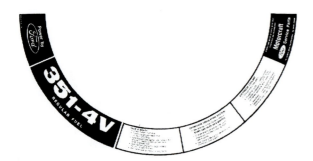

The 1972 Mustang 351-4V Regular Fuel Air Cleaner decal (white/blue) (DF0256).

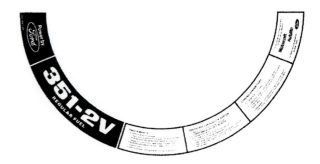

The 1973 Mustang 351-2V Regular Fuel Air Cleaner decal (white/blue) (DF0668).

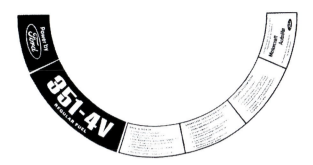

The 1973 Mustang 351-4V Regular Fuel Air Cleaner decal (white/blue) (DF0804).

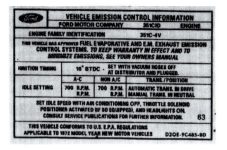

The 1972 Mustang 351C-4V AT Late Emission decal (medium orange) (DF1414).

The 1972 Mustang 302-2V AT/MT Emission decal (dark orange) (DF0843).

The 1973 Mustang 302-2V AT/MT Emission decal (yellow/black) (DF0641).

The 1972 Mustang 351C-2V AT/MT Emission decal (dark orange) (DF0594).

The 1973 Mustang 351C-2V AT Emission decal (yellow/black) (DF1248).

The 1972 Mustang 351C-4V CJ AT Emission decal (dark yellow) (DF0534) and 351C-4V AT Early Emission decal (dark yellow) [D2OE-9C485-HA] (DF0534).

The 1973 Mustang 351C-4V AT/MT Emission decal (before 1/1/73) (yellow/black) (DF0638).

VEHICLE EMISSION CONTROL INFORMATION		
FUEL EVAPORATIVE AND EXHAUST EMISSION CONTROL		

The 1971 Mustang Boss 351 Engine Code decal (DF0930).

The 1973 Mustang 351C-4V MT Late Emission decal (after 1/1/73) (yellow/black) (DF0582).

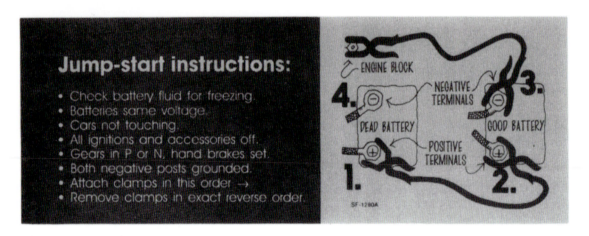

The 1971 Mustang Jump Start Instructions decal SF-4280-A (DF1316).

The 1971-1972 Mustang Autolite Sta-Ful Battery tag (DF784).

The 1971 Mustang Boss 351 PCV plastic ring (DF0985).

The 1971 Mustang 429 CJ/SCJ PCV plastic ring (DF0984).

SPACE SAVER SPARE REMINDER CARD

Dear Customer:

Our records indicate that you may be a Space Saver Spare owner and have not responded to our certified letter advising of our free tire inspection to detect possible product abuse. The problem is caused by improper mounting or subsequent remounting of the tire on the rim or by excessive air pressure. Improper mounting or excessive air pressure can cause the tire to explode during inflation.

It is very important that any time the Space Saver Spare tire is used, it must be bolted to the car axle prior to inflation and then inflated only with the approved canister inflator provided for road use.

If for any reason you do not have the certified inspection notice we sent to you, please write to The B.F. Goodrich Co., Customer Relations Department, Dept. 0620 Bldg. 24-E, Akron, Ohio 44318, and a new inspection authorization notice will be remailed to you.

The free inspection program ends June 30, 1975.

B.F.Goodrich Tire Company
A DIVISION OF THE B.F.GOODRICH COMPANY

The 1968-1971 Mustang B. F. Goodrich Space Saver Spare Inspection card (DF0807).

BATTERY OK

CHARGE READING	DATE	BADGE

The 1965-1978 Mustang Battery OK decal (DF0194).

10

The 1971-1973 Mustang Production Day Number (10) Window decal (DF1015).

 UTICA PLANT QUALITY BUILT

The 1965-1973 Mustang Convertible Top Latch Utica Plant decal (DF1090).

The 1964-1975 Mustang Final Inspection Window sticker (red) (DF1055).

The 1964-1975 Mustang Final Inspection Window sticker (green) (DF1056).

Motorcraft
ENG GOV 6150 RPM
D2ZF-12450-BA
7207

The 1972 Mustang 351-HO Rev Limiter decal (DF0917).

The 1967-1972 Mustang Ford Anti-Freeze tag (DF0700).

The 1973 Mustang 302-2V Engine Code decal (DF1410).

K 600 CG

The 1973 Mustang 351C-2V Engine Code decal (DF0926).

K 600 C

The 1973 Mustang 351C-2V w/ A/C Engine Code decal (DF0924).

K 621 A 6

The 1973 Mustang 351C-4V Non/Ram Air Engine Code decal (DF0932).

The 1973 Mustang 351C-4V Ram Air Engine Code decal (DF0925).

The 1973 Mustang Jack Storage Trunk decal (63, 65, after 3/1/73) (DF0931).

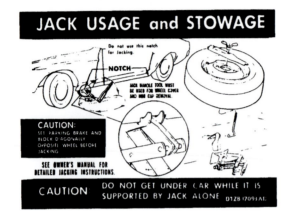

The 1971 Mustang Jack Storage Trunk decal (63, 65, before 4/5/71) (DF0046).

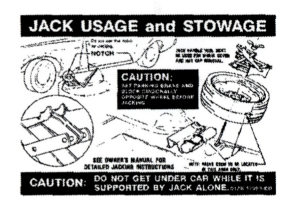

The 1971 Mustang Jack Storage Trunk decal (w/ Comp. Susp., before 4/5/71) (DF0367).

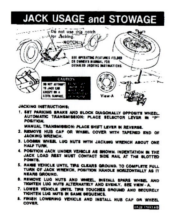

The 1971-1973 Mustang Jack Storage Trunk decal (63, 65, after 4/5/71, before 3/1/73) (DF0413).

The 1971-1972 Mustang Jack Storage Trunk decal (w/ Comp. Susp., after 4/5/71, before 2/5/72) (DF0218).

The 1972-1973 Mustang Jack Storage Trunk decal (w/ Comp. Susp., after 2/5/72, before 3/1/73) (DF0877).

The 1973 Mustang Jack Storage Trunk decal (w/ Comp. Susp., after 3/1/73) (DF0653).

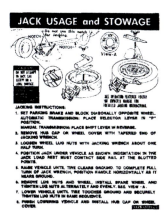

The 1971 Mustang Jack Storage Trunk decal (Convertible) (DF0414).

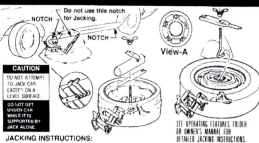

JACK USAGE and STOWAGE

Do not use this notch for Jacking.

CAUTION
DO NOT ATTEMPT TO JACK CAR EXCEPT ON A LEVEL SURFACE.
DO NOT GET UNDER CAR WHILE IT IS SUPPORTED BY JACK ALONE.

SEE OPERATING FEATURES FOLDER OR OWNER'S MANUAL FOR DETAILED JACKING INSTRUCTIONS.

JACKING INSTRUCTIONS:
1. SET PARKING BRAKE AND BLOCK DIAGONALLY OPPOSITE WHEEL. AUTOMATIC TRANSMISSION: PLACE SELECTOR LEVER IN "P" POSITION. MANUAL TRANSMISSION: PLACE SHIFT LEVER IN REVERSE.
2. REMOVE HUB CAP OR WHEEL COVER WITH TAPERED END OF JACKING WRENCH.
3. LOOSEN WHEEL LUG NUTS WITH JACKING WRENCH ABOUT ONE HALF TURN.
4. POSITION JACK UNDER VEHICLE AS SHOWN. INDENTATION IN THE JACK LOAD REST MUST CONTACT SIDE RAIL AT THE SLOTTED POINTS.
5. RAISE VEHICLE UNTIL TIRE CLEARS GROUND. TO COMPLETE FULL TURN OF JACK WRENCH, POSITION HANDLE HORIZONTALLY AS IT NEARS GROUND.
6. REMOVE LUG NUTS AND WHEEL, INSTALL SPARE WHEEL AND TIGHTEN LUG NUTS ALTERNATELY AND EVENLY. SEE VIEW - A.
7. LOWER VEHICLE UNTIL TIRE TOUCHES GROUND AND SECURELY TIGHTEN LUG NUTS IN SAME SEQUENCE.
8. FINISH LOWERING VEHICLE AND INSTALL HUB CAP OR WHEEL COVER.

D2ZB-17093-DA

The 1972 Mustang Jack Storage Trunk decal (Convertible) (DF1239).

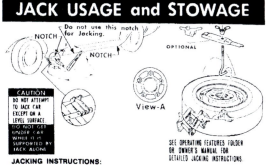

JACK USAGE and STOWAGE

Do not use this notch for Jacking.

CAUTION
DO NOT ATTEMPT TO JACK CAR EXCEPT ON A LEVEL SURFACE.
DO NOT GET UNDER CAR WHILE IT IS SUPPORTED BY JACK ALONE.

SEE OPERATING FEATURES FOLDER OR OWNER'S MANUAL FOR DETAILED JACKING INSTRUCTIONS.

JACKING INSTRUCTIONS:
1. SET PARKING BRAKE AND BLOCK DIAGONALLY OPPOSITE WHEEL. AUTOMATIC TRANSMISSION: PLACE SELECTOR LEVER IN "P" POSITION. MANUAL TRANSMISSION: PLACE SHIFT LEVER IN REVERSE.
2. REMOVE HUB CAP OR WHEEL COVER WITH TAPERED END OF JACKING WRENCH.
3. LOOSEN WHEEL LUG NUTS WITH JACKING WRENCH ABOUT ONE HALF TURN.
4. POSITION JACK UNDER VEHICLE AS SHOWN. INDENTATION IN THE JACK LOAD REST MUST CONTACT SIDE RAIL AT THE SLOTTED POINTS.
5. RAISE VEHICLE UNTIL TIRE CLEARS GROUND. TO COMPLETE FULL TURN OF JACK WRENCH, POSITION HANDLE HORIZONTALLY AS IT NEARS GROUND.
6. REMOVE LUG NUTS AND WHEEL, INSTALL SPARE WHEEL AND TIGHTEN LUG NUTS ALTERNATELY AND EVENLY. SEE VIEW - A.
7. LOWER VEHICLE UNTIL TIRE TOUCHES GROUND AND SECURELY TIGHTEN LUG NUTS IN SAME SEQUENCE.
8. FINISH LOWERING VEHICLE AND INSTALL HUB CAP OR WHEEL COVER.

D3ZB-17093-BA

The 1973 Mustang Jack Storage Trunk decal (Convertible) (DF0465).

EXTERIORS

The appeal of the Mustang was always Style. It is amazing that its unibody structure came from the first Ford Falcon and even more wondrous that it evolved into the larger 1971-1973 design.

The Mustang silhouette expanded slightly in 1967, but to the average viewer only a tape measure would reveal that fact. In 1969 Ford changed the Mustang in a larger way and, in 1971, in response to competition from GM, AMC, and, to a lesser extent, Chrysler, the silhouette would approach the full-sized Ford. Competition also dictated many economies. Exterior changes to the Mustang would be so minor in 1972 that confusion is normal among those attempting to identify and differentiate the 1971 model from the 1972 model. In 1973, the federal 5mph bumper ruling took effect. That change, along with a redesigned grille, grille surround, and headlight area, makes the 1973 models much easier to spot. Even then, the vast number of similarities among the three model years overwhelm the differences.

The volume and appeal of Mustang options also dwindled with simplification. And the 1971-1973 models were produced in smaller numbers. But those who embrace the swan song models of the 1964-1973 period do so with much affection and precision. While the whole philosophy (and size) of the Mustang would regress in 1974, the 1971-1973 era stands as a grand finale to the first generation of Mustangs.

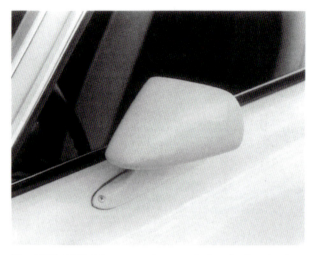

The 1971-1973 Mustang racing-type body color-keyed mirror, rearward view.

The 1972 Mustang "Hockey Stick"-style body-side graphics detail. Note chromed steel front bumper.

The 1971-1973 Mustang racing-type body color-keyed mirror, forward view.

The 1973 Mustang "Hockey Stick"-style bodyside graphics detail. Note body color-keyed front bumper.

Headlight, parking light, grille, and chrome trim details, identical for 1971 and 1972 Mustangs.

The 1973 Mustang headlight, parking light, and body color-keyed trim details.

"USA" rear fender decal on 1972 Mustang "Sprint" Packages A and B.

Rear bumper, taillight, and new-for-1972 "Mustang" script trunk emblem. Note taillight panel painted blue for Sprint Package.

The 1973 Mustang rear bumper, bumper guard, taillight, and trunk spoiler details.

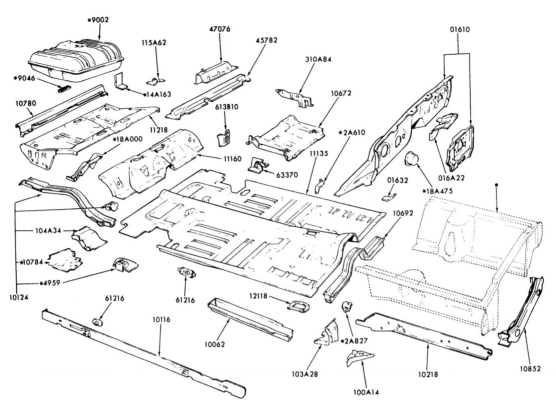

The 1971-1973 Mustang hardtop and SportsRoof underbody structural components and sheet-metal panels.

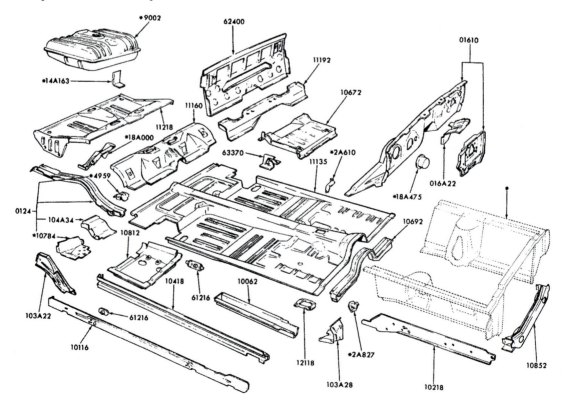

The 1971-1972 Mustang convertible underbody structural components and sheet-metal panels.

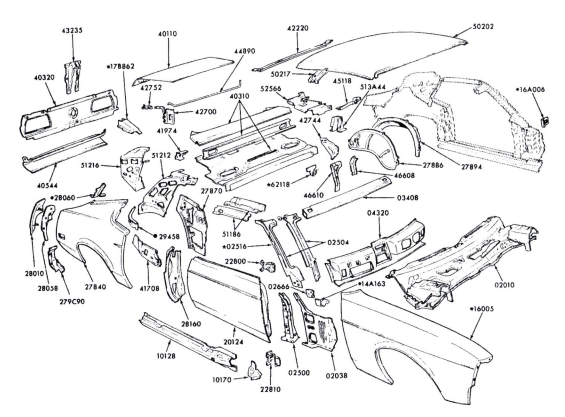

The 1971-1973 Mustang hardtop upper body structural components and sheet-metal panels.

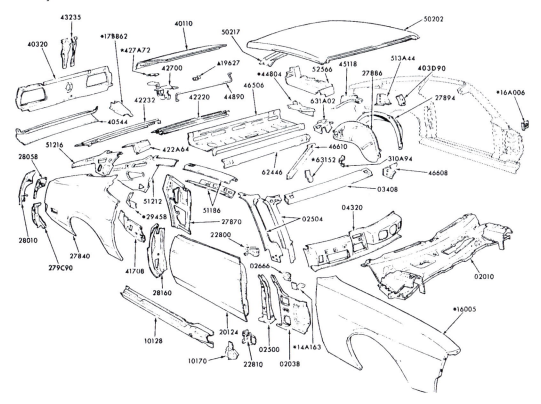

The 1971-1973 Mustang SportsRoof upper body structural components and sheet-metal panels.

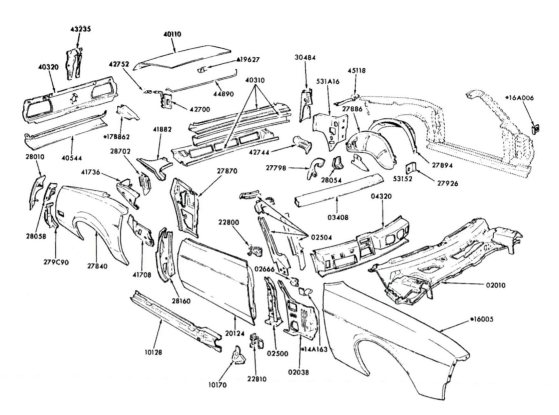

The 1971-1973 Mustang convertible upper body structural components and sheet-metal panels.

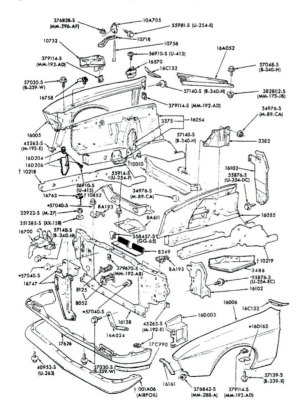

The 1971-1973 Mustang fenders, aprons, and related parts.

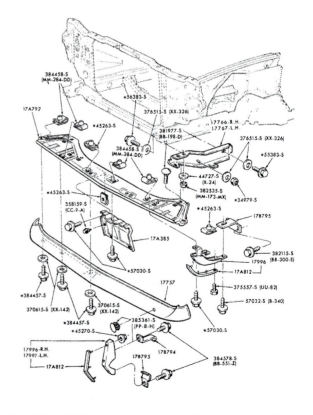

The 1971-1972 Mustang front bumper, lower valance, and related mounting hardware.

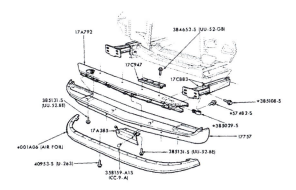

The 1973 Mustang front bumper, lower valance, and related mounting hardware.

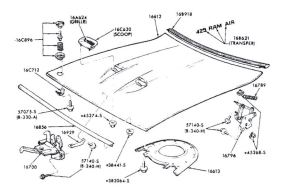

The 1971-1973 Mustang hood and related parts (Ram Air shown).

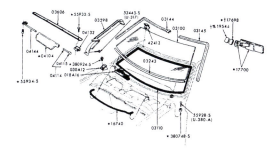

The 1971-1973 Mustang hardtop and SportsRoof windshield, trim, and related parts.

MUSTANG INSIDE REAR VIEW MIRROR APPLICATION CHART, 1971-1973		
Year	Part Number	Description
71	C9AZ-17700-AA	Day/Nite Mirror, 2.45 x 10" with undetachable mounting arm Black vinyl covered - Paint to match.
72/73	D0AZ-17700-A	Day/Nite Mirror, 2.5" x 12", with undetachable mounting arm Black vinyl covered - Paint to match.

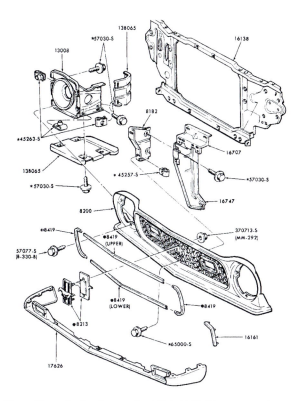

The grille and related parts for 1971-1972 Mustangs with sport lamps.

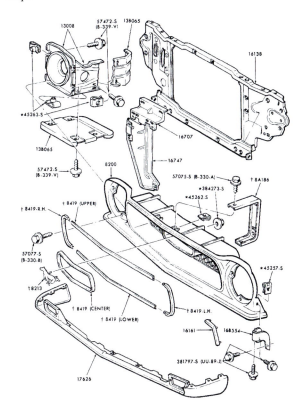

The grille and related parts for 1971-1972 Mustangs without sport lamps.

367

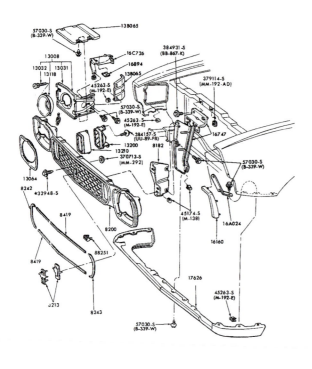

The 1973 Mustang Mach 1 grille and related parts.

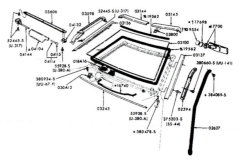

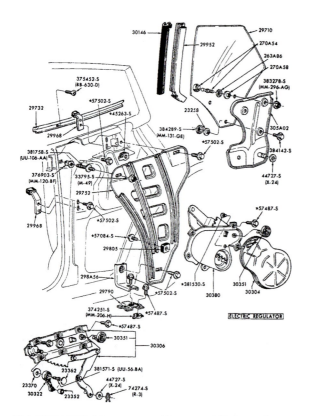

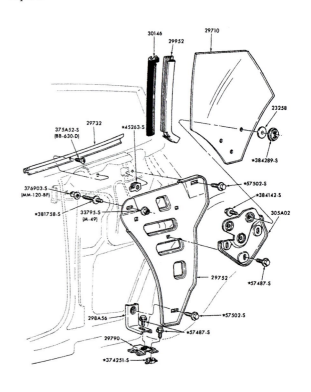

MUSTANG OUTSIDE REAR VIEW MIRROR ASSEMBLY APPLICATION CHART
Please refer to Mirror Type Illustrations, Page 73.

Year	Type	Part Number	Description
71-73	13	D1ZZ-17682-B	RH Manual Racing Type Head, in primer
71-73	9	D1ZZ-17682-A	LH Manual - Rectangular Head I.D. Number: D1ZB-17683-AA
71-73	13	D1ZZ-17682-C	LH Remote Control Racing Type Head, in primer; I.D. Number D1ZB-17683-BW
also:			
71-73	13	D1ZZ-17696-B	Dual Racing Mirrors (kit), in primer.
Consists of:			
	1	D1ZJ-17682-AA	RH Manual Mirror
	1	D1ZJ-17683-AA	LH Remote Control Mirror
	3	D0AJ-17C700-A	Retainer
	2	D1ZZ-17724-B	Gasket
	1	C7SZ-17B732-B	Nut
	1	C8SZ-17B733-C	Plate
	4	387879-S45	Screw #10 - 24 x 1"
	1	382930-S	Clip
	1		Installation Sketch

The 1971-1973 Mustang convertible windshield, trim, and related parts.

The 1971-1973 Mustang movable power and manual quarter window, trim, and related parts.

The 1971-1973 Mustang SportsRoof and Mach 1 stationary quarter window, trim, and related parts.

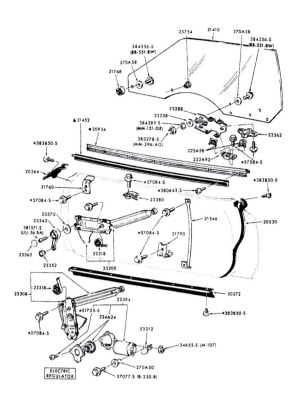

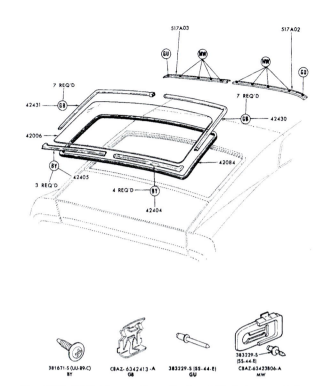

The 1971-1973 Mustang SportsRoof and Mach 1 rear window, exterior trim, and related parts.

The 1971-1973 Mustang door window, mechanism, and related parts.

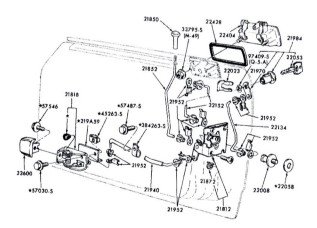

The 1971-1973 Mustang door handle, latch, and related parts.

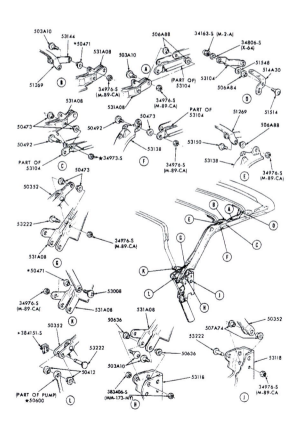

The 1971-1973 Mustang manual folding top and related parts (less trim).

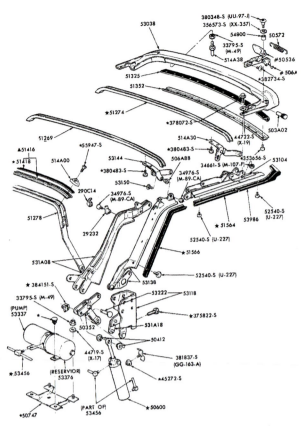

The 1971-1973 Mustang power folding top and related parts (less trim).

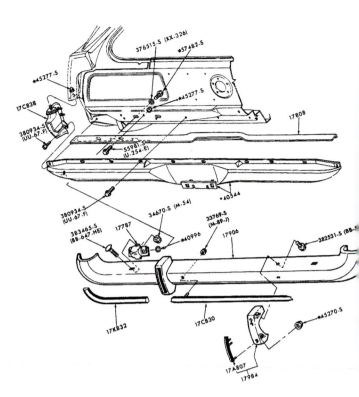

The 1973 Mustang rear bumper, valance, and related parts.

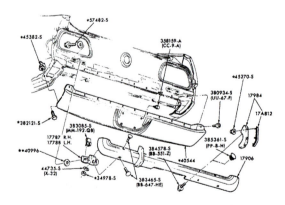

The 1971-1972 Mustang rear bumper, valance, and related parts.

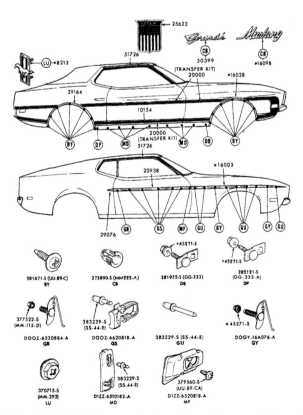

The 1971-1973 Mustang hardtop, Grandé, convertible, and SportsRoof side trim and attaching parts.

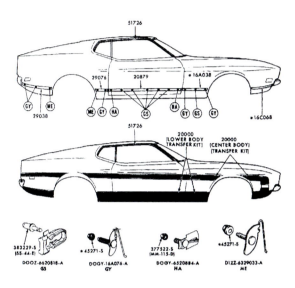

The 1971-1973 Mustang Mach 1 side trim and attaching parts.

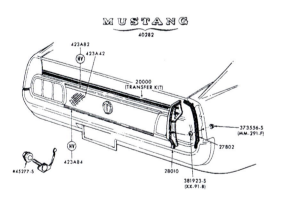

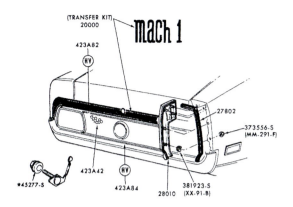

The 1971-1973 Mustang Mach 1 rear trim and attaching parts.

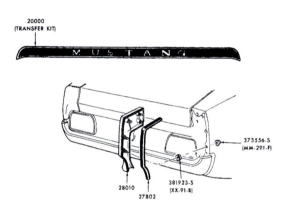

The 1971-1973 Mustang SportsRoof rear trim and attaching parts.

The 1971-1973 Mustang hardtop, Grandé, and convertible rear trim and attaching parts.

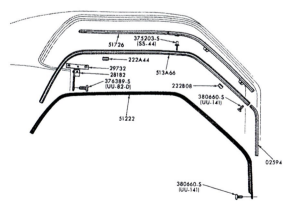

The 1971-1973 Mustang hardtop and Grandé roof side moldings and weather-strips.

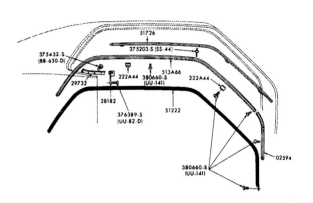

The 1971-1973 Mustang SportsRoof and Mach 1 roof-side moldings and weather-strips.

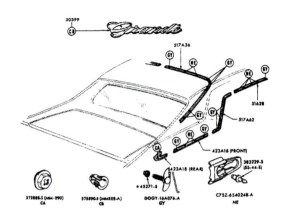

The 1971-1973 Mustang Grandé vinyl roof, moldings, and related parts.

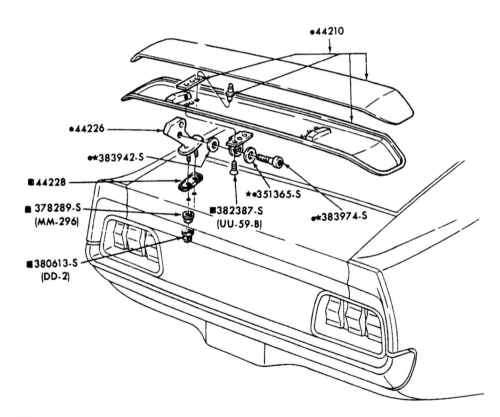

The 1971-1973 Mustang rear spoiler and related parts.

INTERIORS

Mustang interiors always have provided a unique combination of sportiness and luxury. Except for rare bench front seat models in the early years, the Mustang's universal two-seat effect has been one of performance and of differentiation from the norm.

Much of the money spent in Mustang restoration is devoted to interiors. The restorer is always wise to check with concours experts and reputable parts vendors before spending money for interior components and upholstery. Small details such as the texture and grain of vinyl upholstery, the composition of carpet material, the accuracy of seat belt retrofitting, and proper colors of interior paint are best researched before a mistake is made.

For information on 1971-1973 spare tires, jacks, and related parts, please refer to the upper left corner of page 128. For typical retractable and fixed seat belt installation, refer to pages 117, 118, and 119. For 1971-1973 instrument clusters, check the "Wiring and Electrical" section of this chapter.

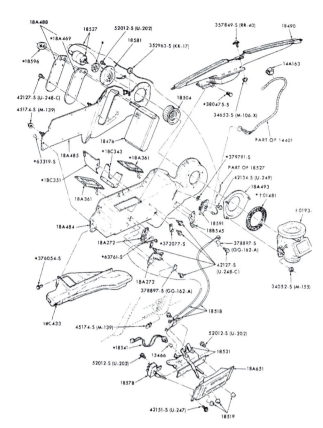

The 1971-1973 Mustang heater, controls, and related parts.

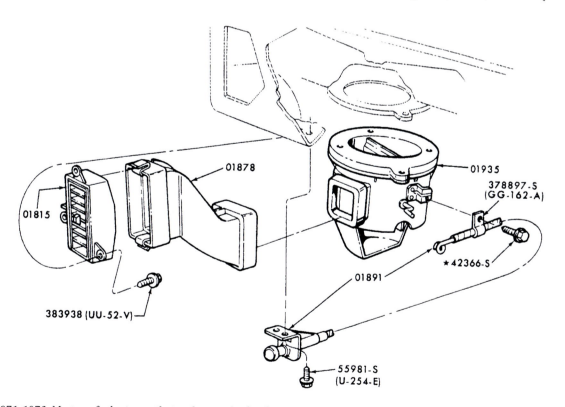

The 1971-1973 Mustang fresh-air ventilating ducts and related parts.

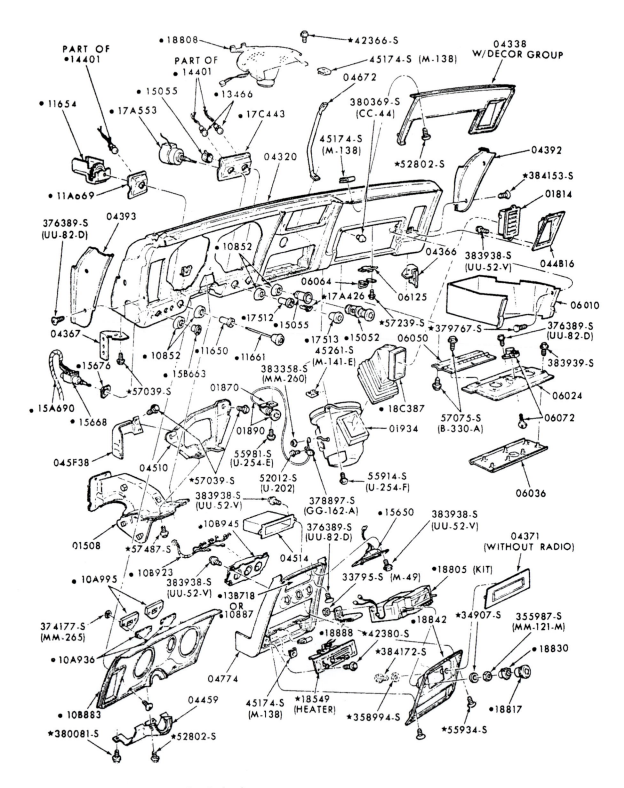

The 1971-1973 Mustang instrument panel and related parts.

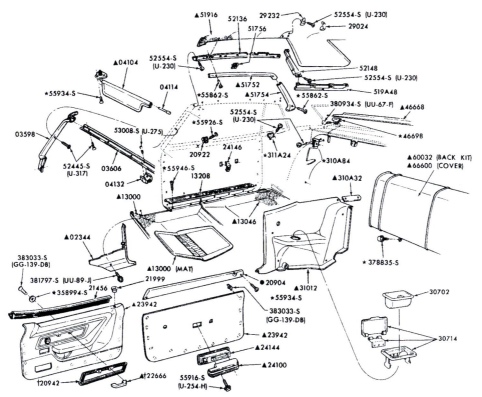

The 1971-1973 Mustang hardtop interior trim and related parts.

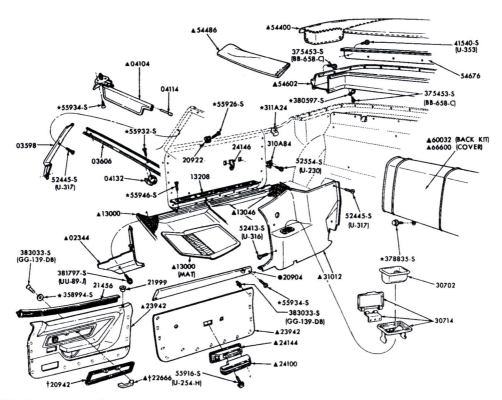

The 1971-1973 Mustang convertible interior trim and related parts.

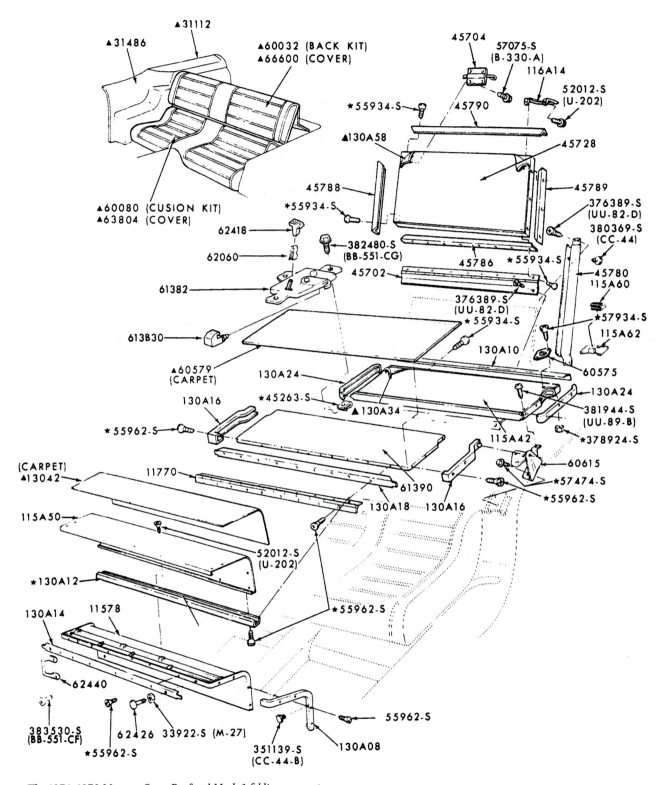

The 1971-1973 Mustang SportsRoof and Mach 1 folding rear seat and related parts.

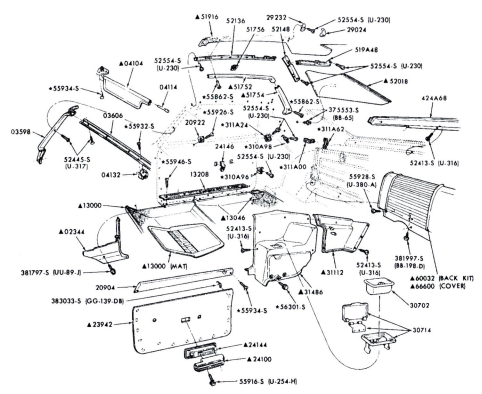

The interior trim and related parts for 1971-1973 Mustang SportsRoof and Mach 1 models with folding rear seat.

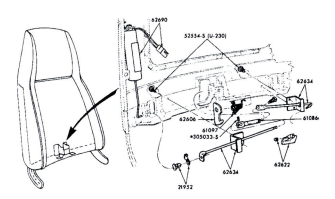

The automatic front-seat back latch mechanism and related parts for 1971-1973 Mustangs with outboard release.

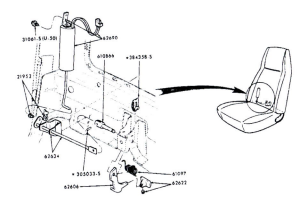

The automatic front-seat back latch mechanism and related parts for 1971-1973 Mustangs with center release.

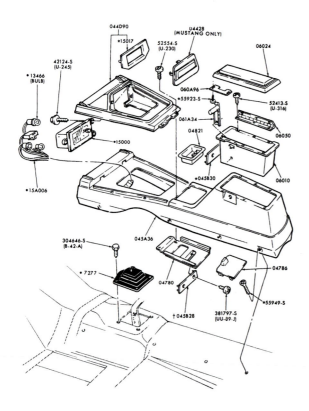

The 1971-1973 Mustang console and related parts.

1971 Mustang Interior Trim Scheme Codes

Code	Body Type	Trim Scheme
1A	63, 65D, 76D	Black, All Vinyl
1B	63, 65D, 76D	Medium Blue, All Vinyl
1E	63, 65D, 76D	Medium Vermilion, All Vinyl
1F	63, 65D	Medium Ginger, All Vinyl
1R	63, 65D, 76D	Medium Green, All Vinyl
1W	63, 65D, 76D	White Vinyl, Black Appointments
2B	63D, 65D	Medium Blue Vinyl & Med. Blue Cloth
2E	63D, 65D	Med. Vermilion Vinyl & Med. Verm. Cloth
2F	63D, 65D	Med. Ginger Vinyl & Med. Ginger Cloth
2R	63D, 65D	Med. Green Vinyl & Med. Green Cloth
Decor Group Interiors:		
3A	63D, 65D	Black, All Vinyl
3W	63D, 65D	White Vinyl, Black Appointments
Grandé Interiors:		
4A	65F	Black Vinyl and Black Cloth
4B	65F	Medium Blue Vinyl & Med. Blue Cloth
4E	65F	Med. Vermilion Vinyl & Med. Verm. Cloth
4F	65F	Med. Ginger Vinyl & Med. Ginger Cloth
4R	65F	Med. Green Vinyl & Med. Green Cloth
Mach 1 Sports Interiors:		
5A	63	Black, All Vinyl
5B	63	Medium Blue, All Vinyl
5E	63	Medium Vermilion, All Vinyl
5F	63	Medium Ginger, All Vinyl
5FA	63	Medium Ginger, All Vinyl
5R	63	Medium Green, All Vinyl
5W	63	White Vinyl, Black Appointments
5WA	63	White Vinyl, Black Appointments
Boss 351 Interiors:		
BB	63D	Medium Blue Vinyl & Med. Blue Cloth
BE	63D, 76D	Med. Vermilion Vinyl & Med. Verm. Cloth
BF	63D, 76D	Med. Ginger Vinyl & Med. Ginger Cloth
BR	63D	Med. Green Vinyl & Med. Green Cloth
Convertible & Boss 351 Interiors:		
CA	63D, 76D	Black, All Vinyl
CW	63D, 76D	White Vinyl, Black Appointments
Convertible Interiors:		
CB	76D	Medium Blue, All Vinyl
CE	76D	Medium Vermilion, All Vinyl
CF	76D	Medium Ginger, All Vinyl
CFA	76D	Medium Ginger, All Vinyl
CR	76D	Medium Green, All Vinyl

1972 Mustang Interior Trim Scheme Codes

Code	Body Type	Trim Scheme
AA, AAB, AAE, AA1	63D, 63R, 65D	Black, All Vinyl
AB, ABB, ABE, AB1	63D, 63R, 65D	Medium Blue, All Vinyl
AE, AEB, AEE, AE1	63D, 63R, 65D	Vermilion, All Vinyl
AF, AFB, AFE, AF1	63D, 63R, 65D	Medium Ginger, All Vinyl
AR, ARB, ARE, AR1	63D, 63R, 65D	Medium Green, All Vinyl
AW, AWB, AWE, AW1	63D, 63R, 65D	White Vinyl, Black Appointments
Convertible Interiors:		
CA, CAA, CAB, CAE	76D	Black Knitted Vinyl
CB, CBA, CBB, CBE	76D	Medium Blue Knitted Vinyl
CE, CEA, CEB, CEE	76D	Vermilion Knitted Vinyl
CF, CFA, CFB, CFE	76D	Medium Ginger Knitted Vinyl
CR, CRA, CRB, CRE, CR1	76D	Medium Green Knitted Vinyl
CW, CWA, CWB, CWE	76D	White Knit Vinyl, Black Appointments
Grandé Interiors:		
FA, FAB, FAE	65F	Black Vinyl & Black Cloth
FB, FBB, FBE	65F	Medium Blue Vinyl & Med. Blue Cloth
FE, FEB, FEE	65F	Med. Vermilion Vinyl & Med. Verm. Cloth
FF, FFB, FFE	65F	Med. Ginger Vinyl & Med. Ginger Cloth
FR, FRB, FRE	65F	Med. Green Vinyl & Med. Green Cloth
Mach 1 Sports Interiors:		
GA, GAA, GAB, GAE	63D, 63R	Black, All Vinyl
GB, GBA, GBB, GBE	63D, 63R	Medium Blue, All Vinyl
GE, GEA, GEB, GEE	63D, 63R	Vermilion, All Vinyl
GF, GFB, GFE	63D, 63R	Medium Ginger, All Vinyl
GR, GRA, GRB, GRE, GR1	63D, 63R	Medium Green, All Vinyl
GW, GWA, GWB, GWE	63D, 63R	White Vinyl, Black Appointments
Sprint Option Interiors:		
HB, HBE, JB, JBE	63D, 65D	Blue Vinyl w/ White & Red Apptmts

Body Style Codes:

65D	Hardtop (Standard)
63D	SportsRoof
76D	Convertible
65F	Hardtop/Grandé
63R	SportsRoof/Mach 1

MUSTANG INSTRUMENT PANEL GLOVE COMPARTMENTS, 1971-1973

Year	Part Number	Description
71-73	D1ZZ-6506010-A	Without A/C
71-73	D1WY-6506010-A	With A/C

INSTRUMENT PANEL GLOVE COMPARTMENT DOOR APPLICATIONS

71-73	D1ZZ-6506024-A	Dashboard, paint to match
71-73	D1ZZ-6506024-B	Console, paint to match

INSTRUMENT CLUSTER HOUSING APPLICATION

71-73	D1ZZ-10838-A	All

1973 Mustang Interior Trim Scheme Codes

Code	Body Type	Trim Scheme
AA	63D, 63R, 65D	Black, All Vinyl
AB	63D, 63R, 65D	Medium Blue, All Vinyl
AF	63D, 63R, 65D	Medium Ginger, All Vinyl
AG	63D, 63R, 65D	Medium Avocado, All Vinyl
AW	63D, 63R, 65D	White Vinyl, Black Appointments

Convertible Interiors:

Code	Body Type	Trim Scheme
CA, CAA	76	Black Knitted Vinyl
CB, CBA	76	Medium Blue Knitted Vinyl
CF, CFA	76	Medium Ginger Knitted Vinyl
CG, CGA	76	Medium Avocado Knitted Vinyl
CW, CWA	76	White Knitted Vinyl, Black Appointments

Grandé Interiors:

Code	Body Type	Trim Scheme
FA	65F	Black Vinyl & Black Cloth
FB	65F	Medium Blue Vinyl & Med. Blue Cloth
FF	65F	Med. Ginger Vinyl & Med. Ginger Cloth
FG	65F	Medium & Light Avocado Vinyl & Medium & Light Avocado Cloth
FU	65F	Tan Vinyl & Tan Cloth (delete 9/25/72)

Mach 1 Sports Interiors:

Code	Body Type	Trim Scheme
GA, GAA	63D, 63R	Black, All Vinyl
GB, GBA	63D, 63R	Medium Blue, All Vinyl
GF, GFA	63D, 63R	Medium Ginger, All Vinyl
GG, GGA	63D, 63R	Medium Avocado & Light Avocado Vinyl
GW, GWA	63D, 63R	White Vinyl, Black Appointments

Body Style Codes:

65D	Hardtop (Standard)
63D	SportsRoof
76D	Convertible
65F	Hardtop/Grandé
63R	SportsRoof/Mach 1

MUSTANG CENTER INSTRUMENT PANEL APPLICATION CHART

Year	Body Type	Description	Part Number
71-73	63D, 63R, 65D, 76D	Black camera case finish, without instrument gauge openings, w/ Mustang name plate.	D1ZZ-6504774-C
		Blue	D1ZZ-6504774-B
		Ginger	D1ZZ-6504774-A
		Green	D1ZZ-6504774-D
71-73	63D, 65D, 76D	Black camera case finish, with instrument gauge openings.	D1ZZ-6504774-J
		Blue	D1ZZ-6504774-K
		Ginger	D1ZZ-6504774-L
		Green	D1ZZ-6504774-M
71-73	63D, 63R, 65F	Black wood grain finish, with instrument gauge openings.	D1ZZ-6304774-A
		Blue	D1ZZ-6304774-B
		Ginger	D1ZZ-6304774-C
		Green	D1ZZ-6304774-D
71-73	65F	Black wood grain finish, without instrument gauge openings, w/ Grandé name plate.	D1ZZ-6504774-E
		Blue	D1ZZ-6504774-F
		Ginger	D1ZZ-6504774-G
		Green	D1ZZ-6504774-H
72	63D, 65D		D2ZZ-6504774-A

MUSTANG FRONT SEAT BELT ASSEMBLY APPLICATION CHART

Note: Base Part Number w/ 76611A72 indicates Convertible models.
Base Part Number w/ 65613B84 indicates Hardtop and SportsRoof models.

Colors and Applicable Part Number Suffixes:

1971	Base Part Number	Black	Blue	Ginger	Parchment	Red	Green	Vermilion
Notes: 1, 4, 8	D0ZZ-65611B84	J	G	H	F	M		
Notes: 1, 4, 8	D1ZZ-65611B84						A	
Notes: 1, 4, 7	D1ZZ-65611B84	D						
Note: 1, 4, 6	D1OZ-65611B84	AA						
Notes: 2, 5, 8	D0ZZ-76611A72	B	A	E			Note 3	
Notes: 2, 5, 8	D1ZZ-76611A72				C		Note 3	E

1972, Before 12/1/71	Base Part Number	Black	Blue	Ginger	Parchment	Red	Green	Vermilion
Notes: 1, 4, 8	D2ZZ-65611B84	H	D	E	B	F	G	C
Notes: 1, 4, 7	D2ZZ-65611B84	A						
Notes: 1,4,6,7	D2ZZ-65611B84	S						
Notes: 1, 4, 9	D2ZZ-65611B84	T						
Notes: 2, 5, 8	D2ZZ-76611B84	A	C	F	G	B	D	E
Notes: 1, 5, 9	D2ZZ-76611B84	S						

1972, After 12/1/71	Base Part Number	Black	Blue	Ginger	Parchment	Red	Green	Vermilion
Notes: 1, 4, 8	D2ZZ-65611B84	R	M	N	K	P	Q	L
Notes: 1, 4, 7	D2ZZ-65611B84	J						
Notes: 1,4,6,7	D2ZZ-65611B84	U						
Notes: 1, 4, 9	D2ZZ-65611B84	V						
Notes: 1, 5, 8	D2ZZ-76611B84	H	L	M	J	N	P	K
Notes: 1, 5, 9	D2ZZ-65611B84	R						

1973	Base Part Number	Black	Blue	Ginger	Avocado
Note: 10	D3ZZ-65611B84	B			
Note: 12	D3ZZ-65611B84	C			
Note: 11	D3ZY-65611B84	E	A	C	B
Note: 12	D3ZZ-76611B84	E			
Note: 11	D3ZZ-76611B84	D	A	C	B

1 - Retractable Harness
2 - Non-Retractable Harness
3 - Use Black
4 - Includes Harness
5 - Does Not Include Harness
6 – Extra Length Belt
7 - Standard Buckle, plastic covered, black.
8 - Deluxe Buckle, Standard Length
9 - Deluxe Buckle, Extra Length Belt
10 - Black Buckle, Extra Length Belt
11 - Bright Finish Buckle
12 - Bright Finish Buckle, Extra Length Belt

MUSTANG REAR SEAT BELT ASSEMBLY APPLICATION CHART

Base Part Number

1971		Black	Green	Blue	Ginger	Parchment	Red	Tobacco	Grey Gold	Vermilion
Note: D	D0MZ-76613B84	A								
Note: S	D1AZ-65613B84	A								
Note: D	D1AZ-76611A72		B						A	E
Note: D	D0MZ-76611A72			J	K	H	L	S		

1972		Black	Green	Blue	Ginger	Parchment	Red
Notes: N, B, S	D2ZZ-65613B84	G					
Notes: R, B, D	D2ZZ-76613B84	F	E	B	C	A	D
Notes: R, A, D	D2ZZ-76613B84	M	L	H	J	G	K
Notes: R, A, S	D2ZZ-65613B84	A					

1973		Black	Avocado	Blue	Ginger	Tan
Notes: R, S	D3ZZ-65613B84	A				
Notes: R, D	D3ZZ-76613B84	E	B	A	C	G

R - Retractable Harness
N - Non-Retractable Harness
B - Before 12/1/71
A - After 12/1/71
S - Standard Buckle, plastic covered, black.
D - Deluxe Buckle, Standard Length

ENGINES

From 1971 through 1973 four engines powered Ford Mustangs, and the 429ci engine was offered only in 1971. Because the 250ci, 302ci, and 351ci engines were offered prior to 1971, their exploded views and options are included in Chapter 4 of this book, beginning on page 129. For reference purposes, the exploded views of the 429ci engine are the same as the smaller 302ci and 351ci Windsor engines.

The musclecar era brought horsepower to the consumer, and larger engines were needed to provide that power. Desiring to offer a big-block engine in 1971, Ford encountered an engine area space problem not unlike that encountered when wedging the wide Boss 429 engine into the 1969 and 1970 Mustangs. The silhouette of the 1971 Mustang had expanded greatly in response to competition from GM, AMC, and, to a lesser extent, Chrysler. But now the FE engine was too high to fit under the long, low hood. The only engine that would work without a cut-to-fit fix was the 429. Alas, emissions and fuel restrictions dictated the deletion of that option in 1972.

Again, let us state that beyond part numbers the value of this information lies in the description, dimension, and application of Ford replacement componentry. Those facts can help anyone gain a better understanding of what was original equipment or what was accepted in the past as original equipment.

The 1971 Mustang 302-2V engine with air conditioning.

The 1971-1973 Mustang standard gas filler cap.

The 1971 and 1972 Mustang Mach 1 "pop-off"-style gas filler cap.

The 1973 Mustang 302-2V engine with air conditioning. Note power steering fluid cooler affixed to A/C compressor. Radiator cap is aftermarket model.

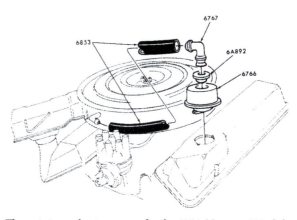

The emission reduction system for the 1971 Mustang 429 Cobra Jet engine.

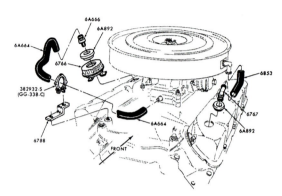

The emission reduction system for the 1971-1972 Mustang 302ci and 351ci engines.

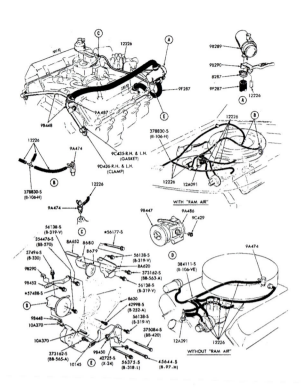

The thermactor emission control system for the 1971 Mustang 429 Cobra Jet engine.

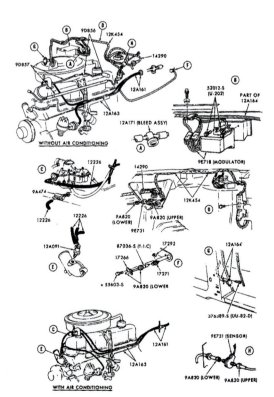

The distributor modulator system for the 1971 Mustang 250ci engine.

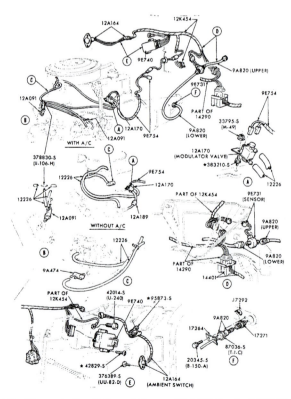

The Electronic Spark Control System (E.S.C.) for the 1972 Mustang 250ci engine.

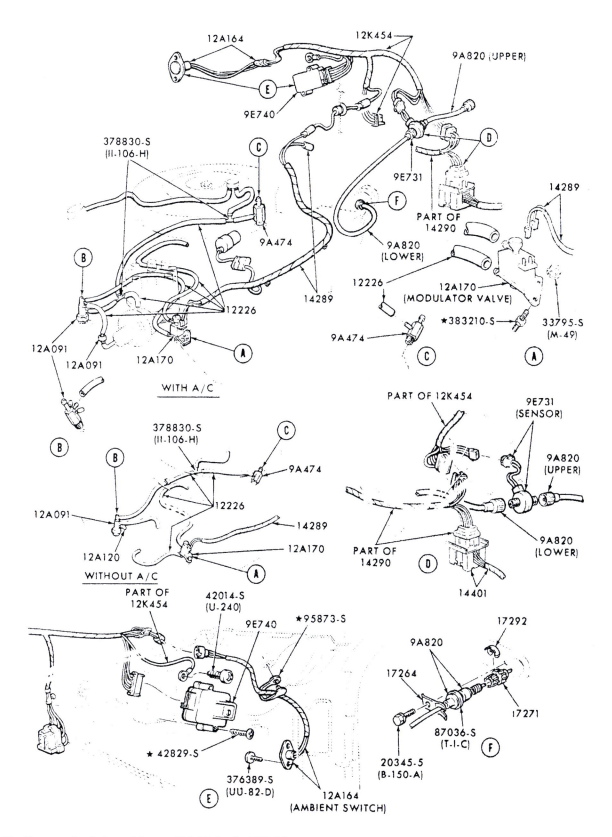

The Electronic Spark Control System (E.S.C.) for the 1972 Mustang 302-2V engine.

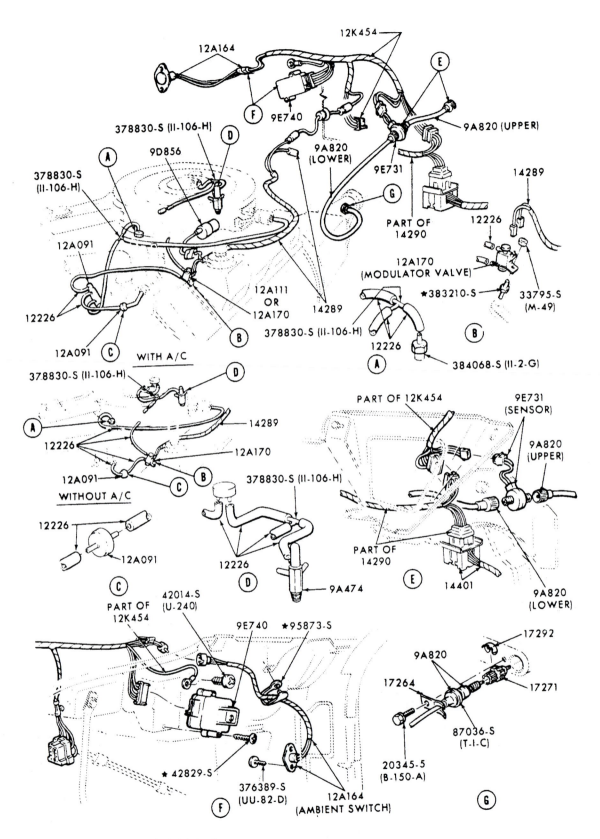

The Electronic Spark Control System (E.S.C.) for the 1972 Mustang 351-4V CJ engine without Ram Air hood.

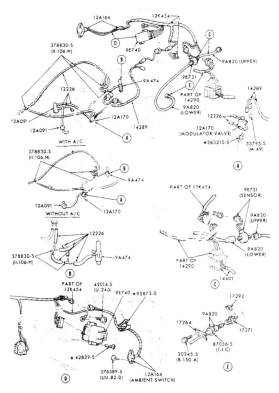

The Electronic Spark Control System (E.S.C.) for the 1972 Mustang 351-4V CJ engine with Ram Air hood.

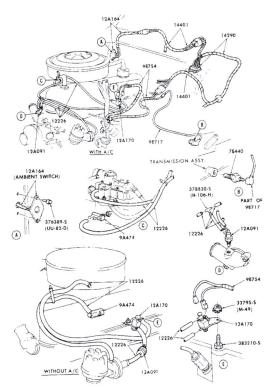

The Transmission Regulated Spark Control System (T.R.S.) for the 1972 Mustang 250ci engine.

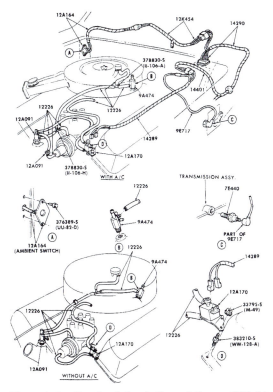

The Transmission Regulated Spark Control System (T.R.S.) for the 1972 Mustang 302-2V engine.

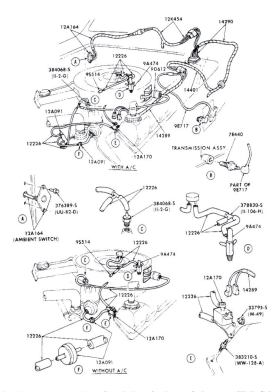

The Transmission Regulated Spark Control System (T.R.S.) for the 1972 Mustang 351-4V CJ engine without Ram Air hood.

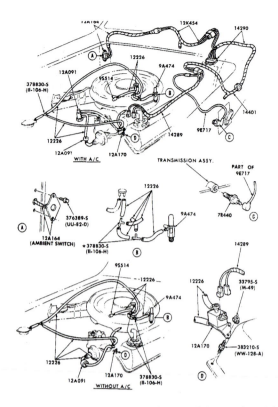

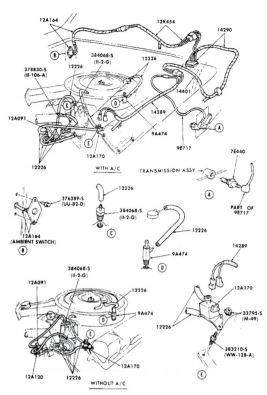

The Transmission Regulated Spark Control System (T.R.S.) for the 1972 Mustang 351-4V CJ engine with Ram Air hood.

The Transmission Regulated Spark Control System (T.R.S.) for the 1972 Mustang 351-2V CJ engine.

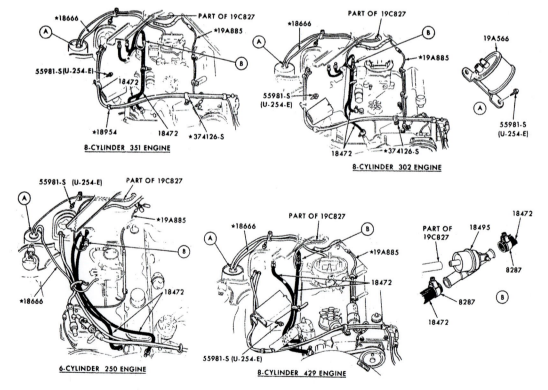

The air conditioning hoses for 1971-1973 Mustangs with all engines and with integral air conditioning.

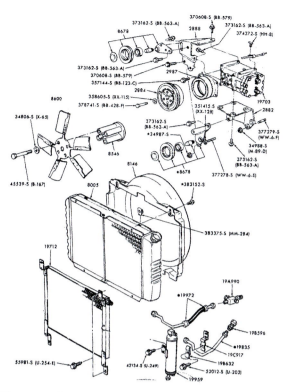

The air conditioning compressor, condenser, and related cooling system parts for 1971-1973 Mustangs equipped with 302ci and 351ci engines and integral air conditioning.

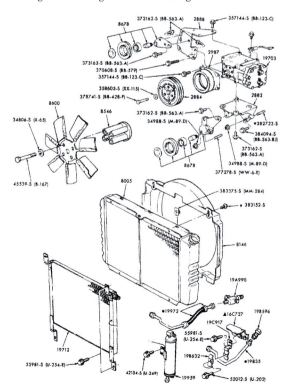

The air conditioning compressor, condenser, and related cooling system parts for 1971 Mustangs equipped with the 429ci engine and integral air conditioning.

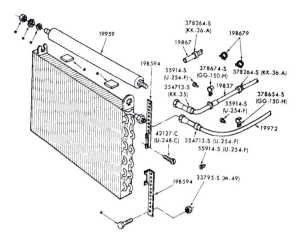

The condenser, dehydrator, and related parts for 1971-1973 Mustangs with 250ci engines and hang-on or dealer-installed air conditioning.

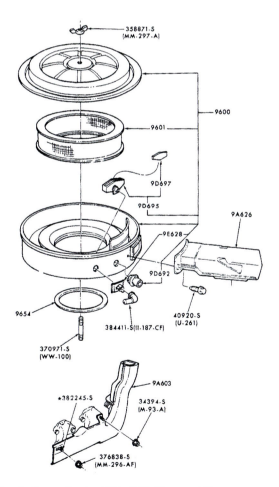

The air cleaner for the 1971-1973 Mustang 302ci engine, except California.

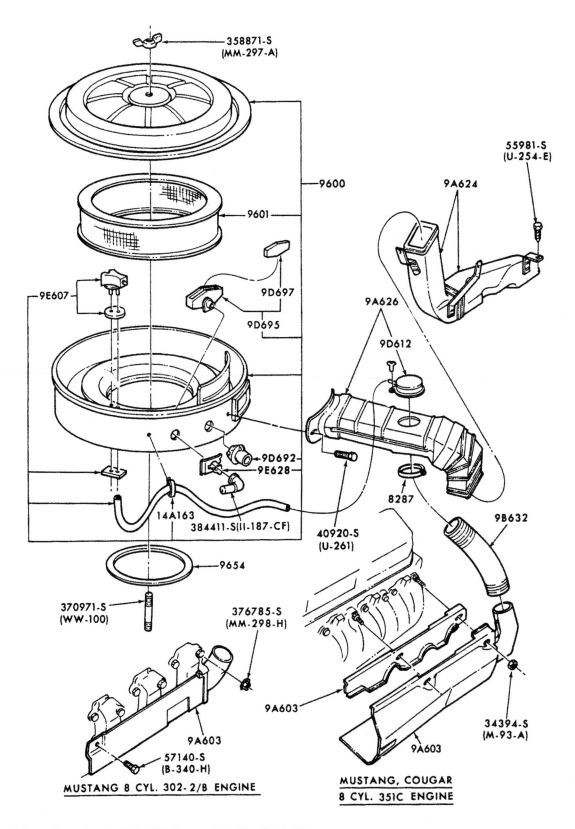

358871-S
(MM-297-A)

9600

9601

9E607

9D697

9D695

55981-S
(U-254-E)

9A624

9A626

9D612

9D692
9E628

8287

9B632

14A163

384411-S(II-187-CF)

40920-S
(U-261)

9654

370971-S
(WW-100)

376785-S
(MM-298-H)

9A603

34394-S
(M-93-A)

9A603

9A603

57140-S
(B-340-H)

9A603

MUSTANG 8 CYL. 302-2/B ENGINE

**MUSTANG, COUGAR
8 CYL. 351C ENGINE**

*The air cleaner for the 1971-1973 Mustang 302-2V and 351-2V
Cleveland engines, California only.*

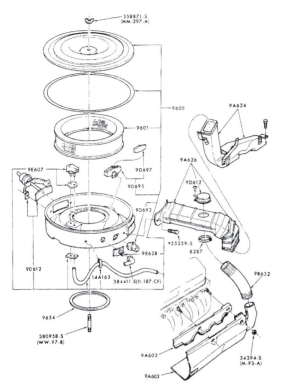

The air cleaner for the 1972 Mustang 351 CJ engine without Ram Air, California only.

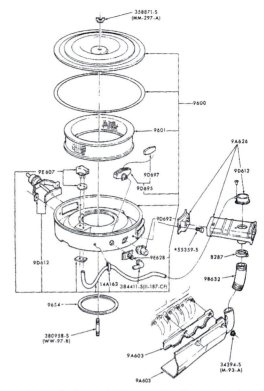

The air cleaner for the 1972 Mustang 351 CJ engine without Ram Air, except California.

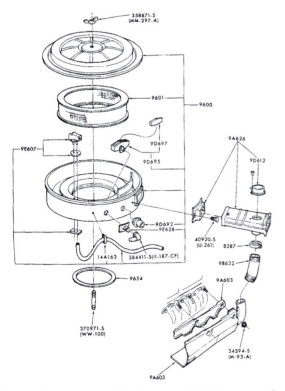

The air cleaner for the 1972 Mustang 351-2V engine without Ram Air, except California.

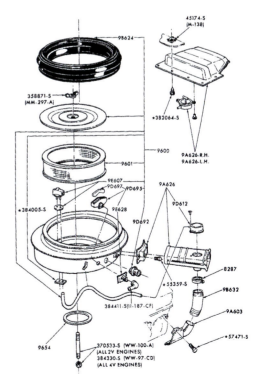

The air cleaner for the 1971-1972 Mustang 351 engine with Ram Air.

389

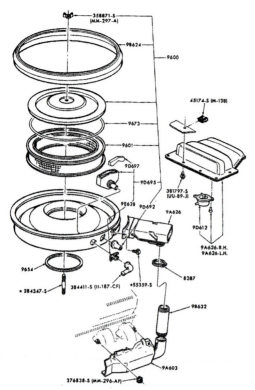

The air cleaner for the 1971 Mustang 429 CJ engine with Ram Air.

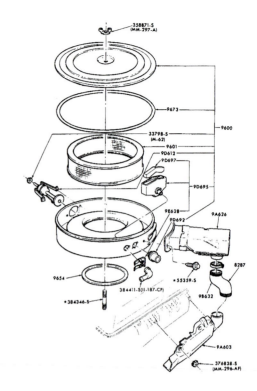

The air cleaner for the 1971 Mustang 429 CJ engine without Ram Air.

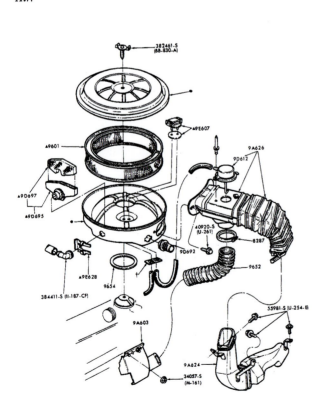

The air cleaner and related parts for 1973 Mustangs equipped with six-cylinder 250ci engines.

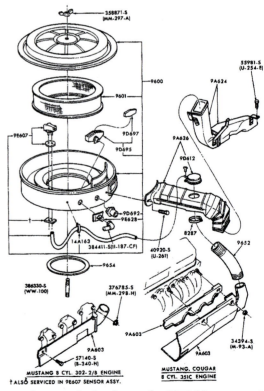

The air cleaner and related parts for 1973 Mustangs equipped with 302ci and 351-2V engines.

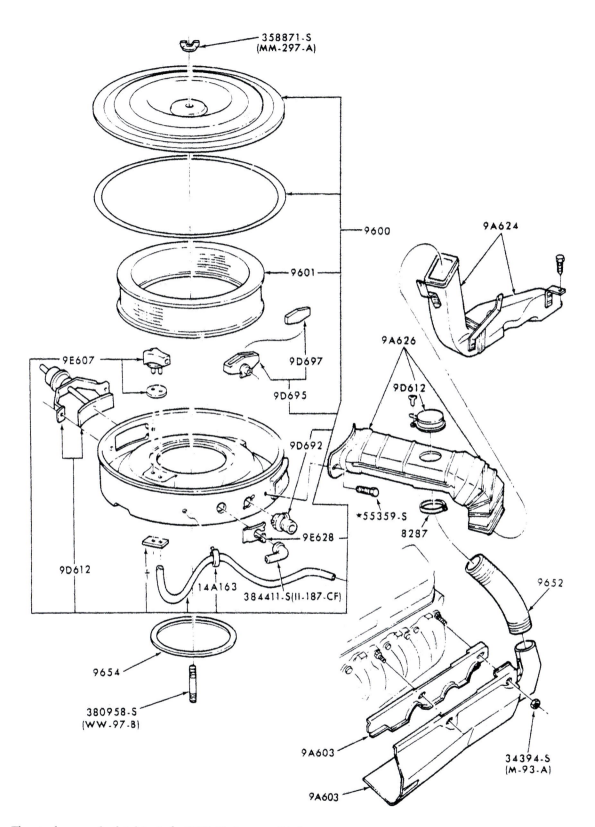

358871-S
(MM-297-A)

9600

9601

9A624

9A626

9D697

9D695

9D612

9E607

9D692

*55359-S

8287

9E628

9D612

14A163

384411-S(II-187-CF)

9652

9654

380958-S
(WW-97-B)

9A603

34394-S
(M-93-A)

9A603

*The air cleaner and related parts for 1973 Mustangs equipped
with eight-cylinder 351-4V engines.*

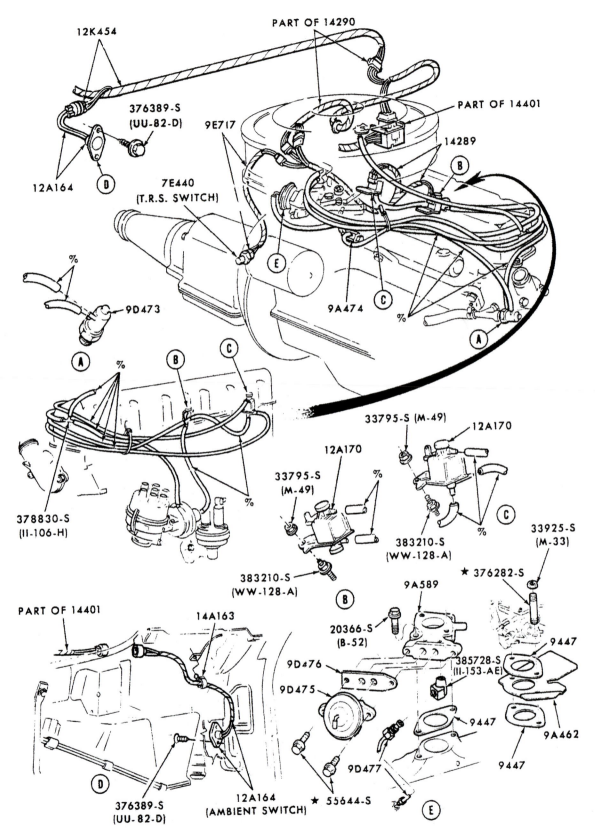

The Exhaust Gas Recirculation (E.G.R.) emissions system and related parts for 1973 Mustangs equipped with 250 six-cylinder engines and manual transmissions.

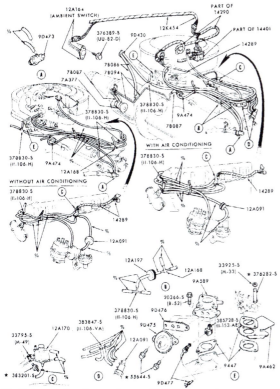

The Exhaust Gas Recirculation (E.G.R.) emissions system and related parts for 1973 Mustangs equipped with 250 six-cylinder engines and automatic transmissions.

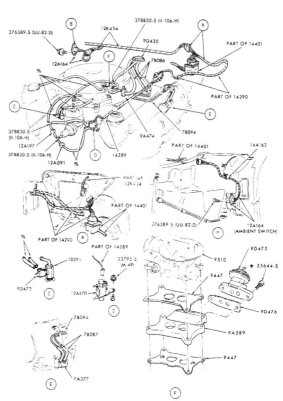

The Exhaust Gas Recirculation (E.G.R.) emissions system and related parts for 1973 Mustangs equipped with 302 eight-cylinder engines.

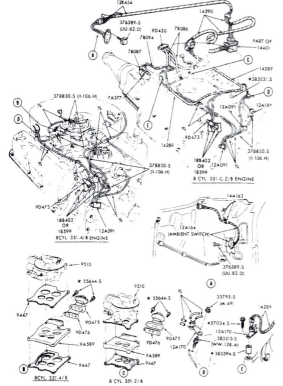

The Exhaust Gas Recirculation (E.G.R.) emissions system and related parts for 1973 Mustangs equipped with 351-2V and -4V eight-cylinder engines and automatic transmissions.

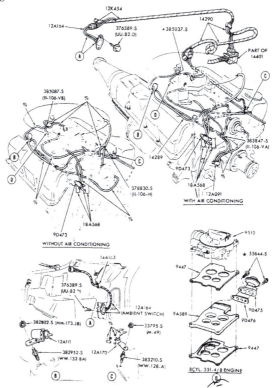

The Exhaust Gas Recirculation (E.G.R.) emissions system and related parts for 1973 Mustangs equipped with 351 eight-cylinder engines and manual transmissions.

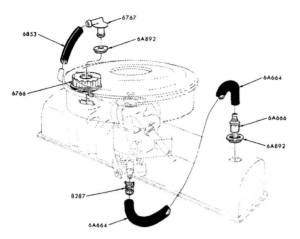

The emission reduction engine crankcase ventilation system for 1973 Mustangs equipped with 250 six-cylinder engines.

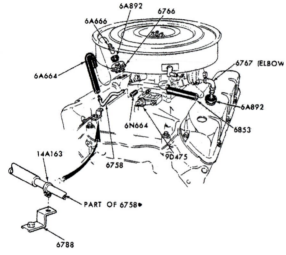

The emission reduction engine crankcase ventilation system for 1973 Mustangs equipped with 302 and 351-2V eight-cylinder engines.

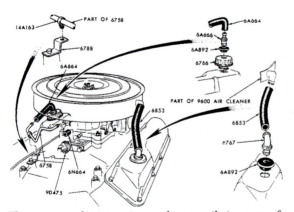

The emission reduction engine crankcase ventilation system for 1973 Mustangs equipped with 351 Cleveland eight-cylinder engines.

YEARS of PRODUCTION, MUSTANG ENGINES

6-Cylinder Engines

CID	1971	1972	1973
250	x	x	x

8-Cylinder Engines

	1971	1972	1973
302	x	x	x
351	x	x	x
351 H.O.	x	x	
429	x		

MUSTANG SPARK PLUG APPLICATION CHART, 1971-1973 8-Cylinder ENGINES

Note: Same part number for Light Service, Normal Service, and Heavy Duty Service Plugs.

Year	CID	I.D.	Part Number
71	302-4V 429	ARF32	C9PZ-12405-A
71	351	ARF42	C9PZ-12405-B
71-73	302-2V	BRF42	D0AZ-12405-A
72/73	351C	ARF42	C9PZ-12405-B

Mustang Exhaust Manifold Application Chart, 1971-1973

For six-cylinder applications:

Year	CID	Part Number
71/72	250	D3BZ-9430-A
73	250	D3DZ-9430-C

For eight-cylinder applications:

Year	CID	Right Hand	Left Hand
71/72	302	D0AZ-9430-C	D0AZ-9431-C
		r/b D4DZ-9430-E &	
		D5DZ-9A603-C(2/75)	
71/72	351/351CJ*	D0AZ-9430-B	D1ZZ-9431-B
71	Boss 351	D1ZZ-9430-B	D1ZZ-9431-D
71/72	351-2V	D2OZ-9430-B	D1ZZ-9431-A
71	429 CJ	D2OZ-9430-C	D1ZZ-9431-C
73	302	D4DZ-9430-E &	D4OZ-9431-B
		D5DZ-9430-C	
73	351-2V	D4AZ-9430-D	D1ZZ-9431-A
73	351-4V	D0DZ-9430-B	D1ZZ-9431-B

* 4v, except Boss

429 CJ and SCJ Engines

Ford's 429 Cobra Jet and Super Cobra Jet propelled the 1971 Mustang to new records, even as the musclecar era sped toward a close. The CJ, SCJ, and the 429 were the most powerful engines ever installed in factory-production Mustangs, and, regrettably, they were the last big blocks. Even though they are the same displacement, CJ and SCJ engines differ greatly from the Boss of all 429s. Although derived from a similar blueprint, a Boss 429 represents the extreme in Ford's 385 Series engine family. CJ and SCJ are equally potent, but unlike the Boss, they are assembled from comparatively common parts.

First installed in 1968, the "Thunder Jet" 429 introduced the buying public to an all new big block. Known as the "Base 429" and engineered to accelerate heavy cars and loaded trucks, they were available with either two- or four-bbl induction. The major differences between a base 429 and the CJ and SCJ installed in the 1971 Mustang are notable.

	Base 429 2V & 4V	CJ 4V	SCJ 4V
Horsepower (bhp @ rpm)	320 @ 4400 2V 360 @ 4600 4V	370 @ 5400 375 @ 5600*	370 @ 5400 375 @ 5600*
Block	2-bolt	4-bolt	4-bolt
Crank	Nodular iron	Nodular iron	Nodular iron
Pistons	Cast, double valve relief	Cast, single valve relief	Forged, single valve relief
Compression Ratio	10.5 2V 11.0 4V	11.3	11.3
Valve Size Intake Exhaust	2.080in 1.650in	2.245in 1.725in	2.245in 1.725in
Cylinder Head Part Number	C0VZ-6049-D	D0OZ-6049-H	D0OZ-6049-H
Port Size ** Intake Exhaust	1.85/2.56 1.43/2.00	2.12/2.86 1.32./2.24	2.12/2.86 1.32./2.24
Combustion Chamber Volume	74.2-77.2cc	71.5-75.5cc	71.5-75.5cc
Camshaft Part Number	C8SZ-6250-A	C9AZ-6250-A	D0AZ-6250-D
Camshaft Type	Hydraulic	Hydraulic	Mechanical
Rocker Arm Ratio	1.75:1	1.73:1	1.73:1
Rocker Arm Type	Forged steel non-adjustable	Stamped steel non-adjustable	Stamped steel adjustable
Intake Manifold Part Number	D0VY-9424-A (1)	D1AZ-9424-B (2)	D0OZ-9424-A (3)

* Drag Pack
** Width x Height in inches
(1) Uses Ford Carburetor
(2) Uses Rochester Carburetor
(3) Uses Holley Carburetor

MUSTANG ENGINE I.D. TAG CODE IDENTIFIER CHART, 1971-1973
Note: Except for 429cid engines, primarily 1973 Warranty Tag Codes.
For additional 1971 and 1972 applications, please refer to charts on ppg. 134, 135.

Tag Code	Cyl.	CID	Carb.	Data Code
K 37	6	250	C-1	L
KK 37	6	250	C-1	L
41*	6	250	C-1	L
42*	6	250	C-1	L
K 46	6	250	C-1	L
KK 46	6	250	C-1	L
K 48	6	250	C-1	L
KK 48	6	250	C-1	L
K 52	6	250	C-1	L
KK 52	6	250	C-1	L
EG 225	6	250	C-1	L
EA 226	6	250	C-1	L
EB 226	6	250	C-1	L
RA 227	6	250	C-1	L
RB 227	6	250	C-1	L
EA 228	6	250	C-1	L
EB 228	6	250	C-1	L
RA 229	6	250	C-1	L
RB 229	6	250	C-1	L
EF 230	6	250	C-1	L
EJ 230	6	250	C-1	L
K 250	8	302	F-2	F
KK 250	8	302	F-2	F
K 252	8	302	F-2	F
KK 252	8	302	F-2	F
K 258	8	302	F-2	F
KK 258	8	302	F-2	F
K 261	8	302	F-2	F
K 262	8	302	F-2	F
KK 262	8	302	F-2	F
K 268	8	302	F-2	F
KK 268	8	302	F-2	F
K 270	8	302	F-2	F
KK 270	8	302	F-2	F
K 271	8	302	F-2	F
K272	8	302	F-2	F
KK272	8	302	F-2	F
K 273	8	302	F-2	F
KK 273	8	302	F-2	F
K 274	8	302	F-2	F
KK274	8	302	F-2	F
K 275	8	302	F-2	F
K 276	8	302	F-2	F
KK 276	8	302	F-2	F
K 287	8	302	F-2	F
KK 287	8	302	F-2	F
K 288	8	302	F-2	F

Tag Code	Cyl.	CID	Carb.	Data Code
KK 288	8	302	F-2	F
K 294	8	302	F-2	F
KK 294	8	302	F-2	F
K296	8	302	F-2	F
KK 296	8	302	F-2	F
K 297	8	302	F-2	F
KK297	8	302	F-2	F
EA 300	8	302	F-2	F
EB 300	8	302	F-2	F
EA 301	8	302	F-2	F
EB 301	8	302	F-2	F
EK 302	8	302	F-2	F
EA 304	8	302	F-2	F
EB 304	8	302	F-2	F
EK 306	8	302	F-2	F
EA 307	8	302	F-2	F
EB 307	8	302	F-2	F
EA 308	8	302	F-2	F
EB 308	8	302	F-2	F
EA 309	8	302	F-2	F
EB 309	8	302	F-2	F
EA 310	8	302	F-2	F
EB 310	8	302	F-2	F
EG 315	8	302	F-2	F
EG 316	8	302	F-2	F
RG 316	8	302	F-2	F
EG 318	8	302	F-2	F
RG 370	8	302	F-2	F
RG 370	8	302	F-2	F
EG 371	8	302	F-2	F
RG 371	8	302	F-2	F
RG 372	8	302	F-2	F
EG 373	8	302	F-2	F
EG 380	8	302	F-2	F
EG 526	8	351C	F-2	H
EK 526	8	351C	F-2	H
EG 528	8	351C	F-2	H
EK 528	8	351C	F-2	H
RG 530	8	351C	F-2	H
RK 530	8	351C	F-2	H
EK 532	8	351C	F-2	H
EK 534	8	351C	F-2	H
EG 560	8	351C	F-2	H
EK 560	8	351C	F-2	H
RG 560	8	351C	F-2	H
RK 560	8	351C	F-2	H
EK 562	8	351C	F-2	H

Tag Code	Cyl.	CID	Carb.	Data Code
EG 570	8	351CJ	F-4	Q
EB 571	8	351CJ	F-4	Q
EG 572	8	351CJ	F-4	Q
K 600	8	351C	F-2	H
K 602	8	351C	F-2	H
KK 602	8	351C	F-2	H
K 603	8	351C	F-2	H
KK 603	8	351C	F-2	H
K 604	8	351C	F-2	H
KK 604	8	351C	F-2	H
K 605	8	351C	F-2	H
K 606	8	351C	F-2	H
K 608	8	351C	F-2	H
KK 608	8	351C	F-2	H
K 610	8	351C	F-2	H
K 612	8	351C	F-2	H
KK 612	8	351C	F-2	H
K 614	8	351C	F-2	H
KK 614	8	351C	F-2	H
K 616	8	351C	F-2	H
K 618	8	351C	F-2	H
KK 618	8	351C	F-2	H
K 620	8	351CJ	F-4	Q
KK 620	8	351CJ	F-4	Q
K 621	8	351CJ	F-4	Q
KK 621	8	351CJ	F-4	Q
K 622	8	351CJ	F-4	Q
K626	8	351CJ	F-4	Q
KK 626	8	351CJ	F-4	Q
K 632	8	351C	F-2	H
KK 632	8	351C	F-2	H
K 634	8	351C	F-2	H
KK 634	8	351C	F-2	H
K 637	8	351C	F-2	H
KK 637	8	351C	F-2	H
824	8	429CJ	F-4	C
826	8	429CJ	F-4	C
829	8	429SCJ	F-4	C
830	8	429SCJ	F-4	C
831	8	429SCJ	F-4	C
832	8	429SCJ	F-4	C
833	8	429CJ	F-4	C
834	8	429CJ	F-4	C
835	8	429SCJ	H-4	C
836	8	429SCJ	H-4	C
837	8	429SCJ	H-4	C
838	8	429SCJ	H-4	C

MUSTANG DISTRIBUTOR APPLICATION and IDENTIFICATION CHART, 1971

For 1971:	I.D.	Service Replacement	Diaphragm 12370	Cam 12210	Primary	Secondary	Vacuum	Stop 12202
					Springs (12191-2)			
250 M/T Calif.	D1OF-12127-AB	D1OZ-12127-A	304	111	241	233	229	7
250 A/T Calif.	D1OF-12127-BB	D1OZ-12127-B	304	117	237	244	225	5
250 A/T, M/T exc. Calif.	D1OF-12127-CA	D1OZ-12127-C	361	111	241	233	218	7
302-2V M/T	D0AF-12127-Y	D0AZ-12127-Y	356	113	236	235	217	1
302-2V A/T	D0AF-12127-T	D0OZ-12127-AL	310	113	236	252	217	3
302-4V M/T w/ T/E	D1FZ-12127-AA	D1ZZ-12127-A	363	112	238	235	225	
	D1FZ-12127-AB	D1ZZ-12127-A	363	112	238	235		
351-2V M/T Imco	D0OF-12127-E, -T	D2ZZ-12127-A	335	107	251	239		
351-2V A/T exc. Calif.	D0OF-12127-U	D0OZ-12127-U	303	107	241	233	217	1
351-4V M/T Imco	D0OF-12127-V	D0OZ-12127-V	356	107	238	233	217	5
351-2V A/T Calif.	D1OF-12127-GA	D2ZZ-12127-C	356	107	241	244	217	9
351-4V A/T exc. Calif.	D0OF-12127-G	D0OZ-12127-T	321	107	241	243	217	2
351-4V A/T	D1OF-12127-GA	D1OZ-12127-L	354	112	236	252	217	2
351-2V A/T Calif.	D2MF-12127-GA	D2MY-12127-G	398	113	238	235		
351-4V CJ	D1ZF-12127-BA	D1ZZ-12127-E, -G	317	112	238	244	229	9
Boss 351-4V M/T Imco	D1ZF-12127-DA	D1ZZ-12127-D	351	112	251	251	229	9
351-4V M/T	D1ZF-12127-EA	D1ZZ-12127-E	358	118	238	244	245	11
351-4V A/T	D1ZF-12127-FA	D1ZZ-12127-G	303	107	238	240	248	2
351-4V CJ A/T	D1ZF-12127-GA	D1ZZ-12127-G	307	107	242	233	250	2
429-S/CJ M/T w/ T/E 429-CJ M/T	D0OF-12127-J, -AA	D0OZ-12127-J	317	112	234	233	225	2
429-S/CJ A/T w/ T/E	D0OF-12127-Y	D0OZ-12127-K	354	108	236	233	247	12
429-S/CJ A/T	D1AF-12127-NA	D1AZ-12127-N	354	107	241	244	218	2

MUSTANG DISTRIBUTOR APPLICATION and IDENTIFICATION CHART, 1972-1973

For 1972:	I.D.	Service Replacement	Diaphragm 12370	Cam 12210	Primary	Secondary	Vacuum	Stop 12202
					Springs (12191-2)			
250 A/T Calif.	D2OF-12127-EA	D2OZ-12127-E	342	111	251	244		
250 A/T exc. Calif.	D2OF-12127-DA	D2OZ-12127-D	339	111	241	244		
250 M/T	D2OF-12127-PA	D2OZ-12127-P	340	110	234	240		
302-2V M/T	D2OF-12127-AA	D2OZ-12127-A	341	107	238	240		
302-2V A/T	D2ZF-12127-LA	D2OZ-12127-A	n/a	107	238	240		
302-2V A/T Calif.	D2OF-12127-JA	D2OZ-12127-J	326	113	237	252		
302-2V A/T exc. Calif.	D2OF-12127-HA	D2OZ-12127-H	326	113	237	252		
351-2V A/T exc. Calif.	D2AF-12127-KA	D2AZ-12127-K	329	107	241	233		
351-2V A/T Calif.	D2ZF-12127-CA	D2ZZ-12127-C	334	107	241	244		
351-2V M/T	D2ZF-12127-AA	D2ZZ-12127-A	335	107	251	239		
351-CJ M/T exc. Calif.	D2ZF-12127-EA	D3OZ-12127-F	399	107				
351-4V CJ M/T Calif.	D2ZF-12127-FA	D2ZZ-12127-F		107				
351-CJ A/T exc. Calif.	D2ZF-12127-GA	D2ZZ-12127-G	348	107	238	240		
351-4V CJ A/T Calif.	D2ZF-12127-HA	D2ZZ-12127-H	348	107	238	240		
	D2ZF-12127-HB	D2ZZ-12127-H	348	108	238	238		
For 1973:								
250 A/T exc. Calif.	D3OF-12127-RA	D3OZ-12127-R	331	103	205	219		
250 M/T	D3OF-12127-BA	D3OZ-12127-B	331	104	204	201		
250 A/T Calif.	D3OF-12127-LA	D3OZ-12127-L	331	104	204	213		
302-2V M/T	D3OF-12127-DA	D3OZ-12127-D	306	101	204	213		
302-2V M/T	D3PE-12127-MA	D3PZ-12127-M	306	101	204	213		
302-2V M/T, A/T	D3OF-12127-HB	D3OZ-12127-H	319	102	206	210		
302-2V A/T w/ 2.79:1, 3.00:1 Axle	D3OF-12127-JA	D3OZ-12127-J	321	102	215	206		
351-2V	D3OF-12127-GA	D3ZZ-12127-G	301	102	215	210		
	D3OF-12127-BA	D3ZZ-12127-B	309	102	202	208		
351-4V M/T	D3PE-12127-PA	D3PZ-12127-P	318	106	205	206		
351-4V A/T	D3OF-12127-GA	D3OZ-12127-G	302	101	205	206		

MUSTANG INTAKE MANIFOLD APPLICATION CHART

Year	Cyl/CID	Part Number
71	351 (See Note 1)	D1ZX-9424-DA
71	Boss 351	D1ZZ-9424-F
71	429 CJ	D1AZ-9424-B
71	429 SCJ	D0OZ-9424-B
71-73	302-2V	D1OZ-9424-A
71-73	351C-2V	D1AZ-9424-D
71	351 CJ	D1ZZ-9424-B
72	351 Special	D1ZZ-9424-B
72	351 CJ	D2ZZ-9424-A
73	302	D3OZ-9424-A
73	351C-2V	D4AZ-9424-C
73	351C-4V	D3ZZ-9424-A

Note 1: Unique Competition Part

MUSTANG WATER PUMP ASSEMBLY APPLICATION CHART, 1971-1973

Year	Engine	Part Number	Description / Notes
71/72	250	D2DZ-8501-A	r/b D5DZ-8501-A
71	302-2V	D0OZ-8501-C	
71	302-4V	D0ZZ-8501-B	
71/72	351	D0AZ-8501-E	Incl. (1) D0AZ-8513-A gasket r/b D2SZ-8501-A (2/75)
71	429	D1VY-8501-B	Incl. (1) ea.: C8VZ-8508-A & C8SZ-8513-A
72	302	D0OZ-8501-C	
72	Off-Hwy.	D0ZX-8501-A	Not Replaced
73	250	D5DZ-8501-A	PW-143
73	302	D6ZZ-8501-B	PW-153
73	351C	D6AZ-8501-A	PW-151

MUSTANG RADIATOR SHROUD APPLICATION CHART, 1971-1973

Year	Engine	Part Number	Description
71-73	250 (2)	D1ZZ-8146-B	Plastic, marked D1ZE-BA & BB D1ZE-BB not replaced.
71-73	302 (4)	D0OZ-8146-B	Plastic, marked D0OE-B
71	302 Special	D3ZZ-8146-A	Plastic - marked D1ZE-AA, D3ZE-AA or D3ZE-AB
71	302 (1)		
71	302 (2)		
72	302 (5)		
73	302 (2)		
71	351 (1)		
71	351 (2)		
71	351 (3)		
72/73	351 (All)		
71	429	D0OZ-8146-D	Plastic, marked D0OE-D; CJ & S/CJ

Notes:
1 - Extra Cooling
2 - w/ A/C
3 - Boss, Std. Cooling
4 - Standard Cooling
5 - w/ A/C & Extra Cooling

MUSTANG RADIATOR APPLICATION CHART, 1971-1973

Year	Engine	Notes	Core Width	Core Height	Core Thickness	Part Number
71	250	1,2,3	21.75	17.875	1.5	D1AZ-8005-B
	302-2V	1	21.75	17.875	1.5	D1AZ-8005-B
	429-CJ	1	26	17.875	2.25	D1VY-8005-A
	302-2V	2	26	17.875	1.5	D2ZZ-8005-C
	351	1, 4	26	17.875	1.5	D2ZZ-8005-C
	351	1,2,3,5	26	17.875	1.5	D2ZZ-8005-C
	351-CJ	1	26	17.875	2.25	D1ZZ-8005-B
	429-S/CJ	1	26	17.875	2.25	D1ZZ-8005-B
	429-CJ	2, 3	26	17.875	2.25	D1ZZ-8005-B
	Boss 351	1	26	17.875	2.25	D1ZZ-8005-B
	351-CJ	3	26	17.875	2.25	D1VY-8005-A
72	250	1,3	21.75	17.875	1.5	D2ZZ-8005-A
	302-2V	1	21.75	17.875	1.5	D2ZZ-8005-A
	302-2V	2,3	26	17.875	1.5	D2ZZ-8005-C
	351-2V	1,2,3	26	17.875	1.5	D2ZZ-8005-C
	351 H.O.	1	26	17.875	2.25	D2ZZ-8005-B
73	250	1,3,6	21.75	17.875	1.5	D3ZZ-8005-B
	302	1,6	21.75	17.875	1.5	D3ZZ-8005-B
	302	2,3,7	26	17.875	1.5	D3ZZ-8005-C
	351-2V	1,2,3,7	26	17.875	1.5	D3ZZ-8005-C
	351-4V	1,2,3,7	26	17.875	1.5	D3ZZ-8005-C

Notes:
1 Standard Cooling
2 Extra Cooling
3 w/ Air Conditioning
4 w/ 3.50:1 rear axle
5 Except CJ
6 Not Replaced (6/2/78)
7 Not Replaced (2/24/81)

MUSTANG FAN BLADE ASSEMBLY APPLICATION CHART, 1971-1973
Note: All assemblies have 5/8-inch hole.

Year	Engine	Notes	Description	Blades	Diameter	Part Number
71-73	250	1	Marked C6AE-E, C9OE-A	4	17-1/2"	C6OZ-8600-A
	302	1, 2				
71	351	1, 2				
73	351	1, 2, 6				
71-73	250	3	Marked C8SE-D, D0ZZ-B	5	17-1/2"	C8SZ-8600-B
71	302/351	3	Marked D0AE-A, D1AE-CA	5	18-1/2"	D0AZ-8600-A
	302 Spec.	2				
	Boss 351	2				
72	351 CJ	1, 4				
71	429 CJ		or S/CJ; Marked D0OE-A	7	19	D0OZ-8600-A
72	302/351	3	Marked D2SE-AA	5	18-1/2"	D2SZ-8600-A
	351 CJ	1, 3, 5				
72	351-2V	1, 2	Marked D2OE-AA,-AB	4	18-1/2"	D2OZ-8600-A
73	351	1, 2, 7				
73	302/351	8	Marked D9AE-EA, D7AE-AA	5	18-1/2"	D9AZ-8600-A
73	302/351	9	Marked D1DE-BA	7	17-9/16"	D3DZ-8600-A

Notes:
1 - Standard Cooling
2 - Extra Cooling
3 - with A/C
4 - with Auto Trans
5 - with Manual Trans
6 - Before 2/19/73
7 - After 2/19/73
8 - w/ Factory-installed A/C
9 - w/ Dealer-installed A/C

MUSTANG RADIATOR HOSE APPLICATION CHART, 1971-1973

Year	Engine	Notes	Int. Diam.	Length	Motorcraft #	Part Number
71/72	250	M, U	1-1/2"	15-9/16"	KM-137	D0OZ-8260-A
		M, L	1-1/2" & 1-7/8"	18-1/4"	KM-374	D1OZ-8286-B
71	250	F, U	1-1/2"	20"	KB-200	C9PZ-8286-L
		F, L	1-1/2" & 1-3/4"	20"	KBC-200	C9PZ-8260-P
71/72	302	M, U	1-1/2"	20-1/2"	KM-136	D0AZ-8260-A
71	302 Spec.	M, L	1-1/2" & 1-3/4"	20-7/8"	KM-383	D1OZ-8286-C
71	302	F, U	n/a			
	302 Spec.	F, L	1-1/2" & 1-3/4"	20"	KBC-200	C9PZ-8260-P
71	351	M, U	1-1/2"	24-15/16"	KM-412	D2OZ-8260-D
		M, L	1-1/2" & 1-3/4"	20-7/8"	KM-383	D1OZ-8286-C
71	351	F, U	1-1/2"	25"	KB-250	C9PZ-8260-Z
		F, L	1-1/2" & 1-3/4"	20"	KBC-200	C9PZ-8260-P
71	429 CJ, S/CJ	M, U	1-3/4"	14-1/2"	KM-297	D1VY-8260-A
		M, L	1-1/2" & 2"	17-9/16"	KM-376	D1SZ-8286-A
71	429 CJ, S/CJ	F, U	1-1/2"	25"	KB-170	C9PZ-8260-L
71/72	351 Spec.	M, U	1-1/2"	24-15/16"	KM-412	D2OZ-8260-D
72	351 CJ	M, L	1-1/2" & 1-3/4"	20-7/8"	KM-383	D1OZ-8286-C
73	250	M, U	1-1/2"	17-15/16"	KM-389	D0OZ-8260-E
		M, L	1-1/2" & 1-7/8"	18-1/4"	KM-374	D1OZ-8286-B
73	302	M, U	1-1/2"	17-15/16"	KM-389	D0OZ-8260-E
		M, L	1-1/2" & 1-3/4"	22"	KM-369	D1AZ-8286-A
73	351	M, U	1-1/2"	24-15/16"	KM-412	D2OZ-8260-D
		M, L	1-1/2" & 1-3/4"	22"	KM-369	D1AZ-8286-A

Notes:
M - Molded Hose
F - Flexible Hose, to be used when Molded hoses are not available.
U - Upper Hose
L - Lower Hose

MUSTANG AIR CONDITIONER COMPRESSOR CLUTCH APPLICATION CHART, 1971-1973

Year	Model	Type	Identification	Part Number	M'craft
71/73	250	5C	C9OA-2981-E	C9OZ-2884-B	YB-34
71	302, 351, Before 10/26/70	5B	D1ZA-2981-AA	D1ZZ-2884-A r/b D1OZ-2884-A	
71/73	302, 351, From 10/26/70	5B	D1OA-2981-AA, -A1A, -A1B, -A2A, -A2B, D2ZZ-2981-A1A, -A1B, -A2A.	D1OZ-2884-A	YB-19
71	429	5A	C9AA-2981-E, -E1, -E2, D0VA-2981-A, D2OA-2981-CA	C9AZ-2884-E r/b C9AZ-2884-K	
72	Use w/ Hang-On A/C	6C	C9RJ-2981-A	C9RZ-2884-A r/b C9AZ-2884-L	
73	Dealer Installed A/C			C9AZ-2884-L r/b D2AZ-2884-A	
73	Dealer Installed, w/ Ogura Clutch & A/C			D2AZ-2884-A	YN-82

MUSTANG AIR CONDITIONER COMPRESSOR CLUTCH & PULLEY I.D. CHART, 1971-1973
Please refer to accompanying A/C Clutch Application Chart
Also, please refer to Reference Illustration, Page 169.

Part Number	Type	A	B	C	D	E	*	Notes
C9OZ-2884-B	5C	6-1/4"	1-7/16"	3/8"	3/8"	1	2	Pitts **
D1ZZ-2884-A	5B	6-5/16"	1-11/16"	3/8"	1/2"	5-1/8"	1	**
D1OZ-2884-A	5B	6-5/16"	1-11/16"	3/8"	1/2"	5-1/8"	1	Pitts **
C9AZ-2884-E	5A	6"	1-3/8"	3/8"	1/2"			Pitts **
C9RZ-2884-A	6C	6-1/8"	1-7/8"	3/8"	3/8"	1-3/8"	2	***
D2AZ-2884-A	3A	6-1/8"	1-7/8"	3/8"	3/8"	1-3/8"	2	***

* - No. of Sheaves
** - use w/ C9AZ-2987-A
*** - use w/ C8SZ-2987-A

ACCELERATOR PEDAL-to-CARBURETOR THROTTLE CABLE ASSEMBLIES, 1971-1973

Year	Engine	Description	Part Number
71	250	Before 4/1/71; 34" long, Identified by color Blue on center conduit. r/b D1ZZ-9A758-E (12/74)	D1ZZ-9A758-C
71/72	250	From 4/1/71 to 7/10/72; 33.50" long.	D1ZZ-9A758-E
72	250	From 7/10/72; 32.50" long.	D3ZZ-9A758-A
71	429 CJ & SCJ	Before 4/1/71; 23.75" long, Identified by color Brown on center conduit. r/b D1ZZ-9A758-G (12/74)	D1ZZ-9A758-A
71	429 CJ & SCJ	From 4/1/71; 23.75" long.	D1ZZ-9A758-A
71/72	302-2V 351-2V, -4V	Before 7/10/72; 22.50" long.	D1ZZ-9A758-H
72	302, 351-2V	From 7/10/72; 23" long.	D3ZZ-9A758-B
72	351-4V	From 7/10/72; 23.25" long.	D3ZZ-9A758-C
73	250	32.50" long, not replaced.	D3ZZ-9A758-A
73	302, 351-2V	23" long, not replaced.	D3ZZ-9A758-B
73	351-4V	23.25" long, not replaced.	D3ZZ-9A758-C

MUSTANG AIR CLEANER ASSEMBLY & ELEMENT APPLICATION CHART, 1971-1973

Year	Engine	Model	Description	Part Number	Element
71/73	250		14.62" diam.; 3.24" high	D1OZ-9600-C	
71	302-2V		17.84" diam.; 4.20" high	D1AZ-9600-G	C8AZ-9601-A (FA-50)
71	351		17.84" diam.; 4.20" high	D1AZ-9600-F	C8AZ-9601-A (FA-50)
71-72	351	w/ Ram Air	19.70" diam.; 6.44" high	D1ZZ-9600-C	C8AZ-9601-A (FA-50)
71	BOSS 351	w/ Ram Air	19.70" diam.; 6.44" high	D1ZZ-9600-C	C8AZ-9601-A (FA-50)
71	429-CJ	w/o Ram Air	17.76" diam.; 4.10" high	D1AZ-9600-H	C8AZ-9601-A (FA-50)
71	429-CJ	w/ Ram Air	18.62" diam.; 4.97" high	D1ZZ-9600-F	D0GY-9601-A (FA-74)
71	429-SCJ	w/o Ram Air	16.79" diam.; 3.66" high	D1AZ-9600-D	B7SZ-9601-A (FA-41)
71	429-SCJ	w/ Ram Air		D1ZZ-9600-A	C8AZ-9601-A (FA-50)
72	302	w/o NOX		D2AZ-9600-A	D2AZ-9601-A (FA-97)
72	302	w/ NOX	14.78" diam.; 4.68" high	D4AZ-9600-A	
72	351-2V		14.78" diam.; 4.68" high	D4AZ-9600-A	
72	351-4V	w/o Ram Air	17.84" diam.; 4.20" high	D1AZ-9600-F	C8AZ-9601-A (FA-50)
72	351-CJ	w/o Ram Air	16.75" diam.; 3.63" high Chrome Cover	D3ZZ-9600-B	
73	250	Man. Trans.		D3DZ-9600-B	D4ZZ-9601-AR
73	250	Auto. Trans.	Before 3/12/73	D3DZ-9600-B	D4ZZ-9601-AR
73	250	Auto. Trans.	After 3/12/73	D3DZ-9600-C	D4ZZ-9601-AR
73	302 351-2V	w/o Ram Air		D3ZZ-9600-AR	D3ZZ-9601-AR
73	351-2V	w/ Ram Air		D3ZZ-9600-C	B7SZ-9601-A (FA-41)
73	351-4V			D4OZ-9600-D	D7AZ-9601-BR

CARBURETOR APPLICATION CHART
Mustang 250 cid 6-Cylinder Engines, 1971-1973

Year	Note	Type	Identification	Part Number	Replaced By:
71	1	C-1	D1ZF-HA	D1ZZ-9510-H	D2OZ-9510-A
71	2	C-1	D1ZF-JA	D1ZZ-9510-J	D2OZ-9510-A
71	3	C-1	D1ZF-KA	D1ZZ-9510-K	D2OZ-9510-A
71	4	C-1	D1ZF-LA	D1ZZ-9510-L	D2OZ-9510-A
71	5	C-1	D1ZF-MA	D1ZZ-9510-M	D2OZ-9510-A
71	6	C-1	D1ZF-NA	D1ZZ-9510-N	D2OZ-9510-A
71		C-1	D1PF-FA	D1ZZ-9510-R	D2OZ-9510-A
72	7	C-1	D2OF-LA	D2OZ-9510-L	D2OZ-9510-A
72	8	C-1	D2OF-MA	D2OZ-9510-M	D2OZ-9510-A
72		C-1	D2PF-BA, D2OF-SA	D2OZ-9510-A	
73	8	C-1	D3OF-CA, -CB, -CC	D3OZ-9510-C	D4PZ-9510-AJ
73	7	C-1	D3OF-BC	D3OZ-9510-B	D4PZ-9510-AJ
73		C-1	D4PE-AJA	D4PZ-9510-AJ	

Notes:

1   Manual Transmission, exc. California
2   C4 - w/o AC, exc. California
3   C4 - w/ AC, exc. California
4   Manual Transmission, California only
5   C4 - w/o AC, California only
6   C4 - w/ AC, California only
7   Manual Transmission
8   Automatic Transmission

CARBURETOR APPLICATION CHART
Mustang 302 cid 8-Cylinder Engines, 1971-1973

Year	Note	Type	Identification	Part Number	Replaced By:
71	1	F-4	D2PF-SA	D2AZ-9510-M	
71	2	F-4	C8ZF-L	C8ZF-9510-L	D2AZ-9510-M
71	1	F-4	C8ZF-A, -B	C8ZF-9510-A	D2AZ-9510-M
71	3	H-4	D0PF-AN	D0PZ-9510-U	not replaced
71	4	H-4	C9OF-R	C9OZ-9510-N	
71	5	F-2	D1AF-BA	D1AZ-9510-B	D2AZ-9510-D
71		F-2	D1AF-DA, D10F-ABA, D10F-AGA, D1ZF-ADA		D2AZ-9510-D
71	6	F-2	D1AF-SA	D1AZ-9510-S	D2AZ-9510-D
71	6	F-2	D1AF-DA, -ZA	D1AZ-9510-D	D2AZ-9510-D
71	7	F-2	D1ZF-AA	D1ZF-9510-A	D2AZ-9510-D
72	5	F-2	D2OF-KA		D2AZ-9510-D
72	8, 9	F-2	D2ZF-FA		D2AZ-9510-D
72		F-2	D2GF-AA, -AB, -AC, -BA, -BB, -BC, D2AF-HB, -HC, D2PF-GA, -GB, D2OF-KB, -VA, D2ZF-FB, -MA, D4PE-FA	D2AZ-9510-D	D2AZ-9510-P
72		F-2	D4PE-EA, -EB, -EC	D2AZ-9510-P	
73	5	F-2	D3OF-AD	D3OZ-9510-A	D4PZ-9510-G
73	10	F-2	D3GF-AD	D3GY-9510-A	D4PZ-9510-G
73		F-2	D3AF-ABA, D3DE-BA D3DF-EA, D3GF-BA, -BB, -BC D3OF-EA, -FA, -JA D3PF-EA, -EB D3ZF-EA, -EB, -GA	D3OZ-9510-D	D4PZ-9510-G
73		F-2	D3ZF-NA, D4PE-CFA	D3PZ-9510-CF	
73		F-2	D3GF-AE, -AF, D4OE-JA D4PE-CGA	D3PZ-9510-CG	

Notes:
1. Open Emission
2. w/ Auto Trans; Open Emission
3. Standard Bowl, 600 cfm
4. Center Pivot, 600 cfm
5. w/ Manual Transmission
6. w/ C/M, C-4, w/o A/C
7. w/ C/M, C-4, w/ A/C
8. w/ A/T & A/C exc. California
9. California only, w/ or w/o A/C
10. w/ Automatic Transmission

CARBURETOR APPLICATION CHART
Mustang 351 cid 8-Cylinder Engines, 1971-1972

Year	Note	Type	Identification	Part Number	Replaced By:
71		F-4	D0PF-AG, D10F-AAA	D00Z-9510-U	D2AZ-9510-M
71	11	H-4	D0PF-AN	D0PZ-9510-U	
71	12	H-4	C9OF-R	C9OZ-9510-N	
71	1	F-2	D10F-PA	D10Z-9510-P	D2AZ-9510-C
71	2	F-2	D1MF-KA, D10F-RA, -YA -ZA, D1ZF-SA, -UA, -ACA	D1ZZ-9510-S	D2AZ-9510-C
71	1	F-4	D10F-EA	D10Z-9510-E	D2AZ-9510-M
71	3	F-4	D10F-FA	D10Z-9510-F	D2AZ-9510-M
71	4	F-2	D1MF-KA, D10F-RA, -YA -ZA, -AHA, -AJA, D1ZF-SA, -UA, -ACA, -AEA	D10Z-9510-C	D2AZ-9510-M
71	5	F-4	D1ZF-FA, -GA	D1ZZ-9510-C	D4OZ-9510-F
71	6	F-4	D1ZF-ZA	D1ZZ-9510-Z	D4OZ-9510-F
71/72		F-4	D4PE-AA, D5PE-GB	D4OZ-9510-F	
72	7	F-2	D2AF-FB, -FC, -FD, -GB, -GC, -GD, D2PF-GA, -GB, D4PE-FA	D2AZ-9510-D	D2AZ-9510-P
72	4	F-2	D2MF-CB, D2OF-PA, -RA, -UA, -UB, -UC, D2PF-HA, -HB, D2WF-CA, -CB, D2ZF-KA, -LA, -LB, LC, D3PF-DA, D4PE-FA, -FB	D2AZ-9510-C	
72	8	F-2	D2OF-JA	D2OZ-9510-J	D2AZ-9510-C
72	7	F-2	D4PE-EA, EB, -EC	D2AZ-9510-P	
72	13	F-4	D2PF-TA, D2ZF-BB	D2AZ-9510-N	D4OZ-9510-F
72		F-4	D2ZF-GA	D2ZZ-9510-G	D4OZ-9510-F
72	13, 1, 10	F-4	D2ZF-AA	D2ZZ-9510-A	D4OZ-9510-F
72	13, 8, 10	F-4	D2ZF-BA	D2ZZ-9510-B	D4OZ-9510-F
72	13, 1, 9	F-4	D2ZF-CA	D2ZZ-9510-C	D4OZ-9510-F
72	13, 8, 9	F-4	D2ZF-DA	D2ZZ-9510-D	D4OZ-9510-F
72	1	F-2	D2ZF-EA	D2ZZ-9510-E	D2AZ-9510-C

Notes:
1. w/ Manual Transmission — F-2 Ford Two-barrel
2. w/ C-4 & C/M — F-4 Ford Four-barrel
3. w/ C-6 — H-4 Holley Four-barrel
4. 351 Cleveland
5. Boss & Cobra Jet
6. Boss
7. 351 Windsor
8. w/ Automatic Transmission
9. California
10. except California
11. w/ Manual, or C-4 & C/M, 600 cfm
12. Center Pivot, 600 cfm
13. Cobra Jet

CARBURETOR APPLICATION CHART
Mustang 429 cid 8-Cylinder Engines, 1971

Year	Note	Type	Identification	Part Number
71	1	R-4	D0OF-B	D0OZ-9510-B
71	2	H-4	D1ZF-YA	D1ZZ-9510-Y
71	3	H-4	D1ZZ-XA	D1ZZ-9510-X

Notes:
1. Cobra Jet
2. Super Cobra Jet w/ Manual Transmission
3. Super Cobra Jet w/ C-6 Transmission
R-4. Rochester Four-barrel Quadra-Jet
H-4. Holley Four-barrel

CARBURETOR APPLICATION CHART
Mustang 351 cid 8-Cylinder Engines, 1973

Year	Note	Type	Identification	Part Number	Replaced By:
73	4	F-2	D3WF-AC	D3WY-9510-A	D4PZ-9510-H
73	7	F-2	D3AF-CE, -DB, -DC, -JA, -KA, -MA, -NA, -PA, -RA -RB, -UA, -XA, -D3PF-FA, -FB, D3WF-CA, D3ZF-FA	D3AZ-9510-E	D4PZ-9510-H
73	1	F-4	D3ZF-BC	D3ZZ-9510-B	D4OZ-9510-F
73	8	F-4	D3ZF-AC	D3ZZ-9510-A	D4OZ-9510-F
73		F-4	D3PF-BA, D3ZF-JA, -KA, -LA, -MA	D3ZZ-9510-E	D4OZ-9510-F
73		F-4	D3ZF-DC	D3ZZ-9510-D	D4OZ-9510-F
73	10	H-4	D8PE-KA	D8PZ-9510-K	
73	9	H-4	D8PE-LA	D8PZ-9510-L	not replaced

Notes:
1. w/ Manual Transmission — F-2 Ford Two-barrel
4. 351 Cleveland — F-4 Ford Four-barrel
7. 351 Windsor — H-4 Holley Four-barrel
8. w/ Automatic Transmission
9. California
10. except California

MUSTANG FUEL PUMP ASSEMBLY CHART, 1971-1973

Year	Cyl/CID	Part Number	Description
71/72	250	C8DZ-9350-A	Carter, identified by 4532-S or 4531-S, stamped on mounting flange. r/b D3TZ-9350-A
71/72	250	D3TZ-9350-A	Carter, identified D3TE-AA and also 6399-S on mounting flange
71	429 S/CJ	C9AZ-9350-A	Carter, identified by 4892-S stamped on mounting flange.
71/72	351	D0AZ-9350-A	Carter, identified D0AE-E and also 6399-S on mounting flange
71/72	302-2V	D0AZ-9350-B	Carter, identified by 4896-S or SA stamped on mounting flange. r/b D3OZ-9350-B
71/72	302-2V	D3OZ-9350-B	Carter, identified by MS-6477-S stamped on mounting flange.
71	429 CJ	D0OZ-9350-A	Carter, identified by 4907-S stamped on mounting flange.
73	250	D3DZ-9350-A	Carter, less filter
73	302	D4OZ-9350-B	Carter
73	351	D0AZ-9350-A	Carter

MUSTANG FUEL TANK FILLER CAP APPLICATION CHART, 1971-1973

Year	Model	Part Number	Description
71-73	All except Mach 1	D2ZZ-9030-A	"Mustang" Emblem
71/72	All except Mach 1	D2PZ-9030-C	Stainless Steel
71/72	Mach 1	D1ZZ-9030-C	Pop-Off Type Cap Assembly
71-73	Except Mach 1	D1PZ-9030-E	Locking

MUSTANG FUEL TANK UNIT GAUGE ASSEMBLY CHART, 1971-1973

Year	Model	Part Number	Description
71/73	250/302/351	D1ZZ-9275-A	Includes C0AF-9276-A Gasket, identified D1ZF-9275-AA, -AB, -AC
71	429	D1ZZ-9275-B	Includes C0AF-9276-A Gasket, identified D1ZF-9275-BA

351 4V, CJ, Boss, and H.O. Engines

Like the 429, CJ, and SCJ, Ford's 335 Series 351-4V, CJ, Boss, and H.O. engines, installed in 1971 and 1972 Mustangs, are a breed apart. Compare the following statistics:

Horsepower (bhp @ rpm)
4V	285 @ 5400
CJ	280 @ 5800
Boss	330 @ 5400
4V/CJ (1972; SAE net)	266 @ 5400
H.O. (1972; SAE net)	275 @ 6000

Torque (lb-ft @ rpm)
4V	370 @ 3400
CJ	345 @ 3800
Boss	370 @ 4000
4V/CJ (1972; SAE net)	301 @ 3600
H.O. (1972; SAE net)	286 @ 3800

Compression Ratio
4V	10.7:1
CJ	9.0:1
Boss	11.7:1
4V/CJ (1972)	9.0:1
H.O. (1972)	9.2:1

Cylinder Head Combustion Chamber Volume (cc)
4V and Boss	64.6-67.6
1971 CJ and 1972 4V/CJ/H.O.	73.9-76.9

Crankshaft Material
Nodular iron/Boss selected for hardness

Connecting Rod Material
All: 1041-H forged steel. Boss and H.O. rods are magnafluxed and shot peened and include 180,000psi nut and bolt.

Piston Material
4V and CJ	Cast aluminum
Boss	Forged aluminum pop-up
H.O.	Forged aluminum flat-top

Cam Timing (open/close, in degrees)
	Intake	Exhaust
4V	14/72	70/20
CJ	18/72	82/28
4V/CJ (1972)	14/76	78/32
Boss	34/76	86/23
H.O. (1972)	17.5/77.5	77.5/17.5

Cam Duration/Overlap (in degrees)
	Intake/Exhaust/Overlap
4V	226/270/34
CJ (1971/1972)	270/290/46
Boss	290/390/58
H.O. (1972)	275/275/35

Valve Lift with 1.73:1 Ratio Rocker Arms (in inches)
	Intake	Exhaust
4V	0.427	0.427
CJ (1971/1972)	0.480	0.488
Boss	0.477	0.477
H.O. (1972)	0.491	0.491

Tappets
Hydraulic	4V and CJ
Mechanical	Boss and H.O.

Block
4V	2-bolt main caps
CJ (1971/1972)	4-bolt main caps
Boss & H.O.	selected for hardness 4-bolt main caps

Cylinder Heads
1971:
4V	Quench combustion chamber, non-adjustable rocker arm pedestal.
CJ	Open combustion chamber, induction hardened exhaust valve seats, otherwise same as 4V.
Boss	Quench combustion chamber, otherwise same as 4V except rocker arm pedestal machined for mechanical lifters.

1972:
CJ	Same as 1971 CJ.
H.O.	Open combustion chamber, otherwise same as 1971 Boss.

Valve Stem Locks
1971:
4V	Multi-groove
CJ	Multi-groove
Boss	Single groove

1972:
CJ	Multi-groove
H.O.	Single groove

Rocker Arm Stud
1971:
4V	5/16in bolt, non-adjustable
CJ	5/16in bolt, non-adjustable
Boss	7/16in threaded, adjustable

1972:
CJ	5/16in bolt, non-adjustable
H.O.	7/16in threaded, adjustable

Distributor
1971:
4V	Single point
CJ	Dual point
Boss	Dual point, same as CJ except for calibration

1972:
CJ	Single point
H.O.	Dual point, same as Boss

Harmonic Balancer
1971:
4V	0.10 inertia, cast-iron hub, cast-iron inertia ring, non-bonded elastic member, 28.2oz-in unbalance
CJ	Same as 4V
Boss	0.14 inertia, nodular iron hub, wider cast-iron inertia ring, bonded elastic member, 27.3oz-in unbalance

1972:
CJ	Same as 4V
H.O.	Same as Boss

Flywheel
1971:
4V	Cast-iron, 28.2oz-in unbalance
CJ	Same as 4V
Boss	Nodular iron, 27.3oz-in unbalance

1972:
CJ	Same as 4V
H.O.	Same as Boss

1971 4V and CJ Comparison:
Compared to the stock 4V, the CJ hydraulic camshaft had more duration and overlap. The 1971 CJ block had four-bolt caps on the number 2, 3, and 4 mains while the 4V has two-bolt caps throughout. CJ heads had the Cleveland 2V open combustion chambers but retained the large 4V valves and gigantic ports.

1972 4V/CJ Comparison:
Ford dropped the Cobra Jet name in 1972. As a result, the 1972 351C-4V is the same as the 1971 Cobra Jet except the engineers retarded the valve timing 4 degrees in 1972.

1971 Boss and 1972 H.O. Comparison:
With some major changes in piston and cylinder head design, the 1971 Boss 351 became the 351C H.O. in 1972. Boss heads featured quench combustion chambers compared to the H.O.'s 2V open chamber design. However, H.O. heads retained the 4V big valves and ports. Also, both heads are machined for adjustable rocker arms to accommodate their solid lifter camshafts. Additionally, Boss pistons have a high dome to increase compression ratio to 11.7:1. The H.O. engines have forged flat-top pistons resulting in a modest 9.2:1 compression ratio. The increased compression combined with a slightly larger camshaft account for the power difference.

DRIVETRAIN

Exploded views of Mustang drivetrains can save a restorer weeks of headaches. While the years 1964 to 1970 gave Mustangers a variety of drivetrain assemblies and components, the years 1971 to 1973 gave us simplification. The Mustang image was one of power and style; the reality gave us compromises that stressed economy and clean air.

As we noted in the introduction to Chapter 5 of this book, the drivetrain can't be seen by the average show judge or admirer. Those viewers cannot know that many restored Mustangs must accommodate replacement assemblies. Compatibility of these assemblies or sub-assemblies is an absolute necessity to the car owner.

Please note that all 1971-1973 manual and automatic transmissions are identical to those covered in Chapter 5 of this book. Similarly, the rear axles, drive shafts, U-joints, and yokes are the same, and can be found in that chapter.

Over the years Ford has managed to maintain a surprisingly broad and complete stock of drivetrain parts. Their decisions to keep such parts in the supply system is based upon supply and demand. Owners have been interested in keeping a significant number of Mustangs on the road. The reader may find, in this section and in Chapter 5, part numbers that still apply and that will be, if not perfectly accurate (due to Ford's consolidation procedures), guidelines to service department personnel in locating needed items.

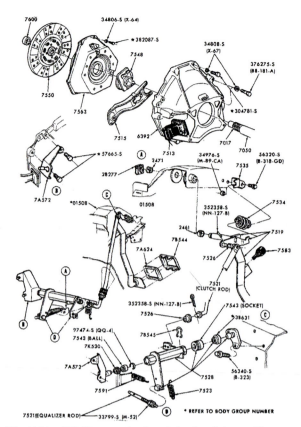

The 1971-1973 Mustang clutch and clutch pedal assembly.

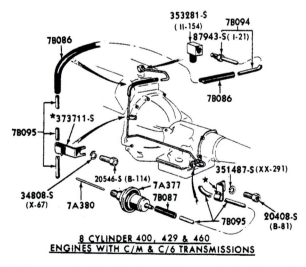

The vacuum throttle valve, lines, fittings, and related parts for 1971 Mustangs equipped with a 429ci engine and C/M or C6 transmission.

MUSTANG AUTOMATIC TRANSMISSIONS, 1971-1973

Year	Transmission Code	Engine CID	Transmission Type
71	PEE-AD2	250	C-4
71 & 72	PEE-AD3-AD4	250	C-4
71	PEE-AC2	302	C-4
71 & 72	PEE-AC3-AC4	302	C-4
71	PHB-E2-E3	351-2V	FMX
71	PGA-AV	351-2V	C-6
71	PGA-AH	351-4V	C-6
71	PGA-AU	351-CJ	C-6
71	PSC-G	429	C-6
72	PEA-BA	351-2V	C-6
72	PHA-H-H1-H2	302	FMX
72	PGA-AV1	351-2V	C-6
71 & 72	PEE-AD3-AD4	250	C-4
71 & 72	PEE-AC3-AC4	302	C-4
72	PHB-E4-E5-E6		FMX
72	PGA-AU1-AU2	351-CJ	C-6
72	PJC-G1	351-4V	C-6
73	PEE-AD6	250	C-4
73	PEE-AC6	302	C-4
73	PHA-H3	302	FMX
73	PHB-E7	351	FMX
73	PCA-AV2	351-C	C-6
73	PGA-AU3	351-CJ	C-6

1971-1973 MUSTANG MANUAL TRANSMISSION TAG CODES by YEAR and DRIVETRAIN

Year	Model	Trans	Part Number	Transmission I.D.
71	6/250	3.03	D0ZZ-7003-A	RAN-AV1
71	6/250	3.03	D2ZZ-7003-A	RAN-BW
71	302-2V	3.03	D0ZZ-7003-B	RAT-BA1
71	302	3.03	D2ZZ-7003-B	RAN-CA
71	302-2V	3.03	D1ZZ-7003-A	RAN-BM
71	302 Spec.; 351-4V; 351 Spec.	F/4/S	D0ZZ-7003-D	RUG-AV1 r/b D2ZZ-D 2.78 1st Gear
71	302 Special; 351-4V	F/4/S	D0ZZ-7003-E	RUG-AW1, 2.32 1st Gear
71	351 CJ & Boss	F/4/S	D2ZZ-7003-D	RUG-BJ, 2.32 1st Gear
71	351-2V	3.03	D0ZZ-7003-C	RAT-BB1; RAT-BB2
71	351-2V	3.03	D2ZZ-7003-C	RAT-BZ
71	429	F/4/S	D0ZZ-7003-H	RUG-AZ1
72	6/250	3.03	D2ZZ-7003-A	RAN-BW; Before 12/1/71
72	6/250	3.03	D2ZZ-7003-E	RAN-BW1; After 12/1/71
72	302	3.03	D2ZZ-7003-B	RAN-CA; Before 12/1/71
72	302	3.03	D2ZZ-7003-F	RAN-CA1; After 12/1/71
72	351-2V	3.03	D2ZZ-7003-C	RAT-BZ; Before 12/1/71
72	351-2V	3.03	D2ZZ-7003-G	RAT-BZ1; After 12/1/71
72	351 CJ	F/4/S	D2ZZ-7003-D	RUG-BJ; Before 12/1/71
72	351 CJ	3.03	D2ZZ-7003-H	RUG-BJ1; After 12/1/71
73	6/250	3.03	D2ZZ-7003-E	RAN-BW1
73	302	3.03	D2ZZ-7003-F	RAN-CA1
73	351 CJ; 351 HO	F/4/S	D2ZZ-7003-H	RUG-BJ1

MUSTANG CLUTCH DISC and PRESSURE PLATE CHART, 1968-1973

Note: Due to error, chart on p. 222 ran only through 1967. Missing items included here.

Year	Model and Description	CID	Trans.	Disc Springs*	Diam.	Matching Disc	Plate
67/70	6 cyl.	200	3.03	6-Pink	9"	C7OZ-7550-C	C6DZ-7563-C
68	8 cyl.	390	All	6L-3S	11"	D1OZ-7550-A	C6OZ-7563-E
68/70	428CJ, SCJ	428	F/4/S	5L-5S	11-1/2"	C6AZ-7550-D	D1OZ-7563-A
68-71	Before 6/15/71	302	All	6L-Pink 6S-Orange	10"	C6OZ-7550-G	C2OZ-7563-F
69	351; 390		All	6L-3S	11"	D1OZ-7550-A	C9OZ-7563-A
69/70	Boss 302	302	F/4/S	8-Gray	10-1/2"	C7ZZ-7550-B	C7ZZ-7563-B
71/72	After 6/15/71	302	All	6L-Pink 6S-Orange	10"	C6OZ-7550-G	C2OZ-7563-A
69/71	Before 6/15/71	250	3.03	6L-6S	10"	C6OZ-7550-G	C9OZ-7563-B
71	After 6/15/71	250	3.03	6L-6S	10"	C6OZ-7550-G	D2OZ-7563-A
71		429	F/4/S	5L-5S	11-1/2"	C5AZ-7550-D	D1OZ-7563-A
71/72	Boss & CJ	351	All	6L-Purple	11"	D2OZ-7550-C	D1ZZ-7563-C
73	6	250	3.03	6L-Orange 4S-Orange	10"	D2OZ-7550-A	D2OZ-7563-A
73	8	351-4V	All	6L-Purple 6S-Green	11"	D2OZ-7550-C	D1ZZ-7563-C
73	8	302	3.03	6L-Pink 6S-Orange	10"	C6OZ-7550-G	D2OZ-7563-A

* If no color noted, color is natural.

MUSTANG SPEEDOMETER CABLE APPLICATION CHART, 1971-1973
For '71-'73 Drive Gear and Driven Gear I.D. Charts, see p. 234. All gears apply.

Year	Model	Trans.	Length	Remarks	Part Number
71	All	C-4	61-1/2"		D1ZZ-17260-G r/b D4FZ-17260-A
71/72	V-8	C-6	61-1/2"	w/o 3.91 or 4.11 Rear	D1ZZ-17260-G r/b D4FZ-17260-A
71	V-8	C-6	57-13/16"	w/ 3.91 or 4.11 Rear C8ZZ-17294-A Adapter Required	D1ZZ-17260-E
71	V-8, exc. Boss & 351-4V Special	4/M/T	66-1/2"	w/o 3.91 or 4.11 Rear	D1ZZ-17260-G
72	V-8, exc. 351 HO	4/M/T	66-1/2"	w/o 3.91 or 4.11 Rear	D1ZZ-17260-G
71	302-4V HO & 351 HO	4/M/T	71-13/16"	w/ 3.91 or 4.11 Rear C8ZZ-17294-A Adapter Required	D1ZZ-17260-F
73	All	3/M/T	54"		D5AY-17260-A
73	All	A/T & 4/M/T	67"	Adapter Required	D4FZ-17260-A
73	351	A/T	49-1/2"	w/ speed control (lower)	D2ZZ-17260-A
73	351-4V	M/T	56"	w/ speed control (lower)	D3ZZ-17260-A
73	All	All	10-1/2"	w/ speed control (upper)	D0ZZ-17260-H

MUSTANG SPEEDOMETER DRIVE GEAR APPLICATION CHART, 1971
Note: For both Drive Gear and Driven Gear Identification Charts, see p. 234.

Axle	Cyl.	CID	Trans.	Tire Size	Drive Gear	Driven Gear
2.75:1	8	351-2V	C4	E70x14	Note: (5)	C7SZ-17271-B
		351-2V	C4	F70x14; F60x15	Note: (5)	C7SZ-17271-A
		351-2V	C4	E78x14	Note: (5)	C7SZ-17271-A
		351-2V	3/M/T	F70x14; F60x15	C8OZ-17285-B	C3DZ-17271-B
		351-2V	3/M/T	E70x14	C8OZ-17285-B	C0DD-17271-B
		351-2V	3/M/T	E78x14	C8OZ-17285-B	C3DZ-17271-B
2.79:1	6/8	250/302	C4	E70x14	Note: (5)	C7SZ-17271-B
	8	302	C4	F60x15	Note: (5)	C7SZ-17271-A
	6/8	250/302	C4	F70x14	Note: (5)	C7SZ-17271-A
	6/8	250/302	3/M/T	E70x14; E78x14	C8OZ-17285-B	C0DD-17271-B
	8	302	3/M/T	F60x15	C8OZ-17285-B	C3DZ-17271-B
	6/8	250/302	3/M/T	F70x14	C8OZ-17285-B	C3DZ-17271-B
3.00:1	6/8	250/302/351	C4	E70x14	8 teeth (5)	C7VY-17271-A
	6/8	250/302/351	C4	F70x14; E78x14	8 teeth (5)	C7VY-17271-A
	6/8	250/302/351	C4	F60x15; F78x14	8 teeth (5)	C7SZ-17271-B
	6/8	250/302/351	3/M/T	F70x14; E78x14	C8OZ-17285-B	C0DD-17271-C
	8	302/351	3/M/T	F60x15	C8OZ-17285-B	C0DD-17271-B
	8	351	4/M/T	F70x14; F60x15; E78x14	C4DZ-17285-A	C2DZ-17271-J
	8	351	4/M/T	E70x14	C4DZ-17285-A	C2DZ-17271-G
3.25:1	8	351	C4, C6	E70x14; E78x14	Note: (5)	D0OZ-17271-A
		351/429	C4, C6	F70x14; F60x15	Note: (5)	C8SZ-17271-B
		351	3/M/T	E70x14; E78x14	C8OZ-17285-B	C4OZ-17271-A
		351	3/M/T	F70x14; F60x15	C8OZ-17285-B	C1DD-17271-A
		351	4/M/T	E70x14; E78x14; F70x14	C4DZ-17285-A	C2DZ-17271-F
		351/429	4/M/T	F60x15	C4DZ-17285-A	C2DZ-17271-G
3.50:1	8	351-4V/429	C6	F70x14; F60x15	8 teeth (5)	D0OZ-17271-A
		351-4V/429	4/M/T (1)	F70x14; F60x15	C4DZ-17285-A	C4DZ-17271-A
		351-4V	4/M/T (2)	F70x14; F60x15	C5ZZ-17285-A	C2DZ-17271-J
		351-4V	4/M/T (1)	E70x14	C4DZ-17285-A	C2DZ-17271-H
		351-4V	4/M/T (2)	E70x14	C5ZZ-17285-A	C2DZ-17271-G
3.91:1	8	429	C6	F60x15	8 teeth (5)	C7SZ-17271-A
		429 (3)	4/M/T (1)	F60x15	C4DZ-17285-A	C2DZ-17271-J
		Boss 351 (3)	4/M/T (1)	F60x15	C4DZ-17285-A	C2DZ-17271-J
4.11:1	8	429 (4)	C6	F60x15	8 teeth (5)	C7SZ-17271-B
		429 (3)	4/M/T	F60x15	C4DZ-17285-A	C2DZ-17271-G

Notes:
1 Except RUG-BA1 Transmission
2 With RUG-BA1 Transmission
3 Requires C9ZZ-17294-A Adapter
4 Requires C8ZZ-17294-A Adapter
5 Part of transmission output shaft

MUSTANG SPEEDOMETER DRIVE GEAR APPLICATION CHART, 1972
Note: For both Drive Gear and Driven Gear Identification Charts, see p. 234.

Axle	Cyl.	CID	Trans.	Tire Size	Drive Gear	Driven Gear
2.75:1	8	351-2V	C4	E70x14; F70x14; F60x15	8 teeth (3)	C7SZ-17271-B
			C4	E78x14	8 teeth (3)	C7SZ-17271-A
			3/M/T	E70x14	C8OZ-17285-B	C0DD-17271-B
			3/M/T	E78x14; F70x14; F60x15	C8OZ-17285-B	C3DZ-17271-B
2.79:1	6/8	250/302-2V	C4	E70x14	8 teeth (3)	C7SZ-17271-B
			C4	E78x14	8 teeth (3)	C7SZ-17271-A
			C4	F70x14	8 teeth (3)	D0OZ-17271-A
			3/M/T	E70x14; F70x14	C8OZ-17285-B	C0DD-17271-B
			3/M/T	E78x14	C8OZ-17285-B	C3DZ-17271-B
			3/M/T	F60x15	C8OZ-17285-B	C3DZ-17271-B
3.00:1	6/8	250/302	C4	E70x14	8 teeth (3)	C8SZ-17271-B
			C4	E78x14; F70x14	8 teeth (3)	C7VY-17271-A
			C4	F60x15	8 teeth (3)	C7SZ-17271-A
			3/M/T	E70X14; E78x14; F70x14	C8OZ-17285-B	C0DD-17271-C
			3/M/T	F60x15	C8OZ-17285-B	C0DD-17271-B
3.25:1	8	351-2V,-4V	C4, C6	E70x14; F70x14; F60x15	8 teeth (3)	C8SZ-17271-B
		351-2V,-4V	C4, C6	E70x14	8 teeth (3)	D0OZ-17271-A
		351-2V	3/M/T	E78x14; F60x15	C8OZ-17285-B	C1DD-17271-A
		351-2V	3/M/T	E70x14	C8OZ-17285-B	C4OZ-17271-A
		351-4V	4/M/T	E70x14; F70x14	D4DZ-17285-A	D2DZ-17271-F
		351-4V	4/M/T	F60x15	D4DZ-17285-A	C2DZ-17271-G
3.50:1	8	351-4V (1)	C6	F60x15	8 teeth (3)	D0OZ-17271-A
		351-4V	C6	E70x14	8 teeth (3)	D0AZ-17271-A
		351-4V	4/M/T	E70x14; F60x15	C4DZ-17285-A	C2DZ-17271-H
3.91:1	8	351 HO (2)	4/M/T	E70x14; F60x15	C4DZ-17285-A	C2DZ-17271-J

Notes:
1 Requires C8ZZ-17294-A Adapter
2 Requires C9ZZ-17294-A Adapter
3 Part of transmission output shaft

MUSTANG SPEEDOMETER DRIVE GEAR APPLICATION CHART, 1973
Note: For both Drive Gear and Driven Gear Identification Charts, see p. 234.

Axle	Cyl.	CID	Trans.	Tire Size	Drive Gear	Driven Gear
2.75:1	8	351-2V	C4	E78x14; F70x14; GR78x14	8 teeth (1)	C7SZ-17271-A
				E70x14	8 teeth (1)	C7SZ-17271-B
2.79:1	6/8	250/302-2V	C4	E78x14; F70x14; GR78x14	8 teeth (1)	C7SZ-17271-A
				E70x14	8 teeth (1)	C7SZ-17271-B
			3/M/T	E78x14; GR78x14	C8OZ-17285-B	C3DZ-17271-B
				F70x14	C8OZ-17285-B	C0DD-17271-C
				E70x14	C8OZ-17285-B	C0DD-17271-B
3.00:1	6/8	250/302-2V	C4	E78x14; F70x14; E70x14; GR78x14	8 teeth (1)	C7VY-17271-A
			3/M/T	E78x14; F70x14; E70x14; GR78x14	C8OZ-17285-B	C0DZ-17271-B
3.25:1	8	351-2V	C4	E78x14; F70x14; GR78x14	8 teeth (1)	C8SZ-17271-B
				E70x14	8 teeth (1)	D0OZ-17271-B
3.50:1	8	351-4V	C6	F70x14	8 teeth (1)	D0OZ-17271-B
			4/M/T	F70x14	C4DZ-17285-A	C4DZ-17271-A

Note:
1 Part of transmission output shaft

MUSTANG REAR AXLE TAG CODE I.D. CHART, 1971-1973
Note: All Removable-Type Carriers

Axle Code	Model Year	Axle Ratio	Ring Gear Diameter	Axle Splines
WDO-M2	71	3.25	9"	31
WES-T2	71/72	2.75	9"	28
WES-AB2	71/72	3.25	9"	28
WES-AD	72/73	3.25	9"	28
WES-AD2	71/72	3.25	9"	28
WES-AE2	71	3.50	9"	31
WES-AE3	71	3.50	9"	28
WES-AJ2	71	3.25	9"	31
WES-AJ3	71	3.25	9"	28
WES-AK	71	3.50	9"	28
WES-AK2	72/73	3.50	9"	28
WFB-C2	71/72	3.25	9"	28
WFB-D2	72	2.75	9"	28
WFD-D2	71/72	3.91	9"	31
WFD-F3	71/73	3.50	9"	28
WFD-M2	71	3.25	9"	31
WFD-M3	71	3.25	9"	28
WCZ-F2	73	3.00	8"	28
WCZ-V	73	2.79	8"	28
WFL-B	73	2.79	8"	28

MUSTANG DRIVESHAFT/REAR AXLE UNIVERSAL JOINT FLANGE ASSEMBLY APPLICATION CHART, 1971-1973 (Note: Use with Illustrations on p. 238)

Year	Ring Gear	Identification	Part Number	Type
67/71	9"	28-spline axles	D2SZ-4851-A	5
67/71	9"	31-spline axles	D2OZ-4851-A	4
72	9"	Industry Desig. 1330	D2OZ-4851-A	
73	9"	WES-T,-AD, WFB	C3OZ-4851-C	2
73	9"	WES-AK, WDF	D4OZ-4851-A	5

MUSTANG DRIVESHAFT ASSEMBLY APPLICATION CHART, 1971-1973

Year	Engine	Trans. Type	Yoke Code	Yoke Type	Part Number	Driveshaft Diam.	Length	U-Joint Front	Rear
71/73	250/302	C4	3	4	D1ZZ-4602-A	3"	51-3/4"	E	F
71/73	351	FMX	2	2	D1ZZ-4602-C	2-3/4"	51-3/32"	E	F
71	351	C6	2	2	D1ZZ-4602-D	3"	47-7/32"	E	F
71/72	351	3/S & 4/S	3	2	D1ZZ-4602-B	2-3/4"	50-13/16"	E	F
71	302/351	4/S	4	2	D1ZZ-4602-E	3"	50-21/32"	G	H
71	351/429	C6	16	2	D1ZZ-4602-F	3-1/2"	47-7/32"	G	H
71	429	4/S	16	2	D1ZZ-4602-G	3"	50-21/32"	G	H
72/73	302	FMX	3	4	D2ZZ-4602-A	3"	52-13/16"	E	F
72	302/351	C6	2	2	D1ZZ-4602-D	3"	47-7/32"	E	F
72	351	4/S	4	2	D1ZZ-4602-E	3"	50-21/32"	G	H
72	351	C6	16	2	D1ZZ-4602-F	3-1/2"	47-7/32"	G	H
73	351 (1)	C6	2	2	D1ZZ-4602-D	3"	47-7/32"	E	F
73	351 (1)	3/S & 4/S	3	2	D1ZZ-4602-B	2-3/4"	50-13/16"	E	F
73	351 (2)	C6	16	2	D1ZZ-4602-F	3-1/2"	47-7/32"	G	H
73	351 (3)	4/S	4	2	D1ZZ-4602-E	3"	50-21/32"	G	H

See related charts and illustrations on pages 239 through 241.

Notes:
1   3.25 ratio and below
2   3.50 ratio
3   3.50 ratio and above

MUSTANG DIFFERENTIAL CASE ASSEMBLY APPLICATION CHART, 1971-1973

Year	Axle I.D.	Notes	Part Number	Description
71/73	WCL, WCZ		D0OZ-4204-A	w/ 8" R/G, Medium Differential Bearing, 2 pinion, conventional
71/72	WFL	1	C9OZ-4204-F	w/ 8" R/G, Medium Differential Bearing, 2 pinion, Traction-Lok
72/73	WFL, WFL-A, WFL-B	2	D3OZ-4204-A	w/ 8" R/G, Medium Differential Bearing, 2 pinion, Traction-Lok
71/73	All		D0OZ-4204-D	w/ 9" R/G, Slim Line Diff. Bearing, 4 pinion, non-locking, w/ 31- or 28-spline axles, includes (2 each) C9AZ-4221-A bearings, C9AZ-4222-A cups, & C9OZ-4228-A washers.
71/73	All	3	D2AZ-4204-A	w/ 9" R/G, Slim Line Diff. Bearing, 2 pinion, non-locking, w/ 28-spline axles.
71/73	All		D0OZ-4204-C	w/ 9" R/G, Slim Line Diff. Brg, 2 or 4 pinion, Traction-Lok, w/ 28- or 31-spline axles, includes (2 each) C9AZ-4221-A bearings, C9AZ-4222-A cups, & C9OZ-4228-A washers.
71/73	All		D0OZ-4204-E	w/ 9" R/G, Slim Line Diff. Brg, no-spin 2-pinion, 31-spline axle shaft. includes (2 each) C9AZ-4221-A bearings, C9AZ-4222-A cups, & C9OZ-4228-A washers.
73	All	4	D3OZ-4204-A	w/ 8" R/G, Traction-Lok
73	All		D3TZ-4204-A	w/ 9" R/G, Traction-Lok

Notes:
1   Before 5/15/72
2   After 5/15/72
3   r/b D0OZ-4204-D (6/83)
4   not replaced

MUSTANG REAR AXLE DIFFERENTIAL SIDE GEAR KIT CHART, 1971-1973

Year	Axle I.D.	Part Number	Description
70/71	WFU-D, -E	C4AZ-4236-A	31 Splines, 4 omitted w/ hub Consists of: (2) C4AW-4236-A gear, (2)C9OZ-4228-A washer.
69/73		C9AZ-4236-A	w/ locking diff., 28-splines, incl.: (1) C9OW-4236-A gear (21/32" long) (r/b D8AW-4236-BA gear), (1) C9OW-4236-B gear (1-3/16" long) (r/b E0EW-4236-AA gear), (2) C9OZ-4228-A washers.
69/73		C9AZ-4236-B	w/ std. diff., 28-splines, incl.: (2) C9OW-4236-B gears (1-3/16" long) (r/b E0EW-4236-AA gears), (2) C9OZ-4228-A washers.
73	All	C8OZ-4236-A	w/ 9" R/G Traction-Lok, R.H. 31 splines, 16 teeth, w/ hub; L.H. 31 splines, 16 teeth, w/o hub. r/b E2UZ-4236-A (6/83)

MUSTANG REAR AXLE DIFFERENTIAL ASSEMBLY APPLICATION CHART, 1971-1973

Year	Axle Tag I.D.	Part Number	Ratio	Gear Size	Locking	Description
67/73	WCZ-V, -V2	C7OW-4200-F	2.79	8"	No	
67/73	WCZ-F, -F2	C7OW-4200-G	3.00	8"	No	
68	WCZ-W	C7OW-4200-H	3.25	8"	No	
68/73	WFD-B, -D, -D2	C8OW-4200-C	3.91	9"	Yes	
69/70	WES-AC	C9OW-4200-D	3.00	9"	No	
69/73	WES-T, -T1, -T2	C9OW-4200-H	2.75	9"	No	
69/73	WES-AA	C9OW-4200-G	3.00	9"	No	
69/73	WES-AD, -AD2	C9OW-4200-K	3.25	9"	No	
69/73	WFB-C, -C2	C9OW-4200-V	3.25	9"	Yes	Traction-Lok
70/73	WFL-A, -A2	D0OW-4200-A	3.00	8"	Yes	Traction-Lok
71	WES-AK	D1ZW-4200-A	3.50	9"	No	
71	WFU-E1	D1ZW-4200-B	4.11	9"	Yes	No-Spin Diff.
71/73	WFD-F3	D1ZW-4200-F	3.50	9"	Yes	

MUSTANG REAR AXLE SEAL ASSEMBLY CHART, 1971-1973

Year	Model	Axle I.D.	Part Number	Description
68/72	7", 8" R/G	All	C2OZ-4676-B	1-13/16" I.D., 2-15/16" Flange Diam. 2-5/8" Seal Diam., 29/64" thick.
71/72	9", 9-3/8" R/G	All	D1UZ-4676-A	1-13/16" I.D., 3-5/16" Flange Diam. 3" Seal Diam., 1/2" thick.
73	8" R/G	All	D9AZ-4676-A	1-13/16" I.D., 3-1/8" Flange Diam. 2-25/32" Seal Diam., 17/32" thick, r/b E3TZ-4676-A
73	8" R/G	All	D9BZ-4676-A	1-13/16" I.D., 2-15/16" Flange Diam. 2-5/8" Seal Diam., 29/64" thick.
73	9" R/G	All	E0TZ-4676-B	1-13/16" I.D., 3-5/16" Flange Diam. 3" Seal Diam., 1/2" thick.

MUSTANG REAR AXLE PINION BEARING RETAINER ASSEMBLY CHART, 1965-1973

Year	Model Appl.	Retainer and Cup Assembly	Cups	Bearings
65/73	8" R/G	C6OZ-4614-B	C0DW-4616-A	C0DW-4621-A
65/73	9" R/G, 28-spline	D2SZ-4614-A	B7A-4616-A	B7A-4621-A
	WES-AD, WES-T, WFB			
67/73	9" R/G, 31-spline	C3AZ-4614-B	B7A-4616-A	B7A-4621-A
	WES-AK, WFD (1)		TBAA-4616-A	TBAA-4621-A

Note: (1) Refer to Ford Motorsport Peformance Equipment Catalog.

MUSTANG REAR AXLE SHAFT ASSEMBLY APPLICATION CHART, 1971-1973

Year	Model	Axle I.D.	Part Number	Description
71	w/ 8" & 9" R/G	All, except: WES-AE3, AJ3 WFD-F3, M3	D0OZ-4234-C	R/H 28-spline, 31-7/8"
			D0OZ-4234-D	L/H 28-spline, 27-13/16"
71	w/ 9" R/G	WES-AE3, AJ3 WFD-F3, M3	D1ZZ-4234-C	R/H 28-spline, 31-49/64" r/b D3ZZ-4234-A (10/74)
			D1ZZ-4234-D	L/H 28-spline, 27-13/16"
71/	w/ 9" R/G		D1ZZ-4234-A	R/H 31-spline, 31-25/32"
			D1ZZ-4234-B	L/H 31-spline, 27-13/16"
72	w/ 8" & 9" R/G	WES (exc. -AK) WCZ, WFL, WFB	D0OZ-4234-C	R/H 28-spline, 31-7/8"
			D0OZ-4234-D	L/H 28-spline, 27-13/16"
72	w/ 9" R/G	WES-AK, WFD-F3	D1ZZ-4234-C	R/H 28-spline, 31-49/64"
			D1ZZ-4234-D	L/H 28-spline, 27-13/16"
73	w/ 8" & 9" R/G	WCZ-F2, V WFL-A, B WES-AD, T1, AK-2 WFB-C, D2 WFD-F3	D3ZZ-4234-A	R/H 28-spline, 31-25/32"
			D3ZZ-4234-B	L/H 28-spline, 27-13/16"

Note: For '71-'73 Rear Axle Differential Bearing Cone Chart (Roller & Cup), please refer to chart on page 246. All 8" and 9" R/G apps carry over.

Note: For '71-'73 Rear Axle Differential Pinion Kit Chart, please refer to chart on page 246. Conventional and Traction-Lok 8" and 9" apps. carry over.

MUSTANG REAR AXLE HOUSING ASSEMBLY APPLICATION CHART, 1971-1973

Year	Model	Axle I.D.	Part Number	Description
71-72	8-inch Ring Gear	WCZ, WFL	D1ZZ-4010-A	Medium Wheel Bearing
71-73	9-inch Ring Gear	WES, WFB, WFD, WFH	D1ZZ-4010-B	Medium Wheel Bearing
73	8-inch Ring Gear		D3OZ-4010-B	Medium Wheel Bearing

8-INCH RING GEAR and PINION SETS APPLICATION CHART, 1971-1973

Year	Ratio	Part Number	Number of Teeth	
			Gear	Pinion
65/71 & 73	2.80/2.79	C4OZ-4209-K	39	14
65/71 & 73	3.00	C4OZ-4209-H	39	13
65/71	4.11	B7AZ-4209-K	37	9
65/73	3.50	C9OZ-4209-A	35	10
67/71	3.00	COOZ-4209-E	39	13
67/72	3.25	B8AZ-4209-C	39	12
68/73	2.75	C7AZ-4209-J	44	16
68/72	3.91	C8OZ-4209-A	43	11
68/71	4.30	C8OZ-4209-B	43	10

MUSTANG LOCKING DIFFERENTIAL I.D. & APPLICATION CHART, 1971-1973

Year	Application	Part Number	Description
71/72	All, 9" R/G	C9OZ-4026-B	Slim-line diff. bearing,
			28-spline shaft, 2- or 4-pinions
71/73	All, 8" R/G	C9OZ-4026-D	Medium diff. bearing,
			28-spline shaft.
71/72	9" R/G	D3TZ-4026-A	Lg. or Slim-line diff. bearing,
			31-spline shaft.
71	9" R/G, WFU-E1	DOOZ-4026-A	Dapco No-spin w/ Lg. or Slim-
			line diff bearing, 31-spline shaft.
73	All, 9" R/G	D4TZ-4026-A	31-spline shaft.
73	All, 9" R/G	D3SZ-4026-A	28-spline shaft.

SUSPENSION, BRAKES, STEERING, WHEELS, AND EXHAUST

The topic groupings in this book are based on Ford's categorization system in their original parts catalogs. For that reason, suspension, brakes, steering, wheels, and exhaust are presented together as general running gear and underchassis. Fortunately, the complications in mixing and matching drivetrain components do not apply here. The reader will find that, in this section, certain applications are narrow, and the possibilities for swaps are reduced by safety considerations or lack of interchangeability.

The value of this section can be found in exploded views where the differences in model years and, especially, body styles become evident. Hobbyists are reminded that any work on the steering or braking systems requires a dedication to safety. Ford's original parts specifications for those systems still apply as minimum requirements. If there are any questions as to brake parts or steering lineage compatibility, the advice of experts should be obtained.

As in other sections of this 1971-1973 addendum, many exploded views from the 1964-1970 chapters apply to the latter model years. Please note these references:

For the typical 1971-1973 Mustang front suspension system, refer to the lower left corner of page 260.

For the 1972-1973 Deluxe two-spoke steering wheel, refer to the bottom of page 272.

For the 1971-1973 Grandé Deluxe three-spoke steering wheel, refer to the lower right corner of page 273.

For the rear sway bar and attaching parts for 1971-1973 Mustangs equipped with the optional handling package, please refer to the center of page 263.

For the 1971-1973 Mustang steering column with tilt wheel, refer to the bottom of page 277.

For the 1971-1973 Mustang steering column with fixed wheel, refer to the top of page 278.

For 1971-1973 Mustang front and rear wheel cylinder assemblies, refer to the top right corner of page 264.

For 1971-1973 Mustang front and rear drum brake assemblies, refer the to top left corner of page 265.

For 1971-1973 Mustang front disc brake details, refer to the top of page 266.

For the 1971-1973 Mustang parking brake system, refer to the bottom of page 269.

For a 1971-1973 Mustang power steering pump exploded view, refer to the top left corner of page 286.

The 1971-1973 Mustang base wheel cover.

The 1971-1973 Mustang sports wheel cover, optional, all models.

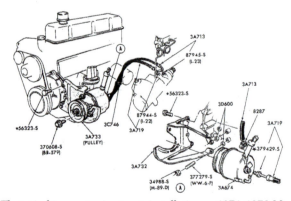

The typical power steering pump installation on 1971-1973 Mustangs with 250ci engines.

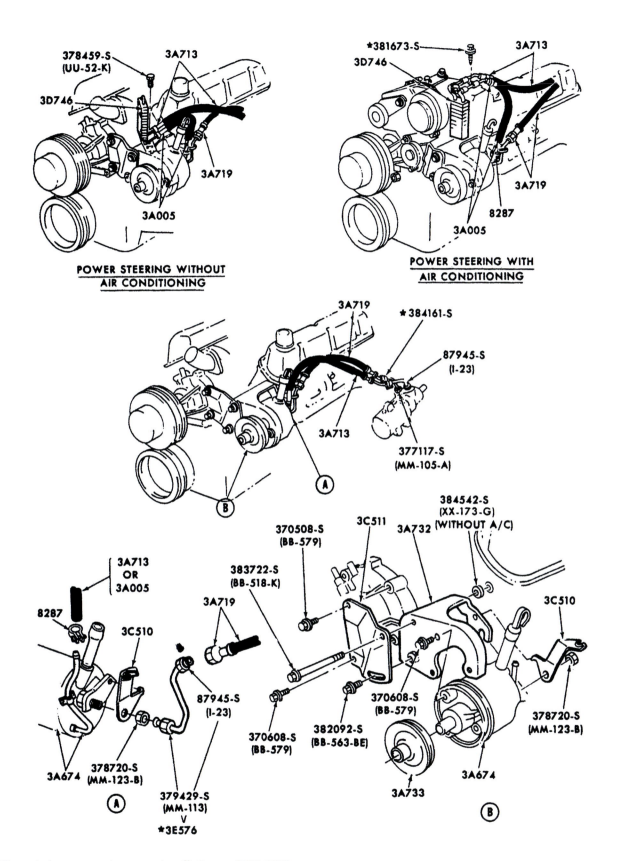

POWER STEERING WITHOUT
AIR CONDITIONING

POWER STEERING WITH
AIR CONDITIONING

*The typical power steering pump installation on 1971-1973
Mustangs with 302ci or 351ci engines.*

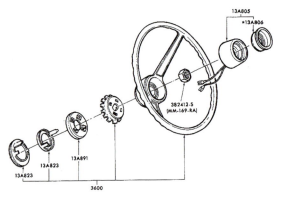

*The standard 1971-1972 Mustang two-spoke steering wheel and
related parts.*

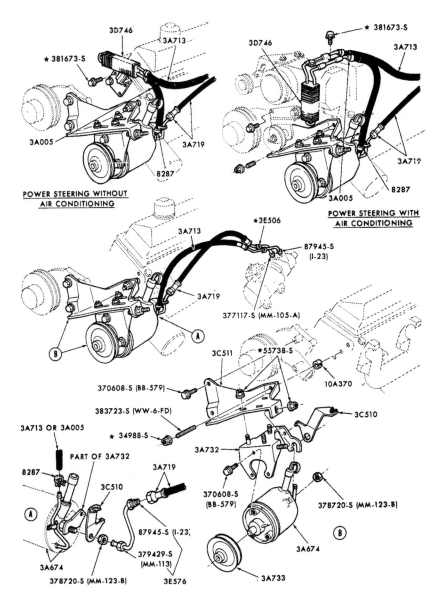

*The typical power steering pump installation on 1971 Mustangs
with 429 engines.*

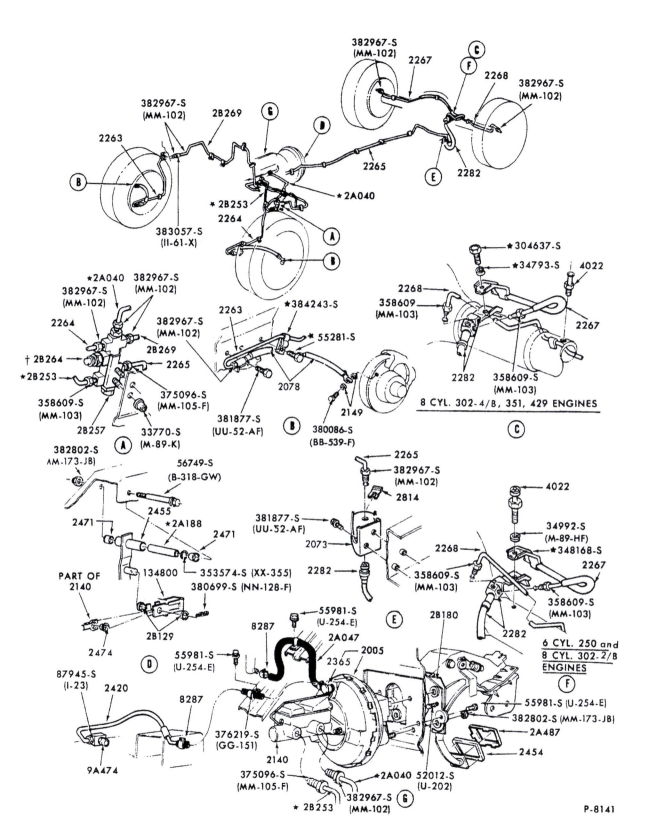

The typical 1971-1973 Mustang disc brake system.

417

MUSTANG FRONT STABILIZER BAR ASSEMBLY CHART, 1971-1973

Note: All '71 through '73 Stabilizer Bar Brackets carry Part Number D0OZ-5486-A

Year	Cyl/CID	Model	Type	Diam.	Ident.	Part Number
71/72	6/250	All	Std	3/4"	3Y, 2Y-1R	D2ZZ-5482-A
71/72	302-2V	All	Std	3/4"	3Y, 2Y-1R	D2ZZ-5482-A
71/72	351-2V	All	Std	3/4"	3Y, 2Y-1R	D2ZZ-5482-A
71	351-4V Exc Boss	w/o Comp Handling	Std	3/4"	3Y, 2Y-1R	D2ZZ-5482-A
71	351-4V Incl. Boss	w/ Comp Handling	Std	7/8"	2Y-1G	D1ZZ-5482-D
71	429	w/ Comp Handling	Std	7/8"	2Y-1G	D1ZZ-5482-D
73	6/250	All	Std	11/16"	3Y	D3ZZ-5482-A
73	302/351-2V	w/o Comp Handling	Std	11/16"	3Y	D3ZZ-5482-A
73	302/351-2V	w/ Comp Handling	Std	3/4"	3Y, 2Y-1R	D2ZZ-5482-A
73	351-4V	w/ Comp Handling	Std	7/8"	2Y-1G	D1ZZ-5482-D

1971 MUSTANG REAR SPRING APPLICATION CHART

Model	Description	Stripes	Part Number
63D: 6 cyl, 302-2V, 351-2V, 65D: 6 cyl, 302-2V, 351-2V, 65F: 6 cyl, 302-2V, 351-2V, Before 10/9/70.	Std. 4-leaf, 560 lb. load rate, w/o Competition Handling Package	1 silver & 2 red	D1ZZ-5560-F
63D: 6 cyl. After 10/9/70, 63D: 351-4V exc. CJ, 76: 6 cyl., 302-2V, 351 exc. CJ Before 10/9/70. 65D: 6 cyl, 302-2V, 351-2V, 65F: 6 cyl, 302-2V, After 10/9/70.	Std. 4-leaf, 595 lb. load rate, w/o Competition Handling Package D1ZA-5556-EA	2 red & 1 pink	D1ZZ-5560-K
63D: 302-2V, 351-2V, 63D: 351-4V exc. CJ, 65D: 351-4V exc. CJ, 65F: 351-2V, 351-4V exc. CJ, 76: 6 cyl., After 10/9/70.	Std. 4-leaf, 625 lb. load rate, w/o Competition Handling Package D1ZA-5556-FA	1 red & 1 pink	D1ZZ-5560-L
63D: 302-2V, 351 exc. CJ, 63R: 302-2V, 351-2V, 65D: 302-2V, 351, 65F: 302-2V, 351-2V, Before 10/19/70. 63D: 351 CJ, 63R: 351-4V, 76: 302-2V, Before 10/9/70.	Std. 4-leaf, 590 lb. load rate, w/ Competition Handling Package	1 violet & 1 pink	D1ZZ-5560-C
63D: 302-2V, 351 exc. CJ, 63D: 429 CJ, 63R: 302-2V, 351-2V, 65D: 302-2V, 351, 429 CJ 65F: 302-2V, 351, 429 CJ After 10/19/70.	Std. 4-leaf, 615 lb. load rate, w/ Competition Handling Package	2 green & 2 gold	D1ZZ-5560-G
63D: 351 CJ, 63R: 351-4V, 429 CJ, 76: 302-2V, 351, 429 CJ, After 10/9/70.	Std. 4-leaf, 654 lb. load rate, w/ Competition Handling Package	2 red & 2 orange	D1ZZ-5560-H
63D: 429 CJ, 65D: 429 CJ, 65F: 351-4V, 429 CJ, Before 10/19/70 63R: 429 CJ, 76: 302-2V, 351, 429 CJ, Before 10/9/70	Std. 4-leaf, 640 lb. load rate, w/ Competition Handling Package	1 green & 2 pink	D1ZZ-5560-E
76: 302-2V, 351 exc. CJ, After 10/9/70.	Std. 4-leaf, 665 lb. load rate, w/o Competition Handling Package D1ZA-5556-GA	2 pink & 1 red	D1ZZ-5560-M

1972 MUSTANG REAR SPRING APPLICATION CHART

Model	Description	Stripes	Part Number
63D: 6 cyl. 65D: 6 cyl., 302, 351-2V 65F: 6 cyl., 8 cyl. 302	Std. 4-leaf, 595 lb. load rate, w/o Competition Handling Package C9ZA-5556-R; D0ZA-5556-E, -F	3 yellow	C9ZZ-5560-H
63D: 302-2V, 351, 351-CJ 65D: 351 CJ 76: 6 cyl.	Std. 4-leaf, 625 lb. load rate, w/o Competition Handling Package D0ZA-5556-A, -B		D0ZZ-5560-A
63D: 302, 351-2V 63R: 302, 351-2V 65D: 302-2V, 351-2V, 351 CJ 65F: 302-2V, 351-2V, 351 CJ	Std. 4-leaf, 615 lb. load rate, w/ Competition Handling Package	2 green & 2 gold	D1ZZ-5560-G
63D: 351 CJ, 63R: 351 CJ, 76: 302, 351-2V, 351 CJ	Std. 4-leaf, 654 lb. load rate, w/ Competition Handling Package	2 red & 2 orange	D1ZZ-5560-H
76: 302, 351-2V, 351 CJ	Std. 4-leaf, 665 lb. load rate, w/o Competition Handling Package D1ZA-5556-CA m/w D1ZZ-5560-M		D1ZZ-5560-J

1973 MUSTANG REAR SPRING APPLICATION CHART

Model	Description	Stripes	Part Number
63D: 250, 302 65D,F: 250, 302, 351-2V	Std. 4-leaf, 639 lb. load rate, w/o Competition Handling Package		D3ZZ-5560-C
63D,R: 302, 351-2V 65D,F: 302, 351-2V 76: 351-2V	Std. 4-leaf, 680 lb. load rate, w/ Competition Handling Package	1 silver & 1 green	D3ZZ-5560-B
76: 302	Std. 4-leaf, 680 lb. load rate, w/o Competition Handling Package	1 silver & 1 green	D3ZZ-5560-B
63D: 351-2V 65D,F: 351-4V (A/T) 76: 250, 302	Std. 4-leaf, 662 lb. load rate, w/o Competition Handling Package	1 silver & 1 pink or 1 silver & 1 red	D3ZZ-5560-D
63D,R: 351-4V 65D,F: 351-4V 76: 351-4V	Std. 4-leaf, 649 lb. load rate, w/ Competition Handling Package	1 silver	D3ZZ-5560-A
63D: 351-4V (A/T) 76: 351-4V (A/T)	Std. 4-leaf, 682 lb. load rate, w/o Competition Handling Package	1 silver & 1 red or 1 silver & 2 orange	D3ZZ-5560-E

MUSTANG REAR SPRING PLATE APPLICATION CHART, 1971-1973

Year	Model	Right Hand	Left Hand
71/72	6/250	D1ZZ-5796-A	D1ZZ-5796-B
71/72	302/351-2V	D1ZZ-5796-A	D1ZZ-5796-B
71/72	351-4V, 429CJ	C8ZZ-5796-A	C8ZZ-5796-B
73	6/250	D3ZZ-5796-A	D3ZZ-5796-B
73	302/351-2V	D3ZZ-5796-A	D3ZZ-5796-B
73	351-4V	D3ZZ-5796-A	D3ZZ-5796-C

MUSTANG BRAKE CYLINDER ASSEMBLY APPLICATION CHART, 1971-1973

FRONT BRAKES:

Year		Brake Size	Diam.	Location	Part Number	Repair Kit
71		10" x 2-1/4"	1-1/8"	R.H.	C3OZ-2061-B	C8UZ-2221-A
		or 2-1/2"		L.H.	C3OZ-2062-B	C8UZ-2221-A
72/73		10" x 2-1/2"	1-1/8"	R.H.	D2ZZ-2061-A	D2AZ-2221-B
				L.H.	D2ZZ-2062-A	D2AZ-2221-B

REAR BRAKES:

Year	Models	Brake Size	Diam.	Location	Part Number	Repair Kit
71	250, 302-2V	10" x 1-3/4"	7/8"	R.H. (1)	C6OZ-2261-A	C6OZ-2128-A
				L.H. (1)	C6OZ-2262-A	C6OZ-2128-A
71	250, 302-2V	10" x 1-3/4"	7/8"	R.H. (2)	D2ZZ-2261-A	D2ZZ-2128-A
				L.H. (2)	D2ZZ-2262-A	D2ZZ-2128-A
71	Boss 302, 351, 429	10" x 2"	29/32"	R.H. (1)	C3OZ-2262-B	C3OZ-2128-B
				L.H. (1)	C3OZ-2262-B	C3OZ-2128-B
71	Boss 302, 351, 429	10" x 2"	29/32"	R.H. (2)	D2ZZ-2262-B	D2ZZ-2128-B
				L.H. (2)	D2ZZ-2262-B	D2ZZ-2128-B
72	250, 302	10" x 1-3/4"	7/8"	R.H.	D2ZZ-2261-A	D2ZZ-2128-A
				L.H.	D2ZZ-2262-A	D2ZZ-2128-A
72	351	10" x 2"	29/32"	R.H.	D2ZZ-2262-B	D2ZZ-2128-B
				L.H.	D2ZZ-2262-B	D2ZZ-2128-B
73	250, 302	10" x 1-3/4" & 2"	7/8"	R.H.	D3ZZ-2261-A r/b D3TZ-2261-A	D3TZ-2128-A
				L.H.	D3ZZ-2262-A	D3TZ-2128-A
73	351	10" x 2"	7/8"	R.H.	D3ZZ-2262-A	D3TZ-2128-A
				L.H.	D3ZZ-2262-A	D3TZ-2128-A

Notes: 1 - Original; 2 - Service Replacement

MUSTANG POWER BRAKE BOOSTER INSTALLATION KIT (Retrofit), 1971-1972

71/72 Before 2/28/72 — Kit Part Number: D1ZZ-2A091-A

Individual Part Number	Descr.	Individual Part Number	Descr.	Individual Part Number	Descr.
D1ZZ-2005-B	Booster	D1ZA-2420-AA	Tube	376428-S8	or
D1ZJ-2A040-AA	Tube	D1ZJ-2B450-AA	Spacers (4)	382984-S2	Clamps (2)
C1AA-2A047-A	Hose	D1ZZ-2455-B	Pedal	378672-S	Clip
C9AZ-2169-F	Piston	55981-S2	Screw	380699-S100	Pin
D1ZJ-2B253-AA	Tube	incl. Installation Sketch		382802-S100	Nuts (6)

1972 After 2/28/72 — Kit Part Number: D2ZZ-2A091-A

Individual Part Number	Descr.	Individual Part Number	Descr.	Individual Part Number	Descr.
D1ZZ-2005-B	Booster	D1ZA-2420-AA	Tube	376428-S8	or
D1ZJ-2A040-AA	Tube	D1ZJ-2B450-AA	Spacers (4)	379059-S2	or
C1AA-2A047-A	Hose	D1ZZ-2455-B	Pedal	382984-S2	Clamps (2)
C9AZ-2169-F	Piston	D1ZZ-13480-B	Switch	380699-S100	Pin
D1ZJ-2B253-AA	Tube	55981-S36M	Screw	382802-S100	Nuts (6)
D2ZJ-2B253-AA	Tube	378672-S	Clip	incl. Installation Sketch	

POWER STEERING INSTALLATION KIT CHART, 1971-1973
(No Linkage Kit Required, 1971-1973.)

Year	Cyl/CID	Pump Kit	P/S to A/C Adapter Kit
71	6/250	D2ZZ-3A635-A	None Required.
	8/302	D1ZZ-3A635-B	None Required.
	8/351	D1ZZ-3A635-D (1)	None Required.
	429CJ	D1ZZ-3A635-F	None Required.
	429SCJ	D1ZZ-3A635-F	None Required.
72	6/250	D2ZZ-3A635-A	None Required.
	8/302	D2ZZ-3A635-B	None Required.
	8/351-2V	D2ZZ-3A635-C	None Required.
	8/351-2V	D2ZZ-3A635-D	D2ZZ-3A635-E
73	8/302	D3ZZ-3A635-B	D3ZZ-3A635-F
	8/351	D3ZZ-3A635-D	D3ZZ-3A635-F

Note (1): For Boss 351 use additional parts, D1ZZ-3A732-A;
D1ZZ-3D746-A; D0ZZ-6A312-A; C9DZ-8620-A and
378459-S36. Improvise oil cooler hoses from bulk
stock C7AZ-3A005-A and C7AZ-3A609-A.

MUSTANG POWER STEERING PUMP ASSEMBLY APPLICATION CHART, 1971-1973

Year	Model	Description / I.D. Marking	Part Number
71/72	All Before 7/1/72	HBA-CG	D1ZZ-3A674-B
72/73	All After 7/1/72	HBA-CN	D3ZZ-3A674-A

MUSTANG POWER STEERING HOSE ASSEMBLY APPLICATION CHART, 1971-1973

Year	Model	Description	Approx. Dev. Length (Inch)	Part Number
71	6/250	From gear to pump (return).		D1ZZ-3A713-A
		From pump to gear (pressure).		D1ZZ-3A719-B
	8 cyl. engines	From gear to pump (return).		D1ZZ-3A713-A
	with oil cooler	From cooler to pump (return).	as required	C7AZ-3A005-A
	with oil cooler	Insulator for above return line.	as required	C7AZ-3A609-A
		Pressure line outlet tube.		D1ZA-3E576-AC
	302, 351	From pump to gear (pressure).		D1ZZ-3A719-C
	429	From pump to gear (pressure).		D1ZZ-3A719-A
72	6/250	From gear to pump (return).		D1ZZ-3A713-A
	Before 5/1/72	From pump to gear (pressure).	71-1/2"	D1ZZ-3A719-D
	After 5/1/72	From pump to gear (pressure).	27-3/4"	D2ZZ-3A719-B
	8 cyl. engines	From gear to pump (return).		D1ZZ-3A713-A
	with oil cooler	From cooler to pump (return).	as required	C7AZ-3A005-A
	with oil cooler	Insulator for above return line.	as required	C7AZ-3A609-A
		Pressure line outlet tube.		D1ZA-3E576-AC
	Before 5/1/72	From pump to gear (pressure).		D1ZZ-3A719-C
	After 5/1/72	From pump to gear (pressure).		D2ZZ-3A719-A
73	6/250	From gear to pump (return).		D1ZZ-3A713-A
		From pump to gear (pressure).		D1ZZ-3A719-B
	8 cyl. engines	From gear to pump (return).		D1ZZ-3A713-A
	with oil cooler	From cooler to pump (return).	as required	C7AZ-3A005-A
		Pressure line outlet tube.		D1ZA-3E576-AC
		From pump to gear (pressure).		D2ZZ-3A719-A

MUSTANG HUB CAP or WHEEL COVER APPLICATION CHART, 1971

Part Number	Identification	Notes	Diam.	Description
C9ZZ-1130-E	none	1	2-3/4"	Use w/ 15x7 Styled Steel wheels, Mustang emblem, black center, before 4/2/71
D1ZZ-1130-G	none	1	2-3/4"	Use w/ 15x7 Styled Steel wheels, Mustang emblem, black center, after 4/2/71
D0AZ-1130-H	D0AA-1130-G D2AA-1130-AA	1	10-1/4"	Plain chrome finish, circ. black stripes imprinted "Ford Motor Company"
D5DZ-1130-B	D00A-1130-K D0ZA-1130-J	1	10-1/4"	Brushed chrome finish, circ. black stripes imprinted "Ford Motor Company" Use with 1210 trim ring.
C6OZ-1130-N	C8OA-1130-M	1	14"	Simulated Mag, Plain Chrome Center
D1ZZ-1130-B	D1ZA-1130-BA	2	14-1/8"	Circular brushed finished, 15 depressions imprinted "Mustang," chrome center
D1ZZ-1130-D	D1ZA-1130-DB	1	15-1/4"	Simulated styled steel, Mustang emblem Black background, use w/ 14x6 wheels.
D1ZZ-1130-C	D1ZA-1130-CB	1	15-1/4"	Simulated styled steel, Mustang emblem Black background, use w/ 14x7 wheels.
D1ZZ-1130-E	D1ZA-1130-EB	1	16-1/4"	Simulated styled steel, Mustang emblem Black background, use w/ 15x7 wheels.

Notes:

1) See illustration on p. 295

2) See accompanying illustrations.

▼□ D0OZ-1130-D (15 1/4")
▼% D0OZ-1130-G (16 1/4")
(RED CENTER)
TORINO
✱□ D1ZZ-1130-C (15 1/4")
✱▲ D1ZZ-1130-D (15 1/4")
✱% D1ZZ-1130-E (16 1/4")
(BLACK CENTER)
MUSTANG

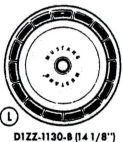

D1ZZ-1130-B (14 1/8")
(PLAIN CENTER)
MUSTANG

C9ZZ-1130-E (2 3/4")
D1ZZ-1130-G (2 3/4")
(BLACK CENTER)
MUSTANG

MUSTANG HUB CAP or WHEEL COVER APPLICATION CHART, 1971

Part Number	Identification	Notes	Diam.	Description
C9ZZ-1130-E	none	1	2-3/4"	Use w/ 15x7 Styled Steel wheels, Mustang emblem, black center, before 4/2/71
D1ZZ-1130-G	none	1	2-3/4"	Use w/ 15x7 Styled Steel wheels, Mustang emblem, black center, after 4/2/71
D0AZ-1130-H	D0AA-1130-G D2AA-1130-AA	1	10-1/4"	Plain chrome finish, circ. black stripes imprinted "Ford Motor Company"
D5DZ-1130-B	D00A-1130-K D0ZA-1130-J	1	10-1/4"	Brushed chrome finish, circ. black stripes imprinted "Ford Motor Company" Use with 1210 trim ring.
C6OZ-1130-N	C8OA-1130-M	1	14"	Simulated Mag, Plain Chrome Center
D1ZZ-1130-B	D1ZA-1130-BA	2	14-1/8"	Circular brushed finished, 15 depressions imprinted "Mustang," chrome center
D1ZZ-1130-D	D1ZA-1130-DB	1	15-1/4"	Simulated styled steel, Mustang emblem Black background, use w/ 14x6 wheels.
D1ZZ-1130-C	D1ZA-1130-CB	1	15-1/4"	Simulated styled steel, Mustang emblem Black background, use w/ 14x7 wheels.
D1ZZ-1130-E	D1ZA-1130-EB	1	16-1/4"	Simulated styled steel, Mustang emblem Black background, use w/ 15x7 wheels.

Notes:
1) See illustration on p. 295
2) See accompanying illustrations.

G
****D0AZ-1130-G (10 1/4")
*D5DZ-1130-B(10 1/4")
*D0AZ-1130-H (10 1/4")
*D2ZZ-1130-B (10 1/4")
(BRUSHED FINISH CENTER)
FORD, MAVERICK, MUSTANG-HUB CAP

D
D2ZZ-1130-A (14 1/8")
(BLACK CENTER)
MUSTANG

B D3ZZ-1130-A(4 3/8")
HUB CAP (RED CENTER)
MUSTANG

MUSTANG HUB CAP or WHEEL COVER APPLICATION CHART, 1973

Part Number	Identification		Diam. (Inch	Description
D1ZZ-1130-G	none	1	2-3/4"	Use w/ 15x7 Styled Steel wheels, Mustang emblem, black center
D0AZ-1130-H	D0AA-1130-G D2AA-1130-AA	1	10-1/4"	Plain chrome finish, circ. black stripes imprinted "Ford Motor Company" Use with 1210 trim ring.
D5DZ-1130-B	D00A-1130-K D0ZA-1130-J	1	10-1/4"	Brushed chrome finish, circ. black stripes imprinted "Ford Motor Company" Use with 1210 trim ring.
D3ZZ-1130-A		2	4-3/8"	Pony Hub - for Forged Aluminum Wheel
D1ZZ-1130-B	D1ZA-1130-BA	2	14-1/8"	Circular brushed finished, 15 depressions imprinted "Mustang," chrome center
D1ZZ-1130-A	D1ZA-1130-AA Grande.	2	14-1/8"	Circular brushed finished, 80 depressions imprinted "Mustang," chrome center
D1ZZ-1130-D	D1ZA-1130-DB	1	15-1/4"	Simulated styled steel, Mustang emblem Black background, use w/ 14x6 wheels.
D0OZ-1130-A			15-3/8"	18 ribs, Ford crest, red background
D1ZZ-1130-E	D1ZA-1130-EB	1	16-1/4"	Simulated styled steel, Mustang emblem Black background, use w/ 15x7 wheels.

Notes:
1) See illustration on p. 295
2) See accompanying illustrations.

WIRING AND ELECTRICAL

For the Mustangs from 1971 through 1973, major wiring harnesses were similar in all body styles. But pigtails and supplementary harnesses were added where needed to adapt accessories. One of the great frustrations in restoring Mustangs is an owner's discovery after a car is assembled that incorrect harness routings or incomplete harnesses are costing either safety or concours points. Add to those problems the possibilities of damaging fire or poor engine performance, and one realizes the importance of getting it right the first time.

This chapter provides cutaway drawings to demonstrate proper placement of the harnesses needed to wire 1971-1973 Mustangs. As a supplement, the reader may wish to obtain model-specific wiring diagrams to assist in a complete rewiring. A good source for such reproduction diagrams is Jim Osborn Reproductions in Lawrenceville, Georgia, (770-962-7556).

Also included in this area are guides to proper bulbs and fuses and a basis for the restorer to plan and establish priorities in budgeting for rebuilding a Mustang.

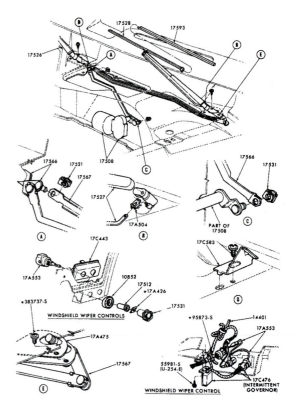

The 1971-1973 Mustang windshield wiper mechanism and electrical system.

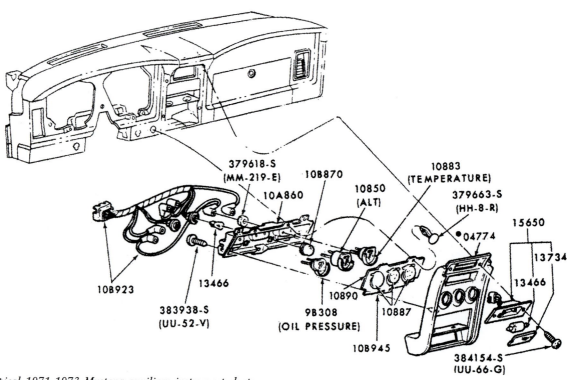

The typical 1971-1973 Mustang auxiliary instrument cluster with gauges.

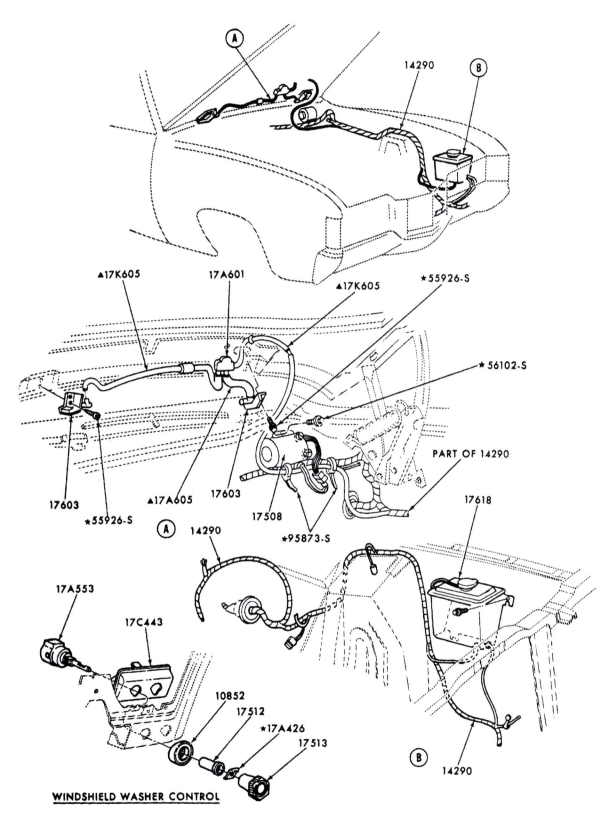

14290

17A601

▲17K605

▲17K605

★55926-S

★56102-S

17603

★55926-S

▲17A605

17603

17508

★95873-S

PART OF 14290

17618

14290

17A553

17C443

10852

17512

★17A426

17513

14290

WINDSHIELD WASHER CONTROL

The 1971-1973 Mustang windshield washer system.

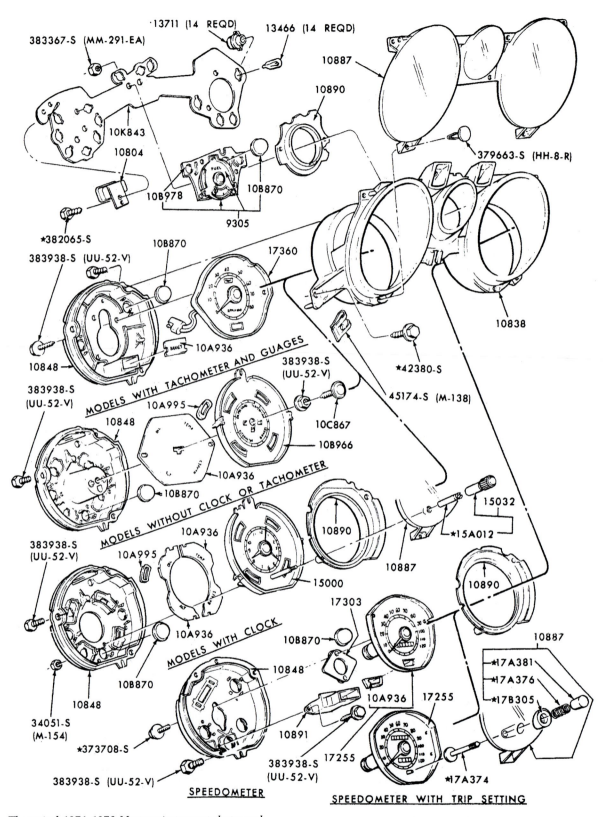

383367-S (MM-291-EA)

13711 (14 REQD)

13466 (14 REQD)

10887

10890

10K843

10804

379663-S (HH-8-R)

10B978

10B870

*382065-S

9305

383938-S (UU-52-V)

10B870

17360

382065-S

10838

10848

*42380-S

383938-S (UU-52-V)

MODELS WITH TACHOMETER AND GUAGES

383938-S (UU-52-V)

10A995

45174-S (M-138)

10848

10C867

10A936

10B966

10A936

15032

10B870

MODELS WITHOUT CLOCK OR TACHOMETER

*15A012

10890

10887

383938-S (UU-52-V)

10A936

10890

10A995

10887

10A936

15000

*17A381

MODELS WITH CLOCK

17303

*17A376

10A936

*17B305

10B870

383938-S (UU-52-V)

10848

10848

17255

34051-S (M-154)

10891

10A936

17255

*373708-S

383938-S (UU-52-V)

383938-S (UU-52-V)

*17A374

SPEEDOMETER

SPEEDOMETER WITH TRIP SETTING

The typical 1971-1973 Mustang instrument cluster and related parts.

426

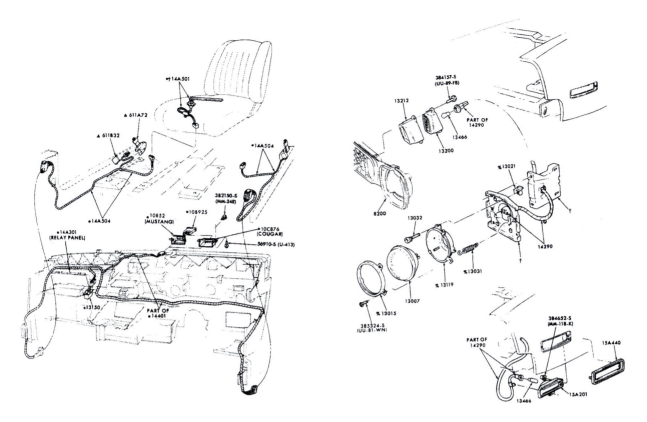

The 1972-1973 Mustang seat belt warning system.

The 1973 Mustang headlamp, parking lamp, fender-side marker lap, and related parts.

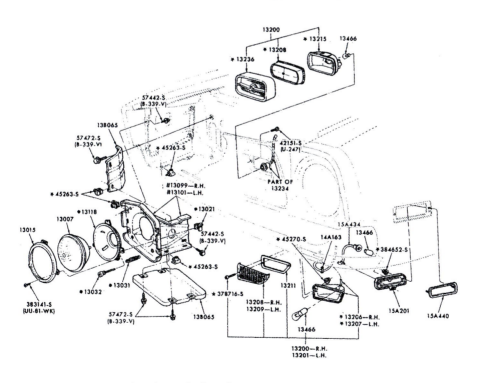

The 1971-1972 Mustang headlamp, parking lamp, fender-side marker lap, and related parts.

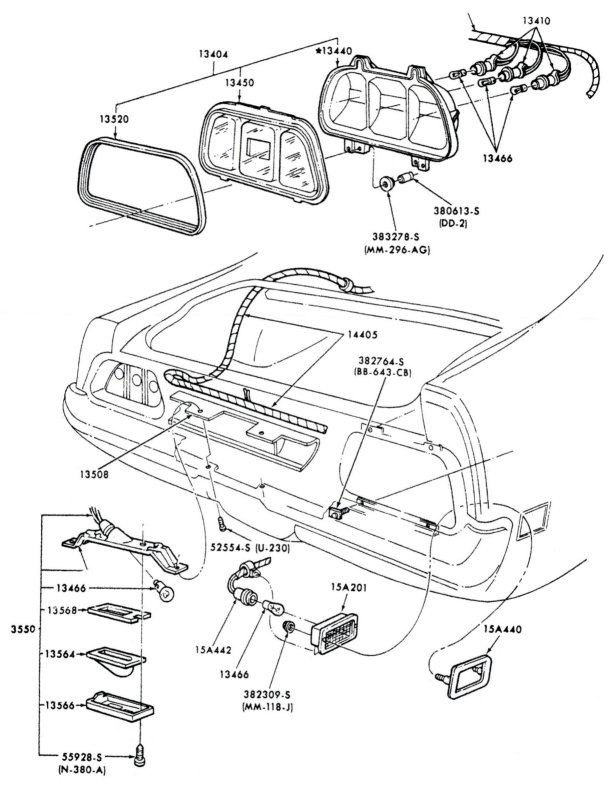

The 1971-1973 Mustang rear lamp, back-up lamp, license plate lamp, and bodyside marker lamp.

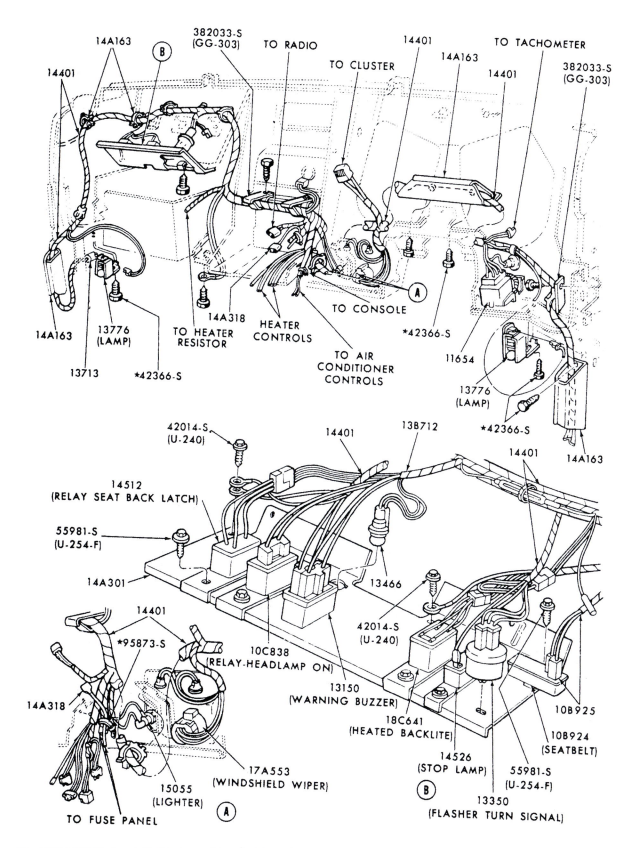

The 1971-1973 Mustang typical instrument panel wiring system.

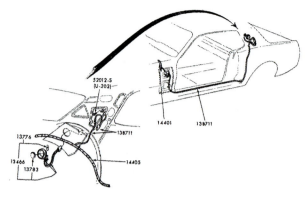

The typical 1971-1973 Mustang pillar-mounted courtesy lamp and related parts.

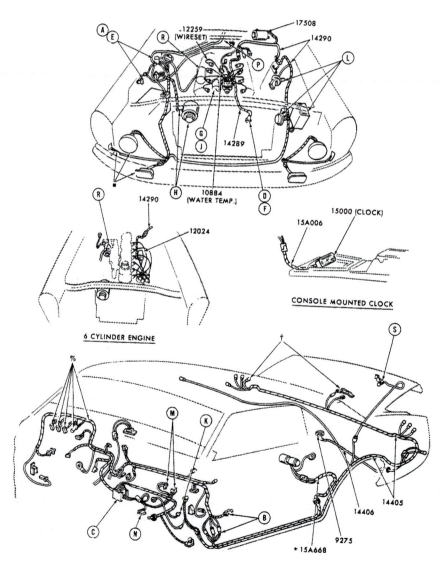

The typical 1971-1973 Mustang overall wiring system.

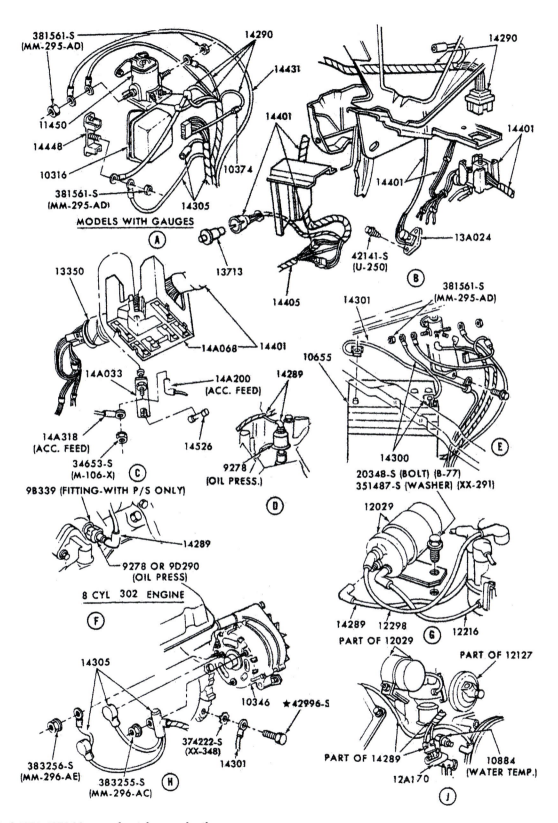

The typical 1971-1973 Mustang electrial system details.

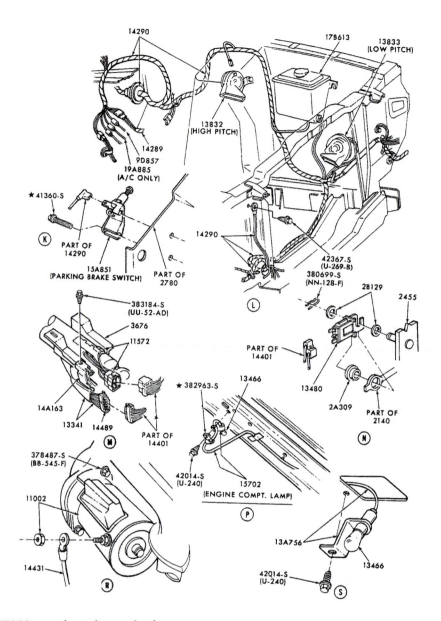

The typical 1971-1973 Mustang electrical system details.

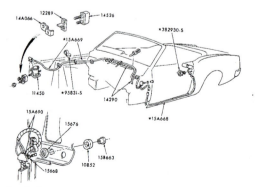

The 1971-1973 Mustang convertible top electrical system.

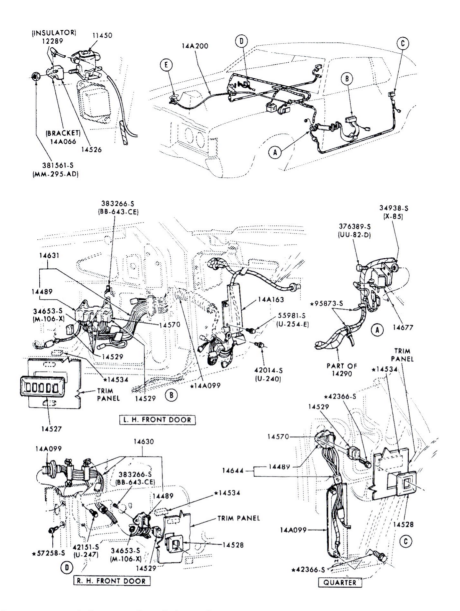

The 1971-1973 Mustang power window controls and electrical system.

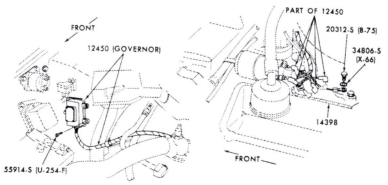

The transistorized engine governor for 1971 Mustangs equipped with 429 CJ and SCJ engines.

MUSTANG BULB CHART, 1971-1973

Year	Function	Industry No.	Part Number	Notes
72/73	Alternator Charge Indicator	194	C2AZ-13466-C	
73	AM Radio Pilot Light	1893	C1VY-13466-A	
73	AM/FM Radio Pilot Light	1892	B9MY-13466-A	
64/73	Ash Tray (Console)	1892	B9MY-13466-A	
71/73	Ash Tray (Instru. Panel)	1445	B6A-13466-B	
71/73	Auto Trans Shift Indicator	1445	D8TZ-13466-A	
71/73	Aux. Instrument Cluster	194	C2AZ-13466-C	
71	Body Side Lamp - Rear	194A	C9DZ-13466-A	
71/73	Back Up Lamp	1156	C3DZ-13466-A	
71/73	Cigar Lighter	1895	C3AZ-13466-B	
71	Clock Lamp	1895	C3AZ-13466-B	
72/73	Clock Lamp	194	C2AZ-13466-C	
71/73	Courtesy Lamp	631	C3VY-13466-A	Instru. Panel
70/73	Courtesy Lamp Pillar	105	D0AZ-13466-A	
71	Dome Lamp	105	D0AZ-13466-A	Before 6/1/71
71/73	Dome Lamp	561	D1AZ-13466-A	After 6/1/71
71/73	Door Ajar Warning Lamp	194	C2AZ-13466-C	
71/73	Engine Compartment	631	C3VY-13466-A	
71	Front Fender Side Lamp	97NA	C8MY-13466-A	Before 8/3/70
71/73	Front Fender Side Lamp	194	C2AZ-13466-C	After 8/3/70
71/73	Fuel Indicator	1895	C3AZ-13466-B	
71/73	Glove Compartment	1895	C3AZ-13466-B	Instru. Panel
73	Heater Control Lamp	1445	D8TZ-13466-A	
71	High Beam Indicator	1895	C3AZ-13466-B	
72/73	High Beam Indicator	194	C2AZ-13466-C	
71/72	Instrument Panel	1895	C3AZ-13466-B	
73	Instrument Panel	194	C2AZ-13466-C	
71/73	Luggage Compartment	631	C3VY-13466-A	
71/73	Map Light	212-1	C6VY-13466-A	Instru. Panel
71	Marker Lamp, Front	97NA	C8MY-13466-A	
72/73	Marker Lamp, Front	194	C2AZ-13466-C	
71	Oil Pressure Warning	1895	C3AZ-13466-B	
72/73	Oil Pressure Warning	194	C2AZ-13466-C	
67/73	Parking Brake Warning	256	C4SZ-13466-A	Option Pkg.
71/73	Parking Lamp	1157NA	C9MY-13466-A	
71/72	Portable Trunk Lamp	1003	B6AZ-13466-A	
71/73	Rear Lamp	1157	C8TZ-13466-A	
71/73	Rear License Plate	97	C3AZ-13466-A	
71	Rear Marker Lamp	97NA	C8MY-13466-A	
72/73	Rear Marker Lamp	194	C2AZ-13466-C	
71/73	Seat Belt Warning Lamp	1445	B6A-13466-B	
71/72	Sport Lamp	94	D0SZ-13466-A	
71	Temperature Indicator	1895	C3AZ-13466-B	
72/73	Temperature Indicator	194	C2AZ-13466-C	
71	Turn Signal Indicator	1895	C3AZ-13466-B	
72/73	Turn Signal Indicator	194	C2AZ-13466-C	
73	Windsh'ld Wiper/Washer Switch	1895	C3AZ-13466-B	

MUSTANG ALTERNATOR to VOLTAGE REGULATOR WIRING ASSEMBLY APPLICATION CHART

Year	Model	Description	Part Number
71	S/R, H/T & Conv w/o Instr Pkg		D1OZ-14305-B
	Before 10/1/70		
	Mach 1 w/o Instr Pkg		
	After 10/1/70		
71	Mach 1 Before 10/1/70		D1ZZ-14305-B
	S/R, H/T & Conv w/ Instr Grp		
	Before 10/1/70		
	S/R, H/T & Conv w/ Std Interior		
	& Instr Pkg After 10/1/70		
	S/R w/ Std Interior & Mach 1 w/		
	Sports Int Pkg After 10/1/70		
	Boss 351 After 10/1/70		
72	All w/ Instr Pkg Before 12/1/71		D2ZZ-14305-B
72	All w/ Instr Pkg	Use w/ 38, 42, 55, 61	D2ZZ-14305-E
	From 12/1/71 to 1/3/72	Amp Ford Alternator	
72	All w/ Instr Pkg	Use w/ 38, 42, 55, 61	D3ZZ-14305-E
	From 1/3/72	Amp Ford Alternator	
72	All w/o Instr Pkg	Use w/ 38, 42, 55, 61	D2ZZ-14305-C
	Before 12/1/71	Amp Ford Alternator	
72	All 8 cyl w/o Instr Pkg	Use w/ 38, 42, 55, 61	D3OZ-14305-B
	After 12/1/71	Amp Ford Alternator	
72	6 cyl w/o Instr Pkg	Use w/ 38, 42, 55, 61	D3DZ-14305-D
	After 12/1/71	Amp Ford Alternator	
72	All w/o Instr Pkg	Use w/ 70 Amp	D2ZZ-14305-G
	Before 7/3/72	Ford Alternator	
72	All w/o Instr Pkg	Use w/ 70 Amp	D3ZZ-14305-C
	After 7/3/72	Ford Alternator	
72	All with Instr Pkg	Use w/ 70 Amp	D2ZZ-14305-H
	Before 7/3/72	Ford Alternator	
72	All with Instr Pkg	Use w/ 70 Amp	D3ZZ-14305-B
	After 7/3/72	Ford Alternator	
73	6 cyl w/o gauges or A/C	Use w/ 42, 55, 61	D3DZ-14305-D
		Amp Ford Alternator	
73	6 cyl w/o gauges or	Use w/ 42, 55, 61	D3DZ-14305-B
	8 cyl with A/C	Amp Ford Alternator	
73	All with gauges	Use w/ 42, 55, 61	D3ZZ-14305-E
		Amp Ford Alternator	
73	All w/o gauges	Use w/ 70 Amp	D3ZZ-14305-C
		Ford Alternator	
73	All with gauges	Use w/ 70 Amp	D3ZZ-14305-B
		Ford Alternator	

INSTRUMENT PANEL to DASH PANEL WIRING ASSEMBLY APPLICATION CHART, 1971-1973

Year	Model	Part Number
71	S/R (incl. Mach 1; exc. Boss) w/o Instr Pkg, Sports Int. or A/C. H/T & Conv w/o Instr Pkg or A/C.	D1ZZ-14401-N
71	S/R, H/T & Conv w/o A/C and w/ Instr Pkg before 10/1/70. Mach 1 & S/R (exc. Boss) w/ Sports Int. and/or Instr Pkg w/o A/C, 10/1/70 to 11/1/70. Boss 351, 10/1/70 to 11/1/70. H/T & Conv w/ Instr Pkg w/o A/C from 10/1/70 to 11/1/70.	D1ZZ-14401-B
71	S/R (exc. Boss) & Mach 1 w/ Sports Int. Pkg and/or Instr Pkg, w/o A/C from 11/1/70 Boss 351 from 11/1/70. H/T & Conv w/ Instr Pkg w/o A/C from 11/1/70.	D1ZZ-14401-H
71	S/R (incl Mach 1), H/T, Conv w/ A/C, w/o Instr Pkg before 10/1/70. Mach 1 & S/R (exc Boss) w/o Instr Pkg and/or Sports Int Pkg, w/ A/C, 10/1/70 to 11/1/70. H/T & Conv w/o Instr Pkg, w/ A/C, 10/1/70 to 11/1/70.	D1ZZ-14401-C
71	S/R (exc. Boss) & Mach 1 w/o Instr Pkg and/or Sports Int. Pkg, w/ A/C, 11/1/70 to 3/1/71. H/T & Conv w/o Instr Pkg, w/ A/C, 11/1/70 to 3/1/71.	D1ZZ-14401-J
71	S/R (exc. Boss) & Mach 1 w/o Instr Pkg and/or Sports Int. Pkg w/ A/C from 3/1/71. H/T & Conv w/o Instr Pkg, w/ A/C from 3/1/71.	D1ZZ-14401-P
71	S/R, H/T & Conv w/ A/C, w/ Instr Pkg before 10/1/70. S/R (exc Boss) w/ Sports Int Pkg, and H/T & Conv, all w/ Instr Pkg, all w/ A/C, 10/1/70 to 11/1/70.	D1ZZ-14401-E
71	S/R (exc Boss) & Mach 1 w/ Instr Pkg, w/ Sports Int Pkg, w/ A/C, 11/1/70 to 3/1/71. H/T & Conv w/ Instr Pkg, w/ A/C, 11/1/70 to 3/1/71.	D1ZZ-14401-L
71	S/R (exc Boss) & Mach 1 w/ Instr Pkg, w/ Sports Int Pkg, w/ A/C from 3/1/71. H/T & Conv w/ Instr Pkg, w/ A/C from 3/1/71.	D1ZZ-14401-R
71	Mach 1 w/o A/C before 10/1/70. S/R (exc Boss) w/ Sports Int Pkg, w/o A/C, 10/1/70 to 11/1/70.	D1ZZ-14401-D
71	S/R (exc Boss) & Mach 1 w/ Sports Int Pkg, w/o A/C, from 11/1/70.	D1ZZ-14401-K
71	Mach 1 w/ A/C before 10/1/70. S/R (exc Boss) w/ Sports Int Pkg, w/ A/C, 10/1/70 to 11/1/70.	D1ZZ-14401-F
71	S/R (exc Boss) w/ Sports Int Pkg, w/ A/C, 11/1/70 to 3/1/71.	D1ZZ-14401-M
71	S/R (exc Boss) w/ Sports Int Pkg, w/ A/C, from 3/1/71.	D1ZZ-14401-Q
72	All body styles w/o tach before 12/1/71	D2ZZ-14401-A
72	All body styles w/o tach after 12/1/71	D2ZZ-14401-E
72	All body styles with tach before 12/1/71	D2ZZ-14401-B
72	All body styles with tach, 12/1/71 to 1/3/72	D2ZZ-14401-D
72	All body styles with tach after 1/3/72	D2ZZ-14401-F
73	All body styles w/o tach and/or gauge pkg	D3ZZ-14401-D
73	All body styles with tach, w/ gauge pkg, before 2/1/73	D3ZZ-14401-B
73	All body styles with tach, w/ gauge pkg, after 2/1/73	D3ZZ-14401-E

MUSTANG DASH to ENGINE GAUGE FEED WIRE ASSEMBLY APPLICATION CHART

Year	Model	Part Number
71	302-2V	D1AZ-14289-B
71	351	D1OZ-14289-C
71	429	D1AZ-14289-D
71	250 (6 cyl)	DODZ-14289-C
72	250 (6 cyl)	D2ZZ-14289-A
72	302, before 10/22/71	D2AZ-14289-B
72	302, after 10/22/71	D2AZ-14289-J
72	351 CJ before 9/15/71	D2AZ-14289-G
	Boss 351 before 2/1/72	
	Boss 351 after 2/1/72	
72	All 351-2V & 351CJ from 9/15/71	D2OZ-14289-D
73	250 (6 cyl) M/T	D3OZ-14289-A
73	250 (6 cyl) A/T before 10/16/72	D3OZ-14289-K
73	250 (6 cyl) A/T, 10/16/72 to 3/12/73	D3OZ-14289-S
73	250 (6 cyl) A/T, from 3/12/73	D3OZ-14289-E
73	302	D3OZ-14289-B
73	351, A/T	D3OZ-14289-C
73	351, M/T	D3OZ-14289-D

MUSTANG ALTERNATOR APPLICATION CHART, 1971
(All Motorcraft Brand)

Year	Engine	Amp Hrs	Service Alternator	Voltage Regulator
71	6/250	38 (1)	D2AZ-10346-C r/b D7AZ-10346-C	C3SZ-10316-B r/b D4TZ-10316-A
71	6/250	55 (2)	D2AZ-10346-F	C3SZ-10316-B r/b D4TZ-10316-A
71	302-2V	38	D2AZ-10346-C r/b D7AZ-10346-C	C3SZ-10316-B r/b D4TZ-10316-A
71	351	38	D2AZ-10346-C r/b D7AZ-10346-C	C3SZ-10316-B r/b D4TZ-10316-A
71	302-2V	42	D2AZ-10346-C r/b D7AZ-10346-C	C3SZ-10316-B r/b D4TZ-10316-A
71	351	42	D2AZ-10346-C r/b D7AZ-10346-C	C3SZ-10316-B r/b D4TZ-10316-A
71	all V8	55	D2AZ-10346-F	C3SZ-10316-B r/b D4TZ-10316-A
71	302-4V	55	DOZZ-10346-B	C3SZ-10316-B r/b D4TZ-10316-A
71	351	55	DOZZ-10346-B	C3SZ-10316-B r/b D4TZ-10316-A
71	429	55	DOZZ-10346-B	C3SZ-10316-B r/b D4TZ-10316-A

Notes: (1) w/o A/C   (2) w/ A/C

MUSTANG ALTERNATOR APPLICATION CHART, 1972
(All Motorcraft Brand)

Year	Engine	Amp Hrs	Service Alternator	Voltage Regulator
72	6/250	38 (1)	D2AZ-10346-C r/b D7AZ-10346-C	C3SZ-10316-B r/b D4TZ-10316-A
72	302/351	38 (1)	D2AZ-10346-C r/b D7AZ-10346-C	C3SZ-10316-B r/b D4TZ-10316-A
72	302/351	42	D2AZ-10346-C r/b D7AZ-10346-C	C3SZ-10316-B r/b D4TZ-10316-A
72	all V8	55	D0AZ-10346-F	C3SZ-10316-B r/b D4TZ-10316-A
72	6/250	55 (2)	D0AZ-10346-F	C3SZ-10316-B r/b D4TZ-10316-A
72	all V8	55	D2AZ-10346-D r/b D7AZ-10346-B	C3SZ-10316-B r/b D4TZ-10316-A
72	6/250	55 (2)	D2AZ-10346-D r/b D7AZ-10346-B	C3SZ-10316-B r/b D4TZ-10316-A
72	351CJ	55 (3)	D0ZZ-10346-B	C3SZ-10316-B r/b D4TZ-10316-A
72	351CJ	55 (4)	D2ZZ-10346-B r/b D7AZ-10346-A	C3SZ-10316-B r/b D4TZ-10316-A
72	302/351	61 (2,3)	D0TZ-10346-C	C3SZ-10316-B r/b D4TZ-10316-A
72	302/351	61 (2,4)	D2TZ-10346-B r/b D7AZ-10346-B	C3SZ-10316-B r/b D4TZ-10316-A

Notes: (1) w/o A/C   (2) w/ A/C
(3) before 12/1/71   (4) after 12/1/71

MUSTANG ALTERNATOR APPLICATION CHART, 1973
(All Motorcraft Brand)

Year	Engine	Amp Hrs	Service Alternator	Voltage Regulator
73	All	38, 42	D2AZ-10346-C r/b D7AZ-10346-C	E2PZ-10316-A
73	exc. 351CJ	55	D2AZ-10346-D r/b D7AZ-10346-B	E2PZ-10316-A
73	351CJ	55 (high temp)	D2ZZ-10346-B r/b D7AZ-10346-A	E2PZ-10316-A
73	All	61	D2TZ-10346-B r/b D7AZ-10346-B	E2PZ-10316-A
73	All	70	D2OZ-10346-B r/b D7OZ-10346-A	E2PZ-10316-A

MUSTANG ALTERNATOR PULLEY APPLICATION CHART, 1971

Engine	Identification	Type	Dimensions: A	B	C	E	F	Amps	Part Number
250	C9AF-10A352-A	3	2.84	.670	.38	1.015		38	C5AZ-10344-K
250	C9AF-10A352-C	6	2.84	.670	.38	1.40	.64	55	C5AZ-10344-L
302	C9AF-10A352-A	3	2.84	.670	.38	1.015		42	C5AZ-10344-K
302-4V	D1ZF-10A352-A	5	3	.670	.38	.91		55	D1ZZ-10344-A
351	C9AF-10A352-A	3	2.84	.670	.38	1.015		42	C5AZ-10344-K
429	D1ZF-10A352-AA	5	3.05	.670	.38	.91		55	D1ZZ-10344-A

MUSTANG ALTERNATOR PULLEY APPLICATION CHART, 1972

Engine	Identification	Type	Dimensions: A	B	C	E	F	Amps	Part Number
250	C9AF-10A352-A	3	2.84	.670	.38	1.015		38	C5AZ-10344-K
250	C9AF-10A352-C	6	2.84	.670	.38	1.40	.64	55	C5AZ-10344-L
250	w/ Hang-On A/C								D2OZ-10344-B
302	C9AF-10A352-A	3	2.84	.670	.38	1		42,61	C5AZ-10344-K
302	D1ZF-10A352-A	5	3	.670	.38	.91		55	D1ZZ-10344-A
351	C9AF-10A352-A	3	2.84	.670	.38	1		42,61	C5AZ-10344-K

MUSTANG ALTERNATOR PULLEY APPLICATION CHART, 1973

Engine	Identification	Type	Dimensions: A	B	C	E	F	Amps	Part Number
250	C9AF-10A352-A	3	2.84	.670	.38	1		38,40,60,70	C5AZ-10344-K
250	C5AF-10A352-J	6	2.84	.670	.38	1.40	.64	55,60,65	C5AZ-10344-L
250	C9AF-10A352-C	6	2.84	.670	.38	1.40	.64	55,60,65	C5AZ-10344-L
250	w/ Hang-On A/C								D2OZ-10344-B
302	C9AF-10A352-A	3	2.84	.670	.38	1		38,40,42,60, 61,70,90,100	C5AZ-10344-K
302	D2OF-10A352-AA	3	3.15	.670	.38	.91		70	D2OZ-10344-A
302	C9AF-10A352-C	6	2.84	.670	.38	1.40	.64	38,40,60,65	C5AZ-10344-L
302	D2ZF-10A352-AA							60,65	D9ZZ-10344-A
351	C9AF-10A352-A	3	2.84	.670	.38	1		40,42,55,60, 61,70,90,100	C5AZ-10344-K
351	D2OF-10A352-AA	3	3.15	.670	.38	.91		70,90,100	D2OZ-10344-A
351	D1ZF-10A352-AA	5	3	.670	.38	.91		55	D1ZZ-10344-A

MUSTANG BATTERY MOUNTING PARTS CHART, 1971-1973

Attention: For '71-'73 Mustang Battery Applications, chart on p. 337 applies through 1973.

Year	Amp Hrs	Bolt Clamp Part Number	Carrier/Tray Part Number	Holddown Clamp Part Number	Brace/Bracket Part Number
71/72	45/55	D4SZ-10756-A	D0OZ-10732-A	D0OZ-10718-A	D0OZ-10A705-A
71	70/80	D4SZ-10756-A	D0OZ-10732-B	D0OZ-10718-A	none
72	70	D4SZ-10756-A	D0OZ-10732-B	D0OZ-10718-A	D0OZ-10A705-A
73	42/45	D4SZ-10756-A	D0OZ-10732-B	D0OZ-10718-A (1)	D0OZ-10A705-A
73	45	D4SZ-10756-A	D0OZ-10732-B	D3OZ-10718-B (2)	D0OZ-10A705-A
73	70	D4SZ-10756-A	D0OZ-10732-B	D0OZ-10718-A (1)	D0OZ-10A705-A
73	70	D4SZ-10756-A	D0OZ-10732-B	D3OZ-10718-B (2)	D0OZ-10A705-A

Notes:　(1) Before 6/1/73　(2) After 6/1/73

MUSTANG STARTER APPLICATION CHART, 1971-1973

Year	Cyl/CID	Identification No.	Service Starter Ass'y
71	6/250	D0ZF-11001-A	C2OZ-11002-B
71	8/302/351/AT	D0AF-11001-B	D4OZ-11002-A
71	8/302/351/MT	D0AF-11001-C	C5TZ-11002-D
71	8/429	C9AF-11001-A	C8VY-11002-C
72	6/250	D2ZF-11001-AA	D4OZ-11002-A
72	8/302/351/AT	D2ZF-11001-CA	D4OZ-11002-A
72	8/302/351/MT	D2AF-11001-DA	C5TZ-11002-D
72	8/429	D2AF-11001-EA	C8VY-11002-C
73	6/250	D2AF-11001-CA	D6OZ-11002-A
73	8/302/AT	D2AF-11001-CA	D6OZ-11002-A
73	8/302/351/MT	D2AF-11001-DA	E4TZ-11002-A
73	8/351/AT	D2AF-11001-CA	D6OZ-11002-A

MUSTANG RADIO ANTENNA KIT APPLICATION CHART

Year	Part Number	Description
67-73	C1SZ-17696-B	F/B, H/T - Univ. Electric Type, Rear Qutr Mount
71-72	D3AZ-18813-C	R/H Manual Front
73	C7AZ-18813-C	Electric
73	D7AZ-18813-A	Manual

MUSTANG WINDSHIELD WIPER MOTOR ASSEMBLY APPLICATION, 1971-1973

Year	Part Number	Description
71/73	D1ZZ-17508-A (WM-254)	Used w/ 2-speed or intermittent wipers

MUSTANG SPEEDOMETER ASSEMBLY APPLICATION CHART, 1971-1973

Year	Model	Description	Part Number
71/73	All	Miles, w/o Tripodometer	D1ZZ-17255-A
71/73	All	Miles, w/ Tripodometer	D1ZZ-17255-B

MUSTANG ELECTRICAL CIRCUIT BREAKER ASSEMBLY APPLICATION CHART, through 1973

Year	Model	Amp	Length	Width	Mark Color	Part Number
65/72	Convertible Top Control	20	1.07"	.40"	Red	C4DZ-14526-C
71/73	Marker, Parking & Tail Lamps	15	1.27"	.79"		D1MY-14526-C
71/73	Heated Backlite, Power Top Power Windows, and Auto Seat Back Latch	20	1.07"	.40"	Red Dot	D1AZ-14526-A

MUSTANG GLASS TUBE FUSE APPLICATION CHART, 1965-1973
Note: The 1964-1970 section of this chart omitted from First Edition.

Year	Function	Length	Industry No.	Part Number
65	Air Conditioner	1.25"	AGC-15	A2AZ-14526-A
69/73	Air Conditioner	1.00"	AGX-30	C8OZ-14526-A
65/70	Back-up Lamp	1.06"	SFE-14	A0AZ-14526-A
69	Back-up Lamp	1.25"	SFE-20	A0AZ-14526-B
71/73	Back-up Lamp	1.25"	AGC-15	A2AZ-14526-A
65/71	Cigar Lighter	1.06"	SFE-14	A0AZ-14526-A
72	Cigar Lighter	1.00"	AGX-20	C5AZ-14526-B
73	Cigar Lighter	1.25"	SFE-20	A0AZ-14526-B
72	Clock	1.06"	SFE-14	A0AZ-14526-A
69	Clock Illumination	.84"	AGW-4	C0LY-14526-B
72/73	Clock Illumination	.62"	SFE-4	C9SZ-14526-C
69/73	Courtesy Lamp	1.06"	SFE-14	A0AZ-14526-A
68	Defogger	1.25"	SFE-20	A0AZ-14526-B
69	Defogger	1.25"	AGC-15	A2AZ-14526-A
70/73	Defogger	1.25"	SFE-20	A0AZ-14526-B
65/69	Dome Lamp	.88"	SFE 7-1/2	B6AZ-14526-A
70/73	Dome Lamp	1.06"	SFE-14	A0AZ-14526-A
68	Electric Antenna	1.06"	SFE-14	A0AZ-14526-A
65/68	Emergency Flasher	1.00"	AGX-20	C5AZ-14526-B
69	Emergency Flasher	1.25"	SFE-20	A0AZ-14526-B
69	Fuel Level System	1.25"	SFE-20	A0AZ-14526-B
70/73	Glove Comp. Lamp	1.06"	SFE-14	A0AZ-14526-A
72/73	Heated Backlite	1.25"	SFE-20	A0AZ-14526-B
65/73	Heater	1.06"	SFE-14	A0AZ-14526-A
69	Heater Illumination	.84"	AGW-4	C0LY-14526-B

MUSTANG GLASS TUBE FUSE APPLICATION CHART, Continued.

Year	Function	Length	Industry No.	Part Number
73	Heater Control Lamp	.62"	SFE-4	C9SZ-14526-C
70/73	Ignition Key Warning	1.06"	SFE-14	A0AZ-14526-A
70/73	Instr. Clust Warn Lgts.	.62"	SFE-4	C9SZ-14526-C
65/68	Instr. Panel Illumination	.62"	1AG 2-1/2	C4GY-14526-A
69/73	Instr. Panel Illumination	.62"	SFE-4	C9SZ-14526-C
72/73	Luggage Comp. Lamp	1.06"	SFE-14	A0AZ-14526-A
69/73	Park Brake Warn Lamp	1.25"	SFE-20	A0AZ-14526-B
73	Park Brake Warn Lamp		AGA 7-1/2	C7VY-14526-A
69/73	Power Window Relay	1.25"	SFE-20	A0AZ-14526-B
69	Radio	1.25"	SFE-20	A0AZ-14526-B
65/68	Radio Lamp (8 tube)	.88"	SFE 7-1/2	B6AZ-14526-A
69	Radio Illumination	.84"	AGW-4	C0LY-14526-B
72/73	Radio Illumination	.62"	SFE-4	C9SZ-14526-C
65	Rr. Seat Speak. Switch	.88"	SFE 7-1/2	B6AZ-14526-A
66/73	Seat Belt Warn Lamp or Buzzer	1.06"	SFE-14	A0AZ-14526-A
69	Seat Belt Warn Lamp	1.25"	SFE-20	A0AZ-14526-B
69	Speed Control	1.25"	SFE-20	A0AZ-14526-B
65/72	Spot Lamp	.88"	SFE 7-1/2	B6AZ-14526-A
68/72	Transm. Selector Lamp	1.25"	SFE-20	A0AZ-14526-B
69	Turn Signal	1.25"	SFE-20	A0AZ-14526-B
72/73	Turn Signal	1.25"	AGC-15	A2AZ-14526-A
65	Windshield Washer	1.06"	SFE-14	A0AZ-14526-A
69	Windshield Washer	1.25"	SFE-20	A0AZ-14526-B
71/73	Windshield Washer	1.25"	AGC-15	A2AZ-14526-A

MUSTANG FUSIBLE LINK WIRE TYPE FUSE BREAKER I.D. & APPLICATIONS, through 1973

Year	Model	Description	Part Number
69/72	w/55, 61 OR 65 amp Ford Alternator	9" long - 14 Gauge wire r/b D3AZ-14526-D (4-74)	C9AZ-14526-D
69/72	w/ 38, 42 OR 45 amp Ford Alternator	9" long -16 Gauge Wire (Alternator Protection)	C9AZ-14526-E
73	As Required	9" long - 14 Gauge wire, Green 1 end stripped, 1 end eyelet	D3AZ-14526-D
73	As Required	9" long - 16 Gauge wire, Orange 1 end stripped, 1 end eyelet	D3AZ-14526-T
73	As Required	9" long - 18 Gauge wire, Red 1 end stripped, 1 end eyelet	D3AZ-14526-F
73	As Required	9" long - 20 Gauge wire, Blue 1 end stripped, 1 end eyelet	D3AZ-14526-G
73	As Required	9" long - 20 Gauge wire, Blue both ends stripped	D3AZ-14526-M
73	As Required	9" long - 14 Gauge wire, Green both ends stripped	D3AZ-14526-H
73	As Required	9" long - 16 Gauge wire, Orange both ends stripped	D3AZ-14526-J
73	As Required	9" long - 17 Gauge wire, Yellow both ends stripped	D3AZ-14526-N
73	As Required	9" long - 18 Gauge wire, Red both ends stripped	D3AZ-14526-L

MUSTANG REAR LAMP WIRING HARNESS APPLICATION CHART, 1971-1973

Year	Model	Description	Part Number
71	Before 11/1/70		D1ZZ-14405-A
71/72	From 11/1/70 to 10/18/71		D1ZZ-14405-B
72/73	From 10/18/71	Incl. (1) D1ZZ-15B411-A Wire	D1ZZ-14405-C

MUSTANG DASH PANEL TO HEADLAMP JUNCTION WIRE APPLICATION CHART, 1971-1973

Year	Model	Part Number
71	SportsRoof w/ 302-2V w/o Instr Pkg, before 10/1/70. Hardtop and Convertible w/o Instrument Package. SportsRoof (exc Boss), Hardtop, Convertible w/o Instr Pkg, Sports Int. Pkg, or Spec Value Pkg from 10/1/70.	D1ZZ-14290-B
	SportsRoof w/ 302-2V w/ Instr Pkg, before 10/1/70. Hardtop and Convertible w/ Instrument Package. SportsRoof (exc Boss), Hardtop, Convertible w/ Instr Pkg or Sports Interior Package, from 10/1/70.	D1ZZ-14290-C
	SportsRoof w/ 302-4V w/o Instr Pkg before 10/1/70. Mach 1 w/o Instrument Package. SportsRoof (exc Boss), & Hardtop, w/ Spec Value Pkg Mach 1 w/o Instr Pkg or Sports Int. Pkg from 10/1/70.	D1ZZ-14290-D
	SportsRoof w/ 302-4V w/ Instr Pkg before 10/1/70. Mach 1 w/ Instr Pkg, or Sports Int Pkg, or Special Value Package, from 10/1/70. Boss 351	D1ZZ-14290-A
72	SportsRoof, Hardtop, Convertible w/o Instr Pkg, Sports Interior Pkg, or Special Value Pkg before 12/1/71.	D2ZZ-14290-C
	SportsRoof, Hardtop, Convertible w/o Instr Pkg, Sports Interior Pkg, or Special Value Pkg, from 12/1/71.	D2ZZ-14290-L
	SportsRoof, Hardtop, Convertible w/ Instr Package before 12/1/71. SportsRoof w/ Sports Int Pkg but w/o Instr Package or Special Value Package, before 12/1/71.	D2ZZ-14290-D
	SportsRoof, Hardtop, Convertible w/ Instr Package from 12/1/71. SportsRoof w/ Sports Int Pkg but w/o Instr Package or Special Value Package, from 12/1/71.	D2ZZ-14290-M
	SportsRoof w/ Instrument Package, or Sports Interior Package, or Special Value Package, before 12/1/71. Mach 1 w/ Instr Pkg or Sports Int Pkg, before 12/1/71. Conv. w/ Sports Int Pkg and Instr Pkg, before 12/1/71.	D2ZZ-14290-B
	SportsRoof w/ Instrument Package, or Sports Interior Package, or Special Value Package, from 12/1/71. Mach 1 w/ Instr Pkg or Sports Int Pkg, from 12/1/71. Conv. w/ Sports Int Pkg and Instr Pkg, from 12/1/71.	D2ZZ-14290-K
	SportsRoof and Mach 1 w/ Spec Value Pkg, but w/o Instr Pkg or Sports Int Pkg, before 12/1/71. Hardtop w/ Spec Value Pkg, but w/o Instr Pkg, before 12/1/71. Conv. w/ Sports Interior Pkg, before 12/1/71.	D2ZZ-14290-E
	SportsRoof and Mach 1 w/ Spec Value Pkg, but w/o Instr Pkg or Sports Int Pkg, from 12/1/71. Hardtop w/ Spec Value Pkg, but w/o Instr Pkg, from 12/1/71. Conv. w/ Sports Interior Pkg, from 12/1/71.	D2ZZ-14290-N
73	All, without gauges or tachometer	D3ZZ-14290-C
	All, with gauges and tachometer	D3ZZ-14290-B

OPTIONS

From the first Mustangs of 1964, Ford offered options so that a prospective owner might "customize" his or her purchase. Those options were always numerous and exciting, though, by the 1970s, a few became standard Mustang equipment. Still, restorers are constantly tempted by the idea of adding luxury, convenience, or personality options to their cars.

Many of the options offered from 1971 through 1973 are depicted in Chapter 8 of this book. The reader should also note that this section does not cover options covered in previous chapters or sections such as radios, brakes, upholstery, exterior trim, air conditioning, and power steering. Also, the following items should be referenced:

For the optional hang-on stereo tape deck, speakers, and wiring for 1971-1973 Mustangs, please refer to the top right corner of page 346.

For the optional integral AM stereo tape player and AM/FM multiplex radio and speakers for 1971-1973 Mustangs, refer to the bottom of page 347.

For the optional 1971 Mustang hang-on or dealer-installed Slimline air conditioning parts, refer to the lower right corner of page 351.

For the optional trunk-mounted luggage carrier, refer to page 343.

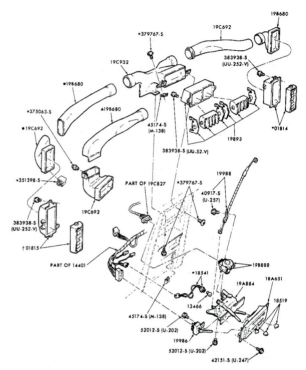

The 1971-1973 Mustang integral air conditioning controls and related parts.

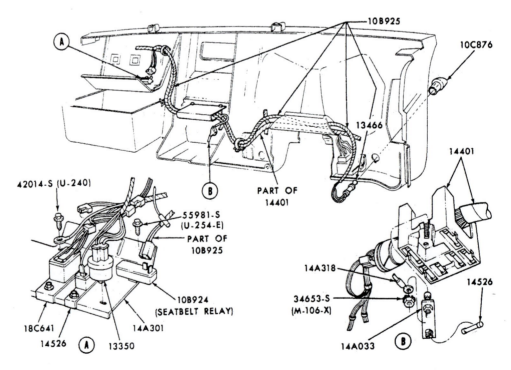

The 1971-1973 Mustang seat belt warning lamp wiring.

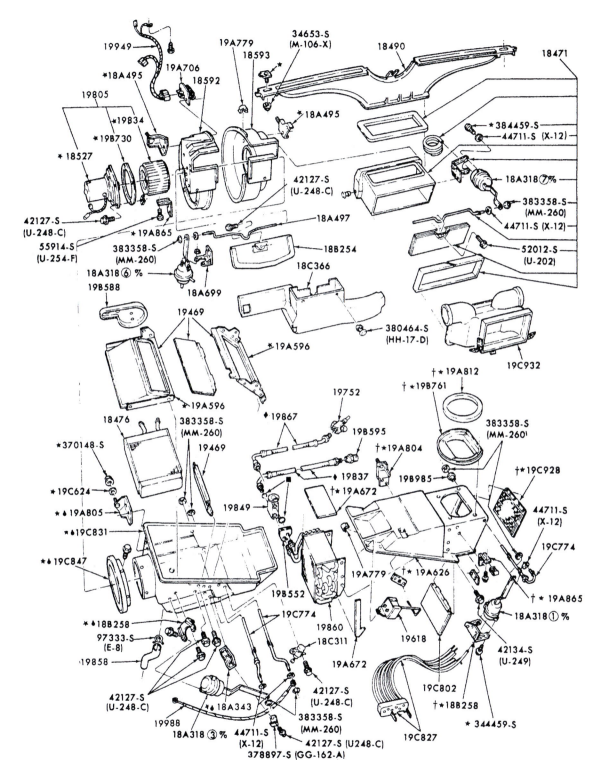

The 1971-1973 Mustang integral air conditioning controls and related parts.

445

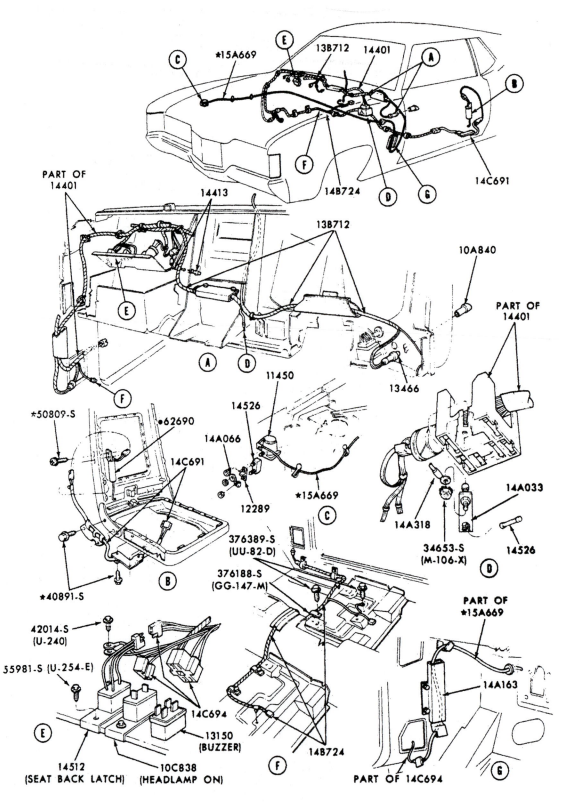

The *1971-1973 Mustang safety/convenience warning indicator system.*

446

Hellbent for Cooking

THE HEAVY METAL COOKBOOK

ANNICK "MORBID CHEF" GIROUX

Second printing, 2010. First edition published in 2009 by

BAZILLION POINTS BOOKS
61 Greenpoint Ave. #504
Brooklyn, NY 11222
United States
www.bazillionpoints.com

HELLBENT FOR COOKING: The Heavy Metal Cookbook

Written by Annick Giroux, with some biographies by Ian Christe
Cover, introduction, and flap photos by Andy Ryan
Food photography and food styling by Annick Giroux (except where noted)
Drawings by Nagawika
Graphic design by Annick Giroux

Edited by Polly Watson

Recipes were kindly given by the bands to the author between May 2007 and August 2009.

ISBN 978-1-935950-00-4

Printed in China

A HUGE THANKS TO THE FOLLOWING MORTALS

Ian Christe for the amazing support, kindness, giant garlic hamburgers, and Ethiopian food; my family and friends for their encouragement; all the bands that have kindly contributed; Julien Nagawika for the mind-blowing drawings; Andy Ryan for the photos; François for washing the dishes, proofreading, and overall help; Adam Parsons of Singerman Entertainment, Sean "Pellet" of Season of Mist, Agnieszka of Metal Mind Productions, Carol Kaye of Kayos Productions, Chris Johnson of Rage Productions, Costa of Iron Pegasus, and Marc of Morbid Moon Records for their help with contacting bands; Arnaud Labelle for cooking with me; Sean Clark and Arturo for the translations; Janick and the Katacombes venue staff; Yvon and Andrée for the kitchen; and finally, King Diamond for making me laugh: "I don't have any recipes, I'm a horrible cook, and I can assure you that if I had a recipe, you would not want it."

DEDICATED TO GRAND-MAMAN HUGUETTE, THE BEST GRANDMOTHER IN THE WORLD!

The Headbanger's Menu

ACKNOWLEDGMENTS 2

INTRODUCTION 6

1. WEAPONS OF MASS NUTRITION 10

2. APPETIZERS AND SIDE DISHES

AUTOPSY / Mummified Jalapeño Bacon Bombs 14

SLAUGHTER / Incinerator Chicken Wings 16

RIGOR MORTIS / Rolled Swamp Bombs 18

GWAR / Candied Sweetbreads on Bed of Seared Heart 20

DEVASTATION / Istrian Manestra 22

DENIAL OF GOD / Fried Egg Rigor Mortis Cure 24

WITCHFYNDE / Devil's Porridge 26

ABIGAIL / War Miso War Soup 28

L'IMPERO DELLE OMBRE / Focaccia Pugliese 30

ARMORED SAINT / Maria del Carmen Guacamole 32

DUSK / Atomic Aalu Power 34

STÍNY PLAMENŮ / Marinated Hermelín Cheese 36

DESOLATION ANGELS / Yorkshire Pudding 38

ENVENOM / Roti Jala (Net Pancake) 40

CAULDRON/GOAT HORN / Welfare Nachos 42

GRIMORIUM VERUM / Llapingachos 44

3. BEEF

SEPULTURA / Churrasco in Soy Sauce 48

TOXIC HOLOCAUST / Bondage Rolled Steak 50

ANTHRAX / Stuffed Cabbage 52

SIGH / Habañero Gyūdon 54

MASTER'S HAMMER / Bull Testicle Surprise 56

SHACKLES / Hamburgers of Devastation 58

CRUACHAN / Irish Beef Stew 60

WEAPON / Bengal Beef Curry 62

REPULSION / Mushroom Steak à la Jack Daniel's 64

MIDNIGHT / Midnight 7" Metaloaf 66

PAGAN ALTAR / Pagan Pie 68

OBSCURITY / Råbiff (Swedish Steak Tartare) 70

ACCEPT/U.D.O. / Roast Beef with Green Beans 72

THE GATES OF SLUMBER / The Stew of True Doom 74

ANVIL / Thundering Beef Brisket 76

MASTER / Speckmann's Chili Mac 78

ROOT / Guláš à la Root 80

4. PORK

MÜTIILATION / BBQ Pork Ribs 84

THIN LIZZY / Black Rose Jambalaya 86

JUDAS PRIEST/HOLY RAGE / Gray Peas and Bacon 88

SKYFORGER / Latvian Countryside Ribs 90

COUNTESS / Macaroni Against Monotheism 92

IMPALER / Bloody Intestines and Worms 94

MESSIAH / Infernal Swiss Alps Macaroni and Cheese 96

FUNEROT / Pizza Cake (A Dangerous Eating) 98

PROCESSION / Pork of Disease (Citrus Style) 100

ELIXIR / Sausage Meat Pie 102

WITCHTRAP / Frijoles Borrachos (Drunk Beans) 104

DEIPHAGO / Sinigang Na Baboy (Pork in Sour Broth) ... 106

ZEMIAL / Spetsofai 108

DISSECTION / Genocide Yellow Pea Soup 110

5. LAMB

THIN LIZZY / Sunday Brunch Lamb Roast 114

NECROMANTIA / Youvetsi Hellfire 116

MAYHEM / Fårikål 118

URIAH HEEP / Ali Baa Baa (Moroccan Lamb) 120

ROTTING CHRIST / Country Lamb Exohiko 122

WARPIG / Lamb Shanks Braised in Burgundy 124

P. 32   P. 110   P. 134   P. 176   P. 182   P. 200   P. 217

6. POULTRY

PENTAGRAM / Delicious Oriental Chicken Casserole..........128

BLASPHEMY / Misanthrope's Last Supper 130

XIBALBA / Mucbipollo: A Dish for the Dead 132

THE RODS / Full Throttle Chicken Curry..........................134

ARPHAXAT / Pictavian Chicken with Mojhéte Beans 136

NECROSADIST / Tomato Chicken Necrocasserole..........138

TYGERS OF PAN TANG / Pan Tang Stew 140

MINOTAUR / Paprika Cream of Chicken 142

ORODRUIN / Witchfinder Grinder Turkey Club................144

TROUBLE / Ronnie Cole's Turkey Chili 146

ELECTRIC WIZARD / Rook Pie..148

7. SEAFOOD

AMEBIX / Amebix Prawn Bisque 152

DESTRUCTION / Pizza Tonno à la Chef 154

TRENCH HELL / Beer-Battered Fish Filets with Prawns 156

THE LAMP OF THOTH / Black Pudding and Squid 158

"THE LORD WEIRD" SLOUGH FEG / Adrian's Ceviche 160

SIR LORD BALTIMORE / Flounder Filet Oreganato 162

GORGOROTH / Shellfish Crossfire....................................164

BUDGIE / Garlic and Coriander King Prawns...................166

BLACKFIRE / Malaya Fried Mee 168

MANTAK / Nasi Lemak (Coconut Milk Rice Meal)...........170

FAUSTCOVEN / Whisky Demon Bacalao 172

BULLDOZER / Spaghetti Barracuda....................................174

MELECHESH / Superb Salmon Filet....................................176

8. VEGETARIAN

KREATOR / Vegan Oatmeal Burgers 180

CHILDREN OF TECHNOLOGY / Nuclear Yellow Pepper Pizza.. 182

AFTER THE BOMBS / Speed Metal Vegan Tofu 184

ATOMIZER / Vegetarian "Beef" Masala 186

EXCITER / Recipe for Disaster/Tour Bus Molotov Cocktail ... 188

EYEHATEGOD / New Orleans Blood Red Beans and Rice ...190

DEADMASK / Tortilla de Patatas (Spanish Omelette)....192

TANKARD / Beer Pizza Crust 194

9. DESSERTS

INEPSY / Thermonuclear Date Squares 198

SADISTIK EXEKUTION / Black Metal Berry Pie................200

POSSESSED / Strawberry Jell-o Pretzel Salad Cake 202

DEATH SS / Chocolate Pudding "Devil" Style 204

BASTARDATOR / Maple Syrup Pudding Cake..................206

WARLOCK/DORO / Doro's Black Forest Cake 208

THE OBSESSED/SAINT VITUS/WINO / Soul Brownies.....210

THANATOS / Dutch Space Cake 211

10. DRINKS

DEATH/CONTROL DENIED / The Viking Testicle 214

REVEREND BIZARRE/LORD VICAR / Peter's Rusty Nail ...215

HOLOCAUSTO / Caipirinha..216

OBITUARY / Good Margarita..217

NUCLEAR ASSAULT / Parrot Bay Coconut Rum and Punch... 218

PILEDRIVER / The Piledriver 219

ALCOHOLIC RITES / Destructive Semen 220

DANTESCO / Coquito (Rum Eggnog) 221

MORTAL SIN / Mayhemic Destruction Fuel 222

11. MORBID CHEF'S TIPS AND TRICKS..................223

BAND INDEX..................224

Introduction

Greetings! My name is Annick, and I have a lethal addiction to heavy metal and heavy rock. I am a music-obsessed record hunter—and I happen to be just as obsessed with cooking and traveling. About six years ago, a friend and I started the *Morbid Tales* metal fanzine, and I started getting in touch with like-minded individuals from the four corners of the planet, getting letters from distant lands.

When I moved to Montreal after graduating college, my interest in different cultures was magnified by Montreal's international cuisine. Growing bored of eating just the same basic meals at home, I picked up an Indian recipe cookbook, and the results were surprising—I was amazed how easy it was to cook authentic food. I started making different recipes almost every day (to my boyfriend's delight), and my cooking abilities grew with practice.

Learning to cook is a bit like learning to play guitar: You can get really good playing by yourself, but you learn much quicker when you jam with somebody else. In my case, what helped the most was cooking with my grandmother, and with friends who worked in restaurants. I then got into trying different local dishes that were eaten every day by my favorite bands around the world… Maybe it sounds strange, but it was another way for me to travel, and to understand a bit where they come from.

Many recipes later, while totally hungover one Sunday morning, I left my house to go shopping for records and used cookbooks. Suddenly, I got the idea to make my own cookbook with recipes from my favorite metal bands, and voilà—*Hellbent for Cooking* was born!

With this book, I want to show that all metalheads need to eat to stay alive—and that food is genuinely a part of the metal lifestyle. Although metal fans have heavy metal and its attitudes in common, each of our own cultures is very different. This book illustrates our incredible cultural diversity. And I hope it wipes out the stupid myth that all metalheads are culinary degenerates who only eat junk food. Death to false meals!

When I started sending requests to bands for recipes, I wasn't too sure how many would cooperate. Let's face it—cooking is not traditionally seen as a "manly" thing (unless you are into haute cuisine), so I was greatly surprised by the overwhelming positive reaction.

I picked the contributors, some of them totally unknown, because I wanted to expose important bands that play good metal—whether they are well-known, or more underground. For example, Sir Lord Baltimore is the first band ever to be labeled "heavy metal," even if they never obtained worldwide commercial success like Black Sabbath. Or in Grimorium Verum's case, they are Ecuador's very first black metal band. Above all, it was essential for the book to have an international flavor in order to show people that metal is a worldwide subculture.

If I couldn't make it myself, I didn't include it in the book. I tested and perfected every recipe (well, almost!), adjusting some, and found substitutes for strange ingredients that could not be found in my area. I also photographed the dishes to show how they are supposed to look—and, of course, to rouse your appetite. On top of it, huge photos of the dishes should make it easy to picture what will soon be on your plate!

Of course, as metal music can be quite extreme, some bands replied with outrageous recipes, like "Stewed Dog (Wedding Style)," from Canada's Piledriver—but obviously there was no way I could kill a dog to eat it. The band Goat Semen wanted to give a guinea pig dish, which is extremely common in their home country, Peru. Unfortunately, I couldn't see myself at the pet store buying a few of those furry things with the intention of eating them! Likewise for "Raw/Fresh Heart of Cobra with Whiskey" from Thailand's Surrender of Divinity. Even though it's a common snack in Vietnam and Thailand—often served still beating with a chaser of the snake's own blood—I had no idea where to find a cobra, let alone how to kill one!!

I found fascinating how well the recipes offered by so many bands reflect their music: Beer-based batter from thrashers; vegan dishes from politically aware bands; and fiery hot and spicy plates from wild-eyed satanic bands. Most importantly, I was able to make almost everything, and I don't have any proper culinary training. Also, cooking dishes from all these different regions was like traveling from my own kitchen. Eventually, I would like to make a lengthy trip around the world to try these dishes firsthand, meet the metalheads I have corresponded with all these years, and see local shows in South America, Australia, Asia, North Africa, and Europe.

Now, to the battlefield! Go to your kitchen, grab your weapons of mass nutrition, and attack these recipes on full speed at high volume. The instructions are in the bands' own words, with comments in the corner of each page from the Morbid Chef to help. Make sure you read the entire page before starting. And don't forget—making a meal is a great excuse for drinking and listening to metal!

—Annick Giroux, "The Morbid Chef"

Weapons of Mass Nutrition

To wage war against junk food, you will need the following weapons:

OVEN MITTS
To remove hot items
from oven

FRYING PAN
For frying, sautéeing,
making omelettes
and sauces

WOK
For making stir-fries

BIG POT

SMALL POT
For soups, couscous

CUTTING BOARD
Use wood for veggies, and

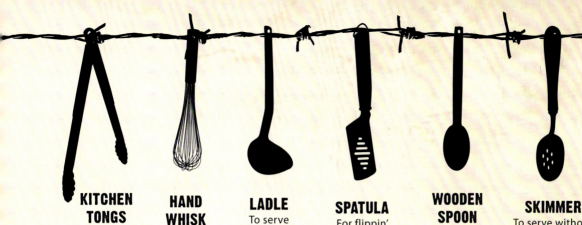

KITCHEN TONGS
To handle hot food

HAND WHISK
To whisk eggs, batter, and sauces

LADLE
To serve soups, beans, and sauces

SPATULA
For flippin' burgers and omelettes

WOODEN SPOON
To mix, stir, and scramble

SKIMMER
To serve without liquid

VEGETABLE PEELER
To peel veggies and make chocolate shavings

SCISSORS
To cut packages and tough pieces of meat

MIXING BOWL
You will need more than one!

KITCHEN SCALE
To measure ingredients perfectly

COLANDER
To drain liquid from food and rinse beans, pasta, etc.

CHEF'S KNIFE
To cut meat and vegetables

BREAD KNIFE
To cut bread

MEASURING CUP
Have two sizes: one to measure 1 cup and the other 2 cups

MEASURING SPOONS
To measure small quantities

GRATER
To grate cheese, carrots, and zucchini

Appetizers and Side Dishes

MUMMIFIED JALAPEÑO BACON BOMBS | INCINERATOR CHICKEN WINGS | ROLLED SWAMP BOMBS
CANDIED SWEETBREADS ON A BED OF SEARED HEART | ISTRIAN MANESTRA | FRIED EGG RIGOR MORTIS CURE
DEVIL'S PORRIDGE | WAR MISO WAR SOUP | FOCACCIA PUGLIESE | MARIA DEL CARMEN GUACAMOLE
ATOMIC AALU POWER | MARINATED HERMELÍN CHEESE | YORKSHIRE PUDDING | ROTI JALA (NET PANCAKE)
WELFARE NACHOS | LLAPINGACHOS (POTATO AND CHEESE CAKES)

"I usually manage to eat myself sick on these when they are around..."

Mummified Jalapeño Bacon Bombs

by Chris Reifert of AUTOPSY / ABSCESS

PREPARATION: 25 MINS

COOKING: 20 MINS

PORTIONS: DEPENDS ON YOU

INGREDIENTS

> Whole raw jalapeños (as many as you want to make)
> Raw bacon strips (the same amount as peppers you want to make)
> 1 block/tub of cream cheese
> 1 block of pepper Monterey Jack cheese

OTHER STUFF YOU WILL NEED

> Toothpicks
> Baking tray or cookie sheet
> Cooling rack
> Aluminum foil

PREPARATION

1. Cut stems completely off of jalapeños. You'll have to cut a bit of the pepper off to do so. Cut jalapeños in half lengthwise. Scoop out seeds with a small spoon (you can dry the seeds out and plant your own jalapeño plants with 'em!)

2. Cut pepper Monterey Jack cheese into slices small enough to fit into pepper halves, filling them about halfway up. With a butter knife, fill up peppers the rest of the way with cream cheese.

3. Cut raw bacon strips in half widthwise. Wrap each bacon strip half around the cheese-filled pepper, covering the pepper as best as possible. Stick a toothpick through the top until it comes out of the bottom, to hold the bacon in place.

4. Heat oven to 400°F (175°C). While oven is heating, place aluminum foil over baking tray or cookie sheet. Place cooling rack on top of foil-covered tray so bacon grease collects on the foil. Place peppers on cooling rack so they are not touching each other. Bake in oven for approximately 15 minutes. Check at 10 minutes. May take up to 20 minutes—just keep checking until the bacon is fully cooked.

Morbid Chef Notes

Damn, these things smelled so good while cooking, it was ridiculous. The taste was of course just mind-blowing! I ate about eight of them all at once. Ha ha. To my great surprise, they were not hot at all! To maximize the cheese stuffing, grate the Monterey Jack instead of cutting it so you can fit more inside those tiny peppers.

AUTOPSY / ABSCESS

The legendary Autopsy was formed by drummer/vocalist Chris Reifert in 1987 after he left Death. Until 1995, the Bay Area sickos marched to their own beat, churning out a thick, molasseslike variety of death metal that became the central influence on Sweden's death metal scene. Reifert then formed the more punkish Abscess, who continued to explore vile themes on a series of albums and split releases. Autopsy unexpectedly regrouped for a 2009 single, with a return to the stage expected to follow.

"One-two, fuck you!"

Incinerator Chicken Wings

by Dave Hewson of SLAUGHTER

PREPARATION: 30 MINS
COOKING: 15 MINS
PORTIONS: 2

WINGS

> 2 lbs (900 g) wings, thawed
> 2 cups (220 g) all-purpose flour
> 1 large bottle canola oil
  (or any oil but olive oil)

SEASONING SAUCE

> 6 oz (177 ml) hot sauce
> ½ tsp red pepper flakes, crushed
> ½ tsp cayenne pepper
> ¾ tsp smoked paprika
> 1 tsp garlic powder
> ¼ cup (60 ml) apple cider vinegar
> 2 tbsp butter

BLUE CHEESE DIPPING SAUCE

> ¾ cup (180 ml) sour cream
> 1 clove garlic, minced
> 3 tbsp apple cider vinegar
> 2 tbsp fresh dill
> ⅓ cup (50 g) gorgonzola cheese,
  crumbled
> ½ cup (125 ml) mayonnaise
> Salt and pepper, to taste

> 12 pack of ice-cold Heineken beer

PREPARATION

1. Start drinking Heineken beer.

2. In a large bowl, mix all the seasoning sauce ingredients together.

3. In another bowl, mix all dipping sauce ingredients together. Refrigerate until ready to use.

4. Dredge chicken wings in flour.

5. Heat oil in a large cooking pot, then drop wings into it.

6. Fry wings on medium to low heat for 10 to 15 minutes or until golden brown.

7. Mix chicken wings with sauce in a big bowl. Serve with blue cheese dipping sauce and more beer.

Morbid Chef Notes

WOW! I can't believe I did chicken wings! I was very excited, because these tasted just like in pubs!! You can serve them with carrots and celery sticks for a more authentic feel.

SLAUGHTER

Formed in 1984 by Terry Sadler (vocals, bass) and Dave Hewson (vocals, guitar) in Toronto, Slaughter was an extreme thrash metal band. Their handful of demos tapes were very popular among tape traders, and their only full-length release, *Strappado*, is now considered legendary. The "Surrender or Die" demo features the very first example of evil chain-saw riffing in metal.

"This recipe—stolen (with permission) from my first ex-wife, Kellie Burton-Orr-Pittman—placed in a Tabasco cook-off and was a finalist in the Food Network's *Ultimate Recipe Challenge*. Didn't make it on the show, but it was selected!"

Rolled Swamp Bombs

by Casey Orr of RIGOR MORTIS

PREPARATION: 25 MINS
COOKING: 40 MINS
PORTIONS: 6

RÉMOULADE SAUCE

> 1 tsp Worcestershire sauce
> ½ tsp fresh parsley
> 3 green onions, chopped (tops only)
> 1 celery stalk
> 1 tsp lemon juice
> 1 clove garlic
> 2 tbsp Zatarain's Creole Mustard
> 1 cup (250 ml) mayo
> 3 tbsp ketchup
> Crystal hot sauce

BOMBS

> ¼ lb (115 g) andouille sausage or smoked sausage, finely chopped
> 1 lb (450 g) fresh raw shrimp, peeled and deveined
> ¾ lb (340 g) cooked crawfish meat
> 1 green bell pepper, finely chopped
> 1 red bell pepper, finely chopped
> ½ med white onion, finely chopped
> 2 cloves garlic, minced
> 1 tbsp fresh parsley, minced
> 1 tbsp fresh coriander, minced
> 1 tbsp Creole seasoning with salt
> 2 tbsp Crystal hot sauce
> 6 oz (170 g) pepper jack cheese
> 20 egg roll wrappers, 5" (13 cm) square
> 1 bottle peanut or vegetable oil
> Cayenne pepper

PREPARATION OF SAUCE

1. Mix Worcestershire sauce, parsley, green onion, celery, lemon juice, garlic, and mustard in blender or small food processor until smooth. Pour mixture into mixing bowl. Add mayo and ketchup, and stir until well blended, adding Crystal hot sauce to taste. Place in refrigerator to chill while you make the Swamp Bombs.

PREPARATION OF BOMBS

1. In a large skillet, cook andouille sausage over medium heat until most of the fat is rendered. Pour andouille and fat onto a plate with paper towels to drain.

2. Add ½ tbsp of oil to skillet at medium-high heat. Add shrimp. When the shrimp is almost cooked, stir in crawfish, Creole seasoning, Crystal hot sauce, and cayenne to taste. Remove from heat when the crawfish is hot. Transfer to a plate or cookie sheet, and spread in a single layer to cool.

3. Add ½ tbsp of oil to skillet. Add peppers, onion, and garlic. Sweat until onion is almost clear. Do not overcook. The onion should still be a bit firm. Transfer to mixing bowl to cool.

4. Finely chop cooled shrimp/crawfish mixture and add to mixing bowl with vegetables. Shred pepper jack cheese. Add the coriander, parsley, andouille, and shredded cheese. Stir together.

5. Use mixture and wrappers to make "egg rolls" using about 1½ to 2 tbsp of the filling. You could try larger rolls, but I don't think they're as good. Using the full-size wrapper to make these smaller rolls gives the outside a great texture. Lightly squeeze the filling together in your hand before placing on wrapper to get the air out of the filling.

6. Deep-fry in 375°F (190°C) oil until golden brown. Makes 18 to 20.

Morbid Chef Notes

These are like some kind of spicy imperial rolls. They taste awesome! Put a bit of water on the egg roll wrapper edges to seal them before frying.

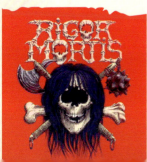

RIGOR MORTIS

Texas metallers Rigor Mortis were formed in 1983 by heavy metal and horror/gore movie fanatics Harden Harrison, Casey Orr, and Mike Scaccia. With vocalist Bruce Corbitt, they played a unique style of raw thrash metal, often borderline death metal. They signed to Capitol Records in 1987 and released a flawless self-titled debut album in 1988. The band broke up in 1991, but since 2005 they've played several shows together.

"Sweetbreads are my all-time favorite food. This dish is a savory, bloody, sweet escape from the ordinary. If I was in charge, I would consider this a dessert, but for now let's just call it a romantic appetizer for the gastronomically sadistic."

Candied Sweetbreads on a Bed of Seared Heart

A Valentine's Day Appetizer by Balsac the Jaws of Death of GWAR

PREPARATION: 12 HRS (including soaking of sweetbreads and heart marinade)

COOKING: 1 HR

PORTIONS: 4

SWEETBREADS

> ½ lb (225 g) lobe of veal sweetbreads (thymus and pancreas glands)
> Whole milk or half-and-half
> 2 sprigs fresh thyme
> 1 slice thick-cut applewood-smoked bacon (or any good-quality thick bacon)
> Olive oil

SEARED HEART

> ½ lb (225 g) beef heart
> ½ cup (125 ml) red wine
> 4 cloves garlic, crushed and minced
> 1 sprig fresh thyme (leaves stripped from the stalk)
> 2 tbsp olive oil
> Salt and pepper (freshly cracked), generous pinch

SAUCE

> ¼ cup (60 ml) chicken stock (if you have veal stock, use it—and you are a badass)
> ¼ cup (60 ml) pure maple syrup
> ¼ cup (60 ml) orange juice
> ½ fresh lemon zest
> 1 vanilla bean pod (or ¼ tsp vanilla flavoring)
> ¼ cup (60 ml) Grand Marnier
> 1 tbsp kneaded butter (flour and butter mixed together)

PASTRY HEARTS

> Puff-pastry sheet, thawed
> Heart-shaped cookie cutter

PREPARATION

1. To prepare, soak sweetbreads in the milk and thyme for 6 to 12 hours. When done, drain and simmer just under a boil in salted water for 2 to 3 minutes. Cool in an ice-water bath, then remove excess membrane and fat.

2. Break the sweetbreads into bite-size portions. The natural nodules of the sweetbreads should want to break into nuggets—think Chicken McNugget–size. Cut when necessary. Season with salt and cracked pepper and then roll in flour. Shake off excess flour.

3. Cut bacon into lardons (make thick matchstick cuts across the grain). Cook over medium-high heat until crisp. Remove and set aside. If necessary, add olive oil to rendered bacon fat so that a thin layer of fat covers the bottom of the pan.

4. Increase heat to high, add sweetbread nuggets, and sauté, turning occasionally until golden brown and crispy. Remove sweetbreads and keep warm in the oven on low.

5. Clean heart of excess fat and slice into ½" (1.3 cm) slices. Put the heart in a ziplock bag and add red wine, garlic, thyme, olive oil, and salt/pepper. Squeeze the air out of the bag and let heart marinate in the refrigerator for about 6 hours. When done, remove heart from marinade and pat dry.

6. Heat a cast-iron or other thick pan to smoking temperature. Add heart and cook no more than 30 seconds per side, then move it to a cutting board while you finish the sauce.

7. With chicken stock, deglaze the pan that was used to cook sweetbreads. Add maple syrup, orange juice, lemon zest, and seeds from split vanilla bean. Bring to a boil, and thicken for 3 minutes.

8. Add kneaded butter and continue boiling until sauce thickens to a thick syrup. Add Grand Marnier and flambé (light it on fire!). Return sweetbreads to pan and stir to coat.

9. Using a heart-shaped cookie cutter, cut thawed pastry into 8 hearts.

10. Bake pastry hearts in a 400°F (200°C) oven for 8 minutes.

11. Slice beef heart into thin strips. Arrange around two pastry hearts.

12. Top with the sweetbreads, and drizzle sauce around the outside of plate. If you are feeling fancy, make lemon zest hearts.

If this dish doesn't get you laid, your girlfriend is a prude or a vegan!

Photo by Balsac the Jaws of Death

GWAR

The fluid-splattered mutants in Gwar have been a touring mainstay since the late 1980s, when their slime-ridden metal carnival first touched down in Richmond, VA. Twice nominated for Grammy awards, these scumdogs of the universe have released over a dozen albums and nearly twice as many home videos documenting their extremely messy theatrical stage show.

CROATIA

"First of all, I must introduce you to this beautiful part of this planet, Istria. It is a region of Croatia, located on the upper coast. Its capital town, Pula, is one of the metalest cities in the Balkans, and its culinary culture is incredibly tasty."

Istrian Manestra

by Alex Bijažic of DEVASTATION

PREPARATION: 8 HRS (Including soaking of the beans)
COOKING: 1 HR 15 MINS
PORTIONS: 6

INGREDIENTS

> 7 oz (200 g) dried brown beans
> 1¼ lbs (550 g) dried/cured ham with bone (a meat made in Istria, and even there it costs a fortune. If you cannot find some, it would be best to use smoked prosciutto or any smoked ham with bone.)
> Salt and pepper
> 1 cup (100 g) smoked ham, cubed
> 1 garlic clove, sliced in three
> 3 bay leaves
> 2 medium tomatoes, chopped (Italian tomatoes will work well)
> 7 oz (200 g) fresh or frozen corn
> 3½ oz (100 g) pasta shells, cooked
> 2 potatoes, cut into small cubes
> 1 tbsp parsley, minced
> 1 tbsp fennel, chopped
> 2 tbsp olive oil
> 2 tbsp vinegar

PREPARATION

1. Put the beans in the water and let them soak in the water overnight. Rinse beans.

2. Put beans in a pot filled with water, then when the water starts to boil, take the beans out of that water and put them to cook in new fresh water—at least 8 cups (2 liters).

3. Put dried ham with bone in the water, and then add salt, pepper, smoked ham cut into small cubes, garlic, bay leaves, and tomatoes, and let it cook for at least an hour.

4. When the beans are nearly cooked, add in corn, potatoes, fennel, parsley, and olive oil. Let it cook, and when the potatoes are ready, add cooked pasta. Let cook for another 5 minutes, then take the dried ham and bone out, and add two spoons of vinegar to the soup. Bon appetit!

Morbid Chef Notes

I'm a sucker for Eastern European food. I wish I had made this recipe in double, because it was really, really killer! Try sprinkling a bit of dill in your soup; it adds a wonderful taste. Mmmm!

DEVASTATION

Devastation were one of the first speed metal bands in Croatia. In 1986, Alex Bijažic, his brother Chriss, and guitarist Marko—all inspired by the sounds of German bands—formed Their Satanic Majesty, which quickly changed to Devastation. They played many shows and released two demos, recently reissued by Chinese label AreaDeath Productions. The band played through the '90s under the name Hatröss, then reformed as Devastation in 2007.

DENMARK

"This is an excellent hangover cure. The good thing with this is you can add anything you want, pretty much. Garlic and sausages are good with it too!"

Fried Egg Rigor Mortis Cure

by Ustumallagam of DENIAL OF GOD

PREPARATION: 30 MINS
COOKING: 30 MINS
PORTIONS: 4

THE POISON INGREDIENTS

> 4 eggs
> 1 onion, chopped
> ¾ cup (180 ml) milk
> 3 cups (250 g) mushrooms, chopped
> 8 oz (250 g) bacon, diced into pieces
> 2 slices cheese
> 8 hash browns
> Paprika, to taste
> Salt and pepper, to taste
> All-purpose spice seasoning, to taste

PREPARATION

1. Preheat oven to 475°F (250°C). Throw the onion, mushrooms, and diced bacon pieces on a bloody hot frying pan, and cook them until they look done or burnt to a crisp. It's all up to you.

2. While working with the frying pan, put the hash browns in the pre-heated oven until they look crunchy.

3. Crush the eggs into a bowl and mix in the milk. Stir it together for a little while, and then pour the mixture into the frying pan on top of the stuff you already cooked. Put in the cheese at the same time. Eventually scramble it up a bit too.

4. Keep on stirring until the eggs become all hard and look ready. Don't forget to use salt, pepper, paprika, and whatever spices you like along the way.

Serve this meal on a plate accompanied with the hash browns, some spicy ketchup, garlic dressing, maggots, or whatever you think suits the meal.

The pain of being dead will be gone in a moment.

Morbid Chef Notes

Ahhh, nothing better to cure a bad hangover than coating your stomach with some good ol' grease. This recipe tastes good, although I felt guilty after eating it all by myself. Ha ha!

DENIAL OF GOD

Denial of God plays unique black metal with horror lyrics. Formed in 1991 by brothers Ustumallagam and Azter, they are heavily influenced by Alice Cooper, King Diamond, Death SS, Mayhem, Bathory, and Hellhammer— as well as supernatural and occult subjects. They recorded many demos and EPs, finally releasing their long-awaited debut album, *The Horrors of Satan*, in 2006 after fifteen years together!

"I came across a munitions factory in Gretna, Scotland, where they used to make an explosive paste for WWI. Sir Arthur Conan Doyle, the creator of Sherlock Holmes, had named it Devil's Porridge. That's where I got the name for my concoction. Believe me, a bowl of it has exactly the same explosive effect on your bodily functions!"

Devil's Porridge

by Montalo of Witchfynde

PREPARATION: 1 MIN
COOKING: 5 MINS
PORTIONS: 1

INGREDIENTS

> ½ cup (45 g) oatmeal
> 1¼ cups (310 ml) goat's milk (or cow's milk, but it may lack a little devilish naughtiness)
> 1–2 tbsp brown sugar or molasses
> 7 dried or fresh dates (stoned and pitted, of course)
> 7 shelled Brazil nuts

PREPARATION

1. Here it goes, hold on tight! Place the oats and milk in a cauldron (or pan, if civilized). Bring to a boil and cook for 1 minute. Simmer for 3 minutes.

2. Let stand for 1 minute, and then add the brown sugar or molasses to taste.

3. Add dates and nuts.

Enjoy, and prepare for action! Blessed be, Montalo

Morbid Chef Notes

This luckily had no *explosive* effects on me, but it was very good-tasting and really filling. I made this a few times already. Make sure to mix everything with the oats before you eat!

WITCHFYNDE

NWOBHM forerunners Witchfynde were formed in 1975, in Nottingham, UK, by lead guitarist Montalo, bassist Andro Coulton, and drummer Gra Scoresby. They played progressive heavy rock, laced with far more severe satanic imagery then their contemporaries. The band was put on hold in 1984 after releasing four albums, and was resurrected in 2001.

JAPAN

War Miso War Soup

by Yasuyuki Suzuki of ABIGAIL

PREPARATION: 20 MINS
COOKING: 15 MINS
PORTIONS: 4

INGREDIENTS

> ½ package tofu, soaked in a generous amount of water and cut into small cubes
> ¾ oz (20 g) wakame seaweed, cut into bite-size pieces
> 4 cups (1 L) dashijiru (fish soup stock)
> 3 tbsp miso (soybean paste)
> ½ green onion, sliced
> ½ package fried tofu, pre-boiled, drained in a strainer, and cut into ¾" (2 cm) sections
> 8 small taro roots (go to your local Chinatown!)

PREPARATION

1. Boil dashijiru.

2. Add taros and miso, and dissolve completely. Be careful not to overcook, otherwise the miso flavor will weaken.

3. Simmer gently about 3 minutes, then add wakame seaweed, fried bean curd, and soybean curd.

4. Boil for a while.

5. Turn off the heat and add chopped green onions, then serve.

Morbid Chef Notes

Miso soup is a traditional Japanese dish, often eaten at breakfast. This particular recipe is very tasty and really healthy. If taros cannot be found, they can be replaced with potatoes —or completely removed. You can add many other ingredients such as mushrooms, shrimp, fish, and sliced daikon (icicle radish).

ABIGAIL

Creeping from the depths of Tokyo's red-light district, Abigail was formed in 1992 by Yasuyuki, Yasunori, and Youhei. Influenced by Bathory, Venom, Sodom, Bulldozer, Hellhammer, and NME, the band's early pure evil black metal, heard on 1997's *Intercourse and Lust*, gradually shifted toward thrash metal by the time of 2009's *Sweet Baby Metal Slut*.

"This is a special bread from Puglia in the south of Italy, our region. Very good for eating at all times, especially in the heart of the night after a headbangers' concert with many, many beers! *Buon appetito!!*"

Focaccia Pugliese

by Giovanni "John Goldfinch" Cardellino of L'IMPERO DELLE OMBRE

PREPARATION: 4 HRS
COOKING: 25 MINS
PORTIONS: 4

INGREDIENTS

> 3 small potatoes, cooked and mashed into liquid (keep warm)
> 3 tsp yeast
> 1¼ cups (310 ml) warm water
> 3¾ cups (480 g) durum flour (or regular white flour)
> 2 tsp salt
> 3 tbsp olive oil
> 8 grape tomatoes, cut in threes
> 16 sun-dried black olives, cut in halves
> ½ tsp salt
> 2 tsp oregano, dried
> 1 sprig fresh rosemary (leaves only)

PREPARATION

1. Pour warm water into a large mixing bowl, then stir in yeast. Mix until completely dissolved. Add the flour, liquefied potatoes, and salt in two additions. Mix together and then knead for 10 minutes.

2. Place dough in a bowl, cover, and let rise until doubled (1 to 2 hours).

3. Divide the dough in half and shape into a ball. Place each ball into a well-oiled 9" (23 cm) round baking pan, and stretch the dough toward the edges. Cover, let sit for 10 minutes, and then stretch a little more. Cover again, and leave until it has doubled (1 or 2 hours).

4. Preheat the oven to 400°F (175°C). Make small holes in the dough with a finger. Place tomatoes and olives in the holes.

5. In a small bowl, mix oregano, rosemary leaves, salt, and olive oil. Baste mixture on top of focaccia, then bake for 25 minutes until golden.

Morbid Chef Notes

The dough took pretty long to make, but was well worth it! Make sure that the yeast is perfectly dissolved in the water, or else you will fuck up your entire recipe. Enjoy as an entrée with some Italian doom metal, pasta, and red wine!

L'IMPERO DELLE OMBRE

L'Impero Delle Ombre ("The Empire of Shadows") was founded by
Giovanni Cardellino in 1995. They play a fine mixture of dark progressive
rock and traditional doom metal, with an Italian vibe along the lines
of cult heroes Paul Chain, Death SS, and Antonius Rex. The band has
released two haunting full-lengths to date.

"I named this recipe after my mother, the master chef Maria del Carmen Sandoval. She literally taught me everything I know. I love her so much! Thank you, Ma!"

Maria del Carmen Guacamole

by Gonzo Sandoval of ARMORED SAINT

PREPARATION: 15 MINS
COOKING: —
PORTIONS: 6–8

INGREDIENTS

> 4–8 avocados (depending on size)
> 2 tomatoes, chopped
> 1 onion, chopped
> 3 cloves of garlic, minced
> Small bunch of coriander, chopped
> Salt, to taste
> Juice of 1 lime
> 1–2 large jalapeños, chopped

PREPARATION

1. Do the vegetable preparation work and cut avocados in half. Save the pits for later.

2. Scoop the avocado meat from the skin and put in a large serving bowl. Wash the pits.

3. Add chopped tomatoes, onions, jalapeños, and garlic. Mix all ingredients together, then add lime juice and salt to taste.

4. Place the pits on top of the guacamole, and then spread the coriander sparingly. The pits and lime juice help the guacamole not brown as fast.

Photo by gonzosandoval.com

Morbid Chef Notes

Guacamole is an ancient Aztec side dish. I thought my own guacamole was pretty hard to beat, but this one kicks its ass! You can replace the onion with green onion if you wish. You can also put some in burritos, or just eat it on its own. It's that good.

ARMORED SAINT

Formed in 1982 in Los Angeles, Armored Saint was a European-style heavy metal band that had nothing to do with the trendy local glam metal scene around them. They released five albums, then went on hiatus during most of the 1990s while singer John Bush joined Anthrax. They returned to action in the 2000s, and continue to release new material.

PAKISTAN

"This is a traditional Pakistan dish named *aalu ki tarkari*. Many people like to eat this with their fried eggs and bread for breakfast. The kalonji seeds, or nigella, might not be very easy to find at times, so one can do an equally delicious dish without them!"

Atomic Aalu Power

by Babar "Iron" Sheikh of DUSK

PREPARATION: 15 MINS
COOKING: 30 MINS
PORTIONS: 2

INGREDIENTS

> ½ cup (125 ml) cooking oil
> 2 medium onions, diced
> 4 medium potatoes, cut in bite-size pieces
> 2–3 tomatoes, chopped in little pieces
> ½ tsp coriander powder
> ½ tsp red chili powder
> ½ tsp turmeric powder
> ½ tsp kalonji seeds (nigella)
> 4–5 green chilies, crushed
> Salt, to taste
> Coriander leaves, to garnish

PREPARATION

1. Pour oil into a saucepan or cooking dish and heat it up on a medium flame for 3 to 5 minutes.

2. Add diced onions to the oil and fry them until they start to change color. Add chopped tomatoes, then masala (all the spices) to the dish— one after the other you can add the chili powder, coriander powder, turmeric powder, green chilies, and salt. Stir all these ingredients constantly.

3. After 5 minutes, add the potatoes, the kalonji seeds, and 3 cups of water. Cover the pot and turn the heat to low. Let the dish cook until the potatoes are tender and the water reduced to a thick gravy. (About 20 to 30 minutes).

Garnish with coriander leaves and serve!

Morbid Chef Notes

Man, if this what is eaten in Pakistan for breakfast, I'm moving there for good! Seriously, these are some great potatoes with a very exotic taste. An atomic kick start to a day!

DUSK

Started in 1994 by Babar Sheikh under the name Carcinogenic, Dusk is considered the first metal band from Pakistan. Throughout the years, they have evolved through many styles—ranging from death, experimental, and doom to progressive metal. After an adventurous 360-degree journey, Dusk returned to their initial style, playing apocalyptic raw bestial metal—third-world thunder thrash!

"We have a special cheese called *hermelín*, which is made in the city of Sedlčany. This cheese is slightly different from Camembert, and according to our opinion is much better—especially for this recipe. So if you want real marinated hermelín, you have to get this cheese from Sedlčany! Good luck!"

Marinated Hermelin Cheese

By Lord Oblomov of STÍNY PLAMENŮ

PREPARATION: 15 MINS
MARINATING: 4 DAYS
PORTIONS: 4

INGREDIENTS

> 4 whole Camembert wheels
> 2 onions
> 4 cloves of garlic
> Salt
> Bay leaves
> 15 peppercorns
> 5 whole allspice (available at any bulk or health food store)
> Sweet and hot paprika
> Hot peppers
> Oil

PREPARATION

1. Cut the cheese to pieces horizontally and spread the garlic and salt mixture (the garlic can be also sliced), paprika, and pepper on the inner sides of the cheese. Interlay with sliced onion, and then put cheese back together.

2. Put the cheeses into a large glass or a tall bowl, and during this process interlay the completed cheeses with onion, whole allspice, and bay leaves. You can add several hot peppers.

3. Pour oil over everything. Close the glass tightly and leave it for 4 days (or more, depends on your taste) to ripen in the fridge.

Serve it with bread on a sewer lid platter and wash down with beer. This last notice is very important: DO NOT FORGET THE BEER!

Morbid Chef Notes

This recipe, which is typically found at pubs in the Czech Republic, is really fucking tasty. Stupidly, I thought that leaving the jar in some shade would be okay, but it was a total mess; the cheese kind of exploded and invaded the marinating oil. Good thing I had tasted some before that happened! Leave the jar in your fridge and it should be fine. Many thanks to Lord Oblomov for sending me a picture of his dish!

STÍNY PLAMENŮ

This unusual Czech band emerged from the wastewaters of Plzen in 1998. This highly original black metal band's Czech lyrics deal solely with their city's underground sewers—even their name ("shadows of flames") refers to the flickering fire that illuminates the sewer expanses. Their unique sound has never been copied. Their most essential album is *Ve Spine Je Pravda*—which features a drum machine!

UNITED KINGDOM

Yorkshire Pudding

by DESOLATION ANGELS

PREPARATION: 40 MINS
COOKING: 10–15 MINS
PORTIONS: 4–6

INGREDIENTS

> 1¼ cup (300 ml) milk
> 4 oz (110 g) plain flour
> 1 egg
> Oil, lard, or roast drippings

PREPARATION

1. Place the flour in a bowl, then make a well in the center and break in the egg. Mix in half the milk using a wooden spoon, work the mixture until smooth, then add the remaining milk.

2. Beat or whisk until fully combined and the surface is covered with tiny bubbles. Allow to rest for 15 to 30 minutes, whisk again before use. Preheat oven to 425°F (220°C).

3. Place a teaspoon of fat into 12 individual deep bun tins or put same amount into a single large tin, and place in the oven until the fat is very hot.

4. Pour the batter into the tins and bake for 10 to 15 minutes for individual puddings (30 to 35 minutes if using a large tin), or until risen and golden brown.

Serve with roast beef, mashed potatoes, and peas.

Morbid Chef Notes

I've been craving these ever since I went to England in 2007, so I was stoked to make some! Usually, Yorkshire pudding tends have some kind of "hole" in the middle where you pour your gravy, but these were too crispy for that to happen. The hole took shape only when I reheated them in the microwave. Try using two eggs instead of one—it might turn out even better!

DESOLATION ANGELS

East London NWOBHM band Desolation Angels were formed in early 1981 by guitarists Robin Brancher and Keith Sharp. Early in their career, they established their name by gigging relentlessly across the UK. They played a few gigs in the United States in the 1980s and early 1990s. The band's entire discography has recently been reissued as a triple-CD box set.

Roti Jala (Net Pancake)

by Istaroth of ENVENOM

PREPARATION: 10 MINS
COOKING: 20 MINS
PORTIONS: 4

INGREDIENTS

> 1¼ cups (165 g) wheat flour
> 2 eggs
> ¾ cup (180 ml) water
> ¾ cup (180 ml) canned
  coconut milk (or milk of
  ½ piece of coconut)
> ½ tsp turmeric powder
> ½ tsp salt

> Roti jala mold (see Morbid
  Chef Notes)

PREPARATION

1. Mix wheat flour, eggs, turmeric powder, coconut milk, water, and salt in a large bowl. Pass through colander if it has lumps—the batter should be moderately fluid.

2. Apply small amount of oil on the surface of a flat-bottomed frying pan and heat it. Put the batter into a roti jala mold and form a thin pattern in the pan by having it leak in a circular motion. The faster you go, the lacier the pancake will be. Cook until it's crisp.

3. Lift the roti jala and fold it in quarters or whatever pattern you like. He he. Repeat the same process until you finish frying all the batter.

Serve it with chicken curry.

Morbid Chef Notes

Unless you are Malaysian, or know Malaysian people, you might not be able to find a roti jala mold. There is one easy way of replacing it: You can put the batter in a squeeze bottle (like an empty mustard bottle). In any case, I am not a big fan of coconut, but these tasted really good, especially dipped in curry sauce!

ENVENOM

Forged in 2002 by the hammers of two worshippers of the black arts, Envenom hail from the capital of Malaysia, Kuala Lumpur. They play a mixture of fast black metal and raw thrash metal with absolutely no compromise, and they are a terror to wimps and posers.

CANADA

"What I do is mock a dish they make at Sneaky Dee's, a Toronto Mexican restaurant and live concert venue. I make the welfare version. It works really well on a day off, or if you're hungover—which is usually my day off."

Welfare Nachos

by Jason Decay of CAULDRON / GOAT HORN

PREPARATION: 25 MINS
COOKING: 20 MINS
PORTIONS: DEPENDS ON YOU

INGREDIENTS

> 1 bag nacho chips
> 1 can refried beans
> Favorite vegetables—I usually uses tomatoes, onion, and green pepper, but you could be budget and just use a jar of salsa
> Shredded cheese
> Fried egg
> Hot sauce

PREPARATION

1. Line a glass bowl with nacho chips and throw in a big scoop of refried beans.

2. Chop your favorite vegetables and throw them on top.

3. Shred some cheese on top and throw it in the toaster oven on like 500°F (260°C) for 10 minutes.

4. Top with a fried egg (or not), and douse it in some hot sauce.

That's it! Or if you're rich, just take a cab to Sneaky Dee's in Toronto and order the "Traditional."

Morbid Chef Notes

You can't go wrong with a recipe like this—it always tastes good. The egg thing is a bit weird, though. I had never heard of putting that on nachos before. Must be a welfare breakfast thing. Great with beer, and lots of it (Pabst Blue Ribbon preferred).

CAULDRON / GOAT HORN

Birthed in 2006 in Pembroke, a small town close to Ottawa, Cauldron was spawned from the demise of heavy doom metal band Goat Horn. The band plays a traditional, fist-raising style of anthemic heavy metal.

"Llapingachos are one of the most typical and delicious recipes in Ecuadorian cooking. They're like little potato cakes mixed with cheese. Surprise your friends with a few good llapingachos in practically a moment's time!"

Llapingachos (Potato and Cheese Cakes)

by GRIMORIUM VERUM

PREPARATION: 40 MINS

COOKING: 10–15 MINS

PORTIONS: 4–6

INGREDIENTS

> 2¼ lbs (1 kg) russet potatoes, previously boiled
> Salt
> Pepper
> ¼ cup (20 g) freshly shredded cheese (mozzarella or other)
> 1 onion, finely chopped
> 4 tbsp peanut butter
> 2 tbsp milk or cream
> 4 tbsp cooking oil

> Cold beers

PREPARATION

1. Fry the chopped onion with the oil and a pinch of pepper.

2. Peel the pre-boiled potatoes, then mash them until you get a creamy puree.

3. Mix the creamy potato puree with the fresh shredded cheese, fried onion, oil, pinch of pepper, and pinch of salt until the mixture becomes very homogeneous.

4. Make little cakes with the mixture, in a diameter of 2.75" x .25" (7 cm x 1 cm).

5. Fry the llapingachos in a frying pan over low-medium heat for 10 to 15 minutes, until golden or roasted.

6. Mix peanut butter and milk together to form a cream of peanut, and pour that on top of the golden llapingachos.

Serve the llapingachos with lettuce, sliced cooked carrot, sliced tomatoes, meat, and avocado.

Do not forget the almighty cold beers!

Morbid Chef Notes

I had quite a lot of trouble making these little cakes, as the "broiled" part kept sticking to the pan! I didn't realize that my heat was too high. Make sure you put just a little oil, and leave it on low-medium heat. The result is really tasty, especially with the peanut cream on top! It's totally worth the effort. You can add a little bit of achiote or paprika for color, also.

GRIMORIUM VERUM

Grimorium Verum was formed in 1993 in Quito, Ecuador, by Lucifeid and Equidnos. They mix extreme raw black metal with a tinge of thrash, and refrain from having any song titles at all, using only numbers in some cases. They are considered the first Ecuadorian black metal band.

Beef

CHURRASCO IN SOY SAUCE | BONDAGE ROLLED STEAK | STUFFED CABBAGE | HABAÑERO GYŪDON
BULL TESTICLE SURPRISE | HAMBURGERS OF DEVASTATION | IRISH BEEF STEW | BENGAL BEEF CURRY
MUSHROOM STEAK À LA JACK DANIEL'S | MIDNIGHT 7" METALOAF | PAGAN PIE
RÅBIFF (SWEDISH STEAK TARTARE) | ROAST BEEF WITH GREEN BEANS | THE STEW OF TRUE DOOM
THUNDERING BEEF BRISKET | SPECKMANN'S CHILI MAC | GULÁŠ À LA ROOT

BRAZIL

"Churrasco is a very popular way of cooking meat in Brazil, Argentina, and Uruguay. It is a kind of barbecue. We in Brazil have the best meat coming from the south, and we do it like this."

Churrasco in Soy Sauce

by Andreas Kisser of SEPULTURA

PREPARATION: 10 MINS
COOKING: 30 MINS
PORTIONS: 1

INGREDIENTS

> 1 big fat steak,
  3–4" (7.5–10 cm) thick
> 1 cup (250 ml) soy sauce
> 2 tbsp butter
> Coarse rock salt, to taste

> Large frying pan
> BBQ grill

PREPARATION

1. Choose the meat you like the most: T-bone steak, rump steak, filet mignon, etc.

2. In a small bowl, mix butter and soy sauce with a fork, then add rock salt as you like. Mix them well, and then spread the paste around in a pan. Melt on medium heat.

3. Take the steak and throw in the pan with the sauce just before putting on the grill. Don't let the meat sit too long in the sauce; otherwise the steak will be too salty.

4. Grill the steak on a BBQ grill as you like—I prefer medium rare— and enjoy with a green salad, some potatoes, and a cold beer. Cooking it first in the sauce adds a different spice to your meat with a touch of an oriental taste. Hope you all enjoy!

Morbid Chef Notes

Traditionally, the meat is impaled on a sword and cooked upwards, roasting on top of a fire. I made the meat on the BBQ, as I didn't have the proper equipment. Also, I thought the salt would have been way too much, but one could hardly taste it on the cooked meat. The flavor was great! I suggest smothering the grilling steak once in a while with the soy mixture.

SEPULTURA

This Brazilian horde of headbangers started out in the mid-1980s, just as Brazil's military dictatorship gave way to a free society. They brought thrash metal up a notch with *Morbid Visions*, truly one of the first death metal albums. The band is revered around the world as the first hugely successful metal act from a developing nation. Classics like *Arise* and *Chaos AD* have cumulatively sold more than 15 million copies worldwide.

"This is my favorite recipe by far. The meat gets so tender! It goes great with beer—it's a German recipe, after all."

Bondage Rolled Steak

by Joel Grind of TOXIC HOLOCAUST

PREPARATION: 5 MINS
COOKING: 3 HRS
PORTIONS: 2

INGREDIENTS

> 2 large thin flank steaks
> 8 slices bacon
> 1 medium onion, chopped

> Cooking string
> Roasting pot

PREPARATION

1. Put bacon slices on thin flank steaks. Add cut-up onions on top.

2. Roll each steak and tie with string.

3. Dip each roll in flour.

4. Put floured rolls in roasting pot and fill pot with water.

5. Cover with aluminum foil.

6. Bake in oven at 350°F (175°C) for about three hours. Make sure you check that the water does not evaporate.

Morbid Chef Notes

What a delicious and really tender recipe! The meat will completely melt under your fork. I suggest adding some beef broth instead of water when you cover up the rolled steaks. Yum. Serve with red cabbage and potatoes for a true German "delicacy"!

TOXIC HOLOCAUST

In 1999, Joel Grind—totally possessed by Bathory, Exodus, English Dogs, and Discharge—formed his own one-man band. In the beginning, Joel wrote and recorded everything himself in his DIY home studio in Portland, OR. His highly praised debut album, *Evil Never Dies,* arrived in 2003, followed by exhaustive worldwide touring with a full live band, and more killer post-apocalyptic recordings. Toxic Holocaust is now a full living, breathing band, signed to Relapse Records.

"Here's my mom's recipe for stuffed cabbage. It comes from my grandmother, so it's old-school Russian New York style. It's great!"

Stuffed Cabbage

by Scott Ian of ANTHRAX

PREPARATION: 30 MINS

COOKING: 2 HRS

PORTIONS: 6 LARGE APPETITES

INGREDIENTS

> 2 lbs (900 g) ground meat
> ⅓ cup (65 g) uncooked rice
> Salt and pepper, to taste
> Garlic powder, to taste
> 1 raw egg
> ½ cup (70 g) dried raisins
> ¼ cup (25 g) uncooked oatmeal (you can use bread crumbs instead)
> 1 small onion, diced
> Anything else you like in your meatloaf
> 1 very large head of cabbage or two mediums (I always make more than I need in case I run out)
> 1 big bottle of ginger ale
> Ketchup

PREPARATION

1. Start a very large pot of water boiling. (Leave room in the pot for spillage, because you have to put the cabbage in.)

2. In a mixing bowl, combine uncooked rice, salt and pepper, garlic powder, egg, raisins, uncooked oatmeal, and diced onions with the meat and set aside.

3. Cut the core(s) out of the bottom(s) of the cabbage(s). Put cabbage(s) in the water to boil, usually one head per boiling pot. Boil for about 10 to 20 minutes. Don't over-boil. Test them with a fork every once in a while. The point is to get the inner leaves soft enough to manipulate without the outer leaves getting too soft and splitting when you roll the cabbage. This comes with practice. It's better to undercook. Take the cabbage(s) out when you think it/they look done and place core side down in the sink so that the water can drain out and cool off.

4. Peel off one outer leaf at a time. Flatten out. Put a small handful of meat (shaped into a small log) on the core end of the leaf. Roll the leaf over the meat once or twice, then tuck in the sides so the meat is entirely covered. Continue rolling until the leaf is used up. The leaves will get smaller and less soft as you get deeper into the cabbage head. At some point, you won't have big enough leaves. Hopefully one head will do all your meat—if not, use the second head. Keep the leftover cabbage.

5. Cut up the leftover boiled cabbage. Layer the bottom of a pot with some of the cabbage. The pot should be large enough to fit the cabbage rolls in 2 to 4 layers, leaving the top half of the pot still free. Put more of the chopped-up cabbage on top of the rolls.

6. Mix equal parts (this is the most important—the measurements should be exactly equal) ginger ale and ketchup, enough to cover the rolls. Pour the mixture over the rolls. It doesn't have to cover the leftover chopped-up cabbage, just the rolls. Cover the pot tightly.

7. Bring to a boil, lower the heat to a simmer, and simmer for 2 hours. Don't take the cover off often, as it cooks better in the heat, and we don't want the steam to get out.

That's it! It's much easier to learn by watching it being done. Good luck!

Morbid Chef Notes

Who knew ketchup and ginger ale could taste so good together? This recipe is killer, on top of being dirt cheap to make. I always had trouble with cabbage rolls before, but this one is foolproof— a real keeper!

ANTHRAX

Anthrax, formed in 1981 by guitarist Scott Ian and bassist Danny Lilker, was one of the "big four" of thrash metal in the 1980s. Once drummer Charlie Benante joined the band, they pioneered the merger of NY-style hardcore into heavy metal, made "mosh" a household word, and became an MTV and concert staple, thanks to speedy music and quick wit.

"Since I moved to the United States, Japanese beef bowl, called *gyūdon* in Japanese, is the food I miss the most. This dish is usually served in fast-food restaurants, but can be also cooked at home. Black rice is available at a Korean market."

Habañero Gyūdon

by Dr. Mikannibal of SIGH

PREPARATION: 15 MINS
COOKING: 25 MINS
PORTIONS: 2

INGREDIENTS

> 1 tsp beef lard
> 1 tbsp sesame oil
> 1 clove garlic, minced
> 1 tsp ginger, grated
> 7 oz (200 g) thinly sliced fatty beef
> ½ onion, sliced
> 1 bowl steamed black rice
> 1 whole habañero, sliced
> ½ cup (125 ml) water
> ¼ cup (60 ml) red wine
> ¼ beef bouillon cube
> 1½ tsp brown sugar
> 1 tsp mirin (or sweet wine)
> 2 tsp soy sauce
> ¼ tsp salt
> ¼ tsp black pepper
> 1 tsp MSG

PREPARATION

1. Brown ginger and garlic with beef lard and sesame oil in a pan at medium heat.

2. Add onion and beef, and stir fry them at high heat until the color changes.

3. Add the rest of ingredients in a pot, and simmer at medium heat for 10 minutes or until well thickened.

4. Serve hot steamed rice in a deep rice bowl, and put the beef topping on the top of rice.

Morbid Chef Notes

I am a total Japanese food junkie, and this one, my friends, this "beef bowl" recipe is the type of food that you eat once and crave forever. It was so insanely good, I couldn't believe my taste buds. Far better than all the teppanyaki places I've tried in the past put together. I didn't add MSG, though, so I suppose that is quite optional!

SIGH

Far Eastern extreme metal pioneers Sigh formed in Tokyo in 1990. They recorded their first record, *Scorn Defeat*, in 1993 for DSP—the Norwegian label founded by Euronymous of Mayhem. From bashing out Venom covers during early sets, the band soon expanded beyond basic black metal to offer wildly unpredictable kaleidoscope platters animated by Moog analog synths, saxophones, and the spirit of macabre cabaret.

"This is delicious and aphrodisiac food!"

Bull Testicle Surprise

by Tomáš "Necrocock" Kohout of MASTER'S HAMMER

PREPARATION: 3 HRS
COOKING: 30 MINS
PORTIONS: 2

INGREDIENTS

> 4 bull testicles
> Mixed together:
>> ½ tsp black pepper
>> 3 tbsp coarsely ground nuts (cashews, almonds, or sunflower seeds)
>> 1 tbsp fresh coriander, finely chopped
>> 1 tsp fennel seeds, ground
> 3 tbsp pickled fish
> Olive oil

PREPARATION

1. Put testicles in frozen water, and let sit in it for 3 hours. When ready, quickly plunge testicles in simmering water.

2. Completely remove skin, then slice the testicles in two.

3. Sprinkle the center with black pepper, nuts, coriander, and fennel seeds.

4. Tie testicles back together, then fry them in the olive oil along with the pickled fish until brown. Turn the oven on to 350°F (175°C).

5. Put testicles in an oven dish, then roast in oven for 30 minutes, until tender.

Morbid Chef Notes

Worshipped by cowboys, bikers, and Serbians, bull testicles (or prairie oysters/Rocky Mountain oysters) are considered a real delicacy. I ate a small bite, and it tasted and felt slightly like liver. The texture is very soft, so be careful with your ball handling! Testicles were available from *halal* butcher shops where I live. *Dobrou chuť!*

MASTER'S HAMMER

Master's Hammer was a distinctive black metal band formed in 1983 in Prague. They produced several extremely dark demos before releasing their great debut album, *Ritual*, in 1990. Two years later they completed the operetta *Jilemnice Occultist*, followed by the even stranger album *Slágry*, which drifted almost completely away from metal. Intense timpani drums, Franta's screechy vocals, Necrocock's complex riffs, and thick analog production make their music absolutely perfect.

AUSTRALIA

"This is the traditional Australian version of a universal favorite. Very messy, but also very tasty and easy to make. And yes, we do put beets and beetroot on our burgers. This recipe should not be made without it!"

Hamburgers of Devastation

by Ian Belshaw of SHACKLES

PREPARATION: 15 MINS
COOKING: 20 MINS
PORTIONS: 3–6

RISSOLES/PATTIES

> 1 lb (450 g) minced beef/kangaroo/venison
> 1 egg
> ½ onion (finely chopped)
> 2 cloves of garlic (finely chopped)
> A handful of bread crumbs
> Mixed herbs (basil, oregano)
> Salt and pepper

BURGERS/FILLING

> 6 toasted hamburger buns or 12 slices of toast
> 6 fried rashers (strips) of bacon (rinds cut off)
> 6 fried eggs
> ½ onion (fried, in rings)
> 6 slices of cheese
> 6 pineapple rings
> Sliced canned beetroot
> Sliced fresh tomato
> 6 lettuce leaves
> Tomato sauce
> Mayonnaise or butter

PREPARATION

1. Mix rissole ingredients in a bowl—best to use your hands for this. Divide into 6 equal portions and mold into rissoles/patties in your hands. Fry for about 3 minutes each side or until cooked.

2. Construct burgers by spreading mayo or butter on the buns (if you choose), then add cheese, rissoles, tomato sauce, bacon, onion, egg, pineapple, beetroot, tomato, and lettuce.

3. It will look like you'll need a mouth as big as Steven Tyler's to bite the sucker, but sing a couple of lines of "Dream On" and you'll be fine. Best served with a Foster's Lite Ice shandy (70% beer, 30% Schweppes lemonade).

Two, four, six, eight—bog in, don't wait!

Morbid Chef Notes

I really don't like the taste of beets (I had a total *borsch* overdose a couple of years ago!) so I cheated and removed them. Sorry, Ian! The sweetness of the pineapple was a good match with the meat, though, and the rest just simply tasted amazing together. Yum!

SHACKLES

Shackles formed in Sydney in 2000, and their early demos generated
a worldwide reputation for high-energy, raw death/thrash metal.
They released their debut album, *Traitors' Gate*, in 2009 but sadly
broke up since.

IRELAND

Irish Beef Stew

by Keith Fay of CRUACHAN

PREPARATION: 20 MINS
COOKING: 2 HRS 30 MINS
PORTIONS: 4–6

INGREDIENTS

> 2 lbs (900 g) large-size chunks of beef
> 4 large potatoes, peeled
> 2 large onions
> 3–4 medium carrots, peeled
> 4 cups (1 L) cold water
> ½ cup (125 ml) Guinness stout
> 2 beef stock cubes (or preferably real beef stock)
> 1 pack Knorr oxtail soup mix (or vegetable beef soup mix, goulash soup mix, or an extra beef stock cube)
> Parsley, to taste
> Thyme, to taste
> Salt and pepper, to taste

PREPARATION

1. Cut the vegetables into large-size chunks.

2. Choose a pot with a lid and put in the ingredients.

3. Add the cold water, Guinness, stock, and soup mix and season to taste.

4. Cover and put on a low heat for about two and half hours until the meat is tender and the potatoes have thickened the liquid.

An old Irish tradition is to prepare the stew a day before you intend to eat it and leave it in the pot for 24 hours, then reheat and serve.

Morbid Chef Notes

For a more traditional taste (and an excellent variation), you can replace the beef with lamb or mutton. I also recommend browning the meat and cooking onions with vegetable oil before throwing in the rest of the ingredients.

CRUACHAN

Cruachan was formed in 1992 by Keith Fay after the demise of Minas Tirith. They combined raw black metal with a passion for Celtic music and mythology in a completely new way. In 1995, they released their debut album, *Tuatha na Gael*, and they've since released a prolific outpouring of music combining Celtic sounds and traditional heavy metal.

"This is what I consider comfort-luxury-mandatory eating. It's a staple in my home, no matter where I am residing. Perhaps this dish will be a tad too *exotic* for the average mac 'n' cheese degenerate, so I recommend it for aficionados of tantalizing pleasures."

Bengal Beef Curry

by Vetis Monarch of WEAPON

PREPARATION: 4 HRS
COOKING: 50 MINS
PORTIONS: 6

INGREDIENTS

> 2 lbs (900 g) beef (either with bone or boneless)
> 3–4 potatoes
> ½ onion, chopped
> ½ cup (125 ml) vegetable oil
> Spices
>> 2½ tbsp turmeric powder
>> 1 tsp hot chili powder
>> ½ tsp cardamom (or 2 whole cardamom seeds)
>> 1 tsp ginger powder
>> 2 tsp garlic powder
>> 1 tsp cumin (or cumin seeds)
>> 1 tsp garam masala powder
>> 1½ tsp table salt
> 2 cups (200 g) basmati rice

MIXING AND MARINATING

1. Put all the spices, the chopped onion, and vegetable oil into a blender. Mix until the ingredients turn into a liquidy paste.

2. Rinse and peel the potatoes and cut them into medium-size cubes. Place the beef and potatoes in a large bowl and cover them with the paste. Mix vigorously, making sure all the meat and potatoes are evenly covered. Once they are thoroughly mixed, cover the bowl with plastic wrap and place in the fridge. The preparation now needs to marinate for *at least* 2 hours. The longer you do it, the better it will turn out. (Suggested marinating time is 4 hours.)

COOKING

1. Pour the marinated ingredients into a large pot. Make sure to get as much of the paste in there as you can! Add one cup of water. Stir the mixture slowly on high heat until it starts to boil.

2. Once boiling, stir vigorously for a few minutes and turn the heat down to medium low. Cover the pot with a lid and cook for 50 minutes. At this point, the potatoes should be soft (test by poking with a knife). Remove pot from heat, but keep covered.

PREPARATION OF BASMATI RICE

1. In a medium-size pot, add rice and 4 cups cold water. Bring to boil on high heat. Once boiling, turn down to minimum and stir thoroughly. Cover and simmer for approximately 20 minutes (or until all water has been absorbed).

SERVING

1. Traditionally, your plate should have a little more rice than meat. In Bengali culture, rice is the principal item, while the meat, potatoes, and gravy, etc., are meant to accompany the rice. Interestingly, the beef curry leftovers will taste even better the next day, when all the juices have been sitting for a significant period of time.

Morbid Chef Notes

This four-star beef curry recipe is really satisfying, and just perfectly spicy! Afterwards, I tried it as leftovers, and it's true that it tastes better the next day. Oh, also—you can freeze the remains, but be aware that the texture of the potatoes will slightly change; they'll become grainy.

WEAPON

Bangladeshi émigré Vetis Monarch formed Weapon in Calgary in 2003. As a three-piece, they wrote harsh black metal dealing heavily with the occult. The first EP, recorded in Bangladesh, was more black/death metal, while the later material is doomier and stronger. Every release grows darker, more original, and thicker in gloomy atmosphere.

Mushroom Steak à la Jack Daniel's

By Matt Olivo of REPULSION

PREPARATION: 30 MINS
COOKING: 10 MINS
PORTIONS: 2

INGREDIENTS

> 1 package tenderizing beef marinade
> 1 package au jus sauce mix
> 2 tsp Jack Daniel's whiskey (I prefer 2 shots of it!)
> Two 1 lb (450 g) spencer/ rib-eye steaks
> 5 medium-size white mushrooms
> Butter

PREPARATION

1. Prepare the marinade as per directions, but add two shots of Jack Daniel's whiskey. Let the steaks sit in the marinade for at least 30 minutes.

2. Slice and sauté the mushrooms in butter, then add the au jus mix to the pan. Simmer for 5 minutes, then set aside. You can add shrimp or lobster pieces to make this even more tasty.

3. Grill the steaks 10 to 15 minutes per side—depending on fire size and how you like it done.

4. Serve with the mushrooms over the steaks with a potato and cold beer. Enjoy!

Morbid Chef Notes

Oooohhh, wow, these steaks were so killer! The mushrooms and sauce tasted amazing over those fine pieces of meat (which you better get on sale, or it'll cost you an arm and a leg!) A real gem of a recipe!

REPULSION

Repulsion came of age in Flint, MI, during the mid-1980s, a ferocious countercurrent of vitality amidst the rusting, hulking wreckage of the industrial age. Their earliest songs about zombies, radiation, and butchery in 1985 brought a raw, blasting edge to early death metal, predating British grindcore by years and making Repulsion founding fathers of extreme metal. They have regrouped in the 2000s several times to perform classic material, like their posthumously released landmark album *Horrified*.

"I cannot cook at all and am lucky if i can make a bowl of cereal—so I got something from my mama. She can really cook, that's why I never had to learn!"

Midnight 7" Metaloaf

by Athenar of MIDNIGHT

PREPARATION: 15 MINS
COOKING: 1 HR
PORTIONS: 4–6

INGREDIENTS

> 2 lbs (900 g) ground beef
> ½ onion, finely chopped
> 1½ green peppers, finely chopped
> 1 large carrot, grated
> 2 eggs, slightly beaten
> 1 cup (60 g) bread crumbs
> ½ cup (50 g) grated parmesan cheese
> Salt, pepper
> ¼ cup (60 ml) milk or tomato sauce
> 2 tbsp Worcestershire sauce
> Tomato sauce or ketchup

PREPARATION

1. Mix all the ingredients together.

2. If too wet, add more bread crumbs, but still keep it moist.

3. Shape into 7" (18 cm) loaf pan or similar.

4. Bake at 350°F (175°C) for between 1 and 1½ hours.

5. Top when cooking with tomato sauce or ketchup.

Morbid Chef Notes

Meatloaf has been a standard American main dish since the 1800s. This old-school Ohio version is quite healthy, as not only do you get your protein and carbs but it's also full of veggies! On top of that, it tastes just awesome. Try to add the tomato sauce near the end only, as it might burn while cooking. All hail hell!

MIDNIGHT

Midnight first struck out from Cleveland in 2003. Originally this one-man-band project by Athenar—who has also been a member of Destructor and Boulder—only planned one EP. As as public outcry grew to deafening levels, Midnight kept going with more releases. They play a killer Motörhead-style black metal.

> "You can write what I know about cooking on a postage stamp in foot-high letters, but here is a thing both Alan—my son—and I like...so here goes!"

Pagan Pie
by Terry Jones of PAGAN ALTAR

PREPARATION: 30 MINS

COOKING: 30 MINS

PORTIONS: 6

INGREDIENTS

> 1 can corned beef (canned ground meat)
> Enough potatoes for your family/guests/self (if there are an awful lot of you, increase the number of tins of corned beef—you can decide this later!)
> Milk
> Butter or margarine
> Can of baked beans (tomato-baked, if available)
> 19 oz (540 ml) canned tomatoes, drained
> Salt, to taste
> Pepper, to taste
> Any old herbs you like!

PREPARATION

1. Peel and cook the potatoes as if you're doing mashed potatoes, which you are—so boil or steam them, with salt if you desire.

2. Empty the corned beef, baked beans, tomatoes, and any old herbs you like into a reasonable-size ovenproof dish. Mix up together thoroughly and smooth the mixture out evenly in the dish.

3. Once the potatoes are cooked, mash them like mash—add milk and butter if you normally do, don't if you don't.

4. Carefully spread the mash over the top of the corned beef, etc., trying not to get the whole thing mixed up. Level off the potato mash. Draw a smiley face on it (optional).

5. Place in a preheated oven at a low heat. Cook through for however long you like—I'd recommend at least half an hour, or until the top has gone golden brown. Actually, I prefer it almost burnt to a crisp, or so hot you have to eat it with asbestos gloves—but that's just me!

Morbid Chef Notes

I was a bit skeptical of this one at first—as you can tell, most of the ingredients are packaged in metal cans... Turns out, to my surprise, this meal is quite delicious, cheap, and easy to make! Those without access to corned beef (some kind of finely ground canned beef) and baked beans could simply replace them with minced cooked beef and a can of navy beans.

PAGAN ALTAR

Formed in 1976, England's Pagan Altar recorded one album in 1982 that wasn't properly released until 1998. The immense popularity of that recording led to a reformation in 2004. As if they had never stopped, the band continues to record ghostly doom metal classics to this very day.

SWEDEN

"This dish was quite common in Sweden about thirty years ago. Nowadays I never see it. I had to check some of the ingredients in an old Swedish cookbook."

Råbiff (Swedish Steak Tartare)

by Jörgen Lindhe of OBSCURITY

PREPARATION: 15 MINS
COOKING: —
PORTIONS: 4

INGREDIENTS

> 1 lb (450 g) *very fresh* beef, minced
> 1 yellow onion, chopped
> 2 marinated beetroots, chopped
> 2 shot glasses of capers
> 4 raw egg yolks

PREPARATION

1. Shape the meat into 4 portions.

2. Mix the onion, beetroots, and capers, and put the ingredients together with the yolk on top of the raw beef.

3. Served with salt and pepper, butter, and toast.

Smaklig måltid! Enjoy the food!

Morbid Chef Notes

This is a Swedish variation of steak tartare. I had never actually tried it before, and to my surprise this was absolutely amazing! The toppings added many dimensions to the taste. I used top sirloin steak and ground the meat myself for perfect taste. Can't wait to make this again!

OBSCURITY

Obscurity started in Malmö in the south of Sweden in 1985 with Dani Vala, Jörgen Lindhe, and Janne Johansson. This very early extreme band released two savage demos in the mid-1980s. Together with Mefisto and Bathory, they represent the origin of Swedish death metal—a great band of a kind that is now extinct. In 2007, Obscurity got together again with a new drummer, and played their first shows since the beginning of their career.

Roast Beef with Green Beans

by Udo Dirkschneider of ACCEPT / U.D.O.

PREPARATION: 15 MINS
COOKING: 1 HR
PORTIONS: 4–6

ROAST BEEF

> 2¼ lbs (1 kg) completely trimmed, flat roast beef
> Mixed fresh herbs (thyme, rosemary, parsley, chervil, tarragon)
> ¾ cup (170 g) softened butter
> ¾ cup (45 g) bread crumbs
> Salt and pepper
> 2 tbsp olive oil
> ½ cup (50 g) Parmesan, grated
> Olive oil and balsamic vinegar to sprinkle over the top

GREEN BEANS

> 1¼ lbs (600 g) green beans, washed, cleaned, and dried
> Salt
> 1 bunch of fresh thyme
> 1 bunch of fresh green onions
> 4 tbsp olive oil

CROUTONS

> 4 pieces white bread, cubed
> 1 clove garlic, peeled and halved
> 2 tbsp olive oil

PREPARATION OF ROAST BEEF

1. Preheat your oven to 350°F (180°C).

2. To prepare the crust, wash and dry all herbs and chop finely. Beat the butter and mix in the herbs. Add the bread crumbs and mix together. Add salt and pepper for seasoning. Gently pat the roast beef dry and sprinkle on both sides with salt and pepper.

3. Add some olive oil to an ovenproof frying pan and heat well. Sear all sides of the meat in the pan and coat in the previously prepared herb mix. Leave roast beef in the pan and put into the oven for 25 minutes.

PREPARATION OF GREEN BEANS

4. Boil beans in salt water for 6 to 8 minutes or until they are soft enough to bite. Rinse, cool, drain, and put aside.

5. Separate the thyme from the stem and chop roughly. Clean the spring onions, cut into rings, and sear with olive oil along with the thyme in a frying pan. Add the beans and heat once more.

FINAL PREPARATION

6. Heat the garlic in the olive oil and add the bread cubes. Gently stir-fry the cubes until they are golden brown. Remove from the pan and let them dry on a paper towel.

7. Slice the roast beef and lay on a large plate. Sprinkle the beans and croutons over the roast beef and top with the parmesan cheese.

8. Drizzle with a bit of olive oil and balsamic vinegar and serve with a good red wine (merlot).

Morbid Chef Notes

This is a different take on roast beef (the German way?), and it is really killer. I ate this one with a friend, and we both agreed the best parts were the ones with the crust.

ACCEPT / U.D.O.

Udo Dirkschneider formed Accept in Solingen, Germany, in 1971. The band pioneered a heavier form of metal, and found international success with albums like the pounding *Restless and Wild* and the seamless *Balls to the Wall*. In 1987, unhappy with the state of the band, Udo formed U.D.O.—his own vehicle with which to carry forward the broiling torch of heavy metal.

"A basic browned stew would be one cooked in water and seasoned with salt and pepper. But it should be tasty as well, so this one includes broth, red wine, and vegetables. "

The Stew of True Doom

by Karl Simon of THE GATES OF SLUMBER

PREPARATION: 30 MINS
COOKING: 2 HRS 30 MINS
PORTIONS: 6

INGREDIENTS

> 2 lbs (900 g) boneless beef shoulder in 1½" (4 cm) cubes
> 1 tbsp butter
> 1 tbsp cooking oil (more if needed)
> 2 tbsp flour
> 2 cloves garlic, chopped
> 1 tsp salt
> ½ tsp thyme
> 2 tsp finely chopped parsley
> 5–6 grinds of pepper
> 1 bay leaf
> 1 cup dry red wine (Beaujolais, California Mountain Red, pinot noir)
> 1 cup canned beef broth
> 4 medium carrots in ½" (1.3 cm) diagonal slices
> 2 medium onions cut in 8 wedges
> 4–6 medium potatoes, halved
> ¾ cup (110 g) green peas
> 1½ tsp salt
> ¼ tsp pepper

PREPARATION

1. Heat oven to 325°F (162°C). Dry the meat in paper towels. It won't brown when wet.

2. In a heavy skillet heat the butter and oil, and carefully brown the beef pieces a few at a time. If they are too close together, they will not sear, and the juice will run out. As the pieces are done, remove them to a heavy, lidded flameproof casserole, with a very low flame under it.

3. Sprinkle flour on the meat in the casserole, and stir with a wooden spoon until the flour is absorbed.

4. Mash the garlic with salt on a saucer using a strong fork. Add to the casserole with the other seasonings.

5. Add the wine, and allow stew to heat for 5 minutes. Add the beef broth to barely cover. Bring to a simmer, cover, and place in the oven. Turn down to 300°F (149°C), or whatever temperature to maintain simmer.

6. Cook 1 to 1½ hours, or until beef is beginning to tender. Check the stew occasionally to make sure it is not too dry. Add hot water to bring it back to original level.

7. Add the veggies except for the peas, and sprinkle with salt and pepper. Cover and cook for ¾ hours, or until meat and veggies are tender. Tip pot to skim off fat. Check and correct seasoning to taste.

8. Add the peas, sprinkle parsley all over. Serve with a hearty ale or stout beer while *Holy Diver* is playing.

Note: For later serving, allow to cool with lid askew so the stew will not continue to cook in its own heat. Cover and refrigerate. Reheat by first bringing to room temperature. Place pot in an oven preheated to 325°F (162°C) for 30 to 45 minutes or until stew is just bubbling and warmed through.

A lettuce salad served after the stew in the French way, followed by a soft Brie or fontina with the last of the wine, could round out the meal—with fresh fruit of the season to top it off.

Morbid Chef Notes

This is by far the best stew I have ever tasted. I almost had a heart attack when plunging my teeth into this baby! The meat melts in your mouth, and the wine-flavored stock makes the veggies taste hellishly good. I suggest preparing this on a weekend because it takes a bit longer, but trust me—it's worth the wait!

THE GATES OF SLUMBER

The Gates of Slumber, from Indianapolis, plays a doomy style of traditional heavy metal in the vein of early Saint Vitus, Omen, Cirith Ungol, and Manilla Road. Their powerful, pounding approach first earned them a devout following in Europe, with America since taking notice.

Thundering Beef Brisket

by Steve "Lips" Kudlow of ANVIL

PREPARATION: 5 MINS
COOKING: 3 HRS 30 MINS
PORTIONS: 4–6

INGREDIENTS

> 1½ lbs (675 g) beef brisket
> 6–7 cloves of fresh garlic, crushed
> 2 onions, sliced and diced
> 1 package of Lipton onion soup mix

> Roasting pot

PREPARATION

1. Fill roasting pot with 1 cup (250 ml) of water and one pack of Lipton's onion soup mix.

2. Using a garlic press, crush up about 6 or 7 cloves of garlic and put them on the meat and into the soup mix. If you really like garlic, use more. Place meat into roasting pot.

3. Place sliced and diced onions into the soup mix and on the meat.

4. For added interest, cut up potatoes into medium to large pieces and put in all around the meat and in the soup mix.

5. Place in oven at 350°F (180°C) for 3½ hours, periodically basting the meat with the soup. Keep covered, and add water if necessary.

Morbid Chef Notes

This is an easy and great beef brisket recipe which unfortunately can only be done in the winter, as butchers usually don't carry that cut of meat in the summer. If not possible to obtain onion soup mix, replace the water in step 1 with a small chopped onion, 1 cup beef stock, 1 tsp celery salt, and 1 tsp sugar.

ANVIL

Best known for early '80s fist-pumping albums like *Metal on Metal* and *Forged in Fire*, these true-blue Toronto 'bangers returned to the limelight in 2008 via the heartfelt documentary *Anvil: The Story of Anvil*. Apart from screen success, Anvil remains one of Canada's longest-running metal bands, boasting thirteen albums and still pounding!

UNITED STATES

Speckmann's Chili Mac

by Paul Speckmann of MASTER

PREPARATION: 30 MINS

COOKING: 3 HRS

PORTIONS: 4–6

INGREDIENTS

> 2 tbsp vegetable oil
> Either 1 lb (450 g) ground beef/ pork/misc. meat and a few turkey sausages or *klobasa* (slovak sausages) and 2 breasts of boneless chicken
> 2 large onions, chopped
> 4 cloves garlic, chopped
> Regular peppers: 1 green, 1 red
> Hot/jalapeño/habañero peppers: 1 red, 1 green, 1 yellow; or can of hot peppers, diced
> 16 oz (500 ml) can tomato sauce
> 16 oz (500 ml) can corn
> 28 oz (830 ml) can whole tomatoes
> 32 oz (950 ml) canned kidney, white, or red beans
> 12 oz (370 ml) can tomato paste
> 1 tsp sugar
> 1 tsp salt
> ¼ tsp pepper
> Few tbsp of chili powder or chili con carne mix

PREPARATION

1. Add onions to the pan with a few tablespoons of oil and garlic. Cook over medium heat. When onions are soft, add diced peppers.

2. I live in Europe, so I use *klobasa* sausage, chicken, ground meat, pork, beef—whatever I can find. Otherwise, one pound of ground beef and a few turkey sausages ground up are the best. Add to the veggies.

3. Cook for about 45 minutes or until tender. Get rid of the grease if you care; I usually don't bother. Add all of the contents of the cans as well as one can of water. After mixing, add the sugar, salt, pepper, and chili powder.

4. After about an hour, check the flavor, as you might need more salt or chili powder. Don't overdose on the salt because it can be a difficult thing to judge. Two to three hours of stirring is the best advice I can give. I think great food takes time, so be patient. Optional: Serve with macaroni, cheese, and sour cream.

Morbid Chef Notes

I had never added sausage to a chili before, and it simply kicks ass!! Overall, this recipe was really delicious. I will make it again for sure. It freezes well and lasts very long.

MASTER

Formed in Chicago in the early 1980s, Master is one of the true old-school pioneers of death metal music. Their intended 1985 debut album remained unreleased until 2003, when it took its rightful place alongside other primitive death metal greats. Bassist/vocalist and bandleader Paul Speckmann has resided in the Czech Republic for many years.

"Good black appetite—from Big Boss and Root."

Guláš à la Root

by Jirí "Big Boss" Valter of ROOT

PREPARATION: 15 MINS
COOKING: 1 HR 30 MINS
PORTIONS: 4-6

INGREDIENTS

> 2.2lb (1 kg) of large beef cubes
> 4 big onions, diced
> 5 big mushrooms, diced
> 1 sack (10 tbsp / 50 g) of sweet paprika
> Pepper
> Salt
> Marjoram

PREPARATION

1. Put the onions in a pot with heated oil, and let them fry. Add the meat to the pot, add salt, and braise with the onions for approximately 40 mins.

2. Add diced mushrooms, the whole sack of sweet paprika, pepper and marjoram according to taste, and simmer, covered, for 30 mins or until done. Then you can serve the Goulash à la Root.

For the trimmings, serve potatoes or *knedliky* dumplings (see below)—but fresh bread will also work.

KNEDLIKY DUMPLING RECIPE

For me, having goulash with dumplings is sacred. They are a pain to make, but they soak up the gravy and just taste incredible. Start this recipe approx 1 hour before cooking the goulash. Enjoy!

INGREDIENTS: 3 1/2 cup (385 g) white flour, 1 tsp dry yeast, 1 cup whole milk, 2 whole beaten eggs, 1 tsp salt, 2 tbsp lukewarm water

1. In a large bowl, mix lukewarm water with dry yeast, then add 1 cup (110 g) flour and whisk in milk. Let rest for 1 hour.

2. Mix in beaten eggs, then add remaining flour. Knead dough until it does not stick to your hands (it should be elastic - add more flour or milk if needed). Roll dough into four long baguette shapes, then lest rest for another 1 1/2 hours or until they have doubled in size.

3. About 20 minutes before serving goulash, bring a large pot 3/4 full of salty water to boil. Place loaves into water, cover pot and cook 13 minutes. Retrieve dumplings and immediately stab dumplings 3 times on each side. Allow dumplings to rest for 5 minutes. Slice crosswise just before serving.

Morbid Chef Notes

This great Slovak Guláš recipe will please any meat lover. I suggest adding some water or beer (Czech pilsner), if you feel it needs more liquid. Also, try adding whole caraway seeds for a variation. Serve with fine Czech beer—I recommend a glass of the ultra-evil Velkopopovický Kozel!

ROOT

Root was formed in Brno, Czech Republic, in 1987. Lead by Jiri "Big Boss" Valter's deep as-the-abyss vocals, their evil, excentric black metal grew more melodic over the years, while always retaining its heaviness and uniqueness.

Pork

BBQ PORK RIBS | BLACK ROSE JAMBALAYA | GRAY PEAS AND BACON | LATVIAN COUNTRYSIDE RIBS
MACARONI AGAINST MONOTHEISM | BLOODY INTESTINES AND WORMS | INFERNAL SWISS ALPS MACARONI
AND CHEESE | PIZZA CAKE (A DANGEROUS EATING) | PORK OF DISEASE (CITRUS STYLE)
SAUSAGE MEAT PIE | FRIJOLES BORRACHOS (DRUNK BEANS) | SINIGANG NA BABOY (PORK IN SOUR BROTH)
SPETSOFAI | GENOCIDE YELLOW PEA SOUP

BBQ Pork Ribs

by Meyhna'ch of MÜTIILATION

PREPARATION: 30 MINS
COOKING: 2 HRS 30 MINS
PORTIONS: 4

INGREDIENTS

> 2¼ lbs (1 kg) thick pork ribs (do not separate)
> 2 fist-size onions, finely diced
> 6 shot glasses ketchup
> 6 shot glasses water
> 2 shot glasses balsamic vinegar
> 2 shot glasses sugar or honey
> 1 tbsp powdered cinnamon
> 1 tsp salt
> 2 or 3 garlic bulbs, minced

(1 shot glass = 1 oz / 5 cl / 50 ml)

PREPARATION

1. Put ribs fat side up in a large oven dish and cook for 30 minutes at 480°F (250°C).

2. While the ribs are cooking, prepare the marinade: Dice onions in small pieces, then put them in a bowl. Add vinegar, ketchup, sugar, water, cinnamon, salt, and garlic. Mix everything with a fork, crushing the onions a little bit.

3. Take the ribs out of the oven and get rid of the extra fat. Soak the ribs in marinade until they are completely drenched with it.

4. Put the ribs back in the oven at 280°F (175°C) for 2 hours, turning them from time to time. The marinade should not evaporate too fast. Baste with more marinade if needed.

Enjoy with red wine.

Morbid Chef Notes

This is a fucking awesome BBQ ribs recipe. The meat gets really tender, and the sauce is incredibly tasty. And it can be used on steaks and chicken, as well! Baste the meat often to get as much BBQ sauce on it as you can.

MÜTIILATION

Mütiilation is a one-man black metal band formed in 1991 by Meyhna'ch.
His project was affiliated with the notorious French black metal circle
Les Légions Noires (LLN). Mütiilation released many demos and the
legendary 1995 debut album *Vampires of Black Imperial Blood*, and is still
around today, releasing great and elaborate black metal albums.

Black Rose Jambalaya

by Scott Gorham of THIN LIZZY

PREPARATION: 5 MINS
COOKING: 30 MINS
PORTIONS: 6

INGREDIENTS

> 1 tsp oil
> 1 pack chorizo sausage, sliced
> 12 free-range chipolatas
> 2 cups (370 g) long-grain rice
> 6 tomatoes, chopped
> 2 cups (480 ml) vegetable stock
> 2 peppers (1 red and 1 green), deseeded and cubed
> 1 bunch green onions, chopped
> 1 tbsp chili powder (optional)

PREPARATION

1. Heat oil in large pan and cook chorizo for 2 to 3 minutes. Add chipolatas and cook for a further 3 to 4 minutes until lightly browned. Tip in the rice and stir until coated in the oil.

2. Add tomatoes and vegetable stock, cover, and simmer for 15 minutes, stirring occasionally.

3. Add peppers and salad onions, cover, and cook for a further 10 minutes until rice is tender and most of the liquid has been absorbed. Those of you who want your Black Rose Jambalaya to blow your heads off, add a tablespoon of hot chili powder.

Morbid Chef Notes

Chipolatas are hard to find outside of Europe—they are thin pork sausages, similar to breakfast sausages, but not as bland tasting. They could be easily replaced by merguez or Italian sausages. Even chicken pieces would be nice! Overall, this is a fast and filling meal, great for busy days.

THIN LIZZY

Throughout the 1970s and early 1980s, Dublin's Thin Lizzy issued album after album of romantic street-fighting anthems such as "Whiskey in the Jar," "The Boys Are Back in Town," "Jailbreak," and "Emerald." The late Phil Lynott's soulful croon and the band's twin-guitar harmonies were a significant influence on early heavy metal. Californian guitarist Scott Gorham joined in 1974 and stayed through the band's demise in 1983. In 1996, he resurrected Thin Lizzy in tribute to Lynott.

UNITED KINGDOM

"Pronounced *gray pays 'n' bearcun*, this dish is a traditional Black Country meal. I have known some people to put in a little Worcestershire sauce, but not me. Be warned, this dish can cause flatulence!"

Gray Peas and Bacon

A Feast for the Priest by Al Atkins, ex–JUDAS PRIEST / HOLY RAGE

PREPARATION: 8 HRS (including soaking of the beans overnight)

COOKING: 3 HRS 15 MINS

PORTIONS: 6

INGREDIENTS

> 1 lb (450 g) dried gray/pigeon peas
> 3 oz (90 g) barley
> 1lb (450 g) smoked streaky bacon
> 1 large onion, sliced up in small pieces
> Salt and pepper
> 1 tsp bicarbonate of soda
> Water

> Saucepan

PREPARATION

1. Put peas and barley in a large saucepan, add teaspoon of bicarbonate, cover in water, and let them soak overnight—this makes them swell. Add a little more water if needed.

2. The next day, carefully rinse soaked peas. Cut up the smoked streaked bacon into small pieces and fry until it becomes crispy. Add both to the saucepan, along with sliced onion and the barley. Cover in water, and then bring to a boil, adding some salt and pepper to taste.

3. Cover and let simmer for about 3 hours. Keep checking the pan and top it up with more water if needed.

4. When cooked, serve with crispy toasted bread. Lovely!

Morbid Chef Notes

This is extremely cheap and killer comfort food. You get all your needed protein, fibers, and carbs in this very dish! Great for students!

JUDAS PRIEST / HOLY RAGE

Al Atkins formed Judas Priest in the British Midlands in 1967. He recruited local heavy rockers K. K. Downing and Ian Hill in 1970, and the group soon recorded a demo tape with the help of Black Sabbath's Tony Iommi. Atkins left Judas Priest in 1973 and remained active in British groups such as Lion during the 1970s. Recently, he has resurfaced with Holy Rage, performing among other songs some early versions of Judas Priest material he helped write in their original bluesy hard rock style.

"This is a typical Latvian-style dinner, whose recipe was obtained from a very old cookery book."

Latvian Countryside Ribs

by Peter of SKYFORGER

PREPARATION: 15 MINS
COOKING: 40 MINS
PORTIONS: 4

RIBS

> 2¼ lbs (1 kg) pig ribs
> Mustard
> Mayonnaise
> 2 garlic cloves, crushed
> 2 onions, chopped

> Aluminum foil

SAUTÉED SAUERKRAUT

> 2¼ lbs (1 kg) sauerkraut (fermented shredded cabbage)
> 1 tbsp pig roast drippings or butter
> 1 onion, chopped
> 2 medium-size carrots, shredded (optional)
> 1 tbsp flour, diluted with water
> Salt
> ¼ cup (50 g) sugar (caramelized, if possible)

> 2¼ lbs (1 kg) small potatoes
> Good beer
> Fresh dill
> Fresh tomatoes (optional)
> Cucumbers (optional)

PREPARATION

1. Start by making the sautéed sauerkraut. Take onions and fry them into the fat until they become golden. Add cabbage and its liquid, then simmer until the cabbage is almost soft (about one hour).

2. Add diluted flour mixture, salt, and sugar, then keep simmering for another hour. Add shredded carrots about 20 minutes before it is ready.

3. Heat oven to 475°F (250°C).

4. In a bowl, mix mustard, mayonnaise, garlic, and onions. Baste the ribs with this nice mixture.

5. Take a large piece of aluminum foil, fold it in two, and then form an envelope shape. Put ribs inside, then seal aluminum completely. Put aluminum envelope on baking tray.

6. Roast ribs for about 40 minutes, or until the meat is falling apart. When the time is over, cut the foil and leave ribs in the open for few minutes. The ribs will get a golden color and a nice brown touch.

Serve with boiled baked potatoes, fresh dill, celery, fresh tomatoes, cucumbers, and good beer. Latvia has many great local breweries with hundreds of years' beer-making experience and traditions, and Skyforger don't like to drink shitty beer. The ones we normally drink and suggest also to you are these four: Tērvetes, Bauskas, Užavas, and Piebalgas. Check them out when you're in Latvia, they all rule!

Morbid Chef Notes

To make caramelized sugar, put sugar in a frying pan on medium heat. Stir constantly with a wooden spoon until it reaches a boil. Swirl the pan around to keep the syrup moving until it begins to turn amber brown. Never stop stirring, or you will burn it!

Photo by Gerda Buša and Andy "Hopkins"

SKYFORGER

Emerging in the mid-'90s, Skyforger are one of the most unique bands from the pagan/folk metal genre. They have written numerous masterpieces, ranging from old-style black metal to more classic heavy metal styles, always combining them with traditional Baltic instrumentation. Skyforger calls their music "Latvian pagan metal."

NETHERLANDS

"Though I am certainly a gourmet these days and enjoy few things more than a really fine meal, this recipe is the quintessence of raw, simple, filthy food. Yeah—just like my music."

Macaroni Against Monotheism

by Count Orlok of COUNTESS

PREPARATION: —
COOKING: 25 MINS
PORTIONS: 10+

INGREDIENTS

> 2¼ lbs (1 kg) cheap macaroni
> 1½ lbs (666 g) ground pork
> ¾ lb (333 g) ground beef of the lowest possible quality
> Powdered pasta sauce

PREPARATION

1. Okay, here we go! Take equal amounts of macaroni (the cheapest you can find) and meat. Fry the meat, grinding it while you do, and simultaneously boil the macaroni. Do the macaroni a little too well (more than al dente), to get the exact result we're looking for here.

2. At the same time, prepare a sauce, based on the cheapest little bag of powder-based sauce you can find in a supermarket, the kind that you have to add water to, and then boil. Use just a bit of sauce in comparison to the amounts of macaroni and meat.

3. Once everything is done, throw it all in a single pan. Do not add anything else, and most certainly not fresh vegetables or herbs or anything that will refine the taste. Then mix it all together and serve.

Consume with large quantities of the cheapest beer (preferably pilsner) you can find in a proletarian supermarket (the kind vagrants drink), and while listening to some orthodox black metal. Enjoy!

ORLOK RECALLS HIS STUDENT DAYS...

This recipe goes back to my days as a student, when of course I had very little money and was too busy either studying or partying to pay much attention to food. I used to cook simple meals in large quantities (so that I could eat off it for three or four days). Sometimes I ate this particular meal every single day for weeks in succession. The taste should be really primitive because of the equal amounts of meat and macaroni and the very limited presence of the sauce.

Morbid Chef Notes

I don't think I ever made such a big meal before! Orlok wasn't kidding when he said he had enough for weeks. This recipe is not *that* bad actually, and will certainly help with some of us who would rather spend money on records than on food!

COUNTESS

Dutch black metal band Countess formed in 1992, and as a trio recorded their debut album, *The Gospel of the Horned One,* in 1993. Today, the sole remaining member is Orlok, who bears the challenge and earns the glory of Countess's truly great orthodox metal. In fact, the later you go in this band's discography, the better it gets. Hail Countess!

UNITED STATES

Bloody Intestines and Worms

Just kidding! Italian sausage, peppers, and onions by Bill Lindsey of IMPALER

PREPARATION: 5 MINS
COOKING: 30 MINS
PORTIONS: 6

INGREDIENTS

> 1 lb (450 g) hot or sweet Italian sausage
> 3 tbsp extra-virgin olive oil
> 3 cloves garlic, thinly sliced
> 1 red bell pepper—seeded and sliced
> 1 green bell pepper—ditto
> 1 large onion in ½″ (1.3 cm) slices
> ¼ cup (60 ml) tomato sauce thinned slightly with water
> Pinch of salt and pepper

PREPARATION

1. Preheat oven to 425°F (215°C). Place sausages on a baking sheet and drizzle extra-virgin olive oil over them.

2. Place in hot oven and roast until casings are crisp and juices run clear (15 to 20 minutes).

3. While sausages roast, heat skillet with 3 tablespoons extra-virgin olive oil and thin-sliced garlic for 2 to 3 minutes, and add peppers and onions. Turn the heat up a notch, and cook until veggies are tender (5 to 6 minutes).

4. Add thinned-out tomato sauce, pinch of salt and pepper, and mix through veggies.

5. Take sausages from oven and pour veggies over the top. Serve with favorite dinner bread. Rock on!!!

Morbid Chef Notes

This is a delicious ultra-quick recipe. I would eat some every day of the week! Add chili flakes for extra spiciness.

IMPALER

Minneapolis shock rockers Impaler fed bloody 1970s punk and metal to voracious mid-1980s thrash metal audiences. Their classic Combat Records releases like *Rise of the Mutants* were loaded with fast, catchy songs about whips, guts, brains, and gore—a perfect side dish for horror videos and late-night creature features. They survive in the 2000s and continue to devour the living.

SWITZERLAND

"Please serve *no* starters and *no* dessert with this meal, for having more space for Brögi's infernal macaronis of the Swiss Alps! Enjoy it with cider!"

Infernal Swiss Alps Macaroni and Cheese

by Brögi of MESSIAH

PREPARATION: 30 MINS (depending on your mental state and blood alcohol level)

COOKING: 20 MINS (10 if you listen to our song "Messiah" or 40 if you are at "Total Maniac")

EATING: 5 MINS

SHITTING: 1 HR (or if prepared with onions, one full day every 10 to 20 minutes, farts not included)

PORTIONS: 8

INGREDIENTS

> 1 lb (450 g) uncooked macaroni
> 1¾ lbs (800 g) potatoes, skinned and diced in small pieces
> 9 oz (250 g) bacon, diced (can be replaced with country ham)
> ¾ cup (180 ml) cream
> 2 cups (250 g) Parmesan, grated
> 2¼ lbs (1 kg) onions, skinned and cut in rings
> Pepper, ground
> Nutmeg, ground
> Unsweetened applesauce

PREPARATION

1. First you need a feeling of high mountains and cow ringing bells. You also have to listen to our album *Thrashing Madness* while you prepare the onions and potatoes: Put the onions into a pan and let them roast until they are brown but not burned. The Swiss name of these onions is now *zwiebele Schweiz*.

2. Cook potatoes in salted water for 12 minutes. While you do that, bring the macaroni to a boil in well-salted water and cook 10 minutes.

3. Take a second big frying pan and heat up some cooking fat or oil. Put the bacon cubes and the boiled potatoes into the pan, and stir all together. Flavor with pepper and nutmeg.

4. Add the boiled macaroni and stir once again. Add the cream and Parmesan cheese and stir all together until the cheese is melted. Put the onions over the macaroni mixture and serve with the applesauce separately.

Morbid Chef Notes

That recipe made tons of leftovers, but I didn't mind because it's the best mac 'n' cheese recipe I've ever eaten! The flavors of this are just fantastic. Totally recommended!

MESSIAH

MESSIAH emerged from Switzerland in 1984 and pioneered an underground path from insane thrash metal to bizarre, cryptic death metal. Their several albums over the following ten years are packed with original ideas, and remain cult favorites. Notably, their *Extreme Cold Weather* LP is a unique example of a heavy metal album cover featuring a photo of a polar bear.

"Here's a little horror helping for those who crave a 666-megaton gutbomb. Like a regular pizza pie, this is a simple base which can be easily altered to suit your taste; and to transform any casual, respectable metalhead into a drooling hesher!"

Pizza Cake (A Dangerous Eating)
by Reuben Storey of FUNEROT

PREPARATION: 10 MINS
COOKING: 45 MINS
PORTIONS: 4 LUNATICS

INGREDIENTS

> 4 frozen party pizzas
> 3 cups (240 g) mozzarella, grated
> 1 lb (450 g) pork sausage, minced
> 1 small can tomato paste

> 4 cookie sheets (or fewer, but it will take more time to bake all 4 pizzas)

PREPARATION

1. Preheat your oven to 450°F (225°C). Unwrap party pizzas and place each on a cookie sheet. Cook each of them halfway.

2. Brown the sausage. Drain fat and gradually mix in spoonfuls of tomato paste. Be cautious of how much you add, as too much will result in, heh, runny gravy.

3. Set the first pie on a cookie sheet and apply a healthy layer of gravy. Lay the next pizza on top. Repeat until all four pizzas are stacked with layers of gravy in between. The pizza is the "cake" and the sausage is the "frosting."

4. Pack the grated mozzarella on all sides and top of the cake. Don't be afraid to get your hands dirty on this step. Make sure it sticks.

5. Bake an additional 15 to 25 minutes or until the cheese is golden brown. Refrigerate for 5 minutes, and then slice into quarters and serve.

Morbid Chef Notes

Okay, I admit I didn't make this one! It's a good thing Reuben has victims—er, friends—who helped him finish this monster. Supposedly, they passed out and never woke up!

Photo by Reuben Storey

FUNEROT

Formed in 2003 in Shoreline, WA, Funerot is a refreshing high-energy thrash metal band with punkish vocals—a mix of Slayer, Tankard, and Voïvod. Skillful solos appear in every song, joining poetic lyrics about diseases, mutations, and weird human experimentation. They released many splits and demos before their first album, *Invasion from the Death Dimension*, arrived in 2006.

CHILE

"Enter the circle of lemon, burn the holy chili and the sacred oregano, worship the beer, and sacrifice the pork meat—because this flesh is the essence of disease!"

Pork of Disease (Citrus Style)

by Felipe Plaza Kutzbach of PROCESSION

PREPARATION: 45 MINS
COOKING: 40 MINS
PORTIONS: 4

"VICTIM"

> 2¼ lbs (1 kg) fresh, young, and virgin pork meat (filet, tenderloin, half leg, or similar)

BATH MARINADE

> 6 pilsner beers—two for the meat, the other ones for the cook!
> 8 lemons, squeezed
> Oregano
> Chili powder
> Salt
> Pepper

SPECIAL GUESTS

> Knack sausages
> Pagan Altar, *Mythical and Magical*

PREPARATION

1. So, you want to experience the disease? Here it goes… First of all, you'll need some music—what about Pagan Altar? Ufff, first tune, we are also getting thirsty, right? So open one of the beers and we are ready for the food metal alchemy!

2. You can start with the liquids. Go find a big bowl and mix two beers with the juice of 8 lemons; then add as much oregano, chili powder, and pepper as you want, as well as loads of salt. Let it rest for 5 minutes.

3. Meanwhile, we can prepare our pink friend for his bath; so, take the ritual knife and cut off 80% of the fat on it. Not everything—because fat gives pork the oily taste we are looking for.

4. Cut the pork in slices (you'll get maybe 4 or 5), and put them into the bowl, under the beer mixture. You should wait from 15 to 30 minutes for the pork to enjoy his tasty last bath, while you can start warming up the oven at 350°F (180°C) and open another beer for Satan's sake!

5. After his bath, the pork shall say (with his smell), "I'm ready… Take me to the oven!" So put some baking paper over the plate and lay down the slices over it, in a circle (if you want). Put in oven.

6. Spend 40 minutes praising Satan (with necessary pauses for more beer, vinyl, farts, etc.).

7. Now I think you're thinking: "What about the sausages?" Pfff! Go and eat some! This is taking too long! (Yes, we thought about everything!)

8. Okay, time's up! Run to the kitchen, open the oven, and say the magic words: "Fuck! It burns!"

9. You will now surrender to this tasty, delicious, mighty (and superior) piece of corpse. It fits perfectly also with some garlic mayonnaise or gypsy sauce. Now *beware*! After one or two slices, your blood will start running slow, and you'll eventually spend the whole afternoon without moving from the couch… Satisfied?

Morbid Chef Notes

I used fresh pork tenderloin to make this recipe, and it turned out perfectly moist. I also made my own garlic mayonnaise, by mixing (in this order): 1 tbsp fresh lemon juice, 2 large garlic cloves (crushed), 6 tbsp mayonnaise, and 1 tsp extra-virgin olive oil. It is really, really tasty!

PROCESSION

Procession is a young Chilean band that plays epic doom metal. Formed in 2006 in Valparaíso, they released an amazing demo tape in 2008, followed by *The Cult of Disease*, their debut album, a year later. Their recordings created a buzz in the underground, leading to a successful tour in Europe. Their breathtaking approach is characterized by melodic vocals atop neck-breaking barrages of riffs that send shivers down the spines of mortals.

UNITED KINGDOM

"This recipe is our old favorite. We used to have it after rehearsals, with a nice big pile of mashed potatoes and baked beans. My wife, Alison, says that it feeds a band of five with a bit left over for a roadie (or a groupie!)"

Sausage Meat Pie

by Phil Denton of ELIXIR

PREPARATION: 20 MINS

COOKING: 1 HR 15 MINS

PORTIONS: 5 BAND MEMBERS AND A ROADIE OR TWO

INGREDIENTS

> 1 lb (450 g) sausage meat
> 1 medium onion, chopped
> 1 can chopped tomatoes
> 1 lb (450 g) pack puff pastry
> 1 tbsp butter
> 1 tbsp olive oil
> ½ tsp sugar
> Salt and pepper

> Greased baking sheet with a raised edge, approx 13" x 9" (33 cm x 23 cm)
> Mashed potatoes
> Two cans baked beans

PREPARATION

1. Melt butter and oil in a large saucepan, and gently fry onions for 5 minutes. Remove and set aside. Cook sausage meat in same saucepan, stirring frequently, breaking up pieces, for approximately 5 minutes. Add onions to sausage meat, plus tomatoes with juice, sugar, and salt and pepper.

2. Stir, bring to boil, put lid on, and turn down to a simmer. Cook for about 10 minutes, stirring now and then. Meanwhile, remove puff pastry from packet and cut in half along shortest width.

3. Roll out one piece of pastry until it fits the baking sheet. Lay it on tray and, when cooked, add sausage-meat mixture using a slotted spoon—as you don't need much juice—and spread over pastry, leaving about a 1" (2.5 cm) gap around the edges. Wet edges with water.

4. Roll out second piece of pastry—slightly larger than the first—and fold over so the two long edges meet. Make long slits along the folded edge, leaving just under 2" (5 cm) uncut.

5. Open out and place on top of other pastry sheet and sausage-meat mixture. Press edges down, then trim any excess pastry so it fits neatly inside baking sheet.

6. Score edges (i.e., make lots of small horizontal cuts around the two edges of the pastry sides), brush top with milk, and place in oven for about 20 to 25 minutes at 400°F (200°C) until golden brown.

Serve with creamy mashed potatoes and baked beans.

Morbid Chef Notes

This is seriously one of the most artery-clogging dishes I've ever eaten, but it was quite good, especially with mashed potatoes!

ELIXIR

Elixir is a traditional British heavy metal band started in 1983, when the New Wave of British Heavy Metal was already at its peak. They released their own singles before signing to Sonic Records during the late 1980s. After lying low during the 1990s, the original lineup returned in the 2000s to perform and record some old and new classic-sounding material.

COLOMBIA

Frijoles Borrachos (Drunk Beans)

by Hugo Alberto "Witchhammer" Uribe of WITCHTRAP

PREPARATION: 8 HRS (including soaking of the beans)

COOKING: 1 HR 15 MINS

PORTIONS: 3

INGREDIENTS

> 1 bottle of beer
> 1 cup of beans of your choice
> 4 cups (1 L) of water
> 1 big carrot
> ¼ lb (115 g) bacon or ham, cut in small pieces
> Salt

> Plantains, fried
> Guacamole (see recipe in Appetizers section!)

PREPARATION

1. Add beer to beans and leave them to soak overnight.

2. The next day, rinse beans and boil them with 3 big cups of water in a pressure cooker. Add carrot and take it out after 45 minutes.

3. Put carrot in a blender, and add some of the water used to cook the beans. When carrot is completely pulverized, add it back to the beans.

4. In a separate pan, fry some ham or slices of bacon, and add that to the beans at the same time you add the carrot blend.

5. Remove lid from pot, and cook on medium heat until it starts getting thick. It can take from 15 to 30 minutes, depending on how thick you like it. Add salt to taste.

Serve with fried plantains and guacamole.

Morbid Chef Notes

This recipe was pretty good! Unfortunately, I used really cheap beer (a can of Milwaukee's Best Dry), and the aftertaste was really bad. I had to add pieces of onions, ha ha ha! Nevertheless, if you use quality beer (one that doesn't have an aftertaste) it should be killer. In fact, after a few days in the fridge, you could barely taste the beer anymore. Also, the fried plantains were excellent!

WITCHTRAP

Formed in Medellín in 1992 by the two metal maniac brothers Carlos and Hugo Uribe, Witchtrap plays merciless blackened thrash metal. Their path truly took off in the 2000s, when they released *Sorceress Bitch*, their dangerous debut full-length. Witchtrap's irresistible genuine approach and killer songwriting have blasted them to the top of current thrash metal bands.

"A recipe from our pagan fathers. Simple, cannibal-style cooking: all in one pot!"

Sinigang Na Baboy (Pork in Sour Broth)

by Voltaire 666 of DEIPHAGO

PREPARATION: 10 MINS
COOKING: 1 HR 30 MINS
PORTIONS: 4

INGREDIENTS

> 1½ lbs (675 g) pork riblets or pork ribs (country style), cut to pieces
> 5 cups (1¼ L) water
> 4 medium tomatoes, sliced
> 1 medium onion, sliced
> 1½ tsp salt
> 1 medium icicle radish (daikon), cut into 1" (2.5 cm) pieces (or 10 red radishes, pared)
> ¼ lb (115 g) green beans
> ½ lb (225 g) spinach, cabbage, mustard greens, or watercress
> 5 midsize tamarind pods (also available in powdered pkg)
> 1 or 2 hot peppers, both ends removed

PREPARATION

1. In a large pot, bring water and pork to a boil. Add tomatoes, onion, hot peppers, salt, and tamarind. Simmer 1 hour, or until pork is tender.

2. Remove tamarind and mash with some broth. Strain juice back into pot.

3. Taste for seasoning. Bring to a boil. Add green beans and radish. Cook for 10 minutes.

4. Add spinach, cover, and remove from heat. Let stand 5 minutes to finish cooking spinach.

Variations: Beef (stewing, brisket, shank, or plate) may be used instead of pork. Adjust cooking time for each.

Morbid Chef Notes

This easy recipe yielded surprising results! The taste was very different from anything I've ever eaten, and I really enjoyed the experience. The best thing about this soup was the ribs; they were fucking awesome! You might have trouble finding tamarind—go to any Asian grocerer and they should have some. It's that ingredient that gives the "sour" taste to the broth, so it is essential.

DEIPHAGO

Deiphago has existed since 1989. Drawing influence from legendary mid-'80s bestial South American bands and the forefathers of European black metal, they have released a handful of contributions to the black arts. This extreme power trio are currently living in Costa Rica, but they originally hail from the city of Manila in the Philippines

GREECE

"This is a traditional winter course from the mountains of central Hellas. It involves traditional village sausage, capsicum (peppers), onion, olive oil, etc. As you can see, Hellenic cuisine is as broad as can be in terms of the ingredients used—simplicity versus complexity and taste!"

Spetsofai

by Archon Vorskaath (with the help of Melanie) of ZEMIAL

PREPARATION: 15 MINS

COOKING: 1 HR

PORTIONS: 4

INGREDIENTS

> 2¼ lbs (1 kg) sweet peppers; 2 green, 2 orange, 1 red, cut in long ½" (1.3 cm) wide strips
> 1⅔ lbs (750 g) ripe tomatoes, scalded, peeled, and diced (or 2 small cans of diced tomatoes)
> 2 large onions, chopped into small pieces
> 4 large garlic cloves, chopped into small pieces
> 4 traditional Greek, German, or Italian sausages, cut in thick slices
> 9 tbsp olive oil
> 1 tsp thyme
> 1 tsp oregano
> 1 pinch raw/brown sugar
> 1 pinch nutmeg (freshly grated is preferable)
> Salt
> Black pepper (freshly ground if possible)
> 2 tbsp fresh parsley, chopped

PREPARATION

1. Heat up the olive oil in a frying pan on medium flame. (Tip: Never overheat olive oil!)

2. Fry the sliced sausages in the oil for around 7 minutes, or until they are well done on both sides

3. Take them out of the oil and put them aside

4. Fry the pepper slices in the leftover oil from the sausages until they are a bit brown (almost roasted) and very soft. Around 10 minutes on high heat should do it. Take them out of the oil and put them aside.

5. Fry the onion and the garlic in the leftover oil from the capsicum (the peppers) and sausages until the onions are well done/golden-brown. (Tip: Add the garlic after the onions, as garlic cooks much faster.) Add the sugar, herbs, and spices, and then the tomatoes. Cook on low flame in an open pot until the ingredients turn into a thick sauce.

6. Add the capsicum and the sausages, mix them in thoroughly, and cook everything together in the closed pot for around 30 minutes on low/medium heat. The sauce is meant to be thick and chunky, so if it is too juicy, open the lid for the last few minutes to allow the sauce to thicken.

Add a bit of fresh parsley on top and serve with fresh continental bread. Optionally, serve with rice on the side—and accompany with red wine, of course! ΚΑΛΗ ΟΡΕΞΗ! Enjoy!

Morbid Chef Notes

Now that's one hell of a meal! Wow, it was really, really fucking good. Try your best to use real tomatoes for this one, as it does make a huge difference in the taste. You won't regret it!

ZEMIAL

One of the first black/death metal bands to emerge from Greece during the late 1980s/early 1990s was Zemial. Formed in 1989 by Vorskaath, the band released a handful of demos and EPs, but held off creating their first full-length until 2006. For twenty years now, they have stood against the mainstream, allowing the strength of their music and concert performances to speak for itself.

"This soup is great! My stepsister Hélène is a *cordon bleu*, and also a mother of five. Her kids actually prefer eating my soup to hers, even though hers is really good. The secret is the simmering of the ham and other ingredients. Enjoy!"

Genocide Yellow Pea Soup

by Mark Bouffard of DISSECTION

PREPARATION: 8 HRS (including soaking of the peas)
COOKING: 2 HRS 30 MINS
PORTIONS: 10

INGREDIENTS

> 2¼ lbs (1kg) smoked ham w/bone
> 1 lb (450 g) dried yellow peas
> ¼ tsp baking soda
> 2 medium onions, finely chopped
> 4 large carrots, grated or finely chopped
> ½ tsp ground savory
> ½ tsp celery salt
> ½ tsp turmeric powder
> ½ tsp cumin powder
> 1 pinch rosemary
> 2 tsp maple syrup
> Sea salt
> Black pepper, freshly ground
> Water

PREPARATION

1. In a large pot or bowl, cover yellow split peas with 8 cups (2 L) of lukewarm water. Add baking soda and sea salt. Mix well, cover, and let soak for 8 hours.

2. During this time, start to prepare your ham. Cut off visible fat and throw it out, then cut small pieces that you will put on a plate. Do this until you are left with a nice ham bone. Put your ham pieces and bone in the fridge until you are ready to make the recipe.

3. Eight hours later, drain the peas and rinse them with plenty of water. Put peas in a large pot, and add 8 cups (2 L) of cold water.

4. Put ham bone in center of pot, and then gradually add chopped onions, grated carrots, maple syrup, and ham pieces. Follow with savory, celery salt, turmeric powder, cumin, and rosemary. Add salt and pepper to taste.

5. Cover and bring to boil. Lower heat and simmer for 2½ hours. Mix soup from time to time, and make sure you got enough water.

6. Remove from heat, take out bone, mix well, and then serve!

Morbid Chef Notes

Yellow pea soup is a very traditional French-Canadian meal. In fact, we ate so much of it for years that English-speaking Canadians sometimes call us *pea soupers*! Anyway, this recipe is a killer version of the soup—which is unfortunately a bit less common these days with younger people, mainly due to globalization.

DISSECTION

Dissection formed under the name Genocide in Quebec City in 1986. They built a reputation for themselves after playing many shows, and recorded their only album in 1987. They play some sort of progressive thrash metal, which sounds like a strange mixture of *Dimension Hatröss*–era Voivod and fellow Canadians Razor.

#

SUNDAY BRUNCH LAMB ROAST | YOUVETSI HELLFIRE | FÅRIKÅL | ALI BAA BAA (MOROCCAN LAMB)
COUNTRY LAMB EXOHIKO | PROTO METAL LAMB SHANKS BRAISED IN BURGUNDY

IRELAND

"This recipe was one of Philip's favorite dinners."

Sunday Brunch Lamb Roast

by Philomena Lynott, mother of Philip Lynott of THIN LIZZY

PREPARATION: 25 MINS
COOKING: 1 HR 30 MINS
PORTIONS: 6–8

LAMB

> 3½ lbs (1.6 kg) leg/shoulder of lamb
> 1 tbsp olive oil
> 1 tsp cracked black pepper
> 1 tbsp or generous pinch rosemary, chopped
> 1 generous pinch sea salt
> 3–4 lbs (1.4–1.8 kg) potatoes, peeled and thickly sliced
> 6–10 garlic cloves, peeled and left whole

BUTTERED LEEKS

> 6 medium leeks
> 1 oz (30 g) butter
> 2 tbsp water
> Salt and pepper

FRESH MINT SAUCE

> 3 tbsp fresh mint, chopped
> 1 tbsp sugar
> ¼ cup (60 ml) boiling water
> 1 tbsp white wine vinegar

PREPARATION OF LAMB

1. Preheat oven to 450°F (230°C). Prick the lamb about 20 to 30 times. Mix the oil, pepper, and rosemary, and spread all over the lamb—pushing it into the holes. Sprinkle the sea salt over the roast.

2. Place in roasting tray and put into preheated oven. Cook for about 20 minutes.

3. Turn oven down to 350°F (180°C). Remove lamb from tray, and cover the bottom of the tray with the sliced potatoes and garlic. Season with salt and pepper, then place lamb on top. Cook uncovered for another 70 minutes. Turn potatoes while in the tray.

4. When lamb is cooked, remove it. Cover the tray with foil, and allow to rest for 10 minutes. Continue to cook the potatoes until they reach desired consistency.

PREPARATION OF BUTTERED LEEKS

1. Wash leeks and cut into round slices.

2. Melt butter in saucepan with water and add leeks. Season with salt and pepper.

3. Reduce heat, cover with lid, and cook for 10 to 20 minutes. Do not overcook, as they should not lose their fresh green color.

PREPARATION OF FRESH MINT SAUCE

Put sugar and mint into bowl. Add boiling water, stir to dissolve the sugar, and add the vinegar. Let sit for 10 minutes. This is best made on the day you want to eat it.

To serve, place potatoes on large server, and place lamb on top. Pour the cooking juices over the whole meal.

Morbid Chef Notes

Great Irish meal—traditionally eaten on Sundays, but can obviously be eaten anytime! Tie the meat if it is boneless, or else it will lose its shape when cooking.

THIN LIZZY

Throughout the 1970s and early 1980s, Dublin's Thin Lizzy issued album after album of romantic street-fighting anthems such as "Whiskey in the Jar," "The Boys Are Back in Town," "Jailbreak," and "Emerald." The late Phil Lynott's (Aug. 20, 1949–Jan. 4, 1986) soulful croon and the band's twin-guitar harmonies were a significant influence on early heavy metal. In 1996, longtime guitarists Scott Gorham and John Sykes, drummer Brian Downey, and keyboardist Darren Wharton resurrected Thin Lizzy to perform Lynott's songs and honor his memory.

GREECE

"Youvetsi—which means 'pot of clay'—is a lamb stew cooked in a clay pot. You may use veal instead of lamb, but you must add a bit of cinnamon in that case."

Youvetsi Hellfire

by The Magus of NECROMANTIA

PREPARATION: 10 MINS
COOKING: 1 HR 30 MINS
PORTIONS: 4

INGREDIENTS

> 2¼ lbs (1 kg) lamb (chops/neck, whatever)
> 3 onions, sliced
> 2 red chili peppers (sliced if you like it *really* spicy, uncut for milder taste)
> 2 tomatoes (cut in cubes—not too small)
> 4 cups (1 L) tomato puree or tomato paste for cooking
> Some olive oil
> 1 lb (450 g) kritharáki (or orzo) pasta (available in Italian/Greek delicatessens, or in bulk/health food stores)
> Salt and pepper
> Kefalotyri cheese (or Parmesan)

PREPARATION

1. Put the oil in a clay pot (or heavy cast-iron pot), and let heat in an oven at high setting.

2. Take clay pot out from oven. Add the sliced onions and fry until brown.

3. Sprinkle the lamb with salt and pepper, and place in the pot to brown the sides.

4. When the lamb starts cooking, place the tomatoes and the tomato puree over it, drop the peppers in the pot, and cover completely with water. Let it heat for about 1 hour, until the lamb is tender and some of the water has evaporated.

5. Remove from the oven, and add kritharáki (or orzo). Add water if needed. Put back in the oven. Remove after 15 minutes, when the pasta is cooked, and serve hot.

Serve with some grated cheese on top. Greek cheese kefalotyri is the best, but some Parmesan can do too.

Morbid Chef Notes

Youvetsi is a kind of Greek bouillabaisse featuring orzo, a small pasta that looks like large rice. Cooking this dish was very easy, although the pasta was a bit undercooked at the end. I suggest pre-cooking the pasta, and adding it to the dish afterwards, so it is totally foolproof. Enjoy!

NECROMANTIA

Created in 1989 by The Magus on bass and vocals and Baron Blood on eight-string bass, Necromantia is an innovative Athenian black metal band. Their unusual instrumentation—the eight-string bass in place of six-string guitars—generates a very thick-sounding, ritualistic, and sinister sound. Their pioneering records for Osmose Recordings in the 1990s established them as gods of Greek black metal.

NORWAY

"This is the Norwegian national dish, and of course it's my fuckin' favorite food in the world. Want some real black metal food—you try this! It's not for wimps!"

Fårikål

by Jan Axel "Hellhammer" Blomberg of MAYHEM

PREPARATION: 5 MINS

COOKING: 2 HRS

PORTIONS: 6–8

INGREDIENTS

> 2 big heads cabbage, ripped into fist-size pieces
> 4½ lbs (2 kg) of chunks of lamb meat with bones and fat (rip to fist-size if too big)
> 4 cups (1 L) water
> Whole black peppercorns
> Salt
> Cooked unpeeled potatoes

> Big casserole dish, about 10" to 12" (25–30 cm) high

PREPARATION

1. Using a big casserole dish, first put meat with most fat on it at the bottom to avoid burning, then cabbage pieces, layered with salt and peppercorns. It should be: Meat, cabbage, meat, cabbage, meat, and finally cabbage. Cabbage layers should be about 2" (5 cm) thick.

2. Use pepper and lots of salt between the layers.

3. Add the water, and let it cook for about 2 hours. Use a lid on the casserole, and check it now and then so nothing gets burned.

Morbid Chef Notes

Although quite costly if you don't get the lamb meat on sale, this dish is a killer discovery! It has to be one of the easiest and tastiest meals I've ever tried. Perfect to impress your family, or cook a meal for the entire band.

MAYHEM

Formed in Oslo in 1984 by guitarist Øystein "Euronymous" Aarseth, bassist Jørn "Necrobutcher" Stubberud, and drummer Kjetil Manheim, Mayhem is one of the pioneers of extreme, primitive, and violent Norwegian black metal. Jan Axel "Hellhammer" Blomberg took over the drums in 1988. Morbid releases like *Deathcrush*, *Live in Leipzig*, and *De Mysteriis Dom Sathanas* are timeless statements that continue to influence thousands of bands to this day.

"Cooked this meal for ten—all by my good self—at the last recording session in Dairy Cottage Studios. It was a *big* success!"

Ali Baa Baa (Moroccan Lamb)

by Bernie Shaw of URIAH HEEP

PREPARATION: 15 MINS
COOKING: 40 MINS
PORTIONS: 2

INGREDIENTS

> 2 lamb shoulder filets, cubed
> ½ large onion, finely chopped
> 1 tsp thyme
> 1 small bunch fresh mint, finely chopped
> 1 small bunch fresh parsley, finely chopped
> 2 tsp brown sugar
> Splash of red wine
> 1 tin chopped tomatoes, and half tin of water
> Salt and pepper, to taste
> 3 cloves of garlic, crushed
> 1 tsp cinnamon
> 2 tbsp olive oil
> 1 handful pitted prunes
> 2 tbsp tomato puree
> Saffron basmati rice (basmati rice, turmeric powder, and saffron)

PREPARATION

1. Brown lamb and onions in oil for 10 minutes.

2. Add chopped tomatoes, garlic, herbs, cinnamon, salt, pepper, and water, and reduce mixture.

3. Add red wine and sugar, and cook another 20 minutes.

4. Add prunes and tomato puree, cover, and cook further for 10 minutes.

Serve with real saffron rice (basmati, if possible) and watch them lick the plates clean!

Morbid Chef Notes

One of the best lamb recipes I've ever tried! The meat was so soft, it was almost like butter in the mouth. I suggest serving with freshly chopped pieces of mint on top.

URIAH HEEP

Uriah Heep is an English hard rock band. Formed in late 1969, they
contributed to early heavy metal with bombastic songwriting, crushing
organs, and piercing guitars on albums like *Very 'Eavy... Very 'Umble*,
Demons and Wizards, *Abominog*, and the gold album *Uriah Heep Live*.
They recently celebrated forty years in circulation as a band.

GREECE

"There used to be Greek guerrillas—called clefts—living in the countryside. They would steal animals, stuff the inside of the skins with pieces of meat, then roast them in pits with glowing embers (covered with soil so those who chased after them wouldn't find them). This is the modern version of that meal (*kleftiko*)."

Country Lamb Exohiko

by Themis Tolis of ROTTING CHRIST

PREPARATION: 1 HR
COOKING: 2 HRS
PORTIONS: 4

INGREDIENTS

> 2¼ lbs (1 kg) leg of lamb
> 7 tbsp olive oil
> 7 oz (200 g) kefalotyri (white cheese) or regato
> 1 lemon, squeezed
> 1 clove garlic, minced
> ½ lb (225 g) fresh broad beans
> ½ lb (225 g) potatoes
> Salt
> Pepper
> Oregano

> Greaseproof baking paper sheets (parchment paper)

PREPARATION

1. Wash and clean the lamb leg. Cut the meat into small cubes. Marinate the meat in olive oil, lemon juice, seasoning, and the oregano for about 1 hour.

2. Wash clean potatoes and beans, and cut potatoes into small cubes. Lay out 4 sheets of baking paper, brush them with oil, and divide the meat into equal amounts onto each of the sheets. The same procedure is followed for the beans, the potatoes, the garlic, and the cheese—which is also diced into small cubes.

3. After putting all the ingredients onto the sheets of baking paper, roll them into a cylindrical shape. Bake in an oiled baking pan in the oven for about 1½ hours at 350°F (180°C).

Serve in the greaseproof paper cylinders.

Morbid Chef Notes

Whoa, what a cool way to make a meal! Using parchment paper was totally mess-free. What's more, the food stays very hot until you open the "package." The cheese place I went to didn't have the cheeses I was looking for, but they recommended a french Ossau-Iraty cheese, which worked very well.

ROTTING CHRIST

Rotting Christ has been a staple of the international extreme metal scene since forming in Athens, Greece, in the late 1980s. Brothers Sakis and Themis Tolis have blazed a controversial trail, drawing attention with their band name while performing intense, emotional, and dark metal that in later years has taken on elements of religious chant and goth-industrial.

"This is the creation of chef Stephen Huston from Dana's restaurant Little Louis'—an exceptional place with great food, and the recipient of many awards!"

Proto Metal Lamb Shanks Braised in Burgundy

from Dana Snitch of WARPIG

PREPARATION: 30 MINS
COOKING: 2 HRS
PORTIONS: 6

INGREDIENTS

> 6 lamb shanks, 9 oz (250 g) each
> 1 medium onion, chopped
> 2 celery stalks, chopped
> 6 carrots (one per shank), chopped
> ¼ head fennel, chopped
> 12 garlic cloves, chopped
> 1 sprig fresh thyme
> Salt and fresh ground pepper (to taste)
> 2 cups (500 ml) red wine
> 4 cups (1 L) chicken stock
> 4 tbsp tomato paste
> Olive oil

> Baked polenta
> Fresh vegetables

PREPARATION

1. Season shanks with salt and pepper, and brown in olive oil over medium-high heat.

2. Remove shanks from frying pan. Add all the chopped vegetables and sauté until very soft.

3. Add tomato paste and cook to mature, stirring frequently (approximately 10 minutes).

4. Add wine and reduce by half.

5. Add stock and shanks, and bring to a boil.

6. Cover pan loosely with foil and place in a 325°F (162°C) oven to braise until very tender, turning every twenty minutes for 1½ hours.

7. Skim away any fat from the surface and serve 1 shank per person with some of the braising liquid, baked polenta, and fresh vegetables.

Recipe © Stephen Huston c.c.c.

Morbid Chef Notes

Lamb shanks are always very tasty, as the meat is right next to the bone. The braising liquid is simply sublime in this case—everything is caramelized and melts in your mouth. You will feel like a chef, too, after making it! For the polenta—you can find it at Italian/European stores, or use coarse cornmeal. Just mix with water and put in the oven for 10 minutes!

WARPIG

Warpig was a Canadian psychedelic heavy rock band formed in 1968 in Woodstock, Ontario. Their self-titled debut album was recorded and released in late 1970 by independent Fonthill Records. The band recently shook off years of dust and emerged from obscurity. The *Warpig* album has been reissued, and in 2007 the band reunited to work on recording unheard material that was originally written in the 1970s.

Poultry

DEVILISHLY DELICIOUS ORIENTAL CHICKEN CASSEROLE | MISANTHROPE'S LAST SUPPER
MUCBIPOLLO: A TRADITIONAL DISH FOR THE DEAD | FULL THROTTLE CHICKEN CURRY
PICTAVIAN CHICKEN WITH MOJHÉTE BEANS | TOMATO CHICKEN NECROCASSEROLE
PAN TANG STEW | PAPRIKA CREAM OF CHICKEN | WITCHFINDER GRINDER TURKEY CLUB
RONNIE COLE'S TURKEY CHILI | ROOK PIE

UNITED STATES

"Here is a dish my mom has been making for years. It is awesome!"

Devilishly Delicious Oriental Chicken Casserole

by Bobby Liebling of PENTAGRAM, and Diane Liebling

PREPARATION: 15 MINS
COOKING: 40–45 MINS
PORTIONS: 4–6

INGREDIENTS

> 2½ cups (500 g) cooked rice
> 4½ oz (125 g) canned French fried onions (French's brand) or 1 big onion, cut in rings and fried
> 1½ cups (85 g) Chinese fried chow mein noodles (La Choy brand)
> 2 cans undiluted condensed cream of mushroom soup (Campbell's brand)
> 2 tbsp soy sauce
> 1 tsp garlic powder
> 3 cups (650 g) chicken, cut in small pieces (predominantly white meat)
> 1 cup (35 g) cornflake crumbs (or bread crumbs)

> 9" x 13" (23 cm x 33 cm) casserole dish, sprayed with Pam or buttered

PREPARATION

1. Preheat oven to 375°F (190°C). Mix all ingredients except for the cornflake crumbs in large bowl.

2. Pour mixture into buttered dish. Distribute cornflake crumbs evenly on top of mixture in the dish.

3. Sprinkle remaining Chinese noodles on top (if any are left over). Cook approximately 40 to 45 minutes, or until sides are lightly browned.

Sauces like duck sauce, soy sauce, and Chinese mustard may be added for additional flavor post-cooking.

Morbid Chef Notes

This casserole is the definition of *comfort food*. The cream of mushroom soaks into the rice and the chicken and makes everything so moist and tender! Perfect for rainy or cold days.

PENTAGRAM

The legendary Pentagram was formed in Arlington, VA, in 1971.
After several promising starts and the release of a few singles in the
1970s, their self-titled debut album arrived in 1985. Through many
reincarnations with singer Bobby Liebling the only constant member, the
band has summoned haunting doom classics across four decades.

CANADA

"You can either buy boneless or skinless breasts, or bone-in—just peel off the meat at home yourself. (Or keep it intact, if you prefer. It's a little more flavorful but less lean with the skin on.) Also, the chicken will be covered in foil while cooking so the inside of your oven won't get dirty! Fuck cleaning!!!"

Misanthrope's Last Supper

by Deathlord of Abomination and War Apocalypse of BLASPHEMY

PREPARATION: 5 MINS

COOKING: 30 MINS

PORTIONS: 4

INGREDIENTS

> 6 chicken breasts
> Olive oil
> Dash of kosher salt (or any type of table salt)
> Dash of freshly ground pepper (or any type of ground pepper)
> Dash of dried basil, rosemary, Cajun spice, Montreal chicken seasoning, or favorite herbs

> Roasting pan
> Aluminum foil
> Store-bought potato salad
> Instant rice (optional)

PREPARATION

1. Preheat oven to 350°F (175°C).

2. Wash off chicken breasts (peel and debone if necessary), then place them in a roasting pan.

3. Lightly coat all the chicken breasts with olive oil.

4. Add a dash of kosher salt and freshly ground pepper on each breast.

5. Now get a little creative, and add a dash of dried basil, rosemary, Cajun spice, Montreal chicken seasoning, or your favorite herbs.

6. Cover roasting pan (not individual chicken breasts) with aluminum foil, and cook for 30 minutes.

After the breasts are cooked (and they'll be perfectly cooked and very moist after exactly 30 minutes, guaranteed!), you can use them in many different ways. Either on a plate with store-bought potato salad, or perhaps some instant rice. You may also add some store-bought pesto, pasta sauce, BBQ sauce, or sweet chili sauce as a topping to your chicken. Or you can chop it up and place it on top of an easy-made salad with your favorite dressing. (I prefer balsamic vinegar.)

This recipe was written for bachelors and bachelorettes. Living alone or with roommates usually leads to poor eating habits. Eating healthier will help you get a focused mind and stronger body for maximum evil and violence!

Morbid Chef Notes

I often make chicken breasts, but honestly, I never thought of covering the pot with aluminum foil. Awesome trick! The chicken is indeed very juicy and tender, and turns out great. In fact, I must have made this meal about five or six times already. It rules!

BLASPHEMY

Blasphemy was formed in Burnaby, BC, in 1984. They were the first band playing black metal in Canada, at a time when few metal scenes around the world had even heard of the genre. Their riffs, solos, and fast drumming are pure black metal, but the vocals have a death metal edge similar to Sarcófago, Vulcano, or Von. Their subgenre is now called *war metal*. Their 1990 debut album, *Fallen Angel of Doom…,* is one of the most intense and unholy albums ever recorded, and the metal world awaits their next strike.

MEXICO

Mucbipollo: A Traditional Dish for the Dead

by XIBALBA

PREPARATION: 1 HR
COOKING: 1 HR 30 MINS
PORTIONS: 10

INGREDIENTS

> 10 cups (1¼ kg) corn flour (corn masa mix)
> 10 cups (2.5 L) hot water
> 7 oz (200 g) lard or shortening
> 2¼ lbs (1 kg) chicken breast, diced in 1" (2.5 cm) pieces
> 1 lb (450 g) pork meat, diced in 1" (2.5 cm) pieces
> Achiote, to taste (optional)
> Salt, to taste
> 1 package banana leaves
> 3 red tomatoes, diced
> 1 large onion, finely diced
> 1 little branch of epazote
> Habañero chili, minced, to taste

> Aluminum foil

PREPARATION

1. Simmer enough water in a stockpot to cover meat; add pork meat first, and then chicken meat, in order to prepare a broth with the juice of both meats. Meat has to be half-cooked already. You can also add some achiote (a natural red plant) to give color to the broth.

2. Add a touch of salt, and some corn flour to thicken the broth. Bring to a boil. When the broth is thick enough, it will be ready to use in our main dish.

3. Put corn flour in large bowl and add water. Let rest for 20 minutes, and then mix. Slowly add lard or shortening until it becomes a thick dough. Shape corn dough as a circle, and place it in the center of a banana leaf. Don't cover the whole leaf, as you will later have to fold it in half. Mold the edges to create some kind of little wall all around the dough. It will prevent the thick broth from running out of the corn dough.

4. Put broth and meat in the center of the corn dough circles, then add onions, diced tomatoes, chili, and some epazote leafs. You can put in other things you like, like ham or cheese, or whatever you think of.

5. Cover the whole thing by placing a second circle of corn dough on top of your first circle. Press to prevent leaking of the broth. Fold the banana leaf to close it, then wrap in foil to prevent burning of the leaf.

6. Bake about 1½ hours at 400°F (200°C). The traditional way in Mexico is to dig a hole in the ground, and then burn wood inside. When the wood is lit, you have to fill the hole with stones, so they can get the heat. Place the *mucbi* on a pot over the stones, and then cover that hole with oak leaves and the soil you removed in the first place. Wait approximately 1½ hours.

7. Open the grave of your dead relatives, wash their bones, and replace the blanket that guards them with a new one. To wash their bones symbolizes that you give the dead a shower, and to change the blanket is to offer a change of clothes. This way, the dead are ready for supper.

8. The final step is to put the mucbi as an offering on the altar (*ofrenda*). The dead will extract its essence, and once they're done, the mucbi is all yours to enjoy. We—Xibalba—haven't dug the graves of our relatives yet, but there's always a first time for everything, don't you think?

Morbid Chef Notes

These gigantic round *tamales* took a long time to make, but tasted great and yielded *tons* of leftovers. Some ingredients might be a bit hard to find if you are not familiar with South American cooking. Go to Asian/Latin grocers and you should find everything you need. Have a good celebration of the Day of the Dead!

XIBALBA

Inspired by ancient Mayan culture and a wide range of metal bands from Bathory to Voivod, Xilbalba is a black metal band formed in 1992 in Mexico City. Their *Ah Dzam Poop Ek* debut in 1994 is a mix of intense, fast black metal with some pre-Hispanic elements. They broke up in 1996, but reunited in 2008 and have played a few select shows.

"This is a favorite dish of mine. Enjoy!"

Full Throttle Chicken Curry

by David "Rock" Feinstein of THE RODS

PREPARATION: 15 MINS

COOKING: 1 HR

PORTIONS: 4–6

INGREDIENTS

> 2 lbs (900 g) chicken breast, cut into small chunks
> 3 or 4 cloves of garlic, chopped
> 1 large onion, sliced
> 1 medium tomato, diced
> 1 green pepper, diced
> 2 tbsp curry powder
> Salt and pepper (add more to taste later if you choose)
> 1 tbsp vegetable oil
> Cooked rice (optional)

> Pot with lid

PREPARATION

1. Sauté the onion and garlic in oil at medium heat. Immediately add the curry powder and black pepper.

2. When onions are brown or caramelized, add the chunks of chicken and mix well. Stir occasionally and cover pot. Cook for about 10 minutes, or until the chicken is cooked.

3. Add tomato and green pepper with ¼ cup (125 ml) of water. Cover and cook for 45 minutes on low to medium heat. Stir occasionally, and add other vegetables (carrots, celery, or potatoes) if desired.

Serve over rice (optional).

Morbid Chef Notes

This is a basic and easy-to-make chicken curry. It tastes good, although I suggest adding a little bit of cumin, garam masala, and chili flakes to increase the hotness and spiciness! Besides that, it's awesome.

THE RODS

After Cortland, NY's hard rock hopes Elf folded, Ronnie James Dio joined Rainbow while his cousin David "Rock" Feinstein formed the Rods in order to kill disco once and for all. The classic louder-than-hell Rods power trio lineup of Feinstein, Gary Bordonaro, and Carl Canedy were stalwarts of the early American independent metal scene. They shared stages with notable bands including Judas Priest, Iron Maiden, Ozzy, Motörhead, and Metallica. For well over a decade, Feinstein has operated the Hollywood, a restaurant in his hometown.

FRANCE

"The chicken in this recipe can be replaced with rabbit. Enjoy this dish with a bottle of Gouverneur red wine (from the island of Ré, west of Pictavia), aged in oak barrels. A wine from the Poitou region (Pictavia) will do as well."

Pictavian Chicken with Mojhéte Beans

by Shaxul of ARPHAXAT

PREPARATION: 8 HRS (including soaking of the beans)
COOKING: 1 HR 30 MINS
PORTIONS: 3

INGREDIENTS

> 3 chicken drumsticks
> 5 oz (140 g) smoked streaky bacon
> 5 shallots (can be replaced with very small onions), minced
> 1¼ cups (300 ml) white wine (from the Charentes region in France, if possible)
> 14 oz (400 g) mojhéte beans (or white navy beans)
> 2 bouquets garnis (thyme, bay leaves, and sage tied together)
> 4 stalks of green/baby garlic
> ⅓ cup (80 ml) walnut oil
> Salted butter (if possible, *du beurre* AOC Charentes-Poitou)
> Salt and pepper

PREPARATION

1. Brown chicken drumsticks in a pot, using a nut-size chunk of salted butter and walnut oil. Fry until you obtain a nice golden color.

2. Add shallots or onions, as well as bacon. Cover and cook for 20 minutes.

3. Add white wine and one bouquet garni. Cover and simmer for 1½ hours on medium heat. At the same time, prepare the mojhéte beans. This word in Pictavian language refers to white beans, typical from the Poitou region, growing in its swamps. Put the beans in a pot and cover with cold water, up to 2" (5 cm) above the beans. Slowly bring to a boil. When it is boiling, quickly drain the mojhéte beans. Then add hot water and the other bouquet garni, and simmer on medium heat for 1 hour.

4. Remove bouquet garni from the mojhéte bean pot. Add freshly ground salt and pepper, as well as a big nut-size chunk of salted butter. Keep cooking for a few minutes more.

5. Remove bouquet garni from chicken, and serve with the mojhéte beans as a side dish. Garnish the beans with green garlic.

Morbid Chef Notes

Unholy shit, what an amazing recipe! As you can see from the photo, the chicken is basically falling apart. It is almost like butter. After about an hour of cooking, the bacon, wine, and onion fuse together and create some sort of paste that tastes simply out of this world. It is one hell of a delight!

ARPHAXAT

Arphaxat is primitive French black metal, hailing from the Poitou region. Formed by Shaxul (also a founding member of Deathspell Omega) and Draken (ex-Putrefactor), Arphaxat delivers raw and merciless metal that uses no guitar at all, only highly distorted bass, pounding drums, and abysmic vocals. Shaxul also operates Legion of Death Records.

"Tomato Chicken Necrocasserole is one of my personal favorite dishes. It is based partially on a typical Greek Cypriot chicken casserole dish. Not only does it taste great, it is also easy and relatively quick to prepare. *Bon appetit*, motherfuckers!"

Tomato Chicken Necrocasserole

by A. Dictator of NECROSADIST

PREPARATION: 10 MINS
COOKING: 20 MINS
PORTIONS: 2

INGREDIENTS

> 1 boneless chicken breast maliciously mutilated into 1" (2.5 cm) cubes
> 1 fresh onion
> 1 fresh tomato (viciously peeled and violently grated)
> ½ cup (125 ml) tomato puree
> 1 vegetable/chicken stock cube (whichever you prefer)
> Salt and pepper
> 2 tbsp cooking oil
> Cooked rice

PREPARATION

1. Angrily dice the onion into small pieces and sauté vengefully in 2 tablespoons of cooking oil in a medium-size pot. Don't sauté the onions for too long, just until they begin to shrivel.

2. Remove the onions from the pot, and toss in the chicken. Fry until just cooked—but not golden.

3. Throw the sautéed onions back into the pot with the chicken, stir well, and add the grated tomato, stock, and puree. Add a little warm water, enough to just cover the chicken and lower the temperature slightly. Add salt and pepper to taste.

4. Let the pot simmer until most of the water has evaporated, leaving a third of the water remaining—and the mixture has become a runny sauce.

5. Serve with rice.

Morbid Chef Notes

I love that he uses a real tomato in this particular dish—it makes such a difference in the overall taste. This killer recipe is really fast to make; perfect for impatient cooks! (You know who you are…)

Photo by A. Dictator

NECROSADIST

Necrosadist was formed in Nicosia, Cyprus, in 2005. The founders Dictator, Blackvein, and Betrayer sought to capture a higher sense of self-negation and death in the vein of early European black metal movements and North American death and thrash metal. Frustrated with the stagnation of the local scene, Dictator consequently decided to relocate to the UK, and recruited Menthor to play drums.

UNITED KINGDOM

"Very important: Don't forget to serve this rocker's meal with alcohol, and lots of it!"

Pan Tang Stew
by Robb Weir of TYGERS OF PAN TANG

PREPARATION: 15 MINS
COOKING: 50 MINS
PORTIONS: 4–5

INGREDIENTS (STEW)

> 4 chicken breasts, cut into chunks; or meatballs (see preparation and ingredients below)
> 3 medium onions, diced
> 4 garlic cloves, crushed or chopped
> 2 cans plum tomatoes, chopped
> 1 tbsp tomato puree
> 1 tsp mixed herbs
> 1 tsp sugar
> 4½ lbs (2 kg) potatoes, cut into chunks
> Water (enough to cover all the potatoes)
> Salt and pepper
> Oil

INGREDIENTS (if using meatballs)

> 1 small egg
> 1 lb (450 g) lean ground beef
> 1 large onion, finely chopped
> 4 garlic cloves, crushed
> 2 tbsp fresh parsley, chopped
> Salt and pepper

PREPARATION

1. In a casserole dish, put 2 tablespoons of oil. Heat and fry the onions and garlic until soft.

2. Add the chicken pieces or meatballs, and fry until colored.

3. Add the chopped tomatoes, tomato puree, mixed herbs, and sugar. Stir all together.

4. Add potato chunks, and cover with water.

5. Add salt and black pepper.

6. Cook in a moderate oven until the chicken is cooked and the potatoes are tender.

PREPARATION (IF USING MEATBALLS)

7. Beat the egg, then combine all the ingredients in a large mixing bowl. Get your hands in there and mix well.

8. When the mixture is together, oil your hands and make small meatballs.

9. Add these to a frying pan with a little sunflower oil in the bottom. Gently sauté them. When browned off, you can add them to the main stew.

10. Adjust the seasoning to your taste, and serve with lots of crusty bread or rice.

Morbid Chef Notes

I made the chicken version of this stew. It was easy and cheap to prepare, but a little bit mild for my taste. Next time, I will try the meatballs! The stew was great with bread, as you could dip it in the sauce. Very comforting!

TYGERS OF PAN TANG

Tygers of Pan Tang are a New Wave of British Heavy Metal band formed in 1978. Originating from Whitley Bay, Tyne and Wear, they were the first band signed to classic NWOBHM label Neat Records—and they released the successful *Wild Cat* on MCA in 1980. Their second album, the excellent *Spellbound*, featured John Sykes, later of Thin Lizzy and Whitesnake. Their galloping, melodic sound has been cited as an influence by tons of later bands, including Metallica.

Paprika Cream of Chicken

by Jörg Bock of MINOTAUR

PREPARATION: 2 HRS (including marinating the meat)
COOKING: 20 MINS
PORTIONS: 4–5

INGREDIENTS

> 1¾ lbs (800 g) chicken breast filets, cut in small cubes
> 1 Spanish onion, finely chopped
> 2 tsp curry powder
> 4 tsp spicy red chili powder
> 8 tbsp olive oil
> Salt
> Pepper, freshly ground
> 3 big peppers (red, yellow, green)
> 2 bags Knorr or Maggi brand paprika cream chicken sauce seasoning, prepared (or see recipe below if not findable).
> Chicken broth (optional)

PREPARATION

1. In large bowl, mix together onions, curry powder, hot chili powder, and olive oil. Add chicken breast cubes, and marinate for 1 to 2 hours.

2. Meanwhile, cut the peppers into slices. When the meat is ready, add pepper slices, and braise lightly.

3. Pour in already prepared sauce, and let simmer for a short time until ready.

4. Add salt and pepper, and/or chicken broth, as you wish.

To garnish, noodles or spaetzle and salad are perfect.

*PAPRIKA CREAM CHICKEN SAUCE SEASONING

This seasoning can be found in German delis, but you can make your own (which is even more delicious).

INGREDIENTS: 2 tbsp flour, 1/2 tbsp garlic powder, 2 tbsp spicy paprika, 3 tbsp butter, 1 cup (250 ml) beef stock, 1/2 cup (125 ml) heavy/sour cream

1. Mix together flour, garlic powder, and spicy paprika in a bowl. In a pan, melt butter, then add the powder mix to it. It will form what we call a roux.

2. Mix until smooth, then gradually add beef stock, whisking all the while. Continue to stir the sauce until smooth, then bring to a simmer and cook for about 15 minutes, or until thickened.

3. Strain the sauce using a colander (to remove any chunks) and return the liquid to the pan. Stir in cream or sour cream. Gently heat, and it's ready to use!

Morbid Chef Notes

This dish—which seems to be a variant on chicken *paprikash*—is a real discovery. I made my own sauce, as I couldn't find the seasoning, and it was truly excellent!

MINOTAUR

Minotaur emerged from Hamburg during the heyday of evil German thrash metal. Following an initial run of demo tapes and vinyl releases, the group disbanded in 1992, but they have returned in the 2000s to fly the flag full force for classic Teutonic speed metal intensity.

UNITED STATES

Witchfinder Grinder Turkey Club

by John Gallo of ORODRUIN

PREPARATION: 5 MINS

COOKING: 5 MINS

PORTIONS: 1

INGREDIENTS

> 2 slices Italian bread
> 6 slices sliced turkey cold cuts
> 2 slices provolone cheese
> 2 tsp mayonnaise
> 3 squirts mustard
> Dash fresh ground pepper
> Dash garlic powder
> 2 leaves fresh spinach

PREPARATION

1. Stack turkey slices evenly on top of each other on a cutting board.

2. With a knife, start at one end and cut the turkey into very thin long strips. Now, using the same technique, cut up the slices of provolone cheese, and put both cheese and turkey into a bowl.

3. Add mayo and mustard, and stir the condiments into the shredded contents.

4. Add a dash of fresh ground pepper, and a little garlic powder into the mix for the final inquisition.

5. Lightly toast the two pieces of Italian bread. Slap them around the contents in the bowl, add a couple leaves of fresh spinach, and cut the sandwich diagonally—there you go!

Shredded witch meat in a torture device!

Morbid Chef Notes

This is a great sandwich when you are in a hurry. The turkey tastes awesome, or you can make it with chicken cold cuts instead. That's my personal choice!

ORODRUIN

Traditional doom metal band Orodruin—named after J.R.R. Tolkien's feared Mount Doom—was founded by guitarist John Gallo in 1998 in Rochester, NY. Their debut album, *Epicurean Mass*, received incredible feedback from the doom metal scene upon its release in 2003. Other recordings followed, including a split with Finland's Reverend Bizarre. Orodruin plays heavy true doom metal, with insane solos and epic riffs.

"It's a football thing. You start one hour before kickoff, and you are eating at halftime."

Ronnie Cole's Turkey Chili
by Ron Holzner of TROUBLE

PREPARATION: 1 HR
COOKING: 1 HR 30 MINS
PORTIONS: 10

INGREDIENTS

> 2 tbsp olive oil
> 1 green pepper
> 1 lb (450 g) ground turkey
> 2 cloves garlic, minced
> 1 medium onion, chopped
> 1–2 serrano or jalapeño peppers, stemmed, seeded, and chopped
> ½ tsp salt
> ½ tsp pepper
> 6 oz (180 ml) can tomato paste
> 14 oz (450 ml) can chili beans (mild)
> 14 oz (450 ml) can chili beans (hot & spicy)
> 28 oz (900 ml) can whole tomatoes
> ½ tbsp parsley
> 2 tbsp chili powder
> 1 tbsp cumin
> ¼ tsp cayenne pepper
> ½ tbsp Worcestershire sauce

> Cheddar cheese
> Sour cream
> Chopped onions
> Hot sauce

PREPARATION

1. Dice and seed green pepper and hot peppers. Add oil to pot, then add chopped green pepper. Sauté them at medium heat for 2 minutes. Add onions, garlic, and hot peppers. Sauté 1 minute.

2. Add turkey, salt, pepper, and parsley. Sauté until turkey is browned. Stir in tomato paste.

3. Add beans (and add a little water to cans to loosen residue), and stir well. Add juice from can of whole tomatoes.

4. Cut up tomatoes into chunks, add to pot, and stir. Add chili powder and cumin, and turn heat to simmer.

5. Add cayenne and Worcestershire sauce. Stir the chili at every commercial break. Simmer till halftime, and serve with cheddar cheese, sour cream, chopped onions, and hot sauce!

Morbid Chef Notes

This recipe was so easy to make; still, I managed to burn the bottom of it—got to stir! Anyway, adding poultry to a chili made for a much lighter taste than usual, which I really, really loved.

TROUBLE

Formed in Chicago in 1979, Trouble started on Metal Blade Records as a crushingly heavy doom band with mournful twin guitars and apocalyptic imagery. After signing to Def American, they began introducing psychedelic sounds. While Trouble are still going strong after thirty years, bassist Ron Holzner left in 2002, joining forces with members of Saint Vitus and Eyehategod in Debris Inc.

UNITED KINGDOM

Rook Pie

by Liz Buckingham of ELECTRIC WIZARD

PREPARATION: 1 HR
COOKING: 1 HR 30 MINS
PORTIONS: 5–6

INGREDIENTS

> 6 rooks (or quails or pigeons)
> 1 bunch fresh thyme
> 1 bunch fresh marjoram
> 1 bunch fresh sage
> 1 onion, chopped
> 4 hard-boiled eggs, sliced in rings
> ½ oz (14 g) powdered gelatin

SHORTCRUST PASTRY

> ½ lb (225 g) frozen savory shortcrust or puff pastry, *or:*

> 4 cups (500 g) plain flour
> 1 cup (200 g) lard, cut into cubes
> ½ cup (40 g) grated cheddar cheese
> Sea salt
> Few sprigs of thyme
> 2 large eggs, beaten
> Splash of milk
> Flour, for dusting

PREPARATION

1. Pluck and dress rooks, chop off wings, heads, and feet. Skin and throw away all but the breasts and legs—nothing else is any good.

2. Put pieces in a large saucepan of cold water with a bunch of thyme, marjoram, sage, and chopped onion. Cook slowly until meat comes off bones.

3. To make shortcrust pastry from scratch: Mix flour, lard, cheese, and sea salt until crumbly and fine, then add thyme leaves. Add beaten eggs and milk to mixture, then place onto floured board and pat together a bit until compact, flat, and round (do not knead). Wrap in cling film (plastic wrap) and refrigerate for at least half an hour.

4. Take all meat off breasts and legs, and put in layers in a Pyrex glass dish, putting rings of hard-boiled eggs between.

5. Heat enough of the cooking liquid to cover meat and egg. Add powdered gelatin to liquid, and pour into pie to cover all.

6. When ready, roll out pastry and use to cover pie (cover only—this traditional farmhouse pie does not have a bottom). Trim excess dough, crimp edges, and brush with beaten egg. (You can use any kind of pastry preferred).

7. Bake until brown (about 1½ hours in a medium-hot oven).

Leave until next day until quite cold. Cut in wedges, and serve with a green salad and a bottle of Blandford Fly ale.

Morbid Chef Notes

Rooks have a similar flavor to pigeon (or squab)—a wonderful gamey flavor. They should be hunted when still young, as older rooks supposedly have a poor flavor. Good luck!

Photo by Liz Buckingham

ELECTRIC WIZARD

Since the mid-1990s, Electric Wizard has unfolded its slow, crushing doom tones over a range of releases like *Supercoven*, *Dopethrone*, and *Witchcult Today*. In 2003, the Dorset, UK, group was joined by American guitarist Liz Buckingham, formerly of Sourvein and 13.

Seafood

AMEBIX PRAWN BISQUE | PIZZA TONNO À LA CHEF | BEER-BATTERED FISH FILETS WITH GARLIC PRAWNS
BLACK PUDDING AND SQUID IN ITS OWN INK | ADRIAN'S CEVICHE | FLOUNDER FILET OREGANATO
SHELLFISH CROSSFIRE | GARLIC AND CORIANDER KING PRAWNS | MALAYA FRIED MEE
NASI LEMAK (COCONUT MILK RICE MEAL) | WHISKY DEMON BACALAO
SPAGHETTI BARRACUDA | SUPERB SALMON FILET

UNITED KINGDOM

"This is a recipe I made up myself, based loosely around lobster bisque. This utilizes Skye prawns, or *langoustines*, as they are known in France. It is also a way of recycling!"

Amebix Prawn Bisque

by Rob "The Baron" Miller of AMEBIX

PREPARATION: 20 MINS
COOKING: 2 HRS 30 MINS
PORTIONS: 6

INGREDIENTS

> 24 prawns
> 2 tbsp garlic butter
> 1 medium-size onion, sliced
> 2 garlic bulbs, minced
> 2 sweet potatoes, peeled and cut in chunks
> 3 carrots, peeled and cut in chunks
> Salt
> Pepper
> 1 glass white wine/dry vermouth
> ½ lb (225 g) whitefish (cod or haddock), cut in chunks
> 5 mussels
> 1 tbsp crème fraîche (or sour cream)
> Sprig parsley

PREPARATION

1. Blanch prawns for 2 minutes in boiling water, then smear the undersides with garlic butter, place onto the barbecue for a couple of minutes, and then eat them! But that's not the recipe. The trick is to save all the shells—heads included—and store them in the fridge whilst you consume many units of alcohol and forget until tomorrow.

2. Return to fridge with hangover next day, place all the shells and stuff on a baking tray, and bake in the oven for 20 minutes or so on a low heat, until the claws begin to get a bit of color. This also makes the shells brittle.

3. Take out and put in a pot. Crush them up a bit with whatever you have on hand, and then almost cover with water. Bring to boil, and simmer for an hour or so.

4. Strain off the water. What you have now is now a superb prawny stock.

5. Fry onion and garlic gently in another pan. Add chunks of peeled sweet potato, carrots, salt and pepper, and then about 2 pints (950 ml) of water to the stock; add a glass of white wine or dry vermouth and bring the fucker back to boil gently for 20 minutes—or until the sweet potato is soft.

6. Stick a hand blender in and blend everything into a thickish soup; taste—then add salt or pepper to suit your taste.

7. Add chunks of whitefish, such as cod or haddock—or smoked fish if you have it—plus a few mussels, and allow to gently heat throughout. Serve with a dollop of crème fraîche and a sprig of parsley if you want to be a clever bastard, and eat with fresh crusty bread. Delicious!

Morbid Chef Notes

This "Ame-bisque" will seriously blow you away. It barely tastes like seafood, as the *langoustine* broth is very subtle compared to the intense flavors of onions, garlic, and sweet potato. You may replace the broth with fish broth if you wish. This is a great recipe to make when hosting guests. Eat and be merry, for tomorrow you may die!

AMEBIX

Amebix were formed in 1978 in Devon, UK, and are pioneers of the doomy apocalyptic brew now called crust punk—a mix of anarcho-punk, hardcore, and metal riffing. Their *Arise* LP from 1985 remains a timeless statement, and the band has lately been active reissuing archive recordings and new material, and playing a few rib-crushing shows. Vocalist Rob Miller now works as a swordsmith on the Isle of Skye.

GERMANY

"Do you like it spicy and crusty? This is my all-time favorite pizza. I am a professional baker, and had my own pizzeria for many years. My customers would have killed for this recipe. The only thing you need is time, and a good oven."

Pizza Tonno à la Chef

by Schmier "The Mad Baker" of DESTRUCTION

PREPARATION: 2 HRS
COOKING: 30 MINS
PORTIONS: 6

DOUGH

> 2¼ lbs (1 kg) wheat flour, type 450 (cake flour) or 550 (all-purpose)
> 5 tbsp yeast
> 3 big tsp sea salt
> 1 big tbsp brown sugar
> 2–3 tbsp native olive oil
> 1¾ to 2 cups (440 to 500 ml) warm water

SAUCE

> 1 can sliced tomatoes
> 1 tube tomato paste (or 1 small can)
> 1 shot extra-virgin olive oil
> Salt and pepper
> Sugar
> 1 hot pepper
> Fresh Italian herbs (oregano, rosemary, and thyme); if you are lazy, use dried herbs

TOPPINGS

> 2 cans high-quality "dolphin-friendly" tuna fish
> ¾ cup (200 g) sour cream or crème fraîche (10% is healthier!)
> Mozzarella and Gouda, grated
> Two onions, sliced
> Garlic
> Fresh hot peppers of any kind

Morbid Chef Notes

Who needs drugs when you have pizza like this? Biting into this monster brings you to another world. The taste is absolutely unreal.

PREPARATION

1. First of all: Put on your favorite metal album, and open a bottle of wine.

2. Prepare the dough at least 4 hours before you start cooking. My advice is to prepare it one day before. Put it in a big bowl with a kitchen dish towel over it, and refrigerate. Put the yeast in the warm water first, then add the other ingredients. Make sure the yeast and the salt do not touch each other directly, otherwise the yeast will die. Yes—like all the posers at a Manowar show! :)

3. Knead the dough with your hands or a machine. My hint: Use your hands. Why? Try, and you will see when the dough gets solid and tight. No lumps, please. Hit it with your hand—if it feels like a hot butt, you did well.

4. Put a big moist dish towel over the dough, and let it rest for an hour. It needs to be fully covered! Then make little ball portions (approximately ½ lb / 225 g each). Cover with dish towel again, and wait another 30 to 40 minutes. The room needs to be warm, otherwise the dough won't rise. Put the leftover pizza dough in the freezer for your next pizza party.

5. To make the pizza sauce, fry the hot peppers, herbs, and then the tomato concentrate in hot olive oil. Add sliced tomatoes, sugar, and spices. Cook for 10 minutes. At the end, add some spoons of olive oil. Put aside.

6. For the toppings, stir garlic, hot pepper, and salt into the sour cream.

7. Get rid of the oil or water in the tuna, and squeeze the liquid out of the tuna chunks with your hands.

8. Put baking paper on your metal oven plate to get the best crust, and to make sure that your pizza does not burn.

9. Heat up the oven to the maximum. Best would be 575°F (300°C) to 480°F (250°C) minimum; both top and bottom grills need to be on max—the heat underneath is very important.

10. Roll out the dough as thin as you can. Put it on the metal oven plate with baking paper. Add sauce, and then spread the tuna on the sauce. Put drops of sour cream on top. Then onions, cheese, and, at the end, peppers.

11. Put the pizza in the center of the oven, so the cheese can melt and the heat underneath creates a perfect crust from below. Depending on the heat, make your first check after 6 to 10 minutes. Your pizza is done when the cheese is golden and the crust has a nice Brazilian tan. If you lift it up with a big knife, it should not deform!

If you did it right, you will enjoy the best pizza of your life. If not, it's time to get wasted now!

DESTRUCTION

Destruction are bullet-belted legends of German speed metal. Their earliest records, *Sentence of Death* in 1984 and *Infernal Overkill* in 1985, spearheaded Europe's response to American Bay Area thrash, and ultimately inspired the wave of bands that would form the earliest death and black metal bands. They have released more than ten albums and a handful of EPs, including the infamous *Mad Butcher*. Schmier grew up with his family in the restaurant business, and for many years he ran his own kitchen in his hometown.

AUSTRALIA

Beer-Battered Fish Filets with Garlic Prawns

by Hexx of TRENCH HELL

PREPARATION: 45 MINS
COOKING: 15 MINS
PORTIONS: 2

INGREDIENTS

> 1½ cups (375 ml) beer of choice (I use Coopers Pale Ale)
> 4 skinless, boneless saltwater fish filets (I use flathead)
> 30 raw prawns
> 2 cups (500 ml) cooking oil
> 1 egg
> 1¾ cups (230 g) self-rising flour
> 2 garlic cloves
> 2 tbsp butter
> Salt and pepper

> 6 cooking skewers

PREPARATION

1. First, put the flour into a mixing bowl, add one egg, and start to mix slowly, adding your chosen beer. Add beer until you have a nice smooth batter. Set the batter aside for at least half an hour, or it will not stick to the fish properly when cooking.

2. Now peel some raw prawns and put them onto skewers; marinate in garlic, butter, oil, and pepper; three skewers per person with about five or six prawns on each is good. Set aside until ready to cook.

3. Put the rest of the unpeeled prawns into boiling water, and cook for normally around 2 to 3 minutes until they turn bright orange; then throw the prawns into cold water and set them aside.

4. Cut your fish filets into large chunks, and check for any bones. Then coat them in batter, and put them straight into a frying pan with enough oil to cover half the filet. Normally cook for about 2 to 3 minutes per side; once golden turn them over and cook reverse side until golden. Take them from the pan and place on absorbent grease towel in oven to keep warm and crispy.

5. Add the garlic prawn skewers to the oil, and cook for 1 to 2 minutes per side, then also add them to the absorbent grease towel in the oven.

6. While cooking your skewers, fry some garlic and butter in another small pan to make ready a nice garlic butter sauce for serving.

7. Place fish, prawn skewers, and cooked prawns onto plate. Pour garlic sauce on fish, and then dig in!

Morbid Chef Notes

Great recipe overall; I especially love the beer batter! Of course, you can't taste the beer much, but it surely adds something. I will be using this one from now on for more than fish—beer tempura, anyone?

TRENCH HELL

Trench Hell emerged from Brisbane, Australia, in 2004, with the release of the *Alcoholic Disaster* demo. Hexx relocated the band to Melbourne in 2005 and recorded the killer *Southern Cross Ripper* EP in 2008. The band plays a dirty mix between early Celtic Frost, Destruction, Motörhead, and Razor, and their interests include serial killers.

UNITED KINGDOM

Black Pudding and Squid in Its Own Ink

by Simon Strange of THE LAMP OF THOTH

PREPARATION: 45 MINS

COOKING: 1 HR

PORTIONS: 2

SQUID

> 2 lbs (900 g) small fresh whole squid with ink sacs
> 1 onion, finely chopped
> 1 clove garlic, finely chopped
> Olive oil for frying
> Yorkshire (flat) parsley
> Chopped bread crumbs

SAUCE

> 1 onion, finely chopped
> 1 clove garlic, finely chopped
> Crust of bread
> ½ cup (125 ml) fish broth
> Ink from the squid sacs
> 2–3 tbsp tomato puree
> 1 potato
> 9 oz (250 g) black pudding
> Salt and freshly ground black pepper
> A quarter of hashish (or the finest Chinese opium)

PREPARATION OF SQUID

1. Take apart and clean the fresh squid, taking care to remove the ink sacs without breaking them. Set the ink sacs aside. Cut the tentacles into 1" (2.5 cm) chunks.

2. Fry one onion and one garlic clove in olive oil. When the onion begins to take on color, add the chunks of squid tentacles, and cook slowly while stirring in the oil. Add the chopped parsley and bread crumbs, and stir until well thickened.

3. Stuff the squid tails with this mixture, being careful not to overfill. Seal the openings with a toothpick. Fry the stuffed tails in a small amount of olive oil, turning gently until golden in color. Meanwhile, make the ink sauce.

PREPARATION OF INK SAUCE

1. Brown the other onion and garlic clove in olive oil, and add a crust of bread. Place the fish broth in a small bowl. Place the reserved ink sacs in a fine sieve (a strainer) over the bowl and puncture carefully. Blend the ink and broth. Add this liquid to the onion and garlic, and cook slowly. Add the tomato puree, and continue to simmer for a short time.

2. Run the mixture through a blender. Place the sauce in a large skillet, add the fried, stuffed squid and simmer for 15 minutes.

3. Peel and dice the potato, and cook in a pan of salted boiling water until tender. Add this and the hashish to the black pudding, and continue to fry for 2 to 3 minutes. Season.

Consume, and enter a world of nightmarish gastric visions. Lament on the appetites of man which chain him to this cold earth. As Nietzsche said: "The belly is why man does not readily mistake himself for a god!"

Morbid Chef Notes

Can you guys believe I actually made this one? It was a long process, and looked very good at the end. Unfortunately, I don't like squid at all. So I made it for a friend of mine—but he never showed up. I wonder why? Ha!

THE LAMP OF THOTH

After lying dormant for over a century, the Hermetic Order of the Lamp of Thoth came back to life in 2006 as an eccentric traditional doom metal group. This extremely proficient West Yorkshire, UK, band consists of The Overtly Melancholic Lord Strange on bass/vocals, Randolf Tiberius Reaper on guitar, and Lady Pentagram on drums.

The Lamp of Thoth

Adrian's Ceviche

by Adrian Maestas of "THE LORD WEIRD" SLOUGH FEG

PREPARATION: 8 HRS (including marinating time)

COOKING: —

PORTIONS: 6–8

INGREDIENTS

> 1 lb (450 g) fresh fish, cut in small bite-size pieces (I like to use a combination of halibut or red snapper and scallops)
> 1 cup (250 ml) freshly squeezed lime juice
> 1 cup tomatoes, diced
> 1 cup red onion, minced
> ½ cup (30 g) fresh coriander, chopped
> ¼ cup (15 g) fresh parsley, chopped
> 1 jalapeño pepper, diced
> 1 cucumber, diced (no seeds)
> 1 avocado, chopped
> 2 cloves garlic
> 2 tbsp olive oil
> Sea salt
> Pepper, freshly ground
> Some beer
>
> Shallow baking dish

PREPARATION

1. Mix the lime juice and olive oil in a plastic bowl. Add small fish pieces and a generous pinch of sea salt. Cover with plastic wrap, and put in fridge.

2. Meanwhile, chop all your other stuff, and maybe pour a little beer in the fish mixture.

3. Pour the fish mix into a shallow baking dish, and then add the other ingredients, one at a time, stirring to coat. When you are finished adding everything, put in another pinch of sea salt, and add some freshly ground pepper.

4. Cover with plastic wrap and put in the fridge for at least a couple hours—overnight is best to let all the flavors come together.

Enjoy with chips, lettuce cups, or whatever you like! I like to cut the avocado in half, stuff the ceviche in the half avocado, and scoop out with a spoon. I also like to add a couple squirts of my favorite hot sauce, Tapatio!

Morbid Chef Notes

Ceviche is a kind of citrus-based "cooking" or marinating method used in Latin America for centuries. This particular recipe is mind-numbingly good. I brought the leftovers to work, and they were gone in a matter of minutes!

"THE LORD WEIRD" SLOUGH FEG

"The Lord Weird" Slough Feg are a unique and noble Celtic-tinged metal tribe. Hailing from Pennsylvania, they relocated to the nonconformist stronghold San Francisco in 1990, and set about reviving the honor of neglected classic early 1980s heavy metal. Their efforts have since been recognized internationally, and 2000s albums like *Hardworlder* are impeccably crafted bastions of almost completely reinvented traditional metal.

Flounder Filet Oreganato

by John Garner of SIR LORD BALTIMORE

PREPARATION: 10 MINS
COOKING: 10 MINS
PORTIONS: 4

INGREDIENTS

> 4 flounder filets (or sole, or any other flat whitefish)
> 3 eggs, beaten
> 4 cups (240 g) flavored bread crumbs
> 2 cloves of garlic, minced
> Dash white wine
> Extra-virgin olive oil
> Salt
> Pepper
> Fresh basil or parsley, or both

PREPARATION

1. Dip your flounder filets in beaten egg, then dip them in ready-flavored bread crumbs. Salt and pepper to taste.

2. Fry the filets in white wine, extra-virgin olive oil, and minced garlic. Do not overdo the frying or the wine.

3. Garnish with either basil leaf or parsley or both, and have a little taste of heaven.

Serve with a salad and mashed potatoes.

ITALIAN-FLAVORED BREAD CRUMBS

If this item can't be found in your local grocery store, you can use this recipe instead. It is really, really good!

INGREDIENTS: 4 cups (240 g) bread crumbs, 2 tsp salt, 2 tsp parsley flakes, 1 tsp oregano, 1 tsp garlic powder, 1 tsp sugar

1. Mix together with a fork or a wooden spoon, and voila!

Morbid Chef Notes

Who said that complicated recipes were the best? This breaded fish recipe is far from being plain. The juice of the fish stays trapped until the filet is cut with your fork; then everything melts in your mouth. Mmm!

SIR LORD BALTIMORE

The first band ever to be described as "heavy metal" (in an infamous *Creem* magazine article often credited for coining the phrase), Sir Lord Baltimore from Brooklyn, NY, released two heavier-than-boulders albums in 1970 and 1971 before disbanding. Their masterpiece, *Kingdom Come*, has since propelled them to cult status. Members John Garner and Louis D'ambra recently reformed and recorded a third album, *III Raw*.

NORWAY

Shellfish Crossfire

From King ov Hell of GOD SEED / ex-GORGOROTH

PREPARATION: 10 MINS
COOKING: 15 MINS
PORTIONS: 6

INGREDIENTS

> 14 oz (400 g) noodles, cooked
> 30 shellfish
> 30 tiger shrimps
> 1 pepper, cut into pieces
> 1 onion, chopped
> 1 pack spicy wok chili sauce
> Vegetable oil

PREPARATION

1. Put everything together in a wok. Fry for 5 minutes and eat it.

Morbid Chef Notes

Here's a quick and simple seafood recipe. I made my own wok sauce by mixing fish sauce, chili paste, shrimp paste, and a bit of teriyaki sauce. I used scallops as the shellfish, and it turned out really killer!

GOD SEED / GORGOROTH
Gorgoroth is a Norwegian black metal band formed by Infernus in 1992.
Their early albums *Pentagram* (1994) and *Antichrist* (1996) are regarded as
classics of the genre. King ov Hell joined as bassist in 1999, and in the fall of
2007, he and Gaahl (vocalist since 1998) waged an unsuccessful legal battle
against founding member Infernus. Afterwards, the pair thus went on to
form God Seed, until Gaahl "retired from metal" in 2009.

WALES

Garlic and Coriander King Prawns

by Steve Williams of BUDGIE

PREPARATION: 10 MINS
COOKING: 30 MINS
PORTIONS: DEPENDS ON YOU

INGREDIENTS

> King prawns
> 2 cloves garlic, crushed
> 1 shallot, finely chopped
> Fresh coriander, roughly chopped
> Single cream
> White wine
> Salt
> Pepper
> Oil

PREPARATION

1. Gently sauté shallot pieces in a little oil until soft. Add prawns, turn up the heat, and stir-fry until they turn pink. Remove prawns (nothing worse than overcooked shrimp), cover, and set aside.

2. Reduce heat. Add garlic and wine and gently simmer until liquid is reduced by two thirds. Slowly stir in cream.

3. Add coriander and reintroduce prawns to mixture. Season to taste and remove from heat.

Serve with brown rice, a fresh green salad, and a cold glass of chardonnay.

Morbid Chef Notes

Another simple yet marvelous recipe. The great thing about this is that you can easily modify it depending on how many people are eating it. I made this one for a friend, and he said it was "fucking good." So there you go!

BUDGIE

Formed in Wales in 1967, Budgie is a great heavy rock/proto metal band that plays simple yet effective heavy songs, characterized by eccentric lyrics, crunchy guitars, and high-pitched vocals. The band broke up in the early 1980s, reformed briefly in the 1990s, and recently released brand-new material. Notable songs include "Breadfan" and "Crash Course in Brain Surgery"—both covered by Metallica; and "In for the Kill," which was covered by Van Halen during their club days.

MALAYSIA

"A few years ago, I was living on an unstable salary together with some friends in a rented house in the capital city of Malaysia, Kuala Lumpur. We rehearsed with our bands almost every night. As we were running out of cash at the end of every month, I invented this recipe as the cost is fucking cheap!"

Malaya Fried Mee
by Rammy Azmi of BLACKFIRE

PREPARATION: 10 MINS
COOKING: 10 MINS
PORTIONS: 2–3

INGREDIENTS

> 2 spoons vegetable cooking oil
> 2 garlic bulbs, crushed
> 2 spoons chili paste
> 4 chicken sausages, sliced
> 1 tsp salt
> 2 spoons chili sauce
> 5 spoons soybean ketchup (sweet soy sauce)
> 5 oz (140 g) boiled squid, sliced (don't throw away the water)
> 7 oz (200 g) Chinese noodles (you can replace with macaroni, too)
> 3 eggs
> Mustard greens or any suitable vegetable

PREPARATION

1. Fry garlic, then sausages and squids together in oil until halfway cooked. Add 2 spoons of chili paste. Be careful; if you do not fry it well enough, this may cause you a terrible stomachache. Use medium heat.

2. As the "hellish" stench arises, pour half cup of boiled squid's water. Add a pinch of salt, soybean ketchup, and chili sauce accordingly.

3. Add noodles and stir. Then add eggs. Lastly, after the mee or noodles look like 95% ready, throw in mustard or vegetables as per your taste. If you like, add some oyster sauce.

4. Ready to serve. Enough for two metalheads; maybe an additional omelette on each plate will make this look like heavy metal meals!

Morbid Chef Notes

Okay, this recipe is a bit spicy—depending on which size spoons you use, I suppose!—but it is quite okay in small portions. It's a great way of making stir-fried noodles! Don't forget to mix vigorously when you add the eggs, or you'll end up with an omelette stuck between your noodles!

BLACKFIRE

Blackfire was the first extreme metal band in Southeast Asia, and the first to sing Malay lyrics. They were first known as as Metal Ghost in 1982, but soon became Blackfire in 1984. This legendary group never had their songs properly recorded until 2006, when they made *Lahir Dari Api*, but they were well known by doing shows and rock fests around Malaysia in the 1980s.

MALAYSIA

Nasi Lemak (Coconut Milk Rice Meal)

by Naz of MANTAK

PREPARATION: 25 MINS
COOKING: 40 MINS
PORTIONS: 2

RICE

> 1 cup (200 g) rice, washed and drained
> 1 small can of coconut milk
> 1 pandan/screw-pine leaf, tied in knot
> ¼ tsp salt

PRAWN SAMBAL

> 10–12 prawns or shrimps, prepared
> 1 small red onion, sliced into rings
> ¼ tsp salt
> 1 tsp sugar
> 2 tsp tamarind pulp
> 2 tbsp cooking oil
> Pound together in a paste:
>> 2 dried chilis and 2 fresh chilis
>> 3 shallots/green onions
>> Small piece Thai ginger
>> 4 cloves garlic, chopped
>> 2 thumb-size lumps of shrimp paste (belacan)
>> 2 candle nuts or macadamia nuts
> 2 hard-boiled eggs, cut in half
> ¼ cucumber, thinly sliced
> 1 cup (50 g) kangkong/river spinach, quickly boiled (can be replaced with spinach)
> Small handful roasted peanuts

PREPARATION

1. Put rinsed rice in a small pot, and add coconut milk and pandan leaf. Bring to a boil.

2. When the rice begins to boil, lower the heat, and simmer gently for 10 to 15 minutes until all the milk has been absorbed. Remove from heat. Be careful not to burn the rice!

3. Loosen rice grains with chopsticks. Cover up pot, and allow rice to rest in its own steam for 10 to 15 minutes.

4. Meanwhile, in a frying pan or wok, heat oil and fry the onions until slightly brown.

5. Add the pounded ingredients and fry until fragrant. Add prawns or shrimps and fry for 2 to 3 minutes.

6. Add sugar, salt, and tamarind pulp. Allow to cook for another 4 to 5 minutes and serve with the rice and other garnishings.

Morbid Chef Notes

Traditionally sold wrapped in banana leaves, nasi lemak is usually served for breakfast in Malaysia, Singapore, and Southern Thailand. It is the national dish of Malaysia, and it turned out to be absolutely delicious.

MANTAK

Mantak is a blackened thrash metal band from Kota Kinabalu, Sabah, in eastern Malaysia. Formed in 1995, they are considered the most successful metal band on the island of Borneo. They are the first Malaysian band to ever release a vinyl record, and to be signed to a well-known black metal label. They have released several full-lengths, alongside numerous split albums and EPs.

NORWAY

"This was a Portuguese recipe, originally. The saying goes that to be a good Portuguese wife, you should be able to make 365 different versions of *bacalao*, one for each day of the year; but my recipe is traditionally based on a Norwegian raw material—stockfish from Lofoten archipelago in Norway."

Whisky Demon Bacalao

by Gunnar Hansen of FAUSTCOVEN

PREPARATION: 24 HRS (including soaking of stockfish)

COOKING: 1 HR 30 MINS

PORTIONS: 8

INGREDIENTS

> 7–8 large potatoes, peeled and sliced in ½" (1.3 cm) pieces
> 1 lb (450 g) good stockfish (dried and salted cod), cut in pieces
> 1 large onion, chopped
> ¾ cup (180 ml) olive oil
> 1 box or can tomatoes, sliced
> 1 chili, chopped (add more chilis if you like things spicy)
> Dash of grated Parmesan
> Black pepper
> Bread
> Basil leaf (optional)
> 2 tbsp Islay whisky (optional)

> Hellhammer, "Triumph of Death" on repeat

PREPARATION

1. The stockfish needs to be soaked overnight. Depending on how big the piece is, or how salty, you would minimally need 12 hours, and change water at least one time. If it's one massive piece, and very salted, up to 24 hours with two to three water changes can be needed.

2. Now for the twist: To the last soak, add smoky Islay whisky. This is optional of course, but if you want real Whisky Demon Bacalao, you need this.

3. To a large pot, add fine olive oil, and then potatoes, pieces of the fish (cut it up prior to adding, of course), onions, and chili in layers. After everything is in there, empty a box or can of sliced tomatoes into the pot.

4. This should be brought to a simmer, and stand there lightly boiling for 1½ hours. Make sure that the potatoes are sufficiently tender; if they are still too hard, leave it on longer. Now and then you need to create some movement in the pot, so that the bacalao doesn't get burned, but you don't want to stir this with a spoon or anything like this, 'cause if you do, you'll just make mashed potatoes. Instead, from time to time, forcefully rotate the entire pot to move the contents around. Note: You should also make sure that Hellhammer's "Triumph of Death" is played constantly, giving small, evil vibrations to the stew.

5. Once the dish is finished, sprinkle some freshly grated Parmesan cheese over each portion, and some freshly ground black pepper. Add a leaf of fresh basil, and serve with newly baked bread.

Morbid Chef Notes

This fish stew was a big success with everyone who tried it. It is especially nice on a cold day, with tons of bread to dip in the sauce!

FAUSTCOVEN

Faustcoven is a Norwegian band that plays blackened doom metal with the most cavernous sound. They mix old Bathory and Black Sabbath with ancient barbaric vocals. If Black Sabbath were formed in Norway nowadays, they would probably sound like this, too! They have released two albums during the 2000s—both come highly recommended to connoisseurs.

"This is a very hot and simple invention of mine. The taste is good!"

Spaghetti Barracuda

by A. C. Wild of BULLDOZER

PREPARATION: 15 MINS

COOKING: 20 MINS

PORTIONS: 8

INGREDIENTS

> 1 lb (450 g) spaghetti
> ¾ lb (340 g) barracuda filets cut in pieces ½" (1.3 cm) size
> 4 tbsp olive oil
> 3 garlic bulbs, minced
> 4 tomatoes, diced
> 4–5 fresh red chili peppers cut in pieces (if possible from Calabria—very hot!!)
> White wine
> Fresh basil leaves

PREPARATION

1. Pour the olive oil into a large pot and fry the garlic for 90 seconds, medium heat.

2. Add the barracuda meat and fry for few minutes, until the meat turns crispy on the outside. Add some white wine to get a better taste.

3. Add fresh tomatoes and fresh hot chili peppers. Cook for another 2 minutes, maximum.

4. Cook spaghetti Italian al dente style (firm in center). As soon as the spaghetti is ready, put it in the pot and mix together with the rest of the ingredients. Serve with some fresh leaves of basil.

5. Serve with white wine.

Morbid Chef Notes

Barracuda fish has a delicious medium-strength flavor. If impossible to find in your area, it can be substituted with marlin, sea trout, or cobia.

Photo by A. C. Wild

BULLDOZER

Ripping apart the roads paved by Motörhead and Venom, Bulldozer roared out of Italy in the early 1980s packing a dangerous payload of vicious, dirty, and occult-tinged heavy metal. Their wild rumbling sound summoned the mood and atmosphere of classic Italian horror movies, and proved enduring enough to demand a comeback during the 2000s.

ISRAEL

Superb Salmon Filet

by Ashmedi of MELECHESH

PREPARATION: 5 MINS

COOKING: 15–20 MINS
(depending on thickness of filet, pan base, and stove type)

PORTIONS: 4

INGREDIENTS

> 2¼ lbs (1 kg) salmon filet, skinned, or with skin only on bottom side
> 1 tbsp light olive oil (virgin olive oil might be too strong)
> ½ tbsp butter
> 1 tsp sea salt
> ½ tsp freshly ground pepper
> 1 tbsp lemon zest (shredded lemon peel)
> 1–2 rosemary sprigs
> 1–2 garlic cloves (make a small incision to let out gentle flavor)
> 4 lemon slices (optional)
> 1½ tsp Worcestershire sauce
> 2–3 tbsp white dry sherry (cooking wine)
> 1 tbsp lemon juice (optional)

PREPARATION

1. Heat olive oil and butter in a large frying pan, preferably covered to allow the steam and flavors to mix. Add salmon and then sprinkle salt, freshly ground pepper, and lemon zest on it. Add rosemary sprigs to the pan at medium heat. Cover. Steam will work its magic!

2. In about 6 to 7 minutes, add garlic cloves to the pan and lemon slices on top of the salmon; then put Worcestershire sauce and sherry all over the pan. Shake the pan gently in order to mix the liquids. Cover. Steam will again work its magic!

3. After approximately 5 to 6 minutes, add a tablespoon of lemon juice, depending on your taste. Cover again until it is cooked to perfection. Stop cooking as soon as the fish turns from orange to pink. Don't forget that the salmon will keep cooking after stove is turned off, and if the filet is of uneven thickness the edges might cook before the center. Do not overcook!

4. You can mix honey and mustard to make a sauce for the side, but it is not necessary.

This can be served with grilled Italian-style veggies—eggplant, zucchini, bell peppers, onions, even small potatoes with balsamic vinegar; or a veggie platter baked in the oven with an herb (for example, thyme) and olive oil seasoning; and whatever potatoes you like as a side.

Pour yourself a nice glass of white wine and... enjoy!

Morbid Chef Notes

This is a an incredibly tasty way of making a nice filet and seriously showing off your heavy metal cooking skills! I made the dipping sauce using all the cooking ingredients (olive oil, garlic, some rosemary, lemon zest, lemon juice, Worcestershire sauce, and sherry) blended with Dijon mustard, white wine, and honey. It was really, really great!

MELECHESH

Melechesh is a black metal band formed in Jerusalem by Ashmedi during the early 1990s. The group fled Israel in 1998, and at times were living as far spread apart as Holland, France, and Texas. Nevertheless, they succeeded in producing a slew of impressive albums notable for their speed, crisp songwriting, and evocative use of Sumerian and Mesopotamian melodies and themes in a metal format.

Vegetarian

VEGAN OATMEAL BURGERS | NUCLEAR YELLOW PEPPER PIZZA | SPEED METAL VEGAN TOFU
VEGETARIAN "BEEF" MASALA | RECIPE FOR DISASTER / TOUR BUS MOLOTOV COCKTAIL
NEW ORLEANS BLOOD RED BEANS AND RICE | TORTILLA DE PATATAS (SPANISH OMELETTE)
BEER PIZZA CRUST

GERMANY

"The burger, veggies, and 'schlock' go on one plate, no buns! The burgers are actually not your regular burger bun size either, but smaller."

Vegan Oatmeal Burgers

by Mille Petrozza of KREATOR

PREPARATION: 30 MINS
COOKING: 30 MINS
PORTIONS: 4

OATMEAL BURGER PATTY

> 4 cups (320 g) oatmeal
> 2 onions
> 2½ cups (600 ml) vegetable broth
> Salt and pepper, to taste
> Paprika, to taste
> Curry powder, to taste
> 3 tsp sesame oil

SOY YOGURT "SCHLOCK"

> 1½ cups (500 g) soy yogurt
> ½ cup fresh parsley, minced
> ½ cup fresh coriander, minced
> 2 tsp lemon juice
> 2 tsp olive oil
> Salt and pepper, to taste

RIOT OF VEGETABLES

> 1 zucchini, cut in small pieces
> 2 peppers (red and yellow), cut in small pieces
> 7 oz (200 g) mixed mushrooms, cut in small pieces
> 2 tsp garlic, minced
> 4 tsp sweet soy sauce
> 5 tsp sesame oil
> ½ cup (125 ml) red wine
> Salt and pepper, to taste

PREPARATION

1. Start with the oatmeal burger. Peel the onions, cut into small pieces, and sauté in a pan. Add oatmeal and vegetable broth. Bring to a boil.

2. Stir well while still boiling so it turns into a thick mash. Add salt, paprika, curry, and pepper, and let it cool down.

3. Form small burger patties, and fry them in sesame oil until brown.

4. For the soy yogurt "shlock," mix soy yogurt, fresh parsley, coriander, lemon juice, and olive oil. Season to taste with salt and pepper.

5. To stir-fry your vegetables, start by heating up the sesame oil, then add the minced garlic. Next, put in the rest of the vegetables and fry until the peppers begin to brown.

6. Extinguish with red wine, add soy sauce, and season to taste with salt and pepper.

Morbid Chef Notes

I had strange vibes about the idea of oatmeal burgers, but these turned out to be awesome! They were even better after reheating in the oven—they became crunchier and also more delicious.

KREATOR

Formed by Mille Petrozza in 1984, Kreator was one of the first and most violent German thrash metal bands of its era. Their neck-breaking classics *Endless Pain* in 1985 and *Pleasure to Kill* in 1986 proved to be a solid ground for inspiring the nascent death metal of a few years later. They have furiously delivered the goods without interruption ever since, fueled by Petrozza's creative guitar and socially aware lyrics.

ITALY

"All the people I know from other countries tell me that they love pizza and want to come to Italy to eat some. Maybe if they have the right recipe, they can cook it at their home!"

Nuclear Yellow Pepper Pizza

by Goddess of Hammering Chaos of CHILDREN OF TECHNOLOGY

PREPARATION: 2 HRS 30 MINS
COOKING: 10–20 MINS
PORTIONS: 2

CRUST

> 2½ cups (350 g) flour
> 1 sachet (8 g) dry yeast
> ½ cup (125 ml) lukewarm water
> 1 tsp salt
> 1 tsp sugar
> 3 tbsp extra-virgin olive oil

SAUCE AND TOPPINGS

> 7 oz (200 g) tomato pulp/sauce
> 9 oz (250 g) mozzarella, sliced
> A few Emmental cheese slices
> 1 yellow pepper, finely chopped
> Veggie sausage, cut into thin rounds

PREPARATION

1. In a small bowl, mix yeast with sugar. Dissolve in half cup of warm water.

2. Pour the flour in a large bowl. Shape it as a small mountain and then make a hole in the middle. In the center, add olive oil and yeast mixture.

3. Begin to mix with your hands, then add salt. You have to get a soft dough, easy to work with and smooth. The amount of water needed will vary from time to time. Work it vigorously until there are no more traces of dough from fingers. The dough should be soft but also elastic. Shape the "blob" into a ball, cover with flour, and then cover with a towel. Let rise in a warm place for at least 2 hours, or until the dough doubles in volume.

4. Turn the oven to 425°F (220°C). Fry the peppers in olive oil until they are half soft. Stretch the risen dough with a rolling pin (I use a bottle) or your fingers, until you have more or less 2–3 mm thickness and 12" (30 cm) in diameter

5. Put stretched dough on a well-oiled baking dish. Garnish with the tomato sauce, mozzarella, cooked peppers, Emmental cheese, and the sausage for those who eat them. Bake for 10 to 20 minutes, but it's best to check because the cooking time may vary.

Morbid Chef Notes

I had a pretty bad cold when I cooked this thing, so besides burning my tongue on the cheese, I couldn't taste anything! I froze the leftovers, and then finally got to taste it a week later! It was really, really good; I couldn't believe I had made that all from scratch. The Emmental cheese was a great addition, also!

CHILDREN OF TECHNOLOGY

The Italian road warriors Children of Technology started in mid-2007 with the intention of making a mutant new hybrid of speed/thrash metal and crust punk. Joining Splatterhead on guitars and his brother Thermo Nuclear Thrashard on bass, the drummer Goddess of Hammering Chaos and the singer Astolfi are taking the survival lessons of early Onslaught, Discharge, Warfare, Tank, English Dogs, and Motörhead several steps farther into the wasteland.

"Thanks to Emma for this recipe!"

Speed Metal Vegan Tofu

by Janick Langlais of AFTER THE BOMBS

PREPARATION: 15 MINS
COOKING: 20 MINS
PORTIONS: 2

TOFU

> 1 lb (450 g) firm tofu, rinsed
> ½ cup (65 g) unbleached flour
> ⅔ cup (166 ml) soy milk
> 2 tsp lemon juice
> 1 tbsp cooking oil

SPICE MIX

> 1½ cups (140 g) nutritional yeast
> 2 tsp salt
> 1 tsp garlic powder
> 1 tsp onion salt
> 1 tsp dry parsley
> ½ tsp paprika
> ½ tsp estragon
> ½ tsp basil leaves
> ½ tsp dill weed
> ½ tsp curry powder
> ¼ tsp dry mustard
> ¼ tsp dried oregano
> ¼ tsp dried rosemary
> ¼ tsp celery seeds

> Baked potatoes
> Vegan gravy (see recipe)

PREPARATION

1. Mix all the spices and nutritional yeast together in a bowl.

2. Mix the soy milk and lemon juice together in another bowl.

3. Cut the tofu in pieces (triangular or rectangular, as you prefer).

4. Pour the flour into a separate bowl.

5. Dip the tofu in the soy milk and lemon juice mixture, then dip it in the flour, then dip it again in the liquid mix, and then in the nutritional yeast and seasoning mix. Put aside and fry in a pan or bake in the oven.

Serve with baked potatoes and vegan gravy. Yummy!

Morbid Chef Notes

Wow, this is a really kick-ass recipe! I tried both fried and baked versions, and the fried one is by far superior. It almost tastes like chicken nuggets!

VEGAN GRAVY

This animal-free gravy can be used on potatoes, in poutine, with stuffing, etc. It really tastes like a normal gravy!

INGREDIENTS: 1/2 cup (125 ml) vegetable oil, 5 cloves garlic (crushed), 3 slices onion (chopped), 1/2 cup (65 g) white flour, 4 tsp nutritional yeast, 6 tbsp soy sauce, 2 cups (480 ml) water, 1/2 tsp sage, 1/4 tsp black pepper, 1/2 tsp salt, 5 or 6 white mushrooms (optional), extra flour/cornstarch (optional)

1. Fry onion and garlic in oil for about 2 minutes on medium heat, until the onion is a bit tender and translucent.

2. Add flour, yeast, and soy sauce to make a paste. Add the water gradually, stirring constantly. Bring the gravy to a boil on medium heat, stirring constantly. The gravy has to boil for it to thicken. Add pepper and salt. If the gravy is too thin, add flour or cornstarch.

AFTER THE BOMBS

Montreal's After the Bombs was born in 2004 from the ashes of crust-core band Hellbound. Influenced by bands like Sacrilege UK, Antisect, and Axegrinder, they play a very epic style of crust metal with raging female vocals and angry political lyrics.

AUSTRALIA

"It's not that Australia has no culture, but unless I was going to prescribe a recipe for witchery grubs and damper, anything else considered intrinsically Australian is purely derivative. I have selected a vegetarian masala, which is essentially a pastelike mixture of spices a little drier in texture and without doubt more exotic in taste than curry."

Vegetarian "Beef" Masala

by Jason Healey of ATOMIZER

PREPARATION: 30 MINS
COOKING: 45 MINS
PORTIONS: 6

INGREDIENTS

> 2 medium brown onions, coarsely chopped
> 4 cloves garlic, finely chopped
> Olive oil
> 1 tbsp cumin seeds
> 1 tsp coriander powder
> 1 tsp cumin powder
> 1 tsp garam masala powder
> 2 tsp sabji masala powder
> 4 tbsp tomato paste
> 1 lb (450 g) vegetarian beef chunks
> 1 cup (250 ml) natural European-style yogurt
> 5 small potatoes (white, washed, with skin on)
> 1 medium to large carrot chopped into thin pieces
> ½ head broccoli, chopped
> 1 fistful of green long beans, sliced into 1" (2.5 cm) pieces
> ½ head cauliflower (optional), chopped
> 10 small mushrooms (optional)
> 6 medium red tomatoes, chopped
> Jasmine rice for 6

Morbid Chef Notes

This recipe might have a lot of ingredients, but I assure you that it tastes really incredible! If you don't feel like buying tons of veggies and don't have time to cut them all, you can use a bag of California blend frozen vegetables.

PREPARATION

1.   In a large, uncovered saucepan, place olive oil on medium to high heat. Add cumin seeds and fry for about 30 seconds, until the aroma of the cumin seeds is present. Careful not to burn them, as this is detrimental to the success of the dish. Add the onion and garlic to the pan, and stir ingredients for about 5 minutes. During this time, the onion should have browned, and we're ready to progress.

2.   Chop the potatoes into halves, and boil in a saucepan until soft. Ensure they aren't falling apart but are soft enough to eat. They will be cooked a little further, but not significantly so.

3.   Steam all the vegetables until soft, but don't overdo it. They too will be cooked a little further beyond the steaming process.

4.   Once the onion has browned, reduce the heat to a simmer and add coriander powder, cumin powder, garam masala, and sabji masala powder to your saucepan. Add another 2 tbsp of oil and simmer ingredients down for approx 5 minutes. Stir rigorously as ingredients are added. Our quest is to reach a nice paste-like consistency. Don't be concerned if the onions don't break right down, but if you achieve that, great stuff. Ensuring that your saucepan remains uncovered, add the tomatoes. You can engage a little more heat at this stage, and shift up to a low-medium range.

5.   Add tomato paste. This aids in the thickening process, and provides an element of sweetness. Cook on a low-medium heat for approximately 15 minutes, and be sure to stir frequently.

6.   Throw your vegetarian beef chunks into a frying pan with some oil (a spray-on olive oil is best), and fry up till they are crispy.

7.   Add yogurt to the paste, stirring as you go. Once mixed through, it's time to add the mock beef chunks, vegetables, and potato. Lower the heat back to a simmer, and allow to cook through for another 5 minutes. Be sure to stir the vegetables and beef through the paste, and ensure everything is coated thoroughly.

8.   Serve on a bed of rice, and voilà—you have a kick-ass masala! This could be served as a vegan dish by leaving out the yogurt, or by substituting with a soy yogurt. This dish serves 6, but freezes extremely well, and tastes even better after a stint in the freezer. Also, the spices should be available from any authentic Indian grocery store, and the mock beef is most commonly found in Asian groceries.

ATOMIZER

This bad-ass black metal/thrasher/rock 'n' roll band from Melbourne, Australia, formed in summer of 1998. They went through many lineup and stylistic changes, always releasing quality material. Unfortunately, Atomizer called it quits in 2008, leaving behind plenty of demos, a handful of EPs, and four full-lengths for posterity.

CANADA

Recipe for Disaster / Tour Bus Molotov Cocktail

by Dan Beehler of EXCITER / BËEHLER

PREPARATION: 20 MINS
COOKING: —
PORTIONS: 1

INGREDIENTS

> 6 large eggs
> 1 loaf high-fiber bread
> 2 large, strong, eye-cryin'
  onions from hell
> 1 garlic clove, crushed
> 1½ tbsp mayonnaise
> One large glass chocolate milk

PREPARATION

1. Boil eggs.

2. Mix cooked eggs, onions (from hell!), mayo, and garlic in a big bowl.

3. Make sandwiches.

4. Drink chocolate milk.

5. Eat sandwiches.

6. Powermix—and watch out tonight!!!

DAN RECALLS HIS TOURING DAYS...

In 1987 we, Exciter, toured with an opening act called Crypt, from
Montreal (awesome band). Both bands and crews shared a bus. Crypt's
soundman, Sylvain (who was massive), had his own little recipe. He would
say, in his French accent, "Me, I'm take the chocolate milk, then I'm
take the egg-salad sandwich, then I'm powermix," moving his hips in a
circular motion (like a hula-hoop). Then he would eye his victim and he
would say: "Watch out tonight, boy." Even our bass player, Allan Johnson
(Gaseous Maximus in all his rancidness), couldn't compete, although he
tried for years. So remember, never choose the bottom bunk.

Morbid Chef Notes

So you want to know if it
works? Well, it sure does!
This is a very effective
stomach bomb, for the
most sadistic of creatures.

EXCITER / BËEHLER

One of the first speed metal bands, Ottawa's Exciter was formed in 1978 by Dan Beehler, John Ricci, and Allan Johnson. After a great deal of success with their song "World War III" on the *US Metal Vol. II* compilation in 1982, they signed to Shrapnel Records and released their heavily influential debut album, *Heavy Metal Maniac*. Since then, the band—which released 10 albums—has been carried on by John Ricci, the only remaining original member. In 2002, Dan and Allan formed Bëehler, which carries the torch of the original Exciter sound.

New Orleans Blood Red Beans and Rice

by Mike IX Williams of EYEHATEGOD

PREPARATION: 10 HRS (including soaking of the beans)

COOKING: 2 HRS

PORTIONS: 6

INGREDIENTS

> 1 lb (450 g) dry red beans
> 1 medium yellow onion, diced
> 3–4 bay leaves
> A lot of spicy cayenne pepper
> 2 tsp salt
> Creole seasoning (Tony Chachere preferred)
> 1 tsp black pepper
> 1 tsp onion powder
> 1 tsp garlic powder
> 1 tsp Creole mustard
> One stick butter
> Crystal hot sauce
> White or brown rice
> One fifth of vodka (to drink)

MUSIC

> Slayer, *Reign in Blood*
> Dwarves, *Blood Guts & Pussy*
> Sabbath, *Sabbath Bloody Sabbath*
> Misfits, *Wolfs Blood*
> Exodus, *Bonded by Blood*
> AC/DC, *If You Want Blood…*
> Bathory, *Blood Fire Death*

PREPARATION

1. Rinse red beans in colander. Place in large pot and cover with 2 to 3 inches of water (above beans). Add 1 tsp of salt. Bring to a heavy Iron Maiden rolling boil. Put on *Reign in Blood* by Slayer. Once boiled hard for 15 to 20 minutes, cover, and turn heat off. Drink vodka, pass out, and let beans soak overnight.

2. Wake up and put on the Dwarves LP and start the boil again. When the record is over in 15 or so minutes, remove the lid, and add more water. Keep boiling, adding water as needed as you boil the beans down.

3. Add onion, along with bay leaves, black pepper, onion powder, garlic powder, Creole mustard, a dash of Tony Chachere's seasoning, and as much spicy cayenne pepper as you think you can handle. Turn down the temperature, cover pot, then put on *Sabbath Bloody Sabbath* and let beans slow boil for 1 to 1½ hours—adding water as needed—until beans are boiled down to a creamy consistency. Stir often.

4. Add another teaspoon of salt and the whole stick of butter to beans, and separately start your rice. Slow boil beans for another 15 minutes, while cranking up the Misfits' *Wolfs Blood*. Turn off red beans and serve over rice. Add Crystal hot sauce to taste. While you are eating, listen to Exodus's *Bonded by Blood*, AC/DC's *If You Want Blood…*, and Bathory's *Blood Fire Death*.

Stolen from Kitten IX!

Morbid Chef Notes

Red beans and rice is a dish that has grown to legendary status. This authentic New Orleans dish is so simple to make, yet tastes soooo good. If the beans don't fall apart into a nice creamy consistency, mash them up a little bit, add a bit of water, and then return to the pot for a few minutes.

EYEHATEGOD

For twenty years, Eyehategod has been synonymous with the sludge, sickness, corruption, vice, and twisted romance of their home city, New Orleans. Former youth offenders turned veteran survivors, the band stirs up a thick Sabbath-y din that summons the most corrosive elements of heavy metal, crust punk, doom, and Delta blues.

SPAIN

Tortilla de Patatas (Spanish Omelette)

by Nuria of DEADMASK

PREPARATION: 20 MINS
COOKING: 20 MINS
PORTIONS: 4–6

INGREDIENTS

> 5 eggs, beaten in small bowl
> One small onion, chopped
> 2¼ lbs (1 kg) potatoes, sliced in thin pieces
> Olive oil
> Salt

> 9" (23 cm) or so frying pan

PREPARATION

1. Fry the potatoes in very hot oil in a frying pan until they're well fried and soft (but not crunchy); then drain them and put them into a big bowl.

2. Mix everything—potatoes with eggs and raw onion. Add salt to this mix.

3. Put the frying pan on the stovetop. Add only a little oil, just to cover the surface. When it's hot, put the mix in the pan and cook while you briefly remove the pan from the heat every few minutes.

4. Look under the omelette. When it is golden, turn the tortilla this way: Take a big plate and put it over the frying pan. Take the pan and the plate firmly with your hands and turn it upside down, so you finish with the tortilla on the plate. Then put the pan again on the stovetop and slip the raw side of the tortilla on it. Repeat this action a couple more times until the whole thing gets a golden color. That's all! Enjoy the tortilla!

The tortilla "turning" technique!

Morbid Chef Notes

This meal is so delicious! The ingredients are very simple, but produce intense flavors. It kind of tastes like a cross between french fries and an omelette. Yum!

DEADMASK

Born in 2007, Deadmask is a duet formed by Nuria of Electricats and Dopi of Machetazo. Their haunting traditional doom metal sound stems from their passion for 1970s occult rock, cemeteries, and, of course, classic doom metal bands. Nuria does all vocals, while Dopi takes care of all instruments.

GERMANY

"This has been tested with German beer conforming to the purity law from 1516! I don't know what will happen if you use beer that contains chemical flavors and preservatives. Enjoy your meal!"

Beer Pizza Crust

by Olaf Zissel of TANKARD

PREPARATION: 2 HRS 30 MINS
COOKING: 10–20 MINS
PORTIONS: 2

INGREDIENTS

> 2 cups (500 ml) wheat beer, warmed
> 5 cups (600 g) white flour
> 1 cube yeast (or 2 packs dry yeast)
> 1 tbsp salt
> 1 tsp sugar

PREPARATION

1.   In a large bowl, mix the yeast, the sugar, and the salt into the warm wheat beer, and wait until the yeast is dissolved. You won't taste the sugar later on—it's just for keeping the yeast going.

2.   Knead the flour into the bowl until you have fluffy-soft dough. Now, I usually let the stuff rest for an hour—so if you bought more beer, you can lean back and have some.

3.   After that break, the dough will need a little kneading again, and another 20-minute break. (Any beer left?) It is possible to repeat this process for 6 hours or more, but 'cause of all the beers you're drinking, it gets a little dangerous, okay?

4.   Again a short kneading, and then we roll the dough on a baking tray. Put the tray in the oven, and bake it for about 2 minutes at 480°F (250°C).

5.   Take pizza dough out from oven, and put on top everything you like (if you still can). Return the tray to the oven at 430°F (220°C) for 5 to 10 minutes. I prefer it simple—with tomato, cheese, and garlic.

Morbid Chef Notes

Eating pizza and drinking beer is always a treat, but I never thought of mixing both together so completely! This pizza crust is just killer; it rises perfectly and has great texture. I did three rises, and before putting it in the oven, I brushed some beaten egg on the dough to give it a nice golden glaze. The crust had a very faint, but distinctive, beer taste.

TANKARD

Tankard emerged on the 1980s German speed metal scene with steins of ale in their right hands and backup pints of pilsner in the other. While other thrashers sang about chemical warfare and deals with the devil, Tankard lifted high its glasses to toast Gambrinus, the patron saint of beer. After polishing off two six-packs of releases filled with every possible kind of song about beer, Tankard cracked open its thirteenth album, *Thirst*, in 2008.

HELLBENT FOR COOKING | DESSERTS

Desserts

THERMONUCLEAR DATE SQUARES | BLACK METAL BERRY PIE | STRAWBERRY JELL-O PRETZEL SALAD CAKE
CHOCOLATE PUDDING, "DEVIL" STYLE | MAPLE SYRUP PUDDING CAKE | DORO'S BLACK FOREST CAKE
SOUL BROWNIES | DUTCH SPACE CAKE

CANADA

"This is an easy recipe for date squares with pineapple. It's amazingly good! I double the ingredients and it lasts me for a week. I eat it for breakfast and lunch."

Thermonuclear Date Squares

by Chany Pilote of INEPSY

PREPARATION: 10 MINS
COOKING: 25 MINS
PORTIONS: 6

INGREDIENTS

> 1 cup (250 ml) crushed pineapple
> 1 cup (170 g) dates, seeded and roughly chopped
> ½ cup (125 ml) water
> 1¾ cups (175 g) oatmeal
> 1½ cups (187 g) whole wheat flour
> 1 cup (200 g) brown sugar
> ½ cup (115 g) butter or margarine at room temperature
> ½ tsp baking soda
> ½ tsp baking powder
> 1 egg, beaten (or vegan egg substitute)

PREPARATION

1. In a pan, cook pineapple and dates in water for around 10 minutes, until they reach a paste consistency.

2. In a large bowl, mix flour, baking soda, baking powder, and sugar, and slowly add butter.

3. Add oatmeal and brown sugar. Mix, and then add the egg. This should look like a a nice crumble.

4. Put half of the dry crumble mix on the bottom of an 8" (20 cm) long glass dish.

5. Spread fruit mix evenly over crumble layer, and then sprinkle remaining crumb mixture over date filling.

6. Bake in the oven on 325°F (162°C) for about 25 minutes, or until lightly browned.

Morbid Chef Notes

This nontraditional date square recipe (usually there are no other fruits in these) tastes less sugary than usual. It's great, because you don't get sick of them if you eat a ton! They taste just right, and make great midday snacks. I suggest eating 'em while drinking coffee or tea (but not with beer!)

INEPSY

INEPSY is a Montreal, Canada, four-piece playing an apocalyptic mix of Motörpunk, D-beat, NWOBHM, and raunchy rock 'n' roll. They are the pride of their home city, and with good reason! Formed ten years ago, they have since played all over Europe, laying waste to the system with tracks from their best albums, *R'n'R Babylon* and *City/Weapons*.

AUSTRALIA

Black Metal Berry Pie

by Reverend Kriss Hades of SADISTIK EXEKUTION

PREPARATION: 45 MINS

COOKING: 1 HR

PORTIONS: 6

FILLING

> 4 small baskets of blackberries (or as many as you like)
> 1 small basket of blueberries
> 2 tsp powdered sugar (more sugar if you want it sweeter)
> 2 tsp cornstarch
> 2 tsp blackberry jam
> Some water

PASTRY

> 2½ cups (315 g) self-rising flour
> ¾ cup (170 g) butter
> ¼ cup (60 ml) water
> 3 tsp powdered sugar
> Belgian chocolate, melted (optional)

> Pie tray (Pyrex preferred)

PREPARATION

1. It is preferable to make your own pastry, or you can buy readymade stuff if you are poser. If you are making the pastry, ask a girl how to put it together. Then knead it into a ball, and leave in fridge until the berry filling is ready.

2. Cook the filling until it is not too runny—on the way to jelly. It is possible to add secret ingredients to the filling. Once the berries are ready, turn off heat and get the pastry out of fridge (pastry posers need not be reading this part).

3. Get your pie tray. Roll out pastry with rolling pin, using flour to stop sticking.

4. Roll out pastry onto cling wrap or something similar. Three things are made from pastry: bottom of pie, top of pie, and decorations. Use your brain to work out how much for each thing. This task will show if you are an elite metal overlord of hell's kitchen, or just a mere mortal. After rolling the bottom of the pie out to the size of tray, you transfer the layer by flipping the pastry over onto tray and then peeling off cling wrap.

5. Put filling in, as much as you have or like. I prefer as much as possible. Roll out top of pie, similar process to bottom. Cut edges with knife, and press the edges of the top down to seal firmly.

6. Use the rest of the pastry for decorations, using your brain again for the types of things you want. To make barbed wire, roll out two long thin worms, twist them together, then wrap shorter pieces around that for the barbs. I melted Belgian chocolate into liquid and used it like paint. Painting before cooking or after has different effects. I painted mine after it was cooked.

7. Sprinkle sugar on the pie, then place it in a hot oven for 30 to 35 minutes until it is golden.

REVEREND KRISS HADES RECALLS A STORY ABOUT THIS PIE...

"Years ago in the Blue Mountains, I visited three sisters who all looked similar-except for their long hair, which was different colors: black, purple, and dark blue (their names were Sabbath, Deep, and Cheer!) I could get assistance from them when cooking, as well as talking about weird topics of life, death, and beyond. They lived in a large house with interesting things everywhere, many rooms, and especially an excellent kitchen. The parents were never home; seemingly always on a holiday trip somewhere else. On one occasion, we made a pie similar to this one and the topic of conversation was 'human sacrifice.' When thick black smoke with some blue flames started emanating from the inside of my pie slice, seeping slowly from the filling and rolling downwards toward the floor and filling the room until waist high, I realized that I somehow had ingested probably the most toxic amount of LSD possible. The sisters seemed to be floating around the room in strange circles, wielding sharp and shining implements of a hypnotic design that curved back and forward like metal snakes. Needless to say, I was out the window and running fast as lightning to hide from them, and whatever else might emerge from that blackberry pie. I spent the night in the Blue Mountains' forests for safety (which is another story entirely)."

Photo by Reverend Kriss Hades

SADISTIK EXEKUTION

Sadistik Execution is a hyper-creative and sociopathic Australian cabal that has tormented the world with fast, chaotic, and abusive sound since the early 1990s. Despite their total hatred of everything and album titles like *We Are Death... Fukk You!,* their total dedication to all-encompassing aggression and maniacal attention to grisly details have attracted admiring legions of thrill-seekers and daredevils.

UNITED STATES

Strawberry Jell-o Pretzel Salad Cake

by Jeff Becerra of POSSESSED

PREPARATION: 1 HR
COOKING: 10 MINS
PORTIONS: 6–8

INGREDIENTS

> 2⅔ cups (300 g) broken unsalted pretzel sticks
> 1½ cups (375 ml) butter, melted
> 12 oz (340 g) cream cheese, softened
> ½ cup (100 g) sugar
> 12 oz (340 g) container whipped topping, thawed
> 6 oz (85 g) package of strawberry Jell-o
> 2 cups (500 ml) pineapple juice
> 3 cups (500 g) fresh strawberries, sliced—or 1 large package of sliced frozen strawberries

PREPARATION

1. Place broken pretzels and butter in a 9" x 12" (23 cm x 30 cm) pan.

2. Bake 10 minutes at 400°F (200°C). Cool down.

3. Cream together cream cheese, whipped topping, and sugar. Spread over the top of lukewarm pretzel mix. Chill.

4. Dissolve Jell-o mix in boiling pinapple juice (no water). Stir in strawberries. Chill to thicken until almost jellied.

5. Spread topping over everything and refrigerate.

Morbid Chef Notes

This three-layer salad is great for metal potlucks. The crunchy pretzel crust is a perfect contrast to the tangy cream cheese filling and the strawberry top layer—incredible!

POSSESSED

The ultra-young Possessed formed in 1983 in San Francisco, and soon took the famed Bay Area thrash metal sound in a much more deathly direction. Famed for Jeff Becerra's guttural vocals, chaotic speed, and ultra-evil lyrics and imagery, the band recorded its landmark *Seven Churches* LP in 1985, opening the floodgates for the rise of death metal. In 1989, Jeff Becerra was paralyzed from the chest down after a tragic shooting. In 2007, he brought Possessed back; the new lineup includes all the members of long-running LA death metal band Sadistic Intent.

ITALY

"This is an authentic and old recipe, very famous in the south of Italy. Nowadays, I know it is not so simple to find pork blood, so many people prefer to do the recipe without it. It could be substituted with lots of bitter cocoa powder and milk."

Chocolate Pudding "Devil" Style

by Steve Sylvester of DEATH SS

PREPARATION: 30 MINS
COOKING: 5 HRS
PORTIONS: 6

INGREDIENTS

> ½ cup (125 ml) pork blood (collected on the day, and shaken vigorously to avoid lumps) or milk
> 1 cup (250 ml) warmed grape juice
> ½ cup (115 g) lard
> 1½ lbs (666 g) melting chocolate
> Lemon peel
> 1 stick of cinnamon
> Tuscany hot pepper
> ½ cup (85 g) sugar
> ¼ cup (30 g) powdered bitter cocoa powder

Note: The original recipe calls for quantities eight times greater!

PREPARATION

1. In a pot, using a strainer/colander, filter the blood and cooked grape juice. Melt the lard, let it cool down, and then add it to the mix using a wooden spoon.

2. Next, add the cocoa powder and the stick of cinnamon. Put it on low heat, and stir the mix constantly to avoid it sticking to the pot.

3. At the halfway point, when the mix starts getting thick (after around 2½ hours), add the sugar, the chocolate flakes, hot pepper, and the lemon peel.

4. Continue cooking, always stirring the mix, arriving finally at the consistency of a thick cream, after 2½ hours.

During preparation, never stop stirring and don't increase the heat. The help of a second person, preferably a virgin, is advised to avoid exhaustion.

The end result is great spread on crackers, preferably on a night of the full moon.

Morbid Chef Notes

This recipe is for total chocolate and/or blood maniacs. I made my version without blood, as it is quite difficult to find (legally), but it tastes really great anyway! The end result is a very thick and rich fudge-like cream. Try to eat it while still warm, and you will not be deceived!

DEATH SS

The legendary Death SS (In Death of Steve Sylvester) was formed in 1977 by Paul Chain and Steve Sylvester. They combined elements of horror, the occult, and heavy metal into a style they called *horror metal*. They were quite obscure in their early days, and only released a few singles and demos with the original lineup. The avant garde tracks on the amazing *The Story of Death SS 1977–1984* compilation album have influenced untold numbers of bands, and still entrance listeners to this day.

CANADA

Maple Syrup Pudding Cake

by Patrick Pageau of BASTARDATOR

PREPARATION: 15 MINS
COOKING: 45 MINS
PORTIONS: 6

INGREDIENTS

> 2¼ cups (540 ml) maple syrup
> 1 cup (250 ml) water
> ¾ cup (150 g) sugar
> 2 cups (500 g) flour
> 3 tsp baking powder
> 1 tsp salt
> 1 egg
> ½ cup (115 g) shortening (or butter/margarine)
> ¾ cup (185 ml) milk
> ½ tsp vanilla extract (optional)

> Large pot

PREPARATION

1. Add water and maple syrup to a large pot. Heat up, but do not boil. Turn the oven on to 350°F (175°C).

2. In a large bowl, use a hand mixer to mix butter and sugar until you get a light paste. Add eggs and vanilla, and mix again. In another bowl, mix flour, salt, and baking powder. Add dry mix to liquid mix, then slowly add milk. Mix properly until you get a nice, smooth texture.

3. Carefully add batter on top of hot syrup using a large spoon. Cover the syrup completely.

4. Cover and place in oven for 45 minutes. The cake will be ready when it has risen and reaches a golden-brown color. If that is not the case, bake it uncovered until it reaches that color.

Serve with a dash of rich table cream.

Morbid Chef Notes

This cake—a variation of the popular Québec dish *pouding chômeur*—was created by female factory workers in 1929 during the Great Depression. The original version contained no maple syrup, but instead used cheaper ingredients, like brown sugar. Patrick's version is a delicious maple syrup–soaked cake, which is just sugary enough.

BASTARDATOR

Formed in Ottawa in 2006, Bastardator continuously seek to annihilate the modern conception of metal. Playing a powerful mix of speed/thrash metal, hardcore, and classic NWOBHM, they are true warriors in the great Canadian metal tradition.

GERMANY

"If you want an extra kick in this, add a little alcohol we call *kirschwasser* to the cake mix. That's the real German way, and it'll taste even better. Just a little spirit—try it, I know you'll love it! With love, Doro Pesch."

Doro's Black Forest Cake

by Doro Pesch of WARLOCK / DORO

PREPARATION: 40 MINS
COOKING: 45 MINS
PORTIONS: 8

INGREDIENTS

> 1 package chocolate cake mix
> 2 big cans tart pitted cherries (cherry pie filling)
> 1¼ cup (225 g) granulated sugar
> ¼ cup (20 g) cornstarch
> 2 tsp vanilla
> 3 cups cold whipping cream
> ⅓ cup (40 g) powdered sugar
> Chocolate shavings
> 8 maraschino cherries (or another red fruit)
> Kirschwasser, German cherry brandy, to taste (optional)
> Butter

> 1 chilled mixing bowl (for the whipped cream)
> 1 large mixing bowl (for the cake mix)
> Two 9" (23 cm) wide round cake pans
> 1 saucepan

PREPARATION

1. Preheat oven to 350°F (175°C). Grease and flour the two cake pans and set them aside. Prepare the cake mix and bake 30 to 35 minutes. Let it cool off completely.

2. Put canned cherries, sugar, and cornstarch in a saucepan, and cook over low heat until it thickens. Stir well. Stir in vanilla and kirschwasser (if desired) at the end.

3. For the frosting, mix cold whipping cream and powdered sugar in a chilled bowl. Put your mixer on high speed until it gets stiff.

4. Cut the cooled cake into layers and put cherry mix and frosting between layers of cake (about 2 to 3 times more cake than cherries and frosting).

5. Now make it look nice, and be creative! Frost the side of this beauty with remaining frosting, and put some chocolate crumbs/shavings on the side, too.

6. Put cherries on top of the cake in the center, and put some whipped cream or remaining frosting into a pastry bag. Have fun with it. Decorate as you like. Oh, it looks wonderful! Magic!

Morbid Chef Notes

I used two packages of cake mix instead of one, but this cake is really great! For the decorations, I bought a 70% dark chocolate bar and made shavings using a vegetable peeler. It works perfectly! Also, I added some red currants instead of cherries on top. The sourness combined with sugar was a huge success.

WARLOCK / DORO

Dorothee Pesch was born in Düsseldorf, Germany. Between 1983 and 1987, she led the heavy metal band Warlock from the European underground to international success with classics like 1984's *Burning the Witches* and 1986's *True as Steel*. Since then, Doro has pursued a successful solo career under the name Doro.

UNITED STATES

"These will store unrefrigerated for several weeks if not months. Wait until completely cool, though, before bagging or mold may appear. If this happens, you can throw 'em out or eat 'em anyway!"

Soul Brownies

by Scott "Wino" Weinrich of THE OBSESSED / SAINT VITUS / WINO

PREPARATION: 5 MINS
COOKING: 1½–2 MINS
PORTIONS: 6

INGREDIENTS
> Store-bought brownie mix
> 1 egg
> 2 g medicinal cannabis, sifted

> Small microwave-proof dish

PREPARATION

1. Fill the dish halfway with store-bought brownie mix. Add one egg, stir until creamy.

2. Add sifted cannabis. Stir in well.

3. Put in microwave on high for between 1½ to 2 minutes. It should rise up.

4. Let cool. Take knife, and push down side of dish and around brownie.

WINO

A fixture on the Maryland/Washington, DC, doom and punk scenes since the late 1970s, Scott "Wino" Weinrich has fronted a succession of essential doom metal / hard rock projects, all characterized by his haunting voice, wailing guitar solos, and spiritual lyrics. Seeing him play live is always an intense experience!

"There are several ways to bake such a cake, but this is the best one!"

Dutch Space Cake

by Stephan Gebédi of THANATOS

PREPARATION: 5 HRS (including space butter preparation)

COOKING: 1 HR 20 MINS

PORTIONS: 8

INGREDIENTS

> 3 complete eggs
> 3 egg yolks
> 1 cup (200 g) sugar
> 1 tbsp lemon juice
> 1 cup (225 g) butter, soft and creamy
> 1 cup (200 g) flour, sifted
> 5–10 g medicinal cannabis, chopped

PREPARATION

1. Boil a couple quarts of water in a pot, then put the butter in it. Add the cannabis. Simmer over a low flame for several hours, then let the mixture completely cool down. The oils of the medicinal cannabis have now dissolved.

2. Gently separate the butter from the water (butter floats!) until all water has been filtered out. Now you have space butter (which is also nice on a sandwich.)

3. Gently grease a baking tin. Let space butter melt.

4. Mix egg, sugar, and lemon juice. Heat to approx 75°F (23°C), then whip until you get a light texture. Add heated butter; mix, and slowly add flour.

5. Pour everything into a baking pan, then place in oven at 200°F (175°C) for 30 to 40 minutes—until you poke the cake with a toothpick and it comes out clean.

THANATOS

Holland's first extreme metal band, Thanatos, was formed by Stephan Gebédi (guitar/vocals) in 1984. They released demos every year until 1990, when they finally recorded their first full-length. Another LP followed, but they broke up in 1992. Stephan resurrected the band in 1999, and Thanatos has since released three killer albums. They play a very violent and ancient breed of death and thrash metal, and are definitely not for the weak.

Drinks

THE VIKING TESTICLE | PETER'S RUSTY NAIL | CAIPIRINHA | GOOD MARGARITA
PARROT BAY COCONUT RUM AND PUNCH | THE PILEDRIVER | DESTRUCTIVE SEMEN
COQUITO (RUM EGGNOG) | MAYHEMIC DESTRUCTION FUEL

UNITED STATES

The Viking Testicle

by Richard Christy, ex–DEATH / CONTROL DENIED

INGREDIENTS

> 1 part Stoli Vanilla vodka
> 1 part pineapple juice
> 1 part champagne

> 1 part listen to "Under the Northern Star" by Amon Amarth while you make the drink

PREPARATION

Mix ingredients together. Serve in a chalice-made-of-the-bones-of-a-Nordic-woolly-mastodon—or, if you can't find one of those, a martini glass will do.

And—*wallah!*—you have a Viking Testicle.

Enjoy responsibly!

DEATH

Death was the brainchild of the late Chuck Schuldiner; he launched the band in Florida in 1983, embarking on a lifelong metal journey that ended when he succumbed to brain stem cancer in 2001. Though early members of Death also spearheaded legendary extreme groups including Autopsy, Repulsion, Cynic, and Massacre, the band Death itself eventually grew out of its screaming gory roots and found enlightenment in progressive metal. The final lineup of Death—including drummer Richard Christy—became Control Denied, who remained active until the tragic death of their leader.

FINLAND

"It's a fucked-up drink, but it does the job. After ten of these, anyone learns to speak Finnish. And the Finns forget how."

Peter's Rusty Nail

by Father Peter Vicar of REVEREND BIZARRE / LORD VICAR

INGREDIENTS

> 2 parts Grant's Blended Scotch Whisky
> 1 part Southern Comfort

PREPARATION

Mix in a glass and serve.

REVEREND BIZARRE

Reverend Bizarre was one of the biggest names of the traditional doom metal wave of the new millennium, with good reason! Formed in Lohja, Finland, in 1995, they released three albums and one very long EP of crushing doom with dramatic vocals. The band sadly broke up in 2007, and its members formed their own new bands. Guitarist Peter Vicar launched Lord Vicar. He also played in the Orne, a killer dark progressive rock band.

BRAZIL

Caipirinha
by HOLOCAUSTO

INGREDIENTS

> 1 lime
> 5 spoons of fine sugar
> Cachaça (sugarcane brandy)
> Ice to your liking

PREPARATION

These ingredients are the traditional ones. Take a lime, cut the tips, and then cut the lime in half lengthwise. Take out the middle white "lines" (to prevent the drink from becoming bitter), cut into wedges, then throw into the bottom of a glass. Add the fine sugar, mash the contents of the glass with a pestle or a wooden spoon, and then fill up the glass with crushed ice and cachaça. Put the contents in one glass, take another glass (same type of glass), put it on top upside down, and then shake the drink like a cocktail. Serve.

HOLOCAUSTO

Hailing from Belo Horizonte, Brazil—also the home city of Sepultura—Holocausto are among the fiercest of an epidemic of warlike Brazilian thrash bands to emerge during the mid-1980s. Their mixture of hardcore punk and death metal is a favorite South American recipe.

"I'm a Budweiser man, and believe it or not, you don't taste the beer at all in this recipe. Corona would also work—just don't use a dark or heavy beer!"

Good Margarita

by John Tardy of OBITUARY

INGREDIENTS

> 12 oz (360 ml) tequila
> 12 oz (360 ml) beer
> 12 oz (360 ml) frozen limeade
> 12 oz (360 ml) ginger ale
> 2–3 fresh limes, sliced
> 2 fresh oranges, sliced (optional)
> Salt

PREPARATION

Mix liquids together in a large pitcher. Add salt and fresh limes (you can also add fresh orange slices). Serve in salted-rim glasses with lots of ice, and garnish with fresh lime and orange slices.

OBITUARY

Obituary is one of the original Florida death metal bands. Formed in 1985 by guitarist Trevor Peres and the Tardy brothers Donald and John, the band combined graphic gore and horror imagery with a slow, groovy, heavy sound often compared to the alligator-filled swamps near their Tampa home. Their classic cut "Chopped in Half" has been an inspiration to sous-chefs everywhere.

UNITED STATES

Parrot Bay Coconut Rum and Punch
by Danny Lilker of ANTHRAX / NUCLEAR ASSAULT / S.O.D. / BRUTAL TRUTH

INGREDIENTS
> 4 parts punch
> 1 part coconut rum
> Ice (optional)

PREPARATION
Mix in a tall glass.

NUCLEAR ASSAULT
With one foot planted in heavy metal and the other in New York City's hardcore scene, Nuclear Assault were one of the most unique and influential groups of the 1980s thrash metal era. Featuring former Anthrax members Danny Lilker and John Connelly, the band assaulted social issues at full speed, but never shirked their duty to write ten-second joke songs in the same vein as Lilker's infamous project band S.O.D.

CANADA

"There are variations, but here's the simplest recipe, happily with Coke instead of the prune juice that is usually found in the original Piledriver recipe…"

The Piledriver

by Gord "Piledriver" Kirchin of PILEDRIVER

INGREDIENTS

> 2 parts dark rum
> 2 parts vodka
> 1 part Coca-Cola
> 1 part orange juice

PREPARATION

1. Add rum and vodka to a beer mug. Top with Coca-Cola and orange juice, and add ice if possible.

2. Drink as many as humanly possible, and fall down a lot… Now get up and flip the album over to side two without drunkenly scratching the hell out of it, cuz it's like, a classic, right!? Hmm… How many of these have I drunk now?… I'm not as think as you drunk I am… Theesh thingsh are fukkkin' strooong, dude!… Hey… Wait… We should get a pizza or shumthin'… Ooh… I love thish part… Danh dan dan dandanna haaanndaaaaahnn… Daaaaa daaaaaah daaaaa dant! Dant dant!!! Daaaaaaah!!!!

PILEDRIVER

Canada's Piledriver was a powerhouse studio project put together in the mid-1980s by Gord Kirchin and an ace team of incognito metal hotshots. Their debut album, *Metal Inquisition*, overwhelmed the metal world with meaty chops and bombastic lyrics about fornication, UFOs, and carnage. In particular, the line "we sentence you to death—by guillotine" has secured the band's place in metal lore. Piledriver resurfaced during the 2000s to perform its first-ever concerts.

"This cocktail, which has no name, is not very common. It is very brutal, because you can mix a product of the coast region—coconuts—with the best rum of the Andean region. We can call it Destructive Semen if that is the case, ha ha! Cheers, metalians!!"

Destructive Semen

by ALCOHOLIC RITES

INGREDIENTS

> 4 cups (1 L) of aguardiente or rum, better if its process of fermentation is not by yeast
> 4 ripe coconuts
> 4 corks

PREPARATION

1. Perforate the coconuts carefully with a lesser diameter than the corks.

2. Pour the aguardiente or rum inside the coconuts. Mix with the juice of the coconuts; then close the holes with the corks.

3. Bury the coconuts very deep for 20 days.

4. To finish the recipe, dig up the coconuts and clean them (to avoid the sand falling into the elixir) and serve! The result will be a sweet drink with a great aroma, and with an astonishing alcoholic power!!!

ALCOHOLIC RITES

Formed in Quito, Ecuador, in 2002, Alcoholic Rites is an ugly drunken death/thrash metal band that breathes, pisses, shits, and pukes metal. Their sole purpose is to get drunk and write hymns about alcohol. You can almost smell the booze evaporating from the *Metal Alcoholico Destructivo* EP. The band sounds like alcohol-soaked early 1980s German thrash metal, lit on fire and fed speed pills. Yeah!

PUERTO RICO

Coquito (Rum Eggnog)

By Erico la Bestia from DANTESCO

INGREDIENTS

> 1 cup (250 ml) coconut milk
> 1 cup (250 ml) white rum, or to taste. Yeah, 3 cups for me!
> 4 egg yolks, well beaten
> 1 cup (250 ml) sweetened condensed milk
> 1 cup (250 ml) water
> 1 cup (250 ml) evaporated milk
> 3 cinnamon sticks
> Ground cinnamon for garnish

PREPARATION

1. Combine all of the milks and the rum in a blender or food processor. Set aside.

2. Boil the water with the cinnamon sticks. Cool to room temperature. Discard the cinnamon sticks.

3. Next, combine all the ingredients except the ground cinnamon, and beat well in a blender or food processor in batches. Pour the eggnog into glass bottles and refrigerate until ready to use.

To serve, transfer the eggnog to a punch bowl and sprinkle the cinnamon on top.

DANTESCO

What happens when a fistfight breaks out between Conan the Barbarian and Satan in a tropical setting? Dantesco, of course! Born in 2003 in the city of Cayey, Puerto Rico, this epic doom metal band is influenced by leaders like Candlemass, Black Sabbath, Dio, Omen, and Mercyful Fate. Their unique, hair-raising epic metal is magnificently enhanced with Erico "La Bestia"'s over-the-top operatic vocals. A real treat, just like their *coquito* recipe!

AUSTRALIA

Mayhemic Destruction Fuel

by Andy Eftichiou of MORTAL SIN

INGREDIENTS

> 1 btl Jack Daniel's
> 1 btl Southern Comfort
> 1btl sour apple schnapps
> 1 btl top-shelf vodka
> 1 btl Bacardi white rum
> 1 gal (4 L) fresh orange juice
> 2 gals (8 L) tropical fruit juice
> 2 cans orange juice concentrate
> 10 peeled and sliced oranges
> 4 honeydew melons, cubed
> 6 limes (skin on), sliced
> 2 pineapples, chopped into pieces
> ½ cup (65 g) castor (fine) sugar
> Many bottles of frozen spring water, sealed

> 5–6 gal (20 L) cooler

PREPARATION

1. Combine all spirits and liquor in a large cooler. Stir well.

2. Toss half the fruit into the cooler with the alcohol, and let sit for 4 to 6 hours.

3. Add the tropical fruit juice, fresh orange juice, and orange juice concentrate. Mix well, and let sit overnight.

4. An hour or two before serving, combine the remaining fruit and sugar in a bowl (remove skin from lime slices), and bash into a rough puree. Stir into the fruit-and-alcohol mixture.

5. Toss in several bottles of frozen spring water to chill. Serve in cups.

MORTAL SIN

Australia's Mortal Sin were the most polished of a rash of Australian contributions to the golden era of thrash metal in the late 1980s. The inroads they made then have ensured that Mortal Sin patches remain mainstays on the denim jackets of headbangers everywhere. Today, Mortal Sin continues to record, tour, and appear at summer metal festivals.

Morbid Chef's Tips and Tricks

CUTTING VEGGIES

When I started cooking for real, my grandmother thought it was important for me to learn how to cut properly. I guess that listening to too much Autopsy made me want to cut ferociously without any thinking! The trick is to follow the blade of your knife—lower the tip of the blade first, and follow the rounded shape. Oh, yeah—and get your knives sharpened!

CHOPPING ONIONS WITHOUT TEARS

Yeah, onions will burn your eyes and make you cry, so here is a trick to not look like a sissy while cutting them. Put your cutting board on the front burner of your stove, and light the rear burner. Electric or gas flames will both work. Apparently, the convection from the source of heat moves the air containing the sulphur compounds away. No more tears!

HANDLING EXTRA-HOT PEPPERS

I suggest wearing thin surgical gloves when handling really hot peppers. I've had my fingers and eyes burn really badly for a few hours before I figured out this piece of advice!

FREEZING YOUR FOOD

I often make recipes in double, in order to have leftovers that I can freeze and eat later. This is especially great if you're really busy and don't have too much time to cook. Pretty much everything freezes well, except for potatoes (which change texture), and most cream/milk dishes. If you're making a creamy vegetable soup, for example, add the cream after you reheat. If you have leftover vegetables, quickly boil them, and remove as much air as possible from package before freezing. Finally, do not refreeze thawed meats! If you thaw frozen meat and don't know what to do with it—cook it, and then it can be refrozen.

MEASURES

1 tsp is 1 teaspoon (small spoon), 1 tbsp is 1 tablespoon (big spoon). All the recipes in this book have been tested with Canadian measuring cups (250 ml). The US ones have 10 ml less, so if you are using 'em, just add around 1 tbsp more of the ingredient to each measure—but it's not the end of the world if you don't.

YEAST ACTIVATION

Yeast converts the fermentable sugars in dough into CO_2. The dough will rise as the CO_2 forms bubbles. When the bread is baked, the bubbles "set," making the bread much fluffier. Sugar (or natural sugar from potatoes and eggs) helps activate the yeast, while salt and fats slow it down. Therefore, when a certain recipe asks for yeast, put it in a small bowl with a bit of warm water (not boiling—just warm), and mix in a little bit of sugar. Mix until you get a homogenous liquid. It will work wonders!

My favorite pot... get one if you can! You can cook everything in it.

Band Index

A

Abigail (Japan) 28
Abscess (USA) 14
Accept (Germany) 72
After the Bombs (Canada) 184
Alcoholic Rites (Ecuador) 220
Amebix (UK) 152
Anthrax (USA) 52, 218
Anvil (Canada) 76
Armored Saint (USA) 32
Arphaxat (France) 136
Atomizer (Australia) 186
Autopsy (USA) 14

B

Bastardator (Canada) 206
Bëehler (Canada) 188
Blackfire (Malaysia) 168
Blasphemy (Canada) 130
Brutal Truth (USA) 218
Budgie (Wales) 166
Bulldozer (Italy) 174

C

Cauldron (Canada) 42
Children of Technology (Italy) 182
Control Denied (USA) 214
Countess (Netherlands) 92
Cruachan (Ireland) 60

D

Dantesco (Puerto Rico) 221
Deadmask (Spain) 192
Death (USA) 14, 214
Death SS (Italy) 204
Deiphago (Philippines) 106
Denial of God (Denmark) 24
Desolation Angels (UK) 38
Destruction (Germany) 154
Devastation (Croatia) 22
Dissection (Canada) 110
Doro (Germany) 208
Dusk (Pakistan) 34

E

Electric Wizard (UK) 148
Elixir (UK) 102
Envenom (Malaysia) 40
Exciter (Canada) 188
Eyehategod (USA) 190

F

Faustcoven (Norway) 172
Funerot (USA) 98

G

Gates of Slumber, The (USA) 74
Goat Horn (Canada) 42
Gorgoroth (Norway) 164
Grimorium Verum (Ecuador) 44
Gwar (USA / Antarctica) 20

H

Holocausto (Brazil) 216
Holy Rage (UK) 88

I

Impaler (USA) 94
Inepsy (Canada) 198

J

Judas Priest (UK) 88

K

Kreator (Germany) 180

L

Lamp of Thoth, The (UK) 158
L'Impero Delle Ombre (Italy) 30
Lord Vicar (Finland) 215

M

Mantak (Malaysia) 170
Master (USA) 78
Master's Hammer (Czech Republic) 56
Mayhem (Norway) 118
Melechesh (Israel) 176
Messiah (Switzerland) 96
Midnight (USA) 66
Minotaur (Germany) 142
Mortal Sin (Australia) 222
Mütiilation (France) 84

N

Necromantia (Greece) 116
Necrosadist (Cyprus) 138
Nuclear Assault (USA) 218

O

Obituary (USA) 217
Obscurity (Sweden) 70
Obsessed, The (USA) 210
Orodruin (USA) 144

P

Pagan Altar (UK) 68
Pentagram (USA) 128
Piledriver (Canada) 219
Possessed (USA) 202
Procession (Chile) 100

R

Repulsion (USA) 64
Reverend Bizarre (Finland) 215
Rigor Mortis (USA) 18
Rods, The (USA) 134

Root (Czech Republic) 80
Rotting Christ (Greece) 122

S

Sadistik Exekution (Australia) 200
Saint Vitus (USA) 210
Sepultura (Brazil) 48
Shackles (Australia) 58
Sigh (Japan) 54
Sir Lord Baltimore (USA) 162
Skyforger (Latvia) 90
Slaughter (Canada) 16
"The Lord Weird" Slough Feg (USA) 160
S.O.D. (USA) 52, 218
Stíny Plamenů (Czech Republic) 36

T

Tankard (Germany) 194
Thanatos (Netherlands) 211
Thin Lizzy (Ireland) 86, 114
Toxic Holocaust (USA) 50
Trench Hell (Australia) 156
Trouble (USA) 146
Tygers of Pan Tang (UK) 140

U

U.D.O. (Germany) 72
Uriah Heep (UK) 120

W

Warlock (Germany) 208
Warpig (Canada) 124
Weapon (Canada) 62
Wino (USA) 210
Witchfynde (USA) 26
Witchtrap (Colombia) 104

X

Xibalba (Mexico) 132

Z

Zemial (Greece) 108